The Supreme Court and American Democracy

THE SUPREME COURT AND AMERICAN DEMOCRACY

CASE STUDIES ON JUDICIAL REVIEW AND PUBLIC POLICY

Earl E. Pollock

GREENWOOD PRESS
Westport, Connecticut · London

Library of Congress Cataloging-in-Publication Data

Pollock, Earl E.
   The Supreme Court and American democracy : case studies on judicial review and public policy /
Earl E. Pollock.
     p. cm.
   Includes bibliographical references and index.
   ISBN 978–0–313–36525–6 (alk. paper)
   1. Judicial review—United States—History. 2. Civil rights—United States—History. I. Title.
KF4575.P598   2009
347.73'12—dc22   2008034766

British Library Cataloguing in Publication Data is available.

Library of Congress Catalog Card Number: 2008034766
ISBN: 978–0–313–36525–6

First published in 2009

Greenwood Press, 88 Post Road West, Westport, CT 06881
An imprint of Greenwood Publishing Group, Inc.
www.greenwood.com

Printed in the United States of America

The paper used in this book complies with the
Permanent Paper Standard issued by the National
Information Standards Organization (Z39.48-1984).

10 9 8 7 6 5 4 3 2 1

Contents

Preface

The republic established by the Framers of the U.S. Constitution is based on two opposing principles. The first is *majority rule*—the principle that the majority determines government policy through legislation enacted by their elected representatives. The second principle is *fundamental law*—the principle that there are nonetheless some things that the Constitution forbids even a majority to do. These two principles come into direct collision when it is claimed that legislation enacted by majority rule is "unconstitutional"—that the legislation violates the provisions of the Constitution.

The primary responsibility of seeking to reconcile those two principles rests today on the nine Justices of the Supreme Court. Although theoretically the three branches of the federal government are equal under the Constitution, the nation's acceptance of judicial supremacy has made the Court the final arbiter of the Constitution's interpretation.

From the birth of the nation to the present day, as shown in the recent debates over the selection of new Justices, the Court's role has been a subject of intense debate. At the heart of the controversy is a wide variety of views concerning whether, in a democratic society, critical issues of national policy should be decided by an unelected body.

Constitutional law cases are not "legal" in a conventional sense but instead often involve issues arising in the political arena. "There is almost no political question in the United States," Alexis de Tocqueville said, "that is not resolved sooner or later into a judicial question." [1] As (later Justice) Robert Jackson pointed out: "Struggles over power that in Europe call out regiments of troops, in America call out battalions of lawyers." [2]

This book examines, in relation to the frequently controversial role of the Supreme Court, a wide variety of such public policy issues—including abortion, gay rights, physician-assisted suicide, racial segregation, affirmative action, elections and voting,

---

[1] *Democracy in America* [Chicago 2000]: 257.
[2] *The Struggle for Judicial Supremacy* [Knopf 1941]: xi).

freedom of expression, church and state, the powers of the president, capital punishment, and the taking of private property.

The extensive commentary summarizes the basic constitutional law principles, explains the Court's function and its work, and recounts the background—and in several instances the contentious aftermath—of the principal decisions.

Each case digest sets forth the central facts, the main issue (or issues) before the Court, what the Court (that is, the majority of the Justices) concluded, and, in addition, condensations of all the opinions (including individual Justices' concurrences and dissents) filed in the case. The key passages of each opinion have been generally retained in the Justice's own words.

In the early years of the Court's history, the "Opinion of the Court" in any case was usually short by current standards and joined by all the Justices. Today, by contrast, the opinions announcing the Court's decisions are likely to be very lengthy, express the views of only a majority (and sometimes only a plurality) of the Justices, and be accompanied by several opinions of individual Justices. In addition, each opinion typically contains numerous case citations plus extensive footnotes.

As a result, particularly when a significant constitutional question is involved, it is not unusual for the opinions in a single case to exceed 100 pages in aggregate. For example, in the Court's 2003 *McConnell* decision (sustaining 5-to-4 the McCain-Feingold campaign finance legislation), eight opinions were filed, totaling 286 pages in the official report. However, in order to understand the issues in a case and the possible alternative ways of resolving those issues, it is not essential that the opinions be read in their entirety. On the other hand, newspaper accounts of Supreme Court decisions often provide only superficial reports of the Court's ultimate conclusions, with little or no explanation of the various Justices' divergent views.

In preparing the digests, I have tried to steer a middle course between those two approaches by editing the opinions to a more manageable length without sacrificing their substance. Most of the digests are relatively short. A few, because of the disputes still swirling about the issues, are somewhat longer—for example, the 2007 decision on racial balancing (*Parents Involved in Community Schools v. Seattle School District No. 1*) and the 2008 decision on Guantánamo detainees (*Boumedienne v. Bush*).

Appendix A contains a complete copy of the Constitution of the United States; provisions that are particularly relevant to the digested decisions are italicized for your convenience. Appendix B is the Index of Case Digests. Appendix C is the Table of Case References by Justice.

1

The Constitution and the Supreme Court

The Making of the Constitution

In 1781, shortly after the Revolutionary War ended (although the formal peace treaty was not signed until two years later), the 13 colonies ratified the Articles of Confederation, creating a loose confederation among the new "States" with very little power in the central government.

The Articles of Confederation declared that "each State retains its sovereignty, freedom, and independence, and every Power, Jurisdiction, and right, which is not by this confederation expressly delegated to the United States, in Congress assembled." There was no national executive or judiciary. Although there was a Congress, its powers were sharply limited; it had, for example, no power to tax or to regulate commerce among the States. When, as might have been expected, States adopted laws that discriminated against goods and services from other States and erected trade barriers to advance their own economic interests, the then-existing Congress was powerless to stop it. And, without a national executive or judiciary, there was no way to obtain compliance with laws adopted by Congress.

The Constitutional Convention met in Philadelphia from May 25 until September 17, 1787. Although the Convention's mandate was merely to propose revisions of the Articles of Confederation, the first vote at the Convention was the adoption of a resolution "that a national government ought to be established consisting of a supreme legislative, judiciary and executive." That action declared an intention to abandon, rather than just revise, the Articles of Confederation, and instead to develop a fundamentally different charter of government.

On September 17, 1787, after extensive deliberation and numerous compromises, the members of the Convention approved the proposed Constitution and (with some exceptions) returned home to fight for its ratification. One key compromise was to create two houses in Congress: one with proportional representation based on population and one in which each State would have equal representation. Another compromise was to provide for a Supreme Court and to leave it up to Congress to decide whether to create lower federal courts.

There were heated debates in many States over whether to ratify the Constitution. Support for ratification was led by the so-called "Federalists," and the most celebrated defense of the Constitution was a series of 85 essays known as "The Federalist Papers," written by Alexander Hamilton, James Madison, and John Jay. Those opposing ratification, the "Anti-Federalists," feared the enhanced powers of the new national government and the impact on the sovereignty of the States. The Anti-Federalists also objected to the absence of an enumeration of individual rights in the Constitution.

Article VII of the proposed Constitution provided that "The Ratification of the Conventions of nine States, shall be sufficient for the establishment of this Constitution between the States so ratifying the same." By June 1788, ten States had ratified, one more than the nine required by Article VII. The other three States soon followed.

Article III of the Constitution provided for establishment of a federal judiciary system, including a Supreme Court, but left the details (including the number of Justices) to determination by Congress. Article III (§1) states:

> The judicial Power of the United States, shall be vested in one supreme Court, and in such inferior Courts as the Congress may from time to time ordain and establish. The Judges, both of the supreme and inferior Courts, shall hold their Offices during good Behaviour, and shall, at stated Times, receive for their Services, a Compensation, which shall not be diminished during their Continuance in Office.

Article III (§2) specifies the types of cases over which the Supreme Court has "original jurisdiction" (cases that may be commenced in the Supreme Court rather than appealed from a lower court)—for example, actions brought by one State against another State. In all other cases, the Supreme Court is granted "appellate jurisdiction" subject to "such Exceptions and under such regulations as Congress shall make."

In the Judiciary Act of 1789, the newly formed Congress created two types of inferior courts. Thirteen district courts were created with jurisdiction over minor federal criminal cases and in areas such as admiralty and bankruptcy. Three circuit courts (the forerunners of the present courts of appeals) were established to exercise appellate jurisdiction over district court decisions and original jurisdiction in diversity cases (between citizens of different States) and major federal criminal prosecutions.

The Judiciary Act of 1789 provided that the Supreme Court would be composed of six Justices—a Chief Justice and five Associate Justices. In addition to performing their Supreme Court duties, each of the Justices was required by the Act to "ride the circuit"—to participate with local district judges as members of one of the circuit courts.

In 1789, in response to a widespread demand to supplement the original Constitution to protect individual rights from the new national government, Congress (under the leadership of James Madison, then in the House of Representatives) proposed a series of amendments known as the Bill of Rights. Congress approved 12 of the proposals, and 10 of the 12 were ratified by the States, thereby enacting Amendments 1 through 10. With Virginia's ratification on December 15, 1791, the Bill of Rights became part of the Constitution.

In addition to protecting against congressional infringement of basic liberties such as freedom of religion and freedom of speech, the Bill of Rights prescribed constitutional procedures for operation of the newly created judiciary. The Amendments required warrants for searches and seizures. A grand jury indictment was made a prerequisite to criminal trial except in certain specified instances. The Amendments barred putting any person in jeopardy twice for the same offense and compelling any person in any criminal case to be a witness against himself. Excessive bail and cruel and unusual punishments were forbidden. The right of jury trial was guaranteed in most civil cases. Private property could not be taken for public use without just compensation to the owners. And (in language that in 1868 was also included in the Fourteenth Amendment) the Fifth Amendment provided that no person shall be deprived of "life, liberty, or property, without due process of law."

Since 1791, 17 more Amendments have been added to the Constitution. Clearly the most important are the Reconstruction Amendments adopted after the Civil War. They fundamentally changed the nature of the Constitution and the function of the Supreme Court. Not only did the Reconstruction Amendments repudiate the original document's implicit acceptance of slavery, but what had been a document that (with very few exceptions) only protected individuals against action by the national government was now expanded to include important protection against action *by the States* as well.

The Early Years of the Supreme Court

The power and prestige of the Supreme Court, as we view it today, were certainly not foreseen by the Framers of the Constitution.

In 1788, in the *Federalist Papers* (No. 78), Alexander Hamilton declared that "the judiciary is beyond comparison the weakest of the three departments of power." "The Executive," he pointed out, "not only dispenses the honors, but holds the sword of the community. The legislature not only commands the purse, but prescribes the rules by which the duties and rights of every citizen are to be regulated. *The judiciary, on the contrary, has no influence over either the sword or the purse. . . .*" (Italics added.)

At its beginning, the Supreme Court had very little to do, and appointment to the Court was not regarded as a particularly great honor. One reason was that, in addition to performing their other duties, Supreme Court Justices were required to "ride circuit." (This "circuit-riding" requirement was not fully eliminated until 1891.)

Congress increased the number of Justices from six to seven in 1807, to nine in 1837, and to ten in 1864. In 1866, Congress reduced the number to seven. In 1869, after Ulysses Grant succeeded the unpopular Andrew Johnson as President, Congress increased the number to nine, where it has remained ever since. (A quorum requires participation by six Justices.)

The Supreme Court was first convened in February 1790 in the Merchants Exchange Building in New York City, then the nation's Capitol. The Court heard and decided its first case in 1792.

In the Court's early years, getting someone to be Chief Justice proved to be difficult; it seemed that no one really wanted the job. The first Chief Justice was John Jay; he resigned in 1795 to become governor of New York. Alexander Hamilton declined Washington's offer to take Jay's place. Washington then gave John Rutledge a recess appointment while Congress was not in session and Rutledge briefly served as Chief Justice, but the Senate refused to confirm him. Washington then appointed William Cushing, who was immediately confirmed by the Senate but declined to accept. Washington then offered the post to Patrick Henry, who declined because of age. Washington then appointed Oliver Ellsworth, who presided over the Court until his retirement in 1800.

Washington's successor, John Adams, offered the position once again to John Jay, and Jay's nomination was confirmed by the Senate. But on learning of the nomination,

Jay sent a letter to Adams declining the office. Jay blamed the Court's failure to "acquire the public confidence and respect which, as the last resort of the justice of the nation, it should possess." Jay's letter to Adams arrived only a few weeks before Adams's term was to end and before Thomas Jefferson was to take office. Adams then turned to his Secretary of State, John Marshall, who accepted the appointment and served as Chief Justice for 35 years, until 1835.

Marshall was the first Chief Justice to preside over the Supreme Court when the government moved to Washington. Since no provision had been made for a separate building for the Court, it was obliged to conduct its sessions in one of the rooms on the first floor of the Capitol. The room assigned to the Court, and in which it met until 1808, was located on the ground floor of the north wing, adjacent to the main staircase. Benjamin Latrobe, the Capitol architect, described it as noisy, "a half-finished committee room meanly furnished, and very inconvenient." Even these quarters were not reserved for the Supreme Court exclusively but had to be shared with the other courts of the District of Columbia. Initially there was no bench for the Justices, and they sat at individual desks placed on a raised platform. In addition, the Court then had no library, no office space, and no clerks or secretaries.[1] Despite this inauspicious start, "It was to the efforts of Marshall, over a period of more than a third of a century, that the establishment of the prestige of the highest tribunal in the land was largely due."[2]

The Work of the Supreme Court

The current members of the Court are Chief Justice John G. Roberts and Associate Justices John Paul Stevens, Antonin E. Scalia, Anthony M. Kennedy, Stephen G. Breyer, Ruth Bader Ginsburg, David H. Souter, Clarence Thomas, and Samuel A. Alito.

Each year the Court's term begins the first Monday in October and usually ends in mid-June.

Almost all Supreme Court cases are appeals from decisions of the lower courts. (There is also occasionally a case invoking the Court's "original jurisdiction"—typically involving a controversy between two or more States, such as a boundary dispute.)

The issues in these appeals may be either *constitutional* (involving the interpretation of the United States Constitution) or *nonconstitutional* (typically involving the interpretation of a federal statute).

The cases come from either a federal court or a state court.

(1) *Federal court route*—A federal action is tried in a U.S. District Court (number of districts: 94; number of judges: 651). The loser may take his or her case to the appropriate U.S. Court of Appeals (12 circuits, 179 judges). For example, Chicago is located in the Northern District of Illinois, which is one of seven judicial districts in the Seventh Circuit (which includes Illinois, Wisconsin, and Indiana).

(2) *State court route*—Decisions of state courts can be appealed to the Supreme Court only if they involve a "federal question," such as the validity of a state statute under the U.S. Constitution, or an alleged violation of a federal constitutional right, or the interpretation of a federal statute. (Thus, a state court decision construing a *state* constitution or statute—for example, the May 2008 decision of the California Supreme Court interpreting the California constitution to require recognition of same-sex marriage in California—is *not* reviewable by the U.S. Supreme Court.)

---

[1] Jean Edward Smith, *John Marshall: Definer of a Nation* [Henry Holt 1996]: 285–286.
[2] Carl Swisher, *American Constitutional Development* [Houghton Mifflin 1943]: 99.

From both routes, a case comes to the Supreme Court (with only a few exceptions) on a "petition for a writ of certiorari"—a brief that sets forth the arguments of the "petitioner" (the party that lost below) why the Court should accept the case for review. The "respondent" (the party that won below) then files a brief setting forth the arguments why review should be denied.

The Court has full discretion to decide which certiorari petitions it will grant and which it will deny. If four Justices (note that a majority is not required) vote to take the case, the petition is granted and the case is scheduled for oral argument (except in a few instances in which the Court summarily affirms or reverses without argument). Otherwise the petition is denied.

If the petition is denied, the denial is *not* a decision "on the merits." It does not mean that the Court agrees with the decision below; it means only that, for whatever reasons, there were not four Justices voting to take the case. Contrary to a widely held misconception, the primary criterion for accepting or denying review is *not* the Justices' view about the correctness of the decision.

Instead, the Court generally accepts only cases presenting questions of federal constitutional or statutory law of general interest: (1) cases raising a federal law question on which a conflict has developed between U.S. Courts of Appeals; (2) cases in which the lower court reached a decision in conflict with governing Supreme Court precedents; and (3) cases that for other reasons present an unusually important issue of federal law.

Over 8,000 certiorari petitions are filed each year. Approximately 2,000 are "paid" petitions (there is a $300 docketing fee). The other petitions—about 6,000 each year—are "in forma pauperis" petitions filed without fee, almost entirely by prisoners complaining of claimed errors in their trials.

Very few certiorari petitions are granted, only about *one percent.*

If certiorari is granted, briefs "on the merits" are filed by the parties on both sides and oral argument is then scheduled. (The petitioner files his or her brief first; the respondent then files a brief answering the petitioner's brief; and the petitioner then gets to file a "reply brief.") Usually only one hour per case—30 minutes for each side—is allowed for oral argument.

After the oral arguments are heard, the Justices meet to decide the cases argued that week. In each case, if the Chief Justice voted with the majority, he determines who among those voting with the majority (including himself) should draft the majority opinion. If the Chief Justice voted with the minority, the most senior Justice in the majority assigns the majority opinion.

If a Justice agrees with the result reached by the majority but bases his or her vote on different grounds (or joins the majority opinion but wishes to express additional views), the Justice may choose to write a separate concurring opinion. And, of course, any Justice who is opposed to the majority's conclusion may choose to file a dissenting opinion.

When the drafting of the opinions is completed, the decision is announced at a public session of the Court and copies are then distributed.

In the 2007–2008 term, the Court issued 67 merits opinions, the lowest number since the 1953–1954 term. The 67 opinions decided 71 cases (including two summary reversals and two summary affirmances without argument). Seventeen percent were decided by a 5-4 vote, compared with approximately twice that percentage in the previous term. In 46 of the merits opinion cases (approximately two-thirds, slightly less than the previous term), the Court reversed or vacated the lower court decision; in approximately one-third, the Court affirmed the lower court decision.

Constitutional Interpretation

How should the Constitution be interpreted?

In a 1936 opinion, Justice Owen Roberts suggested a simple test: "When an act of Congress is appropriately challenged in the courts as not conforming to the constitutional mandate, the judicial branch of the Government has only one duty,—to lay the article of the Constitution which is invoked beside the statute which is challenged and to decide whether the latter squares with the former." United States v. Butler, 297 U.S. 1, 62-63 (1936).

Similarly, in the 2005 Senate Judiciary Committee hearings on his appointment as Chief Justice, John Roberts compared the Supreme Court's function to umpiring in a baseball game. "Judges," he said, "are like umpires. Umpires don't make the rules; they apply them."

In like vein, in the 2004 presidential campaign, *both* the Democratic and Republican candidates promised to appoint Justices who would "apply the law, not create it."

But what is "the law"? Perhaps on some more technical subjects (for example, taxes or estate planning), lawyers can sometimes agree on what is "the law." And on some constitutional questions the answer may be crystal clear. However, in many other cases, as shown by the large number of Supreme Court concurring and dissenting opinions, there may be two or more seemingly reasonable answers. Constitutional interpretation thus involves a process far more complex than either calling balls and strikes or laying a constitutional provision beside a challenged statute.

The root of the matter is the degree of discretion that individual Justices have in deciding cases.

One reason for this is that a typical constitutional case presents not only conventional "legal" issues but also intertwined issues of public policy.

Another reason is that much of the Constitution is written in sweeping language such as "due process," "equal protection," "freedom of speech," "establishment of religion," and "commerce among the states." This kind of language requires interpretation as applied to specific cases and frequently leaves considerable room for good faith disagreement.

Justices may also differ on the proper weight to be given to the text in interpreting the Constitution.[3] No Justice, of course, would deny that the text is relevant, but there is a wide spectrum of views on how controlling it should be.

So-called "textualists" contend that the interpretation of the Constitution should be guided primarily by what the public understood the text to mean when it was ratified; that fundamental changes should be made only through the formal amendment process specified in Article V; and that to ignore the limitations of the text is to convert the Court into a "third legislative chamber." Others, embracing a broader approach (sometimes characterized as "non-interpretivism" or the "living constitution" theory),

---

[3] In this text the term "interpretation" is used in its popular sense of referring to the process of deciding constitutional cases. For purposes of more precise analysis, some commentators choose to use the term "interpretation" more narrowly; they distinguish between "interpretation" and "construction"—using the term "interpretation" to refer to the threshold function of ascertaining the semantic meaning of legal documents, and using the term "construction" to refer to the function of then constructing the legal rules to apply the text to concrete fact situations.

contend that the amendment process is too difficult—and the political branches too unresponsive—to make needed reforms; that the meaning and application of constitutional provisions must evolve; and that interpretation of the Constitution must include reliance on modern values that were not within the contemplation of the Framers or ratifiers. Each side of this controversy vigorously assails the other. For example, textualists charge "living constitutionalists" with seeking to override the Constitution by substituting the policy choices of unelected and unaccountable judges, while living constitutionalists accuse textualists of lacking the flexibility that a changing society requires. These themes have been developed, defended, and attacked in myriad variations.[4]

Differences may exist not only on the primacy of the text but also on (among other factors) the weight that should be given to the views of the document's drafters ("original intent"),[5] the post-enactment history of the text ("tradition"),[6] and the prior decisions of the Court (*stare decisis*).[7]

A Justice may also, of course, be influenced, consciously or unconsciously, by his or her personal ideology—particularly a Justice's view of the proper role of the Supreme Court in a democratic society. Small wonder, then, that any nominee for the Supreme Court will be subjected to rigorous examination in Senate confirmation hearings. But in many instances, once Justices are confirmed, the independence provided by life tenure and the constraints of the Court's traditions tend to subordinate the influence of their private predilections.

That is why many Presidents have subsequently been disappointed with their appointments to the Court. For example, Chief Justice Earl Warren and Justice William Brennan, regarded as among the most liberal Justices to ever serve on the Court, were appointed by a Republican president, Dwight Eisenhower, who later said that the two appointments were the worst mistakes he ever made. Five Republican appointees joined the majority decision in *Roe v. Wade* establishing a right of abortion, and the Court's opinion was written by Justice Harry Blackmun, a Nixon appointee; and Chief Justice Warren Burger, also a Nixon appointee, wrote the Court's opinion unanimously rejecting Nixon's objection to the Watergate subpoena in United States v. Nixon, 418 U.S. 683 (1974). And Justice Felix Frankfurter, an FDR appointee, was widely criticized for having allegedly abandoned his liberal convictions. The history of the Court abounds with similar examples.

As Justice Frankfurter pointed out:[8]

---

[4]E.g., Christopher Wolfe, *The Rise of Modern Judicial Review: From Constitutional Interpretation to Judge-Made Law* [Basic Books 1986]; John Hart Ely, *Democracy and Distrust: A Theory of Judicial Review* [Harvard 1980]; Alexander Bickel, *The Least Dangerous Branch: The Supreme Court at the Bar of Politics* [Bobbs-Merrill 1962]; Antonin Scalia, *A Matter of Interpretation: Federal Courts and the Law* [Princeton 1997]; Stephen Breyer, *Active Liberty: Interpreting Our Democratic Constitution* [Knopf 2005]; Richard Posner, *Law, Pragmatism, and Democracy* [Harvard 2003]; Leonard Levy, *Original Intent and the Framers' Constitution* [Macmillan 1988]; Randy Barnett, *Restoring the Lost Constitution: The Presumption of Liberty* [Princeton 2004]; Herman Belz, *A Living Constitution or Fundamental Law? American Constitutionalism in Historical Perspective* [Rowman & Littlefield 1998]; Raoul Berger, *Government by Judiciary: The Transformation of the Fourteenth Amendment* [Harvard 1977]; Daniel Farber and Suzanna Sherry, *Desperately Seeking Certainty: The Misguided Quest for Constitutional Foundations* [Chicago 2002].
[5]Compare, e.g., Robert Bork, *The Tempting of America: The Political Seduction of the Law* [Simon & Schuster 1990]: 133–178, with Leonard Levy, *Original Intent and the Framers' Constitution* [Macmillan 1988]: 1–29, 322–398.
[6]Compare, e.g., Michael H. v. Gerald D., 491 U.S. 110, 124-128 (1989), with John Hart Ely, *Democracy and Distrust: A Theory of Judicial Review* [Harvard 1980]: 60–63.
[7]See comment "The Amendment Process and *Stare Decisis*" in Chapter 2.
[8]Felix Frankfurter, *Of Law and Men* [Harcourt Brace 1956]: 40–41.

It is asked with sophomoric brightness, does a man cease to be himself when he becomes a Justice? Does he change his character by putting on a gown? No, he does not change his character. He brings his whole experience, his training, his outlook, his social, intellectual, and moral environment with him when he takes a seat on the supreme bench. But a judge worth his salt is in the grip of his function. . . . To assume that a lawyer who becomes a judge takes on the bench merely his views on social or economic questions leaves out of account his rooted notions regarding the scope and limits of a judge's authority. The outlook of a lawyer fit to be a Justice regarding the role of a judge cuts across all his personal preferences for this or that social arrangement.

For example, Justice Oliver Wendell Holmes was politically conservative and doubted the wisdom of social welfare legislation enacted in the early twentieth century, and yet he voted to uphold the constitutionality of such laws. In a letter to a friend, he wrote: "It has given me great pleasure to sustain the constitutionality of laws that I believe to be as bad as possible, because I thereby helped to mark the difference between what I would forbid and what the Constitution permits." [9]

Holmes, however, did not deny there is a proper—albeit limited—role for creativity in judging. As he stated in Southern Pacific Co. v. Jensen, 244 U.S. 205, 221 (1917): "I recognize without hesitation that *judges must and do legislate, but they do so only interstitially.*" (Italics added.) In his celebrated 1921 lectures *The Nature of the Judicial Process,* [10] Benjamin Cardozo concurred: "We must not throw to the winds the advantages of consistency and uniformity to do justice in the instance. *We must keep within those interstitial limits.* . . ." Comparing the limits on legislators and judges, Cardozo pointed out:

> No doubt the limits for the judge are narrower. *He legislates only between gaps. He fills the open spaces in the law.* . . . Even within the gaps, restrictions not easy to define, but felt, however impalpable they may be, by every judge and lawyer, hedge and circumscribe his action.

Cardozo added that "In countless litigations, the law is so clear that judges have no discretion. They have the right to *legislate within gaps,* but often there are no gaps," but that "there is often *greater freedom of choice in the construction of constitutions* than in that of ordinary statutes. Constitutions are more likely to enunciate general principles, which must be worked out and applied thereafter to particular conditions." (Italics added.)

No doubt most Justices would agree with the general principles expounded by Holmes and Cardozo, and yet differ among themselves in applying these principles in particular cases—in determining when there is a "gap" justifying the exercise of judicial discretion and, if so, how it should be filled. The result has been a continuous but uncertain evolution of what we call "the law."

---

[9]Letter to John T. Morse, Jr., November 28, 1926, Oliver Wendell Holmes Papers.
[10][Dover 2005]: 67, 99, 109–110, 125.

2

From *Marbury* to Reconstruction

Marbury v. Madison, 5 U.S. 137 (1803)

FACTS: On February 27, 1801, less than a week before John Adams was succeeded by Thomas Jefferson as President, the lame-duck Federalist Congress passed a statute authorizing the President to appoint justices of the peace in the District of Columbia. On March 2, two days before his term expired, Adams made 42 appointments to that office, and the appointments were confirmed by the Senate the following day. Adams immediately signed the commissions, and John Marshall, then still acting as the Secretary of State, affixed the Great Seal of the United States. However, in the last-minute rush of the transition, the commissions were not delivered.

When Jefferson assumed office, he found them lying on a table in the State Department and directed that they not be delivered. Instead, Jefferson decided to reduce the number of justices of peace from 42 to 30 and gave recess appointments to 30 persons, including 25 of those originally named by Adams, plus five of his own choosing. One of those originally appointed by Adams but not given a Jefferson recess appointment was William Marbury, a prominent Federalist businessman.

Marbury filed a petition in the Supreme Court requesting the Court to issue a writ of mandamus to compel James Madison, Jefferson's Secretary of State, to deliver the Marbury commission signed by Adams. In response to Marbury's petition, the Court issued an order directing Madison to show cause why the requested writ of mandamus should not be granted; Madison, however, ignored the order. The Court conducted a trial on the factual questions presented by Marbury's petition; again Madison declined to participate (although several other officials of the Jefferson administration testified at the trial).

ISSUES: (1) Does Marbury have a right to the commission? (2) If so, and if that right has been violated, is the Secretary of State subject to a court order to deliver the commission? (3) If so, does the Supreme Court have the power to grant such an order?

DECISION (unanimous opinion by *Marshall*): (1) *Yes;* (2) *Yes;* (3) *No* [on the ground that Article III of the Constitution did not authorize Congress to grant the Supreme Court the power to issue a writ of mandamus in the exercise of its original jurisdiction].

(1) *Whether Marbury has a right to the commission*—Mr. Marbury's commission was signed by the President and sealed by the Secretary of State, and the law creating the office gave Mr. Marbury a right to hold the office for five years, independent of the executive. The appointment was therefore not revocable but vested in the officer legal rights that are protected by the laws of his country.

(2) *Whether Marbury is entitled to a remedy to enforce his vested right*—Under the Constitution, the President is invested with certain important political powers, in the exercise of which he is to use his own discretion, and is accountable only to his country in his political character and to his own conscience. To aid him in the performance of these duties, he is authorized to appoint certain officers who act by his authority. In such cases, their acts are his acts; and whatever opinion may be entertained of the manner in which executive discretion may be used, still there exists no power to control that discretion.

But when Congress imposes on that officer other duties, when he is directed peremptorily to perform certain acts, when the rights of individuals are dependent on the performance of those acts, he is amenable to the laws for his conduct and cannot at his discretion sport away the vested rights of others.

We therefore conclude that Mr. Marbury, having already obtained legal title to the office, has a consequent right to the commission, and a refusal to deliver the commission is a plain violation of that right, for which the laws of his country afford him a remedy.

(3) *Whether the Supreme Court can grant a remedy*—The answer to this question depends on (a) the nature of the writ applied for (mandamus) and (b) the jurisdiction of the Supreme Court.

(a) The Secretary of State was directed by law to do an act affecting the rights of individuals, and mandamus is the appropriate remedy for violation of these rights.

(b) In §13 of the Judiciary Act of 1789, after setting forth the scope of the original jurisdiction of the Supreme Court, Congress further provided that

> The Supreme Court shall also have appellate jurisdiction from the circuit courts and courts of the several states . . . ; and shall have power to issue . . . writs of mandamus, in cases warranted by the principles and usages of law, to any . . . persons holding office, under the authority of the United States.

The Secretary of State, being a person holding office under the authority of the United States, is precisely within the letter of that description, and if this Court is not authorized to issue a writ of mandamus to such an officer, it must be because the law is unconstitutional.

Under Article III of the Constitution, the Supreme Court's "original jurisdiction" is limited to "Cases affecting Ambassadors, other public Ministers and Consuls, and those in which a State shall be Party," and in all other Cases "the Supreme Court shall have appellate jurisdiction." It is the essential nature of appellate jurisdiction that it involves review of proceedings previously commenced in a lower court. To issue a writ of mandamus to a government officer to compel delivery of a paper is the same as permitting an original action for that paper, and therefore would not be an exercise of appellate jurisdiction. It therefore becomes necessary to inquire whether a jurisdiction so conferred can be constitutionally exercised.

Either (1) the Constitution is a superior, paramount law, unchangeable by ordinary means, or (2) it is on a level with ordinary legislative acts and is alterable whenever

Congress shall please to alter it. If the first alternative is correct, then a legislative act contrary to the Constitution is not law; if the second alternative is correct, then written constitutions are absurd attempts, on the part of the people, to limit a power in its own nature illimitable.

Certainly all those who have framed written constitutions contemplate them as forming the fundamental and paramount law of the nation, and consequently, the theory of every such government must be that an act of the legislature, if it is repugnant to the constitution, is void. This theory is essentially attached to a written constitution and is, consequently, to be considered, by this court, as one of the fundamental principles of our society.

It is emphatically the province and duty of the judicial department to say what the law is. Those who apply the rule to particular cases must of necessity expound and interpret that rule. If two laws conflict with each other, the courts must decide on the operation of each.

So if a law is inconsistent with the Constitution—if both the law and the Constitution apply to a particular case, so that the case must be decided conformably to the law, disregarding the Constitution, or conformably to the Constitution, disregarding the law—a court must determine which of these conflicting rules governs the case. This is the very essence of judicial duty.

Those then who controvert the principle that the Constitution is to be considered, in court, as a paramount law are reduced to the necessity of maintaining that courts must close their eyes on the Constitution and see only the law. This doctrine would subvert the very foundation of all written constitutions. It would declare that an act which, according to the principles and theory of our government, is entirely void is yet, in practice, completely obligatory. It would declare that if the legislature shall do what is expressly forbidden, such act, notwithstanding the express prohibition, is in reality effectual. It is prescribing limits, and at the same time declaring that those limits may be passed at pleasure.

That it thus reduces to nothing what we have deemed the greatest improvement on political institutions—a written constitution—would of itself be sufficient in America, where written constitutions have been viewed with so much reverence, for rejecting the construction. But the peculiar expressions of the Constitution furnish additional arguments in favor of its rejection.

The judicial power of the United States is extended to all cases arising under the Constitution. Could it be the intention of those who gave this power to say that in using it the Constitution should not be looked into? That a case arising under the Constitution should be decided without examining the instrument under which it arises? This is too extravagant to be maintained.

In some cases, then, the Constitution must be looked into by the judges. And if they can open it at all, what part of it are they forbidden to obey?

There are many other parts of the Constitution that serve to illustrate this subject. It is declared, for example, that "no tax or duty shall be laid on articles exported from any state." Suppose a duty on the export of cotton, of tobacco, or of flour and a suit instituted to recover it. Ought the judges to close their eyes on the Constitution and only see the law?

The Constitution declares that "no bill of attainder or ex post facto law shall be passed." If, however, such a bill should be passed, and a person should be prosecuted under it, must the court condemn to death those victims whom the Constitution endeavors to preserve?

"No person," says the Constitution, "shall be convicted of treason unless on the testimony of two witnesses to the same overt act, or on confession in open court." Here the language of the Constitution is addressed especially to the courts. It prescribes, directly for them, a rule of evidence not to be departed from. If the legislature should change that rule, and declare *one* witness, or a confession *out* of court, sufficient for conviction, must the constitutional principle yield to the legislative act?

From these, and many other selections that might be made, it is apparent that the Framers of the Constitution contemplated that instrument as a rule for the government of *courts,* as well as of the legislature.

Why otherwise does it direct the judges to take an oath to support it? This oath certainly applies to their conduct in their official character. How immoral to impose it on them, if they were to be used as the instruments, and the knowing instruments, for violating what they swear to support?

It is also not entirely unworthy of observation that, in declaring what shall be the *supreme* law of the land, the *Constitution* itself is first mentioned, and not the laws of the United States generally, but those only which shall be made in *pursuance* of the Constitution have that rank.

Accordingly, the writ of mandamus sought by Marbury is denied.

*****

[*Note:* For 54 years after the *Marbury* decision, until the 1857 decision (digested later in this chapter) in *Scott v. Sandford,* the Supreme Court did not declare another Act of Congress unconstitutional.

However, in the period between *Marbury* and *Scott,* several statutes enacted by *state* legislatures were held unconstitutional by the Court. E.g., Fletcher v. Peck, 10 U.S. 87 (1810); Martin v. Hunter's Lessee, 14 U.S. 304 (1816); McCulloch v. Maryland, 17 U.S. 316 (1819); Cohens v. Virginia, 19 U.S. 264 (1821).]

Judicial Review and Judicial Supremacy

The Supreme Court's status as the ultimate arbiter of the interpretation of the Constitution and the constitutional validity of any statute, federal or state, is today firmly established. But that has not always been the case with respect to an Act of Congress.

The "Supremacy Clause" of the Constitution (Article VI) provides that "This Constitution, and the Laws of the United States . . . shall be the supreme Law of the Land . . . *any Thing in the Constitution or Laws of any state to the Contrary notwithstanding.*" By clear implication, in any case in which the "Laws of any state" conflict with the federal Constitution or laws, the Supreme Court is required by the Supremacy Clause to treat the federal Constitution as superior and treat the state law as void—in short, to hold the state law unconstitutional.

But what about laws enacted by Congress? Although the Supremacy Clause makes the federal Constitution and laws superior to state laws, the Constitution says nothing about the Supreme Court's authority to treat an Act of Congress as void. And, even more importantly, it does not answer the far more fundamental question *whether such a decision is binding on Congress and the Executive*—two supposedly coequal branches.

The Founding Fathers expressed divergent views on the subject. In the *Federalist Papers* (No. 78, 1788), Alexander Hamilton argued that judicial enforcement of constitutional limitations on the legislature was indispensable to the new government:

> Limitations of this kind [imposed by the Constitution] can be preserved in practice no other way than through the medium of courts of justice, whose duty it must be to declare all acts contrary to the manifest tenor of the Constitution void. Without this, all the reservations of particular rights or privileges would amount to nothing. . . .
>
> There is no position which depends on clearer principles, than that every act of a delegated authority, contrary to the tenor of the commission under which it is exercised, is void. No legislative act, therefore, contrary to the Constitution, can be valid. To deny this, would be to affirm, that the deputy is greater than his principal; that the servant is above his master; that the representatives of the people are superior to the people themselves; that men acting by virtue of powers, may do not only what their powers do not authorize, but what they forbid. . . .
>
> It is far more rational to suppose, that the courts were designed to be an intermediate body between the people and the legislature, in order, among other things, to keep the latter within the limits assigned to their authority. The interpretation of the laws is the proper and peculiar province of the courts. A constitution is, in fact, and must be regarded by the judges, as a fundamental law. It therefore belongs to them to ascertain its meaning, as well as the meaning of any particular act proceeding from the legislative body. If there should happen to be an irreconcilable variance between the two, that which has the superior obligation and validity ought, of course, to be preferred; or, in other words, the Constitution ought to be preferred to the statute, the intention of the people to the intention of their agents.

James Madison, the "Father of the Constitution" (also one of Hamilton's coauthors of the *Federalist Papers* and later President), took positions on both sides of the issue. In 1788, Madison objected that Hamilton's view would make "the Judiciary Department paramount in fact to the Legislature, which was never intended, and can never be proper."

Yet the following year, in explaining his proposed Bill of Rights amendments to the Constitution, Madison stated: "If they are incorporated into the Constitution, independent tribunals of justice will . . . be an impenetrable bulwark against every assumption of power in the legislative or executive [branch]."

Still later, Madison returned to his earlier view that the courts could not bind the other two branches in interpreting the Constitution. He insisted "that the meaning of the Constitution may as well be ascertained by the legislative as by the judicial authority," and he denied that "any one department draws from the Court greater powers than another, in marking out the limits of the powers of several departments."

Thomas Jefferson, even more emphatically than Madison, opposed any doctrine of judicial review that would make the Court's decisions binding on Congress or the President. Jefferson contended (1801) that each of the three branches

> must have a right in cases which arise within the line of its proper functions, where, equally with the others, it acts in the last resort and without appeal, to decide on the validity of an act according to its own judgment, and uncontrolled by the opinions of any other department.

Jefferson also contended (1804) that "[N]othing in the Constitution has given . . . [the judges] a right to decide for the Executive, more than the Executive to decide for them. Both magistracies are equally independent in the sphere of action assigned to them."

A few went considerably further, arguing (perhaps influenced by the British system that does not allow judicial review of an Act of Parliament) that it is illegitimate for the courts to even question the constitutionality of an Act of Congress.[1] According to this view, the judiciary is not superior to the legislature, and the courts' only proper function is to settle rights between litigants—not to protect the people against alleged abuses of legislative powers.

For example, John Mercer (a Maryland delegate to the Constitutional Convention) "disapproved of the Doctrine that the Judges as expositors of the Constitution should have authority to declare a law void. He thought laws ought to be well and cautiously made, and then to be uncontroulable [*sic*]." Charles Pinckney (who had represented South Carolina at the Convention) contended: "On no subject am I more convinced, that it is an unsafe and dangerous doctrine in a republic, ever to suppose that a judge ought to possess the right of questioning or deciding upon the constitutionality of treaties, laws, or any act of the legislature." Similarly, Senator John Breckenridge (a key Jefferson adviser and later Jefferson's Attorney General) declared that

> The Constitution intended a separation of the powers vested in the three great departments, giving to each *exclusive* authority on the subjects committed to it. . . . The construction of one department of the powers vested in it, is of higher authority than the construction of any other department. *The Legislature have the exclusive right to interpret the Constitution, in what regards the law-making power, and the judges are bound to execute the laws they make.* (Italics added.)

That view was rejected by the Supreme Court in *Marbury v. Madison*. Chief Justice Marshall (in an analysis similar to Hamilton's *Federalist* No. 78) explained that the Court's function necessarily includes the authority to consider the constitutionality of an Act of Congress in cases coming before it:

> It is emphatically the province and duty of the judicial department to say what the law is. Those who apply the rule to particular cases must of necessity expound and interpret that rule. If two laws conflict with each other, the courts must decide on the operation of each.
>
> So if a law is inconsistent with the Constitution—if both the law and the Constitution apply to a particular case, so that the case must be decided conformably to the law, disregarding the Constitution; or conformably to the Constitution, disregarding the law—a court must determine which of these conflicting rules governs the case. This is the very essence of judicial duty.

The decision is of critical importance in the Court's history because it brilliantly expounded the principle of judicial *review*—that an Act of Congress in conflict with the Constitution will not be enforced by the Court. Based on dubious Supreme Court lore,[2] some have contended that *Marbury* also established the modern principle of judicial *supremacy*—that Congress and the President must defer to the Court's

---

[1]The fullest exposition of this doctrine of legislative supremacy in early American history was made by Chief Justice John B. Gibson of the Pennsylvania Supreme Court in Eakin v. Raub, 12 Sergeant & Rawle (Pa.) 330, 343-358 (1825) (dissenting opinion). Although directly concerned only with the Pennsylvania Constitution, Chief Justice Gibson sought to refute Marshall's *Marbury* analysis of judicial review.

[2]A principal source appears to be Albert J. Beveridge, *The Life of John Marshall* [Houghton Mifflin 1916]: Vol. III, 131–132.

decision. But Marshall's opinion provides no substantial basis for such an expansive reading.[3]

The opinion persuasively rejects the argument that, if a conflict arises between an Act of Congress and a provision of the Constitution, "the courts must close their eyes on the Constitution" and "the constitution should not be looked into" in "determining which of these conflicting rules govern the case." But nowhere in the opinion does Marshall assert (contrary to Jefferson's "tripartite" theory) that a judicial interpretation of the Constitution is binding on the other two branches:[4]

- Supporters of a broader reading rely on Marshall's statement that "the province and duty of the judicial department [is] to say what the law is" and to "expound and interpret" legal rules. But that statement merely describes in a very general way what most courts do, quite apart from the effect on the other institutions of government.

- Consistently with Jefferson's theory that each of the three branches may independently interpret the Constitution, the provision that the Court held unconstitutional in *Marbury* related only to the jurisdiction of the judiciary and invalidating the provision did not reduce the power or independence of Congress or the President.

- Not surprisingly, therefore, Marshall's comments on judicial review produced hardly a ripple of protest from Jefferson (although he objected to Marshall's criticism of Jefferson's failure to deliver the commissions) or from newspapers supporting the Jefferson administration.

- Nor is there any external evidence that Marshall intended or expected that the *Marbury* exposition of judicial review would lead to the modern doctrine of judicial supremacy.[5]

Nearly three decades later, the Attorney General under President Andrew Jackson (Roger Taney, later Chief Justice) opined in Jeffersonian terms (1832):

> Whatever may be the force of the decision of the Supreme Court in binding the parties and settling their rights in the particular case before them, I am not prepared to admit that a construction given to the constitution by the Supreme Court in deciding in any one or more cases fixes of itself irrevocably [*sic*] and permanently its construction in that particular and binds the states and the Legislative and executive branches of the General government, forever afterwards to conform to it and adopt it in every other case as the true reading of the instrument although all of them may unite in believing it erroneous.

And, presumably in reliance on his Attorney General's opinion, President Jackson vetoed the bill to recharter the Bank of the United States, stating (1832): "The opinion of the judges has no more authority over Congress than the opinion of Congress has over the judges, and on that point the President is independent of both."

---

[3]Unlike this text, some commentary uses the term "judicial supremacy" interchangeably with the term "judicial review." E.g., Charles G. Haines, *The American Doctrine of Judicial Supremacy* [Russell & Russell rev. ed. 1959], and Robert Jackson, *The Struggle for Judicial Supremacy* [Knopf 1941]. Both authors implicitly accept the premise that the Court's decisions are binding on the other two branches. Jackson uses the term "judicial supremacy" perjoratively to describe what Jackson regards as the *abuse* of judicial review in the New Deal era.

[4]See, e.g., Leonard Levy, *Original Intent and the Framers' Constitution* [MacMillan 1988]: 77; Robert L. Clinton, *Marbury v. Madison and Judicial Review* [University Press of Kansas 1989]; Randy Barnett, *Restoring the Lost Constitution: The Presumption of Liberty* [Princeton 2004]: 143–144; Jean Edward Smith, *John Marshall: Definer of a Nation* [Henry Holt 1996]: 323, 326.

[5]See, e.g., Smith, *John Marshall: Definer of a Nation,* at 326: "With the decision in *Marbury v. Madison,* Marshall was neither embarking on a crusade for judicial supremacy, nor was he charting new territory."

Abraham Lincoln's position was similar. When the Supreme Court announced its *Dred Scott* decision (holding that Congress had no power to regulate slavery), Lincoln (1857) denied that the decision had "established a settled doctrine for the country." After his election, in his First Inaugural Address (1861), Lincoln declared that

> the candid citizen must confess that if the policy of the Government upon vital questions affecting the whole people is to be irrevocably fixed by decisions of the Supreme Court, the instant they are made in ordinary litigation between parties in personal actions, the people will have ceased to be their own rulers, having to that extent practically resigned their Government into the hands of that eminent tribunal.

Unquestionably Marshall's *Marbury* opinion was a major step in the evolution that ultimately led to the Supreme Court's present status as the "first among equals" and the final arbiter in the interpretation of the Constitution. But that development reflects *what the case has now come to stand for*—not what the case actually decided. It was not until well after the Civil War that the more sweeping Hamiltonian view of judicial supremacy (rather than the Jeffersonian "tripartitite" view) became generally accepted and regarded today as if it had always been an integral part of our constitutional system.

What accounts for this evolution? Some of the many contributing factors probably include: (1) the Supreme Court's growing stature among the three branches (enhanced by periodic acrimonious disputes between Presidents and Congress); (2) the widespread perception of the Court as an impartial tribunal engaged in "finding the law"; (3) implicit recognition of the utter impracticality of conflicting "co-equal" constitutional interpretations and the need for a single definitive determination; and (4) the Court's having *chronologically* the "last word" on disputed constitutional issues, since its decisions are typically made after the other branches have offered their interpretations.

By upholding the authority of the Supreme Court to pass on the constitutionality of an Act of Congress, *Marbury* planted the seed that later generations cultivated to become the now widely accepted doctrine of judicial supremacy.

The Slavery Legacy

William Gladstone, the great British statesman and prime minister, described the American Constitution as "the most wonderful work ever struck off at a given time by the brain and purpose of man." [6] It is now the oldest written constitution in the world and has deeply influenced every later attempt to draft a democratically based constitution. It has survived the tribulations of practical politics, the holocaust of the Civil War, and the unrelenting tides of social and economic change.

But the Constitution, even after it was amended in 1791 to add the Bill of Rights, remained a deeply flawed document. This is scarcely surprising in view of the fundamental differences among the 13 original States and the need to reconcile those differences through a series of often painful compromises.

The most famous of these was the so-called Connecticut Compromise, the agreement reached between the larger States and the smaller ones concerning the composition of Congress. Under the compromise, seats in the House of Representatives would be allocated among the States on the basis of their population, but each State regardless of its population would have two members in the Senate.

---

[6]Article in the *North American Review* (September 1878).

The Framers' most infamous compromises, however, were made on the subject of slavery. In order to obtain approval by the Southern States, the Constitutional Convention ultimately agreed to include several provisions recognizing the reality of slavery as it then existed.

Some critics—ranging from abolitionist Wendell Phillips (who called the Constitution a "covenant with death, an agreement with hell") to Justice Thurgood Marshall—have attacked the Constitutional Convention as racist or worse for yielding to the South's conditions. But that criticism overlooks an inescapable fact: if the Framers had not yielded—politics being the art of the possible—there would have been no Constitution and there would have been no United States of America.

As Abraham Lincoln (also tarred as racist by revisionist writers) pointed out: "when we established this government . . . [w]e had slavery among us, we could not get our constitution unless we permitted them to remain in slavery, we could not secure the good we did secure if we grasped for more." [7] Would the slaves have been better off if no agreement had been reached? Would the cause of democracy have been enhanced if no agreement had been reached?

Remarkably, neither the word "slavery" nor "slave" appears in any of the Constitution's slavery provisions. Instead, the Framers resorted to a kind of code as a substitute for the dreaded "S-word." As Lincoln said:[8]

> Thus, the thing is hid away, in the constitution, just as an afflicted man hides away a wen or a cancer, which he dares not cut out at once, lest he bleed to death; with the promise, nevertheless, that the cutting may begin at the end of a given time.

Three provisions of the Constitution dealt with slavery in this artful fashion:

1. Article I §9 barred Congress from prohibiting the importation of slaves until 1808. (The provision cryptically referred to slaves as "such Persons as any of the States now existing shall think proper to admit.") In 1808 Congress did act to adopt such a prohibition, but in the preceding 20 years the South imported more slaves from Africa than in any other 20-year period, and the high birth rate among slaves after 1808 more than satisfied the demand for more slaves.

2. Article IV §2, the fugitive slave provision, required that a slave escaping to a nonslave State must be returned to the slave's owner. (To avoid any reference to the "S-word," the provision referred instead to "Person[s] held to Service or Labour in one State, under the Laws thereof.")

3. Article I §2—the most important of the three provisions—allocated the membership of the House of Representatives among the States. It provided that seats in the House (unlike the Senate) would be allocated on a population basis, but that a State's population would be calculated by adding together its "number of free persons" and "three fifths of *all other persons*"—a euphemistic reference to slaves, who of course had no vote but would nonetheless be fractionally counted to increase the number of House seats allocated to the slave States.[9]

---

[7] Abraham Lincoln, *Selected Speeches and Writings* [Vintage 1992]: 147.
[8] Ibid., at 96–97.
[9] The three-fifths clause was derived from the "federal ratio" utilized in 1783 to allocate the sharing of expense under the Articles of Confederation. After approval of the formula for allocation of House representation, it was agreed to use the same formula for the allocation of "direct taxes." See Don E. Fehrenbacher, *The Slaveholding Republic* [Oxford 2001]: 28–35.

Indeed, the three-fifths clause also furnished the South a positive incentive to *increase* the number of its slaves. The more slaves imported (before 1808) and the more children born into slavery, the greater the power of the slave States in the federal government—all while restricting the vote to free white men.

Particularly in later centuries, the clause would be justly criticized for demeaning blacks as being worth only three-fifths of a white. But if slaves had been counted as whole persons, although the insult to blacks would have been less egregious, the political effect of counting slaves as whole persons would have been to give even greater power to the slave States.[10]

It is difficult to overstate the impact of the three-fifths clause on the nation's history. It took the Civil War and the Reconstruction Amendments to get rid of it. For nearly 75 years, with only minor exceptions, the clause gave the South virtual control of each of the three branches of the federal government.[11]

In Congress, because of the clause, the slave States had approximately one-third more seats in the House of Representatives than their free population warranted—47 seats instead of 33 in 1793, 76 instead of 59 in 1812, and 98 instead of 73 in 1833. In 1800, for example, Massachusetts had a much larger free population than Virginia but Virginia had five more seats because of its nearly 300,000 nonvoting slaves.

From 1789 to 1861, 23 out of the 36 Speakers of the House and 24 of the 36 presidents pro tem of the Senate were from the South. And, of course, Southern control of Congress also gave it control of the lawmaking machinery—including the committees that wrote the bills—and large influence over all federal appointments.

The three-fifths clause also greatly influenced the selection of the President. This was because, under Article II §1 of the Constitution, each State is allocated the same number of electoral votes as the "number of Senators and Representatives to which the State may be entitled in Congress," so that increasing the South's House seats by a third also increased the South's electoral votes by nearly a third.

For example, in the 1800 election—which except for the 1860 election was perhaps the most important in the nation's history—Thomas Jefferson would never have been elected without the "extra" 12 to 16 electoral votes he received on the basis of the three-fifths clause. Instead, John Adams (who lost by only eight electoral votes, 73 to 65) would have been reelected to a second term. The Federalist Party never recovered from their defeat, and many in the Party bitterly scorned Jefferson as the "Negro President" because his election had depended on electoral votes attributable to slaves.[12]

From 1787 to the start of the Civil War in 1861, the President was a Southerner for 49 years—or two-thirds of the time. Nine of the pre–Civil War Presidents (including Washington, Jefferson, Madison, Monroe, and Jackson—the latter had also engaged in slave trading) were slave owners, and only two (John Adams and his son John Quincy Adams) were opponents of slavery. Other Northern Presidents in that period (like Van Buren, Pierce, and Buchanan) were notably friendly to the slave interest.

The three-fifths clause also had a profound impact on the third branch of the government—the Judiciary. By increasing the South's electoral votes by approximately a third in the election of the President (who appointed Justices), the clause

---

[10]See, for example, Akhil Reed Amar, *America's Constitution: A Biography* [Random House 2005]: 89–91.

[11]Garry Wills, *"Negro President": Jefferson and the Slave Power* [Houghton Mifflin 2003]: 1–15, 50–61.

[12]Ibid., at 3–5, 62–72. See also John Ferling, *Adams vs. Jefferson: The Tumultuous Election of 1800* [Oxford 2004]: 47, 168.

led indirectly to Southern dominance of the Supreme Court. Before the Civil War, 20 of the 35 Supreme Court Justices were from the South, and 18 of the 20 had been slaveholders.

The primary threat to Southern domination was the nation's acquisition of huge new territories—the Louisiana Purchase, the annexation of Texas, the Oregon settlement with Britain, the Mexican cession, and the Gadsden Purchase. These acquisitions vastly increased the size of the United States, adding well over two million square miles and resulting by 1850 in the admission of 20 new States.

It was this expansion that increasingly polarized the South and the North over the political issue that ultimately ignited the Civil War—the issue of whether slavery would be permitted in the new States being carved out of the acquired territories.[13]

That issue, and *not* whether slavery could continue in the *existing* slave States, was the key bone of contention. Except for abolitionist groups, the North was generally resigned to accepting slavery in the States where it already existed, but was strongly opposed to allowing its extension beyond those borders. Lincoln, for example, said that "Wrong as we think slavery is, we can yet afford to let it alone where it is, because that much is due to the necessity arising from its actual presence in the nation," but it cannot be allowed "to spread into the National Territories, and to overrun us here in these Free States."[14]

The South, on the other hand, claimed that slaves were merely another form of personal "property" and that the Constitution conferred a right to own and transport such "property" anywhere in the country. And congressional action to limit slavery in the new territories, the South greatly feared, might then lead to congressional action seeking to abolish slavery altogether. The South's highest priorities, therefore, were to establish a cordon of protective slave States surrounding the original slave States and to resist restrictions on the extension of slavery.

In 1820, Congress confronted this issue in the so-called Missouri Compromise. It was agreed to admit both Maine and Missouri as States—a free Maine and a slave Missouri. But even more significantly, as part of the Missouri Compromise, Congress established a formula to govern the subsequent admission of any other States in the massive Louisiana Purchase territory purchased from France in 1803. (The acquired territory included all of present-day Arkansas, Missouri, Iowa, Oklahoma, Kansas, Nebraska, parts of Minnesota south of the Mississippi River, most of North Dakota, nearly all of South Dakota, northeastern New Mexico, northern Texas, the portions of Montana, Wyoming, and Colorado east of the Continental Divide, and Louisiana west of the Mississippi River.) Under the formula, the territory north of the southern ("36-30") boundary of Missouri, excluding Missouri, would be free, and the territory below that line would allow slaves.

However, since the Missouri Compromise by its terms did not apply outside the Louisiana Purchase territory, it left open the question of whether slavery would be permitted in subsequently acquired territories. Acquisitions resulting from the Mexican War in 1846 thrust the issue to the forefront once again. In 1850, Congress provided for the admission of California as a free State and the eventual admission of the New Mexico and Utah territories as States "with or without slavery, as their constitution

---

[13]See Harold M. Hyman and William M. Wiecek, *Equal Justice under Law: Constitutional Development 1835–1875* [Harper & Row 1982]: 129–171.

[14]Abraham Lincoln, *Selected Speeches and Writings* [Vintage 1992]: 251 (Cooper Institute Address, February 27, 1860).

may prescribe" (that is, depending on how their settlers would vote) at the time of admission.

The 1850 New Mexico–Utah precedent led in 1854 to a demand for similar "squatter sovereignty" treatment of the huge Nebraska territory, which was part of the area that the Missouri Compromise had provided would be nonslave. Largely because of Southern opposition, four attempts to organize the Nebraska territory were defeated in Congress. To overcome the stalemate, the law finally adopted by Congress (known as the Kansas-Nebraska Act) divided the territory into two parts: Kansas, lying entirely west of Missouri and therefore convenient for settlement by slaveholding Missourians; and Nebraska, lying west of the free State of Iowa and the free territory of Minnesota. In disregard of the Missouri Compromise formula, the Act left the question of slavery in each of the two territories to the decision of the territorial settlers themselves. In addition, in response to Southern pressure, the Act was amended to include a provision that expressly repealed the Missouri Compromise.

The 1854 Act—which became law only with the benefit of 19 House seats directly attributable to the three-fifths clause—created a political upheaval in the North and led to the formation of the new Republican Party (subsequently led by Abraham Lincoln).

It was against this background that the Supreme Court considered the next-digested case, *Scott v. Sandford*. On the basis of prior decisions, the case could readily have been decided on narrow grounds that would have reduced *Scott* to little more than a footnote in the Court's history. But, not content with that alternative, the majority instead undertook (with disastrous results) to put to rest the festering issue that divided the nation—the scope of congressional power to regulate slavery and, more specifically, whether Congress had the power to prohibit slavery in the territories.[15]

Scott v. Sandford, 60 U.S. 393 (1857)

FACTS: Dred Scott was a slave born in Virginia. He moved with his master to St. Louis, Missouri, where he was sold to Dr. John Emerson, an army surgeon. In 1834, Emerson was transferred to Fort Armstrong, Illinois (near what is now Rock Island), where Emerson and Scott lived for two years. In 1836, Emerson was transferred to Fort Snelling (near what is now St. Paul, Minnesota), located in the northern part of the Louisiana Purchase and designated as free territory by the 1820 Missouri Compromise.

Scott and Emerson lived in Fort Snelling for two years and then returned to St. Louis. Emerson died shortly thereafter and Emerson's wife sold Scott to Sandford, a New York resident.

Scott (after failing to obtain relief in the Missouri state courts) sued Sandford in the St. Louis federal court, seeking his freedom on the ground that he had become free when he lived with Emerson in the free State of Illinois and the free territory of Louisiana. Scott contended that the federal court had jurisdiction of the suit on the basis of diversity of citizenship of the plaintiff and defendant, claiming that he was a Missouri citizen suing a citizen of New York.

In response, Sandford argued (1) that there was no diversity of citizenship because Negroes could not be citizens, and (2) that, on the merits of the suit, Scott's status was controlled by Missouri law under which he was still deemed a slave despite his

---

[15]The classic history of the litigation is Don. E. Fehrenbacher, *The Dred Scott Case* [Oxford 1978].

previously living in free areas. The court agreed with Sandford on the merits and awarded judgment to the defendant.

Scott appealed to the Supreme Court.

ISSUE: Is Scott a Missouri citizen and therefore entitled to bring his case in the federal court?

DECISION (per *Taney,* 7-2, Curtis and McLean dissenting): *No.* Scott's case must be dismissed for lack of federal jurisdiction.

[The "Opinion of the Court" was delivered by Chief Justice Taney. However, each of the other eight Justices (six concurring, two dissenting) also wrote an opinion expressing his individual views. The nine opinions occupy more than 200 pages in the official report of the case.

In holding that Scott's status had not been changed by his residence in territory that the Missouri Compromise had designated to be free, Taney and five of the concurring Justices concluded that Congress did not have the constitutional power to ban slavery in the territories and that therefore the Missouri Compromise was unconstitutional (on that question, Curtis and McLean dissented, and Nelson expressed no view).

On whether Negroes were racially precluded from becoming U.S. citizens, the opinions of only two of the six concurring Justices (Wayne and Daniel) expressed agreement with Taney; the other four concurring opinions were silent on that issue.]

(1) *Negroes' ineligibility to be citizens of the United States*—The rights of citizenship which a State may confer within its own limits must be distinguished from the rights of citizenship as a member of the Union.

Before the adoption of the Constitution of the United States, every State had the undoubted right to confer on whomsoever it pleased the character of citizen and to endow him with all its rights. But he would not be a citizen in the sense in which that word is used in the Constitution of the United States, nor entitled to sue as such in one of its courts, nor to the privileges and immunities of a citizen in the other States. It is very clear, therefore, that no State can, by any act or law of its own passed since the adoption of the Constitution, introduce a new member into the political community created by the Constitution of the United States. It cannot make him a member of this community by making him a member of its own. And for the same reason it cannot introduce any person, or description of persons, who were not intended to be embraced in this new political family, which the Constitution brought into existence, but were intended to be excluded from it.

The question then arises whether the provisions of the Constitution, in relation to the personal rights and privileges to which the citizen of a State should be entitled, embrace a member of the negro African race who is made free in any State. The Court thinks the affirmative of that proposition cannot be maintained. And if it cannot, the plaintiff could not be a citizen of the State of Missouri, within the meaning of the Constitution of the United States, and consequently was not entitled to sue in the federal courts.

At the time the Constitution was established, Negroes were considered as a subordinate and inferior class of beings who had been subjugated by the dominant race, and, whether emancipated or not, yet remained subject to their authority, and had no rights or privileges but such as those who held the power and the government might choose to grant them.

It is not the province of the court to decide upon the justice or injustice, the policy or impolicy, of these laws. The decision of that question belonged to the political or lawmaking power, to those who formed the sovereignty and framed the Constitution. The duty of the court is to interpret the Constitution they framed with the best light we can obtain on the subject, and to administer it as we find it, according to its true intent and meaning when it was adopted.

The legislation and histories of the times show that neither the class of persons who had been imported as slaves nor their descendants, whether they had become free or not, were then acknowledged as a part of the people, nor intended to be included in the general words used in that memorable instrument.

It is difficult at this day to realize the state of public opinion in relation to that unfortunate race, which prevailed in the civilized and enlightened portions of the world at the time of the Declaration of Independence and when the Constitution was framed and adopted. They had for more than a century before been regarded as beings of an inferior order, altogether unfit to associate with the white race either in social or political relations, and so far inferior that they had no rights that the white man was bound to respect and that the negro might justly and lawfully be reduced to slavery for his benefit. He was bought and sold, and treated as an ordinary article of merchandise and traffic whenever a profit could be made by it. This opinion was at that time fixed and universal in the civilized portion of the white race. It was regarded as an axiom in morals as well as in politics, which no one thought of disputing or supposed to be open to dispute, and men in every grade and position in society daily and habitually acted upon it in their private pursuits, as well as in matters of public concern, without doubting for a moment the correctness of this opinion.

The general words of the Declaration of Independence would seem to embrace the whole human family. But it is too clear for dispute that the enslaved African race was not intended to be included, and formed no part of the people who framed and adopted the Declaration, for if the language, as understood in that day, would embrace them, the conduct of the distinguished men who framed the Declaration would have been utterly and flagrantly inconsistent with the principles they asserted, and instead of the sympathy of mankind to which they so confidently appealed, they would have deserved and received universal rebuke and reprobation.

This state of public opinion had undergone no change when the Constitution was adopted, as is equally evident from its provisions dealing with slavery. It is obvious that the negro race was not even in the minds of the Framers of the Constitution when they were conferring special rights and privileges upon the citizens of a State in every other part of the Union.

The legislation of the States further shows in a manner not to be mistaken the inferior and subject condition of that race at the time the Constitution was adopted and long afterwards, throughout the 13 States by which that instrument was framed, and it is hardly consistent with the respect due to these States to suppose that they regarded at that time as fellow citizens a class of beings whom they had thus stigmatized, and upon whom they had impressed such deep and enduring marks of inferiority and degradation. It cannot be supposed that they intended to secure to them rights and privileges in the new political body throughout the Union that every one of them denied within the limits of its own dominion.

More especially, it cannot be believed that the large slaveholding States regarded them as included in the word "citizens," or would have consented to a Constitution that might compel them to receive them in that character from another State. For if they were so received, and entitled to the privileges and immunities of citizens, it would exempt them from the operation of the special laws and from the police regulations that they considered to be necessary for their own safety. It would give to persons of the negro race, who were recognized as citizens in any one State of the Union, the right to enter every other State whenever they pleased, singly or in companies, without pass or passport, and without obstruction, to sojourn there as long as they pleased, to go where they pleased at every hour of the day or night without molestation, unless they committed some violation of law for which a white man would be punished; and it would give them the full liberty of speech in public and in private upon all subjects upon which its own citizens might speak, to hold public meetings upon political affairs, and to keep and carry arms wherever they went. And all of this would be done inevitably producing discontent and insubordination among them, and endangering the peace and safety of the State.

A perpetual and impassable barrier was intended to be erected between the white race and the one that they had reduced to slavery. The change in public opinion and feeling in relation to the African race that has taken place since the adoption of the Constitution cannot change its construction and meaning, and it must be construed and administered now according to its true meaning and intention when it was formed and adopted.

If any of its provisions are deemed unjust, there is a mode prescribed in the instrument itself by which it may be amended; but while it remains unaltered, it must be construed now as it was understood at the time of its adoption. It is not only the same in words, but the same in meaning; it delegates the same powers to the Government, and reserves and secures the same rights and privileges to the citizen; and as long as it continues to exist in its present form, it speaks not only in the same words, but with the same meaning and intent with which it spoke when it came from the hands of its Framers and was voted on and adopted by the people of the United States. Any other rule of construction would abrogate the judicial character of this court and make it the mere reflex of the popular opinion or passion of the day.

Since slaves and their descendants are not citizens of the United States under the meaning of that term in the Constitution, they cannot claim any of the rights and privileges that the Constitution provides to citizens. Scott is not a citizen and therefore cannot invoke diversity of citizenship jurisdiction in order to sue in the federal courts.

(2) *Scott's residence in a free United States Territory*—Scott nevertheless argues that he and his family became entitled to freedom by being taken by their owner to reside in the northern part of the Louisiana Territory, where slavery was then prohibited by the 1820 Missouri Compromise.

[*Note: Although Congress had repealed the Missouri Compromise in 1854 (three years before the Dred Scott decision), Scott relied on his residence in the Louisiana Purchase during the interim prerepeal period when the Missouri Compromise was in effect.*]

When a territory becomes a part of the United States, the government and the citizen both enter it under the authority of the Constitution, with their respective rights defined and marked out; and the federal government can exercise no power over his person or property beyond what that instrument confers nor lawfully deny any right that it has reserved.

The Fifth Amendment to the Constitution provides that no person shall be deprived of life, liberty, and property, without due process of law. And an Act of Congress that deprives a citizen of the United States of his liberty or property merely because he came himself or brought his property into a particular territory of the United States and who had committed no offense against the laws could hardly be dignified with the name of due process of law.

The powers over person and property of which we speak not only were never granted to Congress but are in express terms denied. And if Congress itself cannot do this if it is beyond the powers conferred on the federal government, then Congress could not authorize a territorial government to exercise them. It could confer no power on any local government, established by its authority, to violate the provisions of the Constitution.

It seems, however, to be supposed that there is a difference between property in a slave and other property, and that different rules may be applied to it in expounding the Constitution. However, the right of property in a slave is distinctly and expressly affirmed in the Constitution. The right to traffic in it, like an ordinary article of merchandise and property, was guaranteed to the citizens of the United States, in every State that might desire it, for 20 years. And the government in express terms is pledged to protect it in all future time if the slave escapes from his owner. This is done in plain words, too plain to be misunderstood. And no word can be found in the Constitution that gives Congress a greater power over slave property or that entitles property of that kind to less protection than property of any other description. The only power conferred is the power coupled with the duty of guarding and protecting the owner in his rights.

Upon these considerations, it is the opinion of the Court that the Act of Congress [the Missouri Compromise] that prohibited a citizen from holding and owning property of this kind in a specified portion of the Louisiana territory, is not warranted by the Constitution, and is therefore void; and that neither Dred Scott himself, nor any of his family, were made free by being carried into this territory, even if they had been carried there by the owner, with the intention of becoming a permanent resident.

(3) *Scott's residence in the free State of Illinois*—Scott further contends that he became free by being taken to Rock Island in the free State of Illinois and that, being free on his return to Missouri, he was a Missouri citizen entitled to assert diverse citizenship jurisdiction of the federal courts.

However, whatever Scott's status had been while he was a resident of the free State of Illinois before he returned to Missouri, his status in Missouri depended on the law of that State as interpreted by its own courts. It has been settled by the decisions of the highest court in Missouri that, by the laws of that State, a slave does not become entitled to his freedom where the owner takes him to reside in a State where slavery is not permitted and afterwards brings him back to Missouri. Since Missouri's highest court had declared Scott to be a slave, that decision is controlling.

The case must be dismissed for lack of jurisdiction.

The Reconstruction Amendments

Dred Scott (characterized by a later Chief Justice, Charles Evans Hughes, as one of the Court's "self-inflicted wounds") is widely regarded as the most egregious decision in the Court's history.[16]

Taney and five of the concurring Justices held that the Constitution did not give Congress power to place limits on where slave owners could take their slaves, on the ground that slaves were merely one form of property and that Congress could not

---

[16]See, e.g., Harold M. Hyman and William M. Wiecek, *Equal Justice under Law: Constitutional Development 1835–1875* [Harper & Row 1982]: 172–194.

exercise any more authority over slaves than it could constitutionally exercise over property of any other kind.[17] Therefore, according to the majority, the Missouri Compromise was unconstitutional, the northern territory where Scott had lived had never been "free," and Scott—still being a slave on this analysis—never achieved the status of a "citizen" who is entitled to bring suit in the federal courts.

In his opinion, Taney further wrote that Negroes—whether slaves or freed—were racially ineligible to become "citizens" because, he contended, they had never been regarded as part of the political community created by the Constitution. At the time the Constitution was adopted, according to Taney, Negroes were "considered as a subordinate and inferior class of beings who ... had no rights or privileges but such as those who held the power and the Government might choose to grant them" and that Negroes had been deemed so far inferior "that they had no rights which the white man was bound to respect." (It is unclear how many of the other Justices agreed with Taney on this alternative ground; four of the six concurring opinions were silent on the issue.)

Neither of Taney's two grounds is defensible on the basis of the Constitution's text or history. It is difficult to avoid the impression that the opinion reflected essentially an effort by a southern-dominated Court (five of the Justices in the majority had been slave owners and three of the Justices still owned slaves) to impose the South's view on the issue of Congress's power to regulate slavery. They may have hoped that the decision on the issue would reduce the danger of disunion.[18] But the decision had the directly opposite effect; the result was to inflame the North and divide the country even more.

Instead of settling the matter, the *Dred Scott* decision itself became a key political issue in the 1860 presidential election. As a result, the new Republican Party was vastly strengthened, while the Democratic Party split along sectional lines, leading to Lincoln's election, the Civil War, and then the adoption of the three Reconstruction Amendments of the Constitution:

> The Thirteenth Amendment (1865) prohibits slavery and "involuntary servitude" (thus repealing the three-fifths clause).

---

[17]Two years later, Taney expressed a much broader view of federal authority in Ableman v. Booth, 62 U.S. 506 (1859), enforcing and upholding the Fugitive Slave Act of 1850 that provided for the punishment of persons aiding in the escape of slaves. In his opinion for the Court, Taney stated (p. 517):

> [I]t was felt by the statesmen who framed the Constitution, and by the people who adopted it, that it was necessary that many of the rights of sovereignty which the States then possessed should be ceded to the General Government; and that, in the sphere of action assigned to it, it should be supreme, and strong enough to execute its own laws by its own tribunals, without interruption from a State or from State authorities.

[18]While the opinion was being drafted, the case became embroiled in one of the most notorious chapters in the Court's history. James Buchanan of Pennsylvania had just been elected President in 1856, primarily with southern support. In preparing his inaugural address, he wrote one of the Southern Justices, John Catron, to ask whether the Court's opinion in the case would decide the issue of the constitutionality of the Missouri Compromise. Catron informed Buchanan that the Court would decide the issue and intimated that the Court would hold the Missouri Compromise unconstitutional. Catron also suggested that Buchanan say in his inaugural address that the constitutional question was before the Supreme Court and that the whole matter should be left for its determination. Following Catron's advice, and of course knowing what the decision was going to be, Buchanan disingenuously proclaimed that he would, in common with all good citizens, cheerfully submit to the Court's decision, whatever it may be. See Don E. Fehrenbacher, *The Dred Scott Case* [Oxford 1978]: 307, 309, 312–313; Carl B. Swisher, *American Constitutional Development* [Houghton Mifflin 1943]: 245–247.

The Fourteenth Amendment (1868) declares that "All persons born or naturalized in the United States . . . are citizens of the United States and of the State wherein they reside" (thus overturning the *Dred Scott* decision). The Amendment further provides that no State shall "deprive any person of life, liberty, or property, without due process of law; nor deny to any person within its jurisdiction the equal protection of the laws."

The Fifteenth Amendment (1870) prohibits discrimination in voting "on account of race, color, or previous condition of servitude."

Each of the three Amendments further provides that "The Congress shall have power to enforce this article by appropriate legislation."

The Reconstruction Amendments fundamentally changed the nature and scope of the Constitution—from a document focused primarily on protecting the independence of the States to an evolving charter of individual rights enforceable against the States as well as the federal government. And this "Second American Revolution" enormously expanded the role of the Supreme Court in the resolution of major public policy issues.

The next three chapters deal with the Court's application of the Reconstruction Amendments—particularly the Equal Protection Clause of the Fourteenth Amendment—to government regulation of three types of racial discrimination. Chapter 3 focuses on *governmental* discrimination *against* racial minorities; Chapter 4 deals with racial discrimination by *private* organizations *against* racial minorities; and Chapter 5 relates to *governmental* discrimination *in favor of* racial minorities ("affirmative action").

The Amendment Process and *Stare Decisis*

An interpretation of the Constitution by the Supreme Court can be reversed only in two ways:

(1) Article V of the Constitution (Appendix A) provides a procedure—although a cumbersome one—for amending the Constitution. Under Article V, amendments must be proposed by Congress by a two-thirds vote of both Houses (or by a constitutional convention called at the request of the legislatures of two-thirds of the States) and must be approved by three-fourths of the state legislatures (or by conventions in three-fourths of the States).

Since the ratification of the original Constitution in 1789, only 27 Amendments have been adopted. And since adoption of the first ten Amendments, known as the Bill of Rights, in 1791, only 17 have been approved. Moreover, only four of the 27—and only one in the last 110 years—overruled constitutional decisions of the Supreme Court.

The Eleventh Amendment overruled Chisholm v. Georgia, 2 U.S. 419 (1793), permitting States to be sued in federal courts; the Thirteenth and Fourteenth Amendments overruled Scott v. Sandford, 60 U.S. 393 (1857), holding that Negroes were ineligible for citizenship; the Seventeenth Amendment overruled Pollock v. Farmers' Loan & Trust Co., 158 U.S. 601 (1895), holding the federal income tax invalid; and the Twenty-Sixth Amendment overruled Oregon v. Mitchell, 400 U.S. 112 (1970), holding that Congress could not change the voting age to 18 in state elections.

(2) In the absence of an amendment under Article V, a constitutional decision of the Supreme Court can be reversed only if the Court itself concludes that the decision was erroneous and should be overruled.

Under the doctrine of *stare decisis*—"to stand by things decided"—the Court generally defers to its prior decisions. According such deference helps to maximize stability and certainty in the law. "[T]he rule of law demands that adhering to our prior case law be the norm. Departure from precedent is exceptional, and requires 'special justification.' " Arizona v. Rumsey, 467 U.S. 203, 212 (1984). In addition, "no judicial system could do society's work if it eyed each issue afresh in every case that raised it." [19]

In the application of *stare decisis,* however, there is a crucial distinction between deferring to a prior interpretation of a federal *statute* and a prior interpretation of the Constitution. As Justice Louis Brandeis pointed out, "Stare decisis is usually the wise policy, because in most matters it is more important that the applicable rule of law be settled than that it be settled right. . . . This is commonly true even where the error is a matter of serious concern, provided correction can be had by legislation. *But in cases involving the Federal Constitution, where correction through legislative action is practically impossible, this Court has often overruled its earlier decisions.*" Burnet v. Coronado Oil & Gas Co., 285 U.S. 393, 406-408 (1932) (dissenting opinion).

In addition, while in one sense (as Chief Justice Charles Evans Hughes once commented) "the Constitution is what the judges say it is," the inescapable fact is that a decision of the Court interpreting the Constitution consists only of judge-made gloss on the text. Past judicial decisions are not themselves the law, but rather are only good evidence of the law. Court doctrine does not replace the commands of the Constitution itself.[20]

The Court has overruled its prior constitutional rulings in scores of cases. For example: In Brown v. Board of Education, U.S. (1954), the Court rejected the "separate but equal" doctrine approved in Plessy v. Ferguson, 163 U.S. 537 (1896); in Lawrence v. Texas, 539 U.S. 558 (2003), the Court overruled Bowers v. Hardwick, 478 U.S. 186 (1986), that upheld the validity of antisodomy statutes; and in Planned Parenthood of Southeastern Pennsylvania v. Casey, 505 U.S. 833 (1992), the Court overruled two of its prior decisions invalidating state abortion regulations but declined to overrule "the central holding" in Roe v. Wade, 410 U.S. 113 (1973). Each of these cases is digested in succeeding chapters.

But how is it determined whether and when the Court should or should not repudiate a prior constitutional interpretation? How is it decided that the presumption is overcome by a "special justification"? The Court has pointed to a variety of factors to be considered in determining whether to respect a constitutional precedent.

In their *Casey* plurality opinion (see comment "The Turnabout in *Casey*" in Chapter 7), Justices O'Connor, Kennedy, and Souter invoked *stare decisis* to reaffirm the "central rule" of *Roe v. Wade* irrespective of whether they would have supported it as an original matter. They declared that "a decision to overrule should rest on some special reason over and above the belief that a prior case was wrongly decided" (505 U.S. at 864) and based their decision on

> whether Roe's central rule has been found unworkable; whether the rule's limitation on state power could be removed without serious inequity to those who have relied upon it or significant damage to the stability of the society governed by it; whether the law's growth in the intervening years has left Roe's central rule a doctrinal anachronism discounted by society; and whether Roe's premises of fact have so far changed in the ensuing two decades as to render its central holding somehow irrelevant or unjustifiable in dealing with the issue it addressed. (505 U.S. at 855.)

---

[19]Benjamin Cardozo, *The Nature of the Judicial Process* [Dover ed. 2005]: 149.
[20]Akhil Reed Amar, "The Document and the Doctrine," 114 *Harvard Law Review* 26, 83-84, 87 (2000).

In addition, in a much-criticized portion of the opinion, the *Casey* plurality relied on the need to protect the legitimacy and stature of the Court. According to the opinion:

> overruling Roe's central holding would not only reach an unjustifiable result under principles of stare decisis, but would seriously weaken the Court's capacity to exercise the judicial power and to function as the Supreme Court of a Nation dedicated to the rule of law. . . . Despite the variety of reasons that may inform and justify a decision to overrule, we cannot forget that such a decision is usually perceived (and perceived correctly) as, at the least, a statement that a prior decision was wrong. There is a limit to the amount of error that can plausibly be imputed to prior Courts. If that limit should be exceeded, disturbance of prior rulings would be taken as evidence that justifiable reexamination of principle had given way to drives for particular results in the short term. The legitimacy of the Court would fade with the frequency of its vacillation. . . . Where, in the performance of its judicial duties, the Court decides a case in such a way as to resolve the sort of intensely divisive controversy reflected in Roe and those rare, comparable cases, its decision has a dimension that the resolution of the normal case does not carry. . . . [W]hatever the premises of opposition may be, only the most convincing justification under accepted standards of precedent could suffice to demonstrate that a later decision overruling the first was anything but a surrender to political pressure and an unjustified repudiation of the principle on which the Court staked its authority in the first instance. So to overrule under fire in the absence of the most compelling reason to reexamine a watershed decision would subvert the Court's legitimacy beyond any serious question. (505 U.S. at 866–867.)

Among the many *stare decisis* factors considered in other cases are the following: whether the challenged decision had rejected "an unbroken line of decisions from 1866 to 1960" supported by the "plain meaning" of the constitutional provision, Solorio v. United States, 483 U.S. 435, 439, 450 (1987); whether the decision "departed from our prior cases—and did so quite recently," and the holding of the prior cases is "more embracing in its scope, intrinsically sounder, and verified by experience," Adarand Constructors, Inc. v. Pena, 515 U.S. 200, 231 (1995); whether the decision "contradicted an 'unbroken line of decisions,' contained 'less than accurate' historical analysis, and has produced 'confusion,' " United States v. Dixon, 509 U.S. 688, 720 (1993).

3

Race Discrimination by Government

What Is "Race"?

The Scientific Debate

Terminology such as "racial equality," "racial discrimination," and (a common statutory phrase) "because of such individual's race" presupposes the existence of an accepted definition of the word "race." But the word has been used loosely in many different ways, sometimes suggesting biology ("the Caucasian race"), sometimes ethnicity ("the Hispanic race"), sometimes nationality ("the German race"), sometimes religion ("the Jewish race"), and sometimes *everyone* ("the human race").[1] Even today, there is disagreement and confusion over the definition—and, indeed, whether there is even such a thing as "race."

In the eighteenth century, when America's Constitution was drafted, a different race was considered a different *type* of being—a different species.[2]

As one commentator pointed out:[3]

> The idea that "race" is a crucial and immutable division of mankind is a product of the primitive social science of the nineteenth century. According to theorists of the day, all the peoples of the world were divided into four distinct races: white or "Caucasian," black or "Negroid," yellow or "Oriental," and red or Indian. White, black, yellow, and red people [it was believed] were profoundly different from each other, as different as robins from sparrows, trout from salmon, rabbits from squirrels . . . . If they were to mate across racial lines, their offspring would be biological monstrosities.

This notion gave rise to the infamous "one-drop rule," which defined as black any person with as little as a single drop of "black blood."[4]

Ultimately, because of centuries of immigration and intermarriage, it was recognized that groups have become so intermixed that few people, if any, can claim to be

---

[1]Dinesh D'Souza, *The End of Racism: Principles for a Multiracial Society* [Free Press 1995]: 48.
[2]Ernst Mayr, "The Biology of Race and the Concept of Equality," *Daedalus* (Winter 2002).
[3]Stephan Thernstrom, "The Demography of Racial and Ethnic Groups," in *Beyond the Color Line: New Perspectives on Race and Ethnicity,* ed. Abigail and Stephan Thernstrom [Hoover Press 2002]: 16.
[4]Lawrence Wright, "One Drop of Blood," *The New Yorker,* July 24, 1994. As Wright points out, American Indians were not subject to the rule.

of racially "pure" origins.[5] This research, coupled with revulsion for the earlier association between racism and outdated concepts of "race," led to a widely accepted view that there are no races and that "race" is merely a "social construct"[6] or a "myth."[7] For example, in its 1998 Statement on "Race," the American Anthropological Association declared that "physical variations in the human species have no meaning except the social ones that humans put on them." According to this view, any differences that exist among groups are merely cultural, not biological, and furthermore recognition of "race" only serves to foster prejudice. As David Hollinger succinctly put it: "Racism is real, but races are not."[8]

In the last few years, however, the social construct theory has come under strong attack. As recently as 2001, an editorial in the prestigious journal *Nature Genetics* stated that "scientists have long been saying that at the genetic level there is more variation between two individuals in the same population than between populations, and that there is no biological basis for 'race.'" But only three years later, in 2004, the same journal produced a special supplement containing the views of some two dozen geneticists on the medical uses of racial and ethnic classification. As biologist Armand Marie Leroi observed: "Beneath the jargon, cautious phrases and academic courtesies, one thing was clear: the consensus about social constructs was unraveling. Some even argued that, looked at the right way, genetic data show that races clearly do exist."[9]

The following year in 2005, *The New England Journal of Medicine* reported the news of a "race-based" drug (BiDil) targeted at blacks suffering from certain types of heart failure, and a gene was discovered that raises the risk of heart attack in blacks by more than 250 percent. More recently in 2008, researchers concluded that black patients' different responses to beta blockers was genetic in nature.[10] The September 2008 issue of *Clinical Pharmacology & Therapeutics* is devoted to "Pharmacoethnicity" and examines scientific, ethical, and regulatory considerations arising from new research showing that "Differences in response to medical products have been observed in racially and ethnically distinct subgroups of the US population."

---

[5]Thernstrom, *Beyond the Color Line,* 16.

[6]"The dominance of the social construct theory can be traced to a 1972 article by Dr. Richard Lewontin, a Harvard geneticist, who wrote that most human genetic variation can be found within any given 'race.' If one looked at genes rather than faces, he claimed, the difference between an African and a European would be scarcely greater than the difference between any two Europeans. A few years later he wrote that the continued popularity of race as an idea was an 'indication of the power of socioeconomically based ideology over the supposed objectivity of knowledge.'" Armand Marie Leroi, "A Family Tree in Every Gene," *New York Times,* March 14, 2005.

[7]E.g., Ashley Montagu, *Man's Most Dangerous Myth: The Fallacy of Race* [Columbia 1942]. See also Natalie Angier, "Do Races Differ? Not Really, Genes Show," *New York Times,* August 22, 2000 (stating that Dr. J. Craig Venter, head of the first successful human genome project, and researchers at the National Institutes of Health "had unanimously declared, there is only one race—the human race").

[8]David Hollinger, *Postethnic America: Beyond Multiculturalism,* rev. ed. [Basic Books 2005]: 39. In a "Postscript" included in the 2005 edition of the book, reflecting post-1995 developments, Hollinger acknowledges that "In the meantime, resounding voices in the biomedical sciences insist that the concept of race still has genuine utility after it is separated rigorously from the mistakes and prejudices of old-fashioned racial science" (p. 226).

[9]Leroi, "A Family Tree in Every Gene."

[10]Gina Kolata, "Genes Explain Race Disparity in Response to a Heart Drug," *New York Times,* April 29, 2008; Nicholas Wade, "Genetic Find Stirs Debate on Race-Based Medicine," *New York Times,* November 11, 2005. See also Nicholas Wade, "Race Is Seen as Real Guide To Track Roots of Disease," *New York Times,* July 30, 2002.

Expressing what appears to be an increasingly prevalent view, Harvard professor Ernst Mayr, one of the twentieth century's leading evolutionary biologists, stated:[11]

> There is a widespread feeling that the word "race" indicates something undesirable and that it should be left out of all discussions. This leads to such statements as "there are no human races." *Those who subscribe to this opinion are obviously ignorant of modern biology.* ... Recognizing races is only recognizing a biological fact.
>
> A human race consists of the descendants of a once-isolated geographical population primarily adapted for the environmental conditions of their original home country. [Italics added.]

However, although the classification of races may be pertinent in diagnosing and treating some diseases, it does not follow that races denote essentially different types of people or "species," as racists once insisted. The new scientific research has raised concerns that it might be misapplied to support prejudice. Henry Louis Gates Jr., director of the W. E. B. Du Bois Institute for African and African American Research at Harvard University, cautioned: "We are living through an era of the ascendance of biology, and we have to be very careful. We will all be walking a fine line between using biology and allowing it to be abused." [12]

Government Racial Categories

Science has very little to do with the federal government's classification of racial and ethnic groups. Instead, the categories "are egregiously crude, are susceptible to strategic manipulation, and carry repellant historical associations." [13] As sociologist Nathan Glazer (author with Daniel Patrick Moynihan of *Beyond the Melting Pot*) stated:

> The census questions, whatever we think of their incongruity and irrationality, are the direct result of powerful pressures from the ethnic groups concerned, from Congress, and from the Executive Office. And these are political not only in the sense that political actors are involved, but in the narrower and less respectable sense that they are often motivated by narrow and partisan considerations.[14]

The original census in 1790 had but three racial categories: White, Black, and Indian. These categories were required because of the three-fifths clause in Article I, Section 2, establishing the original formula for the apportionment of representatives and direct taxes among the States. (See comment "The Slavery Legacy" in Chapter 2.) The number of classifications expanded in the late 1800s to account for the increased Chinese and Japanese populations.[15]

The final questionnaires for the 1970 census were already at the printers when, in response to demands of a member of the House Mexican-American Affairs

---

[11]Mayr, "The Biology of Race and the Concept of Equality."
[12]Quoted in Amy Harmon, "In DNA Era, New Worries About Prejudice," *New York Times,* November 11, 2007.
[13]Peter Schuck, *Diversity in America: Keeping Government at a Safe Distance* [Belknap Press 2003]: 25.
[14]Nathan Glazer, "Do We Need the Census Race Questions?" *Public Interest* [Fall 2002]: 21.
[15]See Peter Kirsanow, "2,000 Flavors and Counting," *National Review Online,* April 12, 2006.

Committee, President Richard Nixon ordered the inclusion of a Hispanic-origin category. The result was the addition of a "Hispanic" ethnicity category.[16]

This kind of political intervention has been bipartisan in nature. For example, in the late 1970s, when social scientists and the Census Bureau wanted to remove the "ancestry" census question because it was vague and uninformative (in comparison with the question on birthplaces of respondents' parents which it replaced), the White House insisted that the ancestry question be retained regardless of the objections.[17]

In 1977 the Office of Management and Budget (OMB) issued Directive No. 15, "Race and Ethnic Standards for Federal Statistics and Administrative Reporting," governing race and ethnic standards for federal statistics and administrative reporting. The need for such standards arose because of the passage of several civil rights laws (the Civil Rights Act of 1964, the Voting Rights Act of 1965, the Fair Housing Act of 1968, the Equal Credit Opportunity Act of 1974, the Home Mortgage Disclosure Act of 1975) requiring the federal government to monitor discrimination in a variety of areas. In order to assess discriminatory practices, the various affected agencies first had to specify the relevant protected groups, and this in turn led to the need for a uniform approach on a government-wide basis.[18]

The national impact of the resulting categories has far transcended government matters. As Victoria Hattam has pointed out: "Although the directive was officially limited to federal statistics and administrative reporting, its categories quickly became the de facto standard for American society at large, setting the terms ever since for racial and ethnic classification in the United States." [19]

The OMB's 1977 directive established four racial categories: American Indian or Alaskan Native, Asian or Pacific Islander, Black, and White. In addition, two ethnicity categories were established: Hispanic origin and Not of Hispanic origin. Census respondents—whatever may be their mixed ancestry—were obliged to select one of the permitted boxes. The Directive stated that "These classifications should not be interpreted as being scientific or anthropological in nature."

In 1997, the OMB amended Directive No. 15 to issue slightly revised standards for the 2000 census. Native Hawaiian or Other Pacific Islander was recognized as a fifth race, and Asian (previously linked together with Pacific Islander) now had its own category. There were also two ethnicity categories: Hispanic or Latino (defined as "A person of Cuban, Mexican, Puerto Rican, South or Central American, or other Spanish culture or origin, regardless of race") and Not Hispanic or Latino.[20] The amended Directive also revised the 1977 "not scientific" disclaimer to state: "The categories in this classification are social-political constructs and should not be interpreted as being scientific or anthropological in nature."

---

[16]Glazer, "Do We Need the Census Race Questions?"

[17]Ibid. Glazer points out that even the phrasing of a census race question may be the subject of political interference. Before the 1990 census, both Houses of Congress passed legislation to require that "Taiwanese" be included as one of the "Asian and Pacific Islander" subgroups. The legislation never became law only because of President Reagan's pocket veto.

[18]Victoria Hattam, "Ethnicity and the Boundaries of Race: Rereading Directive 15," *Daedalus* (Winter 2005).

[19]Ibid.

[20]Origin is defined as "the heritage, nationality group, lineage or country of the person or the person's parents or ancestors before their arrival in the United States."

Before the 1997 Directive was adopted, the addition of a "Multiracial" category was strongly urged in public and congressional hearings.[21] In response, civil rights organizations mounted a successful political campaign to oppose any change in the demographic status quo.[22] NAACP leader Julian Bond, for example, declared: "I very much oppose diluting the power and the strength of numbers as they affect legal decisions about race in this country."[23] Similarly, Jon Michael Spencer, a professor of Afro-American Studies at the University of North Carolina, argued that "To relinquish the notion of race—even though it's a cruel hoax—at this particular time is to relinquish our fortress against the powers and principalities that still try to undermine us."[24] As Orlando Patterson has acknowledged, "the orthodox line among Afro-American leaders is now a firm commitment to the one-drop rule."[25]

Although rejecting a "Multiracial" category, the OMB did agree to allow census respondents to "check one or more" of the five categories and also, if they wish, select a sixth racial category "Some Other Race." However, in March 2000, the OMB issued a directive (OMB Bulletin No. 00-02) providing that any response checking one minority race and the white race must be allocated to the minority race for purposes of "civil rights monitoring and enforcement" (i.e., to measure racial composition in education, employment, and public contracting). OMB's directive effectively maximizes the size of minority groups; where previously multiracial individuals chose their own racial identities, the government's allocation rule now decides the matter for them.[26] Respondents who acknowledge that they are not only white but also a member of a "minority race" will—regardless of how they might choose to identify themselves—be counted as belonging to the "minority race."

Based on the 2000 census, the "Some Other Race" category is the third largest race group in the United States. The category was included to reduce the number of nonresponses to questions about race, particularly by Hispanics who do not identify with any of the five major race categories. Continuing efforts by Hispanics to obtain recognition as a separate "race"[27] (rather than only as an "ethnic group") face considerable hurdles

---

[21]See Peter Wood, *Diversity: The Invention of a Concept* [Encounter 2003]: 25–26:

> The idea was to recognize the Tiger Woods phenomenon. In 1997, when the golfer was asked by Oprah Winfrey how he classified himself, Mr. Woods replied that as a teenager he invented the word "Cablinasian"—CAucasian-BLack-INdian-ASIAN—in recognition of his father's mixed Caucasian, Black and Indian ancestry, and his mother's Thai heritage. Despite pressure from many African-Americans, who would prefer that Woods adhere exclusively to an "African-American" identity, he continues to refuse to pigeonhole himself in a single racial category.

See also Stephan and Abigail Thernstrom, *America in Black and White* [Simon & Schuster 1997]: 527.

[22]See, e.g., Thernstrom, *America in Black and White*, 528.

[23]Quoted by Ellis Cose, "One Drop of Bloody History," *Newsweek,* February 13, 1995, 72.

[24]Quoted by Lawrence Wright, "One Drop of Blood," *The New Yorker,* July 24, 1994.

[25]Orlando Patterson, *The Ordeal of Integration: Progress and Resentment in America's "Racial" Crisis* [Civitas 1997]: 71.

[26]Schuck, *Diversity in America,* 144–145; Stephan Thernstrom, "One Drop—Still," *National Review,* April 17, 2000: "If a significant proportion of African Americans reported themselves as partly white, they worried, it could mean fewer affirmative action slots at colleges and universities, fewer jobs for black applicants, a smaller share of public contracts set aside for black-owned businesses, fewer safe black seats on city councils, in state legislatures, and in Congress."

According to various estimates, because of their mixed ancestry, 75–90 percent of those who now check the "Black" box could properly check "Multiracial" if that option were available to them. Wright, "One Drop of Blood."

[27]See, e.g., Ian Haney Lopez, "Race in the 2010 Census: Hispanics and the Shrinking White Majority," *Daedalus* 134 (2005).

because of the extraordinary variety of the Hispanic category. It includes, for example, black Hispanics from the Dominican Republic, Argentines who are almost entirely European whites, and Mexicans who would be counted as American Indians if they had been born north of the Rio Grande.

In preparation for the 2010 census, OMB has rejected the proposed "race" status for Hispanics. The 2010 forms will state that "For this census, Hispanic origins are not races," and the terms changed from "Hispanic or Latino" to "Hispanic, Latino or Spanish origin."

In March 2008, the Census Bureau submitted to Congress the questions it will ask for the 2010 Census. According to the Bureau's submission, "The questions on . . . Race [and] ethnicity . . . are essentially the same as those asked in 2000, with some improvements designed to help reduce respondent confusion." The draft submitted to Congress, however, asks a respondent to "mark one or more boxes" and then sets forth 15 boxes.[28] Presumably the final version will designate some of these boxes as subcategories of the basic five categories recognized in the 2000 census.

Overview of the Equal Protection Clause

The Equal Protection Clause of the Fourteenth Amendment (Appendix A) provides that "No State shall . . . deny to any person within its jurisdiction the equal protection of the laws." But "equal protection" does not require that all persons be treated identically.

Statutory classifications are inherent in the legislative process. Almost every law *classifies*—and in that sense "discriminates"—by imposing special burdens or conferring special benefits on some people and not on others. Generalized "discrimination" of that nature is not sufficient, in itself, to violate the Equal Protection Clause. As the Court stated in Ferguson v. Skrupa, 372 U.S. 726, 732 (1963), "statutes create many classifications which do not deny equal protection; it is only 'invidious discrimination' which offends the Constitution."

But what is "invidious"? The term is only a label that the Court uses to refer to particular types of classifications that have been found to violate (or presumably violate) the Equal Protection Clause.

Until the Court's 1954 decision in Brown v. Board of Education (rejecting the "separate but equal" doctrine in the next-digested case, *Plessy v. Ferguson*), relatively few laws were held unconstitutional under the Equal Protection Clause. However, since *Brown*, the Clause has frequently been invoked to invalidate legislation.

Although primarily designed to benefit Negroes, the Equal Protection Clause was drafted broadly in terms of "any person." In 1873, in the first case in which it was called upon to interpret the Equal Protection Clause, the Court expressed doubt whether "any action of a State not directed by way of discrimination against the negroes as a class, or on account of their race, will ever be held to come within the purview of this provision." Slaughter-House Cases, 83 U.S. 36, 81 (1873). However, in its opinion six years later in Strauder v. West Virginia, 100 U.S. 303, 308 (1879), although the comment was not essential to its decision (striking down a state statute expressly excluding Negroes from serving on juries), the Court rejected the "Negro

---

[28]The 15 are the following: White; Black, African American, or Negro; American Indian or Alaska Native; Asian Indian; Chinese; Filipino; Japanese; Korean; Vietnamese; Native Hawaiian; Guamanian or Chamarro; Samoan; Other Pacific Islander; Other Asian; Some Other Race.

only" limitation suggested in The Slaughter-House Cases. Then, in Yick Wo v. Hopkins, 118 U.S. 356, 369 (1886), the Court upheld an equal protection claim by a group of Chinese laundry owners, declaring that the provisions of the Fourteenth Amendment "are universal in their application, to all persons within the territorial jurisdiction, without regard to any differences of race, of color, or of nationality; and the equal protection of the laws is a pledge of the protection of equal laws." Applying that principle, the Court has held the Equal Protection Clause applicable to a wide variety of groups, both racial (such as Asian Americans) and nonracial (such as women and religious groups).

In the past half-century, in determining whether a claimed discrimination violates the Clause, the Supreme Court has also adopted a set of variable standards of review depending on the nature of the group.

Racial classifications are subjected to a rigorous "strict scrutiny" standard, thereby making far more likely their being held unconstitutional. A discrimination subject to strict scrutiny is, as a practical matter, *presumed* to be invalid; the presumption can be overcome only by showing that the classification is justified by a "compelling" government interest and is narrowly tailored to serve that interest.

In addition to racial classifications, the strict scrutiny standard is also applied to certain other "suspect" classifications, such as discrimination based on national origin and (with some exceptions) discrimination against aliens.

(The Supreme Court has also applied strict scrutiny to Equal Protection Clause claims of violation of "fundamental" rights, such as the right to vote [Reynolds v. Sims, 377 U.S. 533, 562 (1964)] or to procreate [Skinner v. Oklahoma, 316 U.S. 535, 541 (1942)]. See comment "The Substantive Due Process Doctrine" in Chapter 6.)

Classifications based on gender occupy a unique status. Many such classifications are commonly accepted—for example, separate bathrooms for men and women, separate men's and women's sports teams, requiring men but not women to register for the draft, and different penalties and standards for statutory rape depending on sex. To evaluate a law challenged for gender discrimination, the Court generally applies a heightened standard of review but one that is less rigorous than strict scrutiny. Under this standard, a challenged gender classification will not be upheld unless the governmental body demonstrates that the classification is substantially related to an "important" (even though not "compelling") government objective. The Court applied this standard, for example, in United States v. Virginia, 518 U.S. 515 (1996), holding unconstitutional the exclusion of women from the Virginia Military Institute.[29]

All other classifications—all those not subjected to either strict scrutiny or the "intermediate" standard applied to gender classifications—are evaluated under the far more lenient "rational basis" test. This includes all social and economic legislation. Under the rational basis test, whoever challenges the alleged discrimination has the burden of showing that the legislature could have had no rational basis for adopting the classification—a very difficult standard to meet.

The Court has declined to recognize the poor, elderly, or disabled as a suspect classification warranting heightened scrutiny. In addition, although discrimination based on sexual orientation—against homosexual men or lesbian women—shares some characteristics applicable to other classifications that are reviewed under a heightened

---

[29]Because their scope is far broader than the Equal Protection Clause, which applies only to "state action," federal and state laws have become the primary vehicle for regulation of gender and employment discrimination. See comment "Federal Statutes Regulating Private Discrimination" in Chapter 4.

standard, the Court has never held that such discrimination should be judged under the Equal Protection Clause by any standard more exacting than the rational basis test.

In determining what classifications should be deemed "suspect" and therefore entitled to a heightened standard of review, the Court has considered several factors. For example, immutable characteristics like race, national origin, gender, and illegitimate birth—characteristics that the person did not choose and cannot change—may warrant a more rigorous scrutiny than the minimal rational basis standard. Another factor that has been considered is the ability of a group (such as aliens, who lack the right to vote) to protect itself through the political process.

Plessy v. Ferguson, 163 U.S. 537 (1896)

FACTS: An 1890 Louisiana statute required railroad companies to provide "white" and "colored" passengers with "equal but separate accommodations." The statute provided

> that all railway companies carrying passengers in their coaches in this state, shall provide equal but separate accommodations for the white, and colored races, by providing two or more passenger coaches for each passenger train, or by dividing the passenger coaches by a partition so as to secure separate accommodations: provided, that this section shall not be construed to apply to street railroads. No person or persons shall be permitted to occupy seats in coaches, other than the ones assigned to them, on account of the race they belong to.

The statute imposed criminal penalties on passengers using facilities not designated for their race.

Plessy, who alleged that he was only one-eighth African blood, was convicted under the statute for refusing to leave a portion of the train reserved for whites. The Louisiana Supreme Court rejected Plessy's contention that the statute violated the Fourteenth Amendment.

ISSUE: Do state laws requiring the separation of different races in public accommodations violate the Fourteenth Amendment?

DECISION (per *Brown,* 7-1, one Justice not participating): *No.*

A statute that implies merely a legal distinction between the white and colored races—a distinction that is founded in the color of the two races and that must always exist so long as white men are distinguished from the other race by color—has no tendency to destroy the legal equality of the two races.

The object of the Fourteenth Amendment was undoubtedly to enforce the absolute equality of the two races before the law, but, in the nature of things, it could not have been intended to abolish distinctions based upon color, or to enforce social ones, as distinguished from political, equality, or a commingling of the two races upon terms unsatisfactory to either. Laws permitting, and even requiring, their separation, in places where they are liable to be brought into contact, do not necessarily imply the inferiority of either race to the other, and have been generally, if not universally, recognized as within the competency of the state legislatures in the exercise of their police power. The most common instance of this is connected with the establishment of separate schools for white and colored children, which have been held to be a valid exercise of the legislative power even by courts of states where the political rights of the colored race have been longest and most earnestly enforced.

The distinction between laws interfering with the political equality of the Negro and those requiring the separation of the two races in schools, theaters, and railway carriages has been frequently drawn by this Court.

It is claimed by Plessy that the same argument that will justify the state legislature in requiring railways to provide separate accommodations for the two races will also authorize them to require separate cars to be provided for people whose hair is of a certain color, or who are aliens, or who belong to certain nationalities, or to enact laws requiring colored people to walk upon one side of the street and white people upon the other, or requiring white men's houses to be painted white and colored men's black, or their vehicles or business signs to be of different colors, upon the theory that one side of the street is as good as the other or that a house or vehicle of one color is as good as one of another color. The reply to all this is that every exercise of the police power must be reasonable and must extend only to such laws as are enacted in good faith for the promotion of the public good, and not for the annoyance or oppression of a particular class.

So far, then, as a conflict with the Fourteenth Amendment is concerned, the case reduces itself to the question whether the Louisiana statute is a reasonable regulation, and with respect to this there must necessarily be a large discretion on the part of the legislature. In determining the question of reasonableness, it is at liberty to act with reference to the established usages, customs, and traditions of the people, and with a view to the promotion of their comfort and the preservation of the public peace and good order. Gauged by this standard, we cannot say that a law that authorizes or even requires the separation of the two races in public conveyances is unreasonable or more obnoxious to the Fourteenth Amendment than the Acts of Congress requiring separate schools for colored children in the District of Columbia, the constitutionality of which does not seem to have been questioned, or the corresponding acts of state legislatures.

We consider the underlying fallacy of Plessy's argument to consist in the assumption that the enforced separation of the two races stamps the colored race with a badge of inferiority. If this be so, it is not by reason of anything found in the Act, but solely because the colored race chooses to put that construction upon it.

Plessy's argument also assumes that social prejudices may be overcome by legislation and that equal rights cannot be secured to the Negro except by an enforced commingling of the two races. We cannot accept this proposition. If the two races are to meet upon terms of social equality, it must be the result of natural affinities, a mutual appreciation of each other's merits, and a voluntary consent of individuals. Legislation is powerless to eradicate racial instincts or to abolish distinctions based upon physical differences, and the attempt to do so can only result in accentuating the difficulties of the present situation. If the civil and political rights of both races are equal, one cannot be inferior to the other civilly or politically. If one race is inferior to the other socially, the Constitution of the United States cannot put them upon the same plane.

Harlan, dissenting: It was said in argument that the Louisiana statute does not discriminate against either race, but prescribes a rule applicable alike to white and colored citizens. But everyone knows that the statute in question had its origin in the purpose not so much to exclude white persons from railroad cars occupied by blacks as to exclude colored people from coaches occupied by or assigned to white persons. The thing to accomplish was, under the guise of giving equal accommodation for whites and blacks, to compel the latter to keep to themselves while traveling in railroad passenger coaches.

The fundamental objection to the statute is that it interferes with the personal freedom of citizens. If a white man and a black man choose to occupy the same public conveyance on a public highway, it is their right to do so; and no government, proceeding alone on grounds of race, can prevent it without infringing the personal liberty of each.

If a State can prescribe, as a rule of civil conduct, that whites and blacks shall not travel as passengers in the same railroad coach, why may it not so regulate the use of the streets of its cities and towns as to compel white citizens to keep on one side of a street and black citizens to keep on the other? Why may it not, upon like grounds, punish whites and blacks who ride together in street cars or in open vehicles on a public road or street? Why may it not require sheriffs to assign whites to one side of a courtroom and blacks to the other? And why may it not also prohibit the commingling of the two races in the galleries of legislative halls or in public assemblages convened for the consideration of the political questions of the day? Further, if this statute of Louisiana is consistent with the personal liberty of citizens, why may not the State require the separation in railroad coaches of native and naturalized citizens of the United States, or of Protestants and Roman Catholics?

The answer given at the argument to these questions was that regulations of the kind they suggest would be unreasonable, and could not, therefore, stand before the law. Is it meant that the determination of questions of legislative power depends upon the inquiry whether the statute whose validity is questioned is, in the judgment of the courts, a reasonable one, taking all the circumstances into consideration? A statute may be unreasonable merely because a sound public policy forbade its enactment. But I do not understand that the courts have anything to do with the policy or expediency of legislation. There is a dangerous tendency in these latter days to enlarge the functions of the courts, by means of judicial interference with the will of the people as expressed by the legislature. Each of the three departments of government must keep within the limits defined by the Constitution. And the courts best discharge their duty by executing the will of the lawmaking power, constitutionally expressed, leaving the results of legislation to be dealt with by the people through their representatives.

The white race deems itself to be the dominant race in this country. And so it is, in prestige, in achievements, in education, in wealth, and in power. So, I doubt not, it will continue to be for all time if it remains true to its great heritage and holds fast to the principles of constitutional liberty. But in view of the Constitution, in the eye of the law, there is in this country no superior, dominant, ruling class of citizens. There is no caste here. Our Constitution is color-blind and neither knows nor tolerates classes among citizens. In respect of civil rights, all citizens are equal before the law. The humblest is the peer of the most powerful. The law regards man as man, and takes no account of his surroundings or of his color when his civil rights as guaranteed by the supreme law of the land are involved. It is therefore to be regretted that this high tribunal, the final expositor of the fundamental law of the land, has reached the conclusion that it is competent for a state to regulate the enjoyment by citizens of their civil rights solely upon the basis of race.

In my opinion, the judgment this day rendered will, in time, prove to be quite as pernicious as the decision made by this tribunal in the *Dred Scott* case.

The present decision, it may well be apprehended, will not only stimulate aggressions, more or less brutal and irritating, upon the admitted rights of colored citizens, but will encourage the belief that it is possible, by means of state enactments, to defeat the beneficent purposes that the people of the United States had in view when they adopted the recent amendments. Sixty million whites are in no danger from the presence here of eight million blacks. The destinies of the two races, in this country, are indissolubly linked together, and the interests of both require that the common government of all shall not permit the seeds of race hate to be planted under the sanction of law. What can more certainly arouse race hate, what can more certainly create and perpetuate a feeling of distrust between these races, than state enactments that, in fact, proceed on the ground that colored citizens are so inferior and degraded that they cannot be allowed to sit in public coaches occupied by white citizens? That, as all will admit, is the real meaning of such legislation as was enacted in Louisiana.

The sure guaranty of the peace and security of each race is the clear, distinct, unconditional recognition by our governments, national and state, of every right that inheres in civil freedom, and of the equality before the law of all citizens of the United States, without regard to race. State enactments regulating the enjoyment of civil rights upon the basis of race, and cunningly devised to defeat legitimate results of the war, under the pretense of recognizing equality of rights, can have no other result than to render permanent peace impossible and to keep alive a conflict of races, the continuance of which must do harm to all concerned. This question is not met by the suggestion that social equality cannot exist between the white and black races in this country. That argument, if it can be properly regarded as one, is scarcely worthy of consideration; for social equality no more exists between two races when traveling in a passenger coach or a public highway than when members of the same races sit by each other in a street car or in the jury box, or when they stand or sit with each other in a political assembly, or when they use in common the streets of a city or town, or when they are in the same room for the purpose of having their names placed on the registry of voters, or when they approach the ballot box in order to exercise the high privilege of voting.

I am of the opinion that the Louisiana statute is inconsistent with the personal liberty of citizens, white and black, and hostile to both the spirit and letter of the Constitution. If laws of like character should be enacted in the several states of the Union, the effect would be in the highest degree mischievous. Slavery, as an institution tolerated by law, would have disappeared from our country; but there would remain a power in the states, by sinister legislation, to interfere with the full enjoyment of the blessings of freedom, to regulate civil rights, common to all citizens, upon the basis of race, and to place a large body of American citizens in a condition of legal inferiority.

Korematsu v. United States, 323 U.S. 214 (1944)

FACTS: On February 19, 1942, two months after the United States entered World War II, President Franklin Roosevelt issued Executive Order 9066 authorizing United States military commanders to "prescribe military areas [from] which any or all persons may be excluded, and with respect to which, the right of any person to enter, remain in, or leave shall be subject to whatever restriction [the] Commander may impose in his discretion." The Executive Order declared that "the successful prosecution of the war requires every possible protection against espionage and against sabotage to national-defense material, national-defense premises, and national-defense utilities."

On March 21, 1942, Congress passed legislation making it a crime to violate an order of any military commander made pursuant to the Executive Order. On May 3, 1942, under this authority, John DeWitt, the commanding general of the Army Western Command, issued Civilian Exclusion Order No. 34, requiring all persons of Japanese descent living along the West Coast to vacate their homes, report to and temporarily remain in "Assembly Centers," and then be transferred under military control to "Relocation Centers," there to remain for an indeterminate period until released by the military authorities.

Fred Korematsu, a native-born U.S. citizen of Japanese descent, declined to leave his home in San Leandro, California, a designated "Military Area," contrary to Order No. 34. Although no question was raised as to his loyalty to the United States, he was arrested, jailed, tried, and convicted for knowingly and admittedly remaining in San Leandro.

ISSUE: Was the exclusion order in violation of the Due Process Clause of the Fifth Amendment?

DECISION (per *Black,* 6-3): *No.*

All legal restrictions that curtail the civil rights of a single racial group are immediately suspect. That is not to say that all such restrictions are unconstitutional. It is to say that courts must subject them to the most rigid scrutiny. Pressing public necessity may sometimes justify the existence of such restrictions; racial antagonism never can.

A curfew order, which like the exclusion order here was promulgated pursuant to Executive Order 9066, subjected all persons of Japanese ancestry in prescribed West Coast military areas to remain in their residences from 8 P.M. to 6 A.M. In Hirabayashi v. United States, 320 U.S. 81 (1943), the Court sustained a conviction obtained for violation of the curfew order.

In the light of the principles announced in *Hirabayashi,* we are unable to conclude that it was beyond the war power of Congress and the Executive branch to exclude those of Japanese ancestry from the West Coast war area at the time they did. True, exclusion from the area in which one's home is located is a far greater deprivation than constant confinement to the home from 8 P.M. to 6 A.M. Nothing short of apprehension by the proper military authorities of the gravest imminent danger to the public safety can constitutionally justify either. But exclusion from a threatened area, no less than curfew, has a definite and close relationship to the prevention of espionage and sabotage. The military authorities, charged with the primary responsibility of defending our shores, concluded that curfew provided inadequate protection and ordered exclusion.

Korematsu urges that by May 1942, when Order No. 34 was promulgated, all danger of Japanese invasion of the West Coast had disappeared. However, as stated in *Hirabayashi,*

we cannot reject as unfounded the judgment of the military authorities and of Congress that there were disloyal members of that population, whose number and strength could not be precisely and quickly ascertained. We cannot say that the war-making branches of the Government did not have ground for believing that in a critical hour such persons could not readily be isolated and separately dealt with, and constituted a menace to the

national defense and safety, which demanded that prompt and adequate measures be taken
to guard against it.

Like curfew, exclusion of those of Japanese origin was deemed necessary because
of the presence of an unascertained number of disloyal members of the group, most
of whom we have no doubt were loyal to this country. It was because we could not
reject the finding of the military authorities that it was impossible to bring about an
immediate segregation of the disloyal from the loyal that we sustained the validity of
the curfew order as applying to the whole group. In the instant case, temporary exclusion of the entire group was based by the military on the same ground. The judgment
that exclusion of the whole group was for the same reason a military imperative
answers the contention that the exclusion was in the nature of group punishment based
on antagonism to those of Japanese origin. That there were members of the group who
retained loyalties to Japan has been confirmed by investigations made subsequent to
the exclusion. Approximately 5,000 American citizens of Japanese ancestry refused
to swear unqualified allegiance to the United States and to renounce allegiance to the
Japanese Emperor, and several thousand evacuees requested repatriation to Japan.

We uphold the exclusion order as of the time it was made and when Korematsu violated it. In doing so, we are not unmindful of the hardships imposed by it upon a large
group of American citizens. But hardships are part of war, and war is an aggregation of
hardships. All citizens alike, both in and out of uniform, feel the impact of war in
greater or lesser measure. Citizenship has its responsibilities as well as its privileges,
and in time of war the burden is always heavier. Compulsory exclusion of large groups
of citizens from their homes, except under circumstances of direst emergency and
peril, is inconsistent with our basic governmental institutions. But when under conditions of modern warfare our shores are threatened by hostile forces, the power to protect must be commensurate with the threatened danger.

It is said that we are dealing here with the case of imprisonment of a citizen in a concentration camp solely because of his ancestry, without evidence or inquiry concerning
his loyalty and good disposition towards the United States. Our task would be simple,
our duty clear, were this a case involving the imprisonment of a loyal citizen in a concentration camp because of racial prejudice. Regardless of the true nature of the
assembly and relocation centers—and we deem it unjustifiable to call them concentration camps with all the ugly connotations that term implies—we are dealing specifically with nothing but an exclusion order. To cast this case into outlines of racial
prejudice, without reference to the real military dangers that were presented, merely
confuses the issue. Korematsu was not excluded from the military area because of hostility to him or his race. He was excluded because we are at war with the Japanese
Empire, because the properly constituted military authorities feared an invasion of
our West Coast and felt constrained to take proper security measures, because they
decided that the military urgency of the situation demanded that all citizens of Japanese ancestry be segregated from the West Coast temporarily, and, finally, because
Congress, reposing its confidence in this time of war in our military leaders—as inevitably it must—determined that they should have the power to do just this. We cannot,
by availing ourselves of the calm perspective of hindsight, now say that at that time
these actions were unjustified.

Frankfurter, concurring: The provisions of the Constitution that confer on the
Congress and the president powers to enable this country to wage war are as much part

of the Constitution as provisions looking to a nation at peace. And the war power of the government is the power to wage war successfully. Therefore, the validity of action under the war power must be judged wholly in the context of war. That action is not to be stigmatized as lawless because like action in times of peace would be lawless.

The respective spheres of action of military authorities and of judges are, of course, very different. But within their sphere, military authorities are no more outside the bounds of obedience to the Constitution than are judges within theirs. If a military order such as that under review does not transcend the means appropriate for conducting war, such action by the military is as constitutional as would be any authorized action by the Interstate Commerce Commission within the limits of the constitutional power to regulate commerce. And being an exercise of the war power explicitly granted by the Constitution for safeguarding the national life by prosecuting war effectively, I find nothing in the Constitution that denies to Congress the power to enforce such a valid military order by making its violation an offense triable in the civil courts.

Roberts, dissenting: I dissent, because I think the indisputable facts exhibit a clear violation of constitutional rights. This is not a case of keeping people off the streets at night as in *Hirabayashi,* nor a case of temporary exclusion of a citizen from an area for his own safety or that of the community, nor a case of offering him an opportunity to go temporarily out of an area where his presence might cause danger to himself or to his fellows. On the contrary, it is the case of convicting a citizen as a punishment for not submitting to imprisonment in a concentration camp, based on his ancestry, and solely because of his ancestry, without evidence or inquiry concerning his loyalty and good disposition towards the United States. If this be a correct statement of the facts disclosed by this record, and facts of which we take judicial notice, I need hardly labor the conclusion that constitutional rights have been violated.

The liberty of every American citizen freely to come and to go must frequently, in the face of sudden danger, be temporarily limited or suspended. The civil authorities must often resort to the expedient of excluding citizens temporarily from a locality. The drawing of fire lines in the case of a conflagration and the removal of persons from the area where a pestilence has broken out are familiar examples. If the exclusion in question were of that nature, the *Hirabayashi* case would be the authority for sustaining it. But the facts show that the exclusion was but a part of an overall plan for forcible detention. This case cannot, therefore, be decided on any such narrow ground as the possible validity of a temporary exclusion order under which the residents of an area are given an opportunity to leave and go elsewhere in their native land outside the boundaries of a military area. To make the case turn on any such assumption is to shut our eyes to reality.

Murphy, dissenting: This exclusion of "all persons of Japanese ancestry, both alien and non-alien," from the Pacific Coast area on a plea of military necessity in the absence of martial law ought not to be approved.

Being an obvious racial discrimination, the order deprives all those within its scope of the equal protection of the laws as guaranteed by the Fifth Amendment. It further deprives these individuals of their constitutional rights to live and work where they will, to establish a home where they choose, and to move about freely. In excommunicating them without benefit of hearings, this order also deprives them of all their constitutional rights to procedural due process. Yet no reasonable relation to an immediate, imminent, and impending public danger is evident to support this racial restriction, which is one of the most sweeping and complete deprivations of constitutional rights in the history of this nation in the absence of martial law.

In adjudging the military action taken in light of the then apparent dangers, we must not erect too high or too meticulous standards; it is necessary only that the action have some reasonable relation to the removal of the dangers of invasion, sabotage, and espionage. But the exclusion, either temporarily or permanently, of all persons with Japanese blood in their veins has no such reasonable relation. And that relation is lacking because the exclusion order necessarily must rely for its reasonableness upon the assumption that all persons of Japanese ancestry may have a dangerous tendency to commit sabotage and espionage and to aid our Japanese enemy in other ways. It is difficult to believe that reason, logic, or experience could be marshalled in support of such an assumption.

That this forced exclusion was the result in good measure of this erroneous assumption of racial guilt rather than bona fide military necessity is evidenced by the commanding general's final report on the evacuation from the Pacific Coast area. In it he refers to all individuals of Japanese descent as "subversive," as belonging to "an enemy race" whose "racial strains are undiluted," and as constituting "over 112,000 potential enemies . . . at large today" along the Pacific Coast. In support of this blanket condemnation of all persons of Japanese descent, however, no reliable evidence is cited to show that such individuals were generally disloyal, or had generally so conducted themselves in this area as to constitute a special menace to defense installations or war industries, or had otherwise by their behavior furnished reasonable ground for their exclusion as a group.

Individuals of Japanese ancestry are condemned in the report because they are said to be "a large, unassimilated, tightly knit racial group, bound to an enemy nation by strong ties of race, culture, custom and religion." They are claimed to be given to "emperor worshipping ceremonies" and to "dual citizenship." Japanese language schools and allegedly pro-Japanese organizations are cited as evidence of possible group disloyalty, together with facts as to certain persons being educated and residing at length in Japan. It is intimated that many of these individuals deliberately resided "adjacent to strategic points," thus enabling them "to carry into execution a tremendous program of sabotage on a mass scale should any considerable number of them have been inclined to do so."

The main reasons relied upon by those responsible for the forced evacuation, therefore, do not prove a reasonable relation between the group characteristics of Japanese Americans and the dangers of invasion, sabotage, and espionage. The reasons appear, instead, to be largely an accumulation of much of the misinformation, half-truths, and insinuations that for years have been directed against Japanese Americans by people with racial and economic prejudices—the same people who have been among the foremost advocates of the evacuation. A military judgment based upon such racial and sociological considerations is not entitled to the great weight ordinarily given the judgments based upon strictly military considerations.

No adequate reason is given for the failure to treat these Japanese Americans on an individual basis by holding investigations and hearings to separate the loyal from the disloyal, as was done in the case of persons of German and Italian ancestry. All residents of this nation are kin in some way by blood or culture to a foreign land. Yet they are primarily and necessarily a part of the new and distinct civilization of the United

States. They must accordingly be treated at all times as the heirs of the American experiment and as entitled to all the rights and freedoms guaranteed by the Constitution.

Jackson, dissenting: If any fundamental assumption underlies our system, it is that guilt is personal and not inheritable. But here is an attempt to make an otherwise innocent act a crime merely because this prisoner is the son of parents as to whom he had no choice and belongs to a race from which there is no way to resign. If Congress in peacetime legislation should enact such a criminal law, I should suppose this Court would refuse to enforce it.

But the "law" that this prisoner is convicted of disregarding is not found in an act of Congress, but in a military order. Neither the Act of Congress nor the Executive Order of the President, nor both together, would afford a basis for this conviction. It rests on the orders of General John DeWitt. And it is said that if the military commander had reasonable military grounds for promulgating the orders, they are constitutional and become law, and the Court is required to enforce them. I cannot subscribe to this doctrine.

It would be impracticable and dangerous idealism to expect or insist that each specific military command in an area of probable operations will conform to conventional tests of constitutionality. But if we cannot confine military expedients by the Constitution, neither would I distort the Constitution to approve all that the military may deem expedient. This is what the Court appears to be doing, whether consciously or not. Even if the orders of General DeWitt were permissible military procedures, I deny that it follows that they are constitutional. If, as the Court holds, it does follow, then we may as well say that any military order will be constitutional and have done with it.

The limitation under which courts always will labor in examining the necessity for a military order are illustrated by this case. How does the Court know that these orders have a reasonable basis in necessity? No evidence whatever on that subject has been taken by this or any other court. There is sharp controversy as to the credibility of the DeWitt report. So the Court, having no real evidence before it, has no choice but to accept General DeWitt's own unsworn, self-serving statement, untested by any cross-examination, that what he did was reasonable. And thus it will always be when courts try to look into the reasonableness of a military order.

Furthermore, a judicial construction of the due process clause that will sustain this order is a far more subtle blow to liberty than the promulgation of the order itself. A military order, however unconstitutional, is not apt to last longer than the military emergency. But once a judicial opinion rationalizes such an order to show that it conforms to the Constitution, or rather rationalizes the Constitution to show that the Constitution sanctions such an order, the Court for all time has validated the principle of racial discrimination in criminal procedure and of transplanting American citizens. The principle then lies about like a loaded weapon ready for the hand of any authority that can bring forward a plausible claim of an urgent need. All who observe the work of the courts are familiar with what Judge Cardozo described as "the tendency of a principle to expand itself to the limit of its logic." A military commander may overstep the bounds of constitutionality, and it is an incident. But if we review and approve, that passing incident becomes the doctrine of the Constitution.

I do not suggest that the courts should have attempted to interfere with the Army in carrying out its task. But I do not think they may be asked to execute a military expedient that has no place in law under the Constitution. I would reverse the judgment and discharge the prisoner.

*****

[*Note:* In the *Hirabayashi* case cited by the majority, the Supreme Court in 1943 unanimously affirmed the conviction of Kiyoshi Hirabayashi, a Japanese-American college student, for violating a military curfew order on the West Coast. The Court acknowledged that "Distinctions between citizens solely because of their ancestry are by their very nature odious to a free people whose institutions are founded upon the doctrine of equality" and that "racial discriminations are in most circumstances irrelevant and therefore prohibited." Nevertheless, in rejecting the argument that wartime measures could not include a curfew applicable only to persons of a given ancestry, rather than to just those who might be found to be disloyal, the Court stated that "[W]e think that constitutional government, in time of war, is not so powerless and [it] does not compel so hard a choice if those charged with the responsibility of our national defense have reasonable ground for believing that the threat [of sabotage and espionage] is real." Justices Douglas, Murphy, and Rutledge filed concurring opinions.]

The Aftermath of the *Korematsu* Case

In 1980, Congress established an independent commission to review the exclusion and internment program. The commission heard the testimony of more than 720 witnesses, including key officials involved in the issuance and implementation of Executive Order 9066, and reviewed hundreds of documents that had not previously been available. In 1983, after its study of the evidence, the commission unanimously concluded that the factors that shaped the internment decision "were race prejudice, war hysteria, and a failure of political leadership," rather than military necessity.

As Joseph Persico recounted:

> Supposed proof of Japanese sabotage included reports "that ground glass had been found in shrimp canned by Japanese workers and that Japanese saboteurs had sprayed overdoses of arsenic poison on vegetables . . . , a beautiful field of flowers on the property of a Jap farmer near Ventura, California, had been plowed up because it seems the Jap was a fifth columnist and had grown his flowers in a way that when viewed from a plane formed an arrow pointing in the direction of the airport." Where no evidence of sabotage surfaced, a perverse logic provided it anyway. *General DeWitt [the commanding officer on the West Coast] concluded, "The very fact that no sabotage has taken place to date is a disturbing and confirming indication that such action will be taken."* Yet even FBI director J. Edgar Hoover, no civil libertarian or lover of minorities, saw through the calls for rounding up the Japanese. [Hoover said that] "The necessity for mass evacuation is based primarily upon public and political pressure rather than on factual data." (Italics added.)[30]

In 1983, Fred Korematsu filed a petition in federal court to have his conviction set aside for "manifest injustice." The following year, District Judge Marilyn Patel

---

[30]Joseph Persico, *Roosevelt's Secret War* [Random House 2001]: 168; see also Stone, *Perilous Times: Free Speech in Wartime* [Norton 2004]: 286–307.

granted the petition. Judge Patel found that the government, in its presentation of evidence at Korematsu's trial, had knowingly and intentionally failed to disclose critical information that directly contradicted key statements in General DeWitt's "Final Report" that the government had relied upon to justify the mass evacuation.

Four years later, Congress passed and President Ronald Reagan signed the Civil Liberties Act of 1988, which officially declared that the program had been a "grave injustice" that was "carried out without adequate security reasons" and without any documented acts of "espionage or sabotage." The Act included an official apology for the Government's actions and financial reparations for those interned.

Confronting "Separate but Equal"

For over half a century *Plessy v. Ferguson* remained the controlling precedent on the constitutionality of racial segregation. However, starting in the 1930s, the application of the "separate but equal" doctrine was challenged in a series of Supreme Court cases involving segregation of black students at university graduate schools.

In Missouri ex rel. Gaines v. Canada, 305 U.S. 337 (1938), the University of Missouri law school refused to admit a qualified black applicant, but the State offered to pay his tuition at an out-of-state law school. In both Sipuel v. Oklahoma Board of Regents, 332 U.S. 631 (1948), and Sweatt v. Painter, 339 U.S. 629 (1950), state law schools refused to admit qualified black applicants because the State would soon open separate law schools for blacks. In McLaurin v. Oklahoma, 339 U.S. 637 (1950), a black student seeking a doctorate in education was admitted to Oklahoma University but was required to sit in a separate row in class and to sit at separate tables in the library and cafeteria. In each of these cases, the Supreme Court sustained the equal protection claim on the ground that the education offered to the Negro plaintiff was not equal, and therefore found it unnecessary to pass on the validity of the "separate but equal" doctrine.

In 1952 the Supreme Court agreed to review five cases (which became known as *Brown v. Board of Education,* the title of one of the five cases) challenging the constitutionality of legally enforced segregation in public schools. Unlike the earlier graduate school cases, these cases squarely presented the issue whether the "separate but equal" doctrine should be overruled.

According to Justice William Douglas:[31]

When the cases had been argued in December of 1952, only four of us—Minton, Burton, Black and myself—felt that segregation was unconstitutional. Vinson was Chief Justice and he seemed to be firm that *Plessy* v. *Ferguson* should stand, and that the states should be allowed to deal with segregation in their own way and should be given time to make the black schools equal to those of the whites. Justice Reed held that segregation was on its way out and over the years would disappear, and that meanwhile the states should be allowed to handle it in their own way.

Frankfurter's view was that it was not unconstitutional to treat a Negro differently from a white but that the cases should be reargued. Jackson felt that nothing in the Fourteenth Amendment barred segregation and that it "would be bad for the Negroes" to be put in white schools, while Justice Clark said that since we had led the states to believe segregation was lawful, we should let them work out the problem by themselves.

[31]William Douglas, *The Court Years 1939–1975* [Random House 1980]: 113.

It was clear that if a decision had been reached in the 1952 Term, we would have had five saying that separate but equal schools were constitutional, that separate but unequal schools were not constitutional, and that the remedy was to give the states time to make the two systems of schools equal.

Douglas's counting of probable votes and his characterization of the positions of Frankfurter and Jackson (with both of whom Douglas was frequently at odds) is open to question. According to Richard Kluger, the preeminent historian of the *Brown* decision:[32]

Frankfurter thought the Court was divided five-to-four in favor of reversing *Plessy,* with himself in the majority. Burton thought the Court stood at six-to-three for reversing. Jackson counted anywhere from two to four dissenters if the Court voted to reverse, with himself in the majority camp, provided that an opinion palatable to him was drafted by Black or whoever might write for the Court.

In any event, regardless of which of these several predictions would have proved correct if the vote had actually been taken at that time, the result would have been a seriously divided Court on a critical national issue with potentially disastrous consequences.

Fortunately, any decision was deferred by the Court's agreement in June 1952 to order reargument in the following term. For this purpose, counsel were instructed to express their views in further briefs on several questions concerning the legislative history of the Fourteenth Amendment, the judicial power of the judiciary to abolish segregation in public schools, and implementation of any decree in the event the Court found segregation invalid.

The reargument was scheduled for October 1953. In September, one month before the reargument, Chief Justice Fred Vinson died, and President Dwight Eisenhower promptly filled the vacancy by appointing Earl Warren, then governor of California, as Chief Justice. The reargument was rescheduled for December 7–9, 1953.

Douglas stated:[33]

On December 12, 1953, at the first Conference after the second argument, Warren suggested that the cases be discussed informally and no vote be taken. He didn't want the Conference to split up into two opposed groups. Warren's approach to the problem and his discussions in Conference were conciliatory; not those of an advocate trying to convince recalcitrant judges. Frankfurter maintained the position that history supported the conclusions in *Plessy* that segregation was constitutional. Reed thought segregation was constitutional, and Jackson thought the issue was "political" and beyond judicial competence. Tom Clark was of the opinion that violence would follow if the Court ordered desegregation of the schools, but that while history sanctioned segregation, he would vote to abolish it if the matter was handled delicately.

As Warren recounted:[34]

We decided not to make up our minds on that first conference day, but to talk it over, from week to week, dealing with different aspects of it—in groups, over lunches, in conference. It was too important to hurry it.

---

[32]Richard Kluger, *Simple Justice* [Knopf 1975]: 614. Other books detailing the background of the *Brown* case include Jim Newton, *Justice for All: Earl Warren and the Nation He Made* [Riverhead 2006]: 309–325, and *Super Chief: Earl Warren and His Supreme Court* [NYU Press 1983]: 72–127.
[33]Douglas, *The Court Years 1939–1975,* at 114.
[34]Kluger, *Simple Justice,* at 683.

Warren similarly explained:[35]

we were all impressed with their importance and the desirability of achieving unanimity if possible. Realizing that when a person once announces he has reached a conclusion it is more difficult for him to change his thinking, we decided that we would dispense with our usual custom of formally expressing our individual views at the first conference and would confine ourselves for a time to informal discussion of the briefs, the arguments made at the hearing, and our own independent research on each conference day, reserving our final opinions until the discussions were concluded.

We followed this plan until the following February [other indications suggest this was later than February], when it was agreed that we were ready to vote. On the first vote, we unanimously agreed that the "separate but equal" doctrine had no place in public education. The question then arose as to how this view should be written—as a *per curiam* (by the Court) or as a signed, individualized opinion. We decided that it would carry more force if done through a signed opinion, and, at the suggestion of some of the Justices, it was thought that it should bear the signature of the Chief Justice.

Warren's draft of the *Brown* opinion was circulated to the other Justices on Saturday, May 8, together with a short cover memo from Warren (dated May 7) stating that the opinion was prepared on the theory that it "should be short, readable by the lay public, non-rhetorical, unemotional and, above all, non-accusatory." [36]

An earlier *undistributed* draft of Warren's cover memo, dated May 5, listed additional "considerations which caused me to make this approach to the problem." Among other points, this undistributed draft of the cover memo states that "On the question of segregation in education, this should be the end of the line ... but we should not go beyond that. The applicability of the ['separate but equal'] doctrine in other contexts must await future decision." The draft further observed: "No section of the country and no segment of our population can justly place full responsibility for segregation on others. They must assume a measure of that responsibility themselves." [37]

The changes requested by the other Justices were primarily editorial in nature. (Douglas responded: "I do not think I would change a single word.") However, when the next draft of the *Brown* opinion was circulated, a sentence concerning *Plessy v. Ferguson* was revised. The initial draft stated that "In so far as there is language in *Plessy v. Ferguson* contrary to this finding with respect to public education, that case is overruled." In the draft sent on May 12 to the Court's print shop, that sentence (perhaps in recognition of the fact that *Plessy* involved segregation in transportation, not education) was changed to read that "Any language in *Plessy v. Ferguson* contrary to this finding is rejected." [38]

After a few further editorial changes, the Court's unanimous opinion—the next-digested case—was delivered on May 17, 1954.

Brown v. Board of Education, 347 U.S. 483 (1954)

FACTS: The four cases decided in this opinion came from the States of Kansas, South Carolina, Virginia, and Delaware. In each of the cases, minors of the Negro race

---

[35]Earl Warren, *The Memoirs of Chief Justice Earl Warren* [Doubleday 1977]: 285.
[36]Papers of Earl Warren, Library of Congress, Box 571.
[37]Ibid.
[38]Ibid.

(through their legal representatives) sued in the lower courts to obtain admission to the public schools of their community on a nonsegregated basis. In each instance, they had been denied admission to schools attended by white children under state laws requiring or permitting segregation according to race.

The plaintiffs attacked the constitutional validity of the "separate but equal" doctrine upheld in the Supreme Court's decision in Plessy v. Ferguson, 163 U.S. 537 (1896). They contended that segregated public schools are not "equal" and cannot be made "equal," and that hence they were being deprived of the equal protection of the laws under the Fourteenth Amendment.

The cases were initially argued before the Supreme Court in its 1952 Term and then reargued the following term.

ISSUE: Does state-imposed racial segregation of public schools violate the Equal Protection Clause of the Fourteenth Amendment?

DECISION (unanimous opinion by *Warren*): *Yes.*

Reargument was largely devoted to the circumstances surrounding the adoption of the Fourteenth Amendment in 1868. It covered exhaustively consideration of the Amendment in Congress, ratification by the States, then existing practices in racial segregation, and the views of proponents and opponents of the Amendment. This discussion and our own investigation convince us that, although these sources cast some light, it is not enough to resolve the problem with which we are faced. At best, they are inconclusive. The most avid proponents of the postwar amendments undoubtedly intended them to remove all legal distinctions among "all persons born or naturalized in the United States." Their opponents, just as certainly, were antagonistic to both the letter and the spirit of the amendments and wished them to have the most limited effect. What others in Congress and the state legislatures had in mind cannot be determined with any degree of certainty.

An additional reason for the inconclusive nature of the Amendment's history, with respect to segregated schools, is the status of public education at that time. In the South, the movement toward free common schools, supported by general taxation, had not yet taken hold. Education of white children was largely in the hands of private groups. Education of Negroes was almost nonexistent, and practically all of the race were illiterate. In fact, any education of Negroes was forbidden by law in some States. Today, in contrast, many Negroes have achieved outstanding success in the arts and sciences as well as in the business and professional world. It is true that public school education at the time of the Amendment had advanced further in the North, but the effect of the Amendment on Northern States was generally ignored in the congressional debates. Even in the North, the conditions of public education did not approximate those existing today. The curriculum was usually rudimentary; ungraded schools were common in rural areas; the school term was but three months a year in many states; and compulsory school attendance was virtually unknown. As a consequence, it is not surprising that there should be so little in the history of the Fourteenth Amendment relating to its intended effect on public education.

In the first cases in this Court construing the Fourteenth Amendment, decided shortly after its adoption, the Court interpreted it as proscribing all state-imposed discriminations against the Negro race. The doctrine of "separate but equal" did not make its appearance in this Court until 1896 in *Plessy v. Ferguson,* involving not education but transportation. American courts have since labored with the doctrine for over half a century. In this Court, there have been six cases involving the "separate but equal" doctrine in the field of public education. In Cumming v. County Board of Education, 175 U.S. 528, and Gong Lum v. Rice, 275 U.S. 78, the validity of the doctrine itself was not challenged. In more recent cases, all on the graduate school level, inequality was found in that specific benefits enjoyed by white students were denied to Negro students of the same qualifications. Missouri ex rel. Gaines v. Canada, 305 U.S. 337; Sipuel v. Oklahoma, 332 U.S. 631; Sweatt v. Painter, 339 U.S. 629; McLaurin v. Oklahoma State Regents, 339 U.S. 637. In none of these cases was it necessary to reexamine the doctrine to grant relief to the Negro plaintiff. And in Sweatt v. Painter, the Court expressly reserved decision on the question whether Plessy v. Ferguson should be held inapplicable to public education.

In the instant cases, that question is directly presented. Here, unlike Sweatt v. Painter, there are findings below that the Negro and white schools involved have been equalized, or are being equalized, with respect to buildings, curricula, qualifications and salaries of teachers, and other "tangible" factors. Our decision, therefore, cannot turn on merely a comparison of these tangible factors in the Negro and white schools involved in each of the cases. We must look instead to the effect of segregation itself on public education.

In approaching this problem, we cannot turn the clock back to 1868 when the Amendment was adopted, or even to 1896 when Plessy v. Ferguson was written. We must consider public education in the light of its full development and its present place in American life throughout the nation. Only in this way can it be determined if segregation in public schools deprives these plaintiffs of the equal protection of the laws.

Today, education is perhaps the most important function of state and local governments. Compulsory school attendance laws and the great expenditures for education both demonstrate our recognition of the importance of education to our democratic society. It is required in the performance of our most basic public responsibilities, even service in the armed forces. It is the very foundation of good citizenship. Today it is a principal instrument in awakening the child to cultural values, in preparing him for later professional training, and in helping him to adjust normally to his environment. In these days, it is doubtful that any child may reasonably be expected to succeed in life if he is denied the opportunity of an education. Such an opportunity, where the state has undertaken to provide it, is a right that must be made available to all on equal terms.

We come then to the question presented: Does segregation of children in public schools solely on the basis of race, even though the physical facilities and other "tangible" factors may be equal, deprive the children of the minority group of equal educational opportunities? We believe that it does.

In Sweatt v. Painter, in finding that a segregated law school for Negroes could not provide them equal educational opportunities, this Court relied in large part on "those qualities which are incapable of objective measurement but which make for greatness in a law school." In McLaurin v. Oklahoma State Regents, the Court, in requiring that a Negro admitted to a white graduate school be treated like all other students, again resorted to intangible considerations: "his ability to study, to engage in discussions and exchange views with other students, and, in general, to learn his profession." Such considerations apply with added force to children in grade and high schools. To separate them from others of similar age and qualifications solely because of their race generates a feeling of inferiority as to their status in the community that may affect their hearts and minds in a way unlikely ever to be undone. The effect of this separation on their educational opportunities was well stated by a finding in the Kansas case by a court that nevertheless felt compelled to rule against the Negro plaintiffs:

> Segregation of white and colored children in public schools has a detrimental effect upon the colored children. The impact is greater when it has the sanction of the law; for the policy of separating the races is usually interpreted as denoting the inferiority of the negro group. A sense of inferiority affects the motivation of a child to learn. Segregation with the sanction of law, therefore, has a tendency to [retard] the educational and mental development of negro children and to deprive them of some of the benefits they would receive in a racial[ly] integrated school system.[39]

Whatever may have been the extent of psychological knowledge at the time of *Plessy v. Ferguson,* this finding is amply supported by modern authority.[40] Any language in *Plessy v. Ferguson* contrary to this finding is rejected.

We conclude that in the field of public education the doctrine of "separate but equal" has no place. Separate educational facilities are inherently unequal. Therefore, we hold that the plaintiffs and others similarly situated for whom the actions have been brought are, by reason of the segregation complained of, deprived of the equal protection of the laws guaranteed by the Fourteenth Amendment.

Because of the wide applicability of this decision, and because of the great variety of local conditions, the formulation of decrees in these cases presents problems of considerable complexity. In order that we may have the full assistance of the parties in formulating decrees, the cases will be restored to the docket, and the parties are requested to present further argument the following term on the question of how the Court's decision should be implemented.

*****

[*Note:* In a companion case decided the same day, involving segregated schools in the federally regulated District of Columbia, the Court held that such segregation was invalid under the Due Process Clause of the Fifth Amendment. Unlike the Fourteenth Amendment, which applies only to the States, the Fifth Amendment does not contain an equal protection clause. The Court declared: "In view of our decision [in *Brown*] that the Constitution prohibits the States from maintaining racially segregated schools, it would be unthinkable that the same Constitution would impose a lesser duty on the Federal Government." Bolling v. Sharpe, 347 U.S. 497 (1954).]

---

[39][Court Footnote] A similar finding was made in the Delaware case: "I conclude from the testimony that in our Delaware society, State-imposed segregation in education itself results in the Negro children, as a class, receiving educational opportunities which are substantially inferior to those available to white children otherwise similarly situated." 87 A. 2d 862, 865

[40][Court Footnote] K. B. Clark, Effect of Prejudice and Discrimination on Personality Development (Midcentury White House Conference on Children and Youth, 1950); Witmer and Kotinsky, Personality in the Making (1952), c. VI; Deutscher and Chein, The Psychological Effects of Enforced Segregation: A Survey of Social Science Opinion, 26 J. Psychol. 259 (1948); Chein, What are the Psychological Effects of Segregation Under Conditions of Equal Facilities?, 3 Int. J. Opinion and Attitude Res. 229 (1949); Brameld, Educational Costs, in Discrimination and National Welfare (MacIver, ed., (1949), 44-48; Frazier, The Negro in the United States (1949), 674–681. And see generally Myrdal, An American Dilemma (1944).

Racial Segregation Cases after *Brown*

The following term, after hearing further argument, the Court issued its ruling (sometimes referred to as *Brown II*) on implementation of its May 1954 decision holding public school segregation unconstitutional. The lower courts were directed to require compliance "with all deliberate speed." 349 U.S. 294 (1955). They should, the Court stated, "require that the defendants make a prompt and reasonable start toward full compliance," although "[o]nce such a start has been made," some additional time might be warranted if on inquiry delay were found to be "in the public interest and [to be] consistent with good faith compliance . . . to effectuate a transition to a racially nondiscriminatory school system."

Not surprisingly, as the next digested case (*Cooper v. Aaron*) indicates, southern states did not readily comply. Many of the affected school districts resorted to a wide variety of devices to block desegregation, such as school closings, pupil placement laws, and residential zoning, as well as (in some instances) pressure and intimidation. The elimination of government-required racial segregation in public schools was accomplished only after enactment of the 1964 Civil Rights Act expanding the Department of Justice's authority to file school desegregation suits.

The only type of racial segregation addressed in *Brown* was segregation in the public schools. But in 1955, in two brief orders issued without opinion, the Court unanimously affirmed a Fourth Circuit decision holding that the equal protection principle underlying *Brown* also prohibited Baltimore's segregation of its public beaches, Mayor v. Dawson, 350 U.S. 877 (1955), and unanimously reversed a Fifth Circuit decision allowing a segregated municipal golf course in Atlanta, Holmes v. Atlanta, 350 U.S. 879 (1955).

The following year, without hearing oral argument, the Supreme Court summarily affirmed a decision striking down the segregated bus system in Montgomery, Alabama. Gayle v. Browder, 352 U.S. 903 (1956).

In subsequent decisions, the Court held that racial segregation was invalid in all public buildings, housing, transportation, and recreational and eating facilities. By 1963, the Court could declare categorically that "it is no longer open to question that a State may not constitutionally require segregation of public facilities." Johnson v. Virginia, 373 U.S. 61, 64 (1963).

These decisions were followed shortly by enactment of the Civil Rights Act of 1964, which (in addition to provisions prohibiting racial discrimination in public accommodations) prohibited racial discrimination by schools receiving federal funds and authorized the Department of Justice to intervene in school desegregation suits.

In 1967, in Loving v. Virginia, 388 U.S. 1 (1967), the Court held (9-0) that state antimiscegenation laws were also unconstitutional, rejecting the argument that the restriction against interracial marriage did not segregate the races and applied equally to both blacks and whites. According to the unanimous opinion, "equal application does not immunize the statute from the very heavy burden of justification that the Fourteenth Amendment has traditionally required of state statutes drawn according to race" (p. 9). The Court declared that "The clear and central purpose of the Fourteenth Amendment was to eliminate all official state sources of invidious racial discrimination in the States," that racial classifications are subjected to the most rigid scrutiny and cannot be upheld unless they are "necessary to the accomplishment of some permissible state objective independent of the racial discrimination which it was the object of the Fourteenth Amendment to eliminate," and that "There is patently no legitimate overriding purpose independent of invidious racial discrimination which justifies this classification" (pp. 10–11).

Cooper v. Aaron, 358 U.S. 1 (1958)

FACTS: Shortly after the *Brown* decision, a plan of gradual desegregation of the races in the public schools of Little Rock, Arkansas, was developed by the Little Rock School Board and approved by the lower courts. Under the plan, Negro children were ordered admitted to a previously all-white high school at the beginning of the 1957–1958 school year.

However, because of actions by the legislature and governor of the State and resulting threats of mob violence, Negro children were not able to attend the school until after troops were sent and maintained there by the federal government for the children's protection.

Finding that these events had resulted in chaos and turmoil disrupting the educational process, the District Court granted the school board's request that operation of their plan of desegregation be suspended for two and one-half years, and that the Negro students be sent back to segregated schools. The Court of Appeals reversed, and the school board applied to the Supreme Court for a stay.

In order to permit arrangements to be made for the beginning of the school year, the Court convened a special session on August 28, 1958, and scheduled oral argument for September 11.

ISSUE: Should the District Court's order delaying desegregation be upheld?

DECISION: *No.* [On September 12, the day after oral argument, the Court issued a *per curiam* order unanimously affirming the Court of Appeals decision and requiring immediate reinstatement of the earlier orders enforcing the school board's original desegregation plan. The order stated that the Court's opinion would be issued later. On September 29, in a unanimous opinion signed by each of the Justices, the Court explained the basis of its *per curiam* order.]

In affirming the judgment of the Court of Appeals, we have accepted the findings of the District Court as to the conditions at Central High School during the 1957–1958 school year, and also the findings that the educational progress of all the students, white and colored, of that school has suffered and will continue to suffer if the conditions that prevailed last year are permitted to continue. The significance of these findings, however, is to be considered in light of the fact, indisputably revealed by the record before us, that the conditions they depict are directly traceable to the actions of legislators and executive officials of the State of Arkansas, taken in their official capacities, which reflect their own determination to resist this Court's decision in the *Brown* case and which have brought about violent resistance to that decision in Arkansas.

The constitutional rights of respondents are not to be sacrificed or yielded to the violence and disorder that have followed upon the actions of the governor and legislature. Law and order are not here to be preserved by depriving the Negro children of their constitutional rights. The record before us clearly establishes that the growth of the board's difficulties to a magnitude beyond its unaided power to control is the product of state action. Those difficulties can also be brought under control by state action.

The controlling legal principles are plain. The prohibitions of the Fourteenth Amendment extend to all actions of the state denying equal protection of the laws, whatever the agency of the state taking the action, or whatever the guise in which it is taken. In short, the constitutional rights of children not to be discriminated against in school admission on grounds of race or color declared by this Court in the *Brown* case can neither be nullified openly and directly by state legislators or state executive or judicial officers nor be nullified indirectly by them through evasive schemes for segregation whether attempted ingeniously or ingenuously.

What has been said, in the light of the facts developed, is enough to dispose of the case. However, we should answer the premise of the actions of the governor and legislature that they are not bound by our holding in the *Brown* case. It is necessary only to recall some basic constitutional propositions that are settled doctrine.

Article VI of the Constitution makes the Constitution the "supreme Law of the Land." In 1803, Chief Justice John Marshall, speaking for a unanimous Court, referring to the Constitution as "the fundamental and paramount law of the nation," declared in the notable case of Marbury v. Madison, 1 Cranch 137, 177, that "It is emphatically the province and duty of the judicial department to say what the law is." This decision declared the basic principle that the federal judiciary is supreme in the exposition of the law of the Constitution, and that principle has ever since been respected by this Court and the country as a permanent and indispensable feature of our constitutional system. It follows that the interpretation of the Fourteenth Amendment enunciated by this Court in the *Brown* case is the supreme law of the land, and Article VI of the Constitution makes it of binding effect on the States "any Thing in the Constitution or Laws of any State to the Contrary notwithstanding." Every State legislator and executive and judicial officer is solemnly committed by oath taken pursuant to Article VI, cl. 3, "to support this Constitution."

No state legislator or executive or judicial officer can war against the Constitution without violating his undertaking to support it. Chief Justice Marshall spoke for a unanimous Court in saying that: "If the legislatures of the several States may, at will, annul the judgments of the courts of the United States, and destroy the rights acquired under those judgments, the constitution itself becomes a solemn mockery. . . ." United States v. Peters, 5 Cranch 115, 136. A governor who asserts a power to nullify a federal court order is similarly restrained. If he had such power, said Chief Justice Charles Evans Hughes, in 1932, also for a unanimous Court, "it is manifest that the fiat of a state Governor, and not the Constitution of the United States, would be the supreme law of the land; that the restrictions of the Federal Constitution upon the exercise of state power would be but impotent phrases. . . ." Sterling v. Constantin, 287 U.S. 378, 397-398.

It is, of course, quite true that the responsibility for public education is primarily the concern of the States, but it is equally true that such responsibilities, like all other state activity, must be exercised consistently with federal constitutional requirements as they apply to state action. The Constitution created a government dedicated to equal justice under law. The Fourteenth Amendment embodied and emphasized that ideal. State support of segregated schools through any arrangement, management, funds, or property cannot be squared with the Amendment's command that no State shall deny to any person within its jurisdiction the equal protection of the laws. The right of a student not to be segregated on racial grounds in schools so maintained is indeed so fundamental and pervasive that it is embraced in the concept of due process of law. Bolling v. Sharpe, 347 U.S. 497. The basic decision in *Brown* was unanimously reached by this Court only after the case had been briefed and twice argued and the issues had been given the most serious consideration. Since the first *Brown* opinion three new Justices have come to the Court. They are at one with the Justices still on the Court who participated in that basic decision as to its correctness, and that decision is now unanimously reaffirmed. The principles announced in that decision and the obedience of the States to them, according to the command of the Constitution, are indispensable for the protection of the freedoms guaranteed by our fundamental charter for all of us. Our constitutional ideal of equal justice under law is thus made a living truth.

Frankfurter, while joining in the Court's opinion, also filed a concurring opinion.

*****

[*Note: Cooper v. Aaron,* however, did not stop efforts in the South to circumvent *Brown* and prevent desegregation.

In Griffin v. County School Board, 377 U.S. 218 (1964), the Court held unconstitutional the decision of Prince Edward County, Virginia, to close its school system rather than comply with a desegregation order. The Court ordered the schools reopened and held that, "[w]hatever nonracial grounds might support a State's allowing a county to abandon public schools, the object must be a constitutional one, and grounds of race and opposition to desegregation do not qualify as constitutional." The Court also expressed its frustration with the delay in desegregation and declared that "[t]here has been entirely too much deliberation and not enough speed."

In Green v. County School Board, 391 U.S. 430 (1968), the Court held unconstitutional a Virginia county's "freedom of choice plan" under which students could choose what school to attend. The Court declared that "[i]t is incumbent upon the school board to establish that its proposed plan promises meaningful and immediate progress toward disestablishing state-imposed segregation" and that school boards have "the affirmative duty to take whatever steps might be necessary to convert to a unitary system in which racial discrimination would be eliminated root and branch."]

The Discriminatory Purpose Requirement

If a law itself classifies on the basis of race, an additional showing of a discriminatory purpose for the classification is unnecessary; in those circumstances, a discriminatory purpose is implicit in the classification.

But what if a law is race-neutral on its face? Such a law is not necessarily immunized from challenge. On the other hand, to establish a violation of the Equal Protection Clause, a racially discriminatory *impact* alone is insufficient. It must also be shown that a facially neutral law has a discriminatory *purpose*.[41]

In some instances, however, the surrounding circumstances of the discrimination may provide a basis for inferring a discriminatory purpose. For example, in Yick Wo v. Hopkins, 118 U.S. 356 (1886), a San Francisco ordinance—containing no reference to race—required that laundries be located in brick or stone buildings unless a waiver

---

[41] Such a purpose of the law should be distinguished from the subjective *motives* of the legislators who enacted the law. As Justice Hugo Black stated in Palmer v. Thompson, 403 U.S. 217, 225 (1971): "It is difficult or impossible for any court to determine the 'sole' or 'dominant' motivation behind the choices of a group of legislators." See also Justice Antonin Scalia dissenting in Edwards v. Aguillard, 482 U.S. 578, 636 (1987): "[W]hile it is possible to discern the objective "purpose" of a statute (i.e., the public good at which its provisions appear to be directed), or even the formal motivation for a statute where that is explicitly set forth . . . , discerning the subjective motivation of those enacting the statute is, to be honest, almost always an impossible task."

was obtained from the board of supervisors. A Chinese alien who had operated a laundry for many years was refused a permit and was convicted and imprisoned for illegally operating his laundry in violation of the ordinance. In a habeas corpus proceeding, the defendant challenged the ordinance as racially discriminatory, on the ground that over 200 petitions by those of Chinese ancestry had been denied but all but one of the petitions filed by non-Chinese applicants had been granted. The Supreme Court unanimously reversed the conviction, stating (page 373):

> [T]he facts shown establish an administration directed so exclusively against a particular class of persons as to warrant and require the conclusion, that, whatever may have been the intent of the ordinances as adopted, they are applied by the public authorities charged with the administration, and thus representing the State itself, with a mind so unequal and oppressive as to amount to a practical denial by the State of equal protection of the laws.

Gomillion v. Lightfoot, 364 U.S. 339 (1960), involved a challenge to a law enacted by the Alabama law legislature redrawing the boundaries of the city of Tuskegee. As a result of the change, the city was transformed from a square shape into a 28-sided figure. The law contained no reference to race, but its effect was to place virtually all of the 400 blacks in the city—but no whites—outside its boundaries. The Court held that in these circumstances the "conclusion would be irresistible, tantamount for all practical purposes to a mathematical demonstration, that the legislature is solely concerned with segregating white and colored voters by fencing Negro citizens out of town so as to deprive them of their preexisting municipal vote."[42] (Page 341.)

By contrast, for example, statistical evidence was found insufficient in McCleskey v. Kemp, 481 U.S. 279 (1987), holding (5-4) that proof of discriminatory impact in the past administration of the death penalty in the State of Georgia was insufficient to show an equal protection violation. A study of over 2000 Georgia murder cases found that the death penalty was imposed in 22 percent of the cases involving black defendants and white victims; in 8 percent of the cases involving white defendants and white victims; in 1 percent of the cases involving black defendants and black victims; and in 3 percent of the cases involving white defendants and black victims. The study further found that prosecutors sought the death penalty in 70 percent of the cases involving black defendants and white victims; 15 percent of the cases involving black defendants and black victims; and 19 percent of the cases involving white defendants and black victims. The study concluded that black defendants charged with killing white victims were 4.3 times as likely to receive a death sentence as defendants charged with killing blacks. The Court nevertheless held that the study was not relevant to determining the validity of the specific death penalty in the case under review. The Court stated: "Each jury is unique in its composition, and the Constitution requires that its decision rest on consideration of innumerable factors that vary according to the characteristics of the individual defendant and the facts of the particular capital offense." (Page 294.)

Similarly, Washington v. Davis, 426 U.S. 229 (1976), rejected a challenge to a written personnel test that applicants for the police force in Washington, D.C., were

---

[42]The *Gomillion* majority resolved the case under the Fifteenth Amendment (342–348). In a concurring opinion, however, Justice Charles Evans Whittaker concluded that the "unlawful segregation of races of citizens" into different voting districts was cognizable under the Equal Protection Clause (349). In Shaw v. Reno, 509 U.S. 630 (1993), the Court noted that "This Court's subsequent reliance on *Gomillion* in other Fourteenth Amendment cases suggests the correctness of Justice Whittaker's view."

required to take. The test was administered generally to prospective government employees to determine whether applicants meet a uniform minimum standard of literacy—a requirement clearly relevant to the police function. Statistics showed that blacks failed the test much more often than whites, and it was contended on that basis that the test was racially discriminatory. The Supreme Court, however, held that the evidence of disparity in results, without more, was insufficient to demonstrate a discriminatory purpose.

To relieve plaintiffs of the burden of proving discriminatory purpose under the Equal Protection Clause, Congress in some civil rights statutes has provided a less stringent standard to establish claims under those statutes. For example, as amended in 1982, the Voting Rights Act of 1965 provides that a violation may be established "based on the totality of circumstances" and that "[t]he extent to which members of a protected class have been elected to office [is] one circumstance which may be considered." (See comment "The Federal Voting Rights Act" in Chapter 15.)

4

Race Discrimination by Private Persons

The Fourteenth Amendment "State Action" Requirement

The Equal Protection Clause of the Fourteenth Amendment provides that "No *State* shall . . . deny to any person within its jurisdiction the equal protection of the laws." (Italics added.) The Clause thus expressly requires proof of state action—usually consisting (as in the cases reviewed in the previous chapter) of enactment of legislation or issuance of an agency order. In short, the Equal Protection Clause does not apply to truly "private" conduct.

But conversely, even where it is an ostensibly private organization that engages in the challenged conduct (such as racial discrimination), the state action requirement may nevertheless be met depending on the degree of government responsibility for the conduct.

For example, the "White Primary" cases decided in 1944 involved efforts of the Texas Democratic Party to exclude blacks from participating in political primary elections. The Party claimed that it was a private association entitled to determine its own rules of eligibility. The Supreme Court rejected that argument, holding that running an election for government office is very much a "public function" and must comply with the Constitution. Smith v. Allwright, 321 U.S. 649 (1944).

A private organization may also be found to engage in state action (and therefore subject to the Fourteenth Amendment) if there is such a close relationship between the organization and the state that the private and public aspects are virtually intertwined. For example, in Burton v. Wilmington Parking Authority, 365 U.S. 715 (1961), the Court held that a restaurant on leased premises in a parking building owned and operated by the city could not exclude African Americans. It was emphasized that the restaurant was an integral part of the complex, that the restaurant and the parking facilities complemented each other, that the parking authority had regulatory power over the lessee, and that the financial success of the restaurant benefited the governmental agency.

However, the state action requirement is not met merely by showing that an otherwise private entity receives some governmental benefit or service. Nor is the state action requirement satisfied merely by showing that the otherwise private entity is to some extent regulated by the State.

For example, in Moose Lodge No. 107 v. Irvis, 407 U.S. 163 (1972), the Court rejected a claim that a private club's state liquor license barred the club from engaging in racial discrimination. The license required the club to make such physical alterations in its premises as the state liquor board might require, file a list of the names and addresses of its members and employees, and keep extensive financial records. In addition, the board was authorized to inspect the premises at any time when patrons, guests, or members are present. The Court held (6-3) that "the operation of the regulatory scheme enforced by the [board] does not sufficiently implicate the State in the discriminatory guest policies of Moose Lodge to make the latter 'state action' within the ambit of the Equal Protection Clause of the Fourteenth Amendment."

Nor is the state action requirement met just by showing that the State provided financial assistance or tax benefits. For example, in Rendell-Baker v. Kohn, 457 U.S. 830 (1982), a private school for "problem" students referred by public institutions was heavily regulated by the State and received almost all of its operating budget from public funds. When the school fired a teacher for making political speeches, she claimed that her dismissal violated the First Amendment. The Supreme Court, however, held that government funding, by itself, is not a basis for finding state action and that the Constitution did not apply without a showing that the State was involved in the dismissal, either through coercion or encouragement of the private entity to engage in the challenged conduct.

Nor is it sufficient that the organization enjoys a monopoly granted by the State such as a public utility. In Jackson v. Metropolitan Edison Co., 419 U.S. 345 (1978), it was contended that the utility was performing a "public function" by providing electrical services. But the Court held that the "public function" exception applied only to tasks that have *both traditionally and exclusively* been done by government.

In the next-digested case, *Shelley v. Kraemer* (1948), the Court held that an injunction enforcing an agreement between private parties to exclude blacks from the purchase of property would constitute impermissible state action violating the Equal Protection Clause. The decision has had an important impact in expanding the scope of the Fourteenth Amendment.

Although truly private discrimination (i.e., not shown to involve the requisite degree of state action) is not subject to the Fourteenth Amendment, it may in certain instances be prohibited by federal or state *statutes*. The power of Congress to enact such federal statutes is addressed later in this chapter.

Shelley v. Kraemer, 334 U.S. 1 (1948)

FACTS: Negro purchasers contracted with white sellers to buy homes in violation of racially restrictive covenants. The restrictive covenants, providing that the houses could only be occupied by Caucasians, were part of an agreement that had been executed by owners of properties in the neighborhood. The Negroes were willing purchasers with adequate finances and the white owners were willing sellers. However, before the sales could be completed, owners of the neighboring properties (which also were subject to the covenants in the agreement) sued in state courts to enjoin the sales.

The state courts, treating the controversy as only a private dispute and therefore not subject to the Equal Protection Clause of the Fourteenth Amendment, enforced the restrictive covenants and enjoined the sales. The Negro purchasers appealed to the Supreme Court.

ISSUE: Does a state court's enforcement of a racially restrictive covenant agreed to by private parties constitute state action subject to the Equal Protection Clause?

DECISION (per *Vinson,* 6-0, Reed, Jackson, Rutledge not participating): *Yes.*

Equality in the enjoyment of property rights was regarded by the framers of the Fourteenth Amendment as an essential precondition to the realization of other basic civil rights and liberties that the Amendment was intended to guarantee. Thus, §1 of the Civil Rights Act of 1866 [now codified as 42 U.S.C. §1982], which was enacted by Congress while the Fourteenth Amendment was also under consideration, provides: "All citizens of the United States shall have the same right, in every State and Territory, as is enjoyed by white citizens thereof to inherit, purchase, lease, sell, hold, and convey real and personal property."

It is likewise clear that restrictions on the right of occupancy of the sort sought to be created by the private agreements in these cases could not be squared with the requirements of the Fourteenth Amendment if imposed by state statute or local ordinance. But the present cases do not involve action by state legislatures or city councils. Here the particular patterns of discrimination and the areas in which the restrictions are to operate were determined, in the first instance, by the terms of agreements among private individuals. Participation of the State consists in the enforcement of the restrictions so defined.

Thus the crucial issue with which we are here confronted is whether this distinction removes these cases from the operation of the prohibitory provisions of the Fourteenth Amendment.

Since this Court's decision in the Civil Rights Cases, 109 U.S. 3 (1883), the principle has become firmly embedded in our constitutional law that the action inhibited by the first section of the Fourteenth Amendment is only such action as may fairly be said to be that of the States. That Amendment erects no shield against merely private conduct, however discriminatory or wrongful.

Therefore, the challenged restrictive agreements—standing alone—cannot be regarded as a violation of any rights guaranteed to petitioners by the Fourteenth Amendment. So long as the purposes of those agreements are effectuated by voluntary adherence to their terms, it would appear clear that there has been no action by the State and the provisions of the Amendment have not been violated.

But here there was more. These are cases in which the purposes of the agreements were secured only by judicial enforcement by state courts of the restrictive terms of the agreements.

It has long been established by decisions of this Court that the action of state courts and of judicial officers in their official capacities is to be regarded as action of the state within the meaning of the Fourteenth Amendment. These cases demonstrate, also, the early recognition by this Court that state action in violation of the Amendment's provisions is equally repugnant to the constitutional commands whether directed by state statute or taken by a judicial official in the absence of statute.

Thus, in Strauder v. West Virginia, 100 U.S. 303 (1880), this Court declared invalid a state statute restricting jury service to white persons as amounting to a denial of the equal protection of the laws to the colored defendant in that case. Similarly, the action of state courts in imposing penalties or depriving parties of other substantive rights without providing adequate notice and opportunity to defend has, of course, long been regarded as a denial of the due process of law. And, in numerous cases, this Court has reversed criminal convictions in state courts for failure of those courts to provide the essential ingredients of a fair hearing.

The short of the matter is that, from the time of the adoption of the Fourteenth Amendment until the present, it has been the consistent ruling of this Court that the action of the States to which the Amendment has reference includes action of state courts and state judicial officials.

We have no doubt that there has been state action in these cases in the full and complete sense of the phrase. The undisputed facts disclose that the petitioners were willing purchasers of properties upon which they desired to establish homes. The owners of the properties were willing sellers; and contracts of sale were accordingly consummated. It is clear that, but for the active intervention of the state courts, supported by the full panoply of state power, the petitioners would have been free to occupy the properties in question without restraint.

These are not cases, as has been suggested, in which the States have merely abstained from action, leaving private individuals free to impose such discriminations as they see fit. Rather, these are cases in which the States have made available to such individuals the full coercive power of government to deny to petitioners, on the grounds of race or color, the enjoyment of property rights in premises that petitioners are willing and financially able to acquire and that the grantors are willing to sell.

It is contended, however, that there is no inequality since the state courts stand ready to enforce restrictive covenants excluding white persons from the ownership or occupancy of property covered by such agreements, and that therefore enforcement of covenants excluding colored persons should not be deemed a denial of equal protection. This contention does not bear scrutiny. No case has been called to our attention in which a court, state or federal, has been called upon to enforce a covenant excluding members of the white majority from ownership or occupancy of real property on grounds of race or color. But, more fundamentally, the rights created by the Fourteenth Amendment are guaranteed to the individual and are personal in nature. It is, therefore, no answer to these petitioners to say that the courts may also be induced to deny white persons rights of ownership and occupancy on grounds of race or color. Equal protection of the laws is not achieved through indiscriminate imposition of inequalities.

*****

[*Note:* In a companion case, the Court held that District of Columbia courts could not constitutionally enforce racial covenants even though the Fourteenth Amendment is not applicable to the federal government. Hurd v. Hodge, 334 U.S. 24 (1948). The Court stated that such enforcement would violate the Civil Rights Act and would also be contrary to the public policy of the United States.]

Application of the *Shelley* Doctrine

In Barrows v. Jackson, 346 U.S. 249 (1953), relying on the *Shelley* decision, the Court held (6-1) that the Fourteenth Amendment also precluded an action for *damages* by a white homeowner against another white homeowner for selling to a black purchaser in violation of a racial covenant. The majority noted that permitting damage judgments would deter prospective sellers from selling to non-Caucasians. The only dissenter was the author of the *Shelley* opinion, Chief Justice Vinson, who contended that, unlike the innocent black purchaser in *Shelley,* the white homeowner who had agreed to the racial covenant lacked the requisite standing to claim the protection of the Fourteenth Amendment.

In Batson v. Kentucky, 476 U.S. 79 (1986), the Court applied the *Shelley* rationale to a prosecutor's use of "peremptory challenges" (requests to remove particular members of a proposed jury panel without the need to show cause for the removal). The Court held (7-2) that, if a prosecutor used peremptory challenges to exclude blacks from the jury in a criminal action against a black defendant, the prosecutor could be required to justify his peremptory challenges on "neutral" nonracial grounds.

In later decisions, the Court expanded the *Batson* holding to apply to peremptory challenges of black jurors by the *defense* attorney in a criminal case and by attorneys for both plaintiffs and defendants in civil cases. *Batson* has also been extended to other ethnic minorities as well as to women.

A variant of the *Shelley* doctrine was applied in New York Times Co. v. Sullivan, 376 U.S. 254 (1964), holding (9-0) that the First Amendment prevents a "public official from recovering damages for a defamatory falsehood relating to his official conduct unless he proves that the statement was made with 'actual malice.'" Although not citing *Shelley,* the Court stated:

> Although this is a civil lawsuit between private parties, the Alabama courts have applied a state rule of law which petitioners claim to impose invalid restrictions on their constitutional freedoms of speech and press. . . . The test is not the form in which state power has been applied but, whatever the form, whether such power has been exercised.

The scope of the *Shelley* doctrine was sharply contested in the "sit-in" cases of the 1960s. In many instances, when "white-only" restaurants called the police to evict demonstrators protesting the restaurant's racial policy, the demonstrators were arrested and convicted of trespassing—presenting a difficult question: Does the *Shelley* rationale bar enforcement of these trespass laws against persons excluded from private property when the exclusion by the restaurant owner is based on racial grounds?

That question remains undecided by the Supreme Court. In some of the sit-in cases, the convictions were set aside on the ground that the states had implicitly supported the restaurants' discrimination policies. In Bell v. Maryland, 378 U.S. 226 (1964), the case was remanded to the state courts for reconsideration in the light of intervening legislation prohibiting discrimination in public accommodations.

But the Justices' individual opinions in *Bell* demonstrated a fundamental difference of views. Three Justices (Douglas, Goldberg, and Warren) would have found a violation of equal protection under the Fourteenth Amendment; three Justices (Black, Harlan, and White) would have upheld the property right of the restaurant owner to choose his customers and exclude those he declined to serve; and the other three Justices (Brennan, Clark, and Stewart) made no comment on the constitutional issue.

In his concurring opinion, Douglas (joined by Goldberg) contended that a business generally open to the public—like a restaurant—should not be able to invoke a state trespassing law in such circumstances. Goldberg also filed an opinion (joined by Warren) supporting reversal on that ground.

Black (joined by Harlan and White) dissented, insisting that the Fourteenth Amendment "does not of itself, standing alone, in the absence of some cooperative state action or compulsion, forbid property holders, including restaurant owners, to ban people from entering or remaining upon their premises, *even if the owners act out of racial prejudice.*" Black added that

> [R]eliance [on *Shelley*] is misplaced. [The] reason judicial enforcement of the restrictive covenants in Shelley was deemed state action *was not merely the fact that a state court*

had acted, but rather that state enforcement of the covenants had the effect of *denying to [two willing] parties their federally guaranteed right* to own, occupy, enjoy, and use their property without regard to race or color. . . . But equally, when one party is unwilling, as when the property owner chooses *not* to sell to a particular person or *not* to admit that person, then [he] is entitled to rely on the guarantee of due process of law [to] protect his free use and enjoyment of property. (Italics added.)

The unresolved constitutional issue in the *Bell* case was to a large extent rendered moot by the enactment of the 1964 Civil Rights Act (upheld by the Court in the *Heart of Atlanta Motel* and *McClung* decisions, digested in this chapter), which prohibits almost all restaurants from refusing to serve customers on a racially discriminatory basis.

The Civil Rights Act of 1875

Each of the Reconstruction Amendments—Thirteenth, Fourteenth, and Fifteenth—provides, in addition to its substantive terms, that "Congress shall have power to enforce this article by appropriate legislation." Relying on the grant of that constitutional authority, Congress soon enacted a series of civil rights statutes to further implement the Amendments.

The 1875 Civil Rights Act made racial discriminations in public accommodations illegal. Section 1 provided

> That all persons within the jurisdiction of the United States shall be entitled to the full and equal enjoyment of the accommodations, advantages, facilities, and privileges of inns, public conveyances on land or water, theatres, and other places of public amusement, subject only to the conditions and limitations established by law and applicable alike to citizens of every race and color, regardless of any previous condition of servitude.

Section 2 imposed criminal penalties for

> denying to any citizen, except for reasons by law applicable to citizens of every race and color, and regardless of any previous condition of servitude, the full enjoyment of any of the accommodations, advantages, facilities, or privileges in said section enumerated, or by aiding or inciting such denial.

However, in the next-digested decision, the *Civil Rights Cases,* the Supreme Court declared both Sections 1 and 2 unconstitutional. According to the decision, the provisions were not "appropriate legislation" within the scope of Congress's enforcement authority under either the Thirteenth or the Fourteenth Amendment.

The Court held that the Fourteenth Amendment (unlike the Thirteenth and Fifteenth Amendments) only prohibits actions by the States, as distinguished from actions by private parties. While recognizing that the Thirteenth Amendment prohibition against "involuntary servitude" is not limited to actions by the States and also applies to actions by private parties, the Court held that the Thirteenth Amendment did not support the public accommodations law because the amendment did not extend to what the Court characterized as "social" discrimination.

The Court's decision has had a profound effect in limiting—although not ultimately preventing—adoption of federal legislation prohibiting race discrimination by private parties. See comment "Federal Statutes Regulating Private Discrimination" following the *Civil Rights Cases* digest.

Civil Rights Cases, 109 U.S. 3 (1883)

FACTS: These five consolidated cases were founded on Sections 1 and 2 of the Civil Rights Act of 1875 (entitled "An Act to protect all citizens in their civil and legal rights"), imposing criminal penalties on anyone

> denying to any citizen, except for reasons by law applicable to citizens of every race and color, and regardless of any previous condition of servitude, the full enjoyment of any of the accommodations, advantages, facilities, or privileges in said section enumerated, or by aiding or inciting such denial.

In enacting the statute, Congress relied on the Thirteenth and Fourteenth Amendments of the Constitution. §2 of the Thirteenth Amendment and §5 of the Fourteenth Amendment each provides that Congress shall have the power to enforce the Amendment "by appropriate legislation."

Four of the five cases involved criminal actions. Stanley and Nichols were indicted for denying hotel accommodations to a colored person. The actions against Ryan and Singleton involved denying accommodations of a theatre—the information against Ryan being for refusing a colored person a seat in the dress circle of Maguire's theatre in San Francisco, and the indictment against Singleton was for denying another person (whose color was not stated) the full enjoyment of the accommodations of the Grand Opera House in New York.

The fifth case was a civil action brought by Robinson and his wife against the Memphis and Charleston R. R. Company to recover the penalty of $500 provided by §2 of the Act. The complaint charged that the conductor of the railroad company had refused to allow Mrs. Robinson to ride in the ladies' car, for the reason that she was a person of African descent.

ISSUE: Do the Thirteenth and Fourteenth Amendments give Congress the power to prohibit discrimination by private individuals in providing access to public accommodations?

DECISION (per *Bradley*, 8-1): *No.*

§§ 1 and 2 of the Civil Rights Act of 1875 are unconstitutional, not being authorized by either the Thirteenth or Fourteenth Amendment.

(1) The Fourteenth Amendment only prohibits actions by the States, and the only legislation it authorizes Congress to enact to enforce the Amendment (§5) is legislation prohibiting state action of a particular character.

Individual invasion of individual rights is not the subject matter of the Fourteenth Amendment. It has a deeper and broader scope. It nullifies and makes void all state legislation and state action of every kind, which impairs the privileges and immunities of citizens of the United States or which injures them in life, liberty, or property without due process of law, or which denies to any of them the equal protection of the laws. It not only does this, but §5 of the Fourteenth Amendment invests Congress with power to enforce it by appropriate legislation. To enforce what? To enforce the prohibition. To adopt appropriate legislation for correcting the effects of such prohibited state laws and state acts, and thus to render them effectually null, void, and innocuous. This is the legislative power conferred upon Congress, and this is the whole of it. It does not invest Congress with power to legislate upon subjects that are within the domain of state legislation, but to provide modes of relief against state legislation, or state action, of the kind referred to.

It does not authorize Congress to create a code of municipal law for the regulation of private rights, but to provide modes of redress against the operation of state laws and the action of state officers, executive or judicial, when these are subversive of the fundamental rights specified in the Fourteenth Amendment. Positive rights and privileges are undoubtedly secured by the amendment, but they are secured by way of prohibition against state laws and state proceedings affecting those rights and privileges, and by power given to Congress to legislate for the purpose of carrying such prohibition into effect, and such legislation must necessarily be predicated upon such supposed state laws or state proceedings and be directed to the correction of their operation and effect.

Civil rights, such as are guaranteed by the Constitution against state aggression, cannot be impaired by the wrongful acts of individuals, unsupported by state authority in the shape of laws, customs, or judicial or executive proceedings. The wrongful act of an individual, unsupported by any such authority, is simply a private wrong, or a crime of that individual. If not sanctioned in some way by the state, or not done under state authority, the injured party's rights remain in full force and may presumably be vindicated by resort to the laws of the state for redress. An individual cannot deprive a man of his right to vote, to hold property, to buy and sell, to sue in the courts, or to be a witness or a juror; he may, by force or fraud, interfere with the enjoyment of the right in a particular case; he may commit an assault against the person, or commit murder, or use ruffian violence at the polls, or slander the good name of a fellow citizen; but, unless protected in these wrongful acts by some shield of state law or state authority, he cannot destroy or injure the right; he will only render himself amenable to satisfaction or punishment; and amenable therefor to the laws of the state where the wrongful acts are committed.

If this legislation is appropriate for enforcing the prohibitions of the Fourteenth Amendment, it is difficult to see where it is to stop. Why may not Congress, with equal show of authority, enact a code of laws for the enforcement and vindication of all rights of life, liberty, and property? If the States may deprive persons of life, liberty, and property without due process of law, why should not Congress proceed at once to prescribe due process of law for the protection of every one of these fundamental rights, in every possible case, as well as to prescribe equal privileges in inns, public conveyances, and theatres. The implication of a power to legislate in this manner is based upon the assumption that power is conferred upon Congress to legislate generally upon the subject, and not merely power to provide modes of redress against such state legislation or action. The assumption is certainly unsound. It is repugnant to the Tenth Amendment of the Constitution, which declares that powers not delegated to the United States by the Constitution, nor prohibited by it to the states, are reserved to the States, respectively, or to the people.

Of course, these remarks do not apply to those cases in which Congress is clothed with direct and plenary powers of legislation over the whole subject, accompanied with an express or implied denial of such power to the states, as in the regulation of commerce among the several states. In these cases Congress has power to pass laws for regulating the subjects specified, in every detail, and the conduct and transactions of individuals' respect thereof. But where a subject is not submitted to the general legislative power of Congress, any legislation by Congress in the matter must necessarily be corrective in its character, adapted to counteract and redress the operation of prohibited state laws or proceedings of state officers.

(2) The Thirteenth Amendment is not a mere prohibition of state laws establishing or upholding slavery, but is instead an absolute declaration that slavery or involuntary servitude shall not exist in any part of the United States. Is the denial to any person of admission to the accommodations and privileges of an inn, a public conveyance, or a theatre a form of servitude, or does it tend to fasten upon him a badge of slavery?

In answering that question, we must not forget that the province and scope of the Thirteenth and Fourteenth Amendments are different. What Congress has power to do under one, it may not have power to do under the other. Under the Thirteenth Amendment, so far as necessary or proper to eradicate all forms and incidents of slavery and involuntary servitude, legislation may be direct and primary, operating upon the acts of individuals, whether sanctioned by state legislation or not. Under the Fourteenth, as we have already shown, it must necessarily be, and can only be, corrective in its character, addressed to counteract and afford relief against state regulations or proceedings.

On the basis of the Thirteenth Amendment, prior to adoption of the Fourteenth Amendment, Congress enacted the civil rights bill of 1866 to secure to all citizens of every race and color, and without regard to previous servitude, those fundamental rights that are the essence of civil freedom, namely, the same right to make and enforce contracts, to sue, be parties, give evidence, and to inherit, purchase, lease, sell, and convey property, as is enjoyed by white citizens. But Congress did not assume, under the authority given by the Thirteenth Amendment, to adjust what may be called the social rights of men and races in the community, such as the rights claimed in these cases. The denial of equal accommodations in inns, public conveyances, and places of public amusement imposes no badge of slavery or involuntary servitude but at most infringes rights that are protected from state action by the Fourteenth Amendment.

It would be running the slavery argument into the ground to make it apply to every act of discrimination that a person may see fit to make as to the guests he will entertain, or as to the people he will take into his coach or cab or car, or admit to his concert or theater, or deal with in other matters of intercourse or business. Innkeepers and public carriers, by the laws of all the states, so far as we are aware, are bound, to the extent of their facilities, to furnish proper accommodation to all unobjectionable persons who in good faith apply for them. If the state laws themselves make any unjust discrimination, amenable to the prohibitions of the Fourteenth Amendment, Congress has full power to afford a remedy under that amendment and in accordance with it.

When a man has emerged from slavery, and by the aid of beneficent legislation has shaken off the inseparable concomitants of that state, there must be some stage in the progress of his elevation when he takes the rank of a mere citizen, and ceases to be the special favorite of the laws, and when his rights as a citizen, or a man, are to be protected in the ordinary modes by which other men's rights are protected. There were thousands of free colored people in this country before the abolition of slavery, enjoying all the essential rights of life, liberty, and property the same as white citizens; yet no one, at that time, thought that it was any invasion of their personal status as freemen or a badge of slavery because they were not admitted to all the privileges enjoyed by white citizens, or because they were subjected to discriminations in the enjoyment of accommodations in inns, public conveyances, and places of amusement.

We are forced to the conclusion that such discrimination has nothing to do with slavery or involuntary servitude, and that if it is violative of any person's right, his redress is to be sought under the laws of the state; or, if those laws are adverse to his rights and do not protect him, his remedy will be found in the corrective legislation that Congress has adopted, or may adopt, for counteracting the effect of state laws, or state action, prohibited by the Fourteenth Amendment.

Harlan, dissenting: The opinion in these cases proceeds upon grounds entirely too narrow and artificial. The substance and spirit of the recent amendments have been sacrificed by a subtle and ingenious verbal criticism.

Constitutional provisions, adopted in the interest of liberty and for the purpose of securing, through national legislation, if need be, rights inhering in a state of freedom and belonging to American citizenship have been so construed by the Court as to defeat the ends the people desired to accomplish, which they attempted to accomplish, and which they supposed they had accomplished by changes in their fundamental law. By this I do not mean that the determination of these cases should have been materially controlled by considerations of mere expediency or policy. I mean only to express an earnest conviction that the court has departed from the familiar rule requiring, in the interpretation of constitutional provisions, that full effect be given to the intent with which they were adopted.

The statute of 1875, now adjudged to be unconstitutional, is for the benefit of citizens of every race and color. What the nation, through Congress, has sought to accomplish in reference to the black race is what had already been done in every State of the Union for the white race—to secure and protect rights belonging to them as freemen and citizens, nothing more. The one underlying purpose of Congressional legislation has been to enable the black race to take the rank of mere citizens. The difficulty has been to compel a recognition of the legal right of the black race to take the rank of citizens, and to secure the enjoyment of privileges belonging, under the law, to them as a component part of the people for whose welfare and happiness government is ordained.

By the enactment of the Fourteenth Amendment, the supreme law of the land has decreed that no authority shall be exercised in this country upon the basis of discrimination, in respect of civil rights, against freemen and citizens because of their race, color, or previous condition of servitude. To that decree—for the due enforcement of which, by appropriate legislation, Congress has been invested by §5 with express power—everyone must bow, whatever may have been, or whatever now are, his individual views as to the wisdom or policy either of the recent changes in the fundamental law or of the legislation that has been enacted to give them effect.

The first sentence of §1 of the Fourteenth Amendment is of a distinctly affirmative character. It declares that "All persons born or naturalized in the United States . . . are citizens of the United States and of the State wherein they reside." The citizenship thus acquired may be protected, not alone by the judicial branch of the government, but under §5 by congressional legislation of a primary direct character, because the power of Congress is not restricted to the enforcement of prohibitions upon state laws or state action. It is, instead, to enforce "the provisions of this article," not simply those of a prohibitive character, but all of the provisions—both affirmative and prohibitive—of the Amendment. It is, therefore, a grave misconception to suppose that §5 has reference exclusively to express prohibitions upon state laws or state action.

In my view, contrary to the decision of the Court majority, the authority of Congress under §5 is not restricted to the enactment of laws adapted to counteract and redress the operation of state legislation, or the action of state officers. It was perfectly well known that the great danger to the equal enjoyment by citizens of their rights, as citizens, was to be apprehended not just from unfriendly state legislation, but also from the hostile action of corporations and individuals in the States. And it is to be presumed that it was intended by §5 to clothe Congress with power and authority to meet that danger.

Federal Statutes Regulating Private Discrimination

The *Civil Rights Cases* held that neither the Thirteenth nor the Fourteenth Amendment authorizes Congress to prohibit private discrimination in public accommodations, but noted that it was not passing on the question of whether the Constitution's Commerce Clause would authorize such legislation. Some 80 years later, relying on the Commerce Clause, the Court in *Heart of Atlanta Motel* and *McClung* (the next-digested cases) sustained the 1964 Civil Rights Act similarly prohibiting private discrimination in public accommodations.

In the *Civil Rights Cases,* the Court acknowledged that the Thirteenth Amendment —unlike the Fourteenth Amendment—is not limited to action by States and extends to private parties as well. The Thirteenth Amendment, the Court stated, is "an absolute declaration that slavery or involuntary servitude shall not exist in any part of the United States" and therefore "the power vested in Congress to enforce the [Thirteenth Amendment] by appropriate legislation" includes the power to enact laws "operating upon the acts of individuals, whether sanctioned by state legislation or not."

The Court, however, held that the particular law challenged in that case—the 1875 law prohibiting racial discrimination by inns, transportation companies, and places of public amusement—was beyond the scope of the Thirteenth Amendment because it imposed no badge of slavery or involuntary servitude and was concerned with mere "social rights." The Court distinguished such unprotected "social rights" from the "fundamental rights" protected by Congress in its 1866 civil rights statute under the Thirteenth Amendment—"namely, the same right to make and enforce contracts, to sue, be parties, give evidence, and to inherit, purchase, lease, sell, and convey property, as is enjoyed by white citizens."

Despite the Court's intimation in the *Civil Rights Cases* that these "fundamental rights" fell within the scope of the protection of the Thirteenth Amendment, the 1866 statute remained dormant for nearly a century until the Court's decision in Jones v. Alfred H. Mayer Co., 392 U.S. 409 (1968). In *Jones* an African American couple sued a private real estate developer for discriminatorily refusing to sell them a home. The plaintiffs invoked 42 U.S.C. §1982 (derived from the 1866 statute), providing that all citizens have "the same right, in every State and Territory, as is enjoyed by white citizens thereof to inherit, purchase, lease, sell, hold and convey real and personal property." The Court (7-2) concluded that the statute prohibited private discriminatory refusals to deal and that Congress had authority under the Thirteenth Amendment to adopt the law.

In Runyon v. McCrary, 427 U.S. 160 (1976), the Court (7-2) applied the rationale of *Jones v. Alfred H. Mayer Co.* to hold that a private school's discriminatory refusal to admit qualified African American children violated 42 U.S.C. §1981 (also derived from the 1866 statute). §1981 provides in pertinent part that "[a]ll persons within the jurisdiction of the United States shall have the same right in every State and Territory to make and enforce contracts . . . as is enjoyed by white citizens." The Court stated:

> Just as in *Jones* a Negro's [statutory] right to purchase property on equal terms with whites was violated when a private person refused to sell to the prospective purchaser solely because he was a Negro, so also a Negro's [statutory] right to "make and enforce contracts" is violated if a private offeror refuses to extend to a Negro, solely because he is a Negro, the same opportunity to enter into contracts as he extends to white offerees.

Although §1981 (like §1982) refers only to the discriminatory denial of rights *"enjoyed by white citizens,"* the Court in McDonald v. Santa Fe Trail Transp. Co., 427 U.S. 273 (1976), held (7-2) that §1981 also protects white persons from racial discrimination (in that case, an alleged discriminatory discharge from employment).

Title VII of the Civil Rights Act of 1964 applies to most employers engaged in interstate commerce with more than 15 employees, labor organizations, and employment agencies. The Act prohibits employment discrimination based on race, color, religion, sex, or national origin. Sex includes pregnancy, childbirth, or related medical conditions. It prohibits employers from discriminating in hiring, discharging, compensation, or terms, conditions, and privileges of employment. Employment agencies may not discriminate when hiring or referring applicants. Labor organizations are also prohibited from basing membership or union classifications on race, color, religion, sex, or national origin. The broad scope of Title VII, particularly as administered by the Equal Employment Opportunity Commission, has essentially superseded the Equal Protection Clause in dealing with employment discrimination claims.

Title VI of the 1964 Act and many other federal laws prohibit discrimination on the basis of race or color (as well as national origin, sex, disability, or age) in programs or activities that receive federal financial assistance. Any agency dispensing such funds is authorized to terminate or to refuse to grant assistance to any recipient that is found, after hearing, to have engaged in such discrimination.

Quite apart from federal statutes, many state and local laws prohibit private discrimination not only on the basis of race but also on the basis of criteria that are not covered by federal legislation, such as sexual orientation, weight, appearance, or political affiliation (and even, in Minnesota, membership in a motorcycle gang).

In addition, some state public accommodation laws have been broadly construed by state courts to prohibit private discrimination in a wide variety of organizations not traditionally considered "places of public accommodation." For example, the Little League Baseball organization was held to be a "place of public accommodation" under New Jersey law and was therefore required to admit girls. The New Jersey Supreme Court similarly held that the Boy Scouts of America constituted a "place of public accommodation." Boy Scouts of America v. Dale, 530 U.S. 640 (2000) (digested in Chapter 10).

Heart of Atlanta Motel, Inc. v. United States, 379 U.S. 241 (1964)

FACTS: §201(a) of Title II of the Civil Rights Act of 1964 declares:

> All persons shall be entitled to the full and equal enjoyment of the goods, services, facilities, privileges, advantages, and accommodations of any place of public accommodation, as defined in this section, without discrimination or segregation on the ground of race, color, religion, or national origin.

§201(b) lists four classes of business establishments that fall within the scope of the statute "if [the establishment's] operations *affect commerce...*":

(1) any inn, hotel, motel, or other establishment which provides lodging to transient guests, other than an establishment located within a building which contains not more than five rooms for rent or hire and which is actually occupied by the proprietor of such establishment as his residence;

(2) any restaurant, cafeteria...;

(3) any motion picture house...;

(4) any establishment... which is physically located within the premises of any establishment otherwise covered by this subsection, or... within the premises of which is physically located any such covered establishment.

§201(c) then provides the criteria for determining whether the establishment's operations "affect commerce": "any inn, hotel, motel, or other establishment which provides lodging to transient guests" (category 1) affects commerce *per se;* restaurants and cafeterias (category 2) affect commerce only if they serve or offer to serve interstate travelers or if a substantial portion of the food that they serve or products that they sell have "moved in commerce"; motion picture houses (category 3) affect commerce if they customarily present films, performances, etc., "which move in commerce"; and category 4 establishments affect commerce if they are within, or include within their own premises, an establishment "the operations of which affect commerce."

The Heart of Atlanta Motel, a 216-room motel in Atlanta, Georgia, restricted its clientele to white persons, three-fourths of whom are transient interstate travelers. The owner of the motel sued for declaratory relief and to enjoin enforcement of the act, contending that the prohibition of racial discrimination in places of public accommodation affecting commerce exceeded Congress's powers in violation of the Commerce Clause and the Due Process Clause. The District Court upheld the constitutionality of the challenged provisions and enjoined the motel from refusing to accommodate Negro guests for racial reasons.

ISSUE: Is the public accommodation provision of the Act constitutional as applied to the Heart of Atlanta motel?

DECISION (per *Clark,* 9-0): *Yes.*

1. Title II of the Civil Rights Act of 1964 is a valid exercise of Congress's power under the Commerce Clause as applied to a place of public accommodation serving interstate travelers.

(a) The decision in the Civil Rights Cases, 109 U.S. 3 (1883), is inapposite here. As expressly acknowledged in that decision, the 1875 statute had not been based on the Commerce Clause and the Court did not consider its validity in that regard. In addition, unlike Title II of the present legislation, the 1875 Act did not limit the categories of affected businesses to those impinging upon interstate commerce. Finally, even if certain kinds of businesses in 1875 might not have been sufficiently involved in interstate commerce to warrant bringing them within the ambits of the commerce power, that would not be controlling today in view of the dramatic changes in the conditions of transportation and commerce.

(b) The interstate movement of persons is "commerce," which concerns more than one state.

(c) The protection of interstate commerce is within the regulatory power of Congress under the Commerce Clause whether or not the transportation of persons between states is "commercial."

(d) Congress had power to enact appropriate legislation with regard to a place of public accommodation such as the plaintiff's motel even if it is assumed to be of a purely "local" character, as Congress's power over interstate commerce extends to the regulation of local incidents thereof, which might have a substantial and harmful effect upon that commerce. If it is interstate commerce that feels the pinch, it does not matter how local the operation that applies the squeeze.

(e) We, therefore, conclude that the Act as applied here to a motel, which concededly serves interstate travelers is within the power granted it by the Commerce Clause of the Constitution.

(2) The prohibition in Title II of racial discrimination in public accommodations affecting commerce does not violate the Fifth Amendment as being a deprivation of property or liberty without due process of law.

(3) The legislative history of the Act indicates that Congress based the Act on §5 of the Fourteenth Amendment as well as the Commerce Clause. However, because of our decision upholding the power of Congress under the Commerce Clause, it is unnecessary for us to address the question of whether the Act may also be supported under the Fourteenth Amendment.

Black, concurring: I recognize that every remote, possible, speculative effect on commerce should not be accepted as an adequate constitutional ground to uproot and throw into the discard all our traditional distinctions between what is purely local, and therefore controlled by state laws, and what affects the national interest and is therefore subject to control by federal laws. I recognize too that some isolated and remote lunchroom, which sells only to local people and buys almost all its supplies in the locality may possibly be beyond the reach of the power of Congress to regulate commerce, just as such an establishment is not covered by the present Act.

But in deciding the constitutional power of Congress to enact such legislation, we do not consider the effect on interstate commerce of only one isolated, individual, local event, without regard to the fact that this single local event when added to many others of a similar nature may impose a burden on interstate commerce by reducing its volume or distorting its flow. There are approximately 20,000,000 Negroes in our country. Many of them are able to, and do, travel among the states in automobiles. Certainly it would seriously discourage such travel by them if, as evidence before the Congress indicated has been true in the past, they should in the future continue to be unable to find a decent place along their way in which to lodge or eat. And the flow of interstate commerce may be impeded or distorted substantially if local sellers of interstate food are permitted to exclude all Negro consumers.

Measuring, as this Court has so often held is required, by the aggregate effect of a great number of such acts of discrimination, I am of the opinion that Congress has constitutional power under the Commerce and Necessary and Proper Clauses to protect interstate commerce from the injuries bound to befall it from these discriminatory practices.

Douglas, concurring: While I agree that the Commerce Clause clearly supports the constitutionality of the Act, I would prefer to rest the decision on §5 of the Fourteenth

Amendment. A decision based on that ground would have a more settling effect, making unnecessary litigation over whether a particular restaurant or inn is within the commerce definitions of the Act or whether a particular customer is an interstate traveler. Under my construction, the act would apply to all customers in all the enumerated places of public accommodation.

Goldberg, concurring: In my view, Congress clearly had authority under both §5 of the Fourteenth Amendment and the Commerce Clause to enact the statute.

*****

[*Note:* The next digested case, Katzenbach v. McClung, 379 U.S. 294 (1964), dealing with the application of the 1964 Civil Rights Act to a small restaurant, was announced on the same day as the *Heart of Atlanta Motel* case.]

Katzenbach v. McClung, 379 U.S. 294 (1964)

FACTS: §201(a) of Title II of the Civil Rights Act of 1964 declares that all persons shall be entitled to the full and equal enjoyment of the goods and services of any place of public accommodation without discrimination or segregation on the ground of race, color, religion, or national origin.

Under §§ 201(b)(2) and (c), any "restaurant . . . principally engaged in selling food for consumption on the premises" is covered by the act "if . . . it serves or offers to serve interstate travelers or a substantial portion of the food which it serves . . . has moved in commerce."

Ollie's Barbecue is a family-owned restaurant in Birmingham, Alabama, specializing in barbecued meats and homemade pies, with a seating capacity of 220 customers. It is located on a state highway 11 blocks from an interstate highway and a somewhat greater distance from railroad and bus stations. The restaurant provides a take-out service for Negroes and two-thirds of its employees are Negroes, but the restaurant has refused to serve Negroes in its dining accommodations since it opened in 1927. In the 12 months preceding the passage of the act, the restaurant purchased locally approximately $150,000 worth of food, $69,683 (46 percent) of which was meat that it bought from a local supplier who had procured it from outside the State.

The owners of the restaurant sued to enjoin enforcement of Title II against their restaurant, claiming that such enforcement would be unconstitutional. A three-judge District Court expressly found that a substantial portion of the food served in the restaurant had moved in interstate commerce, but granted the requested injunction. The court held that there was no demonstrable connection between, on the one hand, food purchased in interstate commerce and sold in a restaurant and, on the other hand, Congress's conclusion that discrimination in the restaurant would affect commerce so as to warrant regulation of local activities to protect interstate commerce.

ISSUE: Is application of Title II to the plaintiff's restaurant constitutional?

DECISION (per *Clark,* 9-0): *Yes.*

The basic holding in the companion *Heart of Atlanta Motel* case answers many of the contentions made by the plaintiffs. The Court there outlined the overall purpose and operational plan of Title II and found it to be a valid exercise of the power to regulate interstate commerce insofar as it requires hotels and motels to serve transients without regard to their race or color.

In this case, the sole question narrows down to whether Title II is a valid exercise of Congress's power as applied to a restaurant annually serving about $70,000 worth of food that has moved in interstate commerce.

Both Houses of Congress conducted prolonged hearings on the Act. The record is replete with testimony of the burdens placed on interstate commerce by racial discrimination in restaurants. A comparison of per capita spending by Negroes in restaurants, theaters, and like establishments indicated less spending, after discounting income differences, in areas where discrimination is widely practiced. Moreover, there was an impressive array of testimony that discrimination in restaurants had a direct and highly restrictive effect upon interstate travel by Negroes. This resulted, it was said, because discriminatory practices prevent Negroes from buying prepared food served on the premises while on a trip, except in isolated and unkempt restaurants and under most unsatisfactory and often unpleasant conditions. This obviously discourages travel and obstructs interstate commerce for one can hardly travel without eating.

We believe that this testimony afforded ample basis for the conclusion that established restaurants in such areas sold less interstate goods because of the discrimination, that interstate travel was obstructed directly by it, that business in general suffered, and that as a result many new businesses refrained from establishing there.

It goes without saying that, viewed in isolation, the volume of food purchased by Ollie's Barbecue from out-of-state sources was insignificant when compared with the total foodstuffs moving in commerce. But, as the Court said in Wickard v. Filburn, 317 U.S. 111 (1942): "That [Filburn's] own contribution to the demand for wheat may be trivial by itself is not enough to remove him from the scope of federal regulation where, as here, his contribution, taken together with that of many others similarly situated, is far from trivial."

This Court has held time and again that Congress's power under the Commerce Clause extends to activities of retail establishments, including restaurants, which directly or indirectly burden or obstruct interstate commerce. Here, Congress has determined that refusals of service to Negroes have imposed burdens both upon the interstate flow of food and upon the movement of products generally. Of course, the mere fact that Congress has said when a particular activity shall be deemed to affect commerce does not preclude further examination by this Court. But where we find that the legislators, in light of the facts and testimony before them, have a rational basis for finding a chosen regulatory scheme necessary to the protection of commerce, our investigation is at an end.

Confronted as we are with the facts laid before Congress, we must conclude that it had a rational basis for finding that racial discrimination in restaurants had a direct and adverse effect on the free flow of interstate commerce. Insofar as the sections of the Act here relevant are concerned, §§201(b)(2) and (c), Congress acted well within its power to protect and foster commerce in extending the coverage of Title II only to those restaurants offering to serve interstate travelers or serving food that in a substantial amount has moved in interstate commerce.

In view of the finding of the court below that a substantial portion of the food served by the plaintiffs' restaurant has moved in interstate commerce, the decision below is reversed.

*****

[*Note:* The concurring opinions filed by Justices Black, Douglas, and Goldberg in the companion *Heart of Atlanta Motel* case are also applicable to this case.]

Applying the Commerce Clause to Local Conduct

In sustaining the broad reach of the 1964 Civil Rights Act in the *Heart of Atlanta Motel* and *McClung* cases on the basis of the Commerce Clause, the Court placed heavy reliance on Wickard v. Filburn, 317 U.S. 111 (1942).

Under the Agricultural Adjustment Act challenged in that case, each wheat farmer was assigned an allotment specifying how much wheat he would be allowed to grow. Filburn owned a small dairy farm in Ohio and grew wheat primarily for home consumption and feeding his livestock. His allotment for 1941 was 222 bushels of wheat, but he grew 461 bushels and was fined $117. He claimed that the federal law could not constitutionally be applied to him because the wheat that he grew for home consumption was not a part of interstate commerce. Rejecting that contention, the Court (9-0) relied on the cumulative effect of all homegrown wheat on the national market. Even though the wheat grown by Filburn only had a negligible impact on interstate commerce, the Court stated, his production was still held to be within the scope of federal regulation since "his contribution, taken together with that of many others similarly situated, is far from trivial."

Wickard v. Filburn and similar decisions established the principle that the Commerce Clause gives Congress the power to regulate, not only interstate commerce that actually crosses state lines, but also *intrastate* activities that have a "substantial effect" on interstate commerce. However, even today, what constitutes a substantial effect on interstate commerce remains a contentious issue in some cases.

For over 50 years after *Wickard v. Filburn,* not a single federal law was invalidated by the Court on the ground that the law exceeded the scope of Congress's power under the Commerce Clause.

But then in United States v. Lopez, 514 U.S. 549 (1995), the Court (5-4) struck down the Gun-Free School Zones Act of 1990, which made it a federal offense for an individual to knowingly possess a firearm in a school zone. Lopez, a twelfth grade student, was convicted under the Act for possessing a concealed handgun and bullets at his San Antonio high school. The Court held that Lopez's conduct could not be said to substantially affect interstate commerce, stating:

> Under the theories that the Government presents . . . , it is difficult to perceive any limitation on federal power, even in areas such as criminal law enforcement or education where States historically have been sovereign. Thus, if we were to accept the Government's arguments, we are hard-pressed to posit any activity by an individual that Congress is without power to regulate. . . . To uphold the Government's contentions here, we would have to pile inference upon inference in a manner that would bid fair to convert congressional authority under the Commerce Clause to a general police power of the sort retained by the States.

Five years later, in United States v. Morrison, 529 U.S. 598 (2000), the Court applied the *Lopez* decision in striking down a provision in the Violence against Women Act that authorized a federal civil remedy for the victims of gender-motivated violence. The Court held (again 5-4) that such crimes did not constitute economic or commercial activity and were beyond the power of Congress to regulate under the Commerce Clause. The Court rejected "the argument that Congress may regulate noneconomic, violent criminal conduct based solely on that conduct's aggregate effect on interstate commerce."

In Gonzales v. Raich, 545 U.S. 1 (2005), the question presented was whether the Commerce Clause permitted application of the federal Controlled Substance Act to marijuana grown by two chronically ill patients for their own use for medicinal purposes as recommended by their doctors and pursuant to a California statute authorizing such use. Relying on *Lopez* and *Morrison,* the Ninth Circuit had held that the conduct at issue was completely noneconomic and therefore the aggregation principle of *Wickard v. Filburn* did not apply. The Supreme Court, however, reversed (6-3, Scalia concurring in the judgment). The majority rejected the characterization of the conduct as noneconomic, stating that "In contrast [with *Lopez* and *Morrison*], the CSA regulates quintessentially economic activities: the production, distribution, and consumption of commodities for which there is an established, and lucrative, interstate market." The Court further stated:

> In assessing the scope of Congress' authority under the Commerce Clause, . . . [w]e need not determine whether respondents' activities, taken in the aggregate, substantially affect interstate commerce in fact, but only whether a "rational basis" exists for so concluding. Given the enforcement difficulties that attend distinguishing between marijuana cultivated locally and marijuana grown elsewhere, . . . and concerns about diversion into illicit channels, we have no difficulty concluding that Congress had a rational basis for believing that failure to regulate the intrastate manufacture and possession of marijuana would leave a gaping hole in the CSA. Thus, as in *Wickard,* when it enacted comprehensive legislation to regulate the interstate market in a fungible commodity, Congress was acting well within its authority to "make all Laws which shall be necessary and proper" to "regulate Commerce . . . among the several States."

5

Minority Preferences

Defining "Affirmative Action"

For nearly 100 years after adoption of the Fourteenth Amendment, black leaders and civil rights groups contended that the Equal Protection Clause should be interpreted to prohibit any governmental distinction based on race. That was the view espoused by the first Justice John Marshall Harlan in his celebrated *Plessy* dissent, 163 U.S. at 559: "Our constitution is color-blind, and neither knows nor tolerates classes among citizens. In respect of civil rights, all citizens are equal before the law."

But in the mid-1960s, black leaders and civil rights groups repudiated their long-time support of a color-blind test. Since then, they have contended that achieving legal equality is insufficient and demanded in addition "affirmative action"—minority preferences for blacks (and, later, Hispanics and some other minorities as well) in education, employment, and other areas.[1]

However, sometimes confusingly the term "affirmative action" is also used in many other ways and is often applied to practices that do not present a constitutional issue. For example:

- "Affirmative action" to eliminate racial discrimination against minorities. (This was apparently the way the term was first used in a racial context. Executive Order 10925, issued by President John F. Kennedy on March 6, 1961, required government contractors to "take affirmative action to ensure that applicants are employed, and that employees are treated during employment, without regard to their race, creed, color, or national origin.")
- "Affirmative action" recruiting programs to expand the pool of eligible applicants on a race-neutral basis.
- "Affirmative action" through preferences to the economically disadvantaged on a race-neutral basis.

In addition, as a remedy to eradicate a deeply entrenched pattern of illegal racial discrimination that has been found to violate the Fourteenth Amendment, courts have in some cases ordered racial preferences on a temporary basis (for example, to desegregate a dual school system or a segregated fire department). By contrast, the kind of "affirmative action" addressed in this chapter concerns minority preferences (so-called

---

[1]See, e.g., Andrew Kull, *The Color-Blind Constitution* [Harvard 1992]: 182–201; Terry Anderson, *The Pursuit of Fairness: A History of Affirmative Action* [Oxford 2004].

"reverse discrimination") employed by government institutions as a matter of legislative or administrative policy choice.

Such preferences have taken myriad forms. Examples include:

- *Outright numerical or percentage quotas*—devices widely used in earlier years to limit Jews, Catholics, and Asian Americans, but now used in some instances to benefit other minorities.
- *"Set-asides" or "reserved spots"*—this was the problem in *Bakke,* the next digested case.
- *"Bonus" arrangements*—thus, in *Adarand Constructors, Inc. v. Pena,* the challenged law awarded a contractor a substantial bonus for selecting a minority subcontractor over a non-minority subcontractor (even if the minority subcontractor's bid was higher).
- *"Critical mass" policies*—of the type challenged in *Grutter v. Bollinger.*
- *"Racial balancing"*—school boards' use of race to assign students to schools within a public school system. This practice, a variant of "affirmative action," was recently considered by the Court in the last case digested in this chapter, *Parents Involved in Community Schools v. Seattle School District No. 1.*

As we shall see in this chapter, despite the support of some Justices for a more lenient standard, the Court has held that the Equal Protection Clause requires minority preferences (like other racial classifications) to meet the strict scrutiny standard of review—i.e., whether the preference serves a substantial governmental interest and is narrowly tailored to serve that interest.

Regents of the University of California v. Bakke, 438 U.S. 265 (1978)

FACTS: The Medical School of the University of California at Davis had two admissions programs for the entering class of 100 students—the regular admissions program and a special admissions program. The special program was administered by a separate committee, a majority of whom were members of minority groups. In the entering class, 16 out of 100 places were reserved for members of minority groups ("Blacks," "Chicanos," "Asians," and "American Indians"). These applicants did not have to meet a 2.5 grade point cutoff applied to others and were not ranked against candidates in the general admissions process.

Allan Bakke, a white male, applied to the school in 1973 and 1974, in both years being considered only under the general admissions program. Though he had a score of 468 out of 500 in 1973, he was rejected; at that time four special admission slots were still unfilled. In 1974 Bakke applied early, and though he had a score of 549 out of 600, he was again rejected. In both years special applicants were admitted with significantly lower scores than Bakke's.

After his second rejection, Bakke filed an action in state court for injunctive and declaratory relief to compel his admission. His complaint alleged that the special admissions program operated to exclude him on the basis of his race in violation of the Equal Protection Clause of the Fourteenth Amendment, a provision of the California Constitution, and §601 of Title VI of the Civil Rights Act of 1964 ("No person in the United States shall, on the ground of race, color, or national origin, be excluded from participation in, be denied the benefits of, or be subjected to discrimination under any program or activity receiving Federal financial assistance").

The trial court upheld Bakke's claim, finding that the special program operated as a racial quota because minority applicants in that program were rated only against one another and 16 places in the class of 100 were reserved for them, and that the program therefore violated the federal and state constitutions and Title VI. The California Supreme Court, without passing on the state constitutional or federal statutory grounds, held that the special admissions program violated the Equal Protection Clause and ordered his admission. The university appealed to the U.S. Supreme Court.

ISSUE: Does the special admissions program violate the Equal Protection Clause and/ or Title VI of the Civil Rights Act of 1964?

DECISION: *Yes* (5-4). [Justice Powell announced the judgment of the Court and filed the principal opinion. However, of the five Justices in the majority, Powell was the only justice who relied on the Equal Protection Clause to support Bakke's claim; the other four Justices concurring in that conclusion relied instead on Title VI. The four dissenting Justices disagreed with Powell on the Equal Protection Clause. Thus, none of the other eight Justices joined in the portion of the Powell opinion suggesting the possible applicability of a diversity justification.]

Powell: (1) Under the Equal Protection Clause, racial and ethnic classifications of any sort are inherently suspect and call for the most exacting judicial scrutiny.

The university contends that in past decisions this Court has approved preferential racial classifications without applying that strict standard. However, each of those cases presented a situation materially different from the facts of this case.

In the school desegregation cases following *Brown v. Board of Education,* the racial classifications were designed as remedies for the vindication of clearly determined constitutional violations. Here, there has been no judicial determination of constitutional violation as a predicate for a remedial classification.

Our decisions in employment discrimination cases are also inapposite. In those cases, various types of racial preferences were fashioned as remedies for constitutional or statutory violations resulting in clearly identified race-based injuries.

We have never approved preferential racial classifications in the absence of proved constitutional or statutory violations. It is evident that the Davis special admissions program involves the use of an explicit racial classification never before countenanced by this Court. It tells applicants who are not Negro, Asian, or Chicano that they are totally excluded from a specific percentage of the seats in an entering class. No matter how strong their qualifications, quantitative and extracurricular, including their own potential for contribution to educational diversity, they are never afforded the chance to compete with applicants from the preferred groups for the special admissions seats. At the same time, the preferred applicants have the opportunity to compete for every seat in the class.

The university offers four justifications in support of the "special program": (i) "reducing the historic deficit of traditionally disfavored minorities in medical schools and in the medical profession"; (ii) countering the effects of societal discrimination; (iii) increasing the number of physicians who will practice in communities currently underserved; and (iv) obtaining the educational benefits that flow from an ethnically diverse student body. None of these asserted justifications meets the exacting standard required to support a governmental racial classification.

(i) If the petitioner's purpose is to ensure within its student body some specified percentage of a particular group merely because of its race or ethnic origin, such a preferential purpose must be rejected not only as insubstantial but as facially invalid. Preferring members of any one group for no reason other than race or ethnic origin is discrimination for its own sake. This the Constitution forbids.

(ii) The purpose of helping certain groups perceived as victims of "societal discrimination" does not justify a classification that imposes disadvantages upon persons like Bakke, who bear no responsibility for whatever harm the beneficiaries of the special admissions program are thought to have suffered.

(iii) It may be assumed that in some situations a state's interest in facilitating the health care of its citizens is sufficiently compelling to support the use of a suspect classification. But there is virtually no evidence in the record indicating that the school's special admissions program is either needed or geared to promote that goal.

(iv) Even though the reservation of a specified number of seats in each class for individuals from the preferred ethnic groups would contribute to the attainment of ethnic diversity in the student body, this is not the only effective means of serving the interest of diversity. The diversity that furthers a compelling state interest encompasses a far broader array of qualifications and characteristics; racial or ethnic origin is but a single though important element. The Davis special admissions program, focused solely on ethnic diversity, would hinder rather than further attainment of genuine diversity.

The experience of other university admissions programs, which take race into account in achieving the educational diversity valued by the First Amendment, demonstrates that the assignment of a fixed number of places to a minority group is not a necessary means toward that end. An illuminating example is found in the Harvard College program:

> In recent years Harvard College has expanded the concept of diversity to include students from disadvantaged economic, racial and ethnic groups. Harvard College now recruits not only Californians or Louisianans but also blacks and Chicanos and other minority students. . . .
>
> In practice, this new definition of diversity has meant that race has been a factor in some admission decisions. When the Committee on Admissions reviews the large middle group of applicants who are "admissible" and deemed capable of doing good work in their courses, the race of an applicant may tip the balance in his favor just as geographic origin or a life spent on a farm may tip the balance in other candidates' cases. A farm boy from Idaho can bring something to Harvard College that a Bostonian cannot offer. Similarly, a black student can usually bring something that a white person cannot offer . . . .
>
> In Harvard College admissions the Committee has not set target-quotas for the number of blacks, or of musicians, football players, physicists or Californians to be admitted in a given year. . . . But that awareness [of the necessity of including more than a token number of black students] does not mean that the Committee sets a minimum number of blacks or of people from west of the Mississippi who are to be admitted. It means only that in choosing among thousands of applicants who are not only "admissible" academically but have other strong qualities, the Committee, with a number of criteria in mind, pays some attention to distribution among many types and categories of students.

In such an admissions program, race or ethnic background may be deemed a "plus" in a particular applicant's file, yet it does not insulate the individual from comparison with all other candidates for the available seats. The file of a particular black applicant may be examined for his potential contribution to diversity without the factor of race being decisive when compared, for example, with that of an applicant identified as an Italian-American if the latter is thought to exhibit qualities more likely to promote beneficial educational pluralism. Such qualities could include exceptional personal talents, unique work or service experience, leadership potential, maturity, demonstrated compassion, a history of overcoming disadvantage, ability to communicate with the poor, or other qualifications deemed important. In short, an admissions program operated in this way is flexible enough to consider all pertinent elements of diversity in light of the particular qualifications of each applicant, and to place them on the same footing for consideration, although not necessarily according them the same weight. Indeed, the weight attributed to a particular quality may vary from year to year depending upon the "mix" of both the student body and the applicants for the incoming class.

This kind of program treats each applicant as an individual in the admissions process. The applicant who loses out on the last available seat to another candidate receiving a "plus" on the basis of ethnic background will not have been foreclosed from all consideration for that seat simply because he was not the right color or had the wrong surname. It would mean only that his combined qualifications, which may have included similar nonobjective factors, did not outweigh those of the other applicant. His qualifications would have been weighed fairly and competitively, and he would have no basis to complain of unequal treatment under the Fourteenth Amendment.

It has been suggested that an admissions program that considers race only as one factor is simply a subtle and more sophisticated—but no less effective—means of according racial preference than the Davis program. A facial intent to discriminate, however, is evident in the Davis program. No such facial infirmity exists in an admissions program where race or ethnic background is just one element—to be weighed fairly against other elements—in the selection process. "A boundary line," as Justice Frankfurter remarked in another connection, "is none the worse for being narrow." And a court would not assume that a university, professing to employ a facially nondiscriminatory admissions policy, would operate it as a cover for the functional equivalent of a quota system. In short, good faith would be presumed in the absence of a showing to the contrary.

The fatal flaw in the Davis preferential program is its disregard of individual rights as guaranteed by the Fourteenth Amendment. Such rights are not absolute. But when a state's distribution of benefits or imposition of burdens hinges on ancestry or the color of a person's skin, that individual is entitled to a demonstration that the challenged classification is necessary to promote a substantial state interest. The university has failed to carry this burden. For this reason, that portion of the judgment below holding Davis's special admissions program invalid under the Fourteenth Amendment must be affirmed.

(2) In enjoining Davis from ever considering the race of any applicant, however, the court below failed to recognize that the State has a substantial interest that legitimately may be served by a properly devised admissions program involving the competitive consideration of race and ethnic origin. For this reason, so much of the judgment as enjoins Davis from any consideration of the race of any applicant must be reversed.

Brennan, White, Marshall, and *Blackmun* (jointly concurring in part and dissenting in part) agreed with Powell's opinion that Davis should not be enjoined from any consideration of race, but they dissented from Powell's opinion finding a violation of the Equal Protection Clause:

In our view, racial classifications designed to further remedial purposes are not fore-closed by the Constitution under appropriate circumstances. The position that our Constitution is color-blind has never been adopted by this Court as the proper meaning of the Equal Protection Clause.

Even ostensibly benign racial classifications could be misused and produce stigma-tizing effects and therefore must be searchingly scrutinized to ferret out these in-stances. But benign racial preferences, unlike invidious discriminations, need not be subjected to strict scrutiny; instead, intermediate scrutiny would do. As applied, then, this review would enable the Court to strike down any remedial racial classification that stigmatized any group, that singled out those least well represented in the political process to bear the brunt of the program, or that was not justified by an important and articulated purpose.

In the present case, the purpose of overcoming substantial, chronic minority under-representation in the medical profession was sufficiently important to justify the uni-versity's remedial use of race as a factor in admission, and therefore the judgment below should be reversed in all respects.

Stevens, concurring in the judgment in part and dissenting in part (joined by Burger, Stewart, and Rehnquist), filed a separate opinion contending that Title VI applies; that the California Supreme Court held that Bakke was excluded from Davis in violation of Title VI; and that whether race can ever be a factor in an admissions policy is therefore not an appropriate issue here.

White, concurring in the judgment in part and dissenting in part, filed a separate opin-ion expressing the view that Title VI did not authorize a private cause of action.

Marshall, concurring in the judgment in part and dissenting in part, filed a separate opinion rejecting the view that the medical school's admission policy violated the Equal Protection Clause:

Neither its history nor our past cases lend any support to the conclusion that a uni-versity may not remedy the cumulative effects of society's discrimination by giving consideration to race in an effort to increase the number and percentage of Negro doctors.

There is thus ample support for the conclusion that a university can employ race-conscious measures to remedy past societal discrimination, without the need for a find-ing that those benefited were actually victims of that discrimination.

It is unnecessary in twentieth-century America to have individual Negroes demon-strate that they have been victims of racial discrimination; the racism of our society has been so pervasive that none, regardless of wealth or position, has managed to escape its impact. The dream of America as the great melting pot has not been realized for the Negro; because of his skin color he never even made it into the pot.

It is because of a legacy of unequal treatment that we now must permit the institu-tions of this society to give consideration to race in making decisions about who will hold the positions of influence, affluence, and prestige in America. For far too long, the doors to those positions have been shut to Negroes. If we are ever to become a fully integrated society, one in which the color of a person's skin will not determine the opportunities available to him or her, we must be willing to take steps to open those doors.

Blackmun, concurring in the judgment in part and dissenting in part, filed a separate opinion rejecting the Equal Protection Clause claim:

At least until the early 1970s, approximately three-fourths of our Negro physicians were trained at only two medical schools. If ways are not found to remedy that situation, the country can never achieve its professed goal of a society that is not race conscious.

I yield to no one in my earnest hope that the time will come when an "affirmative action" program is unnecessary, and I hope that we could reach this stage within a decade at the most. But the story of Brown v. Board of Education, 347 U.S. 483 (1954), suggests that that hope is a slim one. At some time, however, the United States must and will reach a stage of maturity where persons will be regarded as persons.

The number of qualified, indeed highly qualified, applicants for admission to existing medical schools in the United States far exceeds the number of places available. Wholly apart from racial and ethnic considerations, therefore, the selection process inevitably results in the denial of admission to many qualified persons. Obviously, it is a denial to the deserving. This inescapable fact is brought into sharp focus here because Bakke is not himself charged with discrimination and yet is the one who is disadvantaged.

The administration and management of educational institutions are beyond the competence of judges and are within the special competence of educators, provided always that the educators perform within legal and constitutional bounds. For me, therefore, interference by the judiciary must be the rare exception and not the rule.

I suspect that it would be impossible to arrange an affirmative-action program in a racially neutral way and have it successful. In order to get beyond racism, we must first take account of race. There is no other way. And in order to treat some persons equally, we must treat them differently. We dare not let the Equal Protection Clause perpetuate racial supremacy.

*****

[*Note:* Four years before the *Bakke* decision, the Court faced—but did not decide—a similar issue in DeFunis v. Odegaard, 416 U.S. 312 (1974). After being denied admission to the University of Washington law school, DeFunis brought suit in the Washington state courts, claiming that the school's admissions policy racially discriminated against him in violation of the Equal Protection Clause. The trial court agreed and ordered the school to admit him. After his admission, however, the trial court's decision was reversed by the Washington Supreme Court, but that judgment was stayed by Justice Douglas pending the U.S. Supreme Court's final disposition of the case. By the time that the Court heard oral argument in the case, DeFunis had nearly completed his senior year in the law school, and the Court (5-4) dismissed the case on the ground of mootness. In his dissent, in addition to disagreeing that the case was moot, Justice Douglas forcefully contended that the law school's admissions policy was unconstitutional, stating in part: (416 U.S. at 336-337):

There is no constitutional right for any race to be preferred. . . . There is no superior person by constitutional standards. A DeFunis who is white is entitled to no advantage by reason of that fact; nor is he subject to any disability, no matter what his race or color. Whatever his race, he had a constitutional right to have his application considered on its individual merits in a racially neutral manner.

The following year, Justice Douglas retired from the Court.]

Racial Preferences in Employment

The preference challenged in Wygant v. Jackson Board of Education, 476 U.S. 267 (1986), was a collective-bargaining agreement between a school board and a teachers' union providing that teachers with the most seniority would be retained if it became necessary to lay off teachers, except that at no time would there be a greater percentage of minority personnel laid off than the percentage of minority personnel employed at the time of the layoff. During certain school years, white teachers were laid off, while black teachers with less seniority were retained. White teachers who had been displaced brought suit, alleging violations of the Equal Protection Clause. The Court (5-4) struck down the challenged provision.

The Court held that the level of scrutiny does not change depending on which racial group is benefited or burdened by a racial preference and that such a preference can be justified only by showing that it serves a compelling governmental purpose and is narrowly tailored to effectuate that purpose. No such showing, the Court held, had been made by the school board.

Justice Powell's plurality opinion stated: "This Court never has held that societal discrimination alone is sufficient to justify a racial classification" (page 274). In addition, the plurality rejected the theory that the preferences for black teachers were justified to provide additional "role models" for black students; such a theory, it was stated, "has no logical stopping point" and "allows the Board to engage in discriminatory hiring and layoff practices long past the point required by any legitimate remedial purpose" (pages 275–276).

Unlike the Equal Protection Clause, Title VII of the Civil Rights Act of 1964 (see comment "Federal Statutes Regulating Private Discrimination" in Chapter 4) applies to private employers. In addition, unlike the Equal Protection Clause, Title VII—despite remarkably clear statutory language to the contrary—has been construed not only to authorize affirmative action in employment but indeed to require it. Whatever may have been its original purpose, Title VII has resulted in a widespread system of minority preferences.

Title VII broadly prohibits an employer

(1) to fail or refuse to hire . . . any individual . . . because of such individual's race, color, religion, sex or national origin; or (2) to . . . classify his employees . . . in any way which would deprive or tend to deprive any individual of employment opportunities because of such individual's race, color, religion, sex, or national origin.

The Act further specifically provides that

Nothing contained in this title shall be interpreted to require any employer . . . to grant preferential treatment to any individual or to any group because of the race . . . of such individual or group on account of an imbalance which may exist with respect to the total number or percentage of persons of any race . . . employed by any employer . . . in comparison with the total number or percentage of persons of such race . . . in any community . . . or in the available work force in any community.

Seemingly in the face of this express limitation, for the purpose of determining whether an employer should be charged with violating the Act, the primary criterion applied by the Equal Employment Opportunities Commission (EEOC) is statistical analysis of the racial composition of the employer's workforce. The Commission's guidelines, for example, provide that a "disparate impact" may be assumed if the employer's rate of selection for any protected group is less than 80 percent of the rate for the most successful racial group. (29 CFR 1607.4.D.) Implicitly, the guidelines signal to any litigation-shy employer how to avoid EEOC difficulties.[2]

In 1971, accepting the EEOC's "strict liability" interpretation of the Act, the Supreme Court held (8-0) that an intent to discriminate is not necessary for a violation. Griggs v. Duke Power Co., 401 U.S. 424 (1971). According to the decision, in enacting Title VII, Congress had been concerned about "the consequences of employment practices, not simply the motivation" (p. 432). On that basis, the Court concluded that the employer could not require a high school diploma or passing a standardized intelligence test as a condition of employment—even in the absence of any discriminatory intent—because disproportionate numbers of black applicants lacked a high school diploma and failed the tests. The Court stated (p. 431):

> The touchstone is business necessity. If an employment practice which operates to exclude Negroes cannot be shown to be related to job performance, the practice is prohibited. . . . [G]ood intent or absence of discriminatory intent does not redeem employment procedures or testing mechanisms that operate as "built-in headwinds" for minority groups and are unrelated to measuring job capability.

Although the 1964 Act expressly approved employers' use of "any professionally developed ability test" that is not "designed, intended or used to discriminate because of race," the Court held that such a test is permissible only if the employer demonstrated that it is essential to determine fitness for the specific job (p. 436).[3]

In 1989, the Court temporarily retreated from the numbers approach that it had approved in *Griggs*. In Wards Cove Packing Company v. Atonio, 490 U.S. 642 (1989), in an opinion by Justice Byron White (who had joined the *Griggs* opinion), the Court (5-4) reversed the Court of Appeals' decision that a prima facie case of "disparate impact" had been established solely on the basis of a statistical analysis of the racial composition of two different groups of employees. The Court stated (p. 652):

> The Court of Appeals' theory, at the very least, would mean that any employer who had a segment of his work force that was—for some reason—racially imbalanced, could be haled into court and forced to engage in the expensive and time-consuming task of defending the "business necessity" of the methods used to select the other members of his work force. The only practicable option for many employers would be to adopt racial quotas, insuring that no portion of their work forces deviated in racial composition from the other portions thereof; this is a result that Congress expressly rejected in drafting Title VII.

---

[2]See, e.g., Stephan and Abigail Thernstrom, *America in Black and White: One Nation Indivisible* [Simon & Schuster 1997]: 431:

> If a firm's workforce was racially balanced—if the numbers were "right"—the expense of hiring experts to justify particular employment criteria as matters of "business necessity" could be spared. This was also the obvious way to keep litigators at bay. For those who wished to avoid an expensive, time-consuming, and image-damaging battle in the courts, the best defense was a good offense: anticipatory race-conscious hiring.

[3]See Andrew Kull, *The Color-Blind Constitution* [Harvard 1992]: 202–207; Thernstrom, *America in Black and White,* 427–434.

The Court further held that the plaintiffs "will also have to demonstrate that the disparity they complain of is the result of one or more of the employment practices that they are attacking here," because "To hold otherwise would result in employers being potentially liable for 'the myriad of innocent causes that may lead to statistical imbalances in the composition of their work forces' " (p. 657).

The retreat from *Griggs,* however, was short-lived. The *Wards Cove* decision was the main impetus behind Congress's passage of the Civil Rights Restoration Act of 1991, which reinstated the earlier standards on business necessity, disparate impact, and discrimination without intent.

Concurrently the broad antidiscrimination provisions of Title VII were held to be inapplicable to employment affirmative action plans favoring minorities or women. In United Steelworkers of America v. Weber, 443 U.S. 193 (1979), a white employee of Kaiser Steel brought a class action charging that his union and Kaiser had violated Title VII by entering into an affirmative action agreement designed to eliminate racial imbalances in Kaiser's plants. Under the agreement, 50 percent of the openings in craft-training programs would be reserved for black employees until the percentage of black craftworkers in a plant is commensurate with the percentage of blacks in the local labor force. Although acknowledging that the plaintiff's reliance on the literal language of Title VII "is not without force," the Supreme Court (7-2) sustained the agreement, holding that "The prohibition against racial discrimination in . . . Title VII must therefore be read against the background of the legislative history . . . and the historical context from which the Act arose" and that a literal "interpretation of the sections that forbade all race-conscious affirmative action would 'bring about an end completely at variance with the purpose of the statute' and must be rejected" (p. 201). Eight years later, in Johnson v. Transportation Agency, 480 U.S. 616 (1987), the Court (6-3) similarly rejected a Title VII challenge to an affirmative action giving employment preferences to women.

Racial Preferences in Public Contracts

In Fullilove v. Klutznick, 448 U.S. 448 (1980), the Supreme Court upheld a federal law requiring that 10 percent of grants to state and local public works projects be set aside for "minority-owned businesses" (owned by "Negroes, Spanish-speaking, Orientals, Indians, Eskimos, and Aleuts"). Six Justices voted to uphold the requirement, although no more than three joined any single opinion. Although *Fullilove* has not been expressly overruled, it has in effect been superseded by later decisions, particularly Richmond v. J. A. Croson Co., 488 U.S. 469 (1989).

In *Croson,* the Court held that the city failed to establish the type of identified past discrimination in the city's construction industry that would allow race-based relief under the strict scrutiny standard of review. The Court stated (488 U.S. at 498-499):

> Like the "role model" theory employed in *Wygant,* a generalized assertion that there has been past discrimination in an entire industry provides no guidance for a legislative body to determine the precise scope of the injury it seeks to remedy. It "has no logical stopping point" (*Wygant*). "Relief" for such an ill-defined wrong could extend until the percentage of public contracts awarded to MBE's in Richmond mirrored the percentage of minorities in the population as a whole. . . .
> Like the claim [in *Bakke*] that discrimination in primary and secondary schooling justifies a rigid racial preference in medical school admissions, an amorphous claim that there

has been past discrimination in a particular industry cannot justify the use of an unyielding racial quota. It is sheer speculation how many minority firms there would be in Richmond absent past societal discrimination, just as it was sheer speculation how many minority medical students would have been admitted to the medical school at Davis absent past discrimination in educational opportunities. Defining these sorts of injuries as "identified discrimination" would give local governments license to create a patchwork of racial preferences based on statistical generalizations about any particular field of endeavor.

The Court held that, before a local jurisdiction could use racial classifications for awarding public contracts, it is necessary to make

> proper findings . . . to define the scope of the injury and the extent of the remedy necessary to cure its effects. Such findings also serve to assure all citizens that the deviation from the norm of equal treatment of all racial and ethnic groups is a temporary matter, a measure taken in the service of the goal of equality itself. (p. 510)

The Court further noted that the judiciary would have a responsibility to closely examine those findings (p. 493):

> Absent searching judicial inquiry into the justification for such race-based measures, there is simply no way of determining what classifications are "benign" or "remedial" and what classifications are in fact motivated by illegitimate notions of racial inferiority or simple racial politics.

Since the *Croson* decision, the result has been to create a virtual industry devoted to the preparation of so-called "disparity studies" seeking to demonstrate that a sufficient evidentiary basis exists to initiate, maintain, or expand MBE programs. Very few of these disparity studies have been found to meet the *Croson* standard.[4]

Croson was followed by the next-digested case, *Adarand Constuctors, Inc. v. Pena,* involving the grant of a federal subsidy for race preferences.

Adarand Constructors, Inc. v. Pena, 515 U.S. 200 (1995)

FACTS: A branch of the United States Department of Transportation awarded a highway construction project to Mountain Gravel and Construction Company. Mountain then solicited bids from subcontractors for the guardrail portion of the project. Adarand submitted the low bid. Gonzalez Construction Company also submitted a bid.

The contract between the government and Mountain provided that Mountain would receive additional compensation if it hired subcontractors that were certified as small businesses controlled by "socially and economically disadvantaged individuals." The contract also provided:

> The contractor shall presume that socially and economically disadvantaged individuals include Black Americans, Hispanic Americans, Native Americans, Asian Pacific Americans, and other minorities, or any other individual found to be disadvantaged by the Small Business Administration pursuant to section 8(a) of the Small Business Act.

Gonzalez—but not Adarand—was certified as controlled by "socially and economically disadvantaged individuals" within that definition. Mountain awarded the

---

[4]See George R. La Noue, "Discrimination in Public Contracting," in *Beyond the Color Line: New Perspectives on Race and Ethnicity in America* [Hoover Press 2002]: 200, 203.

subcontract to Gonzalez, but would have awarded it to Adarand, the low bidder, if it had not been for the additional payment Mountain would receive by selecting Gonzalez instead.

Adarand filed suit against federal officials, claiming that the race-based presumption required by §8(a) of the Small Business Act violates the equal protection component of the Fifth Amendment's Due Process Clause. The District Court rejected Adarand's claim and granted the defendants summary judgment. In affirming the rejection of Adarand's claim, the Court of Appeals assessed the constitutionality of the challenged presumptions under a more lenient standard than the "strict scrutiny" standard applied to discrimination against minorities.

ISSUE: Are federal racial preferences subject to strict scrutiny review?

DECISION (per *O'Connor*): *Yes* (6-3).

In Regents of University of California v. Bakke, 438 U.S. 265 (1978), the Court confronted the question whether race-based governmental action designed to benefit minority groups should also be subject to "the most rigid scrutiny." Although the case did not produce an opinion joined by a majority, Justice Powell's opinion announcing the Court's judgment rejected the argument. In a passage joined by Justice White, Justice Powell wrote that "[t]he guarantee of equal protection cannot mean one thing when applied to one individual and something else when applied to a person of another color." 438 U.S. at 289-290. He concluded that "[r]acial and ethnic distinctions of any sort are inherently suspect and thus call for the most exacting judicial examination." Id. at 291.

Similarly, in Wygant v. Jackson Board of Education, 476 U.S. 267, 273 (1986), involving another form of remedial racial classification, Justice Powell's plurality opinion observed that "the level of scrutiny does not change merely because the challenged classification operates against a group that historically has not been subject to governmental discrimination."

The Court's failure in those cases to produce a majority opinion left temporarily unresolved what standard must be applied in analyzing remedial race-based governmental action. But, at least with respect to state and local governments, the Court resolved that issue in Richmond v. J. A. Croson Co., 488 U.S. 469 (1989), in which a majority of the Court held that the standard of review under the Equal Protection Clause is not dependent on the race of those burdened or benefited by a particular classification, and that the standard should be "strict scrutiny." While *Croson* did not consider what standard of review the Fifth Amendment requires for such action taken by the federal government, we believe that the Due Process Clause of the Fifth Amendment requires application of the same strict scrutiny standard in such cases.

The Court's cases through *Croson* had established three general propositions with respect to governmental racial classifications: First, skepticism: "[a]ny preference based on racial or ethnic criteria must necessarily receive a most searching examination," *Wygant,* 476 U.S. at 273 (plurality opinon of Powell, J.); McLaughlin v. Florida, 379 U.S. 184, 192 (1964) ("[R]acial classifications [are] 'constitutionally suspect' "); Hirabayashi v. United States, 320 U.S. 81, 100 (1943) ("Distinctions between citizens solely because of their ancestry are by their very nature odious to a free people"). Second, consistency: "the standard of review under the Equal Protection Clause is not dependent on the race of those burdened or benefited by a particular classification," Croson, 488 U.S. at 494 (plurality opinion); see also *Bakke,* 438 U.S. at 289-290 (opinion of Powell, J.). And third, congruence: "[e]qual protection analysis in the Fifth Amendment area is the same as that under the Fourteenth Amendment," Buckley v. Valeo, 424 U.S. 1, 93 (1976); Bolling v. Sharpe, 347 U.S. 497, 500 (1954). taken together, these three propositions lead to the conclusion that any person, of whatever race, has the right to demand that any governmental actor subject to the Constitution justify any racial classification subjecting that person to unequal treatment under the strictest judicial scrutiny.

However, a year after the *Croson* decision, the Court took a surprising turn. Metro Broadcasting, Inc. v. FCC, 497 U.S. 547 (1990), involved a Fifth Amendment challenge to two race-based policies of the Federal Communications Commission. In *Metro Broadcasting,* the Court repudiated the long-held notion that "it would be unthinkable that the same Constitution would impose a lesser duty on the Federal Government" than it does on a State to afford equal protection of the laws (*Bolling,* supra, 347 U.S. at 500). Even though *Croson* had recently concluded that racial classifications enacted by a State must satisfy strict scrutiny, the Court held in *Metro Broadcasting* that benign federal racial classifications need only satisfy intermediate scrutiny. Applying that test, the Court upheld the FCC policies, concluding that they served the "important governmental objective" of "enhancing broadcast diversity," and that they were "substantially related" to that objective.

By adopting intermediate scrutiny as the standard of review for congressionally mandated benign racial classifications, *Metro Broadcasting* departed from our prior decisions in two significant respects. First, it turned its back on *Croson*'s explanation of why strict scrutiny of all governmental racial classifications is essential. Second, *Metro Broadcasting* squarely rejected one of the three propositions established by the Court's earlier equal protection cases, namely, congruence between the standards applicable to federal and state racial classifications, and in so doing also undermined the other two—skepticism of all racial classifications, and consistency of treatment irrespective of the race of the burdened or benefited group.

The three propositions undermined by *Metro Broadcasting* all derive from the basic principle that the Fifth and Fourteenth Amendments to the Constitution protect persons, not groups. It follows from that principle that all governmental action based on race—a group classification long recognized as "in most circumstances irrelevant and therefore prohibited," *Hirabayashi,* supra, at 100—should be subjected to detailed judicial inquiry to ensure that the personal right to equal protection of the laws has not been infringed.

These ideas have long been central to this Court's understanding of equal protection, and holding benign state and federal racial classifications to different standards does not square with them. A free people whose institutions are founded upon the doctrine of equality should tolerate no retreat from the principle that government may treat people differently because of their race only for the most compelling reasons. Accordingly, we hold today that all racial classifications, imposed by whatever federal, state, or local governmental actor, must be analyzed by a reviewing court under strict scrutiny. To the extent that *Metro Broadcasting* is inconsistent with that holding, it is overruled.

Because our decision today alters the playing field in some important respects, we think it best to remand the case to the lower courts for further consideration in light of the principles we have announced. The Court of Appeals did not decide the question whether the interests served by the use of subcontractor compensation clauses are properly described as "compelling." It also did not address the question of narrow tailoring in terms of our strict scrutiny cases, by asking, for example, whether there was any consideration of the use of race-neutral means to increase minority business participation in government contracting, or whether the program was appropriately limited such that it will not last longer than the discriminatory effects it is designed to eliminate. Moreover, unresolved questions remain concerning the details of the complex regulatory regimes implicated by the use of subcontractor compensation clauses.

The case is remanded to the lower courts for further consideration.

Scalia, concurring: I join the opinion of the Court except insofar as it may be inconsistent with my view that government can never have a "compelling interest" in discriminating on the basis of race in order to "make up" for past racial discrimination. Under our Constitution there can be no such thing as either a creditor or a debtor race. That concept is alien to the Constitution's focus upon the individual and its rejection of dispositions based on race. To pursue the concept of racial entitlement—even for the most admirable and benign of purposes—is to reinforce and preserve for future mischief the way of thinking that produced race slavery, race privilege, and race hatred. In the eyes of government, we are just one race here. It is American.

Thomas, concurring: Strict scrutiny applies to all government classifications based on race. Contrary to the suggestion of the dissents, there is no racial paternalism exception to the principle of equal protection. The paternalism that appears to lie at the heart of the program here is at war with the principle of inherent equality that underlies and infuses our Constitution. That principle recognizes that racial classifications are ultimately destructive to the individual and to society. So-called "benign" discrimination teaches the majority that minorities cannot compete without the patronizing indulgence of the majority, and will inevitably engender attitudes of superiority and resentment. These programs stamp minorities with a badge of inferiority and promote a mind-set of entitlement and dependency.

Stevens, dissenting (joined by Ginsburg): The problem with the Court's view of consistency is that it assumes there is no difference between the majority imposing a burden upon the members of a minority race and the decision by the majority to provide a benefit to certain members of that minority.

An attempt by the majority to exclude members of a minority race from a regulated market is fundamentally different from a subsidy that enables a relatively small group of newcomers to enter that market. The desire for consistency does not justify treating differences as though they were similarities. I believe that we can tell the difference between "invidious" and "benign" discrimination. Therefore, we need not treat dissimilar race-based classifications as though they were similar.

I also take issue with the Court's concept of congruence because it ignores the difference between a decision of Congress and a decision by a state or municipality. Federal affirmative action programs represent the will of our entire nation's elected representatives, whereas a state or local program may have an impact on nonresident entities who played no part in the decision to enact it. Congressional deliberations about a matter as important as affirmative action should be accorded far greater deference than those of a state or municipality.

Souter, dissenting (joined by Ginsburg and Breyer): As the Court today reiterates, there are circumstances in which government may, consistently with the Constitution, adopt programs aimed at remedying the effects of past invidious discrimination. When the extirpation of lingering discriminatory effects is thought to require a catch-up mechanism, like the racially preferential inducement under the statutes considered here, the result may be that some members of the historically favored race are hurt by that remedial mechanism, however innocent they may be of any personal responsibility for any discriminatory conduct. When this price is considered reasonable, it is in part because it is a price to be paid only temporarily; if the justification for the preference is eliminating the effects of a past practice, the assumption is that the effects will themselves recede into the past, becoming attenuated and finally disappearing.

Ginsburg, dissenting (joined by Breyer): In view of the considerable attention that the political branches are giving to affirmative action, I see no reason for the Court to have interfered the way that it did today. We owe deference to Congress's institutional competence and constitutional authority to overcome historic racial subjugation. Courts need not review all benign racial classifications by a standard that is strict in theory and fatal in fact. I would not disturb the programs challenged in this case and would leave their improvement to the political branches.

The Aftermath of the *Adarand* Decision

In its 1995 *Adarand* decision, the Supreme Court determined that federal minority preferences in public contracting are subject to strict scrutiny review but, by remanding the case to the lower courts, avoided a decision on the merits of the constitutional issues—whether the preferences are unconstitutional on their face or as applied by the implementing jurisdiction.

On remand, the Court of Appeals for the Tenth Circuit concluded that the Equal Protection Clause was violated by the preferences for "disadvantaged" small businesses that were in force at the time of the Supreme Court's 1995 decision. But the Tenth Circuit held that the program, as revised and amended in 1997, was narrowly tailored to serve a compelling governmental interest and passed constitutional muster.

However, by the time the case returned to the Supreme Court in 2001, the legal and factual framework of the case had been substantially altered by changes in the plaintiff's legal standing, the details of the challenged federal program, and the Clinton administration's regulatory reforms to "amend, not end" federal affirmative action. After hearing oral argument, the Court dismissed the case as "improvidently granted" because of several technical flaws making the case inappropriate for deciding the constitutional issues. Adarand Constructors, Inc. v. Mineta, 534 U.S. 103 (2001).

In 2004 the Court declined to revisit these issues when it denied review of the Eighth Circuit's ruling in Sherbrooke Turf, Inc. v. Minnesota Department of Transportation, 345 F.3d 964 (8th Cir. 2003), cert. denied, 541 U.S. 1041 (2004).[5]

[5]Since *Adarand,* while generally concluding that the federal government had a compelling interest for adopting such a program, the lower federal courts have disagreed on whether states or localities must independently justify the use of racial preferences to implement federal mandates within their individual jurisdictions. See, e.g., Western States Paving Co., Inc. v. Washington State Department of Transportation, 407 F.3d 983 (9th Cir. 2005); Rothe Development Corporation v. U.S. Department of Defense, 262 F.3d 1306 (Fed. Cir. 2001).

Under the revised Small Business Administration regulations, the list of groups "presumed" to be "socially and economically disadvantaged"[6] remains the same (13 CFR 124-8(2)-124.104):

> Black Americans; Hispanic Americans; Native Americans (American Indians, Eskimos, Aleuts, or Native Hawaiians); Asian Pacific Americans (persons with origins from Burma, Thailand, Malaysia, Indonesia, Singapore, Brunei, Japan, China (including Hong Kong), Taiwan, Laos, Cambodia (Kampuchea), Vietnam, Korea, The Philippines, U.S. Trust Territory of the Pacific Islands (Republic of Palau), Republic of the Marshall Islands, Federated States of Micronesia, the Commonwealth of the Northern Mariana Islands, Guam, Samoa, Macao, Fiji, Tonga, Kiribati, Tuvalu, or Nauru); Subcontinent Asian Americans (persons with origins from India, Pakistan, Bangladesh, Sri Lanka, Bhutan, the Maldives Islands or Nepal); and members of other groups designated from time to time by SBA.

In September 2005, the U.S. Commission on Civil Rights issued a report concluding that, ten years after the *Adarand* decision, federal agencies still largely failed to comply with the strict scrutiny standard.

Racial Preferences in College Admissions

Starting with the *Bakke* case, the constitutional battle over affirmative action under the Equal Protection Clause has primarily been waged over admissions to state universities.[7]

The issues arise from an effort to bridge the tragic achievement gap, in terms of averages, between black and Hispanic students, on the one hand, and whites and Asian Americans on the other, even among children from families of similar income.

By the twelfth grade of high school, although obviously there are many outstanding black students (and many white students who do very poorly), black students *on average* are nearly *four years* behind whites and Asian Americans, and Hispanics do not do much better.[8]

The racial gap among college-bound seniors is only somewhat smaller. The SAT averages of blacks are over 22 percent lower than white averages, and Hispanic

---

[6]The Small Business Act, 15 U.S.C. 637(a)(5), defines "socially disadvantaged individuals" as "those who have been subjected to racial or ethnic prejudice or cultural bias because of their identity as a member of a group without regard to their individual qualities."

[7]Admission programs of private colleges and universities generally do not involve "state action" subject to the Fourteenth Amendment. See comment "The Fourteenth Amendment 'State Action' Requirement" in Chapter 4. However, Title VI of the Civil Rights Act of 1964 prohibits discrimination on the basis of race, color, or national origin by all colleges and universities—including private ones—that receive federal financial assistance from the Department of Education. Enforcement of Title VI is the responsibility of the Department's Office of Civil Rights, which only rarely has taken any action against minority preferences. A still pending OCR investigation of Princeton was initiated in 2006 concerning alleged discrimination against Asians. Jennifer Rubin, "The New Jews? Asian Admissions at the Ivies," *Weekly Standard,* September 1, 2008.

[8]Abigail and Stephan Thernstrom, *No Excuses—Closing the Racial Gap in Learning* [Simon & Schuster 2003]: 12; John T. Yun and Chungmei Lee, "O'Connor's Claim—The Educational Pipeline and *Bakke,*" in *Realizing Bakke's Legacy* [Stylus 2008]: 78: "In general, the research literature has come to a consensus that the Black-White test score gap has been difficult to narrow on nearly all longitudinal test-based measures of student achievement." Since the 1980s, the gap has not significantly narrowed, Jaekyung Lee, "Racial and Ethnic Achievement Gap Trends: Reversing the Progress Toward Equity," *Educational Researcher,* Vol. 31, 3–12 (2002), notwithstanding the federal No Child Left Behind Act. Jaekyung Lee, *Tracking Achievement Gaps and Assessing the Impact of NCLB on the Gaps: An In-depth Look into National and State Reading and Math Outcome Trends* [Harvard Civil Rights Project 2006].

averages are only slightly higher.[9] Moreover, "at every SAT score level, the test, which has long been criticized as being culturally biased against blacks, in fact *over-predicts their actual academic performance.*"[10]

The causes of the racial gap are much debated. Most scientists attribute the gap wholly or partly to cultural and environmental factors.[11] Among those factors, poverty is important but does not account for the large disparity.[12] Indeed, the average SAT scores of black students from families in the *top* income bracket are *lower* than those of white students from families in the *bottom* income bracket.[13]

Nor is the large disparity explainable on the basis of differences in the schools attended.[14] Improved schools will, of course, improve the education of their students, whatever their race, but have not been shown to substantially narrow the racial gap.

The gap, however, does not preclude black or Hispanic high school graduates from going to college. Almost all high school graduates—even without any racial preferences—have a choice of several accredited colleges to attend, and the number of minority students attending college has skyrocketed to over 1.4 million.

In 1978 approximately 160,000 black, 56,000 Hispanic, and 1.3 million white students enrolled in college within a year of high school graduation. In 2004, the

---

[9]In 2008 the racial breakdown of SAT *averages* among all college-bound high school seniors was as follows: Asian Americans, 1610; whites, 1583; and blacks, 1280—an average of 303 points lower than whites and 330 lower than Asian Americans. The Hispanic averages are only slightly better than the black averages. See also Stephan and Abigail Thernstrom, *America in Black and White* [Simon & Schuster 1997]: 398–399; Peter H. Schuck, *Diversity in America* [Harvard University Press 2003]: 148–149.

[10]Schuck, *Diversity in America,* 148 (italics in original). See also William G. Bowen and Derek Bok, *The Shape of the River* [Princeton 1998]: 77: "The average rank in class for black students is appreciably lower than the average rank in class for white students *within each SAT interval*" (italics in original).

[11]The 1994 publication of *The Bell Curve: Intelligence and Class Structure in American Life* [Free Press] by Richard Herrnstein and Charles Murray created a national furor because of their conclusion that racial differences in IQ are genetically based (pp. 269–368). The book led to an avalanche of harsh criticism. See Dinesh D'Souza, *The End of Racism: Principles for a Multiracial Society* [Free Press 1995]: 431–437. The controversy—although now somewhat more subdued—still continues. See, e.g., David L. Kirp, "After the Bell Curve," *New York Times,* July 23, 2006.

[12]Richard Rothstein, *Class and Schools* [Columbia 2004]: 47–50 ("An aspect of the black-white gap that puzzles many observers is its persistence even for whites and blacks from families whose incomes are similar"). See also, e.g., Thernstrom, *No Excuses,* at 129. ("After taking full account of racial differences in poverty rates, parental education, and place of residence, roughly two-thirds of the troubling racial gap remains.") Students admitted to colleges through affirmative action usually do not come from the ghetto but instead are children of middle-class or upper-middle-class families; John H. McWhorter, *Losing the Race* [Free Press 2000]: 167–168; Schuck, *Diversity in America,* at 159, 175.

[13]Thernstrom, *Black and White,* at 404–405 (1995 data); Shelby Steele, "The Age of White Guilt and the Disappearance of the Black Individual," *Harper's Magazine,* November 30, 1999 (2000 data).

[14]Rothstein, *Class and Schools,* 13–14:

So Congress then ordered a study to prove, once and for all, that blacks attended inferior schools and that this caused their relatively low achievement. Most people thought the proposed study was somewhat silly: after all, why prove once again that blacks attended inferior schools? But James S. Coleman, a sociologist then at Johns Hopkins University, accepted the charge and concluded, to his own consternation, that variation in school resources had very little—almost nothing—to do with what we now term the test score gap between black and white children.... [S]cholarly efforts over four decades have consistently confirmed Coleman's core finding.

For example, a 1998 study of the well-financed schools in Shaker Heights, an affluent Cleveland suburb, left "the school administrators totally baffled. About half of the students in the Shaker Heights school system are black, but blacks are 7 percent of those in the top fifth of their class, and 90 percent of those in the bottom fifth." Abigail and Stephan Thernstrom, *Beyond the Color Line: New Perspectives on Race and Ethnicity* [Hoover Press 2002]: 264. See also Sam Dillon, "Schools Slow in Closing Gaps Between Races," *New York Times,* November 20, 2006.

comparable numbers that year for blacks and Hispanics had increased to approximately 250,000 and 180,000, while the number of whites remained about the same.[15] Today blacks and Hispanics attend college at nearly the same rate as whites (but only 17 percent graduate—about half the white rate[16]).

The constitutional issue is therefore not "college versus no college"; instead, the issue arises only when minorities apply to so-called "highly selective" state schools —the relatively few that receive far more applications than they can accept.

In selecting applicants, these "highly selective" schools typically place heavy emphasis on objective standards—grade point averages and tests like the SAT. As a result, if the same rigorous standards are applied to all applicants, the percentage of black and Hispanic students who would be admitted would almost invariably be far below the percentage of blacks and Hispanics in the population.[17]

If they seek to increase the percentage of their minority enrollment, these schools (apart from, e.g., race-neutral outreach programs) are confronted with a difficult dilemma—they must either lower their admission standards for all applicants or else make exceptions for minority students.

But if a state school applies a double standard to admit some applicants *on a racial basis,* a significant constitutional issue is then presented under the Equal Protection Clause; for, in those circumstances, it necessarily follows that the school is thereby excluding *on a racial basis* some nonminority applicants who are more qualified on the basis of the school's ostensible high standards. Since the capacity of each "highly selective" school is limited, race preferences do not merely add minority applicants to the student body. Instead, for every winner, there is also a loser—an applicant denied admission who otherwise would have been admitted.

As already pointed out, the Supreme Court has repeatedly refused to apply a less strict standard to so-called "benign" racial discrimination (what others label "reverse discrimination"). All racial classifications—whether benign or otherwise—must "be subjected to the 'most rigid scrutiny,' " rendering any racial classification invalid unless the government demonstrates not only that the classification serves a "compelling" governmental interest but also that the restriction is "narrowly tailored" to further that interest.[18] The Court furthermore has

---

[15]Catherine L. Horn and John T. Yun, "Is 1500 the New 1280," in *Realizing Bakke's Legacy* [Stylus 2008]: 154; Thernstrom, *No Excuses,* at 33.

[16]Rothstein, *Class and Schools,* at 30.

[17]See, e.g., Schuck, *Diversity in America,* at 148–149:

> A recent study of forty-seven public institutions, moreover, found that the odds of a black student being admitted compared to a white student with the same SAT and GPA were 173 to 1 at Michigan and 177 to 1 at North Carolina State. . . . The leading study of law school admissions in the early 1990s found that only a few dozen of the 420 blacks admitted to the eighteen most selective law schools would have been admitted to those schools absent affirmative action.

[18]The Court held that the validity of a racial classification "is not dependent on the race of those burdened or benefited by a particular classification," McLaughlin v. Florida, 379 U.S. 184, 192 (1964), and that "the Fourteenth Amendment 'protect[s] *persons, not groups,' "* Loving v. Virginia, 388 U.S. 1, 11 (1967) (italics the Court's). Applying those principles, the Court struck down a variety of allegedly "benign" racial preferences in several governmental contexts, including: a state medical school's reserving 16 out of 100 places in an entering class for certain minorities (*Bakke*); a city's requirement that 30 percent of the dollar amount of each city contract go to "[a] business at least fifty-one (51) percent of which is owned and controlled . . . [by] Blacks, Spanish-speaking, Orientals, Indians, Eskimos, or Aleuts" (*Croson*); a federal subsidy to general contractors if they engaged subcontractors controlled by designated minorities (*Adarand*); and a school board's layoff policy favoring the retention of minority teachers over nonminority teachers with greater seniority (*Wygant*).

held that racial preferences cannot be justified as restitution for "historic societal discrimination." [19]

It was against this background that the Court in 2003 decided two important affirmative action cases involving the admission policies of the University of Michigan.

The University of Michigan Affirmative Action Cases

One of the two cases involved undergraduate admissions; the other involved admissions to the law school. The plaintiffs in both cases alleged that they had been denied admission because of the university's affirmative action policies in violation of the Equal Protection Clause of the Fourteenth Amendment and Title VI of the Civil Rights Act of 1964.

The university admitted the use of race preferences but, relying on Justice Powell's comments on diversity in the *Bakke* case, sought to justify the preferences on the ground that increased enrollment of three "under-represented groups"—African Americans, Hispanics, and Native Americans—would enhance diversity in the student body.

In the undergraduate case, Gratz v. Bollinger, 539 U.S. 244 (2003), applicants for admission were evaluated on the basis of a "point system" assigning to each applicant a certain number of points for SAT scores, high school grade averages, and other academic credentials. In addition, an automatic "bonus" of 20 points was given to any applicant from one of the three favored groups. The result of the bonus was to admit almost every applicant from the three groups that met minimal standards; by contrast, a Caucasian or Asian American of equal qualifications would have only about a 1-in-3 chance of admission.

The Supreme Court held (6-3) that the "bonus" for minorities violated the equal protection of the laws. In an opinion by Chief Justice Rehnquist, the Court rejected the university's effort to justify its undergraduate policy on the basis of the diversity rationale suggested by Justice Powell in *Bakke*:

> Justice Powell's opinion in *Bakke* emphasized the importance of considering each particular applicant as an individual, assessing all of the qualities that individual possesses, and in turn, evaluating that individual's ability to contribute to the unique setting of higher education. The admissions program Justice Powell described, however, did not contemplate that any single characteristic automatically ensured a specific and identifiable contribution to a university's diversity.... Instead, under the approach Justice Powell described, each characteristic of a particular applicant was to be considered in assessing the applicant's entire application. The [University's undergraduate] policy does not provide such individualized consideration.... The only consideration that accompanies this distribution of points is a factual review of an application to determine whether an individual is a member of one of these minority groups.

Three Justices dissented, including Justice Ginsburg, whose opinion predicted that colleges and universities—despite the majority decision—would still seek to maintain minority enrollment "through winks, nods, and disguises."

On the same day, in the next-digested case, *Grutter v. Bollinger,* a differently constituted majority (now including Justice O'Connor, who had joined the *Gratz* majority to strike down the Michigan undergraduate policy) voted 5 to 4 to uphold the law school's admission program.

---

[19] Wygant v. Jackson Board of Education, 476 U.S. 267 (1986); Shaw v. Hunt, 517 U.S. 898, 909-912 (1967).

Grutter v. Bollinger, 539 U.S. 306 (2003)

FACTS: The University of Michigan Law School has sought to enroll at least 10 percent of its students from members of three minority groups—African American, Hispanic, and Native American. Despite (on average) their substantially lower GPA and LSAT scores, the preference given to these three minority groups has greatly increased the odds of their admission in comparison with Caucasian Americans and Asian Americans with equal or superior academic qualifications.

The result was to increase the law school's minority admissions by 400 percent, and the percentage of minority enrollment remained virtually identical year after year. In addition, in each year in the 1995–2000 period, the percentage of admitted applicants of each of the three minority groups was approximately the same as the percentage of applications by members of that minority. In 1995, for example: 9.7 percent of the applicants were African American, and 9.4 percent of those admitted by the law school were African American; 5.1 percent of the applicants were Hispanic, and 5.0 percent of those admitted by the law school were Hispanic; 1.1 percent of the applicants were Native American, and 1.1 percent of the applicants admitted by the law school were Native American.

Barbara Grutter is a white Michigan resident with a 3.8 GPA and a 161 LSAT score. When the law school denied her application for admission, she filed suit, alleging that her academic qualifications were substantially superior to many of the applicants admitted from the three minority groups and that the school had thereby discriminated against her on the basis of race in violation of the Equal Protection Clause of the Fourteenth Amendment and Title VI of the Civil Rights Act of 1964.

The law school defended its admission policy on diversity grounds. The school contended that African Americans, Hispanics, and Native Americans were "underrepresented minorities" and that the School gave special consideration to applicants from those groups in order to achieve a "critical mass" of students in each of the three minorities.

ISSUE: Is the law school's admission policy unconstitutional?

DECISION (*O'Connor,* 5-4): *No.*

The law school's use of race in admissions decisions to further a compelling interest in obtaining the educational benefits that flow from a diverse student body is not prohibited by the Equal Protection Clause or Title VI.

(a) In his opinion in the landmark *Bakke* case, Justice Powell expressed his view that an admissions policy aimed at attaining a diverse student body could in some circumstances justify consideration of race. The Court endorses Justice Powell's view that student body diversity is a compelling state interest.

(b) All government racial classifications must be analyzed by a reviewing court under strict scrutiny. But not all such uses are invalidated by strict scrutiny. Race-based action necessary to further a compelling governmental interest does not violate the Equal Protection Clause so long as it is narrowly tailored to further that interest.

(c) The Court defers to the law school's educational judgment that diversity is essential to its educational mission. The Court's scrutiny of that interest is no less strict for taking into account complex educational judgments in an area that lies primarily within the university's expertise. The law school's good faith is presumed absent a showing to the contrary.

Enrolling a "critical mass" of minority students simply to ensure some specified percentage of a particular group merely because of its race or ethnic origin would be patently unconstitutional. But the law school defines its "critical mass" concept by reference to the substantial, important, and laudable educational benefits that diversity is designed to produce, including cross-racial understanding and the breaking down of racial stereotypes.

The school's claim is further bolstered by expert studies and reports showing that such diversity promotes learning outcomes and better prepares students for an increasingly diverse workforce, for society, and for the legal profession. Major American businesses have made clear that the skills needed in today's increasingly global marketplace can only be developed through exposure to different cultures, ideas, and viewpoints. In addition, as high-ranking retired officers and civilian leaders of the United States military assert in briefs submitted to the Court, a "highly qualified, racially diverse officer corps . . . is essential to the military's ability to fulfill its principal mission to provide national security" and cannot be achieved "unless the service academies and the ROTC used limited race-conscious recruiting and admissions policies."

(d) The law school's admissions program bears the hallmarks of a narrowly tailored plan. To be narrowly tailored, as Justice Powell pointed out in *Bakke,* a race-conscious admissions program cannot insulate each category of applicants with certain desired qualifications from competition with all other applicants. Instead, it may consider race or ethnicity only as a "'plus' in a particular applicant's file"; i.e., it must be "flexible enough to consider all pertinent elements of diversity in light of the particular qualifications of each applicant, and to place them on the same footing for consideration, although not necessarily according them the same weight." It follows that universities cannot establish quotas for members of certain racial or ethnic groups or put them on separate admissions tracks. The law school's admissions program, like the Harvard plan approved by Justice Powell, satisfies these requirements.

Moreover, the program is flexible enough to ensure that each applicant is evaluated as an individual and not in a way that makes race or ethnicity the defining feature of the application. The law school engages in a highly individualized, holistic review of each applicant's file, giving serious consideration to all the ways an applicant might contribute to a diverse educational environment. In the law school program (unlike the undergraduate program involved in the *Gratz* case), there is no policy, either *de jure* or *de facto,* of automatic acceptance or rejection based on any single "soft" variable.

The law school's admissions program, like the Harvard plan described by Justice Powell, does not operate as a quota. Some attention to numbers, without more, does not transform a flexible admissions system into a rigid quota.

The Court rejects the argument that the law school was obliged to use other race-neutral means to obtain the educational benefits of student body diversity, such as a lottery system or decreasing the emphasis on GPA and LSAT scores. These alternatives would require a dramatic sacrifice of diversity, the academic quality of all admitted students, or both. Narrow tailoring does not require exhaustion of every conceivable race-neutral alternative or mandate that a university choose between maintaining a reputation for excellence or fulfilling a commitment to provide educational opportunities to members of all racial groups.

Finally, race-conscious admissions policies must be limited in time. We take the law school at its word that it would "like nothing better than to find a race-neutral admissions formula" and will terminate its race-conscious program as soon as practicable. It has been 25 years since Justice Powell in *Bakke* first approved the use of race to further an interest in student body diversity in the context of public higher education. Since that time, the number of minority applicants with high grades and test scores has indeed increased. We expect that 25 years from now the use of racial preferences will no longer be necessary to further the interest approved today.

(e) Because the law school's use of race in admissions decisions is not prohibited by the Equal Protection Clause, the statutory claims based on Title VI also fail.

Ginsburg, concurring (joined by Breyer): It remains the current reality that many minority students encounter markedly inadequate and unequal educational opportunities. Despite these inequalities, some minority students are able to meet the high threshold requirements set for admission to the country's finest undergraduate and graduate educational institutions. From today's vantage point, one may hope, but not firmly forecast, that over the next generation's span, progress toward nondiscrimination and genuinely equal opportunity will make it safe to sunset affirmative action.

Rehnquist, dissenting (joined by Scalia, Kennedy, and Thomas): The law school's means are not narrowly tailored to the interest it asserts. Stripped of its "critical mass" veil, the law school's program is revealed as a naked effort to achieve racial balancing.

Before the Court's decision today, we consistently applied the same strict scrutiny analysis regardless of the government's purported reason for using race and regardless of the setting in which race was being used. Although the Court recites the language of our strict scrutiny analysis, its application of that review is unprecedented in its deference.

In practice, the law school's program bears little or no relation to its asserted goal of achieving "critical mass." The university contends that the law school seeks to accumulate a "critical mass" of *each* underrepresented minority group. But the record demonstrates that the law school's admissions practices with respect to these groups differ dramatically and do not support the school's "critical mass" theory.

From 1995 through 2000, the law school admitted between 1,130 and 1,310 students. Of those, between 13 and 19 were Native American, between 91 and 108 were African American, and between 47 and 56 were Hispanic. If the law school admits between 91 and 108 African Americans in order to achieve "critical mass," surely a number of the same order of magnitude would be necessary to accomplish the same purpose for Hispanics and Native Americans. Thus, to sustain the law school's critical mass explanation, one would have to believe that critical mass objectives are achieved with only *half* the number of Hispanics and *one-sixth* the number of Native Americans as compared to African Americans. But the university offers no explanation of why the critical mass concept is applied differently among the three minority groups.

The law school's disparate admissions practices with respect to these minority groups demonstrate that its alleged goal of critical mass is simply a sham. The correlation between the percentage of the law school's pool of applicants who are members of the three minority groups and the percentage of the admitted applicants who are members of these same groups is far too precise to be dismissed as merely the result of the school paying "some attention to [the] numbers," as the majority opinion suggests.

I do not believe that the Constitution gives the law school such free rein in the use of race. We are bound to conclude that the law school has managed its admissions program, not to achieve a critical mass, but to admit members of selected minority groups in proportion to their statistical representation in the applicant pool. But this is precisely the type of racial balancing that the Court itself calls "patently unconstitutional."

Kennedy, dissenting: Justice Powell's *Bakke opinion* is based on the principle that a university admissions program may take account of race as one, nonpredominant factor in a system designed to consider each applicant as an individual, provided the program can meet the test of strict scrutiny by the judiciary. The Court today, however, does not apply strict scrutiny, and instead undermines both the test and its own controlling precedents.

The Court takes the first part of Justice Powell's rule but abandons the second. Having approved the use of race as a factor in the admissions process, the majority proceeds to nullify the essential safeguard Justice Powell insisted upon as the precondition of the approval. The safeguard was rigorous judicial review, with strict scrutiny as the controlling standard. As Justice Powell emphasized in *Bakke* and as this Court has restated in subsequent cases: "Racial and ethnic distinctions of any sort are inherently suspect and thus call for the most exacting judicial examination." The Court confuses deference to a university's definition of its educational objective with deference to the implementation of this goal.

The Court, in a review that is nothing short of perfunctory, fails to confront the reality of how the law school's admissions policy is implemented. As Chief Justice Rehnquist demonstrates, the concept of critical mass is a delusion used by the law school to mask its attempt to make race an automatic factor in most instances and to achieve numerical goals indistinguishable from quotas. And an effort to achieve racial balance among the minorities the school seeks to attract is, by the Court's own admission, "patently unconstitutional."

The law school has not demonstrated how individual consideration is, or can be, preserved at this stage of the application process given the instruction to attain what it calls "critical mass." In fact, the evidence shows otherwise. There was little deviation among admitted minority students during the years from 1995 to 1998. The percentage of enrolled minorities fluctuated only by 0.3 percent, from 13.5 percent to 13.8 percent. The number of minority students to whom offers were extended varied by just a slightly greater magnitude of 2.2 percent, from the high of 15.6 percent in 1995 to the low of 13.4 percent in 1998.

To be constitutional, a university's compelling interest in a diverse student body must be achieved by a system where individual assessment is safeguarded through the entire process. An educational institution must ensure that each applicant receives individual consideration and that race does not become a predominant factor in the admissions decision making. The law school failed to comply with this requirement, and by no means has it carried its burden to show otherwise by the test of strict scrutiny.

Scalia (joined by Thomas), dissenting: As Chief Justice Rehnquist demonstrates, the law school's mystical critical mass justification for its discrimination by race challenges even the most gullible mind. The admissions statistics show it to be a sham to cover a scheme of racially proportionate admissions.

As Justice Thomas points out, the allegedly "compelling state interest" at issue here is not the incremental "educational benefit" that emanates from the fabled critical mass of minority students, but rather Michigan's interest in maintaining a "prestige" law school whose normal admissions standards disproportionately exclude blacks and other minorities. If that is a compelling state interest, everything is.

The educational benefit that the law school seeks to achieve by racial discrimination consists, according to the Court, of "cross-racial understanding" and "better prepar [ation of] students for an increasingly diverse workforce and society." This is not, of course, an educational benefit on which students will be graded on their law school transcript (Works and Plays Well with Others: B+) or tested by the bar examiners (Q: Describe in 500 words or less your cross-racial understanding). For it is a lesson of life rather than law—essentially the same lesson taught in institutions ranging from Boy Scout troops to public-school kindergartens. If properly considered an educational benefit at all, it is surely not one that is either uniquely relevant to law school or uniquely "teachable" in a formal educational setting.

And therefore: If it is appropriate for the law school to use racial discrimination for the purpose of putting together a critical mass that will convey generic lessons in socialization and good citizenship, surely it is no less appropriate for the civil service system of the State of Michigan to do so. There, also, those exposed to critical masses of certain races will presumably become better Americans, better Michiganders, better civil servants. The nonminority individuals who are deprived of a legal education, a civil service job, or any job at all by reason of their skin color will surely understand.

Unlike a clear constitutional holding that racial preferences in state educational institutions are impermissible, or even a clear anticonstitutional holding that racial preferences in state educational institutions are OK, today's *Grutter-Gratz* split double header seems perversely designed to prolong the controversy and the litigation. Some future lawsuits will presumably focus on whether the discriminatory scheme in question contains enough evaluation of the applicant "as an individual," and sufficiently avoids "separate admissions tracks," to fall under *Grutter* rather than *Gratz*. Some will focus on whether a university has gone beyond the bounds of a "good faith effort" and has so zealously pursued its critical mass as to make it an unconstitutional *de facto* quota system, rather than merely "a permissible goal." Other lawsuits may focus on whether, in the particular setting at issue, any educational benefits flow from racial diversity. Still other suits may challenge the bona fides of the institution's expressed commitment to the educational benefits of diversity that immunize the discriminatory scheme in *Grutter*. (Tempting targets, one would suppose, will be those universities that talk the talk of multiculturalism and racial diversity in the courts but walk the walk of tribalism and racial segregation on their campuses—through minority-only student organizations, separate minority housing opportunities, separate minority student centers, even separate minority-only graduation ceremonies.) I do not look forward to any of these cases.

The Constitution proscribes government discrimination on the basis of race, and state-provided education is no exception.

Thomas (joined by Scalia), dissenting: The Constitution does not tolerate racial discrimination. Nor does the Constitution countenance the unprecedented deference the Court gives to the law school, an approach inconsistent with the very concept of "strict scrutiny."

No one would argue that a university could set up a lower general admission standard and then impose heightened requirements only on black applicants. Similarly, a university may not maintain a high admission standard and grant exemptions to favored races. The law school, of its own choosing, and for its own purposes, maintains an exclusionary admissions system that it knows produces racially disproportionate results. Racial discrimination is not a permissible solution to the self-inflicted wounds of this elitist policy.

The majority upholds the law school's racial discrimination, not by interpreting the people's Constitution, but by responding to a faddish slogan of the cognoscenti.

(1) The Constitution abhors classifications based on race, not only because those classifications can harm favored races or are based on illegitimate motives but also because every time the government makes race relevant to the provision of burdens or benefits, it demeans us all.

(2) The law school adamantly rejects any race-neutral alternative that would reduce "academic selectivity." The law school thus seeks to improve the education it offers without sacrificing too much of its exclusivity and elite status. In the name of "diversity," the Court upholds the use of racial discrimination as a tool to advance the law school's interest in offering a marginally superior education while maintaining an elite institution.

(3) Michigan has failed to demonstrate a cognizable state interest in having an elite law school. The law school, however, does precious little training of those attorneys who will serve the citizens of Michigan. In 2002, graduates of the law school made up less than 6 percent of applicants to the Michigan bar, and less than 16 percent of the law school's graduating class elect to stay in Michigan.

(4) With the adoption of different admissions methods, such as accepting all students who meet minimum qualifications, the law school could achieve its vision of the racially aesthetic student body without the use of racial discrimination. The law school concedes this, but the Court holds, implicitly, that the law school has a compelling state interest in doing what it wants to do. I cannot agree.

First, under strict scrutiny, the law school's assessment of the benefits of racial discrimination and devotion to the admissions status quo are not entitled to any sort of deference.

Second, even if its "academic selectivity" must be maintained at all costs along with racial discrimination, the Court ignores the fact that other top law schools (e.g., Boalt Hall at the University of California) have succeeded in meeting their aesthetic demands without racial discrimination.

(5) In any event, there is nothing especially honorable or constitutionally protected about "selective" admissions. Since its inception, selective admissions has been the vehicle for racial, ethnic, and religious tinkering by university administrators. Columbia, Harvard, and others infamously determined that they had "too many" Jews, just as today the law school argues it would have "too many" whites if it could not discriminate in its admissions process.

Similarly, no modern law school can claim ignorance of the poor performance of blacks on the Law School Admissions Test (LSAT). Nevertheless, law schools continue to use the test and then attempt to "correct" for black underperformance by using racial discrimination in admissions so as to obtain their aesthetic student body. Having decided to use the LSAT, the law school must accept the constitutional burdens that come with that decision.

(6) Nowhere in any of the many filings in this case is there any evidence that the purported "beneficiaries" of this racial discrimination perform at (or even near) the same level as those students who receive no preferences. The law school tantalizes

unprepared black students with the promise of a University of Michigan degree. These overmatched students take the bait, only to find that they cannot succeed in the cauldron of competition. While these students may graduate with law degrees, there is no evidence that they have received a qualitatively better legal education (or become better lawyers) than if they had gone to a less "elite" law school for which they were better prepared.

It is uncontested that each year the law school admits blacks who would not be admitted in the absence of racial discrimination. Who can differentiate between those who belong there, on the basis of merit, and those who do not? The majority of blacks are admitted to the law school because of discrimination against nonblacks, and because of this policy all are tarred as undeserving. The result is to unfairly stigmatize blacks who would succeed without such help.

(7) The Court suggests that in 25 years racial discrimination in admissions would no longer be acceptable. In my view, the practices of the law school are illegal now. The majority has placed its *imprimatur* on a practice that can only weaken the principle of equality embodied in the Declaration of Independence and the Equal Protection Clause.

*****

[*Note:* In November 2006 Michigan voters adopted a state constitutional amendment that, in effect, overruled the *Grutter* decision insofar as it would apply to Michigan schools and public facilities. The amendment (like similar referendums in California and Washington and an executive order in Florida) "prohibit[s] state and local government from discriminating against or granting preferential treatment to any individual or group based on race, sex, color, ethnicity or national origin in the areas of public employment, public contracting and public education." In November 2008 Nebraska voters approved a similar measure.]

Racial Balancing within a Public School System

The *Gratz* and *Grutter* decisions have by no means ended the debate over the validity and scope of affirmative action—particularly in view of later changes in the membership of the Court. The authors of both opinions—O'Connor and Rehnquist—have now been replaced by Roberts and Alito. But, even if *Grutter* is not overruled, questions may be raised whether other affirmative action plans are sufficiently "individualized" (and therefore valid under *Grutter*) or too much like a quota (and therefore invalid under *Gratz*).

In addition, controversy will continue on a closely related issue concerning the validity of "racial balancing"—the assignment of students to public elementary and secondary schools on a racial basis for the purpose of avoiding an "imbalance" of minority students in some schools.

In *Grutter,* the Court stated that "[O]utright racial balancing . . . is patently unconstitutional." And in the *Bakke* case Justice Powell stated: "If petitioner's purpose is to assure within its student body some specified percentage of a particular group merely because of its race or ethnic origin, such a preferential purpose must be rejected not as insubstantial but as facially invalid. . . . This the Constitution forbids."

Nevertheless, even in the absence of any background of government-imposed discrimination, many public school districts have sought to use assignment systems to correct what they perceive as "imbalances" between white and minority students. These imbalances arise primarily from neighborhood housing patterns but also from

the ever-declining percent of white students attending public schools. White enrollment in 25 of the 26 largest urban school districts averaged a mere 17 percent in
2000–2001 (and is undoubtedly less now). Whites made up only 10 percent of the public school students in Los Angeles, 17 percent in Philadelphia, 15 percent in New York
City, 11 percent in Miami, 10 percent in Chicago and in Houston, 8 percent in Dallas,
and 4 percent in New Orleans and Detroit.[20]

The constitutionality of two racial balancing plans was considered by the Court in
the next-digested case, *Parents Involved in Community Schools v. Seattle School District No. 1,* decided in June 2007. Because of the great importance of this decision in
the interpretation of the Equal Protection Clause, and because of the length of the opinions (totaling nearly 200 pages in the official report), the digest is longer than others
in this text.

Parents Involved in Community Schools v. Seattle School District No. 1, ___ U.S. ___, 127 S.Ct. 2738 (2007)

FACTS: The Seattle and Jefferson County (Louisville) school districts chose voluntarily to adopt student assignment plans based on race. Both plans were challenged
in lawsuits brought by the parents of students who were denied assignment to particular schools solely because of their race. In each case, the plaintiffs contended that the
plan violated the Equal Protection Clause.

Seattle—The Seattle school district, which has never been racially segregated by
law or been subject to court-ordered desegregation, classifies all students entering high
school as either "white" or "nonwhite." It includes in the nonwhite category not only
African Americans but also Asian Americans, Latinos, and Native Americans. Each
student is counted as white or nonwhite according to the race specified in the student's
registration materials (but if no race is specified in the student's registration materials,
the district classifies the student through "a visual inspection" of the student's color).
On the basis of this methodology, 59 percent are nonwhite and 41 percent are white.
The district seeks a diverse composition in each high school that reflects, as closely
as possible, this 59/41 ratio.

Students entering the ninth grade may request any of the Seattle's ten high schools
and, if space allows, will be assigned to their first choice. But the ability of any student
to attend an oversubscribed school (unless the student's brother or sister is already
enrolled there) will depend on whether he or she is deemed nonwhite or white. If an
oversubscribed high school is considered "racially imbalanced" by the district's criteria (i.e., if the nonwhite/white makeup of the school's student body differs by more
than 15 percent from the desired 59/41 ratio), a white student will be rejected if
the imbalance is white and a nonwhite student will be rejected if the imbalance is
nonwhite.

The Court of Appeals for the Ninth Circuit *en banc* upheld the Seattle plan by a
7-4 vote.

Jefferson County—This case is similar to the Seattle case except that the Jefferson
County schools, unlike the Seattle schools, had once been racially segregated under
legal compulsion and had previously been the subject of a desegregation decree. In
2000, the district court dissolved the decree after finding that the district had eliminated the vestiges of prior segregation.

---

[20]Abigail & Stephan Thernstrom, "Have We Overcome?" *Commentary* (November 2004).

In 2001, the Jefferson County district adopted its racial balancing plan. Students are classified as either "black" (African American) or "other" (all races, including Asian American).

Approximately 34 percent of the district's 97,000 students are black; most of the remaining 66 percent are white. The plan requires that schools maintain a black enrollment of no less than 15 percent and no more than 50 percent.

Assignments are made on the basis of available space within the schools and the district's racial guidelines. If a school has reached a "black/other" ratio exceeding the racial guidelines, a student whose race would add to the school's racial imbalance will be denied assignment there.

The Jefferson County plan was upheld by the Court of Appeals for the Sixth Circuit.

ISSUE: Do the racial balancing plans violate the Equal Protection Clause?

DECISION (*Roberts,* 5-4): *Yes*

[Part I of Roberts's opinion was joined by Scalia, Kennedy, Thomas, and Alito; the rest of the opinion was joined by Scalia, Thomas, and Alito. Kennedy and Thomas filed concurring opinions. Breyer filed a dissenting opinion, joined by Stevens, Souter, and Ginsburg. Stevens also filed a dissenting opinion.]

I.

Both cases present the same underlying legal question—whether a public school that had not operated legally segregated schools or has been found to be unitary may choose to classify students by race and rely upon that classification in making school assignments.

In the Seattle case, for example, Andy Meeks's mother sought to enroll him in a special program because he suffered from attention deficit hyperactivity disorder and dyslexia. He was found qualified for the program but was denied admission because of his race. Similarly, in the Jefferson County case, for example, when his family moved into the school district, Joshua McDonald was assigned to a kindergarten class in a school located ten miles from his home. When his mother sought a transfer to a school only a mile from his new home, space was available but his transfer was denied because, in the school district's words, it "would have an adverse effect on desegregation compliance."

It is well established that, when the government distributes burdens or benefits on the basis of individual racial classifications, that action is reviewed under strict scrutiny. As the Court recently reaffirmed in the *Gratz* case, "racial classifications are simply too pernicious to permit any but the most exact connection between justification and classification." In order to satisfy this searching standard of review, the school districts must demonstrate that the use of individual racial classifications in the assignment plans here under review is "narrowly tailored" to achieve a "compelling" government interest. E.g., Adarand Constructors, Inc. v. Pena, 515 U.S. 200, 224 (1995).

Although courts may in some instances employ racial balancing on a temporary basis to eradicate the effects of past intentional discrimination, no such compelling interest is involved here. The Seattle schools were never segregated by law nor subject to court-ordered desegregation, and the Jefferson County desegregation decree had previously been dissolved.

In *Grutter,* the interest in diversity "in the context of higher education" was recognized by the Court as compelling for purposes of strict scrutiny. However, the diversity interest upheld there was not focused on race alone but encompassed "all factors that may contribute to student body diversity" and "many possible bases for diversity admissions," such as overcoming personal adversity and family hardship and exceptional records of extensive community service. Quoting Justice Powell's articulation of diversity in the *Bakke* case, the Court in *Grutter* noted that "'it is not an interest in simple ethnic diversity, in which a specified percentage of the student body is in effect guaranteed to be members of selected ethnic groups,' that can justify the use of race," but "a far broader array of qualifications and characteristics of which racial or ethnic origin is but a single though important element."

The entire gist of the analysis in *Grutter* was that the admissions program at issue there focused on each applicant as an individual, and not simply as a member of a particular racial group. The classification of applicants by race was only as part of a "highly individualized, holistic review." As the Court explained, "[t]he importance of this individualized consideration in the context of a race-conscious admissions program is paramount." The point of the narrow tailoring analysis in which the *Grutter* Court engaged was to ensure that the use of racial classifications was indeed part of a broader assessment of diversity, and not simply an effort to achieve racial balance, which the Court explained would be "patently unconstitutional."

In the present cases, by contrast, race is not considered as part of a broader effort to achieve "exposure to widely diverse people, cultures, ideas, and viewpoints." Instead, for some students, race is determinative standing alone. The districts argue that other factors, such as student preferences, affect assignment decisions under their plans, but under each plan when race comes into play, it is decisive by itself. It is not simply one factor weighed with others in reaching a decision, as in *Grutter;* it is *the* factor. Like the University of Michigan undergraduate plan struck down in *Gratz,* the plans here "do not provide for a meaningful individualized review of applicants."

Even when it comes to race, the plans here employ only a limited notion of diversity, viewing race exclusively in white/nonwhite terms in Seattle and black/other terms in Jefferson County. We are a Nation not of black and white alone, but one teeming with divergent communities knitted together with various traditions and carried forth, above all, by individuals. Yet, under the Seattle plan, a school with 50 percent Asian American students and 50 percent white students but no African American, Native American, or Latino students would qualify as "balanced," while a school with 30 percent Asian American, 25 percent African American, 25 percent Latino, and 20 percent white students would not. It is hard to understand how a plan that could allow these results can be viewed as being concerned with achieving enrollment that is "broadly diverse" (*Grutter*).

Moreover, in upholding the admissions plan in *Grutter,* this Court relied upon considerations unique to institutions of higher education, noting that in light of "the expansive freedoms of speech and thought associated with the university environment, universities occupy a special niche in our constitutional tradition." The Court repeatedly noted that it was addressing the use of race "in the context of higher education."

The present cases are not governed by *Grutter*. The Court in *Grutter* expressly articulated key limitations on its holding—defining a specific type of broad-based diversity and noting the unique context of higher education—but these limitations were largely disregarded by the courts below in extending *Grutter* to uphold race-based assignments in elementary and secondary schools.

II.

The parties dispute whether racial diversity in schools in fact has a marked impact on test scores and other objective yardsticks or achieves intangible socialization benefits. The debate is not one we need to resolve, however, because it is clear that the racial classifications employed by the districts are not narrowly tailored to the goal of achieving the educational and social benefits asserted to flow from racial diversity. In design and operation, the plans are directed only to racial balance, pure and simple, an objective this Court has repeatedly condemned as illegitimate.

In *Grutter,* the number of minority students the school sought to admit was an undefined "meaningful number" necessary to achieve a genuinely diverse student body. Although this was the subject of disagreement on the Court, the majority concluded that the law school did not count back from its applicant pool to arrive at the "meaningful number" it regarded as necessary to diversify its student body. Here the racial balance the districts seek is a defined range set solely by reference to the demographics of the respective school districts.

This working backward to achieve a particular type of racial balance, rather than working forward from some demonstration of the level of diversity that provides the purported benefits, is a fatal flaw under our existing precedent. As Justice Powell pointed out in *Bakke:* "If petitioner's purpose is to assure within its student body some specified percentage of a particular group merely because of its race or ethnic origin, such a preferential purpose must be rejected . . . as facially invalid." *Grutter* itself reiterated that "outright racial balancing is patently unconstitutional."

Accepting racial balancing as a compelling state interest would justify the imposition of racial proportionality throughout American society, contrary to our repeated recognition that "[a]t the heart of the Constitution's guarantee of equal protection lies the simple command that the Government must treat citizens as individuals, not as simply components of a racial, religious, sexual or national class." Miller v. Johnson, 515 U.S. 900, 911 (1995). Allowing racial balancing as a compelling end in itself would effectively ensure that race will always be relevant in American life and that the ultimate goal of eliminating entirely from governmental decision making such irrelevant factors as a human being's race will never be achieved.

The principle that racial balancing is not permitted is one of substance, not semantics. Racial balancing is not transformed from "patently unconstitutional" to a compelling state interest simply by relabeling it "racial diversity." While the school districts use various verbal formulations to describe the interest they seek to promote—racial diversity, avoidance of racial isolation, racial integration—they do not define it in any way that differs from racial balance.

Moreover, narrow tailoring requires "serious, good faith consideration of workable race-neutral alternatives" (*Grutter*). Both districts have failed to show that they considered methods other than explicit racial classifications to achieve their stated goals.

III.

Justice Breyer's dissent selectively relies on inapplicable precedent and even dicta while dismissing contrary holdings, alters and misapplies our well-established legal framework for assessing equal protection challenges to racial classifications, and greatly exaggerates the consequences of today's decision.

To begin with, Justice Breyer seeks to justify the plans at issue on the basis of precedents recognizing the compelling interest in remedying past intentional discrimination. Not even the school districts go this far, and for good reason. The distinction between segregation by state action and racial imbalance caused by other factors has been central to our jurisprudence for generations. The dissent elides this distinction between *de jure* and *de facto* segregation, casually intimates that Seattle's school attendance patterns reflect illegal segregation, and fails to credit the judicial determination—under the most rigorous standard—that Jefferson County had eliminated the vestiges of prior segregation before adopting its present plan. The dissent thus alters in fundamental ways not only the facts presented here but the established law.

Justice Breyer's dissent also asserts that these cases are controlled by *Grutter,* claiming that the existence of a compelling interest in these cases "follows *a fortiori*" from *Grutter,* and accusing us of tacitly overruling that case. However, *Grutter* itself recognized that using race simply to achieve racial balance would be patently unconstitutional. The Court was exceedingly careful in describing the interest furthered in *Grutter* as "not an interest in simple ethnic diversity" but rather a "far broader array of qualifications and characteristics" in which race was but a single element. We simply do not understand how Justice Breyer can maintain that classifying every schoolchild as black or white, and using that classification as a determinative factor in assigning children to achieve pure racial balance, can be regarded as "more narrowly tailored" than the consideration of race in *Grutter,* where the Court stated that "[t]he importance of . . . individualized consideration" in the program was "paramount," and consideration of race was but one factor in a "highly individualized, holistic review." In light of the foregoing, Justice Breyer's appeal to *stare decisis* rings particularly hollow.

At the same time it relies on inapplicable desegregation cases, the dissent candidly dismisses the significance of this Court's repeated *holdings* that all racial classifications must be reviewed under strict scrutiny, arguing that a different standard of review should be applied here because the districts use race for beneficent rather than malicious purposes. But our decisions clearly reject the argument that motives affect the strict scrutiny analysis. See, e.g., Johnson v. California, 543 U.S. 499, 505 (2005) ("We have insisted on strict scrutiny in every context, even for so-called 'benign' racial classifications").

Justice Breyer speaks of bringing "the races" together (putting aside the purely black-and-white nature of the plans) as the justification for excluding individuals on the basis of their race. Again, this approach to racial classifications is fundamentally at odds with our many precedents making clear that the Equal Protection Clause "protect[s] *persons,* not *groups*" (*Adarand,* italics in original).

Justice Breyer's position comes down to a familiar claim: The end justifies the means. He admits that "there is a cost in applying 'a state-mandated racial label,'" but he is confident that the cost is worth paying. Our established strict scrutiny test for racial classifications, however, insists on detailed examination as to both ends *and* means. Simply because the districts may seek a worthy goal does not mean they are free to discriminate on the basis of race to achieve it, or that their racial classifications should be subject to less exacting scrutiny.

Without any detailed discussion of the operation of the plans, the students who are affected, or the districts' failure to consider race-neutral alternatives, the dissent concludes that the districts have shown that these racial classifications are necessary and urges deference to local school boards on these issues. Such deference is fundamentally at odds with our equal protection jurisprudence. We put the burden on state actors to demonstrate that their race-based policies are justified. As the Court stated in Richmond v. J. A. Croson, 488 U.S. 469, 501 (1989), "The history of racial classifications in this country suggests that blind judicial deference to legislative or executive pronouncements of necessity has no place in equal protection analysis."

Justice Breyer also suggests that other means for achieving greater racial diversity in schools must necessarily be unconstitutional if the racial classifications in these cases cannot survive strict scrutiny. These other means—for example, where to construct new schools, how to allocate resources among schools, and which academic offerings to provide to attract students to certain schools—implicate different considerations than the explicit racial classifications at issue in these cases, and we express no opinion on their validity. Rather, we employ the familiar and well-established analytic approach of strict scrutiny to evaluate the plans at issue today, an approach that in no way warrants the dissent's cataclysmic concerns. Under that approach, the school districts have not carried their burden of showing that the ends they seek justify the particular extreme means they have chosen—classifying individual students on the basis of their race and discriminating among them on that basis.

*****

In Brown v. Board of Education, 347 U.S. 483 (1954), we held that segregation deprived black children of equal educational opportunities regardless of whether school facilities and other tangible factors were equal, because government classification and separation on grounds of race denoted inferiority. It was the fact of legally separating children on the basis of race on which the Court relied. And the following year in *Brown II* the Court emphasized that what was required was "determining admission to the public schools *on a nonracial basis*." (Italics added).

What do the racial classifications do in these cases, if not determine admission to a public school on a racial basis? Before *Brown,* schoolchildren were told where they could and could not go to school based on the color of their skin. The school districts in these cases have not carried the heavy burden of demonstrating that we should allow this once again—even for very different reasons. The way to stop discrimination on the basis of race is to stop discriminating on the basis of race.

The judgments of the Courts of Appeals for the Sixth and Ninth Circuits are reversed.

Kennedy, concurring in part and concurring in the judgment: I join Part I of the Chief Justice's opinion. However, my views do not allow me to join the balance of the opinion. Justice Breyer's dissenting opinion, on the other hand, rests on what I believe is a misuse and mistaken interpretation of our precedents. As a result, this separate opinion is necessary to set forth my different conclusions.

I.

The dissent finds that the school districts have identified a compelling interest in increasing diversity, including for the purpose of avoiding racial isolation. The plurality, by contrast, does not acknowledge that the school districts have identified a compelling interest here. Diversity, depending on its meaning and definition, is in my view a compelling educational goal that a school district may pursue.

When as here a governmental policy is subjected to strict scrutiny, the government has the burden of proving that racial classifications are narrowly tailored measures that further compelling governmental interests. And the inquiry into less restrictive alternatives demanded by the narrow tailoring analysis requires a thorough understanding of just how a plan works. The government bears the burden of justifying its use of racial classifications. As part of that burden it must establish, in detail, how decisions based on an individual student's race are made in a challenged governmental program.

Jefferson County has wholly failed to meet that threshold mandate. Jefferson County's explanation of how and when it employs these classifications is so broad and imprecise that it cannot withstand strict scrutiny. While it acknowledges that racial classifications are used to make assignments, it fails to make clear, for example, who makes the decisions; what, if any, oversight is employed; the precise circumstances in which an assignment decision will or will not be made on the basis of race; or how it is determined which of two similarly situated children will be subjected to a race-based decision. Jefferson County fails to make clear—even in the limited respects implicated by Joshua's initial assignment and transfer denial—whether, in fact, it relies on racial classifications in a manner narrowly tailored to the interest in question, rather than in the far-reaching, inconsistent, and *ad hoc* manner that the record would suggest. When a court subjects governmental action to strict scrutiny, it cannot construe ambiguities in favor of the state.

As for the Seattle case, the school district has gone further in describing the methods and criteria used to determine assignment decisions. The district, nevertheless, has wholly failed to explain why, in a district composed of a diversity of races, with fewer than half of the students classified as white, it has employed the crude racial categories of "white" and "nonwhite" as the basis for its assignment decisions. Far from being narrowly tailored to its purposes, the district has provided no convincing explanation for its design. As the district fails to account for the classification system it has chosen, despite what appears to be its ill fit, Seattle has not shown its plan to be narrowly tailored to achieve its own ends; and thus it fails to pass strict scrutiny.

II.

I believe that parts of the Chief Justice's opinion imply an all-too-unyielding insistence that race cannot be a factor in instances when, in my view, it may be taken into account. The plurality opinion is too dismissive of the legitimate interest government has in ensuring all people have equal opportunity regardless of their race. The plurality's postulate that "[t]he way to stop discrimination on the basis of race is to stop discriminating on the basis of race" is not sufficient to decide these cases. The plurality opinion is at least open to the interpretation that the Constitution requires school districts to ignore the problem of *de facto* resegregation in schooling. I cannot endorse that conclusion. To the extent the plurality opinion suggests the Constitution mandates that state and local school authorities must accept the status quo of racial isolation in schools, it is, in my view, profoundly mistaken.

The statement by Justice Harlan that "[o]ur Constitution is color-blind" was most certainly justified in the context of his dissent in Plessy v. Ferguson, 163 U.S. 537 (1896). The Court's decision in that case was a grievous error it took far too long to overrule. As an aspiration, Justice Harlan's axiom must command our assent. In the real world, it is regrettable to say, it cannot be a universal constitutional principle.

In the administration of public schools by the state and local authorities, it is permissible to consider the racial makeup of schools and to adopt general policies to encourage a diverse student body, one aspect of which is its racial composition. If school authorities are concerned that the student-body compositions of certain schools interfere with the objective of offering an equal educational opportunity to all of their students, they are free to devise race-conscious measures to address the problem in a general way and without treating each student in different fashion solely on the basis of a systematic, individual typing by race.

School boards may pursue the goal of bringing together students of diverse backgrounds and races through other means, including strategic site selection of new schools; drawing attendance zones with general recognition of the demographics of neighborhoods; allocating resources for special programs; recruiting students and faculty in a targeted fashion; and tracking enrollments, performance, and other statistics by race. These mechanisms are race-conscious but do not lead to different treatment based on a classification that tells each student he or she is to be defined by race, so it is unlikely any of them would demand strict scrutiny to be found permissible. Executive and legislative branches, which for generations now have considered these types of policies and procedures, should be permitted to employ them with candor and with confidence that a constitutional violation does not occur whenever a decision maker considers the impact a given approach might have on students of different races. Assigning to each student a personal designation according to a crude system of individual racial classifications is quite a different matter; and the legal analysis changes accordingly.

In the cases before us, it may well be that the schools could have achieved their stated ends through different means. These include the facially race-neutral means set forth above or, if necessary, a more nuanced, individual evaluation of school needs and student characteristics that might include race as a component. The latter approach would be informed by *Grutter,* though, of course, the criteria relevant to student placement would differ based on the age of the students, the needs of the parents, and the role of the schools.

III.

Justice Breyer's dissent rests on the assumptions that sweeping race-based classifications of persons are permitted by existing precedents; that endorsement of race categories for each child in a large segment of the community would present no danger to individual freedom in other prospective realms of governmental regulation; and that the racial classifications used here cause no hurt or anger of the type the Constitution prevents. Each of these premises is, in my respectful view, incorrect.

The dissent's reliance on this Court's precedents to justify the explicit classwide racial classifications at issue here is a misreading of our authorities and contrary to well-accepted principles. And in his critique of the dissent's analysis, I am in many respects in agreement with the Chief Justice. As he points out, the compelling interests implicated in the present cases are distinct from the interests the Court has recognized in remedying the effects of past intentional discrimination and in increasing diversity in higher education. But to the extent the plurality opinion can be interpreted to foreclose any consideration of these interests, I disagree with that reasoning.

As to the dissent, the general conclusions upon which it relies have no principled limit and would result in the broad acceptance of governmental racial classifications in areas far afield from schooling. The dissent's permissive strict scrutiny could invite widespread governmental deployment of racial classifications. There seems to be no principled rule, moreover, to limit the dissent's rationale to the context of public schools. The dissent emphasizes local control, the unique history of school desegregation, and the fact that these plans make less use of race than prior plans, but these factors seem more rhetorical than integral to the analytical structure of the opinion.

This brings us to the dissent's reliance on the Court's decisions in *Gratz* and *Grutter*. To say that we must ratify the racial classifications here at issue on the basis of those decisions is, with all respect, simply baffling.

Gratz involved a system where race was not the entire classification. The procedures in *Gratz* placed much less reliance on race than do the plans at issue here. The issue in *Gratz* arose, moreover, in the context of college admissions where students had other choices and precedent supported the proposition that First Amendment interests give universities particular latitude in defining diversity. Even so the race factor was found to be invalid. If *Gratz* is to be the measure, the racial classification systems here are *a fortiori* invalid. Under no fair reading can *Gratz* be cited as authority to sustain the racial classifications under consideration here.

The same must be said for *Grutter*. There the Court sustained a system that, it found, was flexible enough to take into account "all pertinent elements of diversity" and considered race as only one factor among many. If students were considered for a whole range of their talents and school needs with race as just one consideration, *Grutter* would have some application. That, though, is not the case here.

*****

A school district may consider it a compelling interest to achieve a diverse student population. Race may be one component of that diversity, but other demographic factors, plus special talents and needs, must also be considered. What the government is *not* permitted to do, absent a showing of necessity not made here, is to classify every student on the basis of race and to assign each of them to schools based on that classification. Crude measures of this sort threaten to reduce children to racial chits valued and traded according to one school's supply and another's demand.

The decision today should not prevent school districts from continuing the important work of bringing together students of different racial, ethnic, and economic backgrounds. Because of a variety of factors—some influenced by government, some not—neighborhoods in our communities do not reflect the diversity of our nation as a whole. Those entrusted with directing our public schools can bring to bear the creativity of experts, parents, administrators, and other concerned citizens to find a way to achieve the compelling interests they face without resorting to widespread governmental allocation of benefits and burdens on the basis of racial classifications.

Thomas, concurring: I wholly concur in the Chief Justice's opinion. I write separately to address several of the contentions in Justice Breyer's dissent.

(1) Contrary to the dissent's rhetoric, neither of these school districts is threatened with resegregation, and neither is constitutionally compelled to undertake race-based remediation. Racial imbalance is not segregation, and the mere incantation of terms like "resegregation" and "remediation" cannot make up the difference. To raise the specter of segregation to defend these programs is to ignore the meaning of the word and the nature of the cases before us.

It is important to define segregation clearly and to distinguish it from racial imbalance. In the context of public schooling, segregation is the deliberate operation of a school system to carry out a governmental policy to separate pupils in schools solely on the basis of race. Racial imbalance, on the other hand, is the failure of a school district's individual schools to match or approximate the demographic makeup of the student population at large. Racial imbalance can result from any number of innocent private decisions, including voluntary housing choices. Because racial imbalance is not inevitably linked to unconstitutional segregation, it is not unconstitutional in and of itself.

Although there arguably is a danger of racial imbalance in schools in Seattle and Louisville, there is no resegregation in any constitutional sense. No one contends that Seattle has established or that Louisville has reestablished a dual school system to separate students on the basis of race. Racial imbalance without state action to require racial separation does not amount to segregation.

Not only are the two concepts distinct, but a school cannot "remedy" racial imbalance in the same way that it can remedy segregation. Unlike *de jure* segregation, there is no ultimate remedy for racial imbalance. Individual schools will fall in and out of balance in the natural course with a school district's changing demographics—a continuous process with no identifiable culpable party and no discernable end.

(2) In an effort to justify the plans in issue, the dissent claims that "the law requires application here of a standard of review that is not 'strict' in the traditional sense of that word." That argument cannot be reconciled with the Court's precedents. We have made it clear that strict scrutiny applies to *every* racial classification. Purportedly "benign" race-based decision making suffers the same constitutional infirmity as invidious race-based decision making.

Even supposing it were constitutionally relevant, the race-based assignment programs before us are not as benign as the dissent believes. As these programs demonstrate, every time the government uses racial criteria to "bring the races together," someone gets excluded, and the person excluded suffers an injury solely because of his or her race. This type of exclusion is precisely the sort of government action that pits the races against one another, exacerbates racial tension, and "provoke[s] resentment among those who believe that they have been wronged by the government's use of race" (*Adarand*).

(3) In its search for a compelling interest that would satisfy strict scrutiny, the dissent argues that racially balanced schools improve educational outcomes for black children. In support, the dissent uncritically cites certain social science research to support propositions that are hotly disputed among social scientists. Scholars have radically differing opinions as to whether educational benefits arise from racial balancing and whether "integration" is necessary to black achievement. (Indeed, the Seattle school district itself must believe that racial mixing is not necessary for black achievement. Seattle operates a K–8 "African-American Academy," which has a nonwhite enrollment of 99 percent and was founded to "increase academic achievement.")

Given the questionable relationship between forced racial mixing and improved educational results for black children, the dissent argues that the social science evidence should be deemed at least "strong enough to permit a democratically elected school board reasonably to determine that this interest is a compelling one." This assertion is inexplicable. It is not up to the school boards—the very government entities whose race-based practices we must strictly scrutinize—to determine what interests qualify as compelling under the Fourteenth Amendment. Rather, this Court must assess independently the nature of the interest asserted and the evidence to support it in order to determine whether it qualifies as compelling under our precedents. To adopt the dissent's deferential approach would be to abdicate our constitutional responsibilities.

(4) The dissent attempts to find a compelling interest by claiming that it follows *a fortiori* from the interest this Court recognized as compelling in *Grutter*. However, regardless of the merit of *Grutter,* the compelling interest recognized in that case cannot support these plans. *Grutter* recognized a compelling interest in a law school's attainment of a diverse student body. This interest was critically dependent upon features unique to higher education. Only by ignoring *Grutter*'s reasoning can the dissent claim that recognizing a compelling interest in these cases is an *a fortiori* application of *Grutter*.

Stripped of the baseless interests that the dissent asserts on their behalf, the school districts cannot plausibly maintain that their plans further a compelling interest. Accordingly, the districts cannot satisfy strict scrutiny.

(5) My view of the Constitution is Justice Harlan's view in *Plessy:* "Our Constitution is color-blind, and neither knows nor tolerates classes among citizens." And that view was the rallying cry for the lawyers who litigated *Brown* and argued in that case "That the Constitution is color blind is our dedicated belief" and that "The Fourteenth Amendment precludes a state from imposing distinctions or classifications based upon race and color alone."

The dissent appears to pin its interpretation of the Equal Protection Clause to current societal practice and expectations, deference to local officials, and likely practical consequences. Such a view was unfortunately ascendant in this Court's jurisprudence for several decades. In *Plessy,* upholding the notorious "separate but equal" doctrine, the Court stated that "there must necessarily be a large discretion on the part of the legislature," and relied on "the established usages, customs and traditions of the people, and with a view to the promotion of their comfort, and the preservation of the public peace and good order." The segregationists in *Brown* embraced the arguments the Court endorsed in *Plessy*. Though *Brown* decisively rejected those arguments, today's dissent replicates them to a distressing extent.

The plans before us base school assignment decisions on students' race. Because "[o]ur Constitution is color-blind," as Justice Harlan proclaimed in *Plessy,* such race-based decision making is unconstitutional. I concur in the Chief Justice's opinion so holding.

Breyer, dissenting (joined by Stevens, Souter, and Ginsburg): The plurality pays inadequate attention to past opinions' rationales, their language, and the contexts in which they arise. As a result, it reverses course and reaches the wrong conclusion. In doing so, it distorts precedent, it misapplies the relevant constitutional principles, it announces legal rules that will obstruct efforts by state and local governments to deal effectively with the growing resegregation of public schools, and it undermines *Brown*'s promise of integrated primary and secondary education that local communities have sought to make a reality.

The plurality errs in looking simply to whether earlier school segregation was *de jure* or *de facto* in order to draw separate the constitutionally permissible from the constitutionally forbidden use of "race-conscious" criteria. A court finding of *de jure* segregation cannot be the crucial variable.

A long-standing line of legal authority tells us that the Equal Protection Clause permits local school boards to use race-conscious criteria to achieve positive race-related goals, even when the Constitution does not compel it. The plurality says that such cases all "were decided before this Court definitively determined that 'all racial classifications . . . must be analyzed by a reviewing court under strict scrutiny' " (quoting *Adarand*). This Court in *Adarand* added that "such classifications are constitutional only if they are narrowly tailored measures that further compelling governmental interests." And the Court repeated this same statement in *Grutter*.

However, no case—not *Adarand, Gratz, Grutter,* or any other—has ever held that the test of "strict scrutiny" means that all racial classifications, no matter whether they seek to include or exclude, must in practice be treated the same. As the Court in *Grutter* stated: "Although all governmental uses of race are subject to strict scrutiny, not all are invalidated by it." And in *Grutter* the challenged use of race was upheld.

As *Grutter* recognized, "[c]ontext matters when reviewing race-based governmental action under the Equal Protection Clause." And contexts differ dramatically one from the other. Governmental use of race-based criteria can arise in the context of, for example, census forms, research expenditures for diseases, assignments of police officers patrolling predominantly minority-race neighborhoods, efforts to desegregate racially segregated schools, policies that favor minorities when distributing goods or services in short supply, actions that create majority-minority electoral districts, peremptory strikes that remove potential jurors on the basis of race, and others. Given the significant differences among these contexts, it would be surprising if the law required an identically strict legal test for each of them.

Here, the context is one in which school districts seek to advance or to maintain racial integration in primary and secondary schools. This context is *not* a context that involves the use of race to decide who will receive goods or services that are normally distributed on the basis of merit and which are in short supply. It is not one in which race-conscious limits stigmatize or exclude; the limits do not pit the races against each other or otherwise significantly exacerbate racial tensions. They do not impose burdens unfairly upon members of one race alone but instead seek benefits for members of all races alike. The racial limits here seek, not to keep the races apart, but to bring them together.

The standard of review that should apply here is not "strict" in the traditional sense of that word. In my view, a legislature or school district, ultimately accountable to the electorate, could properly conclude that a racial classification sometimes serves a purpose important enough, for example, to help end racial isolation or to achieve a diverse student body in public schools. Nonetheless, even under the more rigorous version of strict scrutiny embodied in *Grutter* and other cases, I conclude that both plans serve a "compelling governmental interest" and are "narrowly tailored" to achieve that interest.

The compelling interest is the interest in promoting or preserving greater racial integration of public schools by increasing the degree to which racial mixture characterizes each of the district's schools. This interest possesses three essential elements: an interest in setting right the consequences of prior conditions of segregation; an interest in overcoming the adverse educational effects produced by and associated with highly segregated schools; and an interest in producing an educational environment that reflects the pluralistic society in which our children will live.

These advantages of integration are supported by many studies. Admittedly there are studies that offer contrary conclusions. However, the evidence is sufficiently strong to permit a school board to determine that this interest is compelling.

In light of this Court's conclusions in *Grutter,* the "compelling" nature of these interests in the context of primary and secondary public education follows *a fortiori.* It was *Brown,* after all, focusing upon primary and secondary schools—not earlier decisions focusing on graduate schools—that affected so deeply not only Americans but the world.

The plans before us are also "narrowly tailored" to achieve these "compelling" objectives. In fact, the defining feature of both plans is greater emphasis upon student choice. Indeed, the plans before us are *more narrowly tailored* than the race-conscious admission plans that this Court approved in *Grutter.* Here, race becomes a factor only in a fraction of the assignments. Moreover, the effect of applying race-conscious criteria here affects potentially disadvantaged students *less severely,* not more severely, than the criteria at issue in *Grutter.* Disappointed students are not rejected from a state's flagship graduate program; they simply attend a different one of the district's many public schools that are substantially equal.

Nor is it relevant that these school districts did not examine the merits of applications "individual[ly]." The context here does not involve admission by merit; a child's academic, artistic, and athletic merits are not at all relevant to the child's placement. These are not affirmative action plans, and hence "individualized scrutiny" is simply beside the point.

The upshot is that these plans' specific features show that the districts' plans are narrowly tailored to achieve their compelling goals. In sum, the districts' race-conscious plans satisfy "strict scrutiny" and are therefore lawful.

It is important to consider the potential consequences of the plurality's approach. Yesterday, school boards had available to them a full range of means to combat segregated schools. Today, they do not. At a minimum, the plurality's views would threaten a surge of race-based litigation. Hundreds of state and federal statutes and regulations use racial classifications for educational or other purposes. In many such instances, the contentious force of legal challenges to these classifications, meritorious or not, would displace earlier calm.

The plurality, or at least those who follow Justice Thomas's "color-blind" approach, may feel confident that, to end invidious discrimination, one must end *all* governmental use of race-conscious criteria, including those with inclusive objectives. By contrast, I do not claim to know how best to stop harmful discrimination; how best to create a society that includes all Americans; how best to overcome our serious problems of increasing *de facto* segregation, troubled inner city schooling, and poverty correlated with race. But, as a judge, I do know that the Constitution does not authorize judges to dictate solutions to these problems. Rather, the Constitution creates a democratic political system through which the people themselves must together find answers. And it is for them to debate how best to educate the nation's children and how best to administer America's schools to achieve that aim. The Court should leave them to their work. And it is for them to decide, to quote the plurality's slogan, whether the best "way to stop discrimination on the basis of race is to stop discriminating on the basis of race."

Brown held out a promise. The plurality's position, I fear, would break that promise. This is a decision that the Court and the nation will come to regret.

Stevens, dissenting: While I join Justice Breyer's eloquent and unanswerable dissent in its entirety, it is appropriate to add these words.

There is a cruel irony in the Chief Justice's reliance on our *Brown* decision. In the last paragraph of his opinion, he states: "Before *Brown,* schoolchildren were told where they could and could not go to school based on the color of their skin." The Chief Justice fails to note that it was only black schoolchildren who were so ordered; indeed, the history books do not tell stories of white children struggling to attend black schools. In this and other ways, the Chief Justice rewrites the history of one of this Court's most important decisions.

The Chief Justice rejects the conclusion that the racial classifications at issue here should be viewed differently than others, because they do not impose burdens on one race alone and do not stigmatize or exclude. However, if we look at cases decided during the interim between *Brown* and *Adarand,* we can see how a rigid adherence to tiers of scrutiny obscures *Brown*'s clear message. It is my firm conviction that no Member of the Court that I joined in 1975 would have agreed with today's decision.

Seeking Other Remedies for Racial Imbalance

In an effort to reduce racial imbalances resulting from demographic housing patterns —where the homes of the students are located—school boards have employed a variety of race-conscious techniques, including the assignment of students on the basis of race. That particular technique, the Court held in *Parents Involved,* violates the Equal Protection Clause. But would the Constitution permit other race-conscious methods to address racial imbalances resulting from housing patterns?

Speaking for the four dissenters, Justice Breyer claimed that "Yesterday, school boards had available to them a full range of means to combat segregated schools. Today, they do not." He added:

> At a minimum, the plurality's views would threaten a surge of race-based litigation. Hundreds of state and federal statutes and regulations use racial classifications for educational or other purposes. . . . In many such instances, the contentious force of legal challenges to these classifications, meritorious or not, would displace earlier calm.

In his opinion Chief Justice Roberts responded that "we employ the familiar and well-established analytic approach of strict scrutiny to evaluate the plans at issue today, an approach that in no way warrants the dissent's cataclysmic concerns." Roberts further stated that the Court was not passing on the validity of considering race in pursuing "other means for achieving greater racial diversity in schools"—in determining "for example, where to construct new schools, how to allocate resources among schools, and which academic offerings to provide to attract students to certain schools." Those issues, according to Roberts, "implicate different considerations than the explicit racial classifications at issue in these cases, and we express no opinion on their validity."

In view of the split of views among the other eight Justices, Justice Kennedy's concurrence constitutes in effect the controlling opinion on the permissible scope of race-conscious methods to increase or maintain diversity in the public schools. While otherwise agreeing with Roberts's opinion, Kennedy in his concurrence objected that Roberts's opinion "is at least open to the interpretation that the Constitution requires school districts to ignore the problem of *de facto* resegregation in schooling." On the other hand, Kennedy rejected the dissenters' apparent willingness to give school boards virtually untrammeled authority to use racial balancing techniques, even to the extent of deciding whether individual students should be admitted on the basis of skin color.

According to Kennedy:

> In the administration of public schools by the state and local authorities, it is permissible to consider the racial makeup of schools and to adopt general policies to encourage a diverse student body, one aspect of which is its racial composition. If school authorities are concerned that the student-body compositions of certain schools interfere with the objective of offering an equal educational opportunity to all of their students, *they are free to devise race-conscious measures to address the problem in a general way and without treating each student in different fashion solely on the basis of a systematic, individual typing by race.*
>
> School boards may pursue the goal of bringing together students of diverse backgrounds and races through other means, including strategic site selection of new schools; drawing attendance zones with general recognition of the demographics of neighborhoods; allocating resources for special programs; recruiting students and faculty in a targeted fashion; and tracking enrollments, performance, and other statistics by race. *These mechanisms are race-conscious but do not lead to different treatment based on a classification that tells each student he or she is to be defined by race, so it is unlikely any of them would demand strict scrutiny to be found permissible.* Executive and legislative branches, which for generations now have considered these types of policies and procedures, should be permitted to employ them with candor and with confidence that a constitutional violation does not occur whenever a decisionmaker considers the impact a given approach might have on students of different races. *Assigning to each student a personal designation according to a crude system of individual racial classifications is quite a different matter; and the legal analysis changes accordingly.* (Italics added.)

Of the nine Justices, Thomas was the only one who explicitly supported a color-blind test. In his concurrence he declared that, "as a general rule, all race-based government decisionmaking—regardless of context—is unconstitutional."[21]

---

[21]See Emily Bazelon, "The Next Kind of Integration," *New York Times Magazine,* July 20, 2008, concerning steps taken by school boards after the *Parents Involved* decision to achieve diversity by a primarily class-based method.

6

Due Process of Law

Procedural Due Process

The Fourteenth Amendment, like the Fifth Amendment in the original Constitution, prohibits denying "any person of life, liberty, or property *without due process of law*." (Italics added.)

As the word "process" clearly connotes, the requirement of "due process" was initially understood to refer exclusively to *procedural* safeguards. This was its well-understood meaning in English and colonial usage when the Constitution was adopted. Alexander Hamilton pointed out (1787) that "The words 'due process' have a precise technical import, and are only applicable to the process and proceedings of the courts of justice; they can never be referred to an act of the legislature."

Procedural due process issues include, for example, whether a defendant in a criminal case was given sufficient notice of the charges, whether the jury was selected on an impartial basis, and whether the defendant was given a reasonable opportunity to defend himself against the charges. Civil and administrative proceedings brought by the government must also comply with procedural due process.

Procedural due process issues are almost invariably "fact-specific"—that is, focused on whether the particular circumstances of a case demonstrate a substantial departure from accepted standards of fairness. The hundreds—probably thousands—of Supreme Court decisions dealing with such procedural issues are beyond the scope of this text, which instead is focused on the judicial review of the constitutionality of federal and state statutes.

Substantive Due Process

Starting in the second half of the nineteenth century, notwithstanding the Framers' understanding of "due process," Supreme Court decisions began to interpret the term to include—in addition to the original procedural element—a *substantive* element as well. While procedural due process regulates *how* a statute enacted by a legislature will be enforced in judicial or administrative proceedings, "substantive due process" addresses the validity of the "substance" of the statute itself.[1] Substantive due process is a judicially created doctrine empowering courts to strike down a statute—*not* because the statute provides for an unfair procedure—but instead on the basis of the

---

[1] As one commentator suggested, "Substantive due process is a contradiction in terms—sort of like 'green pastel redness.'" John Hart Ely, *Democracy and Distrust: A Theory of Judicial Review* [Harvard 1980]: 18.

court's evaluation that the statute unduly restricts "liberty" or "property" of "freedom of contract" or exceeds the state's "police power."

Lochner v. New York, 198 U.S. 45 (1905), was a landmark decision in the development of the substantive due process doctrine. In *Lochner* the Supreme Court (5-4) held unconstitutional a New York statute providing that no bakery employee shall be required or permitted to work more than 60 hours a week or 10 hours a day. According to the majority, the law interfered with "freedom of contract" and was not a valid exercise of a state's police power. The Court stated that "The general right to make a contract in relation to his business is part of the liberty of the individual protected by the Fourteenth Amendment," and "The right to purchase or sell labor is part of the liberty protected by this amendment." The question to be decided, the Court stated, was the following:

> Is this a fair, reasonable and appropriate exercise of the State, or is it an unreasonable, unnecessary and arbitrary interference with the right of the individual to his personal liberty or to enter into those contracts in relation to labor which may seem to him appropriate or necessary for the support of himself and his family?

The Court's answer was that, "There is, in our judgment, no reasonable foundation for holding this to be necessary or appropriate as a health law to safeguard the public health, or the health of the individuals who are following the trade of a baker."

Dissenting, Justice Holmes contended:

> This case is decided upon an economic theory that a large part of the country does not entertain. If it were a question whether I agreed with that theory, I should desire to study it further and long before making up my mind. But I do not conceive that to be my duty, because I strongly believe that my agreement or disagreement has nothing to do with the right of a majority to embody their opinions in law. It is settled by various decisions of this court that state constitutions and state laws may regulate life in many ways which we as legislators might think as injudicious, or if you like as tyrannical, as this, and which, equally with this, interfere with the liberty to contract.
>
> ... A constitution is not intended to embody a particular economic theory, whether of paternalism and the organic relation of the citizen to the state or of laissez faire. It is made for people of fundamentally differing views, and the accident of our finding certain opinions natural and familiar, or novel, and even shocking, ought not to conclude our judgment upon the question whether statutes embodying them conflict with the Constitution.

From *Lochner* to the mid-1930s, the Court relied on the substantive due process doctrine to nullify a large number of statutes regulating business and labor organizations —including, among others, statutes prescribing maximum hours, setting minimum wages, and outlawing "yellow dog" contracts (prohibiting employees from joining unions).

In the New Deal period in the mid-1930s, substantive due process fell into disrepute, at least in the review of economic legislation. Indeed, *Lochner* eventually became one of the most reviled decisions in the Court's history.

West Coast Hotel v. Parrish, 300 U.S. 379 (1937), is a landmark decision initiating the Court's greater deference to economic legislation. The Court (5-4) upheld a Washington state statute requiring a minimum wage for women and minors. Chief Justice Hughes, writing for the majority, repudiated the *Lochner* "freedom of contract" doctrine and stated:

What is this freedom of contract? The Constitution does not speak of freedom of contract. It speaks of liberty and prohibits the deprivation of liberty without due process of law. . . . [R]egulation which is reasonable in relation to its subject and is adopted in the interests of the community is due process.

Regulation, moreover, was not limited to advancing the public safety, public health, or public morals:

The exploitation of a class of workers who are in an unequal position with respect to bargaining power and are thus relatively defenseless against the denial of a living wage is not only detrimental to their health and well being but casts a direct burden for their support upon the community.

Today, in reviewing the validity of economic regulatory statutes, the Court applies a minimal level of review, known as the "rational basis" test. Under that test, a challenged law will be upheld if it is rationally related to a legitimate government purpose and if the means chosen constitute a reasonable way to accomplish the objective. Moreover, the challenger of the law has the burden of proof under the rational basis test, usually leading to the law being sustained.

By contrast, a much more rigorous standard is applied to rights (such as the right to vote and freedom of speech) that have been classified by the Court as "fundamental"— rights that are accepted as being "implicit in the concept of ordered liberty," "deeply rooted in this Nation's history and tradition," or "so rooted in the traditions and conscience of our people as to be ranked as fundamental." Statutes alleged to violate "fundamental" rights (under either the Due Process Clause or the Equal Protection Clause) are reviewed under a "strict scrutiny" standard, requiring a demonstration that the challenged law is "necessary" to achieve a "compelling" government purpose and is "narrowly tailored" to serve that purpose. In a strict scrutiny case, moreover, the government (rather than the challenger) has the burden of proof. Because that burden is a very heavy one, laws subject to the strict scrutiny standard will usually—but not always—fail to pass constitutional muster.

Despite its rejection in the review of economic legislation, substantive due process has continued to be significant in civil liberties cases where the claimed individual right (as in, for example, *Roe v. Wade,* digested and discussed in Chapter 7) is not addressed in any other provision of the Constitution and resort must be had to a theory of denial of "liberty" under the substantive due process doctrine.

Both within and outside the Court, the legitimacy of the substantive due process continues to be a major source of controversy.

"Incorporation" of Rights in Due Process

The first eight Amendments of the Constitution—known as the "Bill of Rights"—provide a variety of protections against governmental abuses. But these Amendments, as originally enacted, were restrictions on actions by the federal government. Conversely, the Fourteenth Amendment is applicable to the States but does not contain any specific provision concerning, for example, the freedoms of speech, press, or religion protected by the First Amendment.

Beginning in the early 1900s, however, a series of Supreme Court decisions held that the Due Process Clause of the Fourteenth Amendment "incorporates" provisions of the first eight Amendments that guarantee "fundamental" personal rights. As a result of their "incorporation," the First Amendment and most of the other provisions of the Bill of Rights apply to the States as well as the federal government.

Other "incorporated" provisions include the Fourth Amendment prohibition of unreasonable searches and seizures, the Fifth Amendment prohibitions against double jeopardy and self-incrimination, the Sixth Amendment requirements in criminal cases of the assistance of counsel (if possible imprisonment is involved) and trial by jury, and the Eighth Amendment prohibition against cruel and unusual punishment.

In determining which provisions of the Bill of Rights are fundamental and therefore incorporated in the Fourteenth Amendment, the Court has articulated varying tests such as, for example, whether a right is "deeply rooted in the Nation's history and tradition" and "implicit in the concept of ordered liberty."

The Fourteenth Amendment also contains the Privileges or Immunities Clause: "No State shall make or enforce any law which shall abridge the privileges or immunities of citizens of the United States." Many historians and some Justices (notably Justice Black) have contended that this Clause was intended to apply the entire Bill of Rights to the States. That view, however, was foreclosed by the highly technical (but never overruled) decision in The Slaughter-House Cases, 83 U.S. 36 (1873), holding (5-4) that the Privileges or Immunities Clause did not confer any new rights against action by a State. This virtual nullification of the Clause may have provided the impetus for the Court's later reliance on the Due Process Clause of the Fourteenth Amendment as the basis for the incorporation doctrine (and also for the development of the substantive due process doctrine).

7

Abortion and the "Right of Privacy"

Emergence of a New Doctrine

The first antiabortion statute in the United States was enacted in 1821 in Connecticut. The statute initially criminalized abortions only if they took place after the "quickening" (the first detectable movement) of the fetus. A New York statute enacted in 1828, however, made abortion at any stage of pregnancy a felony. Then, as described by historian David Garrow:[1]

> starting in the mid-1840s a new wave of pressure for tougher antiabortion statutes, and more serious enforcement efforts began to build, with medical doctors often taking the political lead. By the end of the 1850s, the physicians' antiabortion efforts were making significant headway, and in 1860 Connecticut, again leading the way, passed a comprehensive new law eliminating the quickening distinction, prohibiting any abortion-related advertising, and mandating criminal punishment for a woman who obtained an abortion as well as for whoever performed it. . . . By the final two decades of the nineteenth century an "official consensus against abortion" had solidified in the law of each and every state of the union, with almost all of the prevailing statutes prohibiting all abortions, irrespective of the stage of pregnancy, except in cases where a woman's life was directly at risk.

Constitutional challenges to the abortion statutes began in the 1950s but picked up momentum with the issuance of the opinion in the next-digested case, *Griswold v. Connecticut.* Although it did not involve abortion but instead contraceptives, the Court found in the Constitution a "right of privacy" derived from "penumbras" and "emanations" from various guarantees of the Bill of Rights.

Griswold v. Connecticut, 381 U.S. 479 (1965)

FACTS: Griswold was the executive director of the Planned Parenthood League of Connecticut, and Buxton was a licensed physician who served as medical director for the League. They provided information, instruction, and medical advice to married couples as to the means of preventing conception.

---

[1]David Garrow, *Liberty and Sexuality: The Right to Privacy and the Making of Roe v. Wade* [University of California]: 271–272.

A Connecticut statute prohibited the use of contraceptive devices. Another Connecticut statute provided: "Any person who assists, abets, counsels, causes, hires or commands another to commit any offense may be prosecuted and punished as if he were the principal offender."

Griswold and Buxton were found guilty of violating the latter statute for giving married persons information and medical advice on how to prevent conception and, following examination, prescribing a contraceptive device or material for the wife's use. Each was fined $100. The Connecticut courts upheld the convictions and the two defendants appealed to the Supreme Court.

ISSUE: Is it unconstitutional to prohibit the use of contraceptives by a married couple?

DECISION (per *Douglas,* 7-2): *Yes.*

We are met with a wide range of questions that implicate the Due Process Clause of the Fourteenth Amendment. Overtones of some arguments suggest that Lochner v. New York, 198 U.S. 45 (1905), should be our guide. But we decline that invitation. We do not sit as a superlegislature to determine the wisdom, need, and propriety of laws that touch economic problems, business affairs, or social conditions. This law, however, operates directly on an intimate relation of husband and wife and their physician's role in one aspect of that relation.

The association of people is not mentioned in the Constitution or in the Bill of Rights. The right to educate a child in a school of the parents' choice—whether public or private or parochial—is also not mentioned. Nor is the right to study any particular subject or any foreign language. Yet this Court has construed the First Amendment to include certain of those rights, and we have recognized that "freedom to associate and privacy in one's associations" is a peripheral First Amendment right.

Those decisions suggest that specific guarantees in the Bill of Rights have penumbras, formed by emanations from those guarantees that help give them life and substance. Various guarantees create zones of privacy. The right of association contained in the penumbra of the First Amendment is one, as we have seen. The Third Amendment in its prohibition against the quartering of soldiers "in any house" in time of peace without the consent of the owner is another facet of that privacy. The Fourth Amendment explicitly affirms the "right of the people to be secure in their persons, houses, papers, and effects, against unreasonable searches and seizures." The Fifth Amendment in its Self-Incrimination Clause enables the citizen to create a zone of privacy that government may not force him to surrender to his detriment. The Ninth Amendment provides: "The enumeration in the Constitution, of certain rights, shall not be construed to deny or disparage others retained by the people."

The present case, then, concerns a relationship lying within the zone of privacy created by several fundamental constitutional guarantees. And it concerns a law that, in forbidding the use of contraceptives rather than regulating their manufacture or sale, seeks to achieve its goals by means having a maximum destructive impact upon that relationship. Such a law cannot stand in light of the familiar principle, so often applied by this Court, that a governmental purpose to control or prevent activities constitutionally subject to state regulation may not be achieved by means that sweep unnecessarily broadly and thereby invade the area of protected freedoms. Would we allow the police to search the sacred precincts of marital bedrooms for telltale signs of the use of contraceptives? The very idea is repulsive to the notions of privacy surrounding the marriage relationship.

We deal with a right of privacy older than the Bill of Rights—older than our political parties, older than our school system. Marriage is a coming together for better or for worse, hopefully enduring, and intimate to the degree of being sacred. It is an association that promotes a way of life, not causes; a harmony in living, not political faiths; a bilateral loyalty, not commercial or social projects. Yet it is an association for as noble a purpose as any involved in our prior cases.

Goldberg, concurring (joined by Warren and Brennan): I agree with the Court that Connecticut's birth-control law unconstitutionally intrudes upon the right of marital privacy, and I join in its opinion and judgment.

The "liberty" protected by the Due Process Clause of the Fourteenth Amendment embraces the right of marital privacy. Although that right is not mentioned explicitly in the Constitution, it is supported both by the decisions referred to in the Court's opinion and by the Ninth Amendment.

The language of the Ninth Amendment and its history reveal that the Framers of the Constitution believed that there are additional fundamental rights, protected from governmental infringement, which exist alongside those fundamental rights specifically mentioned in the first eight constitutional amendments. To hold that a right so basic and fundamental and so deep-rooted in our society as the right of privacy in marriage may be infringed because that right is not guaranteed in so many words by the first eight amendments to the Constitution is to ignore the Ninth Amendment and to give it no effect.

I do not mean to imply that the Ninth Amendment is applied against the States by the Fourteenth. Nor do I mean to state that the Ninth Amendment constitutes an independent source of rights protected from infringement by either the States or the Federal Government. Rather, the Ninth Amendment shows a belief of the Constitution's authors that fundamental rights exist that are not expressly enumerated in the first eight amendments and an intent that the list of rights included there not be deemed exhaustive. I do not see how this broadens the authority of the Court; rather, it serves to support what this Court has been doing in other areas in protecting fundamental rights.

In support of the Connecticut birth-control law, the state does not show that the law serves any compelling governmental interest or that it is necessary to the accomplishment of a permissible state policy. The state, at most, argues that there is some rational relation between this statute and what is admittedly a legitimate subject of state concern—the discouraging of extramarital relations. But it is clear that the state interest in safeguarding marital fidelity can be served by a more discriminately tailored statute, which does not, like the present one, sweep unnecessarily broadly, reaching far beyond the evil sought to be dealt with and intruding upon the privacy of all married couples.

Harlan, concurring only in the judgment: While I agree with the result of this case, I cannot join the Court's opinion that the Due Process Clause of the Fourteenth Amendment does not touch this Connecticut statute unless the enactment is found to violate some right assured by the letter or penumbra of the Bill of Rights. The proper inquiry is whether the statute infringes the Due Process Clause because it violates basic values implicit in the concept of ordered liberty.

Connecticut's contraception statute is an intolerable and unjustifiable invasion of privacy in the conduct of the most intimate concerns of an individual's life. In order to be constitutional, the statute must pass a strict scrutiny analysis. Connecticut does not even suggest a justification for the intrusive means it has chosen to effectuate its policy.

White, concurring only in the judgment: The Connecticut statute deprives married couples of liberty without due process. The statute bears a substantial burden of justification when attacked under the Fourteenth Amendment. An examination of the justification cannot be avoided, however, by saying that the statute invades a protected area of privacy. Such statutes, if reasonably necessary for the effectuation of a legitimate and substantial state interest, and not arbitrary and capricious in application, are not invalid.

Connecticut contends the statute serves the state's policy against promiscuous or illicit sexual relationships. But I fail to see how the ban on contraceptives by married couples reinforces the state's ban on illicit sexual relationships. At most, the broad ban is of marginal utility to the declared objective. I find nothing in the record justifying the law's sweeping scope.

Black, dissenting (joined by Stewart): The Connecticut law is every bit as offensive to me as it is to my Brethren. But I cannot join their conclusion.

The Court talks about a constitutional "right of privacy." There are, of course, guarantees in certain specific constitutional provisions that are designed in part to protect privacy at certain times and places with respect to certain activities. But we get nowhere in this case by talk about a constitutional "right of privacy" as an emanation from one or more constitutional provisions. I like my privacy as well as the next one, but I am nevertheless compelled to admit that government has a right to invade it unless prohibited by some specific constitutional provision.

This brings me to the arguments made by my Brothers Harlan, White, and Goldberg. Irrespective of whether based on due process or the Ninth Amendment, their arguments on analysis turn out to be the same thing—merely using different words to claim the power to invalidate any legislative act that judges find irrational, unreasonable, or offensive. If these formulas based on "natural justice" are to prevail, they require judges to determine what is or is not constitutional on the basis of their own individual appraisal of what laws are unwise or unnecessary. The power to make such decisions is that of a legislative body. I do not believe that we are granted this power.

I realize that many good and able men have eloquently spoken and written about the duty of this Court to keep the Constitution in tune with the times. I reject that philosophy. The Constitution makers knew the need for change and provided for it through the amendment process. As *Lochner* illustrates, the Due Process Clause with an "arbitrary and capricious" or "shocking to the conscience" formula was liberally used by this Court to strike down economic legislation in the early decades of this century, threatening, many people thought, the tranquility and stability of the nation. That formula, based on subjective considerations of "natural justice," is no less dangerous when used to enforce this Court's views about personal rights than those about economic rights.

The Ninth Amendment was passed, not to broaden the powers of this Court, but, as every student of history knows, to assure the people that the Constitution in all its provisions was intended to limit the federal government to the powers granted expressly or by necessary implication. Until today, for a period of a century and a half, no serious suggestion was ever made that the Ninth Amendment, enacted to protect state powers against federal invasion, could be used as a weapon of federal power to prevent state legislatures from passing laws they consider appropriate to govern local affairs. Use of any such broad, unbounded judicial authority would make of this Court's members a day-to-day constitutional convention.

The late Judge Learned Hand, after emphasizing his view that judges should not use due process or any other formula like it to invalidate legislation offensive to their "personal preferences," made the statement, with which I fully agree, that: "For myself it would be most irksome to be ruled by a bevy of Platonic Guardians, even if I knew how to choose them, which I assuredly do not." So far as I am concerned, Connecticut's law as applied here is not forbidden by any provision of the Federal Constitution as that Constitution was written.

Stewart, dissenting (joined by Black): I think this is an uncommonly silly law. But we are not asked in this case to say whether we think this law is unwise, or even asinine. We are asked to hold that it violates the Constitution. And that I cannot do.

In the course of its opinion the Court refers to no less than six amendments to the Constitution but does not say which of these amendments, if any, it thinks is infringed by this Connecticut law. We *are* told that the Due Process Clause of the Fourteenth Amendment is not, as such, the "guide" in this case. With that much I agree. As to the First, Third, Fourth, and Fifth Amendments, I can find nothing in any of them to invalidate this Connecticut law. And to say that the Ninth Amendment has anything to do with this case is to turn somersaults with history. The Ninth Amendment, like its companion the Tenth, was simply to make clear that the adoption of the Bill of Rights did not alter the plan that the *federal* government was to be a government of express and limited powers.

What provision of the Constitution, then, does make this state law invalid? The Court says it is the right of privacy "created by several fundamental constitutional guarantees." With all deference, I can find no such general right of privacy in the Bill of Rights, in any other part of the Constitution, or in any case ever before decided by this Court.

From Contraceptives to Abortion

Griswold involved the use of contraceptives by married couples in their homes, not abortions—a distinction that Griswold's counsel emphasized in the Supreme Court oral argument.[2] Nevertheless, the decision inspired numerous suits across the country claiming that abortion was also protected by the newly announced "right of privacy."

---

[2]See Garrow, ibid., at 240:

> Hugo Black broke in with a different question: "Would your argument concerning these things you've been talking about relating to privacy, invalidate all laws that punish people for bringing about abortions?" Tom [Emerson] responded, "No, I think it would not cover the abortion laws or the sterilization laws, your honor. Those—that cconduct does not occur in the privacy of the home." Tom paused, and then reiterated the point. "The conduct that is being prohibited in the abortion cases takes place outside of the home, normally. There is no violation of the sanctity of the home."

The first abortion case to reach the Supreme Court was United States v. Vuitch, 402 U.S. 62 (1971), challenging the validity of a District of Columbia statute prohibiting abortions "unless necessary to preserve the mother's life or health." The District Court had held that the statute was unconstitutional on the ground that the word "health" is too vague to meet due process standards. The Supreme Court reversed 5 to 4. The majority held that the word "health" in the statute, in accord with general usage and modern understanding, includes psychological as well as physical well-being, and as thus construed is not overly vague. Four Justices dissented, contending that the Court lacked jurisdiction to hear the direct appeal from the District Court.[3]

Of the four dissenters, three dissented on jurisdictional grounds. Justice Douglas, while agreeing that the Court had jurisdiction, dissented on the ground that the statute was overly vague. He added:

> Abortion touches intimate affairs of the family, of marriage, of sex, which in Griswold v. Connecticut, 381 U.S. 479, we held to involve rights associated with several express constitutional rights and which are summed up in 'the right of privacy.'. . . There is a compelling personal interest in marital privacy and in the limitation of family size.

While the *Vuitch* case was pending, the Court had deferred consideration of requests for review in other abortion cases. On April 22, 1971, the day after *Vuitch* was decided, the Court agreed to hear both *Roe v. Wade* and *Doe v. Bolton,* both appeals from three-judge district courts sustaining the constitutionality of state abortion statutes.

The Texas statute (similar to those in a majority of the States) challenged in *Roe v. Wade* made it a crime to "procure an abortion" except with respect to "an abortion procured or attempted by medical advice for the purpose of saving the life of the mother." The Georgia law (similar to those in 13 other States) challenged in *Doe v. Bolton* was more complex. It provided additional exceptions (if the physician determined in "his best clinical judgment" that continued pregnancy would endanger a woman's life or injure her health, if the fetus would likely be born with a serious defect, or if the pregnancy resulted from rape), but the law also required that the abortion be performed in an accredited hospital, that the procedure be approved by the hospital staff abortion committee, and that the physician's judgment be confirmed by independent examinations by two other licensed physicians.

Shortly before the beginning of the 1971–1972 term, Justices Black and Harlan retired, and they were replaced in early 1972 by Lewis Powell and William Rehnquist.

On March 22, 1972, the Court decided Eisenstadt v. Baird, 405 U.S. 438 (1972). Although none of the opinions in the case received the support of a majority, the Court (6-1, Powell and Rehnquist not participating because they had not been on the Court when the case was argued) held that the Equal Protection Clause was violated by a Massachusetts statute prohibiting the distribution of contraceptives to *unmarried* persons. Justice Brennan, in an opinion joined by three other Justices, stated:

> It is true that in *Griswold* the right of privacy in question inhered in the marital relationship. Yet . . . [i]f the right of privacy means anything, it is the right of the individual, married or single, to be free from unwarranted governmental intrusion into matters so fundamentally affecting a person as the decision whether to bear or beget a child.

---

[3]Garrow, ibid., at 473–491, describes in detail the Court's lengthy deliberations in seeking to arrive at a decision in *Vuitch.*

The other two Justices in the majority declined to reach that issue and instead concurred on the ground that the record did not support the State's classification of a particular contraceptive as dangerous to health.[4]

The abortion cases were reargued on October 11, 1972, and decided on January 22, 1973. Treating neither the bedroom nor the marriage relation as controlling, the Court extended the "right of privacy" concept to abortion.

In *Roe v. Wade,* the next-digested case, the Court declared that, "This right of privacy ... is broad enough to encompass a woman's decision whether or not to terminate her pregnancy." And, relying on the substantive due process doctrine that Justice Douglas had spurned in *Griswold,* the Court categorized abortion as a "fundamental" right because of "[t]he detriment that the State would impose upon the pregnant woman."

Roe v. Wade, 410 U.S. 113 (1973)

FACTS: Jane Roe, a pregnant single woman, challenged a Texas abortion law making it a crime to procure an abortion except for the purpose of saving the life of the mother. Roe contended, under the First, Fourth, Fifth, Ninth, and Fourteenth Amendments, that the law improperly invaded the constitutional right of pregnant women to choose to terminate their pregnancies. The District Court granted declaratory relief to Roe, holding that the law is unconstitutional under the Ninth and Fourteenth Amendments. The state appealed directly to the Supreme Court.

ISSUE: Does a pregnant woman have a constitutional right to terminate her pregnancy in its early stages?

DECISION (per *Blackmun,* 7-2): *Yes.*

The Constitution does not explicitly mention any right of privacy. But in prior decisions the Court has recognized that a right of personal privacy, or a guarantee of certain areas or zones of privacy, does exist under the Constitution. In varying contexts, the Court or individual Justices have, indeed, found at least the roots of that right in the First Amendment; in the Fourth and Fifth Amendments; in the penumbras of the Bill of Rights (*Griswold*); in the Ninth Amendment (*Griswold*); or in the concept of liberty guaranteed by the Fourteenth Amendment. These decisions make it clear that only personal rights that can be deemed "fundamental" or "implicit in the concept of ordered liberty" are included in this guarantee of personal privacy. They also make it clear that the right has some extension to activities relating to marriage, procreation, contraception, family relationships, and child rearing and education.

This right of privacy, whether it is founded in the Fourteenth Amendment's concept of personal liberty as we feel it is or, as the District Court determined, in the Ninth Amendment, is broad enough to encompass a woman's decision whether or not to terminate her pregnancy. The detriment that the State would impose upon the pregnant woman by denying this choice altogether is apparent. Specific and direct harm medically diagnosable even in early pregnancy may be involved. Maternity, or additional offspring, may force upon the woman a distressful life and future. Psychological harm

---

[4]In Carey v. Population Services International, 431 U.S. 678 (1977), the Court (7-2) declared unconstitutional a New York law prohibiting the sale or distribution of contraceptives to minors under 16, the distribution of contraceptives by anyone other than licensed pharmacists, and the advertising or display of contraceptives. The Court held that the law unduly restricted access to contraceptives and violated the right to control procreation.

may be imminent. Mental and physical health may be taxed by child care. There is also the distress, for all concerned, associated with the unwanted child, and there is the problem of bringing a child into a family already unable, psychologically and otherwise, to care for it. In other cases, as in this one, the additional difficulties and continuing stigma of unwed motherhood may be involved. All these are factors the woman and her responsible physician necessarily will consider in consultation.

On the basis of elements such as these, the plaintiff and some *amici curiae* argue that the woman's right is absolute and that she is entitled to terminate her pregnancy at whatever time, in whatever way, and for whatever reason she alone chooses. With this we do not agree. The Court's decisions recognizing a right of privacy also acknowledge that some state regulation in areas protected by that right is appropriate. A State may properly assert important interests in safeguarding health, in maintaining medical standards, and in protecting potential life. At some point in pregnancy, these respective interests become sufficiently compelling to sustain regulation of the factors that govern the abortion decision. The privacy right involved, therefore, cannot be said to be absolute.

We, therefore, conclude that the right of personal privacy includes the abortion decision, but that this right is not unqualified and must be considered against important state interests in regulation.

The plaintiff claims an absolute right that bars any state imposition of criminal penalties in the area. On the other hand, the State argues that the state's determination to recognize and protect prenatal life from and after conception constitutes a compelling state interest. We do not agree fully with either formulation.

A. The State argues that the fetus is a "person" within the language and meaning of the Fourteenth Amendment. If so, the plaintiff's case, of course, collapses, for the fetus's right to life is then guaranteed specifically by the Amendment. The Constitution does not define "person" in so many words. Section 1 of the Fourteenth Amendment contains three references to "person." "Person" is used in other places in the Constitution. But in nearly all these instances, the use of the word is such that it has application only postnatally. None indicates, with any assurance, that it has any possible prenatal application. All this, together with our observation that throughout the major portion of the nineteenth century prevailing legal abortion practices were far freer than they are today, persuades us that the word "person," as used in the Fourteenth Amendment, does not include the unborn.

B. The pregnant woman, however, cannot be isolated in her privacy. She carries an embryo and, later, a fetus. The situation therefore is inherently different from marital intimacy, or bedroom possession of obscene material, or marriage, or procreation, or education, with which our prior cases were concerned. It is therefore reasonable and appropriate for a State to decide that at some point in time another interest, that of health of the mother or that of potential human life, becomes significantly involved. The woman's privacy is no longer sole and any right of privacy she possesses must be measured accordingly.

Texas urges that, apart from the Fourteenth Amendment, life begins at conception and is present throughout pregnancy, and that, therefore, the State has a compelling interest in protecting that life from and after conception. We need not resolve the difficult question of when life begins. When those trained in medicine, philosophy, and theology are unable to arrive at any consensus, the judiciary, at this point in the development of man's knowledge, is not in a position to speculate as to the answer. It should be sufficient to note the wide divergence of thinking on this most sensitive and difficult question.

Physicians have tended to focus either upon conception, upon live birth, or upon the interim point at which the fetus becomes "viable," that is, potentially able to live outside the mother's womb, albeit with artificial aid. Viability is usually placed at about seven months (28 weeks) but may occur earlier, even at 24 weeks. The modern official belief of the Catholic Church, recognizing the existence of life from the moment of conception, is a view strongly held by many non-Catholics as well and by many physicians. Substantial problems for precise definition of this view are posed, however, by new embryological data that purport to indicate that conception is a "process" over time, rather than an event, and by new medical techniques such as menstrual extraction, the "morning-after" pill, implantation of embryos, artificial insemination, and even artificial wombs. In areas other than criminal abortion, the law has been reluctant to endorse any theory that life, as we recognize it, begins before live birth or to accord legal rights to the unborn except in narrowly defined situations and except when the rights are contingent upon live birth.

In short, the unborn have never been recognized in the law as persons in the whole sense. In view of all this, we do not agree that, by adopting one theory of life, Texas may override the rights of the pregnant woman that are at stake. We repeat, however, that the State does have an important and legitimate interest in preserving and protecting the health of the pregnant woman and that it has still another important and legitimate interest in protecting the potentiality of human life. These interests are separate and distinct. Each grows in substantiality as the woman approaches term and, at a point during pregnancy, each becomes "compelling."

With respect to the interest in the health of the mother, the compelling point, in the light of present medical knowledge, is at approximately the end of the first trimester. This is so because of the now established medical fact that until the end of the first trimester mortality in abortion is less than mortality in normal childbirth. It follows that, from and after this point, a State may regulate the abortion procedure to the extent that the regulation reasonably relates to the preservation and protection of maternal health. Examples of permissible state regulation in this area are requirements as to the qualifications of the person who is to perform the abortion, as to the facility in which the procedure is to be performed, and the like. This means, on the other hand, that, for the period of pregnancy prior to this compelling point, the attending physician, in consultation with his patient, is free to determine, without regulation by the State, that, in his medical judgment, the patient's pregnancy should be terminated. If that decision is reached, the judgment may be effectuated by an abortion free of interference by the State.

With respect to the interest in potential life, the compelling point is at viability. This is so because the fetus then presumably has the capability of meaningful life outside the mother's womb. State regulation protective of fetal life after viability thus has both logical and biological justifications. If the State is interested in protecting fetal life after viability, it may go so far as to proscribe abortion during that period, except when it is necessary to preserve the life or health of the mother. Measured against these standards, the Texas law sweeps too broadly and cannot survive the constitutional attack made upon it here.

Thus, a state criminal abortion statute of the current Texas type that excepts from criminality only a *lifesaving* procedure on behalf of the mother, without regard to pregnancy stage and without recognition of the other interests involved, is violative of due process.

(a) For the stage prior to approximately the end of the first trimester, the abortion decision and its effectuation must be left to the medical judgment of the pregnant woman's attending physician.

(b) For the stage subsequent to approximately the end of the first trimester, the State, in promoting its interest in the health of the mother, may, if it chooses, regulate the abortion procedure in ways that are reasonably related to maternal health.

(c) For the stage subsequent to viability, the State in promoting its interest in the potentiality of human life may, if it chooses, regulate, and even proscribe, abortion except where it is necessary, in appropriate medical judgment, for the preservation of the life or health of the mother.

Our decision leaves the State free to place increasing restrictions on abortion as the period of pregnancy lengthens, so long as those restrictions are tailored to the recognized state interests. The decision vindicates the right of the physician to administer medical treatment according to his professional judgment up to the points where important state interests provide compelling justifications for intervention. Up to those points, the abortion decision in all its aspects is inherently, and primarily, a medical decision, and basic responsibility for it must rest with the physician.

In summary: Abortion is a constitutional right that the States can only abridge after the first six months of pregnancy. More specifically: (1) the right to privacy includes the right to abortion; (2) since abortion is a fundamental right, state regulation must meet the "strict scrutiny" standard, which means the State must show it has a "compelling interest" in having the law; (3) the word "person" in the Fourteenth Amendment does not apply to the unborn; (4) the State has an important interest in both preserving the heath of a pregnant woman and protecting fetal life; (5) the State's interest in maternal health becomes compelling at three months; (6) the State's interest in fetal life becomes compelling at viability—six months; (7) the State may not regulate abortion at all during the first trimester; (8) the State may regulate abortion during the second three months, but only for the protection of the woman's health; (9) the State may regulate or even ban abortion during the third trimester to protect fetal life, subject to the exception for the life or health of the mother.

Burger, concurring: I agree that under the Fourteenth Amendment the Texas statute impermissibly limits the performance of abortions necessary to protect the health of pregnant women, using the term "health" in its broadest medical context. I am somewhat troubled that the Court has taken notice of various scientific and medical data in reaching its conclusion; however, I do not believe that the Court has exceeded the scope of judicial notice accepted in other contexts.

In oral argument, counsel for the State of Texas informed the Court that early abortion procedures were routinely permitted in certain exceptional cases, such as nonconsensual pregnancies resulting from rape and incest. In the face of a rigid and narrow statute, such as that of Texas, no one in these circumstances should be placed in a posture of dependence on a prosecutorial policy or prosecutorial discretion. Of course, States must have broad power, within the limits indicated in the opinions, to regulate the subject of abortions, but where the consequences of state intervention are so severe, uncertainty must be avoided as much as possible. For my part, I would be inclined to allow a State to require the certification of two physicians to support an abortion, but the Court holds otherwise.

I do not read the Court's holdings today as having the sweeping consequences attributed to them by the dissenting Justices; the dissenting views discount the reality that the vast majority of physicians observe the standards of their profession, and act only on the basis of carefully deliberated medical judgments relating to life and health. Plainly, the Court today rejects any claim that the Constitution requires abortions on demand.

Stewart, concurring: In 1963, in Ferguson v. Skrupa, 372 U.S. 726 (1963), this Court purported to sound the death knell for the doctrine of substantive due process. Barely two years later, in the *Griswold* case, the Court held a Connecticut birth control law unconstitutional. In view of what had been so recently said in the *Ferguson* case, the Court's opinion in *Griswold* understandably did its best to avoid reliance on due process. Yet the Connecticut law did not violate any specific provision of the Constitution. So it was clear to me then, and it is equally clear to me now, that *Griswold* can be rationally understood only as a holding that the Connecticut statute substantively invaded "liberty." As so understood, *Griswold* stands as one in a long line of cases decided under the doctrine of substantive due process, and I now accept it as such.

The "liberty" protected by due process covers more than those freedoms explicitly named in the Bill of Rights. In Eisenstadt v. Baird, 405 U.S. 438 (1972), we recognized "the right of the individual, married or single, to be free from unwarranted governmental intrusion into matters so fundamentally affecting a person as the decision whether to bear or beget a child." That right necessarily includes the right of a woman to decide whether or not to terminate her pregnancy. It is evident that the Texas abortion statute infringes that right directly.

The question then becomes whether the state interests advanced to justify this abridgment can survive the "particularly careful scrutiny" that the Fourteenth Amendment here requires. The asserted state interests are legitimate objectives, but as the Court today has demonstrated these state interests cannot constitutionally support the broad abridgment of personal liberty worked by the Texas law.

Douglas, concurring: The Ninth Amendment obviously does not create federally enforceable rights but a catalogue of the rights acknowledged by it includes customary, traditional, and time-honored rights, amenities, privileges, and immunities that come within the sweep of "the Blessings of Liberty" mentioned in the preamble to the Constitution. Many of them in my view come within the meaning of the term "liberty" as used in the Fourteenth Amendment.

First is the autonomous control over the development and expression of one's intellect, interests, tastes, and personality. These are rights protected by the First Amendment and in my view they are absolute. *Second is freedom of choice in the basic decisions of one's life respecting marriage, divorce, procreation, contraception, and the education and upbringing of children.* These "fundamental" rights, unlike those protected by the First Amendment, are subject to some control by the police power. *Third is the freedom to care for one's health and person, freedom from bodily restraint or compulsion, freedom to walk, stroll, or loaf.* These rights, though fundamental, are likewise subject to regulation on a showing of "compelling state interest." A woman is free to make the basic decision whether to bear an unwanted child. Childbirth may deprive a woman of her preferred life style and force upon her a radically different and undesired future. (Italics in original.)

Such reasoning is, however, only the beginning of the problem. The State has interests to protect. Voluntary abortion at any time and place regardless of medical standards would impinge on a rightful concern of society. The woman's health is part of that concern, as is the life of the fetus after quickening. These concerns justify the State in treating the procedure as a medical one.

White, dissenting (joined by Rehnquist): I find nothing in the language or history of the Constitution to support the Court's judgment.

The Court simply fashions and announces a new constitutional right for pregnant mothers and, with scarcely any reason or authority for its action, invests that right with sufficient substance to override most existing state abortion statutes. The upshot is that the people and the legislatures of the 50 States are constitutionally disentitled to weigh the relative importance of the continued existence and development of the fetus on the one hand against a spectrum of possible impacts on the mother on the other hand. As an exercise of raw judicial power, the Court perhaps has authority to do what it does today; but in my view its judgment is an improvident and extravagant exercise of the power of judicial review.

In a sensitive area such as this, involving as it does issues over which reasonable men may easily and heatedly differ, this issue should be left with the people.

Rehnquist, dissenting: I have difficulty in concluding that a right of "privacy" is involved in this case.

A transaction resulting in an operation by a physician is not "private" in the ordinary usage of that word. Nor is the "privacy" that the Court finds here even a distant relative of the Fourth Amendment freedom from searches and seizures. If the Court means by the term "privacy" no more than that the claim of a person to be free from unwanted state regulation of consensual transactions may be a form of "liberty" protected by the Fourteenth Amendment, I agree that "liberty" embraces more than the rights specifically provided in the Bill of Rights. But that liberty is not guaranteed absolutely against deprivation, but only against deprivation without due process of law.

The test traditionally applied in the area of social and economic legislation is whether or not a law such as that challenged has a rational relation to a valid state objective. If the Texas statute were to prohibit an abortion even where the mother's life is in jeopardy, I have little doubt that such a statute would lack a rational relation to a valid state objective under that test. But the Court's sweeping invalidation of any restrictions on abortion during the first trimester is impossible to justify under that test.

As in Lochner v. New York, 198 U.S. 45 (1905) and similar cases applying substantive due process standards to economic and social welfare legislation, the adoption of such a standard here will inevitably require this Court to pass on the wisdom of legislative policies in the very process of deciding whether or not a particular state interest is compelling. For example, breaking the term of pregnancy into three distinct terms and outlining the permissible restrictions the state may impose in each one, as the Court decrees today, partakes more of judicial legislation than it does of a determination of the intent of the drafters of the Fourteenth Amendment.

The fact that a majority of the States have had restrictions on abortions for at least a century is a strong indication, it seems to me, that the asserted right to an abortion is not "so rooted in the traditions and conscience of our people as to be ranked as fundamental." Even today, when society's views on abortion are changing, the very existence of the debate is evidence that the "right" to an abortion is not so universally accepted as the plaintiffs would have us believe. By the time of the adoption of the Fourteenth Amendment in 1868, there were at least 36 laws enacted by state or territorial legislatures limiting abortion. The only conclusion possible from this history is that the drafters did not intend to have the Fourteenth Amendment withdraw from the States the power to legislate with respect to this matter.

*****

[*Note:* In the companion case, Doe v. Bolton, 410 U.S. 179 (1973), decided the same day, all of the principal provisions of the Georgia law were found unconstitutional in an opinion by Justice Blackmun. In striking down Georgia's hospitalization requirement, the Court held that the State had failed to demonstrate that the full resources of a licensed hospital were necessary. Similarly, with regard to the hospital committee authorization mandated by the Georgia law, the Court concluded that "we see no constitutionally justifiable pertinence in the structure for the advance approval by the abortion committee." Lastly, the statute's requirement of endorsement by two other doctors was invalidated because it had "no rational connection with a patient's needs and unduly infringes on the physician's right to practice."]

Reaction to the Decision

Not surprisingly, *Roe v. Wade* was met with a barrage of criticism. The criticism of religious groups, antiabortion organizations, and politicians was to be expected. But what was surprising was the ferocity of the criticism from prominent members of the academic community—men and women who in all probability opposed making abortion illegal.

A particularly influential article was written by John Hart Ely (later to become dean of the Stanford Law School). Ely stated that, "Were I a legislator I would vote for a statute very much like the one that the Court ends up drafting." Nevertheless, "it is a very bad decision," he contended, "because it is bad constitutional law, or rather because it is not constitutional law and gives almost no sense of an obligation to try to be." According to Ely,

> What is frightening about *Roe* is that this superprotected right is not inferable from the language of the Constitution, the framers' thinking respecting the specific problem in issue, any general value derivable from the provisions they included, or the nation's governmental structure. . . . The problem with *Roe* is not so much that it bungles the question it sets itself, but rather that it sets itself a question the Constitution has not made the Court's business.[5]

Other examples of the onslaught: Future Yale Law School dean Guido Calabresi called the *Roe* decision "a disaster." Archibald Cox stated that the Court's "failure to confront the issue in principled terms leaves the opinion to read like a set of hospital rules and regulations, whose validity is good enough this week but will be destroyed with new statistics." William Van Alstyne stated:

> There is no such thing as a personal, free-standing, fundamental right embedded in the Constitution of the United States to kill gestating life. *Roe v. Wade,* in suggesting otherwise, proceeded on an assumption not derived or derivable from *Griswold v. Connecticut,*

---

[5]John Hart Ely, "The Wages of Crying Wolf: A Comment on *Roe v. Wade,*" 82 *Yale Law Journal* 920 (1973), reprinted in John Hart Ely, *On Constitutional Ground* [Princeton 1996]: 285, 289, 293, 296.

from any previous case, or indeed, from any constitutional clause. It was rather judicial legislation.[6]

And Ruth Bader Ginsburg, a future Supreme Court Justice who in 1973 had headed the American Civil Liberties Union's Women's Rights Project, said that the "heavy-handed judicial intervention" in *Roe v. Wade* "was difficult to justify." She criticized *Roe* for going too far too fast and contended that the decision had "halted a political process that was moving in a reform direction and thereby, I believe, prolonged divisiveness and deferred stable settlement of the issue." [7]

Thirty-five years after the decision, the controversy continues. Indeed, the case is viewed by many on both sides as virtually a litmus test for either election to high office or appointment to the Supreme Court.

Abortion Decisions between *Roe* and *Casey*

In the 19 years between *Roe* and the next-digested case, *Planned Parenthood of Southeastern Pennsylvania v. Casey,* the Court struck down a variety of other restrictions on abortions. These included, for example: requiring abortions after the first trimester to be performed in a hospital; requiring a 24-hour waiting period after the patient signs a consent form; requiring the participation of a second physician for post-viability abortions; requiring the attending physician to convey to the patient certain prescribed information about the procedure; and requiring an unmarried woman under 18 to obtain the consent of a parent (unless the statute also provided an alternative judicial procedure to bypass the need for parental consent).

The validity and scope of the *Roe* doctrine continued to be disputed. In Akron v. Akron Center for Reproductive Health, 462 U.S. 416 (1983), rejecting the argument that *Roe* was wrongly decided, the Court (per Powell, 6-3) stated that "the doctrine of *stare decisis,* while perhaps never entirely persuasive on a constitutional question, is a doctrine that demands respect in a society governed by the rule of law. We respect it today, and reaffirm *Roe v. Wade*." The three dissenting Justices (per O'Connor), although not calling for overruling *Roe,* rejected *Roe*'s trimester framework and its strict scrutiny standard of review.

In Thornburgh v. American College of Obstetricians and Gynecologists, 476 U.S. 747 (1986), the U.S. Solicitor General filed an *amicus* brief explicitly urging that *Roe* be overruled. The majority (5-4) again reaffirmed *Roe,* but this time three of the dissenters (including Burger, who had concurred in *Roe*) argued that *Roe* should be overruled. O'Connor also dissented, repeating her objections to *Roe*'s trimester framework and strict scrutiny standard.

In Webster v. Reproductive Health Services, 492 U.S. 490 (1989), the Court (5-4) upheld a Missouri law requiring a viability test after 20 weeks of pregnancy and prohibiting the use of either government funds or public facilities for abortions. Four of the five Justices in the majority (Rehnquist, White, Kennedy, and Scalia) urged that *Roe* be overruled. O'Connor, concurring, stated that it was unnecessary in this case to consider whether *Roe* should be overruled, but she provided the fifth vote to sustain

---

[6]These and other examples of the criticism are contained in Garrow, ibid., at 609–617.
[7]Ruth Bader Ginsburg, "Some Thoughts on Autonomy and Equality in Relation to *Roe v. Wade,*" 63 *North Carolina Law Review* 375 (1985).

the Missouri law on the ground that it did not impose an "undue burden" on access to an abortion.

It was against this background that the Court decided *Casey* in 1992.

Planned Parenthood of Southeastern Pennsylvania v. Casey, 505 U.S. 833 (1992)

FACTS: The Pennsylvania Abortion Control Act of 1982 imposed several restrictions on abortions. The Act required a woman seeking an abortion to be provided with certain information 24 hours prior to the abortion; required the woman to give her informed consent; mandated that a minor could not obtain an abortion without the informed consent of her parents; required a married woman to notify her husband of her intended abortion; and imposed reporting requirements on facilities that provided abortion services. The Act exempted compliance with the regulations only in the event of a medical emergency.

The plaintiff, Planned Parenthood of Southeastern Pennsylvania, challenged the constitutionality of the Act, seeking declaratory and injunctive relief. The District Court held that all of the provisions at issue were unconstitutional under Roe v. Wade, 410 U.S. 113 (1973). The Court of Appeals reversed, upholding all of the provisions except for the husband notification requirement.

ISSUES: (1) Should the central holding of *Roe v. Wade* be retained and reaffirmed? (2) Should *Roe*'s trimester framework be replaced by a different standard? (3) Are the Pennsylvania restrictions valid?

DECISION: (1) *Yes,* (2) *Yes,* (3) *Yes,* except for the husband notification requirement. (None of the several opinions was joined by a majority.)

O'Connor, Kennedy, and *Souter* issued a joint opinion setting forth their views and announced the judgment of the Court:

(1) Some of us as individuals find abortion offensive to our most basic principles of morality, but that cannot control our decision. Our obligation is to define the liberty of all, not to mandate our own moral code. The underlying constitutional issue is whether the State can resolve these philosophic questions in such a definitive way that a woman lacks all choice in the matter, except perhaps in those rare circumstances in which the pregnancy is itself a danger to her own life or health, or is the result of rape or incest.

Roe's essential holding has three parts. First is a recognition of the right of the woman to choose to have an abortion before viability and to obtain it without undue interference from the state. Before viability, the State's interests are not strong enough to support a prohibition of abortion or the imposition of a substantial obstacle to the woman's effective right to elect the procedure. Second is a confirmation of the State's power to restrict abortions after fetal viability if the law contains exceptions for pregnancies that endanger the woman's life or health. And third is the principle that the State has legitimate interests from the outset of the pregnancy in protecting the health of the woman and the life of the fetus that may become a child. We adhere to each of these principles.

Constitutional protection of a woman's right to abortion derives from the term "liberty" in the Due Process Clause of the Fourteenth Amendment. Neither the Bill of Rights nor the specific practices of States at the time of the adoption of the Fourteenth

Amendment mark the outer limits of the substantive sphere of liberty thath the Amendment protects. See U.S. Const., Amdt. 9. The inescapable fact is that adjudication of substantive due process claims may call upon the Court in interpreting the Constitution to exercise that same capacity which, by tradition, courts always have exercised: reasoned judgment.

Our law affords constitutional protection to personal decisions relating to marriage, procreation, contraception, family relationships, child rearing, and education. Our cases recognize the right of the individual, married or single, to be free from unwarranted governmental intrusion into matters so fundamentally affecting a person as the decision whether to bear or beget a child. Our precedents have respected the private realm of family life that the state cannot enter. These matters, involving the most intimate and personal choices a person may make in a lifetime, choices central to personal dignity and autonomy, are central to the liberty protected by the Fourteenth Amendment. At the heart of liberty is the right to define one's own concept of existence, of meaning, of the universe, and of the mystery of human life.

Abortion is a unique act. It is an act fraught with consequences for others: for the woman who must live with the implications of her decision; for the persons who perform and assist in the procedure; for the spouse, family, and society that must confront the knowledge that these procedures exist, procedures some deem nothing short of an act of violence against innocent human life; and, depending on one's beliefs, for the life or potential life that is aborted. Though abortion is conduct, it does not follow that the state is entitled to proscribe it in all instances. That is because the liberty of the woman is at stake in a sense unique to the human condition, and so, unique to the law. The mother who carries a child to full term is subject to anxieties, to physical constraints, to pain that only she must bear. That these sacrifices have from the beginning of the human race been endured by woman with a pride that ennobles her in the eyes of others and gives to the infant a bond of love cannot alone be grounds for the state to insist she make the sacrifice. Her suffering is too intimate and personal for the state to insist, without more, upon its own vision of the woman's role, however dominant that vision has been in the course of our history and our culture. The destiny of the woman must be shaped to a large extent on her own conception of her spiritual imperatives and her place in society.

(2) Several considerations guide our *stare decisis* analysis and lead to the determination that *Roe* should not be overturned: (a) Although controversial, *Roe* has not proven unworkable. (b) *Roe* has caused reliance by people, who have organized intimate relationships and made choices in reliance on the availability of abortion, such that repudiating the decision would cause a great hardship. (c) No constitutional law development has left *Roe* behind as a mere survivor of obsolete constitutional thinking. (d) Although time has overtaken some of *Roe*'s factual assumptions, with technological advances making abortions safe later in pregnancy and advancing viability to an earlier point, these facts go only to the scheme of time limits and have no bearing on *Roe*'s central holding.

Moreover, overruling *Roe* would overtax the country's belief in the Court's good faith and would cause profound and unnecessary damage to the Court's legitimacy. Where, in the performance of its judicial duties, the Court decides a case in such a way as to resolve the sort of intensely divisive controversy reflected in *Roe,* its decision has a dimension that the resolution of the normal case does not carry. It is the dimension present whenever the Court's interpretation of the Constitution calls the contending sides of a national controversy to end their national division by accepting a common mandate rooted in the Constitution.

A decision to overrule is usually perceived (and perceived correctly) as a statement that a prior decision was wrong. There is a limit to the amount of error that can plausibly be imputed to prior Courts. If that limit should be exceeded, disturbance of prior rulings would be taken as evidence that justifiable reexamination of principle had given way to drives for particular results in the short term. The legitimacy of the Court would fade with the frequency of its vacillation and would seriously weaken the Court's capacity to exercise the judicial power and to function as the Supreme Court of a nation dedicated to the rule of law. Only the most convincing justification under accepted standards of precedent could suffice to demonstrate that a decision overruling a decision such as *Roe* was anything but a surrender to political pressure.

We have concluded that it is imperative to adhere to the essence of *Roe*'s original decision.

(3) We conclude the line should be drawn at viability, so that, before that time, the woman has a right to choose to terminate her pregnancy. The concept of viability, as noted in *Roe,* is the time at which there is a realistic possibility of maintaining and nourishing a life outside the womb, so that the independent existence of the second life can, in reason and all fairness, be the object of state protection that now overrides the rights of the woman. The viability line also has, as a practical matter, an element of fairness. In some broad sense, it might be said that a woman who fails to act before viability has consented to the State's intervention on behalf of the developing child.

The *Roe* Court recognized the State's "important and legitimate interest in protecting the potentiality of human life." The weight to be given this state interest, not the strength of the woman's interest, was the difficult question faced in *Roe*. We do not need to say whether each of us, had we been members of the Court when the valuation of the state interest came before it as an original matter, would have concluded, as the *Roe* Court did, that its weight is insufficient to justify a ban on abortions prior to viability. The matter is not before us in the first instance, and we are satisfied that the immediate question is not the soundness of *Roe*'s resolution of the issue, but the precedential force that must be accorded to its holding. And we have concluded that the essential holding of *Roe* should be reaffirmed.

Yet it must be remembered that *Roe* speaks with clarity in establishing not only the woman's liberty but also the State's "important and legitimate interest in potential life." That portion of the decision in *Roe* has been given too little acknowledgment and implementation by the Court in its subsequent cases. Those cases cannot be reconciled with the State's legitimate interests in the health of the woman and in protecting the potential life within her.

The trimester framework established by *Roe* was erected to ensure that the woman's right to choose not become so subordinate to the State's interest in promoting fetal life that her choice exists in theory but not in fact. We do not agree, however, that the trimester approach is needed to accomplish this objective.

Though the woman has a right to choose to terminate or continue her pregnancy before viability, it does not at all follow that the State is prohibited from taking steps to ensure that this choice is thoughtful and informed. Even in the earliest stages of pregnancy, the State may enact rules and regulations designed to encourage her to know that there are philosophic and social arguments of great weight that can be brought to bear in favor of continuing the pregnancy to full term, and that there are procedures and institutions to allow adoption of unwanted children as well as a certain degree of state assistance if the mother chooses to raise the child herself. The Constitution does not forbid a State, through democratic processes, from expressing a preference for normal childbirth.

It follows that States are free to enact laws to provide a reasonable framework for a woman to make a decision that has such profound and lasting meaning. This, too, we find consistent with *Roe*'s central premises, and indeed the inevitable consequence of our holding that the State has an interest in protecting the life of the unborn.

A logical reading of the central holding in *Roe* itself, and a necessary reconciliation of the liberty of the woman and the interest of the State in promoting prenatal life, require, in our view, that we abandon the trimester framework as a rigid prohibition on all pre-viability regulation aimed at the protection of fetal life. The trimester framework suffers from these basic flaws: in its formulation, it misconceives the nature of the pregnant woman's interest; and in practice, it undervalues the State's interest in potential life.

As our jurisprudence relating to all liberties save perhaps abortion has recognized, not every law that makes a right more difficult to exercise is, ipso facto, an infringement of that right. The fact that a law that serves a valid purpose, one not designed to strike at the right itself, has the incidental effect of making it more difficult or more expensive to procure an abortion cannot be enough to invalidate it. Only where state regulation imposes an undue burden on a woman's ability to make this decision does the power of the State reach into the heart of the liberty protected by the Due Process Clause.

All abortion regulations interfere to some degree with a woman's ability to decide whether to terminate her pregnancy. It is, as a consequence, not surprising that, despite the protestations contained in the *Roe* opinion to the effect that the Court was not recognizing an absolute right, the Court's experience applying the trimester framework has led to the striking down of some abortion regulations that in no real sense deprived women of the ultimate decision. Those decisions, such as Akron v. Akron Center for Reproductive Health, 462 U.S. 416 (1983), and Thornburgh v. American College of Obstetrics & Gynecology, 476 U.S. 747 (1986), went too far.

In our view, the undue burden standard is the appropriate means of reconciling the state's interest with the woman's constitutionally protected liberty. A finding of an undue burden is shorthand for the conclusion that a state regulation has the purpose or effect of placing a substantial obstacle in the path of a woman seeking an abortion of a nonviable fetus. A statute with this purpose is invalid because the means chosen by the State to further the interest in potential life must be calculated to inform the woman's free choice, not hinder it. And a statute that, while furthering the interest in potential life or some other valid state interest, has the effect of placing a substantial obstacle in the path of a woman's choice cannot be considered a permissible means of serving its legitimate ends.

On the other hand, regulations that do no more than create a structural mechanism by which the State, or the parent or guardian of a minor, may express profound respect for the life of the unborn are permitted, if they are not a substantial obstacle to the woman's exercise of the right to choose. Unless it has that effect on her right of choice, a state measure designed to persuade her to choose childbirth over abortion will be upheld if reasonably related to that goal. Regulations designed to foster the health of a woman seeking an abortion are valid if they do not constitute an undue burden.

To summarize:

(a) To protect the central right recognized by *Roe v. Wade* while at the same time accommodating the State's profound interest in potential life, we will employ the undue burden analysis as explained in this opinion. An undue burden exists if its purpose or effect is to place a substantial obstacle in the path of a woman seeking an abortion before the fetus attains viability.

(b) We reject the rigid trimester framework of *Roe*. To promote the State's profound interest in potential life, throughout pregnancy, the State may take measures to ensure that the woman's choice is informed, and measures designed to advance this interest will not be invalidated as long as their purpose is to persuade the woman to choose childbirth over abortion.

(c) As with any medical procedure, the state may enact regulations to further the health or safety of a woman seeking an abortion. Unnecessary health regulations that have the purpose or effect of presenting a substantial obstacle to a woman seeking an abortion impose an undue burden on the right.

(d) Our adoption of the undue burden analysis does not disturb the central holding of *Roe* that a State may not prohibit any woman from making the ultimate decision to terminate her pregnancy before viability.

(e) We also reaffirm *Roe*'s holding that, subsequent to viability, the State, in promoting its interest in the potentiality of human life, may, if it chooses, regulate, and even proscribe, abortion except where it is necessary, in appropriate medical judgment, for the preservation of the life or health of the mother.

These principles control our assessment of the Pennsylvania statute, and we now turn to the issue of the validity of its challenged provisions.

(4) The husband notification requirement provides, except in cases of medical emergency, that no physician shall perform an abortion on a married woman without receiving a signed statement from the woman declaring either (a) that she has notified her husband that she is about to undergo an abortion or (b) that her husband is not the man who impregnated her; that her husband could not be located; that the pregnancy is the result of spousal sexual assault that she has reported; or that she believes notifying her husband will cause him or someone else to inflict bodily injury upon her.

This provision imposes an undue burden on the abortion right and is therefore invalid. It cannot be claimed that the father's interest in the fetus's welfare is equal to the mother's protected liberty in view of the impact on the pregnant woman's bodily integrity. The requirement's target is married women seeking abortions who do not wish to notify their husbands of their intentions and who do not qualify for one of the statutory exceptions to the notice requirement. In a large fraction of the cases in which the requirement is relevant, it would operate as a substantial obstacle to a woman's choice to undergo an abortion.

On the other hand, for the reasons already stated, neither the 24-hour waiting period requirement nor the informed consent requirement is an undue burden on a woman's right to decide to terminate a pregnancy.

We also reaffirm that a State may require a minor to obtain the informed consent of her parents, although the State must also provide an adequate judicial bypass procedure enabling the minor to receive authorization if the judge decides that it is in the best interests of the child or that the girl is mature enough to make such a decision herself.

With respect to the facility reporting requirements, we uphold the provisions because they relate to health concerns and do not impose a substantial obstacle to a woman's choice.

Stevens, concurring in part and dissenting in part: The Court is unquestionably correct in concluding that the doctrine of *stare decisis* has controlling significance in a case of this kind, notwithstanding an individual Justice's concerns about the merits. The central holding of *Roe v. Wade* has been a part of our law for almost two decades. The societal costs of overruling *Roe* at this late date would be enormous. *Roe* is an integral part of a correct understanding of both the concept of liberty and the basic equality of men and women.

I disagree with the dismantling of the trimester framework; it is not a contradiction to realize that the state may have a legitimate interest in potential human life and, at the same time, to conclude that that interest does not justify the regulation of abortion before viability. I agree that the State may take steps to ensure that a woman's choice is informed, but serious questions arise when the State attempts to persuade the woman to choose childbirth over abortion. Those sections of the Pennsylvania law requiring a physician to provide the woman with a range of materials designed to persuade her to choose not to undergo the abortion are unconstitutional. The 24-hour waiting period raises even more serious concerns, as there is no evidence that the delay benefits women or that it is necessary to convey any relevant information. The State cannot further its interest in potential life by simply wearing down the ability of the pregnant woman to exercise her constitutional right. The counseling provisions also create an undue burden and do not serve a useful purpose.

Blackmun, concurring in part and dissenting in part: I remain steadfast that the right to reproductive choice is entitled to the full protection afforded by our previous cases. Abortion restrictions should be subjected to the strictest of scrutiny. State restrictions on abortion violate a woman's right of privacy by infringing on her right to bodily integrity and by depriving her of the right to make critical choices about reproduction and family planning. Furthermore, restrictions implicate constitutional guarantees of gender equality, conscripting a woman's body into the state's service. The strict scrutiny standard should stand, along with the trimester framework, instead of the undue burden standard.

Rehnquist, concurring in part and dissenting in part (joined by White, Scalia, and Thomas): The joint opinion of Justices O'Connor, Kennedy, and Souter, following its newly minted variation on *stare decisis,* retains the outer shell of *Roe v. Wade,* but beats a wholesale retreat from the substance of that case. We believe that *Roe* was wrongly decided, and that it can and should be overruled consistently with our traditional approach to *stare decisis* in constitutional cases.

The joint opinion frankly concludes that *Roe* and its progeny were wrong in failing to recognize that the State's interests in maternal health and in the protection of unborn human life exist throughout pregnancy. But there is no indication that these components of *Roe* are any more incorrect at this juncture than they were at its inception.

Nor do the historical traditions of the American people support the view that the right to terminate one's pregnancy is "fundamental." The common law that we inherited from England made abortion after "quickening" an offense. At the time of the adoption of the Fourteenth Amendment in 1868, at least 28 of the then-37 States and

8 territories had statutes banning or limiting abortion. By the turn of the century, virtually every State had a law prohibiting or restricting abortion on its books. By the middle of the present century, a liberalization trend had set in, but in 1973 when *Roe* was decided an overwhelming majority of the States prohibited abortion unless necessary to preserve the life or health of the mother. On this record, it can scarcely be said that any deeply rooted tradition of relatively unrestricted abortion in our history supported the classification of the right to abortion as "fundamental" under the Due Process Clause.

The joint opinion cannot bring itself to say that *Roe* was correct as an original matter, but the authors are of the view that the controlling question is not the soundness of *Roe*'s resolution of the issue but instead the precedential force to be accorded its holding. Although the opinion contains an elaborate discussion of *stare decisis,* it does not apply that principle to the *Roe* decision. *Roe* decided that a woman had a fundamental right to an abortion. The joint opinion rejects that view. *Roe* decided that abortion regulations were to be subjected to "strict scrutiny," and could be justified only by "compelling state interests." The joint opinion rejects that standard. *Roe* analyzed abortion regulation under a rigid trimester framework, a framework that has guided this Court's decision making for 19 years. The joint opinion rejects that framework. In these circumstances, *stare decisis* does not require that any remaining portion of *Roe* be kept intact.

In the end, the joint opinion's *stare decisis* argument is based on general assertions about the nation's psyche, and on the fact that *Roe* is so intensely divisive that it should not be overruled. This is a novel principle. Under this principle, once the Court has ruled on a divisive issue, it is prevented from overruling that decision even if it was incorrect. By that standard, the Court could not have overruled *Plessy v. Ferguson* in *Brown v. Board of Education.*

We think that States should be allowed to regulate abortion procedures in ways rationally related to legitimate state interests. Accordingly, we find that the spousal notification requirement rationally furthers legitimate state interests in protecting the interests of both the father and the potential life of the fetus.

Scalia, concurring in part and dissenting in part (joined by Rehnquist, White, and Thomas): The States may, if they wish, permit abortion on demand, but the Constitution does not require them to do so. The permissibility of abortion, and the limitations upon it, are to be resolved like most important questions in our democracy—by citizens trying to persuade one another and then voting. A State's choice between two positions on which reasonable people can disagree is constitutional even when (as is often the case) it intrudes upon a "liberty" in the absolute sense. Laws against bigamy, for example, intrude upon men and women's liberty to marry and live with one another. But bigamy happens not to be a liberty protected by the Constitution.

That is, quite simply, the issue in this case: not whether the power of a woman to abort her unborn child is a "liberty" in the absolute sense, or even whether it is a liberty of great importance to many women. Of course it is both. The issue is whether it is a liberty protected by the Constitution. I am sure it is not. I reach that conclusion not because of anything so exalted as my views concerning the "concept of existence, of meaning, of the universe, and of the mystery of human life" on which the joint opinion relies. Rather, I reach it for the same reason I reach the conclusion that bigamy is not constitutionally protected—because of two simple facts: (1) the Constitution says absolutely nothing about it, and (2) the long-standing traditions of American society have permitted it to be legally proscribed.

The emptiness of the "reasoned judgment" that produced *Roe* is displayed in plain view by the fact that, after more than 19 years of effort by some of the brightest legal minds in the country, and after more than ten cases upholding abortion rights in this Court, the best the Court can do to explain how it is that the word "liberty" must be thought to include the right to destroy human fetuses is to rattle off a collection of adjectives that simply decorate a value judgment and conceal a political choice. The right to abort, we are told, inheres in liberty because it is among "a person's most basic decisions"; it involves a "most intimate and personal choice"; it is "central to personal dignity and autonomy"; it "originates within the zone of conscience and belief"; it is "too intimate and personal" for state interference, it reflects "intimate views" of a "deep, personal character"; it involves "intimate relationships" and notions of "personal autonomy and bodily integrity"; and it concerns a particularly "important decision."

But it is obvious that the same adjectives can be applied to many forms of conduct that this Court has held are not entitled to constitutional protection—for example, homosexual sodomy, polygamy, adult incest, and suicide, all of which are equally "intimate" and "deeply personal" decisions involving "personal autonomy and bodily integrity." It is not "reasoned judgment" that supports the Court's decision—only personal predilection.

Not only did *Roe* not, as the Court suggests, resolve the deeply divisive issue of abortion; it did more than anything else to nourish it, by elevating it to the national level, where it is infinitely more difficult to resolve. National politics were not plagued by abortion protests, national abortion lobbying, or abortion marches on Congress before *Roe* was decided. Profound disagreement existed among our citizens over the issue—as it does over other issues, such as the death penalty—but that disagreement was being worked out at the state level. Pre-*Roe,* political compromise was possible. *Roe,* however, destroyed the compromises of the past, rendered compromise impossible for the future, and required the entire issue to be resolved uniformly, at the national level. To portray *Roe* as the statesmanlike "settlement" of a divisive issue, a jurisprudential Peace of Westphalia that is worth preserving, is nothing less than Orwellian.

I am appalled by the Court's suggestion that the decision whether to stand by an erroneous constitutional decision must be influenced by the substantial and continuing public opposition the decision has generated. The notion that we would decide a case differently from the way we otherwise would have in order to show that we can stand firm against public disapproval is frightening.

Roe should be overruled, because it was not correctly decided and has not succeeded in producing a settled body of law.

The Turnabout in *Casey*

The *Casey* case, which upheld the "central" abortion right, had come remarkably close to overruling *Roe v. Wade*. The story is related in Linda Greenhouse's biography of Justice Blackmun[8] based on her access to his papers at the Library of Congress.

---

[8]*Becoming Mr. Justice Blackmun* [Time Books 2005].

In Webster v. Reproductive Health Services, 492 U.S. 490 (1989), three years before *Casey,* Chief Justice Rehnquist and Justices White, Scalia, and Kennedy had signaled their desire to overrule *Roe.* In addition, Justice O'Connor had rejected *Roe*'s trimester framework and had proposed that any regulation that did not "unduly burden the right to seek an abortion," even in early pregnancy, should be upheld as long as the state could show a "rational basis" for it. Akron v. Akron Center for Reproductive Health, 462 U.S. 416 (1983); Thornburgh v. American College of Obstetricians & Gynecologists, 476 U.S. 747 (1986).

In the Court's conference following the *Casey* oral argument on April 22, five Justices (Rehnquist, Scalia, White, Kennedy, and Thomas) voted to sustain each of the challenged restrictions in the Pennsylvania statute, including the spousal notice provision (which Stevens, Blackmun, O'Connor, and Souter wanted to strike down). To uphold the waiting period and informed consent provisions, it was understood that the Court would have to overrule the *Akron v. Akron Center for Reproductive Health* and *Thornburgh* decisions that had struck down nearly identical requirements. Rehnquist assigned himself the writing of the majority opinion.

Greenhouse states:[9]

> On May 27, Rehnquist circulated a twenty-seven-page draft majority opinion. . . . All the Pennsylvania law's provisions were upheld. Further, Rehnquist said the Court had been wrong to find "any all-encompassing right of privacy" in the Constitution: "The Court was mistaken in *Roe* when it classified a woman's decision to terminate her pregnancy as a 'fundamental right' that could be abridged only in a manner which withstood 'strict scrutiny.' " As in his *Webster* opinion, he maintained that "States may regulate abortion procedures in ways rationally related to a legitimate state interest." If Rehnquist actually spoke for a majority, *Roe* would effectively be overruled.

"Then," as Greenhouse states, "suddenly, everything changed." [10] In a meeting with Blackmun on May 30,

> Kennedy revealed that he, O'Connor, and Souter had been meeting privately and were jointly drafting an opinion that, far from overruling *Roe,* would save it—not in its details, but in its essence. The *Akron v. Akron Center for Reproductive Health* and *Thornburgh* decisions would be overruled; the waiting period and informed consent provisions of the Pennsylvania law would be held constitutional. The spousal notice provision would fall. The opinion would adopt O'Connor's "undue burden" test, substituting it for *Roe*'s trimester approach. But the constitutional right to abortion was preserved.

The unexpected result: Instead of there being five votes to overrule *Roe,* there were five votes (the three coauthors of the plurality opinion—Kennedy, O'Connor, and Souter—plus Blackmun and Stevens) to uphold *Roe,* albeit in a substantially narrower scope.

"Partial Birth" Abortion

An estimated 1.2 million abortions (the lowest level since 1976) are performed annually in the United States, and 85–90 percent take place in the first trimester of pregnancy.

---

[9]Ibid., 203.
[10]Ibid., 204.

After the first trimester, the most common method is "dilation and evacuation" or "D&E." In this procedure, the doctor dilates the cervix and then inserts surgical instruments into the uterus to grab the fetus and pull it back through the cervix and vagina. The fetus is then usually ripped apart and the pieces are extracted until the fetus has been fully removed.

Another little-used procedure, sometimes called "partial birth abortion," is generally known in the medical community as "intact D&E." According to the Guttmacher Institute, a prominent abortion research organization, only about 30 American doctors use this procedure in approximately 2,200 abortions each year.[11] The main difference between D&E and intact D&E is that in intact D&E a doctor extracts the fetus intact or largely intact, pulling out its entire body instead of ripping it apart. In order to allow the head to pass through the cervix, the doctor typically pierces or crushes the skull.

After *Roe v. Wade,* 31 States enacted legislation prohibiting partial birth abortion without providing an exception for the health of the mother. In 2000, the Nebraska statute was struck down by the Supreme Court (5-4) in Stenberg v. Carhart, 530 U.S. 914 (2000), holding that the statute posed an undue burden because of the trial court's finding that in some instances the banned procedure was less risky for the mother's health.

In his dissenting opinion in *Stenberg,* Justice Kennedy strongly protested that the Court's decision was inconsistent with the controlling *Casey* opinion that he had coauthored together with Justices O'Connor and Souter. He wrote that "When the Court [in *Casey*] reaffirmed the essential holding of *Roe,* a central premise was that the States retain a critical and legitimate role in legislating on the subject of abortion" and that "The Court's decision today . . . repudiates this understanding."

Subsequently, Justice O'Connor was replaced on the Court by Samuel Alito, and John Roberts succeeded William Rehnquist as Chief Justice.

It was against this background that in the next-digested case, *Gonzales v. Carhart,* Justice Kennedy wrote the Court's majority opinion upholding (5-4) the federal Partial-Birth Abortion Ban Act of 2003, designed by Congress to circumvent the *Stenberg* decision.

Gonzales v. Carhart, ___ U.S. ___, 127 S.Ct. 1610 (2007)

FACTS: Three years after the *Stenberg* decision, and after holding hearings and developing a record on the subject, Congress passed the Partial-Birth Abortion Ban Act of 2003. The Act provides criminal penalties for "Any physician who, *in or affecting interstate or foreign commerce,* knowingly performs a partial-birth abortion . . . that is [not] necessary to save the life of a mother."

The Act defines "partial-birth abortion" as a procedure in which a physician:

(A) deliberately and intentionally vaginally delivers a living fetus until, in the case of a head-first presentation, the entire fetal head is outside the [mother's] body . . . , or, in the case of breech presentation, any part of the fetal trunk past the navel is outside the [mother's] body . . . , for the purpose of performing an overt act that the person knows will kill the partially delivered living fetus;

and "(B) performs the overt act, other than completion of delivery, that kills the fetus."

The Act declares that such "abortions involve the killing of a child that is in the process, in fact mere inches away from, becoming a 'person' " and that therefore

---

[11]David Garrow, "Don't Assume the Worst," *New York Times,* April 21, 2007.

"the government has a heightened interest in protecting the life of the partially-born child."

Among its findings set forth in the Act, Congress found that "[a] moral, medical, and ethical consensus exists that the practice of performing a partial-birth abortion . . . is a gruesome and inhumane procedure that is never medically necessary and should be prohibited." Congress also found that, although the Supreme Court in *Stenberg* "was required to accept the very questionable findings issued by the district court judge" in that case, Congress was "not bound to accept the same factual findings."

Before the Act took effect, two actions challenging its validity were filed in Nebraska and California by abortion advocacy groups and abortion physicians (including the doctor who was the principal plaintiff in the *Stenberg* case). Relying on the *Stenberg* decision and the evidence presented at trial, both district courts held the Act invalid on its face, primarily on the ground that it lacked a health exception, and enjoined its enforcement. The Courts of Appeals for the Eighth and Ninth Circuits affirmed, and the Attorney General appealed their decisions to the Supreme Court.

ISSUE: Is the Act unconstitutional on its face because it does not contain a health exception?

DECISION (per *Kennedy,* 5-4): *No.* [The Court also rejected claims that the Act is overbroad and void for vagueness.]

Under the principles that we accept as controlling here, the Act would be unconstitutional "if its purpose or effect is to place a substantial obstacle in the path of a woman seeking an abortion before the fetus attains viability" (*Casey*). We conclude that the Act, measured by its text in this facial attack, does not on its face impose a substantial obstacle, and we conclude the Act should therefore be sustained against the broad attack brought against it.

(1) In *Casey,* the Court reaffirmed what it termed the three-part "essential holding" of *Roe v. Wade:* First, a woman has the right to choose to have an abortion before fetal viability and to obtain it without undue interference from the state. Second, the State has the power to restrict abortions after viability, if the law contains exceptions for pregnancies endangering the woman's life or health. And third, the State has legitimate interests from the pregnancy's outset in protecting the health of the woman and the life of the fetus that may become a child.

Though all three aspects of the *Roe* holding are implicated here, it is the third that requires the most extended discussion. In deciding whether the Act furthers the government's legitimate interest in protecting fetal life, we assume in accord with *Casey* that an undue burden on the pre-viability abortion right exists if a regulation's "purpose or effect is to place a substantial obstacle in the [woman's] path," but that "[r]egulations which do no more than create a structural mechanism by which the State . . . may express profound respect for the life of the unborn are permitted, if they are not a substantial obstacle to the woman's exercise of the right to choose." *Casey* struck a balance that was central to its holding, and the Court applies *Casey*'s standard here.

Under that standard, the plaintiffs have not demonstrated that the Act, as a facial matter, imposes an undue burden on a woman's access to late-term pre-viability abortions.

The prohibition in the Act would be unconstitutional, under precedents we here assume to be controlling, if it subjected women to significant health risks. However, the State's regulatory interest in protecting the life of the fetus cannot be set at naught by interpreting *Casey*'s requirement of a health exception so that it becomes tantamount to allowing a doctor to choose the abortion method he or she might prefer. Where it has a rational basis to act, and it does not impose an undue burden, the State may use its regulatory power to bar certain procedures and substitute others, all in furtherance of its legitimate interests in regulating the medical profession in order to promote respect for life, including life of the unborn.

The evidence presented in the trial courts and before Congress demonstrates that both sides have medical support for their positions. The question thus becomes whether the Act can stand when this medical uncertainty persists. The Court's precedents have given state and federal legislatures wide discretion to pass legislation in areas where there is medical and scientific uncertainty. The law need not give abortion doctors unfettered choice in the course of their medical practice, nor should it elevate their status above other medical experts. Medical uncertainty does not foreclose the exercise of legislative power in the abortion context any more than it does in other contexts. The medical uncertainty over whether the Act's prohibition creates significant health risks provides a sufficient basis to conclude that the Act on its face does not impose an undue burden.

Congress could conclude that the type of abortion proscribed by the Act requires specific regulation because it implicates additional ethical and moral concerns that justify a special prohibition. Congress determined that the abortion methods it proscribed had a "disturbing similarity to the killing of a newborn infant" and was concerned with "draw[ing] a bright line that clearly distinguishes abortion and infanticide." The Court has in the past confirmed the validity of drawing boundaries to prevent certain practices that extinguish life and are close to actions that are condemned.

It is objected that the standard D&E is in some respects as brutal as, if not more than, the intact D&E, so that the legislation accomplishes little. But partial-birth abortion, as defined by the Act, differs from a standard D&E because the former occurs when the fetus is partially outside the mother. It was reasonable for Congress to think that partial-birth abortion, more than standard D&E, "undermines the public's perception of the appropriate role of a physician during the delivery process, and perverts a process during which life is brought into the world."

The conclusion that the Act does not impose an undue burden is supported by other considerations. Alternatives are available to the prohibited procedure. As we have noted, the Act does not proscribe D&E. In addition the Act's prohibition only applies to the delivery of "a living fetus." If the intact D&E procedure is truly necessary in some circumstances, it appears likely an injection that kills the fetus is an alternative under the Act that allows the doctor to perform the procedure.

Whether to have an abortion requires a difficult and painful moral decision, and it seems unexceptionable to conclude (while we find no reliable data to measure the phenomenon) that some women come to regret their choice to abort the infant life they once created and sustained. In a decision so fraught with emotional consequence, doctors may prefer not to disclose precise details of the means that will be used. However, this lack of information concerning the way in which the fetus will be killed is of legitimate concern to the state, and the state has an interest in ensuring so grave a choice is well informed. It is self-evident that a mother who comes to regret her choice to abort must struggle with grief more anguished and sorrow more profound when she learns, only after the event, what she once did not know: that she allowed a doctor to pierce the skull and vacuum the fast-developing brain of her unborn child, a child assuming the human form.

It is a reasonable inference that a necessary effect of the statute's requirement and the knowledge it conveys will be to encourage some women to carry the infant to full term, thus reducing the absolute number of late-term abortions. The medical profession, furthermore, may find different and less shocking methods to abort the fetus in the second trimester, thereby accommodating legislative demand. The state's interest in respect for life is advanced by dialogue concerning the consequences that follow from a decision to elect a late-term abortion.

Interpreting *Stenberg* as leaving no margin for legislative error in the face of medical uncertainty is too exacting a standard. The weighing of marginal safety considerations, including the balance of risks, is within the legislative competence where, as here, the regulation is rational and pursues legitimate ends, and standard, safe medical options are available.

(2) Furthermore, these facial attacks on the Act should not have been entertained in the first instance.

The government has acknowledged that preenforcement as-applied challenges to the act can be maintained. That is the proper manner to protect the health of women if it can be shown that in discrete and well-defined instances a particular condition has or is likely to occur in which the procedure prohibited by the Act must be used. In an as-applied challenge, the nature of the medical risk can be better quantified and balanced than in a facial attack such as made here.

The plaintiffs have not demonstrated that the Act would be unconstitutional in a large fraction of relevant cases. It is neither our obligation nor within our traditional institutional role to consider every conceivable situation that might possibly arise in the application of complex and comprehensive legislation.

With respect to a woman's health, the Act is open to a proper as-applied challenge in a discrete case; and if the Act's prohibition threatens a woman's life, no as-applied challenge would be necessary because the Act already contains a life exception.

Thomas, concurring (joined by Scalia): I join the Court's opinion because it accurately applies current jurisprudence, including *Casey*. I write separately to reiterate my view that the Court's abortion jurisprudence, including *Casey* and *Roe v. Wade,* has no basis in the Constitution. I also note that whether the Act constitutes a permissible exercise of Congress's power under the Commerce Clause is not before the Court. The parties did not raise or brief that issue; it is outside the question presented; and the lower courts did not address it.

Ginsburg, dissenting (joined by Stevens, Souter, and Breyer): Today's decision is alarming. It refuses to take *Casey* and *Stenberg* seriously. It tolerates, indeed applauds, federal intervention to ban a procedure found necessary and proper in certain cases by the American College of Obstetricians and Gynecologists. And, for the first time since *Roe,* the Court blesses a prohibition with no exception safeguarding a woman's health.

Until now, the Court has consistently required that laws regulating abortion, at any stage of pregnancy and in all cases, safeguard a woman's health. We have ruled that a State must avoid subjecting women to health risks not only where the pregnancy itself creates danger but also where state regulation forces women to resort to less safe methods of abortion.

In *Stenberg,* we expressly held that a statute banning intact D&E was unconstitutional in part because it lacked a health exception. We noted that there existed a "division of medical opinion" about the relative safety of intact D&E, but we made clear that a health exception is required as long as "substantial medical authority supports the proposition that banning a particular abortion procedure could endanger women's health."

The congressional findings on which the Partial-Birth Abortion Ban Act rests do not withstand inspection. Congress claimed there was a medical consensus that the banned procedure is never necessary. But the evidence very clearly demonstrates the opposite. Similarly, Congress found that "[t]here is no credible medical evidence that partial-birth abortions are safe or are safer than other abortion procedures." But the congressional record includes letters from numerous individual physicians stating that pregnant women's health would be jeopardized under the Act, as well as statements from nine professional associations, attesting that intact D&E carries meaningful safety advantages over other methods. No comparable medical groups supported the ban.

In contrast to Congress, the district courts in these cases made findings after full trials at which all parties had the opportunity to present their best evidence. The courts had the benefit of much more extensive medical and scientific evidence concerning the safety and necessity of intact D&Es. During the district court trials, numerous accomplished and experienced medical experts explained that, in certain circumstances and for certain women, intact D&E is safer than alternative procedures and necessary to protect women's health. According to their testimony, the safety advantages of intact D&E are marked for women with certain medical conditions (for example, uterine scarring, bleeding disorders, heart disease, or compromised immune systems), for women with certain pregnancy-related conditions, and for women carrying fetuses with certain abnormalities.

Today's opinion supplies no reason to reject the district courts' findings. Nevertheless, in undisguised conflict with *Stenberg,* the Court asserts that the Act can survive "when . . . medical uncertainty persists." This assertion is bewildering. It not only defies the Court's long-standing precedent affirming the necessity of a health exception, but it gives short shrift to the records before us, carefully canvassed by the district courts.

The Court emphasizes that the Act does not proscribe the nonintact D&E procedure. But why not, one might ask. Nonintact D&E could equally be characterized as brutal, involving as it does tearing a fetus apart and ripping off its limbs. The notion that either of these two equally gruesome procedures is more akin to infanticide than the other is simply irrational. Delivery of an intact, albeit nonviable, fetus warrants special condemnation, the Court maintains, because a fetus that is not dismembered resembles an infant. But so, too, does a fetus delivered intact after it is terminated by injection a day or two before the surgical evacuation, or a fetus delivered through medical induction or cesarean. Yet, the availability of those procedures—along with D&E by dismemberment—the Court says, saves the ban on intact D&E from a declaration of unconstitutionality. Never mind that the procedures deemed acceptable might put a woman's health at greater risk. Ultimately, the Court admits that "moral concerns" are at work, concerns that could yield prohibitions on any abortion.

The Court also invokes an antiabortion shibboleth for which it concededly has no reliable evidence—that women who have abortions come to regret their choices, and consequently may suffer from "[s]evere depression and loss of esteem." Because of women's fragile emotional state and because of the "bond of love the mother has for her child," the Court worries, doctors may withhold information about the nature of the intact D&E procedure. This way of thinking reflects ancient notions about women's place in the family and under the Constitution—ideas that have long since been discredited. Though today's majority may regard women's feelings on the matter as self-evident, this Court has repeatedly confirmed that "[t]he destiny of the woman must be shaped . . . on her own conception of her spiritual imperatives and her place in society" (*Casey*).

The Court further confuses our jurisprudence when it declares that "facial attacks" are not permissible in "these circumstances." Without attempting to distinguish *Stenberg* and earlier decisions, the majority asserts that the Act survives review because the plaintiffs have not shown that the ban on intact D&E would be unconstitutional "in a large fraction of relevant cases." But the lack of such a showing affords no basis for rejecting this facial challenge since the very purpose of a health *exception* is to protect women in *exceptional* cases.

If there is anything at all redemptive to be said of today's opinion, it is that the Court is not willing to foreclose entirely a constitutional challenge to the Act. "The Act is open," the Court states, "to a proper as-applied challenge in a discrete case." But the Court offers no clue on what a "proper" lawsuit might look like. Surely the Court cannot mean that no suit may be brought until a woman's health is immediately jeopardized by the ban on intact D&E. A woman suffering from medical complications needs access to the medical procedure at once and cannot wait for the judicial process to unfold.

The Court's allowance only of an "as-applied challenge in a discrete case" jeopardizes women's health and places doctors in an untenable position. Even if courts were able to carve out exceptions through piecemeal litigation for "discrete and well-defined instances," women whose circumstances have not been anticipated by prior litigation could well be left unprotected. In treating those women, physicians would risk criminal prosecution, conviction, and imprisonment if they exercise their best judgment as to the safest medical procedure for their patients. The Court is thus gravely mistaken to conclude that narrow as-applied challenges are "the proper manner to protect the health of the woman."

Though today's opinion does not go so far as to discard *Roe* or *Casey,* the Court, differently composed than it was when we last considered a restrictive abortion regulation, is hardly faithful to our earlier invocations of the rule of law and principles of *stare decisis*. Congress imposed a ban despite our clear prior holdings that the state cannot proscribe an abortion procedure when its use is necessary to protect a woman's health. Although Congress's findings could not withstand the crucible of trial, the Court defers to the legislative override of our Constitution-based rulings. A decision so at odds with our jurisprudence should not have staying power.

In sum, the Act and the Court's defense of it cannot be understood as anything other than an effort to chip away at a right declared again and again by this Court—and with increasing comprehension of its centrality to women's lives.

The Ninth and Tenth Amendments

The Ninth Amendment provides: "The enumeration in the Constitution, of certain rights, shall not be construed to deny or disparage others retained by the people."

The Tenth Amendment provides: "The powers not delegated to the United States by the Constitution, nor prohibited by it to the States, are reserved to the States respectively, or to the people."

The Tenth Amendment has occasionally been invoked to invalidate federal statutes that intrude upon a zone of activity reserved to the States' exclusive control. For example, in Printz v. United States, 521 U.S. 898 (1997), the Court (5-4) relied in part on the Tenth Amendment to invalidate a provision of the Brady Handgun Violence Prevention Act that "commandeered" state and local law enforcement officials to conduct background checks on gun purchasers.

However, with minor exceptions (Goldberg's puzzling *Griswold* concurrence and cryptic references in the *Griswold* and *Roe* majority opinions and the *Casey* plurality opinion), the Court has treated the Ninth Amendment as largely irrelevant to constitutional analysis. According to the widely accepted view, the purpose of the Ninth Amendment (as Justice Black stated in his *Griswold* dissent) was merely "to assure the people that the Constitution in all its provisions was intended to limit the Federal Government to the powers granted expressly or by necessary implication."

When the original Constitution was submitted to the States for ratification, the States demanded adoption of a bill of rights but also expressed concern that such a codification might have the unintended effect of expanding federal power. As James Madison explained:

> It has been objected also against a bill of rights, that, by enumerating particular exceptions to the grant of power, it would disparage those rights which were not placed in that enumeration; and it might follow by implication, that those rights which were not singled out, were intended to be assigned into the hands of the General Government.

To address this concern, Madison drafted what became the Ninth and Tenth Amendments with the specific aim of safeguarding the local autonomy and other rights that were to remain at the state level.

The Fourteenth Amendment narrowed this zone of activity reserved to the States' exclusive control, but it did not in any way alter the purpose of the Ninth and Tenth Amendments—to protect state authority by preventing federal intrusion not authorized by the Constitution. On that premise, it would indeed "turn somersaults with history" (as Justice Stewart stated in his *Griswold* dissent) to convert the Ninth Amendment into an open-ended source of *additional* federal restrictions on the States.[12]

---

[12]For a more expansive view of the Ninth Amendment, see, for example, Randy Barnett, *Restoring the Lost Constitution: The Presumption of Liberty* [Princeton 2004]: 54–60, 224–253.

8

Terminal Illness Issues

The Right to Refuse Treatment

A mentally competent adult is constitutionally entitled to reject unwanted medical treatment even if the refusal will result in the person's death. But other actions taken to terminate the life of oneself or another person are subject to extensive state regulation. There is no general constitutional "right to die."

In Cruzan v. Director, Missouri Department of Health, 497 U.S. 261 (1990), the patient had suffered severe head injuries in an automobile accident and was in a persistent vegetative state with virtually no chance of regaining consciousness. Hospital employees refused, without court approval, to honor the request of Nancy Cruzan's parents to terminate her artificial nutrition and hydration, since that would result in her death. Her parents then asked a Missouri state court to authorize them to remove her feeding tube. The State of Missouri intervened to prevent it, contending that Missouri law required "clear and convincing" evidence that a patient wanted treatment terminated.

The trial court authorized the termination, finding that Cruzan's statement to a former housemate—that she would not wish to continue her life if sick or injured unless she could live at least halfway normally—indicated that she would not want to continue artificial nutrition and hydration. The Missouri Supreme Court reversed, holding that the State's requirement of clear and convincing evidence had not been met.

In affirming, the U.S. Supreme Court unanimously recognized that a competent adult is constitutionally entitled to refuse unwanted medical treatment, and a majority held (5-4) that a State may require clear and convincing evidence that a patient wanted treatment terminated (487 U.S. at 279-281):

[F]or purposes of this case, we assume that the United States Constitution would grant a competent person a constitutionally protected right to refuse lifesaving hydration and nutrition. Petitioners go on to assert that an incompetent person should possess the same right in this respect as is possessed by a competent person. . . .

The difficulty with petitioners' claim is that, in a sense, it begs the question: an incompetent person is not able to make an informed and voluntary choice to exercise a hypothetical right to refuse treatment or any other right. Such a "right" must be exercised for her, if at all, by some sort of surrogate. Here, Missouri has in effect recognized that, under certain circumstances, a surrogate may act for the patient in electing to have hydration and nutrition withdrawn in such a way as to cause death, but it has established a procedural safeguard to assure that the action of the surrogate conforms as best it may to the wishes expressed by the patient while competent. Missouri requires that evidence of the incompetent's wishes as to the withdrawal of treatment be proved by clear and convincing evidence. The question, then, is whether the United States Constitution forbids the establishment of this procedural requirement by the State. We hold that it does not.

Whether or not Missouri's clear and convincing evidence requirement comports with the United States Constitution depends in part on what interests the State may properly seek to protect in this situation. Missouri relies on its interest in the protection and preservation of human life, and there can be no gainsaying this interest. As a general matter, the States—indeed, all civilized nations—demonstrate their commitment to life by treating homicide as serious crime. Moreover, the majority of States in this country have laws imposing criminal penalties on one who assists another to commit suicide. We do not think a State is required to remain neutral in the face of an informed and voluntary decision by a physically able adult to starve to death.

But in the context presented here, a State has more particular interests at stake. The choice between life and death is a deeply personal decision of obvious and overwhelming finality. We believe Missouri may legitimately seek to safeguard the personal element of this choice through the imposition of heightened evidentiary requirements. It cannot be disputed that the Due Process Clause protects an interest in life as well as an interest in refusing life-sustaining medical treatment. Not all incompetent patients will have loved ones available to serve as surrogate decisionmakers. And even where family members are present, "[t]here will, of course, be some unfortunate situations in which family members will not act to protect a patient." ... A State is entitled to guard against potential abuses in such situations. Similarly, a State is entitled to consider that a judicial proceeding to make a determination regarding an incompetent's wishes may very well not be an adversarial one, with the added guarantee of accurate factfinding that the adversary process brings with it.... Finally, we think a State may properly decline to make judgments about the "quality" of life that a particular individual may enjoy, and simply assert an unqualified interest in the preservation of human life to be weighed against the constitutionally protected interests of the individual.

In our view, Missouri has permissibly sought to advance these interests through the adoption of a "clear and convincing" standard of proof to govern such proceedings.

The *Cruzan* decision further held that a State may prevent the patient's family from making the decision to terminate treatment for the patient. Family members may be in a conflict of interest situation, and they may choose to terminate care to relieve their own emotional or financial burdens. Hence "the State may choose to defer only to [the] wishes [of the patient], rather than confide the decision to close family members."

Cruzan did not address questions arising in the situation where a competent adult has designated a surrogate or guardian to make the decision. Nor did the Court resolve what is sufficient to constitute clear and convincing proof of a person's desire to terminate treatment (although obviously the level of proof must be higher than the "preponderance of the evidence" standard typically applied in civil cases).

A few months after the Supreme Court's decision, the parents requested a new evidentiary hearing, after which the trial court found that the evidence of Nancy Cruzan's intent met the clear and convincing standard and authorized removal of the tube. Less than two weeks later, she died.

The *Schiavo* Case

For 15 years after suffering a cardiac arrest in 1990 at the age of 25, Terri Schiavo was confined to nursing homes in a persistent vegetative state.

Her husband, Michael Schiavo, was appointed her legal guardian by a Florida probate court. In 1998, over the objections of Terri's parents, Michael petitioned the probate court to have her feeding and hydration tubes removed. During the course of the subsequent court proceedings, three independent "guardians ad litem" were appointed by the court to protect her interests.

At a trial in 2000, medical experts testified that the overwhelming odds were that she would never emerge from her vegetative state. In addition, although she had never executed a living will, Michael and his brother and sister-in-law testified that Terri had told them in conversations before her collapse that she would never want to be subjected to life-prolonging procedures. At the conclusion of the trial, the probate court found that there was clear and convincing evidence that her condition was terminal and that she would have preferred to die. On that basis, Terri's feeding and hydration tubes were removed in April 2001.

Two days after the tubes were removed, the tubes were reinserted because of an injunction obtained by Terri's parents from another judge. But in June 2003 the Florida District Court of Appeal affirmed the probate court's order allowing removal of the tubes, concluding that "The extensive medical testimony in this record only confirms once again the guardianship's initial decision." On October 15, 2003, the tubes were removed a second time.

However, six days later on October 21, the Florida Legislature passed an emergency bill (widely known as "Terri's Law") to override the probate court's order. The bill provided that the Governor (for 15 days after enactment) could "issue a one-time stay to prevent the withholding of nutrition and hydration from a patient" having the identical medical history as Terri Schiavo. The Governor immediately signed the bill and the tubes were reinserted a second time.

Michael Schiavo then commenced an action in the Florida courts challenging the validity of the statute. In May 2004 the trial judge held that the statute was unconstitutional. On September 23, 2004, the Florida Supreme Court unanimously affirmed, holding that the statute violated Florida's constitutional separation of powers among the legislative, executive, and judicial branches. The court stated that, if the legislature and the Governor could retroactively overturn court rulings, no judgment would ever be final and "vested rights could be stripped away based on popular clamor."

On March 18, 2005, after lengthy further proceedings, the tubes were removed for the third time.

Three days later the U.S. Congress enacted a bill entitled "An Act for the relief of the parents of Theresa Marie Schiavo." The Act provided that

> The United States District Court for the Middle District of Florida shall have jurisdiction to hear, determine, and render judgment on a suit or claim by or on behalf of Theresa Marie Schiavo for the alleged violation of any right of Theresa Marie Schiavo under the Constitution or laws of the United States relating to the withholding or withdrawal of food, fluids, or medical treatment necessary to sustain life.

The Act further provided that

> In such a suit, the District Court shall determine de novo any claim of a violation of any right of Theresa Marie Schiavo within the scope of this act, notwithstanding any prior State court determination and regardless of whether such a claim has previously been raised, considered, or decided in State court proceedings.

The Federal District Court, after reviewing the prior proceedings and considering each of the asserted constitutional claims, found that none of the claims provided a valid basis to enjoin removal of the tubes. The Court of Appeals for the Eleventh Circuit (one judge dissenting) affirmed, stating in conclusion:

> There is no denying the absolute tragedy that has befallen Mrs. Schiavo. . . . However, we are called upon to make a collective, objective decision concerning a question of law. . . . While the position of our dissenting colleague has emotional appeal, we as judges must decide this case on the law.

The parents' petition for certiorari was denied by the Supreme Court.
Terri Schiavo died on March 31, 2005.

Physician-Assisted Suicide and the "Right to Die"

In the next digested case, *Washington v. Glucksburg,* the Supreme Court (9-0) sustained the constitutionality of state laws that prohibit aiding a suicide. The Court held that a person did not have a "fundamental" right under the Fourteenth Amendment to commit suicide or obtain assistance in doing so and that the state prohibition was rationally based on several significant governmental interests.

However, the Constitution does not bar a State from *permitting* assisted suicide. Oregon was the first State to adopt such a statute. It authorizes physicians, under certain conditions, to provide drugs to terminally ill patients that they can use to commit suicide.

In Gonzales v. Oregon, 546 U.S. 243 (2006), the federal government challenged the authority of physicians to prescribe drugs for that purpose under the Oregon statute. The federal Controlled Substances Act (CSA) authorizes physicians to dispense controlled substances only "in the course of professional practice or research." A 1971 regulation under CSA provides that prescriptions for controlled substances are valid only if issued for a "legitimate medical purpose" as part of "professional treatment." In 2001 Attorney General John Ashcroft issued an interpretive ruling that assisted suicide is not a "legitimate medical practice" for "treatment" within the meaning of the 1971 regulation. The case before the Supreme Court did not involve a constitutional issue but instead turned on the interpretation of the federal statute. The Court held (6-3) that the Attorney General's interpretive ruling was based on a misconstruction of CSA and was therefore invalid, with the result that physicians can continue to dispense prescription drugs to terminally ill patients under the Oregon statute.

Washington v. Glucksberg, 521 U.S. 707 (1997)

FACTS: A State of Washington criminal statute provides: "A person is guilty of promoting a suicide attempt when he knowingly causes or aids another person to attempt suicide." "Promoting a suicide attempt" is a felony, punishable by up to five years' imprisonment and up to a $10,000 fine. Dr. Harold Glucksberg and the other three plaintiffs are physicians who practice in Washington and occasionally treat terminally ill, suffering patients whom they would assist in ending their lives if it were not for Washington's assisted suicide ban.

The plaintiffs sued in the U.S. District Court, alleging that the Washington statute is unconstitutional. Relying primarily on Planned Parenthood v. Casey, 505 U.S. 833

(1992), and Cruzan v. Director, Missouri Dept. of Health, 497 U.S. 261 (1990), the District Court agreed and concluded that the statute is unconstitutional because it "places an undue burden on the exercise of a constitutionally protected liberty interest." The District Court's decision was affirmed by the Court of Appeals for the Ninth Circuit.

ISSUE: Does the statute violate the Due Process Clause of the Fourteenth Amendment?

DECISION (per *Rehnquist*, 9-0): *No.*

In almost every State—indeed, in almost every Western democracy—it is a crime to assist a suicide. These laws are long-standing expressions of the States' commitment to the protection and preservation of all human life. Indeed, for over 700 years, the Anglo American common law tradition has punished or otherwise disapproved of both suicide and assisting suicide.

As this Court has frequently held, the Due Process Clause specially protects those fundamental rights and liberties that are, objectively, "deeply rooted in this Nation's history and tradition," "so rooted in the traditions and conscience of our people as to be ranked as fundamental," and "implicit in the concept of ordered liberty," such that "neither liberty nor justice would exist if they were sacrificed." The Fourteenth Amendment forbids the government to infringe "fundamental" liberty interests unless the infringement is narrowly tailored to serve a compelling state interest.

The question before us is whether the "liberty" specially protected by the Due Process Clause includes a right to commit suicide, which itself includes a right to assistance in doing so. We now inquire whether this asserted right has any place in our Nation's traditions. Here, as already pointed out, we are confronted with a generally consistent and almost universal tradition that has long rejected the asserted right, even for terminally ill, mentally competent adults. To accept the plaintiffs' contention, we would have to reverse centuries of legal doctrine and practice, and strike down the considered policy choice of almost every State.

The plaintiffs contend, however, that the constitutional principle that the Court recognized in *Cruzan*—the patient's liberty to direct the withdrawal of artificial life support—applies at least as strongly to the choice to hasten impending death by consuming lethal medication. We do not agree. The right assumed in *Cruzan* was not simply deduced from abstract concepts of personal autonomy. Given the common law rule that forced medication was a battery, and the long legal tradition protecting the decision to refuse unwanted medical treatment, our assumption was entirely consistent with this Nation's history and constitutional traditions. The decision to commit suicide with the assistance of another, although it may be just as personal and profound as the decision to refuse unwanted medical treatment, has never enjoyed similar legal protection.

The plaintiffs also rely on the *Casey* decision. The plurality opinion in that case described, in a general way and in light of our prior cases, those personal activities and decisions that the Court has identified as so deeply rooted in our history and traditions that they are protected by the Fourteenth Amendment. However, the fact that many of the rights and liberties protected by the Due Process Clause found in personal autonomy does not warrant the sweeping conclusion that any and all important, intimate, and personal decisions are so protected, and *Casey* did not suggest otherwise.

Our decisions lead us to conclude that the asserted "right" to assistance in committing suicide is not a fundamental liberty interest protected by the Due Process Clause. But that does not end our inquiry; for, even though the right asserted by the plaintiffs cannot be deemed fundamental, the Constitution also requires that Washington's assisted suicide ban be rationally related to legitimate government interests. That requirement is unquestionably met here.

Washington's assisted suicide ban implicates a number of state interests. In particular, Washington has an unqualified interest in the preservation of human life. The State's prohibition on assisted suicide, like all homicide laws, both reflects and advances its commitment to this interest.

Extensive studies have found that those who attempt suicide—terminally ill or not—often suffer from depression or other mental disorders. Research also indicates that many people who request physician-assisted suicide withdraw that request if their depression and pain are treated. Thus, lawful physician-assisted suicide could make it more difficult for the State to protect depressed or mentally ill persons, or those who are suffering from untreated pain, from suicidal impulses.

The State also has an interest in protecting the integrity and ethics of the medical profession. The American Medical Association, like many other medical and physicians' groups, has concluded that physician-assisted suicide is fundamentally incompatible with the physician's role as healer.

In addition, the State has an interest in protecting vulnerable groups—including the poor, the elderly, and disabled persons—from abuse, neglect, and mistakes. In *Cruzan* we recognized the real risk of subtle coercion and undue influence in end of life situations. If physician-assisted suicide were permitted, many might resort to it to spare their families the substantial financial burden of end of life health care costs.

The State's interest here goes beyond protecting the vulnerable from coercion; it extends to protecting disabled and terminally ill people from prejudice, negative and inaccurate stereotypes, and societal indifference. The State's assisted suicide ban reflects and reinforces its policy that the lives of terminally ill, disabled, and elderly people must be no less valued than the lives of the young and healthy.

Finally, the State may fear that permitting assisted suicide will start it down the path to voluntary and perhaps even involuntary euthanasia. In some instances, the patient may be unable to self-administer the drugs, and not only physicians, but also family members and loved ones, may participate in the process of assisting suicide. Thus, what is now couched as merely a limited right to "physician-assisted suicide" may result, in effect, in a much broader license that could prove extremely difficult to police and contain.

This concern is further supported by evidence about the practice of euthanasia in the Netherlands. The Dutch government's own study revealed that in 1990 there were 2,300 cases of voluntary euthanasia (defined as "the deliberate termination of another's life at his request"), 400 cases of assisted suicide, and more than 1,000 cases of euthanasia without an explicit request. In addition to these latter 1,000 cases, the study found an additional 4,941 cases where physicians administered lethal morphine overdoses without the patients' explicit consent.

We need not weigh exactly the relative strengths of these various interests. They are unquestionably important and legitimate, and Washington's ban on assisted suicide is at least reasonably related to their promotion and protection. We accordingly hold that the statute does not violate the Fourteenth Amendment.

O'Connor, concurring (joined in part by Ginsburg and Breyer): I join the Court's opinions [in this case and the companion *Vacco* case] because I agree that there is no generalized right to commit suicide. I agree that the State's interests in protecting those who are not truly competent or facing imminent death, or those whose decisions to hasten death would not truly be voluntary, are sufficiently weighty to justify a statutory prohibition against physician-assisted suicide.

But the plaintiffs urge that we also address the narrower question whether a mentally competent person who is experiencing great suffering has a constitutionally cognizable interest in controlling the circumstances of his or her imminent death. I see no need to reach that question in the context of the facial challenges to the Washington and New York laws at issue here. The parties agree that in these states a patient who is suffering from a terminal illness and who is experiencing great pain has no legal barriers to obtaining medication, from qualified physicians, to alleviate that suffering, even to the point of causing unconsciousness and hastening death. In this light, even assuming that we would recognize such an interest, there is no need to address the additional question raised by the plaintiffs.

Stevens, concurring in the judgments: Today, the Court decides that Washington's statute prohibiting assisted suicide is not invalid "on its face," that is to say, in all or most cases in which it might be applied. That holding, however, does not foreclose the possibility that some applications of the statute might well be invalid.

History and tradition provide ample support for refusing to recognize an open-ended constitutional right to commit suicide. The State has an interest in preserving and fostering the benefits that every human being may provide to the community. The value to others of a person's life is far too precious to allow the individual to claim a constitutional entitlement to complete autonomy in making a decision to end that life. Thus, I fully agree with the Court that the "liberty" protected by the Due Process Clause does not include a categorical right to commit suicide that itself includes a right to assistance in doing so.

But the State's interests supporting a general rule banning the practice of physician-assisted suicide do not have the same force in all cases. First and foremost of these interests, as *Cruzan* points out, is the "unqualified interest in the preservation of human life," which is equated with "the sanctity of life." Properly viewed, however, this interest is not a collective interest that should always outweigh the interests of a person who because of pain, incapacity, or sedation finds her life intolerable, but rather, an aspect of individual freedom.

Although as a general matter the State's interest in the contributions each person may make to society outweighs the person's interest in ending her life, this interest does not have the same force for a terminally ill patient faced not with the choice of whether to live, only of how to die.

Similarly, the State's legitimate interests in preventing suicide, protecting the vulnerable from coercion and abuse, and preventing euthanasia, do not apply to an individual who is not victimized by abuse, who is not suffering from depression, and who makes a rational and voluntary decision to seek assistance in dying.

Concern is expressed that patients whose physical pain is inadequately treated will be more likely to request assisted suicide. However, an individual adequately informed of the care alternatives thus might make a rational choice for assisted suicide. For such an individual, the State's interest in preventing potential abuse and mistake is only minimally implicated.

The final major interest asserted by the State is its interest in preserving the traditional integrity of the medical profession. But for doctors who have long-standing relationships with their patients, who have given their patients advice on alternative treatments, who are attentive to their patient's individualized needs, and who are knowledgeable about pain symptom management and palliative care options, heeding a patient's desire to assist in her suicide would not serve to harm the physician-patient relationship. Furthermore, physicians are already necessarily involved in making decisions that hasten the death of terminally ill patients—through termination of life support, withholding of medical treatment, and terminal sedation.

There remains room for vigorous debate about the outcome of particular cases that are not necessarily resolved by the opinions announced today. How such cases may be decided will depend on their specific facts. In my judgment, however, the State's interest in the preservation of human life is not always, in itself, sufficient to outweigh the interest in liberty that may justify the only possible means of preserving a dying patient's dignity and alleviating her intolerable suffering.

Souter, concurring in the judgment: A question presented by this case is which institution, a legislature or a court, is relatively more competent to deal with an emerging issue as to which facts currently unknown could be dispositive. The answer has to be that the legislative process is to be preferred.

The experimentation that should be out of the question in the Court's constitutional adjudication is entirely proper, as well as highly desirable, when the legislative power addresses an emerging issue like assisted suicide. The Court should accordingly stay its hand to allow reasonable legislative consideration. While I do not decide for all time that the plaintiffs' claim should not be recognized, I acknowledge the legislative institutional competence as the better one to deal with that claim at this time.

Breyer, concurring: The challenged Washington and New York laws are constitutional because they do not prohibit doctors from providing patients with drugs sufficient to control pain despite the risk that those drugs themselves will cause death. However, I do not believe that the Court need decide whether the right to die is fundamental. There is available in these States palliative care for a dying person who is suffering from severe pain. If the law prevented such palliative care, the law's impact on serious and unavoidable pain would then be at issue.

*****

[*Note:* In a companion case decided the same day, Vacco v. Quill, 521 U.S. 793 (1997), it was contended that a New York law banning assisted suicide violated the Equal Protection Clause because terminally ill patients in New York were allowed to die by letting them refuse life support (as in the *Cruzan* case) but were not allowed to die by receiving a lethal dose of medicine. Applying a rational basis standard, the Court (9-0 *per* Rehnquist) rejected the contention, holding that the distinction between allowing individuals to refuse life support and prohibiting assisted suicide was rationally related to the state's interests in individuals' health and welfare and the ethics of the medical profession. The Court also recognized that there is "a clear line between assisting suicide and [physicians'] withdrawing or permitting the refusal of unwanted lifesaving medical treatment," pointing out that "The law has long used actors' intent or purpose to distinguish between two acts that may have the same result."

In November 2008 Washington voters approved a law, like Oregon's statute, that authorizes physicians under certain conditions to dispense drugs to terminally ill patients for use in committing suicide.]

9

Gay Rights

The Legal Status of Homosexuality

For most of the nation's history, homosexuality has been severely condemned under the law.

When the nation was founded, sodomy was generally punished by the death penalty. In 1777, a committee of the Virginia legislature (including Thomas Jefferson) proposed that the punishment be reduced—to castration for males and the boring of a hole through the nose of a woman. This attempted "reform" was rejected, and the death penalty continued until 1800, when the Virginia legislature reduced the penalty to 1–10 years imprisonment.

When the Fourteenth Amendment was ratified in 1868, 32 of the 37 States had criminal laws prohibiting sodomy performed in private and between consenting adults; by 1961 all 50 States did. By 1986, when Bowers v. Hardwick, 478 U.S. 186 (1986), upheld the constitutionality of these statutes, the number had fallen to 24 and the District of Columbia. By 2003, when *Bowers* was overruled in Lawrence v. Texas, 539 U.S. 558 (2003), the number had further fallen to 13 States (9 of the 13, including Florida, also prohibited heterosexual sodomy).

Neither *Lawrence* nor any other Supreme Court decision has ever held that discrimination based on sexual orientation—unlike discrimination based on race, alienage, national origin, or gender—is subject to "strict scrutiny" or any other heightened level of review. (See comment "Overview of the Equal Protection Clause" in Chapter 3.)

Currently there is no federal statute prohibiting employment discrimination by private employers on the basis of sexual orientation. Title VII of the 1964 Civil Rights Act prohibits a private employer (who has 15 or more employees and is in an industry "affecting commerce") from discriminating on the basis of sex (in addition to race, color, religion, and national origin) but the statute has never been construed to forbid antigay discrimination.

On November 7, 2007, the House of Representatives approved a bill that would amend Title VII to also include antigay discrimination. The bill would make it illegal for an employer "to fail or refuse to hire or to discharge any individual, or otherwise discriminate against any individual with respect to the compensation, terms, conditions or privileges of employment of the individual, because of such individual's actual or perceived sexual orientation."

Another bill currently pending in Congress (known as the Local Law Enforcement Hate Crimes Prevention Act) would expand the scope of federal "hate crime" laws to include violent crimes motivated by the "actual or *perceived* race, color, religion, national origin, *gender, sexual orientation, gender identity or disability of any person*" (additions italicized). The bill has been approved by both the House and the Senate but has not yet been submitted to the President. (See comment "Federal Hate Crime Laws" in Chapter 10.)

An executive order issued by President William Clinton in 1998 prohibits antigay discrimination against federal civilian employees in the Executive Branch. But the military "don't ask, don't tell" policy (supported by President Clinton and codified in a 1998 federal statute) requires the discharge of any member of the armed forces who is openly gay or solicits or engages in homosexual acts.

Nineteen States and the District of Columbia have adopted gay rights laws prohibiting discrimination against homosexuals in employment and housing. In addition, many counties and cities have also adopted ordinances prohibiting discrimination against gays.

Bowers v. Hardwick, 478 U.S. 186 (1986)

FACTS: A Georgia criminal statute prohibited sodomy between any two persons, whether homosexual or heterosexual. Hardwick, an adult male, was charged by police with violating the statute with another adult male in his own bedroom. Although the prosecutor chose not to pursue the charge, Hardwick brought suit for a declaratory judgment in the Federal District Court, challenging the constitutionality of the statute insofar as it criminalized consensual sodomy. He asserted that he was a practicing homosexual, that the Georgia sodomy statute as administered by the defendants placed him in imminent danger of arrest, and that the statute violates the federal Constitution.

The District Court granted the defendant's motion to dismiss for failure to state a claim, but a divided panel of the Court of Appeals reversed, holding that the Georgia statute violated Hardwick's fundamental rights under the Due Process Clause of the Fourteenth Amendment. The case was remanded for trial, at which, to prevail, the state would have to prove that the statute is supported by a compelling interest and is the most narrowly drawn means of achieving that end.

ISSUE: Are acts of homosexual sodomy committed in the privacy of one's home constitutionally protected from state regulation?

DECISION (per *White,* 5-4): *No.*

This case does not require a judgment on whether laws against sodomy between consenting adults in general, or between homosexuals in particular, are wise or desirable. The issue presented is whether the Fourteenth Amendment confers a fundamental right upon homosexuals to engage in sodomy and hence invalidates the laws of the many States that still make such conduct illegal. The case also calls for some judgment about the limits of the Court's role in carrying out its constitutional mandate.

Contrary to the view expressed by the Court of Appeals, this Court's prior decisions have never construed the Constitution to confer a right of privacy that extends to homosexual sodomy. The reach of this line of cases was sketched in Carey v. Population Services International, 431 U.S. 678, 685 (1977), which characterized Pierce v. Society of Sisters, 268 U.S. 510 (1925), and Meyer v. Nebraska, 262 U.S. 390 (1923), as dealing with child rearing and education; Prince v. Massachusetts, 321

U.S. 158 (1944), with family relationships; Skinner v. Oklahoma ex rel. Williamson, 316 U.S. 535 (1942), with procreation; Loving v. Virginia, 388 U.S. 1 (1967), with marriage; Griswold v. Connecticut, supra, and Eisenstadt v. Baird, 405 U.S. 438 (1972), with contraception; and Roe v. Wade, 410 U.S. 113 (1973), with abortion. The latter three cases were interpreted in *Carey* (also dealing with a statutory constraint on contraceptives) as construing the Due Process Clause to confer a fundamental individual right to decide whether or not to have a child.

Accepting the decisions in these cases and the above descriptions of them, we think it evident that none of the rights announced in those cases bears any resemblance to the claimed constitutional right of homosexuals to engage in acts of sodomy. No connection between family, marriage, or procreation on the one hand and homosexual activity on the other has been demonstrated. Moreover, any claim that these cases nevertheless stand for the proposition that any kind of private sexual conduct between consenting adults is constitutionally insulated from state proscription is unsupportable.

Precedent aside, Hardwick would have us announce, as the Court of Appeals did, a fundamental right to engage in homosexual sodomy. This we are quite unwilling to do. It is true that despite the language of the Due Process Clauses of the Fifth and Fourteenth Amendments, which appears to focus only on the processes by which life, liberty, or property is taken, the cases are legion in which those Clauses have been interpreted to have substantive content, subsuming rights that to a great extent are immune from federal or state regulation or proscription. Among such cases are those recognizing rights that have little or no textual support in the constitutional language. *Meyer, Prince,* and *Pierce* fall in this category, as do the privacy cases from *Griswold* to *Carey*.

Striving to assure itself and the public that announcing rights not readily identifiable in the Constitution's text involves much more than the imposition of the Justices' own choice of values on the States and the Federal Government, the Court has sought to identify the nature of the rights qualifying for heightened judicial protection. In previous decisions we have emphasized that this category includes those fundamental liberties that are "implicit in the concept of ordered liberty," such that "neither liberty nor justice would exist if [they] were sacrificed," and that are "deeply rooted in this Nation's history and tradition."

It is obvious to us that none of these formulations would extend a fundamental right to homosexuals to engage in acts of consensual sodomy. Proscriptions against that conduct have ancient roots. Sodomy was a criminal offense at common law and was forbidden by the laws of the original 13 States when they ratified the Bill of Rights. In 1868, when the Fourteenth Amendment was ratified, all but 5 of the 37 States in the Union had criminal sodomy laws. In fact, until 1961, all 50 States outlawed sodomy, and today, 24 States and the District of Columbia continue to provide criminal penalties for sodomy performed in private and between consenting adults. Against this background, to claim that a right to engage in such conduct is "deeply rooted in this Nation's history and tradition" or "implicit in the concept of ordered liberty" is, at best, facetious.

Nor are we inclined to take a more expansive view of our authority to discover new fundamental rights imbedded in the Due Process Clause. The Court is most vulnerable and comes nearest to illegitimacy when it deals with judge-made constitutional law having little or no cognizable roots in the language or design of the Constitution. That this is so was painfully demonstrated by the face-off between the Executive and the

Court in the 1930s, which resulted in the repudiation of much of the substantive gloss that the Court had placed on the Due Process Clauses of the Fifth and Fourteenth Amendments. There should be, therefore, great resistance to expand the substantive reach of those clauses, particularly if it requires redefining the category of rights deemed to be fundamental. Otherwise, the judiciary necessarily takes to itself further authority to govern the country without express constitutional authority. The claimed right pressed on us today falls far short of overcoming this resistance.

Hardwick, however, asserts that the result should be different where the homosexual conduct occurs in the privacy of the home. He relies on Stanley v. Georgia, 394 U.S. 557 (1969), where the Court held that the First Amendment prevents conviction for possessing and reading obscene material in the privacy of one's home. *Stanley* did protect conduct that would not have been protected outside the home, but the decision was firmly grounded in the First Amendment. The right pressed upon us here has no similar support in the text of the Constitution. Moreover, conduct that is otherwise illegal is not always immunized whenever it occurs in the home. Many crimes, such as the possession and use of illegal drugs, do not escape the law when they are committed at home. *Stanley* itself recognized that its holding offered no protection for the possession in the home of drugs, firearms, or stolen goods.

Even if the conduct at issue here is not a fundamental right, Hardwick asserts that there must be a rational basis for the law and that there is none in this case other than the presumed belief of a majority of the electorate in Georgia that homosexual sodomy is immoral and unacceptable. This is said to be an inadequate rationale to support the law. The law, however, is constantly based on notions of morality, and if all laws representing essentially moral choices are to be invalidated under the Due Process Clause, the courts will be very busy indeed. Even Hardwick makes no such claim, but insists that majority sentiments about the morality of homosexuality should be declared inadequate. We do not agree that the sodomy laws of some 25 States should be invalidated on this basis.

Accordingly, the judgment of the Court of Appeals is reversed.

Burger, concurring: The proscriptions against sodomy have ancient roots, firmly rooted in Judeo-Christian moral and ethical standards. To hold that the act of homosexual sodomy is somehow protected as a fundamental right would be to cast aside millennia of moral teaching.

Powell, concurring: I agree that there is no fundamental right—i.e., no substantive right under the Due Process Clause—such as claimed by Hardwick. This is not to say, however, that someone who is convicted under the statute (providing a sentence of up to 20 years for a single act of sodomy) may not be protected by the Eighth Amendment prohibiting cruel and unusual punishment. But in this case Hardwick has not even been tried (let alone convicted) under the statute and therefore the Eighth Amendment issue is not before us.

Blackmun, dissenting (joined by Brennan, Marshall, and Stevens): This case is not about a fundamental right to engage in homosexual sodomy. Rather, this case is about the basic right to be let alone inherent in the constitutional right of privacy.

While our prior decisions construing this right focused on the protection of the family, the right of privacy should extend beyond this boundary. We protect those rights not because they contribute to the general public welfare, but because they form a central part of an individual's life. The Court has failed to realize the fundamental interest all individuals have in controlling the nature of their intimate associations with others.

Moreover, the behavior for which Hardwick faces prosecution occurred in his own home, a place to which the Fourth Amendment attaches special significance. The *Stanley* decision cited by the majority was anchored in the Fourth Amendment's special protection for an individual in his home; it did not rest entirely on the First Amendment. I see no reason for the Court to equate private, consensual sexual activity with the possession in the home of drugs, firearms, or stolen goods to which *Stanley* refused to extend its protection.

That certain religious groups condemn the behavior at issue gives the State no license to impose their judgments on the entire citizenry. The State cannot advance justification for its law beyond its conformity to religious doctrine. The mere fact that sexual activity can be punished when it takes place in public cannot dictate how States can regulate intimate behavior that occurs in intimate places.

Stevens, dissenting: Because the statute at issue and the rationale of the Court's opinion apply equally to all acts of sodomy, regardless of whether the parties are married or unmarried, or are of the same or different sexes, we must consider two questions. First, may a State prohibit all sodomy by means of a neutral law applying to all persons? If not, may the State save the statute by enforcing it only against homosexuals? Our prior decisions demonstrate that the fact that the governing majority in a State has traditionally viewed a practice as immoral is not a sufficient reason for upholding a law prohibiting the practice. In addition, individual decisions by married persons concerning their private sexual activities are a form of liberty protected by due process. This protection extends even to unmarried persons.

The State's attempt to save the statute by enforcing it only against homosexuals must fail. Either homosexuals do not have the same interest in liberty that others have or there must be a reason why the State can selectively apply a neutral law. But the principle that "all men are created equal" must mean that all men have the same interest in liberty.

Furthermore, any policy of selective application must be supported by a neutral and legitimate state interest. Neither the State nor the Court has identified any such interest. The Court has justified the statute on the presumed belief of a majority of the electorate in Georgia that homosexual sodomy is immoral and unacceptable. But the Georgia electorate has expressed no such belief. The law says that all sodomy is immoral and unacceptable. There is no basis to selectively apply the law only to homosexuals.

Romer v. Evans, 517 U.S. 620 (1996)

FACTS: After several Colorado cities had passed ordinances banning discrimination against people on the basis of their sexual orientation in housing, employment, education, public accommodations, and health and welfare services, Colorado voters in a referendum adopted a measure (known as "Amendment 2") that amended the Colorado Constitution to provide the following:

> No Protected Status Based on Homosexual, Lesbian, or Bisexual Orientation. Neither the
> State of Colorado, through any of its branches or departments, nor any of its agencies,

political subdivisions, municipalities or school districts, shall enact, adopt or enforce any statute, regulation, ordinance or policy whereby homosexual, lesbian or bisexual orientation, conduct, practices or relationships shall constitute or otherwise be the basis of or entitle any person or class of persons to have or claim any minority status, quota preferences, protected status or claim of discrimination.

The Colorado Supreme Court held that Amendment 2 violated the Equal Protection Clause on the ground that it infringed the fundamental right of gays and lesbians to participate in the political process and is therefore subject to strict scrutiny analysis. Applying that test, the Colorado Supreme Court concluded that the State had failed to make a sufficient showing of a compelling governmental interest to survive strict scrutiny.

ISSUE: Does a State constitutional amendment prohibiting laws specifically protecting homosexuals from discrimination violate the Equal Protection Clause?

DECISION (per *Kennedy,* 6-3): *Yes.*

(1) The State's principal argument in defense of Amendment 2 is that it puts gays and lesbians in the same position as all other persons and does no more than deny homosexuals special rights. This reading of the amendment's language is implausible. The amendment withdraws from homosexuals, but no others, specific legal protection from the injuries caused by discrimination.

In their public accommodations laws, Colorado's state and local governments have set forth an extensive catalogue of traits that cannot be the basis for discrimination, including age, military status, marital status, pregnancy, parenthood, custody of a minor child, political affiliation, physical or mental disability of an individual or of his or her associates—and, in recent times, sexual orientation. Amendment 2 bars homosexuals from securing protection against the injuries that those public accommodations laws address. Amendment 2 also nullifies specific legal protections for this targeted class in all transactions in housing, sale of real estate, insurance, health and welfare services, private education, and employment. Not confined to the private sphere, Amendment 2 also operates to repeal and forbid all laws or policies providing specific protection for gays or lesbians from discrimination by every level of Colorado government.

The Colorado Supreme Court acknowledged that the amendment was not intended to affect antidiscrimination laws of general application. However, even if homosexuals could find some safe harbor in such laws, we cannot accept the view that Amendment 2's prohibition of specific legal protections does no more than deprive homosexuals of special rights. To the contrary, the amendment imposes a special disability upon those persons alone. Homosexuals are forbidden the safeguards that others enjoy or may seek without constraint. They can obtain specific protection against discrimination only by enlisting the citizenry of Colorado to amend the State Constitution (or perhaps by trying to pass helpful laws of general applicability).

(2) If a law neither burdens a fundamental right nor targets a suspect class, we will uphold the legislative classification so long as it bears a rational relation to some legitimate end. Amendment 2 fails, indeed defies, even this conventional inquiry.

First, Amendment 2 has the peculiar property of imposing a broad and undifferentiated disability on a single named group, an exceptional and invalid form of legislation. Second, its sheer breadth is so discontinuous with the reasons offered for it that the amendment seems inexplicable by anything but animus toward the class that it affects; it lacks a rational relationship to legitimate state interests.

Taking the first point, even in the ordinary equal protection case calling for the most deferential of standards, a law will be sustained if it can be said to advance a legitimate government interest, even if the law seems unwise or works to the disadvantage of a particular group, or if the rationale for it seems tenuous. By requiring that the classification bear a rational relationship to an independent and legitimate legislative end, we ensure that classifications are not drawn for the purpose of disadvantaging the group burdened by the law.

Amendment 2 confounds this normal process of judicial review. It is at once too narrow and too broad. It identifies persons by a single trait and then denies them protection across the board. The resulting disqualification of a class of persons from the right to seek specific protection from the law is unprecedented in our jurisprudence. Central both to the idea of the rule of law and to our own Constitution's guarantee of equal protection is the principle that government and each of its parts remain open on impartial terms to all who seek its assistance. A law declaring that in general it shall be more difficult for one group of citizens than for all others to seek aid from the government is itself a denial of equal protection of the laws in the most literal sense.

A second and related point is that laws of the kind now before us raise the inevitable inference that the disadvantage imposed is born of animosity toward the class of persons affected. Amendment 2, in making a general announcement that gays and lesbians shall not have any particular protections from the law, inflicts on them immediate, continuing, and real injuries that outrun and belie any legitimate justifications that may be claimed for it. We conclude that a law must bear a rational relationship to a legitimate governmental purpose and Amendment 2 does not.

The primary rationale the State offers for Amendment 2 is respect for other citizens' freedom of association, and in particular the liberties of landlords or employers who have personal or religious objections to homosexuality. The breadth of the amendment is so far removed from such a particular justification that we find it impossible to credit it. We cannot say that Amendment 2 is directed to any identifiable legitimate purpose or discrete objective. It is a status-based enactment divorced from any factual context from which we could discern a relationship to legitimate state interests; it is a classification of persons undertaken for its own sake, something the Equal Protection Clause does not permit.

We must conclude that Amendment 2 classifies homosexuals not to further a proper legislative end but to make them unequal to everyone else. A State cannot so deem a class of persons a stranger to its laws. Amendment 2 violates the Equal Protection Clause.

Scalia, dissenting (joined by Rehnquist and Thomas): The constitutional amendment before us here is merely a modest attempt by seemingly tolerant Coloradans to preserve traditional sexual mores against the efforts of a politically powerful minority to revise those mores through use of the laws. Since the United States Constitution says nothing about this subject, it is left to be resolved by normal democratic means, including the democratic adoption of provisions in state constitutions. This Court has no business imposing upon all Americans the resolution favored by the elite class from which the members of this institution are selected, pronouncing that "animosity" toward homosexuality is evil.

(1) In rejecting the State's arguments that Amendment 2 puts gays and lesbians in the same position as all other persons and does no more than deny homosexuals special rights, the Court concludes that this reading of Amendment 2 is "implausible." However, the Supreme Court of Colorado authoritatively construed the amendment as not having any effect on Colorado laws that "currently proscribe discrimination against persons who are not suspect classes, including discrimination based on age...; marital or family status...; veterans' status...; and for any legal, off-duty conduct such as smoking tobacco...." The Colorado Supreme Court further specifically held that "Of course Amendment 2 is not intended to have any effect on this legislation, but seeks only to prevent the adoption of anti-discrimination laws intended to protect gays, lesbians, and bisexuals."

The clear import of the Colorado court's decision is that general laws and policies that prohibit arbitrary discrimination would continue to prohibit discrimination on the basis of homosexual conduct as well. The amendment prohibits special treatment of homosexuals, and nothing more. It would not affect, for example, a requirement of state law that pensions be paid to all retiring state employees with a certain length of service; homosexual employees, as well as others, would be entitled to that benefit. But it would prevent the State or any municipality from making death-benefit payments to the "life partner" of a homosexual when it does not make such payments to the longtime roommate of a nonhomosexual employee. Or again, it does not affect the requirement of the State's general insurance laws that customers be afforded coverage without discrimination unrelated to anticipated risk.

Despite all of the Court's hand-wringing about the potential effect of Amendment 2 on general antidiscrimination laws, the only denial of equal treatment the Court contends homosexuals have actually suffered is that they may not obtain preferential treatment without amending the state constitution. That is to say, the principle underlying the Court's opinion is that one who is accorded equal treatment under the laws, but cannot as readily as others obtain preferential treatment under the laws, has been denied equal protection of the laws. If merely stating this alleged "equal protection" violation does not suffice to refute it, our constitutional jurisprudence has achieved terminal silliness.

The central thesis of the Court's reasoning is that any group is denied equal protection when, to obtain advantage (or, presumably, to avoid disadvantage), it must have recourse to a more general and hence more difficult level of political decision making than others. The world has never heard of such a principle, which is why the Court's opinion is so long on emotive utterance and so short on relevant legal citation. And it seems to me most unlikely that any multilevel democracy can function under such a principle. For whenever a disadvantage is imposed, or conferral of a benefit is prohibited, at one of the higher levels of democratic decision making (i.e., by the state legislature rather than local government, or by the people at large in the state constitution rather than the legislature), the affected group has (under this theory) been denied equal protection.

To take the simplest of examples, consider a state law prohibiting the award of municipal contracts to relatives of mayors or city councilmen. Once such a law is passed, the group composed of such relatives must, in order to get the benefit of city contracts, persuade the state legislature—unlike all other citizens, who need only persuade the municipality. It is ridiculous to consider this a denial of equal protection, which is why the Court's theory is unheard-of.

(2) I turn next to whether there was a legitimate rational basis for the substance of the constitutional amendment—for the prohibition of special protection for homosexuals. It is unsurprising that the Court avoids discussion of this question, since the answer is so obviously yes.

No principle set forth in the Constitution, nor even any imagined by this Court in the past 200 years, prohibits what Colorado has done here. What it has done is not only unprohibited, but eminently reasonable, with close, congressionally approved precedent in earlier constitutional practice.

First, as to its eminent reasonableness. The Court's opinion contains grim, disapproving hints that Coloradans have been guilty of "animus" or "animosity" toward homosexuality, as though that has been established as un-American. Of course, it is our moral heritage that one should not hate any human being or class of human beings. But I had thought that one could consider certain conduct reprehensible—murder, for example, or polygamy, or cruelty to animals—and could exhibit even "animus" toward such conduct. Surely that is the only sort of animus at issue here: moral disapproval of homosexual conduct.

But though Coloradans are, as I say, entitled to be hostile toward homosexual conduct, the Court's portrayal of Coloradans as a society fallen victim to pointless, hate-filled "gay-bashing" is so false as to be comical. Colorado not only is one of the 25 states that have repealed their antisodomy laws, but was among the first to do so. But the society that eliminates criminal punishment for homosexual acts does not necessarily abandon the view that homosexuality is morally wrong and socially harmful; often, abolition simply reflects the view that enforcement of such criminal laws involves unseemly intrusion into the intimate lives of citizens.

There is a problem, however, that arises when criminal sanction of homosexuality is eliminated but moral and social disapprobation of homosexuality is meant to be retained. The problem is that, because those who engage in homosexual conduct tend to reside in disproportionate numbers in certain communities, have high disposable income, and, of course, care about homosexual-rights issues much more ardently than the public at large, they possess political power much greater than their numbers, both locally and statewide. Quite understandably, they devote this political power to achieving not merely a grudging social toleration, but full social acceptance, of homosexuality.

I do not mean to be critical of these legislative successes; homosexuals are as entitled to use the legal system for reinforcement of their moral sentiments as are the rest of society. But they are subject to being countered by lawful, democratic countermeasures as well. That is where Amendment 2 came in. It sought to counter both the geographic concentration and the disproportionate political power of homosexuals by (1) resolving the controversy at the statewide level, and (2) making the election a single-issue contest for both sides. It put directly, to all the citizens of the State, the question: Should homosexuality be given special protection? They answered no. The Court today asserts that this most democratic of procedures is unconstitutional. Lacking any cases to establish that facially absurd proposition, it simply asserts that it must be unconstitutional, because it has never happened before.

As I have noted above, this is proved false every time a state law prohibiting or disfavoring certain conduct is passed, because such a law prevents the adversely affected group—whether drug addicts, or smokers, or gun owners, or motorcyclists—from changing the policy in local areas of the state. What the Court says is even demonstrably false at the constitutional level. The Eighteenth Amendment to the federal

Constitution, for example, deprived those who drank alcohol not only of the power to alter the policy of prohibition locally or through state legislation, but even of the power to alter it through state constitutional amendment or federal legislation.

But there is a much closer analogy, one that involves precisely the effort by the majority of citizens to preserve its view of sexual morality statewide against the efforts of a geographically concentrated and politically powerful minority to undermine it. The constitutions of the States of Arizona, Idaho, New Mexico, Oklahoma, and Utah to this day contain provisions stating that polygamy is "forever prohibited." Polygamists, and those who have a polygamous "orientation," have been "singled out" by these provisions for much more severe treatment than merely denial of favored status; and that treatment can only be changed by achieving amendment of the state constitutions. The Court's disposition today suggests that these provisions are unconstitutional and that polygamy must be permitted in these States on a state-legislated, or perhaps even local-option, basis.

The U.S. Congress, moreover, required the inclusion of these antipolygamy provisions in the constitutions of Arizona, New Mexico, Oklahoma, and Utah, as a condition of their admission to statehood. Thus, this "singling out" of the sexual practices of a single group for statewide, democratic vote—so utterly alien to our constitutional system, the Court would have us believe—has not only happened, but has received the explicit approval of the U.S. Congress.

When the Court takes sides in the culture wars, it tends to reflect the views and values of the lawyer class from which the Court's members are drawn. How that class feels about homosexuality will be evident to anyone who wishes to interview job applicants at virtually any of the nation's law schools. The Association of American Law Schools requires all its member schools to exact from job interviewers "assurance of the employer's willingness" to hire homosexuals. This law-school view of what "prejudices" must be stamped out may be contrasted with the more plebeian attitudes that apparently still prevail in the United States Congress, which has been unresponsive to repeated attempts to extend to homosexuals the protections of federal civil rights laws.

Today's opinion has no foundation in American constitutional law. The people of Colorado have adopted an entirely reasonable provision that does not even disfavor homosexuals in any substantive sense, but merely denies them preferential treatment. Amendment 2 is designed to prevent piecemeal deterioration of the sexual morality favored by a majority of Coloradans and is not only an appropriate means to that legitimate end but a means that Americans have employed before. Striking it down is an act, not of judicial judgment, but of political will. I dissent.

*****

[*Note:* In Boy Scouts of America v. Dale, 530 U.S. 640 (2000) (digested in Chapter 10), BSA had revoked Dale's position as assistant scoutmaster of a New Jersey troop when BSA learned that Dale is an avowed homosexual and gay rights activist. BSA defended the revocation on the ground that homosexual conduct is inconsistent with the system of values that the organization sought to instill in young people. The New Jersey Supreme Court held that the revocation violated the State's public accommodations law and ordered BSA to reinstate Dale. The U.S. Supreme Court reversed (5-4), holding that requiring BSA to retain Dale as an assistant scoutmaster violated BSA's First Amendment right of expressive association.]

Lawrence v. Texas, 539 U.S. 558 (2003)

FACTS: Texas's "Homosexual Conduct Law" imposes criminal penalties on any person who "engages in deviate sexual intercourse with another individual of the same sex." The same conduct by different-sex couples is not prohibited. The statute defines "deviate sexual intercourse" as "(A) any contact between any part of the genitals of one person and the mouth or anus of another person" or "(B) the penetration of the genitals or the anus of another person with an object."

In Houston, police officers were dispatched to a private residence in response to a reported weapons disturbance. They entered an apartment where one of the defendants, John Geddes Lawrence, resided. The officers observed Lawrence and another man, Tyron Garner, engaging in sodomy. Both defendants are adults. They were arrested and charged under the Homosexual Conduct Law. They were found guilty and each was fined $200.

The Texas Court of Appeals rejected the defendants' constitutional arguments and affirmed the convictions, relying primarily on the U.S. Supreme Court's decision in Bowers v. Hardwick, 478 U.S. 186 (1986).

ISSUE: Does the Texas statute violate the Due Process or Equal Protection Clause of the Fourteenth Amendment?

DECISION (*Kennedy,* 6-3): *Yes.*

Liberty protects the person from unwarranted government intrusions into a dwelling or other private places. In our tradition the state is not omnipresent in the home. And there are other spheres of our lives and existence, outside the home, where the state should not be a dominant presence. Freedom extends beyond spatial bounds. Liberty presumes an autonomy of self that includes freedom of thought, belief, expression, and certain intimate conduct. The instant case involves liberty of the person both in its spatial and more transcendent dimensions.

We conclude the case should be resolved by determining whether the petitioners were free as adults to engage in the private conduct in the exercise of their liberty under the Due Process Clause of the Fourteenth Amendment to the Constitution. For this inquiry we deem it necessary to reconsider the Court's holding in *Bowers*.

The Court's beginning of its substantive discussion in *Bowers* ("The issue presented is whether the Federal Constitution confers a fundamental right upon homosexuals to engage in sodomy and hence invalidates the laws of the many States that still make such conduct illegal and have done so for a very long time") discloses the Court's failure to appreciate the extent of the liberty at stake. To say that the issue in *Bowers* was simply the right to engage in certain sexual conduct demeans the claim the individual put forward, just as it would demean a married couple were it to be said marriage is simply about the right to have sexual intercourse. The laws involved in *Bowers* and here are, to be sure, statutes that purport to do no more than prohibit a particular sexual act. Their penalties and purposes, though, have more far-reaching consequences, touching upon the most private human conduct, sexual behavior, and in the most private of places, the home. The statutes do seek to control a personal relationship that, whether or not entitled to formal recognition in the law, is within the liberty of persons to choose without being punished as criminals.

The *Bowers* Court further stated that proscriptions against homosexual sodomy have "ancient roots." At the outset it should be noted that early American sodomy laws were not directed at homosexuals as such but instead sought to prohibit nonprocreative sexual activity more generally. This does not suggest approval of homosexual conduct. It does tend to show that this particular form of conduct was not thought of as a separate category from like conduct between heterosexual persons. And laws prohibiting sodomy do not seem to have been enforced against consenting adults acting in private. Far from possessing "ancient roots," as *Bowers* suggested, American laws targeting same-sex couples did not develop until the last third of the twentieth century. In summary, the historical grounds relied upon in *Bowers* are more complex than the majority indicated.

It must be acknowledged, of course, that the Court in *Bowers* was making the broader point that for centuries there have been powerful voices to condemn homosexual conduct as immoral. The condemnation has been shaped by religious beliefs, conceptions of right and acceptable behavior, and respect for the traditional family. For many persons these are not trivial concerns but profound and deep convictions accepted as ethical and moral principles to which they aspire and which thus determine the course of their lives. These considerations do not answer the question before us, however. The issue is whether the majority may use the power of the State to enforce these views on the whole society through operation of the criminal law.

The sweeping references in *Bowers* to the history of Western civilization and to Judeo-Christian moral and ethical standards did not take account of other authorities pointing in an opposite direction. A committee advising the British Parliament in 1957 recommended repeal of laws punishing homosexual conduct; Parliament enacted the substance of those recommendations ten years later. Of even more importance, almost five years before *Bowers* was decided, the European Court of Human Rights held that the laws proscribing such conduct were invalid under the European Convention on Human Rights. Authoritative in all countries that are members of the Council of Europe (21 nations then, 45 nations now), the decision is at odds with the premise in *Bowers* that the claim put forward was insubstantial in our Western civilization.

In our own constitutional system the deficiencies in *Bowers* became even more apparent in the years following its announcement. The 25 States with laws prohibiting the relevant conduct referenced in the *Bowers* decision are reduced now to 13, of which 4 enforce their laws only against homosexual conduct. In those States where sodomy is still proscribed, whether for same-sex or heterosexual conduct, there is a pattern of nonenforcement with respect to consenting adults acting in private.

Two principal cases decided after *Bowers* cast its holding into even more doubt. In Planned Parenthood of Southeastern Pennsylvania v. Casey, 505 U.S. 833 (1992), the Court again confirmed that our laws and tradition afford constitutional protection to personal decisions relating to marriage, procreation, contraception, family relationships, child rearing, and education. In explaining the respect the Constitution demands for the autonomy of the person in making these choices, we stated as follows:

> These matters, involving the most intimate and personal choices a person may make in a lifetime, choices central to personal dignity and autonomy, are central to the liberty protected by the Fourteenth Amendment. At the heart of liberty is the right to define one's own concept of existence, of meaning, of the universe, and of the mystery of human life. Beliefs about these matters could not define the attributes of personhood were they formed under compulsion of the State.

Persons in a homosexual relationship may seek autonomy for these purposes, just as heterosexual persons do. The decision in *Bowers* would deny them this right.

The second post-*Bowers* case of principal relevance is Romer v. Evans, 517 U.S. 620 (1996). There the Court struck down class-based legislation directed at homosexuals as a violation of the Equal Protection Clause. We concluded that the provision was "born of animosity toward the class of persons affected" and further that it had no rational relation to a legitimate governmental purpose.

As an alternative argument in this case, it is contended that *Romer* provides the basis for declaring the Texas statute invalid under the Equal Protection Clause. That is a tenable argument, but we conclude the instant case requires us to address whether *Bowers* itself has continuing validity. Were we to hold the statute invalid under the Equal Protection Clause, some might question whether a prohibition would be valid if drawn differently, say, to prohibit both same-sex and different-sex sodomy.

If protected conduct is made criminal and the law that does so remains unexamined for its substantive validity, its stigma might remain even if it were not enforceable as drawn for equal protection reasons. When homosexual conduct is made criminal by the law of the state, that declaration in and of itself is an invitation to subject homosexual persons to discrimination both in the public and in the private spheres. The central holding of *Bowers* has been brought in question by this case, and it should be addressed. Its continuance as precedent demeans the lives of homosexual persons.

The doctrine of *stare decisis* is essential to the respect accorded to the judgments of the Court and to the stability of the law, but it is not an inexorable command. The holding in *Bowers* has not induced detrimental reliance comparable to some instances where recognized individual rights are involved. Indeed, there has been no individual or societal reliance on *Bowers* of the sort that could counsel against overturning its holding once there are compelling reasons to do so. *Bowers* itself causes uncertainty, for the precedents before and after its issuance contradict its central holding.

In his dissenting opinion in *Bowers,* Justice Stevens came to these conclusions:

> Our prior cases make two propositions abundantly clear. First, the fact that the governing majority in a State has traditionally viewed a particular practice as immoral is not a sufficient reason for upholding a law prohibiting the practice; neither history nor tradition could save a law prohibiting miscegenation from constitutional attack. Second, individual decisions by married persons, concerning the intimacies of their physical relationship, even when not intended to produce offspring, are a form of "liberty" protected by the Due Process Clause of the Fourteenth Amendment. Moreover, this protection extends to intimate choices by unmarried as well as married persons.

Justice Stevens's analysis, in our view, should have been controlling in *Bowers* and should control here.

Bowers was not correct when it was decided, and it is not correct today. It ought not to remain binding precedent. *Bowers v. Hardwick* should be and now is overruled.

The present case does not involve minors. It does not involve persons who might be injured or coerced or who are situated in relationships where consent might not easily be refused. It does not involve public conduct or prostitution. It does not involve whether the government must give formal recognition to any relationship that homosexual persons seek to enter. The case does involve two adults who, with full and mutual consent from each other, engaged in sexual practices common to a homosexual lifestyle. The petitioners are entitled to respect for their private lives. The state cannot demean their existence or control their destiny by making their private sexual conduct a crime. Their right to liberty under the Due Process Clause gives them the full right to engage in their conduct without intervention of the government. The Texas statute furthers no legitimate state interest that can justify its intrusion into the personal and private life of the individual.

The judgment of the Texas Court of Appeals is reversed.

O'Connor, concurring in the judgment: I joined *Bowers* and do not join the Court in overruling it. Nevertheless, I agree with the Court that Texas's statute banning same-sex sodomy is unconstitutional. Rather than relying on the substantive component of the Fourteenth Amendment's Due Process Clause, as the Court does, I base my conclusion on the Fourteenth Amendment's Equal Protection Clause.

The statute at issue here makes sodomy a crime only if a person "engages in deviate sexual intercourse with another individual of the same sex." Sodomy between opposite-sex partners, however, is not a crime in Texas. That is, Texas treats the same conduct differently based solely on the participants.

While the penalty imposed on the defendants in this case was relatively minor, the consequences of conviction are not. As the Court notes, defendants' convictions, if upheld, would disqualify them from or restrict their ability to engage in a variety of professions.

And the effect of Texas's sodomy law is not just limited to the threat of prosecution or consequence of conviction. Texas's sodomy law brands all homosexuals as criminals, thereby making it more difficult for homosexuals to be treated in the same manner as everyone else, including in the areas of employment, family issues, and housing.

Texas attempts to justify its law, and the effects of the law, by arguing that the statute furthers the legitimate governmental interest of the promotion of morality. In *Bowers,* we held that a state law criminalizing sodomy as applied to homosexual couples did not violate substantive due process. This case raises a different issue than *Bowers:* whether, under the Equal Protection Clause, moral disapproval is a legitimate state interest to justify by itself a statute that bans homosexual sodomy, but not heterosexual sodomy. It is not. Moral disapproval of this group is an interest that is insufficient to satisfy rational basis review under the Equal Protection Clause. And because Texas so rarely enforces its sodomy law as applied to private, consensual acts, the law serves more as a statement of dislike and disapproval against homosexuals than as a tool to stop criminal behavior.

Texas argues, however, that the sodomy law does not discriminate against homosexual persons. Instead, the State maintains that the law discriminates only against homosexual conduct. But Texas's sodomy law is targeted at more than conduct. It is instead directed toward homosexual persons as a class. When a State makes homosexual conduct criminal, and not "deviate sexual intercourse" committed by persons of different sexes, that declaration in and of itself is an invitation to subject homosexual persons to discrimination both in the public and in the private spheres.

That this law as applied to private, consensual conduct is unconstitutional under the Equal Protection Clause does not mean that other laws distinguishing between heterosexuals and homosexuals would similarly fail under rational basis review. Texas cannot assert any legitimate state interest here, such as national security or preserving the traditional institution of marriage. Unlike the moral disapproval of same-sex relations—the asserted state interest in this case—other reasons exist to promote the institution of marriage beyond mere moral disapproval of an excluded group.

I therefore concur in the Court's judgment on the ground that in my view the law banning deviate sexual intercourse between consenting adults of the same sex, but not between consenting adults of different sexes, is unconstitutional.

Scalia, dissenting (joined by Rehnquist and Thomas): Though there is discussion of "fundamental proposition[s]" and "fundamental decisions," nowhere does the Court's opinion declare that homosexual sodomy is a "fundamental right" under the Due Process Clause. Nor does it subject the Texas law to the standard of review that would be appropriate (strict scrutiny) if homosexual sodomy *were* a fundamental right.

Thus, while overruling the *outcome* of *Bowers,* the Court leaves strangely untouched the central legal conclusion of *Bowers:* "[R]espondent would have us announce . . . a fundamental right to engage in homosexual sodomy. This we are quite unwilling to do." In the present case, the Court simply describes defendants' conduct as "an exercise of their liberty"—which it undoubtedly is—and proceeds to apply an unheard-of form of rational-basis review that will have far-reaching implications beyond this case.

Today's approach to *stare decisis* invites us to overrule an erroneously decided precedent *if:* (1) its foundations have been "eroded" by subsequent decisions; (2) it has been subject to "substantial and continuing" criticism; and (3) it has not induced "individual or societal reliance" that counsels against overturning. The problem is that *Roe v. Wade* itself—which today's majority surely has no disposition to overrule—satisfies these conditions to at least the same degree as *Bowers.*

Having decided that it need not adhere to *stare decisis,* the Court still must establish that *Bowers* was wrongly decided and that the Texas statute, as applied to defendants, is unconstitutional.

The Texas statute undoubtedly imposes constraints on liberty. So do laws prohibiting prostitution, recreational use of heroin, and, for that matter, working more than 60 hours per week in a bakery. But there is no right to "liberty" under the Due Process Clause, though today's opinion repeatedly makes that claim. The Fourteenth Amendment *expressly allows* states to deprive their citizens of liberty, *so long as "due process of law" is provided:* "No State shall . . . deprive any person of life, liberty, or property, *without due process of law.*"

Our opinions applying the doctrine known as "substantive due process" hold that the Due Process Clause prohibits states from infringing *fundamental* liberty interests, unless the infringement is narrowly tailored to serve a compelling state interest. We have held repeatedly, in cases the Court today does not overrule, that *only* fundamental rights qualify for this so-called "heightened scrutiny" protection—that is, rights that are "deeply rooted in this Nation's history and tradition." All other liberty interests may be abridged or abrogated pursuant to a validly enacted state law if that law is rationally related to a legitimate state interest.

Bowers held, first, that criminal prohibitions of homosexual sodomy are not subject to heightened scrutiny because they do not implicate a "fundamental right" under the Due Process Clause. The Court today does not overrule this holding. Not once does it describe homosexual sodomy as a "fundamental right" or a "fundamental liberty interest"; nor does it subject the Texas statute to strict scrutiny. Instead, having failed to establish that the right to homosexual sodomy is "deeply rooted in this Nation's history and tradition," the Court applies the rational-basis test and on that basis overrules *Bowers.*

The proposition that there is no rational basis for the Texas statute is so out of accord with our jurisprudence—indeed, with the jurisprudence of *any* society we know—that it requires little discussion.

The Texas statute undeniably seeks to further the belief of its citizens that certain forms of sexual behavior are "immoral and unacceptable" (*Bowers*)—the same interest furthered by criminal laws against fornication, bigamy, adultery, adult incest, bestiality, and obscenity. *Bowers* held that this *was* a legitimate state interest. The Court today reaches the opposite conclusion. The Texas statute, it says, "furthers *no legitimate state interest* which can justify its intrusion into the personal and private life of the individual." The Court embraces instead Justice Stevens's declaration in his *Bowers* dissent that "the fact that the governing majority in a State has traditionally viewed a particular practice as immoral is not a sufficient reason for upholding a law prohibiting the practice." This effectively decrees the end of all morals legislation. If, as the Court asserts, the promotion of majoritarian sexual morality is not even a *legitimate* state interest, none of the above-mentioned laws can survive rational-basis review.

With respect to the defendants' equal-protection challenge—which no member of the Court save Justice O'Connor embraces—the Texas law on its face applies equally to all persons. Men and women, heterosexuals and homosexuals, are all subject to its prohibition of deviate sexual intercourse with someone of the same sex. To be sure, the law does distinguish between the sexes insofar as concerns the partner with whom the sexual acts are performed: men can violate the law only with other men, and women only with other women. But this cannot itself be a denial of equal protection, since it is precisely the same distinction regarding partner that is drawn in state laws prohibiting marriage with someone of the same sex while permitting marriage with someone of the opposite sex.

Since no purpose to discriminate against men or women as a class can be gleaned from the Texas law, rational-basis review applies. That review is readily satisfied here by the same rational basis that satisfied it in *Bowers*—society's belief that certain forms of sexual behavior are "immoral and unacceptable." This is the same justification that supports many other laws regulating sexual behavior that make a distinction based upon the identity of the partner—for example, laws against adultery, fornication, and adult incest, and laws refusing to recognize homosexual marriage.

Justice O'Connor seeks to preserve state laws limiting marriage to opposite-sex couples by the conclusory statement that "preserving the traditional institution of marriage" is a legitimate state interest. But "preserving the traditional institution of marriage" is just a kinder way of describing the state's *moral disapproval* of same-sex couples. Texas's interest in the challenged statute could be recast in similarly euphemistic terms: "preserving the traditional sexual mores of our society." In the jurisprudence Justice O'Connor proposes, judges can validate laws by characterizing them as "preserving the traditions of society" (good); or invalidate them by characterizing them as "expressing moral disapproval" (bad).

Today's opinion is the product of a Court, which is the product of a law-profession culture, that has largely signed on to the so-called homosexual agenda, by which I mean the agenda promoted by some homosexual activists directed at eliminating the opprobrium that has traditionally attached to homosexual conduct.

One of the most revealing statements in today's opinion is the Court's grim warning that the criminalization of homosexual conduct is "an invitation to subject homosexual persons to discrimination both in the public and in the private spheres." It is clear from this that the Court has taken sides in the culture war, departing from its role of assuring, as neutral observer, that the democratic rules of engagement are observed. Many Americans do not want persons who openly engage in homosexual conduct as partners in their businesses, as scoutmasters for their children, as teachers in their children's schools, or as boarders in their homes. They view this as protecting themselves and their families from a lifestyle that they believe to be immoral and destructive. But the Court views it as "discrimination," which it is the function of our judgments to deter.

So imbued is the Court with the anti-anti-homosexual culture that it is seemingly unaware that the attitudes of that culture are not obviously "mainstream"; that in most states what the Court calls "discrimination" against those who engage in homosexual acts is perfectly legal; that proposals to ban such discrimination have repeatedly been rejected by Congress; that in some cases such discrimination is *mandated* by federal statute (e.g., mandating discharge from the armed forces of any service member who engages in or intends to engage in homosexual acts); and that in some cases such discrimination is a constitutional right, as the Court held in Boy Scouts of America v. Dale, 530 U.S. 640 (2000).

I have nothing against homosexuals, or any other group, promoting their agenda through normal democratic means. Social perceptions of sexual and other morality change over time, and every group has the right to persuade its fellow citizens that its view of such matters is the best. But persuading one's fellow citizens is one thing, and imposing one's views in absence of democratic majority will is something else. I would no more *require* a State to criminalize homosexual acts—or, for that matter, display *any* moral disapprobation of them—than I would *forbid* it to do so. What Texas has chosen to do is well within the range of traditional democratic action, and its hand should not be stayed through the invention of a brand-new "constitutional right" by a Court that is impatient of democratic change. It is the premise of our system that those judgments are to be made by the people and not imposed by a governing caste that knows best.

At the end of its opinion—after having laid waste to the foundations of our rational-basis jurisprudence—the Court says that this case "does not involve whether the government must give formal recognition to any relationship that homosexual persons seek to enter." Do not believe it. Today's opinion dismantles the structure of constitutional law that has permitted a distinction to be made between heterosexual and homosexual unions, insofar as formal recognition in marriage is concerned. If moral disapprobation of homosexual conduct is "no legitimate state interest" for purposes of proscribing that conduct; and if, as the Court coos (casting aside all pretense of neutrality), "[w]hen sexuality finds overt expression in intimate conduct with another person, the conduct can be but one element in a personal bond that is more enduring"; what justification could there possibly be for denying the benefits of marriage to homosexual couples exercising "[t]he liberty protected by the Constitution"? This case "does not involve" the issue of homosexual marriage only if one entertains the belief that principle and logic have nothing to do with the decisions of this Court. Many will hope that, as the Court comfortingly assures us, this is so.

Thomas, dissenting: I join Justice Scalia's dissenting opinion. I write separately to note my view that the challenged Texas law is "uncommonly silly," and if I were a member of the Texas Legislature, I would vote to repeal it. Punishing someone for expressing his sexual preference through noncommercial consensual conduct with another adult does not appear to be a worthy way to expend limited law enforcement resources. Notwithstanding this, I recognize that as a member of this Court I am not empowered to help the defendants and others similarly situated. My duty, rather, is to decide cases agreeably to the Constitution and laws of the United States. And I can find neither in the Bill of Rights nor any other part of the Constitution a general right of privacy, or as the Court terms it today, the "liberty of the person both in its spatial and more transcendent dimensions."

10

Freedom of Speech

The Primacy of Freedom of Speech

The next four chapters deal with key aspects of the First Amendment:

> Congress shall make no law respecting an establishment of religion, or prohibiting the free
> exercise thereof; or abridging the freedom of speech, or of the press; or the right of the
> people peaceably to assemble, and to petition the Government for a redress of grievances.

This chapter focuses on freedom of speech; Chapter 11 on freedom of the press;
Chapter 12 on the Establishment Clause; and Chapter 13 on the Free Exercise Clause.

Each of the liberties protected by the First Amendment is an essential element of a
democratic society. But freedom of speech occupies a unique status because it is the
necessary foundation for each of the others (and, indeed, for most other rights protected by the Constitution). As Justice Benjamin Cardozo pointed out: "Freedom of
expression is the matrix, the indispensable condition, of nearly every other form of
freedom." Palko v. Connecticut, 302 U.S. 319, 327 (1937). For example, without freedom of speech, how could there be freedom of religion? Likewise, without freedom of
speech, how could there be a meaningful right to assemble or to petition the
government to redress grievances?

Historians sharply differ on what the framers of the Bill of Rights viewed as the
scope of freedom of speech. Thus, although the question is much disputed, some historians contend that as originally understood the First Amendment only prohibited
"prior restraints" on speech and did not bar prosecutions for sedition or libel against
the government.[1]

Perhaps relying on that view, the Federalist-dominated Congress adopted the infamous Sedition Act of 1798, prohibiting the publication of

> false, scandalous, and malicious writing [against] the Government of the United States, or
> either House of [Congress], or the President, [with] intent to defame [them]; or to bring

---

[1]See, e.g., Christopher Wolfe, *The Rise of Modern Judicial Review: From Constitutional Interpretation to Judge-
Made Law* [Basic Books 1986]: 182–183. Compare, e.g., Ronald Dworkin's comment in Antonin Scalia, *A Matter
of Interpretation: Federal Courts and the Law* [Princeton 1997]: 124–125; Geoffrey Stone, *Perilous Times: Free
Speech in Wartime* [Norton 2004]: 42. ("In fact, the framers of the First Amendment had no common understanding of its 'true' meaning. They embraced a broad and largely undefined constitutional principle, not a concrete,
well-settled doctrine.")

them [into] contempt or disrepute; or to excite against them [the] hatred of the good people of the United States, or to stir up sedition within the United States.

Numerous Jeffersonian Republicans (including their leading newspapers) were prosecuted under the act. Although the Supreme Court was never called upon to rule on the act's constitutionality, it was upheld by several lower federal courts. (The act expired by its own terms in 1801, and all those convicted under it were pardoned by Jefferson on taking office as president.)[2]

Whatever may have been its intended scope when the Bill of Rights was adopted, the freedom of speech guarantee has (starting in the World War I period) received an increasingly expansive interpretation by the Supreme Court. These decisions are reviewed in the succeeding portions of this chapter.

The Court's decisions have emphasized the importance of freedom of speech in advancing knowledge and "truth" in the "marketplace of ideas." In the oft-repeated words of Justice Oliver Wendell Holmes, "the best test of truth is the power of the thought to get itself accepted in the competition of the market. . . . That at any rate is the theory of our constitution." Abrams v. United States, 250 U.S. 616, 630 (1919) (dissenting opinion).

The Court's decisions have also emphasized the function of freedom of speech in facilitating representative democracy and self-government. Thus, in Buckley v. Valeo, 424 U.S. 1, 14 (1976), the Court declared:

> The First Amendment affords the broadest protection to such political expression in order "to assure [the] unfettered interchange of ideas for the bringing about of political and social changes desired by the people." Roth v. United States, 354 U.S. 476, 484 (1957). Although First Amendment protections are not confined to "the exposition of ideas," Winters v. New York, 333 U.S. 507, 510 (1948), "there is practically universal agreement that a major purpose of that Amendment was to protect the free discussion of governmental affairs, . . . of course includ[ing] discussions of candidates. . . ." Mills v. Alabama, 384 U.S. 214, 218 (1966). This no more than reflects our "profound national commitment to the principle that debate on public issues should be uninhibited, robust, and wide-open," New York Times Co. v. Sullivan, 376 U.S. 254, 270 (1964).

But, while "It is no doubt true that a central purpose of the First Amendment 'was to protect the free discussion of governmental affairs' . . . [the Court has] never suggested that expression about philosophical, social, artistic, economic, literary, or ethical matters—to take a nonexclusive list of labels—is not entitled to full First Amendment protection." Abood v. Detroit Board of Education, 431 U.S. 209, 211 (1977).

Freedom of Speech Overview

Although the wording of the First Amendment ("Congress shall make no law . . . abridging the freedom of speech.") expressly applies only to Congress, the Amendment's guarantees have been held to be "incorporated" in the Due Process Clause of the Fourteenth Amendment and are thus equally applicable to the States. (See comment "'Incorporation' of Rights in Due Process" in Chapter 6.)

The First Amendment is stated in absolute terms ("shall make no law"), but it has never been construed to bar every regulation that might be said to involve some form

---

[2]See Stone, *Perilous Times: Free Speech in Wartime,* at 25–76.

of "speech." Examples of speech unprotected by the Amendment include perjury, bribery, and obscenity.

Another category of speech traditionally unprotected by the amendment is speech
that advocates or incites violence or other illegal action. But in *Brandenburg v. Ohio,*
the next digested case, the Court sharply narrowed this category, holding that
government cannot "forbid or proscribe advocacy of the use of force or of law violation except where such advocacy is directed to inciting or producing *imminent* lawless
action *and is likely to incite or produce such action.*" (Italics added.)

The core of freedom of speech, as the Court has frequently declared, is that
government cannot regulate speech based on its *content*—its subject matter, its message, its ideas, its viewpoint. Content-based speech restrictions, unlike content-
neutral restrictions, are tested under a strict scrutiny standard, are presumptively
unconstitutional, and can be sustained only by a demonstration of a "compelling" governmental interest.

The distinction is illustrated in several of the decisions digested in this chapter.
Thus, in the *R. A. V.* case, the challenged statute sought to prohibit a particular kind
of message (addressed to race, color, creed, religion, or gender) and was therefore
content-based and held to be invalid. By contrast, although similarly aimed at the burning of a cross, the statute upheld in *Virginia v. Black* was content-neutral since it
focused on the purpose and effect of the cross burning, quite apart from the nature of
the message.

Content-neutral speech regulations are tested under a less exacting standard of
review than restrictions based on content. A content-neutral regulation can be justified
by a showing that it serves a "substantial" or "significant" governmental interest (as
distinguished from the "compelling" interest needed to justify a content-based speech
regulation).

First Amendment issues frequently arise in connection with government restrictions
on the use of public property—streets, sidewalks, and parks. As the Court recognized
in Cantwell v. State of Connecticut, 310 U.S. 296 (1940),

> a state may by general and non-discriminatory legislation regulate the times, the places,
> and the manner of soliciting upon its streets, and of holding meetings thereon, and may
> in other respects safeguard the peace, good order, and comfort of the community, without
> unconstitutionally invading the liberties protected by the Fourteenth Amendment.

However, such time, place, and manner restrictions must be reasonable "so [that]
that they leave open ample alternative channels for communication of information."
Heffron v. International Society for Krishna Consciousness, Inc., 452 U.S. 640,
648 (1981).

Time, place, and manner restrictions must be content-neutral, serve a substantial
state interest (for example, control of automobile or pedestrian traffic), and provide
objective standards for the granting of licenses or permits. Regulations that allow an
administrative authority to grant or deny permits on the basis of the content of the
applicant's message, or give the administrative authority untrammeled discretion to
grant or deny permits, will almost certainly be found to offend the First Amendment.

For example, in Saia v. New York, 334 U.S. 558 (1948), the Court (6-3) declared
unconstitutional a city's requirement of a permit to operate a sound truck where the
mayor had unlimited discretion whether to grant a permit. But in Kovacs v. Cooper,
336 U.S. 77 (1949), the Court (5-4) upheld an ordinance restricting the decibel level

on sound trucks using public streets. The Court emphasized that the law did not prohibit all such devices, but rather was a reasonable time, place, and manner restriction.

Police Department of Chicago v. Mosley, 408 U.S. 92 (1972), involved an ordinance that barred picketing or demonstrations within 150 feet of a school building while the school was in session, except for peaceful picketing in connection with a labor dispute. The Court (9-0) held that the ordinance, by allowing only labor picketing and not other types of protests, was not content-neutral and was therefore invalid.

In contrast, in Hill v. Colorado, 530 U.S. 703 (2000), the Court (6-3) rejected a challenge by antiabortion groups to a law restricting "oral protest, education, or counseling" on public sidewalks. The law made it unlawful, within 100 feet of the entrance to any health care facility, for any person to "knowingly approach" within 8 feet of another person, without that person's consent, "for the purpose of passing a leaflet or handbill to, displaying a sign to, or engaging in oral protest, education, or counseling with such other person." The majority held that the restriction on speech was content-neutral on the ground that the law applied regardless of the subject or viewpoint of the speech. In his dissent, Justice Scalia argued that the language and history of the law showed that it was a content-based restraint aimed at antiabortion speech.

Symbolic Speech

The "speech" protected by the First Amendment typically involves the use of words, whether written or spoken, to communicate a message. But in many instances *nonverbal* conduct may be employed as a mode of communication.

Marches and picketing are examples of expressive conduct recognized as "speech" under the First Amendment (subject, of course, to reasonable time, place, and manner restrictions explained in the previous comment "Freedom of Speech Overview"). Symbolic conduct in a public place or before an audience may also qualify for constitutional protection. As the Court stated in West Virginia State Board of Education v. Barnette, 319 U.S. 624, 632 (1943), "Symbolism is a primitive but effective way of communicating ideas."

Each of the first five cases digested in this chapter deals with the application of the First Amendment to a particular type of symbolic speech—setting a fire to burn an object (a cross, draft card, or flag) to express a point of view.

In *Brandenburg v. Ohio* the defendant had coupled the burning of a cross with verbal advocacy of illegal action. The Court concluded that the violence urged by the defendant was neither imminent nor likely and held unconstitutional a state syndicalism law prohibiting, e.g., advocacy "of crime, sabotage, or unlawful methods of terrorism as a means of accomplishing industrial or political reform."

In *United States v. O'Brien,* the defendant was charged with burning his draft card in violation of the selective service statute requiring registrants to maintain such cards in their possession. Although acknowledging that the defendant's conduct included "speech elements," the Court held that enforcement of the draft card requirement was justified because the government had a substantial "non-speech" interest in administering and enforcing the selective service program. The defendant was convicted, the Court said, "[f]or the noncommunicative impact of his conduct, and for nothing else" (391 U.S. at 382).

By contrast, in the *Texas v. Johnson* flag-burning case, the palpable purpose of the statute (prohibiting flag mistreatment "in a way that the actor knows will seriously offend one or more persons likely to observe or discover his action") was to restrain communication. The statute, it was held, was not justified by a substantial government interest unrelated to the suppression of free expression.

In the other two "burning" cases—*R. A. V. v. St. Paul* and *Virginia v. Black*—the Court (except for Justice Thomas) accepted cross-burning conduct as "speech" presumptively entitled to First Amendment protection. However, the Court reached opposite conclusions in the two cases; the "speech" claim was rejected in *R. A. V.* and upheld in *Virginia v. Black*. In *R. A. V.* the St. Paul ordinance (prohibiting a cross burning when it "arouses anger, alarm or resentment in others *on the basis of race, color, creed, religion, or gender*") was held to be content-based and therefore invalid because it singled out specific disfavored subjects for punishment. On the other hand, unlike the St. Paul ordinance, the statute upheld in *Virginia v. Black* (prohibiting a cross burning "*with the intent of intimidating any person or group of persons*") was content-neutral because it contains no list of taboo subjects.

Symbolic speech issues frequently arise in the public schools. A leading case is Tinker v. Des Moines Independent Community School District, 393 U.S. 503 (1969), holding it impermissible to bar a student from wearing a black armband to protest the Vietnam War—an action the Court characterized as "closely akin to 'pure speech' " (p. 505). According to the Court: "it can hardly be argued that either students or teachers shed their constitutional rights to freedom of speech or expression at the schoolhouse gate" (p. 506). Generally student speech in public schools can be restricted only if it is vulgar or profane or if there is serious reason to believe that it is likely to cause material disruption. The recent decision in Morse v. Frederick, ___ U.S. ___, 127 S.Ct. 2618 (2007), added that speech (in that case, a banner proclaiming "Bong Hits 4 Jesus" in front of the school during a school-sponsored activity) can also be regulated if it is reasonably perceived by school officials to promote a drug-use message.

Brandenburg v. Ohio, 395 U.S. 444 (1969)

FACTS: Brandenburg, a Ku Klux Klan leader, was indicted under the Ohio Criminal Syndicalism Act for "advocat[ing] . . . the duty, necessity, or propriety of crime, sabotage, violence, or unlawful methods of terrorism as a means of accomplishing industrial or political reform" and for "voluntarily assembl[ing] with any society, group or assemblage of persons formed to teach or advocate the doctrines of criminal syndicalism."

According to the evidence presented at trial, Brandenburg telephoned a reporter on the staff of a Cincinnati television station and invited him to come to a Ku Klux Klan "rally" to be held at a farm. With the cooperation of the organizers, the reporter and a cameraman attended the meeting and filmed the events. Portions of the films were later broadcast on the local station and on a national network. The prosecution's case rested on the films and on testimony identifying Brandenburg as the person who communicated with the reporter and who spoke at the rally. The State also introduced into evidence several articles appearing in the film, including a pistol, a rifle, a shotgun, ammunition, a Bible, and a red hood worn by the speaker in the films.

One film showed 12 hooded figures, some of whom carried firearms. They were gathered around a large wooden cross, which they burned. No one was present other than the participants and the newsmen who made the film. Most of the words uttered during the filmed scene were incomprehensible but scattered phrases could be understood that were derogatory of Negroes and Jews. Another scene on the same film showed the appellant, in Klan regalia, making this speech:

This is an organizers' meeting. We have had quite a few members here today which are—we have hundreds, hundreds of members throughout the State of Ohio. I can quote from a newspaper clipping from the Columbus, Ohio Dispatch, five weeks ago Sunday morning. The Klan has more members in the State of Ohio than does any other organization. We're not a revengent organization, but if our President, our Congress, our Supreme Court, continues to suppress the white, Caucasian race, it's possible that there might have to be some revengeance taken. We are marching on Congress July the Fourth, four hundred thousand strong. From there we are dividing into two groups, one group to march on St. Augustine, Florida, the other group to march into Mississippi. Thank you.

The second film showed six hooded figures, one of whom was Brandenburg repeating a speech very similar to that recorded on the first film. The reference to the possibility of "revengeance" was omittted, and one sentence was added: "Personally, I believe the nigger should be returned to Africa, the Jew returned to Israel." Although some of the persons in the films carried weapons, Brandenburg did not.

Brandenburg was found guilty, fined $1,000, and sentenced to 1 to 10 years' imprisonment. He challenged the constitutionality of the criminal syndicalism statute under the First and Fourteenth Amendments, but his conviction was sustained by the Ohio appellate courts.

ISSUE: Does the statute violate freedom of speech under the First and Fourteenth Amendments?

DECISION (*per curiam*, 9-0): *Yes.*

The Ohio Criminal Syndicalism Act was enacted in 1919. From 1917 to 1920, identical or quite similar laws were adopted by 20 states and 2 territories. In Whitney v. California, 274 U.S. 357 (1927), this Court sustained the constitutionality of California's Criminal Syndicalism Act, the text of which is quite similar to that of the Ohio statute. The Court upheld the statute on the ground that, without more, "advocating" violent means to effect political and economic change involves such danger to the security of the state that the state may outlaw it.

But *Whitney* has been thoroughly discredited by our later decisions. These later decisions have fashioned the principle that the constitutional guarantees of free speech and free press do not permit a state to forbid or proscribe advocacy of the use of force or of law violation except where such advocacy is directed to inciting or producing imminent lawless action and is likely to incite or produce such action. The mere abstract teaching of the moral propriety or even moral necessity for a resort to force and violence is not the same as preparing a group for violent action and steeling it to such action. A statute that fails to draw this distinction impermissibly intrudes upon the freedoms guaranteed by the First and Fourteenth Amendments. It sweeps within its condemnation speech that our Constitution has immunized from governmental control.

Measured by this test, Ohio's Criminal Syndicalism Act cannot be sustained. The Act punishes persons who "advocate or teach the duty, necessity, or propriety" of violence "as a means of accomplishing industrial or political reform"; or who publish or circulate or display any book or paper containing such advocacy; or who "justify" the commission of violent acts "with intent to exemplify, spread or advocate the propriety of the doctrines of criminal syndicalism"; or who "voluntarily assemble" with a group formed "to teach or advocate the doctrines of criminal syndicalism." Neither the indictment nor the trial judge's instructions to the jury in any way refined the stat-ute's bald definition of the crime in terms of mere advocacy, as distinguished from incitement to imminent lawless action.

Accordingly, we are here confronted with a statute which, by its own words and as applied, purports to punish mere advocacy and to forbid, on pain of criminal punish-ment, assembly with others merely to advocate the described type of action. Such a statute falls within the condemnation of the First and Fourteenth Amendments. The contrary teaching of *Whitney v. California* cannot be supported, and that decision is therefore overruled.

Black, concurring: I agree with the views expressed by Justice Douglas in his concur-ring opinion that the "clear and present danger" doctrine should have no place in the interpretation of the First Amendment. I join the Court's opinion, which, as I under-stand it, does not indicate any agreement on the Court's part with the "clear and present danger" doctrine.

Douglas, concurring: While I join the opinion of the Court and believe that *Whitney* is correctly overruled, I desire to enter a caveat.

The "clear and present danger" test was adumbrated by Justice Holmes in Schenck v. United States, 249 U.S. 47 (1919), a case arising in World War I. In that case, the defendant was charged with attempts to cause insubordination in the military and obstruction of enlistment by distributing pamphlets that urged resistance to the draft, denounced conscription, and impugned the motives of those backing the war effort. In rejecting a First Amendment defense in that case, Justice Holmes said:

> The question in every case is whether the words used are used in such circumstances and are of such a nature as to create a clear and present danger that they will bring about the substantive evils that Congress has a right to prevent. It is a question of proximity and degree.

In the following term, the Court applied the *Schenck* doctrine to affirm the convic-tions of other dissidents in World War I. In one such case, Abrams v. United States, 250 U.S. 616 (1919), Justice Holmes (joined by Justice Louis Brandeis) dissented. While adhering to *Schenck,* he did not think that on the facts a case for overriding the First Amendment had been made out:

> It is only the present danger of immediate evil or an intent to bring it about that warrants Congress in setting a limit to the expression of opinion where private rights are not con-cerned. Congress certainly cannot forbid all effort to change the mind of the country.

Dennis v. United States, 341 U.S. 494 (1951), distorted the clear and present danger test beyond recognition. In *Dennis* the prosecution dubbed an agreement to teach the Marxist creed a "conspiracy." The case was submitted to a jury on a charge that the jury could not convict unless it found that the defendants "intended to over-throw the Government 'as speedily as circumstances would permit.' " This Court sus-tained the convictions under that charge, construing it to mean a determination of "whether the gravity of the evil, discounted by its improbability, justifies such invasion of free speech as is necessary to avoid the danger."

I see no place in the regime of the First Amendment for any clear and present danger test, whether strict and tight as some would make it, or freewheeling as the Court in *Dennis* rephrased it.

When one sees when and how the clear and present danger test has been applied, great misgivings are aroused. First, the threats were often loud but always puny and made serious only by judges so wedded to the status quo that critical analysis made them nervous. Second, the test was so twisted and perverted in *Dennis* as to make the trial of those teachers of Marxism an all-out political trial, which was part and parcel of the cold war that has eroded substantial parts of the First Amendment.

Action is often a method of expression and within the protection of the First Amendment. One's beliefs have long been thought to be sanctuaries that government could not invade. The lines drawn by the Court between the criminal act of being an "active" Communist and the innocent act of being a nominal or inactive Communist mark the difference only between deep and abiding belief and casual or uncertain belief. But I think that all matters of belief are beyond the reach of subpoenas or the probings of investigators.

The example usually given by those who would punish speech is the case of one who falsely shouts fire in a crowded theatre. In my view, apart from rare instances of that kind, speech is immune from prosecution. The quality of advocacy turns on the depth of the conviction; and government has no power to invade that sanctuary of belief and conscience.

*****

[*Note:* In the 1951 *Dennis* case, sharply criticized by Justice Douglas in his *Brandenburg* concurring opinion, the defendants were convicted of conspiring in violation of the Smith Act to organize the Communist Party of the United States, which was alleged to be a group that taught and advocated the overthrow of the U.S. government. §2 of the Smith Act made it unlawful for any person "to knowingly or willfully advocate, abet, advise, or teach the duty, necessity, desirability, or propriety of overthrowing or destroying any government in the United States by force or violence, or by the assassination of any officer of such government." §3 of the Act made it "unlawful for any person to attempt to commit, or to conspire to commit, any of the acts" prohibited in §2.

The Supreme Court (6-2, Clark not participating) affirmed the convictions in the *Dennis* case. According to the plurality opinion, written by Chief Justice Fred Vinson (joined by Reed, Burton, and Minton), the appropriate test is the *Schenck* clear and present danger analysis and the government need not

> wait until the putsch is about to be executed, the plans have been laid and the signal is awaited.... The damage which such attempts create both physically and politically to a nation makes it impossible to measure the validity in terms of the probability of success, or the immediacy of a successful attempt.

Frankfurter and Jackson concurred in the judgment; Black and Douglas dissented.[3]

In a post-*Brandenburg* case, the Court reversed a disorderly conduct conviction in Hess v. Indiana, 414 U.S. 105 (1973). After a campus antiwar demonstration during which there had been arrests, over 100 demonstrators blocked the street until they were moved to the curb by the police. Hess, standing off the street, said: "We'll take the

---

[3]Concerning the *Dennis* case, see Stone, ibid., at 395–413.

fucking street later." The Court concluded that "At best, [the] statement could be taken as counsel for present moderation; at worst, it amounted to nothing more than advocacy of illegal action at some indefinite future time."]

United States v. O'Brien, 391 U.S. 367 (1968)

FACTS: O'Brien and three companions burned their Selective Service registration certificates in front of a crowd on the steps of the South Boston Courthouse. Immediately after the burning, members of the crowd began attacking O'Brien and his companions. After being ushered to safety inside the courthouse, informed of his right to counsel, and advised to remain silent, O'Brien stated to FBI agents that he had burned his registration certificate because of his beliefs, knowing that he was violating federal law. He produced the charred remains of the certificate, which, with his consent, were photographed.

O'Brien was indicted for violating the 1965 Amendment of the Universal Military Training and Service Act that imposes criminal penalties on any person "who forges, alters, knowingly destroys, knowingly mutilates, or in any manner changes any such certificate." At his trial, he did not contest the fact that he had burned the certificate. He stated to the jury that he burned the certificate publicly to influence others to adopt his antiwar beliefs, "so that other people would reevaluate their positions with Selective Service, with the armed forces, and reevaluate their place in the culture of today, to hopefully consider my position."

He was found guilty, and his conviction was affirmed by the Court of Appeals.

ISSUE: Was O'Brien's burning of his draft card protected under the First Amendment?

DECISION (per *Warren*, 7-1, Marshall not participating): *No.*

O'Brien argues that the 1965 Amendment is unconstitutional as applied to him because his act of burning his registration certificate was protected "symbolic speech" within the First Amendment. His argument is that the freedom of expression that the First Amendment guarantees includes all modes of "communication of ideas by conduct," and that his conduct is within this definition because he did it in "demonstration against the war and against the draft."

We cannot accept the view that an apparently limitless variety of conduct can be labeled "speech" whenever the person engaging in the conduct intends thereby to express an idea. However, even on the assumption that the alleged communicative element in O'Brien's conduct is sufficient to bring into play the First Amendment, it does not necessarily follow that the destruction of a registration certificate is constitutionally protected activity.

This Court has held that, when "speech" and "nonspeech" elements are combined in the same course of conduct, a sufficiently important governmental interest in regulating the nonspeech element can justify incidental limitations on First Amendment freedoms. To characterize the quality of the governmental interest that must appear, the Court in prior decisions has employed a variety of descriptive terms: compelling; substantial; subordinating; paramount; cogent; strong. Whatever imprecision inheres in those terms, we think it clear that a government regulation is sufficiently justified if it is within the constitutional power of the government; if it furthers an important or substantial governmental interest; if the governmental interest is unrelated to the suppression of free expression; and if the incidental restriction on alleged First Amendment freedoms is no greater than is essential to the furtherance of that interest.

The 1965 Amendment to the Universal Military Training and Service Act meets all of these requirements. The power of Congress to classify and conscript manpower for military service is beyond question. Pursuant to this power, Congress may establish a system of registration for individuals liable for training and service, and may require such individuals within reason to cooperate in the registration system. The issuance of certificates indicating the registration and eligibility classification of individuals is a legitimate and substantial administrative aid in the functioning of this system. And legislation to ensure the continuing availability of issued certificates serves a legitimate and substantial purpose in the system's administration. The registration certificate also serves other purposes; e.g., it proves that the described individual has registered for the draft; it facilitates communication between registrants and local boards; and it provides a reminder that the registrant must notify his local board of changes in address or status.

We think it apparent that the continuing availability to each registrant of his Selective Service certificates substantially furthers the smooth and proper functioning of the system that Congress has established to raise armies. We think it also apparent that the nation has a vital interest in having a system for raising armies that functions with maximum efficiency and is capable of easily and quickly responding to continually changing circumstances. For these reasons, the government has a substantial interest in ensuring the continuing availability of issued Selective Service certificates.

It is equally clear that the 1965 Amendment specifically protects this substantial governmental interest. We perceive no alternative means that would more precisely and narrowly insure the continuing availability of issued Selective Service certificates than a law that prohibits their willful mutilation or destruction. The 1965 Amendment prohibits such conduct and does nothing more. In other words, both the governmental interest and the operation of the 1965 Amendment are limited to the noncommunicative aspect of O'Brien's conduct. The governmental interest and the scope of the 1965 Amendment are limited to preventing harm to the smooth and efficient functioning of the Selective Service System. When O'Brien deliberately rendered unavailable his registration certificate, he willfully frustrated this governmental interest. For this noncommunicative impact of his conduct, and for nothing else, he was convicted.

Here, we find that a sufficient governmental interest has been shown to justify O'Brien's conviction because of the government's substantial interest in insuring the continuing availability of issued Selective Service certificates, because amended §462(b) is an appropriately narrow means of protecting this interest and condemns only the independent noncommunicative impact of conduct within its reach, and because the noncommunicative impact of O'Brien's act of burning his registration certificate frustrated the government's interest.

O'Brien further argues that the 1965 Amendment is unconstitutional as enacted because what he calls the "purpose" of Congress was "to suppress freedom of speech." In support of this argument, Johnson relies on the 1965 Amendment's legislative history containing several adverse comments by some Congressmen on antiwar protesters. We reject this argument because under settled principles the purpose of Congress, as O'Brien uses that term, is not a basis for declaring this legislation unconstitutional.

Inquiries into congressional motives or purposes are a hazardous matter. When the issue is simply the interpretation of legislation, the Court will look to statements by legislators for guidance as to the purpose of the legislature, because the benefit to sound decision making in this circumstance is thought sufficient to risk the possibility of misreading Congress's purpose. It is an entirely different matter when we are asked to void a statute that is, under well-settled criteria, constitutional on its face, on the basis of what fewer than a handful of Congressmen said about it. What motivates one legislator to make a speech about a statute is not necessarily what motivates scores of others to enact it, and the stakes are sufficiently high for us to eschew guesswork.

Harlan, concurring: I join in the Court's opinion but wish to make explicit my understanding that First Amendment claims are not foreclosed in those rare instances when an "incidental" restriction upon expression, imposed by a regulation that furthers an "important or substantial" governmental interest and satisfies the Court's other criteria, in practice has the effect of entirely preventing a "speaker" from reaching a significant audience with whom he could not otherwise lawfully communicate. This is not such a case, since O'Brien manifestly could have conveyed his message in many ways other than by burning his draft card.

Douglas, dissenting: The Court states that Congress's power "to classify and conscript manpower for military service is beyond question." This is undoubtedly true in times when, by declaration of Congress, the nation is in a state of war. The underlying and basic problem in this case, however, is whether conscription is permissible in the absence of a declaration of war. That question has not been briefed nor was it presented in oral argument; but it is, I submit, a question upon which the litigants and the country are entitled to a ruling.

The rule that this Court will not consider issues not raised by the parties is not inflexible and yields in "exceptional cases" to the need to correctly decide the case before the Court. This case should be put down for reargument.

Texas v. Johnson, 491 U.S. 397 (1989)

FACTS: A Texas criminal statute (in language similar to the laws of 47 other States) prohibited desecration of the American flag, making it illegal to "deface, damage or otherwise physically mistreat" a flag "in a way that the actor knows will seriously offend one or more persons likely to observe or discover his action." During the 1984 Republican National Convention in Dallas, Texas, Gregory Lee Johnson participated in a political demonstration to protest the policies of the Reagan administration. After a march through the city streets, Johnson burned an American flag while protesters chanted. No one was physically injured or threatened with injury, although several witnesses were seriously offended by the flag burning.

Johnson was convicted of violating the Texas statute. On appeal, the conviction was reversed by the Texas Court of Criminal Appeals, holding that the State could not, consistent with the First Amendment, punish Johnson for burning the flag in the circumstances involved. The State appealed to the U.S. Supreme Court.

ISSUE: Does Johnson's conviction violate his First Amendment right of free speech?

DECISION (per *Brennan,* 5-4): *Yes.*

The expressive, overtly political nature of Johnson's conduct was both intentional and overwhelmingly apparent. In these circumstances, Johnson's burning of the flag was conduct sufficiently imbued with elements of communication to implicate the First Amendment.

The government generally has a freer hand in restricting expressive conduct than it has in restricting the written or spoken word. It may not, however, proscribe particular conduct because it has expressive elements. It is, in short, not simply the verbal or non-verbal nature of the expression, but the governmental interest at stake, that helps to determine whether a restriction on that expression is valid.

In United States v. O'Brien, 391 U.S. 367 (1968), holding that a federal conviction for burning the defendant's draft card did not infringe the First Amendment, we recognized that where "'speech' and 'nonspeech' elements are combined in the same course of conduct, a sufficiently important governmental interest in regulating the nonspeech element can justify incidental limitations on First Amendment freedoms." However, we have limited the applicability of the relatively lenient *O'Brien* standard to those cases in which the governmental interest is unrelated to the suppression of free expression.

Texas claims that its interest in preventing breaches of the peace justifies Johnson's conviction for flag desecration. However, no disturbance of the peace actually occurred or threatened to occur because of Johnson's burning of the flag. The only evidence offered by the State at trial to show the reaction to Johnson's actions was the testimony of several persons who had been seriously offended by the flag burning. The State's position, therefore, amounts to a claim that an audience that takes serious offense at particular expression is necessarily likely to disturb the peace and that the expression may be prohibited on this basis.

Our precedents do not support such a presumption. On the contrary, they recognize that a principal function of free speech under our system of government is to invite dispute. It may indeed best serve its high purpose when it induces a condition of unrest, creates dissatisfaction with conditions as they are, or even stirs people to anger.

Thus, we have not permitted the government to assume that every expression of a provocative idea will incite a riot, but have instead required careful consideration of the actual circumstances surrounding such expression, asking whether the expression "is directed to inciting or producing imminent lawless action and is likely to incite or produce such action." Brandenburg v. Ohio, 395 U.S. 444, 447 (1969). That standard has not been met here.

The State also asserts an interest in preserving the flag as a symbol of nationhood and national unity. Under our decisions, such a claim must be subjected to the most exacting scrutiny. According to Texas, if one physically treats the flag in a way that would tend to cast doubt on either the idea that nationhood and national unity are the flag's referents or that national unity actually exists, the message conveyed thereby is a harmful one and therefore may be prohibited.

But if there is a bedrock principle underlying the First Amendment, it is that the government may not prohibit the expression of an idea simply because society finds the idea itself offensive or disagreeable. Our decisions have not recognized an exception to this principle even where our flag has been involved. We have held, for example, that a State may not criminally punish a person for uttering words critical of the flag. Nor may the government, we have held, compel conduct that would evince respect for the flag—compel, for example, public school students to salute the flag. West Virginia State Board of Education v. Barnette, 319 U.S. 624 (1943).

We are fortified in today's conclusion by our conviction that forbidding criminal punishment for conduct such as Johnson's will not endanger the special role played by our flag or the feelings it inspires. Our decision is a reaffirmation of the principles of freedom and inclusiveness that the flag best reflects, and of the conviction that our toleration of criticism such as Johnson's is a sign and source of our strength.

Kennedy, concurring: Sometimes we must make decisions we do not like. We make them because they are right, right in the sense that the law and the Constitution compel the result. I do not believe the Constitution gives us the right to rule as the dissenters urge, however painful this judgment is to announce. It is poignant but fundamental that the flag protects those who hold it in contempt. Johnson's acts were speech. I agree he must go free.

Rehnquist, dissenting (joined by White and O'Connor): The American flag, throughout more than 200 years of our history, has come to be the visible symbol embodying our nation. It does not represent the views of any particular political party, and it does not represent any particular political philosophy. The flag is not simply another "idea" or "point of view" competing for recognition in the marketplace of ideas. Millions of Americans regard it with an almost mystical reverence regardless of what sort of social, political, or philosophical beliefs they may have. I cannot agree that the First Amendment invalidates the laws of 48 of the 50 States, which make criminal the public burning of the flag.

But the Court insists that the Texas law infringes on Johnson's freedom of expression. Such freedom, of course, is not absolute. Johnson's public burning of the flag obviously did convey Johnson's bitter dislike of his country. But his act, like the "fighting words" that the Court has repeatedly held fall outside the First Amendment, conveyed nothing that could not have been conveyed just as forcefully in a dozen different ways. As with fighting words, so with flag burning, for purposes of the First Amendment.

Flag burning is the equivalent of an inarticulate grunt or roar that is most likely to be indulged in not to express any particular idea, but to antagonize others. The Texas statute deprived Johnson of only one rather inarticulate symbolic form of protest—a form of protest that was profoundly offensive to many—and left him with a full panoply of other symbols and every conceivable form of verbal expression to express his deep disapproval of national policy. Thus, in no way can it be said that Texas is punishing him because his hearers were profoundly opposed to the message that he sought to convey. It was Johnson's use of this particular symbol, and not the idea that he sought to convey, for which he was punished.

Uncritical extension of constitutional protection to the burning of the flag risks the frustration of the very purpose for which organized governments are instituted. The Court decides that the American flag is just another symbol, about which not only must opinions pro and con be tolerated, but for which the most minimal public respect may not be enjoined. The government may conscript men into the Armed Forces where they may die for the flag, but the government may not prohibit the public burning of the banner under which they fight. I would uphold the Texas statute as applied in this case.

Stevens, dissenting: A country's flag is a symbol of more than nationhood and national unity. It is also a symbol of freedom, of equal opportunity, of religious tolerance, and of goodwill for other peoples who share our aspirations. The value of the flag as a symbol cannot be measured. Even so, I have no doubt that the interest in preserving that value for the future is both significant and legitimate.

The content of Johnson's message has no relevance whatsoever to the case. Moreover, the case has nothing to do with "disagreeable ideas." It involves disagreeable conduct that, in my opinion, diminishes the value of an important national asset. The Court is therefore quite wrong in blandly asserting that Johnson "was prosecuted for his expression of dissatisfaction with the policies of this country." Johnson was prosecuted because of the method he chose to express his dissatisfaction with those policies. Had he chosen to spray-paint his message of dissatisfaction on the facade of the Lincoln Memorial, there would be no question about the power of the government to prohibit his means of expression. Though the asset at stake in this case is intangible, given its unique value, the same interest supports a prohibition on the desecration of the American flag.

*****

[*Note:* In response to the public furor over the decision in this case, Congress quickly adopted the Flag Protection Act of 1989 in an effort to impose a flag-burning prohibition on the federal level. The statute was promptly violated in order to challenge its constitutionality, and the result was United States v. Eichman, 496 U.S. 310 (1990), striking down the 1989 law, once again in a 5-to-4 decision.

Subsequent attempts to adopt a constitutional amendment overruling the *Johnson* and *Eichman* decisions have proved unsuccessful.]

R. A. V. v. St. Paul, 505 U.S. 377 (1992)

FACTS: R. A. V., a teenager, allegedly assembled a crudely made cross out of broken chair legs and burned it inside the fenced yard of an African American family that lived across the street from where he was staying. The City of St. Paul charged R. A. V. with violating the St. Paul Bias-Motivated Crime Ordinance, which provides that

> Whoever places on public or private property a symbol, object, appellation, characterization or graffiti, including, but not limited to, a burning cross or Nazi swastika, which one knows or has reasonable grounds to know arouses anger, alarm or resentment in others on the basis of race, color, creed, religion or gender, commits disorderly conduct and shall be guilty of a misdemeanor.

The trial court dismissed the charges on the ground that the ordinance was substantially overbroad and impermissibly content-based, and therefore facially invalid under the First and Fourteenth Amendments. On appeal, the Minnesota Supreme Court reversed, upholding the validity of the law.

ISSUE: Does the St. Paul ordinance violate the First and Fourteenth Amendments?

DECISION (per *Scalia,* 9-0): *Yes.*

I. Assuming, *arguendo,* that all of the expression reached by the ordinance is proscribable under the "fighting words" doctrine, we nonetheless conclude that the ordinance is facially unconstitutional in that it prohibits otherwise permitted speech solely on the basis of the subjects the speech addresses.

The First Amendment generally prevents government from proscribing speech, or even expressive conduct, because of disapproval of the ideas expressed. Content-based regulations are presumptively invalid. From 1791 to the present, however, our society, like other free but civilized societies, has permitted restrictions upon the content of speech in a few limited areas (such as obscenity, defamation, and fighting words), which are of such slight social value as a step to truth that any benefit that may be derived from them is clearly outweighed by the social interest in order and morality.

We have sometimes said that these categories of expression are "not within the area of constitutionally protected speech," or that the "protection of the First Amendment does not extend" to them. But such statements must be taken in context. What they mean is that these areas of speech can, consistently with the First Amendment, be regulated because of their constitutionally proscribable content—not that they are categories of speech entirely invisible to the Constitution. Thus, the government may proscribe libel, but it may not make the further content discrimination of proscribing only libel critical of the government. Nor could a city council enact an ordinance prohibiting only those legally obscene works that contain criticism of the city government.

The proposition that a particular instance of speech can be proscribable on the basis of one feature (for example, obscenity) but not on the basis of another (for example, opposition to the city government) is commonplace and has found application in many contexts. We have long held, for example, that nonverbal expressive activity can be banned because of the action it entails, but not because of the ideas it expresses—so that burning a flag in violation of an ordinance against outdoor fires could be punishable, whereas burning a flag in violation of an ordinance against dishonoring the flag is not. And just as the power to proscribe particular speech on the basis of a noncontent element (for example, noise) does not entail the power to proscribe the same speech on the basis of a content element, so also the power to proscribe it on the basis of one content element, (for example, obscenity) does not entail the power to proscribe it on the basis of other content elements.

Thus, the exclusion of fighting words from the scope of the First Amendment simply means that, for purposes of that amendment, the unprotected features of the words are, despite their verbal character, essentially a "nonspeech" element of communication. Fighting words are thus analogous to a noisy sound truck: both can be used to convey an idea, but neither has, in and of itself, a claim upon the First Amendment. As with the sound truck, however, so also with fighting words: The government may not regulate use based on hostility—or favoritism—towards the underlying message expressed.

However, even the prohibition against content discrimination is not absolute. When the basis for the content discrimination consists entirely of the very reason the entire class of speech at issue is proscribable, no significant danger of idea or viewpoint discrimination exists. Such a reason, having been adjudged neutral enough to support exclusion of the entire class of speech from First Amendment protection, is also neutral enough to form the basis of distinction within the class.

To illustrate: a State might choose to prohibit only that obscenity which is the most patently offensive in its prurience—i.e., that which involves the most lascivious displays of sexual activity. But it may not prohibit, for example, only that obscenity which includes offensive political messages. And the federal government can criminalize only those threats of violence that are directed against the president, since the reasons why threats of violence are outside the First Amendment have special force when applied to the person of the president. But the federal government may not criminalize only those threats against the president that mention his policy on aid to inner cities.

Another valid basis for according differential treatment to even a content-defined subclass of proscribable speech is that the subclass happens to be associated with particular "secondary effects" of the speech, so that the regulation is "justified without reference to the content of the ... speech," Renton v. Playtime Theatres, Inc., 475 U.S. 41, 48 (1986). A State could, for example, permit all obscene live performances except those involving minors. Moreover, since words can in some circumstances violate laws directed not against speech, but against conduct (a law against treason, for example, is violated by telling the enemy the Nation's defense secrets), a particular content-based subcategory of a proscribable class of speech can be swept up incidentally within the reach of a statute directed at conduct, rather than speech. Thus, for example, sexually derogatory "fighting words," among other words, may produce a violation of Title VII's general prohibition against sexual discrimination in employment practices, 42 U.S.C. 2000e-2; 29 CFR 1604.11 (1991). Where the government does not target conduct on the basis of its expressive content, acts are not shielded from regulation merely because they express a discriminatory idea or philosophy.

II. Applying these principles to the St. Paul ordinance, we conclude that, even as narrowly construed by the Minnesota Supreme Court to apply only to fighting words, the remaining terms of the ordinance make clear that it applies only to fighting words that insult, or provoke violence, "on the basis of race, color, creed, religion or gender." Displays containing abusive invective, no matter how vicious or severe, are permissible unless they are addressed to one of the specified disfavored topics. Those who wish to use fighting words in connection with other ideas—to express hostility, for example, on the basis of political affiliation, union membership, or homosexuality— are not covered. The First Amendment does not permit St. Paul to impose special prohibitions on those speakers who express views on disfavored subjects.

Under the St. Paul ordinance, displays containing some words—odious racial epithets, for example—would be prohibited to proponents of all views. But fighting words that do not themselves invoke race, color, creed, religion, or gender—aspersions upon a person's mother, for example—would seemingly be usable freely by those arguing in favor of racial, color, etc., tolerance and equality, but could not be used by that speaker's opponents. One could hold up a sign saying, for example, that all "anti-Catholic bigots" are misbegotten, but not that all "papists" are, for that would insult and provoke violence "on the basis of religion." St. Paul has no such authority to license one side of a debate to fight freestyle, while requiring the other to follow Marquis of Queensbury Rules.

Finally, St. Paul argues that, even if the ordinance regulates expression based on hostility towards its protected ideological content, this discrimination is nonetheless justified because it is narrowly tailored to serve compelling state interests in protecting the rights of members of groups that have historically been subjected to discrimination. We do not doubt that these interests are compelling, but the dispositive question in this case is whether content discrimination is reasonably necessary to achieve St. Paul's compelling interests; it plainly is not. An ordinance not limited to the favored topics, for example, would have precisely the same beneficial effect. In fact, the only interest distinctively served by the content limitation is that of displaying the city council's special hostility toward the particular biases thus singled out. That is precisely what the First Amendment forbids. The politicians of St. Paul are entitled to express that hostility—but not through the means of imposing unique limitations upon speakers who disagree.

Let there be no mistake about our belief that burning a cross in someone's front yard is reprehensible. But St. Paul has sufficient means at its disposal to prevent such behavior without adding the First Amendment to the fire.

White, concurring (joined by Blackmun and O'Connor and in part by Stevens): I agree with the majority that the judgment below should be reversed. However, our agreement ends there. This case could easily be decided within the contours of established First Amendment law by holding, as the defendant argues, that the St. Paul ordinance is fatally overbroad because it criminalizes not only unprotected expression but expression protected by the First Amendment. The Court instead holds the ordinance facially unconstitutional on a ground that requires serious departures from the teaching of prior cases.

Today, the Court announces that earlier Courts did not mean their repeated statements that certain categories of expression are "not within the area of constitutionally protected speech." The majority holds that the First Amendment protects those narrow categories of expression long held to be undeserving of First Amendment protection— at least to the extent that lawmakers may not regulate some fighting words more strictly than others because of their content. Should the government want to criminalize certain fighting words, the Court now requires it to criminalize all fighting words.

It is inconsistent to hold that the government may proscribe an entire category of speech because the content of that speech is evil, but that the government may not treat a subset of that category differently without violating the First Amendment. The content of the subset is, by definition, worthless and undeserving of constitutional protection.

The Court has patched up its argument with an apparently nonexhaustive list of ad hoc exceptions, in what can be viewed either as an attempt to confine the effects of its decision to the facts of this case, or as an effort to anticipate some of the questions that will arise from its radical revision of First Amendment law.

Thus the Court posits that certain content-based regulations will survive under the new regime if the regulated subclass "happens to be associated with particular 'secondary effects' of the speech . . . ," which the majority treats as encompassing instances in which "words can . . . violate laws directed not against speech, but against conduct. . . ." Under the general rule the Court applies in this case, Title VII hostile work environment claims would suddenly be unconstitutional.

Title VII of the Civil Rights Act of 1964 is similar to the St. Paul ordinance that the majority condemns because it imposes special prohibitions on speakers who express views on disfavored subjects. Under the broad principle the Court uses to decide the present case, hostile work environment claims based on sexual harassment should fail First Amendment review; because a general ban on harassment in the workplace would cover the problem of sexual harassment, any attempt to proscribe the subcategory of sexually harassing expression would violate the First Amendment.

Hence, the exception, which the Court indicates would insulate a Title VII hostile work environment claim from an underinclusiveness challenge because "sexually derogatory 'fighting words'... may produce a violation of Title VII's general prohibition against sexual discrimination in employment practices." But application of this exception to a hostile work environment claim does not hold up under close examination.

First, the hostile work environment regulation is keyed to the impact of the speech on the victimized worker. Consequently, the regulation would no more fall with a secondary effects exception than does the St. Paul ordinance. Second, the majority's focus on the statute's general prohibition on discrimination glosses over the language of the specific regulation governing hostile working environment, which reaches beyond any "incidental" effect on speech. United States v. O'Brien, 391 U.S. 367, 376 (1968). If the relationship between the broader statute and specific regulation is sufficient to bring the Title VII regulation within O'Brien, then all St. Paul need do to bring its ordinance within this exception is to add some prefatory language concerning discrimination generally.

Although I disagree with the Court's analysis, I do agree with its conclusion: the St. Paul ordinance is unconstitutional. However, I would decide the case on overbreadth grounds. A defendant being prosecuted for speech or expressive conduct may challenge the law on its face if it reaches protected expression, even when that person's activities are not protected by the First Amendment. This is because the possible harm to society in permitting some unprotected speech to go unpunished is outweighed by the possibility that protected speech of others may be muted. Although the ordinance, as construed, reaches categories of speech that are constitutionally unprotected, it also criminalizes a substantial amount of expression that —however repugnant—is shielded by the First Amendment.

Blackmun, concurring: I do not see the compromise of First Amendment values in a law that prohibits hoodlums from driving minorities from their homes by burning crosses on their lawns, but I do see harm in preventing St. Paul from punishing race-based fighting words that prejudice the community. I concur in the judgment, however, because I agree that this particular ordinance reaches beyond fighting words to speech protected by the First Amendment.

Stevens, concurring (joined in part by White and Blackmun): I agree that the St. Paul ordinance is overbroad, but I am troubled by the majority's conclusion that the ordinance is an unconstitutional content-based regulation of speech. The Court establishes a near-absolute ban on content-based regulations of expression and holds that the First Amendment prohibits the regulation of fighting words by subject matter. This fails to recognize the role and constitutional status of content-based regulations on speech.

The scope of the First Amendment is determined by the content of expressive activity. Indeed, whether speech falls within one of the categories of unprotected or proscribable expression is determined, in part, by the speech's content. Therefore, it can scarcely be said that the regulation of expressive activity cannot be predicated on its content.

Further, the Court applies the prohibition on content-based regulation to speech that the Court had, until today, considered wholly unprotected. This new absolutism in the prohibition of content-based regulations severely contorts the fabric of settled First Amendment law and gives fighting words more protection than they had before.

I do not believe that all content-based regulations are equally infirm and are presumptively invalid. I would conclude that a more complex and subtle analysis—one that considers the content and context of the regulated speech, and also the nature and scope of the restriction on speech—is necessary. Under such a view, even if the St. Paul ordinance did regulate fighting words based on its subject matter, such a regulation would, in my opinion, be constitutional. Were it not overbroad, I would vote to uphold it.

Virginia v. Black, 538 U.S. 343 (2003)

FACTS: A Virginia statute makes it a felony "for any person. . . , with the intent of intimidating any person or group. . . , to burn . . . a cross on the property of another, a highway or other public place" and provides that "[a]ny such burning . . . shall be *prima facie* evidence of an intent to intimidate a person or group." Barry Black, Richard Elliott, and Jonathan O'Mara were each convicted of violating the statute in two separate incidents.

Black led a Ku Klux Klan rally on an open field just off a state highway. During the rally, attended by 25 to 30 people, Klan members "talked real bad about the blacks and the Mexicans," and "One speaker told the assembled gathering that "he would love to take a .30/.30 and just random[ly] shoot the blacks." At the end of the rally, the crowd circled around a 25- to 30-foot cross located between 300 and 350 yards away from the road. The cross "then all of a sudden . . . went up in a flame."

Elliott and O'Mara attempted to burn a cross on the yard of James Jubilee, an African American who was Elliott's next-door neighbor and had recently moved to Virginia. Before the cross burning, Jubilee asked Elliott's mother about shots being fired from behind the Elliott home. Elliott's mother told Jubilee that her son shot firearms as a hobby and used the backyard as a firing range. Shortly thereafter, Elliott and O'Mara drove a truck onto Jubilee's property, planted a cross, and set it on fire. Their apparent motive was to "get back" at Jubilee for complaining about the shooting in the backyard.

In Black's trial, the trial judge instructed the jury that "the burning of a cross by itself is sufficient evidence from which you may infer the required intent." In Elliott's trial, the judge did not instruct the jury on the meaning of the word "intimidate," nor on the *prima facie* provision of the statute. The juries in both the Black and Elliott cases found the defendants guilty. O'Mara pleaded guilty, but reserved the right to challenge the constitutionality of the statute.

On appeal the Virginia Supreme Court, relying on R. A. V. v. St. Paul, 505 U.S. 377 (1992), held that the statute was unconstitutional under the First Amendment because it discriminates on the basis of content and viewpoint by prohibiting cross burning because of its distinctive message. The court further held that the *prima facie* provision renders the statute overbroad because the enhanced probability of prosecution chills the expression of protected speech.

ISSUES: (1) Is the First Amendment violated by a State's prohibition of the burning of a cross with the intent to intimidate? (2) Is the *prima facie* evidence provision valid?

DECISION: (1) On the first issue, the Court (6-3) held that a State, consistent with the First Amendment, may ban cross burning carried out with the intent to intimidate.

(2) On the second issue, although none of the several opinions was joined by a majority on this issue, the Court (7-2) held that the *prima facie* provision was unconstitutional.

O'Connor (joined by Rehnquist, Stevens, Scalia, and Breyer on the first issue, and joined by Rehnquist, Stevens, and Breyer on the second issue):

(1) Burning a cross in this country is inextricably intertwined with the history of the Ku Klux Klan, which, following its formation in 1866, imposed a reign of terror throughout the South. The Klan has often used cross burnings as a tool of intimidation and a threat of impending violence, although such burnings have also remained potent symbols of shared group identity and ideology, serving as a central feature of Klan gatherings. To this day, however, regardless of whether the message is a political one or is also meant to intimidate, the burning of a cross is a symbol of hate.

The protections the First Amendment affords speech and expressive conduct are not absolute. This Court has long recognized that certain categories of expression may be regulated consistently with the Constitution. For example, the First Amendment permits a State to ban "true threats," which encompass those statements where the speaker means to communicate a serious expression of an intent to commit an act of unlawful violence to a particular individual or group of individuals. The speaker need not actually intend to carry out the threat. Rather, a prohibition on true threats protects individuals from the fear of violence and the disruption that fear engenders, as well as from the possibility that the threatened violence will occur.

Intimidation in the constitutionally proscribable sense of the word is a type of true threat, where a speaker directs a threat to a person or group of persons with the intent of placing the victim in fear of bodily harm or death. As the history of cross burning in this country shows, that act is often intimidating, intended to create a pervasive fear in victims that they are a target of violence.

The First Amendment permits Virginia to outlaw cross burnings done with the intent to intimidate because burning a cross is a particularly virulent form of intimidation. Instead of prohibiting all intimidating messages, Virginia may choose to regulate this subset of intimidating messages in light of cross burning's long and pernicious history as a signal of impending violence.

A ban on cross burning carried out with the intent to intimidate is fully consistent with *R. A. V. v. St. Paul*, 505 U.S. 377 (1992). Contrary to the Virginia Supreme Court's ruling, *R. A. V.* did not hold that the First Amendment prohibits *all* forms of content-based discrimination within a proscribable area of speech. Unlike the ordinance at issue in *R. A. V.,* the Virginia statute does not single out for opprobrium only speech directed toward one of the specified disfavored topics. Under the statute, it does not matter whether an individual burns a cross with intent to intimidate because of the victim's race, gender, or religion, or with intent to intimidate because of the victim's political affiliation, union membership, homosexuality, or any other reason.

(2) However, the Virginia statute's *prima facie* evidence provision is invalid on its face.

As construed by the trial court's instruction in Black's case, the *prima facie* provision permits a jury to convict in every cross-burning case in which defendants exercise their constitutional right not to put on a defense. And even where a defendant like Black presents a defense, the provision makes it more likely that the jury will find an intent to intimidate regardless of the particular facts of the case. It permits the State to arrest, prosecute, and convict a person based solely on the fact of cross burning itself. As so interpreted, it would create an unacceptable risk of the suppression of ideas.

The act of burning a cross may mean that a person is engaging in constitutionally proscribable intimidation, or it may mean only that the person is engaged in core political speech. The *prima facie* provision blurs the line between these meanings, ignoring all of the contextual factors that are necessary to decide whether a particular cross burning is intended to intimidate. The First Amendment does not permit such a shortcut.

Thus, Black's conviction cannot stand, and we accordingly affirm the reversal of his conviction. With respect to Elliott and O'Mara, the judgment below is vacated and the case remanded to the Virginia Supreme Court for its determination whether the *prima facie* provision is severable and if so, whether Elliott and O'Mara could be retried under the statute.

Stevens, concurring: Cross burning with "an intent to intimidate" clearly qualifies as the kind of threat that is unprotected by the First Amendment. For the reasons stated in my separate opinion in *R. A. V.,* that simple proposition provides a sufficient basis for upholding the basic prohibition in the Virginia statute even though it does not cover other types of threatening expressive conduct. With this observation, I join the Court's opinion.

Scalia, concurring in part and (joined by Thomas) dissenting in part: I agree that under *R. A. V.* a state may, without infringing the First Amendment, prohibit cross burning carried out with the intent to intimidate. I believe, however, that there is no justification for the plurality's apparent decision to invalidate the *prima facie* provision on its face.

Souter, concurring in part and dissenting in part (joined by Kennedy and Ginsburg): The Virginia statute makes a content-based distinction within the category of punishable intimidating expression—the very type of distinction we considered in invalidating the law challenged in the *R. A. V.* case. But furthermore, even under a pragmatic recasting of *R. A. V.,* no content-based statute should survive without a high probability that no official suppression of ideas is threatened. I believe the *prima facie* evidence provision stands in the way of finding such a high probability here. Its primary effect is to skew jury deliberations toward conviction in cases where the evidence of intent to intimidate is relatively weak and arguably consistent with a solely ideological reason for burning.

I conclude that the Virginia statute violates the First Amendment. In my view, severance of the *prima facie* provision could not eliminate the invalidity of the whole statute at the time of the defendants' conduct. I would therefore affirm the judgment below reversing all three convictions.

Thomas, dissenting: In every culture, certain things acquire meaning well beyond what outsiders can comprehend. That goes for both the sacred and the profane. I believe that cross burning is the paradigmatic example of the latter.

Although I agree with the majority's conclusion that it is constitutionally permissible to ban cross burning carried out with intent to intimidate, I believe that the majority errs in imputing an expressive component to the activity in question. In my view, whatever expressive value cross burning has, the legislature simply wrote it out by banning only intimidating conduct undertaken by a particular means. A conclusion that this statute sweeps beyond a prohibition on certain conduct into the zone of expression overlooks not only the words of the statute but also reality. Because I would uphold the statute's constitutionality and therefore sustain the three convictions, I respectfully dissent.

Cohen v. California, 403 U.S. 15 (1971)

FACTS: While in a corridor of the Los Angeles County Courthouse, Cohen wore a jacket bearing the words "Fuck the Draft." There were women and children present in the corridor. He was convicted of violating a California state statute that prohibited "maliciously and willfully disturbing the peace or quiet of any neighborhood or person by offensive conduct," and he was sentenced to 30 days in jail.

At his trial, Cohen testified that he wore the jacket as a means of informing others of his deep anti–Vietnam War sentiments. At no time did Cohen engage in or threaten to engage in any act of violence; nor did anyone else engage in such activity as a result of his conduct.

On appeal, Cohen's conviction was affirmed by the California Court of Appeal. The court construed the statutory term "offensive conduct" to mean behavior that has a tendency to provoke others to acts of violence or to in turn disturb the peace, and held that it was reasonably foreseeable that Cohen's wearing the jacket might cause others to commit violent acts against him or attempt forcibly to remove the jacket.

ISSUE: Under the First and Fourteenth Amendments, was the defendant's speech punishable as a disturbance of the peace?

DECISION (per *Harlan,* 5-4): *No.*

Cohen's conviction rests squarely upon his exercise of the "freedom of speech" protected from arbitrary governmental interference by the Constitution and can be justified, if at all, only as a valid regulation of the manner in which he exercised that freedom, not as a permissible prohibition on the substantive message it conveys. This does not end the inquiry, of course, for the First and Fourteenth Amendments have never been thought to give absolute protection to every individual to speak whenever or wherever he pleases, or to use any form of address in any circumstances that he chooses.

In the first place, Cohen was tried under a statute applicable throughout the entire State. Any attempt to support this conviction on the ground that the statute seeks to preserve an appropriately decorous atmosphere in the courthouse where Cohen was arrested must fail in the absence of any language in the statute that would have put appellant on notice that certain kinds of otherwise permissible speech or conduct would nevertheless not be tolerated in certain places.

Second, this is not an obscenity case. It cannot plausibly be maintained that Cohen's vulgar allusion to the Selective Service System would conjure up erotic stimulation in anyone likely to be confronted with Cohen's crudely defaced jacket.

Third, Cohen's jacket plainly does not fall within the exception for so-called "fighting words," those personally abusive epithets that, when addressed to the ordinary citizen, are, as a matter of common knowledge, inherently likely to provoke violent reaction. Here, however, no individual actually or likely to be present could reasonably have regarded the words on Cohen's jacket as a direct personal insult.

Fourth, we do not have here an instance of the exercise of the State's police power to prevent a speaker from intentionally provoking a given group to hostile reaction. There was no showing that anyone who saw Cohen was, in fact, violently aroused or that Cohen intended such a result.

Finally, much has been made of the claim that Cohen's distasteful mode of expression was thrust upon unwilling or unsuspecting viewers, and that the state might therefore legitimately act as it did in order to protect the sensitive from otherwise unavoidable exposure to Cohen's crude form of protest. Of course, the mere presumed presence of unwitting listeners or viewers does not serve automatically to justify curtailing all speech capable of giving offense. While this Court has recognized that government may properly act in many situations to prohibit intrusion into the privacy of the home of unwelcome views and ideas that cannot be totally banned from the public dialogue, we have at the same time consistently stressed that we are often captives outside the sanctuary of the home and subject to objectionable speech. The ability of government, consonant with the Constitution, to shut off discourse solely to protect others from hearing it is, in other words, dependent upon a showing that substantial privacy interests are being invaded in an essentially intolerable manner. Any broader view of this authority would effectively empower a majority to silence dissidents simply as a matter of personal predilections.

In this regard, persons confronted with Cohen's jacket were in a quite different posture than, say, those subjected to the raucous emissions of sound trucks blaring outside their residences. Those in the Los Angeles courthouse could effectively avoid further bombardment of their sensibilities simply by averting their eyes. And, while it may be that one has a more substantial claim to a recognizable privacy interest when walking through a courthouse corridor than, for example, strolling through Central Park, surely it is nothing like the interest in being free from unwanted expression in the confines of one's own home. Given the subtlety and complexity of the factors involved, if Cohen's "speech" was otherwise entitled to constitutional protection, we do not think the fact that some unwilling "listeners" in a public building may have been briefly exposed to it can serve to justify this breach of the peace conviction where, as here, there was no evidence that persons powerless to avoid his jacket did, in fact, object to it, and where the statute on which Cohen's conviction rests indiscriminately sweeps within its prohibitions all "offensive conduct" that disturbs any one.

Against this background, the issue presented here stands out in bold relief. It is whether California can excise, as "offensive conduct," one particular scurrilous epithet from the public discourse, either upon the theory that its use is inherently likely to cause violent reaction or upon a more general assertion that the states, acting as guardians of public morality, may properly remove this offensive word from the public vocabulary.

The rationale of the California court is plainly untenable. We have been shown no evidence that substantial numbers of citizens are standing ready to strike out physically at whoever may assault their sensibilities with execrations like that uttered by Cohen. The argument amounts to little more than the self-defeating proposition that, in order to avoid physical censorship of one who has not sought to provoke such a response, the States may effectuate that censorship themselves.

The principle contended for by the State seems inherently boundless. How is one to distinguish this from any other offensive word? Surely the State has no right to cleanse public debate to the point where it is grammatically palatable to the most squeamish among us. Yet no readily ascertainable general principle exists for stopping short of that result were we to affirm the judgment below. For, while the particular four-letter word being litigated here is perhaps more distasteful than most others of its genre, it is nevertheless often true that one man's vulgarity is another's lyric.

Additionally, we cannot overlook the fact (well illustrated by the episode involved here) that much linguistic expression serves a dual communicative function: it conveys not only ideas capable of relatively precise, detached explication, but otherwise inexpressible emotions as well. In fact, words are often chosen as much for their emotive as their cognitive force. We cannot sanction the view that the Constitution, while solicitous of the cognitive content of individual speech, has little or no regard for that emotive function that may often be the more important element of the overall message sought to be communicated.

Moreover, and in the same vein, we cannot indulge the facile assumption that one can forbid particular words without also running a substantial risk of suppressing ideas in the process. Indeed, governments might soon seize upon the censorship of particular words as a convenient guise for banning the expression of unpopular views.

In sum, absent a more particularized and compelling reason for its actions, a State may not, consistently with the First and Fourteenth Amendments, make the simple public display of this single four-letter expletive a criminal offense.

Blackmun, dissenting (joined by Burger and Black, and by White with respect to Paragraph 2): I dissent for two reasons: First, Cohen's absurd and immature antic, in my view, was mainly conduct and little speech. Further, the case appears to me to be well within the fighting words exception to freedom of speech. As a consequence, the Court's agonizing over First Amendment values seems misplaced and unnecessary. Second, since a later decision of the California Supreme Court adopted what appears to be a narrower interpretation of the statute that Cohen was convicted of violating, this case should be remanded for reconsideration in the light of the later decision.

*****

[*Note:* As pointed out in Justice Harlan's opinion, *Cohen* "is not an obscenity case," for "It cannot plausibly be maintained that Cohen's vulgar allusion to the Selective Service System would conjure up erotic stimulation in anyone likely to be confronted with Cohen's crudely defaced jacket."

Obscene (unlike "offensive" or "indecent") speech is not within the area of constitutionally protected speech or press. To regulate speech as obscene, the government must meet all three of the following tests: (1) "the average person, applying contemporary community standards, would find that the work, taken as a whole, appeals to the prurient interest," *and* (2) "the work depicts or describes, in a patently offensive way, sexual conduct specifically defined by the applicable state law," *and* (3) "the work, taken as a whole, lacks serious literary, artistic political, or scientific value." Miller v. California, 413 U.S. 15 (1973).]

Offensive Speech under the First Amendment

"Cohen's crudely defaced jacket" was clearly expressing a political message, and arguably the case could have been decided on that narrow basis. But the Court's opinion goes beyond the protection of political messages and articulates a far broader principle—that the government may not prohibit or punish speech just because others might find it offensive or indecent.

In an exception to that principle, FCC v. Pacifica Foundation, 438 U.S. 726 (1978), the Court (5-4) upheld the authority of the Federal Communications Commission to prohibit and punish indecent language over federally licensed television and radio frequencies. However, in cases involving other communications media—telephones, cable television, and the Internet—the Court has distinguished its *Pacifica* holding on various grounds and has struck down federal regulations prohibiting indecent speech.

Sable Communications v. FCC, 492 U.S. 115 (1989), invalidated (6-3) a federal statute prohibiting indecent as well as obscene telephone calls. The Court declared that "Sexual expression which is indecent but not obscene is protected by the First Amendment" and that the challenged "statute's denial of adult access to such messages far exceeds that which is necessary to serve the compelling interest of preventing minors from being exposed to the messages."

In United States v. Playboy Entertainment Group, Inc., 529 U.S. 803 (2000), the Court (5-4) held unconstitutional a provision of the federal Cable Act that required cable television channels "primarily dedicated to sexually-oriented programming" to either "fully scramble or otherwise fully block" those channels or to limit their transmission to hours when children are unlikely to be viewing. This provision, the Court held, is a content-based restriction on speech and therefore can stand only if it satisfies strict scrutiny. On that predicate, the majority concluded that the statute was not "narrowly tailored" because the statute's purpose could be effectively achieved by a far less restrictive alternative provided in the act (the option of subscribers to block adult-oriented channels).

In Ashcroft v. American Civil Liberties Union, 542 U.S. 656 (2004), the Court (5-4) held unconstitutional the federal Child Online Protection Act, aimed at protecting children from exposure to sexual material on the Internet. The Court held that the government had failed to meet its burden of showing that less restrictive alternatives (particularly the use of blocking and filtering software) would not be equally effective in achieving Congress's goal.

"Hate Speech"

Offensive speech concerning, for example, race, religion, or gender is sometimes called "hate speech." But calling it "hate speech" does not change the basic constitutional principles or create a category of speech that is more subject to government regulation than other types of offensive speech. Unless it meets the requirements of an established exception to First Amendment protection (e.g., "fighting words," a narrow exception limited to intimidating speech that is directed to a specific individual and tends to cite an immediate breach of the peace), it is entitled to the same protection as other speech.

However, as the next-digested case *Wisconsin v. Mitchell* illustrates, the First Amendment does not preclude imposing a more severe sentence for violent crimes motivated by bias or "hate" against members of racial minorities and other designated groups.

Speech Codes

Notwithstanding *Cohen* and other Supreme Court decisions protecting "offensive speech" under the First Amendment, hundreds of state universities and colleges have adopted "speech codes" prohibiting and penalizing speech that expresses bias or hate or "insensitivity" toward minorities or women.

The University of Michigan, for example, adopted a regulation subjecting individuals to discipline for "[any] behavior, verbal or physical, that stigmatizes or victimizes an individual on the basis of race, ethnicity, religion, sex, sexual orientation, creed, national origin, ancestry, age, marital status, handicap or Viet-Nam era veteran status," which "has the purpose or reasonably foreseeable effect of interfering with an individual's academic efforts, employment, participation in University sponsored extracurricular activities or personal safety." A federal district court held that the regulation was unconstitutional under the First Amendment as overbroad and too vague. Doe v. University of Michigan, 721 F.Supp. 852 (E.D. Mich. 1989).

Similarly, a federal district court struck down a University of Wisconsin speech code that prohibited, among other things, "discriminatory comments" directed at an individual that "intentionally ... demean" the "sex ... of the individual" and "[c]reate an intimidating, hostile or demeaning environment for education, university related work, or other university-authorized activity." UWM Post, Inc. v. Board of Regents of University of Wisconsin System, 774 F. Supp. 1163 (E.D. Wis. 1991). College speech codes have also been struck down by courts in California and Pennsylvania.[4]

Although such speech codes have generally been rejected or withdrawn by public institutions whenever they have been challenged on First Amendment grounds by threat of court action, speech codes in the American workplace are flourishing.

Title VII of the 1964 Civil Rights Act provides that it is an unlawful employment practice for an employer "to discriminate against any individual with respect to his compensation, terms, conditions, or privileges of employment because of such individual's race, color, religion, sex, or national origin." Successful plaintiffs may recover substantial damages; complaints may also be filed with the Equal Employment Opportunities Commission (EEOC).

"Discrimination" under Title VII has been defined to include sexual or racial "harassment"—either (1) "*quid pro quo*" sexual harassment (typically involving a claim that a female employee was pressured by the employer to submit to sexual advances) or (2) sexual or racial harassment creating a "hostile work environment."[5] To be actionable under Title VII, the Supreme Court has held, a hostile work environment must be "sufficiently severe or pervasive to alter the conditions of the victim's employment and create an abusive working environment."[6]

---

[4]Speech codes are also widely prevalent in private universities and colleges (which are not subject to court challenges under the First Amendment). Tufts University, for example, prohibits (among other things) "[h]arassment or discrimination against individuals on the basis of race, religion, gender identity/expression, ethnic or national origin, gender, sexual orientation, disability, age, or genetics," including "*attitudes or opinions that are expressed verbally or in writing*" (italics added). In May 2007, a Tufts disciplinary board (composed largely of faculty members) found that the policy was violated by a student newspaper that criticized the repression of civil liberties in Islamic countries. The board did not question the truth of any of the statements but found that "Muslim students felt psychologically intimidated by the piece," which "created a hostile environment for them."

[5]EEOC Guidelines provide the most commonly accepted definition of "sexual harassment"—"*verbal or physical conduct* of a sexual nature [that] has the purpose or effect of unreasonably interfering with an individual's work performance or creating an intimidating, hostile, or offensive work environment." (Italics added.) This definition has been adapted to fit cases of racial harassment as well.

[6]Meritor Savings Bank v. Vinson, 477 U.S. 57, 67 (1986). In Harris v. Forklift Systems, Inc., 510 U.S. 17 (1993), the Court added the requirement that the challenged conduct must be severe or pervasive enough to create an objectively hostile or abusive work environment that a reasonable person would find hostile or abusive.

Harassment creating a hostile work environment is frequently found on the basis of offensive speech that is not protected by the Amendment, such as sexual demands, threats, obscene propositions, obscene pictures, and "fighting words."

But many cases have also found harassment on the basis (in whole or in substantial part) of offensive speech that the First Amendment, outside the workplace, does protect—including content-based comments, jokes, magazines, and cartoons that insult of annoy women or minorities.[7] Indeed, courts have acknowledged that the very purpose of Title VII is to "prevent . . . bigots from expressing their opinions in a way that abuses or offends their co-workers."[8]

The result is to suppress content-based expression that in other contexts is protected by the First Amendment.[9] Moreover, it is not required that the employer himself have uttered the offensive speech. The employer is held responsible if he knew or should have known of the offensive speech contributing to the hostile work environment and failed to take corrective action. The fear of such liability creates a powerful incentive for employers to censor the speech of their employees.[10]

In an effort to justify the regulation of speech otherwise regarded as protected, offensive speech is sometimes characterized as "conduct" rather than speech.[11] But if offensive speech is protected by the First Amendment—i.e., if it does not fall into one of the traditionally unprotected categories such as obscenity or "fighting words"—changing the label to "conduct" does not change its communicative character. As pointed out in the comment "Symbolic Speech" in this chapter, *nonverbal conduct* may in some instances (e.g., flag burning) be recognized as speech; even more clearly, *verbal conduct* (i.e., speech) constitutes speech.

Nor does it lose its protected status because it offends someone; that indeed is the very nature of offensive speech. For example, "Cohen's crudely defaced jacket" no doubt outraged the sensibilities of some who saw it at the courthouse, and the Nazi march in Skokie, Illinois, was no doubt terrifying to many Skokie residents, but in both cases the courts ruled that the offensiveness musct be tolerated because of the higher demands of the First Amendment.

Nor does offensive speech, if otherwise protected, lose its protection because the effect of the speech—such as a hostile work environment—is legislatively or administratively declared illegal. By that standard, the freedom of speech guaranteed by the Constitution could readily be made a dead letter.

In R. A. V. v. St. Paul, 505 U.S. 377 (1992), digested in this chapter, the Court dealt tangentially with the constitutionality of Title VII. At issue was an ordinance

[7]See, e.g., Eugene Volokh, "What Speech Does 'Hostile Work Environment' Harassment Law Restrict?" 85 *Georgetown Law Review* 627 (1997); Kingsley Browne, "Title VII as Censorship: Hostile-Environment Harassment and the First Amendment," 52 *Ohio State Law Journal* 481 (1991).
[8]Davis v. Monsanto Chemical Co., 858 F.2d 345, 350 (6th Cir. 1988), cert. denied, 490 U.S. 1110 (1989); Andrews v. City of Philadelphia, 895 F.2d 1469, 1486 (3d Cir. 1990) (quoting *Davis*).
[9]Compare, e.g., Hustler Magazine, Inc. v. Falwell, 485 U.S. 46, 52-53 (1988) (holding protected a "parody" portraying the plaintiff as engaged in "a drunken incestuous rendezvous with his mother in an outhouse"); NAACP v. Claiborne Hardware Co., 458 U.S. 886, 921 (1982) (reversing a judgment against the NAACP that had been based upon a boycott against certain white-owned businesses, and holding that a judgment that rests, or might rest in part, upon protected expression is invalid.
[10]Kingsley Browne, "Title VII as Censorship: Hostile-Environment Harassment and the First Amendment," 52 *Ohio State Law Journal* 481, 483 (1991).
[11]Lindemann and Kadue, *Primer on Sexual Harassment* [BNA Books 1992]: 598; Jon Gould, *Speak No Evil: The Triumph of Hate Speech Regulation* [Chicago 2005]: 133; Kingsley Browne, "Title VII as Censorship: Hostile-Environment Harassment and the First Amendment," 53 *Ohio State Law Journal* 481 (1991).

prohibiting a form of "fighting words." Although "fighting words" is a class of speech unprotected by the First Amendment, the majority held that the ordinance was nevertheless invalid because the ordinance (applicable only to disfavored subjects of "race, color, creed, religion, or gender") was content-based. Apparently in response to the dissenters' claim that such an interpretation of the First Amendment would also invalidate Title VII, the majority opinion observed that "a *proscribable* class of speech can be swept up incidentally within the reach of a statute directed at conduct, rather than speech. . . . Thus, for example, sexually derogatory 'fighting words,' among other words, may produce a violation of Title VII's general prohibition against sexual discrimination in employment practices." (Page 389, italics added.) While that may be true of a proscribable (unprotected) class of speech, such as fighting words, the Court's opinion is silent on whether *protected* speech may be similarly utilized.

Although Title VII was enacted nearly half a century ago, there still remains an apparent direct conflict between what Title VII forbids in the workplace and what the Constitution otherwise protects.[12]

Wisconsin v. Mitchell, 508 U.S. 476 (1993)

FACTS: A Wisconsin statute provides that the maximum penalty for an offense shall be increased whenever the defendant "intentionally selects the person against whom the crime . . . is committed . . . because of the race, religion, color, disability, sexual orientation, national origin or ancestry of that person."

Mitchell and several other black men discussed a scene from the motion picture *Mississippi Burning,* in which a white man beat a young black boy who was praying. Mitchell asked the others: "Do you all feel hyped up to move on some white people?" Shortly thereafter, a young white boy approached the group on the opposite side of the street where they were standing. As the boy walked by, Mitchell said: "You all want to fuck somebody up? There goes a white boy; go get him." Mitchell counted to three and pointed in the boy's direction. The group ran towards the boy and beat him severely. The boy was rendered unconscious and remained in a coma for four days.

After a jury trial, Mitchell was convicted of aggravated battery, an offense that ordinarily carries a maximum sentence of two years' imprisonment. But the Wisconsin penalty enhancement law, because the jury found that Mitchell had intentionally selected his victim because of the boy's race, increased the maximum to seven years. The trial court sentenced Mitchell to four years' imprisonment.

On appeal, the Wisconsin Supreme Court reversed the conviction. The court, relying on R. A. V. v. St. Paul, 505 U.S. 377 (1992), held that the statute violates the First and Fourteenth Amendments by punishing what the legislature has deemed to be offensive thought. According to the court, "the Wisconsin legislature cannot criminalize bigoted thought with which it disagrees." The court also held that the statute would have a "chilling effect" on free speech because, in order to prove that a defendant intentionally selected his victim because of the victim's protected status, the state would often have to introduce evidence of the defendant's prior statements, such as racial epithets he may have uttered before the commission of the offense.

[12]See Cynthia Estlund, "Freedom of Expression in the Workplace and the Problem of Discriminatory Harassment," 75 *Texas Law Review* 688 (1997) ("most courts adjudicating harassment suits either avoid the issue or assume that the speech allegedly contributing to a hostile environment is unprotected"); Gould, *Speak No Evil: The Triumph of Hate Speech Regulation,* 30: "[T]here remains a lingering sense that other factors may have driven this doctrinal schism—a view that the courts may have responded as much to extralegal forces as to precedent."

ISSUE: May a state criminal statute constitutionally provide for increased punishment because of the defendant's discriminatory motive or reason for acting?

DECISION (per *Rehnquist,* 9-0): *Yes.*

Under the Wisconsin statute, the same criminal conduct may be more heavily punished if the victim is selected because of his race or other protected status than if no such motive obtained. Thus, although the statute punishes criminal conduct, it enhances the maximum penalty for conduct motivated by a discriminatory point of view more severely than the same conduct engaged in for some other reason or for no reason at all. Because the only reason for the enhancement is the defendant's discriminatory motive for selecting his victim, Mitchell argues (and the Wisconsin Supreme Court held) that the statute violates the First Amendment by punishing offenders' bigoted beliefs.

Traditionally, sentencing judges have considered a wide variety of factors in addition to evidence bearing on guilt in determining what sentence to impose on a convicted defendant. The defendant's motive for committing the offense is one important factor. Thus, in many States, the commission of a murder or other capital offense for pecuniary gain is a separate aggravating circumstance under the capital sentencing statute.

The Constitution does not erect a per se barrier to the admission of evidence concerning one's beliefs and associations at sentencing simply because those beliefs and associations are protected by the First Amendment. Thus, in Barclay v. Florida, 463 U.S. 939 (1983), we held that it was permissible for the sentencing court to consider the defendant's racial animus in determining whether he should be sentenced to death, surely the severest "enhancement" of all. And the fact that the Wisconsin Legislature has decided, as a general matter, that bias-motivated offenses warrant greater maximum penalties across the board does not alter the result here, for the primary responsibility for fixing criminal penalties lies with the legislature.

Mitchell argues that the Wisconsin penalty-enhancement statute is invalid because it punishes the defendant's discriminatory motive, or reason, for acting. But motive plays the same role under the Wisconsin statute as it does under federal and state antidiscrimination laws, which we have previously upheld against constitutional challenge. Title VII of the Civil Rights Act of 1964, for example, makes it unlawful for an employer to discriminate against an employee "because of such individual's race, color, religion, sex, or national origin." In Hishon v. King & Spalding, 467 U.S. 69, 78 (1984), we rejected the argument that Title VII infringed employers' First Amendment rights.

Nothing in our *R. A. V.* decision compels a different result here. That case involved a First Amendment challenge to a municipal ordinance prohibiting the use of "fighting words that insult, or provoke violence, on the basis of race, color, creed, religion or gender." Because the ordinance only proscribed a class of fighting words deemed particularly offensive by the city—i.e., those "that contain . . . messages of bias-motivated hatred," we held that it violated the rule against content-based discrimination. But whereas the ordinance struck down in *R. A. V.* was explicitly directed at expression, the statute in this case is aimed at conduct unprotected by the First Amendment.

Moreover, the Wisconsin statute singles out bias-inspired conduct for enhancement because this conduct is thought to inflict greater individual and societal harm. It is widely believed, for example, that bias-motivated crimes are more likely to provoke retaliatory crimes, inflict distinct emotional harms on their victims, and incite community unrest. The State's desire to redress these perceived harms provides an adequate explanation for its penalty-enhancement provision over and above mere disagreement with offenders' beliefs or biases.

For the foregoing reasons, we hold that Mitchell's First Amendment rights were not violated by the application of the Wisconsin penalty-enhancement provision in sentencing him.

Federal Hate Crime Laws

"Hate crime" laws of the type challenged in *Wisconsin v. Mitchell* do not criminalize conduct that is not already illegal. Instead of adding new prohibitions, such laws *increase the punishment* for violating already-existing criminal statutes of general applicability (statutes that prohibit, for example, homicide or other crime regardless of the identity of the victim) if it is proved that the crime was motivated by bias against a member of one of the protected groups.

In addition to such punishment-enhancing laws, some criminal statutes—also characterized as hate crime laws—specifically prohibit conduct injuring members of certain protected groups.

A federal statute adopted in 1969 (18 U.S.C. 245(b)(2)) provides for prosecution of conduct that "by force or threat of force willfully injures, intimidates or interferes with, or attempts to injure, intimidate or interfere with . . . any person [1] because of his race, color, religion or national origin and [2] because he is or has been" engaging in specified federally protected activities (such as voting, serving on a jury, or traveling in interstate commerce). Penalties for covered offenses involving firearms are prison terms of up to ten years, while offenses involving murder, kidnapping, or sexual assault are subject to life imprisonment or the death penalty.

The 1969 law would be significantly expanded if it were amended by a bill known as the Local Law Enforcement Hate Crimes Prevention Act. The bill would expand present law in two major respects: First, it would eliminate the requirement of the 1969 statute that the victim be engaged in federally protected activity. Second, the bill would expand the current prohibition to cover violent crime motivated by the "actual or *perceived* race, color, religion, national origin, *gender, sexual orientation, gender identity or disability of any person*" (additions italicized).

The bill was approved in 2007 by both the House and Senate. It was passed by the Senate as part of the proposed Defense Authorization Act, which President Bush indicated he would veto if it included the hate crimes provision. In December 2007, while the proposed Defense Authorization Act was under consideration by a Senate-House conference committee, the hate crimes provision was removed before submittal of the legislation to the President for approval.

Freedom of Expressive Association

The First Amendment has been read as implicitly protecting people's right to associate with each other for expressive purposes. The Court has recognized that "freedom to engage in association for the advancement of beliefs and ideas is an inseparable aspect of the 'liberty' assured by the Due Process Clause of the Fourteenth Amendment, which embraces freedom of speech." NAACP v. Alabama ex. rel. Patterson, 357 U.S. 449, 460 (1958).

In that case, the Court held unconstitutional an Alabama law requiring the NAACP to disclose its membership lists. The Court declared: "Inviolability of privacy in group association may in many circumstances be indispensable to preservation of freedom of association, particularly where a group espouses dissident beliefs."

Issues concerning freedom of association arise in a variety of other contexts. For example, in the next digested case, *Boy Scouts of America v. Dale,* the Court held that New Jersey could not require the Boy Scouts to reinstate an openly gay scoutmaster.

On the other hand, in upholding an order under a Minnesota law prohibiting the Jaycees from excluding women from full membership, the Court rejected the claim that the State was violating the members' First Amendment freedom of association. Roberts v. United States Jaycees, 468 U.S. 609 (1984). The Court relied on the very large size of the organization, its nearly indiscriminate membership requirements, and the extensive participation of nonmembers in the group's activities. The Court found that the club did not involve the kind of "intimate or private" relation or expressive activity that warrants constitutional protection.

Freedom of association may also be invoked to protect organizations from state interference in the way they express their views. The *Hurley* case cited in the *Boy Scouts* majority opinion concerned the validity of an order under the Massachusetts antidiscrimination law requiring a veterans group that organized the Boston St. Patrick's Day parade to allow an Irish-American gay group to carry a gay rights banner in the parade. The veterans group contended that allowing such participation would introduce a "sexual theme" into a parade that was intended to focus on "traditional religious and social values." The Supreme Court unanimously held that organizing a parade was an inherently expressive activity and that it violated the First Amendment to require the organizers to promote a message that they did not want to promote.

Boy Scouts of America v. Dale, 530 U.S. 640 (2000)

FACTS: The Boy Scouts of America (BSA) is a private, not-for-profit organization engaged in instilling its system of values in young people and asserts that homosexual conduct is inconsistent with those values. Dale was an assistant scoutmaster of a New Jersey troop. When BSA learned that Dale is an avowed homosexual and gay rights activist, his position as an assistant scoutmaster was terminated.

Dale filed suit in the New Jersey Superior Court, alleging that BSA had violated the New Jersey statute prohibiting discrimination on the basis of sexual orientation in places of public accommodation. The trial court granted summary judgment for BSA, but that decision was reversed by the New Jersey Supreme Court, which concluded that BSA violated the State's public accommodations law by revoking Dale's membership based on his avowed homosexuality. The court held that application of that law did not violate the BSA's First Amendment right of expressive association because Dale's inclusion would not significantly affect members' ability to carry out their purposes and that Dale's reinstatement did not compel BSA to express any message.

ISSUE: Does requiring BSA to retain Dale as an assistant scoutmaster, under New Jersey's public accommodations law, violate BSA's First Amendment right of expressive association?

DECISION (per *Rehnquist,* 5-4): *Yes.*

Intrusion into a group's internal affairs by forcing it to accept a member it does not desire is unconstitutional if the person's presence affects in a significant way the group's ability to advocate public or private viewpoints. However, the freedom of expressive association is not absolute; it can be overridden by regulations adopted to serve compelling state interests, unrelated to the suppression of ideas, that cannot be achieved through means significantly less restrictive of associational freedoms.

The record clearly shows that BSA engages in "expressive association" when its adult leaders inculcate its youth members with its value system. Thus, the Court must determine whether the forced inclusion of Dale would significantly affect BSA's ability to advocate public or private viewpoints.

The Court gives deference to BSA's position that homosexual conduct is inconsistent with the values embodied in the Scout Oath and Law, particularly those represented by the terms "morally straight" and "clean," and that the organization does not want to promote homosexual conduct as a legitimate form of behavior. Dale's presence as an assistant scoutmaster would significantly burden the expression of those viewpoints and interfere with BSA's choice not to propound a point of view contrary to its beliefs.

BSA's ability to disseminate its message would be significantly affected by the forced inclusion of Dale. First, contrary to the New Jersey Supreme Court's view, an association need not associate for the purpose of disseminating a certain message in order to be protected, but must merely engage in expressive activity that could be impaired. Second, even if BSA discourages Scout leaders from disseminating views on sexual issues, its method of expression is protected. Third, the First Amendment does not require that every member of a group agree on every issue in order for the group's policy to be expressive association.

We apply here an analysis similar to the strict scrutiny analysis applied in Hurley v. Irish-American Gay Group of Boston, 515 U.S. 557 (1995), unanimously upholding the First Amendment right of a private sponsor of a Boston St. Patrick's Day parade to exclude an Irish-American gay group from participating in the parade.

A requirement that BSA retain Dale would significantly burden the organization's right to oppose or disfavor homosexual conduct. The State's interests embodied in its public accommodations law do not justify such a severe intrusion on BSA's freedom of expressive association. While the law may promote all sorts of conduct in place of harmful behavior, it may not interfere with speech for no better reason than promoting an approved message or discouraging a disfavored one, however enlightened either purpose may be.

Stevens, dissenting (joined by Souter, Ginsburg, and Breyer): The majority holds that New Jersey's law violates BSA's right to associate and its right to free speech. But that law does not impose any serious burdens on BSA's collective effort on behalf of its shared goals, nor does it force BSA to communicate any message that it does not wish to endorse. New Jersey's law, therefore, abridges no constitutional right of BSA.

First, to prevail on a claim of expressive association in the face of a state's antidiscrimination law, it is not enough simply to engage in *some kind* of expressive activity. Second, it is not enough to adopt an openly avowed exclusionary membership policy. Third, it is not sufficient merely to articulate *some* connection between the group's expressive activities and its exclusionary policy.

The evidence before this Court makes it exceptionally clear that BSA has, at most, simply adopted an exclusionary membership policy and has no shared goal of disapproving of homosexuality. BSA's mission statement and federal charter say nothing on the matter; its official membership policy is silent; its Scout Oath and Law—and accompanying definitions—are devoid of any view on the topic; its guidance for Scouts and Scoutmasters on sexuality declare that such matters are "not construed to be Scouting's proper area," but are the province of a Scout's parents and pastor; and BSA's posture respecting religion tolerates a wide variety of views on the issue of homosexuality. Moreover, there is simply no evidence that BSA otherwise teaches anything in this area, or that it instructs Scouts on matters involving homosexuality in ways not conveyed in the Boy Scout or Scoutmaster Handbooks. In short, BSA is simply silent on homosexuality. There is no shared goal or collective effort to foster a belief about homosexuality at all—let alone one that is significantly burdened by admitting homosexuals.

I am unaware of any previous instance in which our analysis of the scope of a constitutional right was determined by looking at what a litigant asserts in his or her brief and inquiring no further. An organization can adopt the message of its choice, and it is not this Court's place to disagree with it. But we must inquire whether the group is, in fact, expressing a message (whatever it may be) and whether that message (if one is expressed) is significantly affected by a State's antidiscrimination law. More critically, that inquiry requires our *independent* analysis, rather than deference to a group's litigating posture. In this case, it is entirely clear that BSA in fact expresses no clear, unequivocal message burdened by New Jersey's law.

The majority does not rest its conclusion on the claim that Dale will use his position as a bully pulpit to propagate homosexuality. Rather, it contends that Dale's mere presence among the Boy Scouts will itself force the group to convey a message about homosexuality—even if Dale has no intention of doing so. The only apparent explanation for the majority's holding, then, is that homosexuals are simply so different from the rest of society that their presence alone—unlike any other individual's—should be singled out for special First Amendment treatment. Under the majority's reasoning, the openness of an openly gay male is the sole and sufficient justification for his ostracism. Though unintended, reliance on such a justification is tantamount to a constitutionally prescribed symbol of inferiority.

Souter, dissenting (joined by Ginsburg and Breyer): The right of expressive association does not, of course, turn on the popularity of the views advanced by a group that claims protection. Whether the group appears to this Court to be in the vanguard or rearguard of social thinking is irrelevant to the group's rights. I conclude that BSA has not made out an expressive association claim, not because of what BSA may espouse, but because of its failure to make sexual orientation the subject of any unequivocal advocacy, using the channels it customarily employs to state its message. As Justice Stevens explains, no group can claim a right of expressive association without identifying a clear position to be advocated over time in an unequivocal way.

If, on the other hand, an expressive association claim has met the conditions Justice Stevens describes as necessary, there may well be circumstances in which the antidiscrimination law must yield, as he says. It is certainly possible for an individual to become so identified with a position as to epitomize it publicly. When that position is at odds with a group's advocated position, applying an antidiscrimination statute to require the group's acceptance of the individual in a position of group leadership could so modify or muddle or frustrate the group's advocacy as to violate the expressive associational right.

The Aftermath of the *Boy Scouts* Decision

The "FAIR" Case

Because of their opposition to the federal prohibition against gays serving in the armed forces, a large number of colleges and universities prohibited or restricted access on their campuses to military recruiters. In response, Congress enacted a statute known as the Solomon Amendment providing that, as a condition of receiving federal funding, colleges and universities must grant the same access to military recruiters as they do to any other recruiters.

Forum for Academic and Institutional Rights, Inc. (FAIR), is an association of law schools and law faculties, whose members have policies opposing discrimination based on, *inter alia,* sexual orientation. When the schools were threatened with a cutoff of federal funding under the Solomon Amendment, FAIR sued claiming that the law violated their First Amendment rights. Relying primarily on the *Boy Scouts* decision, they claimed that their denial of equal access to military recruiters was a constitutionally protected way of expressing their opposition to the federal policy on gays.

The Court of Appeals for the Third Circuit upheld (2-1) the law schools' contention, but the Supreme Court unanimously reversed (8-0, Alito not participating). Rumsfeld v. Forum for Academic and Institutional Rights, Inc., ___ U.S. ___, 126 S.Ct. 1297 (2006). In an opinion by Chief Justice Roberts, the Court distinguished the *Boy Scouts* decision in rejecting the First Amendment claim.

The Court concluded that "The Solomon Amendment neither limits what law schools may say nor requires them to say anything, all the while maintaining eligibility for federal funds. . . ." According to the Court, the schools are not "speaking" when they host interviews and recruiting receptions. They are instead facilitating recruitment to assist their students in obtaining jobs. Thus, a law school's recruiting services lack the expressive quality of, for example, the Boston gay parade held to be protected communication in Hurley v. Irish-American Gay Group of Boston, 515 U.S. 557 (1995). The Court held that nothing about recruiting suggests that law schools agree with any speech by recruiters, and that nothing in the Solomon Amendment restricts what they may say about the military's policies.

The Court further held that the Solomon Amendment does not violate the law schools' freedom of expressive association. Unlike the order rejected in the *Boy Scouts* case, the Solomon Amendment does not force a law school "to accept members it does not desire." Law schools "associate" with military recruiters only in the sense that they interact with them, but recruiters are not part of the school. They are instead outsiders who come onto campus for the limited purpose of trying to hire students—not to become members of the school's expressive association.

The Boy Scouts of America Equal Access Act

The Supreme Court decision in *Boy Scouts of America v. Dale* sparked efforts in many communities to deny Boy Scouts the use of public facilities for their meetings and activities. Congress responded by passing (as part of the No Child Left Behind Act of 2001) the Boy Scouts of America Equal Access Act. The Act provides that no public school receiving federal financial assistance

> shall deny equal access or a fair opportunity to meet to, or discriminate against, any group officially affiliated with the Boy Scouts of America . . . that wishes to conduct a meeting

within that designated open forum or limited public forum, including denying such access or opportunity or discriminating for reasons based on the membership or leadership criteria or oath of allegiance to God and country of the Boy Scouts of America.

Campaign Regulation and the First Amendment

In recent years one of the most important and controversial issues under the First Amendment has been the constitutionality of various types of restrictions imposed on contributions and expenditures in connection with federal elections.

The three leading cases are Buckley v. Valeo, 424 U.S. 76 (1974), McConnell v. Federal Election Commission, 540 U.S. 93 (2003), and Federal Election Commission v. Wisconsin Right to Life, Inc., ___ U.S. ___, 127 S.Ct. 2652 (2007).

Buckley, involving a challenge to the 1974 amendments to the Federal Election Campaign Act, upheld the principle that contributing or spending money in connection with federal elections is a form of political speech protected by the First Amendment. The Court, however, drew a sharp distinction between contribution limits and the expenditure limits, upholding the former and invalidating the latter. The Court viewed expenditure limits as restricting the nature and quantity of political speech, but saw little direct effect on political speech through limits on contributions and accordingly recognized a broader congressional power to regulate contributions. The Court also emphasized that restrictions on the amount that a person or group could contribute to any particular candidate were justified to prevent "the actuality and appearance of corruption resulting from large individual financial contributions," but that independent expenditures to support a candidate do not have the same risk of corruption or the appearance of corruption.

In 2002, Congress adopted the McCain-Feingold law, known as the Bipartisan Campaign Reform Act (BRCA). A primary purpose of BRCA was to place limits on the use of unregulated "soft money" and to require candidates to finance their campaigns primarily with "hard money"—federally regulated contributions to candidates by individual citizens (not to exceed $2,000 per citizen for each election for each candidate). Toward that end, BRCA establishes a highly detailed code of restrictions governing the financing of campaigns. Violations of the restrictions are subject to heavy criminal penalties.

The two main changes were the following:

1. *Ban on "Soft Money" Contributions:* The amendment prohibits national, state, district or local political party committees from directly or indirectly soliciting funds for, or making or directing contributions to, either

   (1) a political party or other political organization or

   (2) a tax-exempt corporation that makes expenditures in connection with an election for federal office (including but not limited to spending money for voter registration, voter identification, or get-out-the-vote activities, promotion of a political party, or advertising that refers to a clearly identified candidate for federal office and promotes or supports, or attacks or opposes, a candidate for that office).

2. *Ban on "Electioneering Communications":* §203 of the act prohibits all corporations (including nonprofit advocacy groups) and unions from paying for an "electioneering communication," defined as

   (1) a television or radio communication that

(2) refers to a clearly identified candidate for federal office, and

(3) is made within a "blackout period"—60 days before a general election or 30 days before a primary election.

The only ads that §203 allows a corporation or union to run during a "blackout" period are "issue ads" that contain no reference to any candidate.

In addition, any person (not just corporations and unions) who makes disbursements for the cost of "electioneering communications" in the aggregate amount of $10,000 in any calendar year must within 24 hours file with the Federal Election Commission a statement containing full details of the expenditure.

(Excluded from the definition of "electioneering communications" is any "communication appearing in a news story, commentary, or editorial distributed through the facilities of any broadcasting station, unless such facilities are owned or controlled by any political party, political committee, or candidate.")

In 2003 in the *McConnell* case, the Supreme Court by a 5-to-4 decision upheld the constitutionality of these new restrictions "on their face"—i.e., without precluding later challenges to the act as applied in particular circumstances. Because of the complexity of the statute and the variety of views among the justices, the eight opinions in *McConnell* total 298 pages in the official report.

While acknowledging that "Money, like water, will always find an outlet," the majority concluded that "In the main we uphold BCRA's two principal, complementary features: the control of soft money and the regulation of electioneering communications."

In sustaining the §203 prohibition on electioneering communications, *McConnell* held that the First Amendment does not bar the regulation of ads that either expressly support or oppose a candidate's election or are their *functional equivalent.* The decision, however, did not address the question of what criteria should be used in categorizing a specific ad—whether it is a "functional equivalent" of an ad expressly supporting or opposing a candidate's election (and therefore prohibited) or is instead an "issue ad" (and therefore unregulated).

That question was presented in the *Wisconsin Right to Life* case. The ads in question were placed by Wisconsin Right to Life, Inc. (WRTL), a nonprofit corporation engaged in advocacy on political issues. In 2004 WRTL sponsored three radio ads opposing filibusters on federal judicial appointments and urging people to "Contact Senators Feingold and Kohl and tell them to oppose the filibuster." The ads were to be run during a preelection "blackout" period when Feingold, but not Kohl, was running for reelection. Emphasizing the content of the ads, WRTL argued (with the support of such diverse advocacy groups as the American Civil Liberties Union and the National Rifle Association) that the ads were constitutionally protected "grassroots lobbying" on the filibuster issue.

In an opinion by Chief Justice Roberts (joined by Scalia, Kennedy, Thomas, and Alito), the Court (5-4) held that an ad can be deemed the "functional equivalent" of a campaign ad "only if the ad is susceptible of no reasonable interpretation other than as an appeal to vote for or against a specific candidate." According to the majority, "Discussion of issues cannot be suppressed simply because the issues may also be pertinent in an election. Where the First Amendment is implicated, the tie goes to the speaker, not the censor." On that basis, the Court concluded that the three WRTL ads could not be constitutionally prohibited.

In light of that conclusion, Roberts and Alito stated that they found it unnecessary to revisit the *McConnell* holding that §203 on its face does not violate the First Amendment. In a concurring opinion, three justices (Scalia, Kennedy, and Thomas) went further, urging that the *McConnell* §203 ruling be explicitly overruled. And the four dissenters (Stevens, Breyer, Souter, and Ginsburg) claimed that the practical effect of the majority decision, despite its disclaimer, was to overrule the *McConnell* §203 ruling without saying so.

*****

The prediction of the *McConnell* majority that "Money, like water, will always find an outlet"—despite statutory restraints—has since been amply confirmed.

In the 2004 campaign, notwithstanding the 2002 Act, record amounts of funds were spent on behalf of the presidential and congressional candidates. This was accomplished in part through "soft money" raised through so-called "independent" political committees—known as "527 organizations"—dedicated to supporting certain candidates but ostensibly expending funds without coordination with the favored candidates or their parties. Although obliged to disclose their donors and expenditures, these organizations can raise money from corporations, unions, and wealthy individuals without the limits applicable to campaigns and parties.

In the 2004 campaign, 527s spent $550.6 million in support of candidates. At least 46 people contributed $1 million or more to 527s; one of the 46 gave $26 million, and another gave $23 million.[13]

In the 2004 campaign, in addition to the money spent by candidates and 527s, approximately $30 billion ("by conservative estimate") was spent by nonprofit groups—known as "501c organizations"—in promoting voter registration and turnout and in sponsoring political "issue advertising." These 501c organizations are not only tax-exempt but (unlike 527s) are not required to disclose either their expenditures or the sources of their funds.[14]

In the November 2006 midterm election, spending by candidates and 527s reached new records. On advertising alone, more than $2 billion was spent in the campaign—$400 million more than the $1.6 billion spent in the 2004 presidential campaign.[15]

The expenditures for the 2008 presidential and congressional elections are expected to exceed $5.3 billion, and the cost of the presidential race alone will likely exceed $2.4 billion—50 percent more than the 2004 campaign.[16]

---

[13]*New York Times,* December 17, 2004.

[14]*Washington Post,* August 21, 2004.

[15]*Washington Post,* November 3, 2006.

[16]*New York Times,* December 2, 2007; *USA Today,* October 23, 2008.

11

Freedom of the Press

The News Media and the First Amendment

The First Amendment explicitly protects not only freedom of speech but also freedom of the press. In large measure, the standards of constitutionality are the same whether applied to expressive activities of the press or expressive activities of others.

But there are also some constitutional issues that uniquely apply to the press. For example, the Supreme Court has held that taxes aimed specifically at the press are invalid. E.g., Grosjean v. American Press Co., 297 U.S. 233 (1936). An obvious concern is that otherwise the government could use taxes to punish the press for harsh criticism or aggressive reporting.

On the other hand, just as the press should not be saddled with special burdens, the Court has generally taken the view that the press is not entitled to any special rights or protections under the First Amendment. The press therefore can be required to pay taxes applicable generally to all businesses and must likewise comply with other statutes of general applicability (such as the Fair Labor Standards Act and the federal antitrust and labor laws). E.g., Associated Press v. United States, 326 U.S. 1 (1945).

The press has claimed that the First Amendment exempts it from complying with subpoenas that require disclosure of the identity of confidential sources. That position, however, was rejected (5-4) by the Supreme Court in Branzburg v. Hayes, 408 U.S. 665 U.S. (1972), holding that reporters have no special exemption from grand jury subpoenas. The Court concluded that "the public interest in law enforcement" is sufficient "to override the consequential, but uncertain, burden on news gathering that is said to result from insisting that reporters, like other citizens, respond to relevant questions put to them in the course of a valid grand jury investigation or criminal trial." The Court also noted that accepting the argument for a special constitutional privilege would create serious problems in defining who should be regarded as a member of the press and therefore entitled to refuse to answer questions.

A large number of States have enacted "shield laws" that in varying degrees protect reporters from having to disclose their sources. No comparable federal law now exists. However, on October 16, 2007, the House of Representatives approved a bill to protect the confidentiality of reporters' sources in most federal court cases. President Bush, contending that the bill would encourage leaks of classified information, threatened a veto. The Senate has not yet acted on the measure.

Near v. Minnesota, 283 U.S. 697 (1931)

FACTS: A Minnesota law authorized enjoining, as a public nuisance, a "malicious, scandalous and defamatory newspaper, or other periodical." Pursuant to that law, the county attorney for Hennepin County filed an action to stop publication of a Minneapolis newspaper called *The Saturday Press.*

The newspaper had published articles charging in substance "that a Jewish gangster was in control of gambling, bootlegging and racketeering in Minneapolis, and that law enforcing officers and agencies were not energetically performing their duties." The newspaper especially targeted the Minneapolis chief of police, who was charged with several loosely defined offenses, such as "illicit relations with gangsters [and] participation in graft."

A state court perpetually enjoined the defendants from publishing or circulating "any publication whatsoever which is a malicious, scandalous or defamatory newspaper." The Minnesota Supreme Court affirmed.

ISSUE: Does the injunction violate the Fourteenth Amendment?

DECISION (*Hughes,* 5-4): *Yes.*

It is no longer open to doubt that the liberty of the press and of speech is within the liberty safeguarded by the Due Process Clause of the Fourteenth Amendment from invasion by state action.

The object of the statute is not punishment, in the ordinary sense, but suppression of the offending newspaper. The reason given for the enactment is that prosecutions to enforce penal statutes for libel do not result in "efficient repression or suppression of the evils of scandal." The operation and effect of the statute is that public authorities may bring the owner or publisher of a newspaper or periodical before a judge upon a charge of conducting a business of publishing scandalous and defamatory matter, and unless the owner or publisher is able to prove that the charges are true and are published with good motives and for justifiable ends, his newspaper or periodical is suppressed and further publication is made punishable as a contempt. This is of the essence of censorship.

The question is whether a statute authorizing such proceedings is consistent with the conception of the liberty of the press as historically conceived and guaranteed. In determining the extent of the constitutional protection, it has been generally, if not universally, considered that it is the chief purpose of the guaranty to prevent previous restraints upon publication. The struggle in England, directed against the legislative power of the licenser, resulted in renunciation of the censorship of the press. The liberty deemed to be established was thus described by Blackstone: "The liberty of the press is indeed essential to the nature of a free state; but this consists in laying no *previous* restraints upon publications, and not in freedom from censure for criminal matter when published."

The protection even as to previous restraint is not absolutely unlimited. But the limitation has been recognized only in exceptional cases. No one would question but that a government might prevent actual obstruction to its recruiting service or the publication of the sailing dates of transports or the number and location of troops. On similar grounds, the primary requirements of decency may be enforced against obscene publications. The security of the community life may be protected against incitements to acts of violence and the overthrow by force of orderly government. These limitations are not applicable here.

The fact that for approximately 150 years there has been almost an entire absence of attempts to impose previous restraints upon publications relating to the malfeasance of public officers is significant of the deep-seated conviction that such restraints would violate constitutional right. Public officers, whose character and conduct remain open to debate and free discussion in the press, find their remedies for false accusations in actions under libel laws providing for redress and punishment, and not in proceedings to restrain the publication of newspapers and periodicals. The fact that the liberty of the press may be abused by miscreant purveyors of scandal does not make any the less necessary the immunity of the press from previous restraint in dealing with official misconduct. Subsequent punishment for such abuses as may exist is the appropriate remedy, consistent with constitutional privilege.

The statute in question cannot be justified by reason of the fact that the publisher is permitted to show, before injunction issues, that the matter published is true and is published with good motives and for justifiable ends. If such a statute is valid, it would be equally permissible for the legislature to provide that at any time the publisher of any newspaper could be brought before a court, or even an administrative officer, and required to produce proof of the truth of his publication, or of what he intended to publish and of his motives, or stand enjoined. If this can be done, the legislature may provide the machinery for determining in the complete exercise of its discretion what are justifiable ends and restrain publication accordingly. And it would be but a step to a complete system of censorship.

We hold the statute, so far as it authorized these proceedings, to be an infringement of the liberty of the press guaranteed by the Fourteenth Amendment.

Butler, dissenting (joined by Van Devanter, McReynolds, and Sutherland): The *previous restraint* referred to by Blackstone subjected the press to the arbitrary will of an administrative officer. The Minnesota statute does not operate as a *previous restraint* on publication within the proper meaning of that phrase. It does not authorize administrative control in advance such as was formerly exercised by the licensers and censors but prescribes a remedy to be enforced by a suit in equity.

In this case there was previous publication made in the course of the business of regularly producing malicious, scandalous, and defamatory periodicals. The business and publications unquestionably constitute an abuse of the right of free press. There is no question of the power of the state to denounce such transgressions. The restraint authorized in this case relates only to the plaintiff's continuing to do what has already been duly adjudged to constitute a nuisance. It is fanciful to suggest similarity between the decree authorized by this statute to prevent *further* publication of malicious, scandalous, and defamatory articles and the *previous restraint* upon the press as referred to by Blackstone.

It is well known that existing libel laws are inadequate effectively to suppress evils resulting from the kind of publications that are shown in this case. The doctrine of this ruling exposes the peace and good order of every community and the business and private affairs of every individual to the constant and protracted false and malicious assaults of any insolvent publisher who may have purpose and sufficient capacity to contrive and put into effect a scheme or program for oppression, blackmail, or extortion.

New York Times Co. v. United States, 403 U.S. 713 (1971)

FACTS: This case (widely known as the *Pentagon Papers Case*) concerned the government's efforts to prevent newspapers from publishing a top-secret 47-volume study entitled "History of U.S. Decision-Making Process on Vietnam Policy."

The study had been compiled by a group of Pentagon officials. One of the officials, Daniel Ellsberg, unlawfully furnished copies of the study to the *New York Times* and the *Washington Post.* Claiming that public disclosure of the study contents would be injurious to national security, the United States brought injunction actions against both newspapers to prevent them from publishing the material.

In the action against the *New York Times,* the District Court for the Southern District of New York rejected the government's injunction request, but the Court of Appeals for the Second Circuit reversed. In the action against the *Washington Post,* the District Court for the District of Columbia rejected the government's injunction request, and the Court of Appeals for the District of Columbia Circuit affirmed.

ISSUE: Would issuance of the requested injunction constitute an unconstitutional prior restraint in violation of the First Amendment?

DECISION (6-3 *per curiam*): *Yes.* There were ten opinions; each Justice wrote a separate opinion in addition to joining in the following *per curiam* opinion.

PER CURIAM.

We granted certiorari in these cases in which the United States seeks to enjoin the *New York Times* and the *Washington Post* from publishing the contents of a classified study entitled "History of U.S. Decision-Making Process on Viet Nam Policy."

"Any system of prior restraints of expression comes to this Court bearing a heavy presumption against its constitutional validity." Bantam Books, Inc. v. Sullivan, 372 U.S. 58, 70 (1963); see also Near v. Minnesota, 283 U.S. 697 (1931). The Government "thus carries a heavy burden of showing justification for the imposition of such a restraint." Organization for a Better Austin v. Keefe, 402 U.S. 415, 419 (1971). The District Court for the Southern District of New York in the *New York Times* case and the District Court for the District of Columbia and the Court of Appeals for the District of Columbia Circuit in the *Washington Post* case held that the Government had not met that burden. We agree.

The judgment of the Court of Appeals for the District of Columbia Circuit is therefore affirmed. The order of the Court of Appeals for the Second Circuit is reversed and the case is remanded with directions to enter a judgment affirming the judgment of the District Court for the Southern District of New York. The stays entered June 25, 1971, by the Court are vacated. The judgments shall issue forthwith.

*****

[*Note:* Six of the Justices filed concurring opinions. Black and Douglas each categorically condemned any prior restraint. Brennan argued for the use of strict scrutiny for prior restraints and concluded that the attempt to enjoin publication of the Pentagon Papers fell far short of the high standard that needed to be met. Stewart similarly concluded that publication should not be restrained unless it would result in "direct, immediate, and irreparable damage to our Nation or its people." White and Marshall each emphasized the absence of statutory authority for the courts to issue such an injunction.

Each of the three dissenting opinions by Burger, Harlan, and Blackmun supported allowing an injunction until there could be a more thorough review of the material. In addition, Blackmun warned that, if "these newspapers proceed to publish the critical documents and there results therefrom 'the death of soldiers, the destruction of alliances, the greatly increased difficulty of negotiation with our enemies, the inability of our diplomats to negotiate' [as the Government had argued], to which list I might add the factors of prolongation of the war and of further delay in the freeing of United States prisoners, then the Nation's people will know where the responsibility for these sad consequences rests." [1]]

The Prior Restraint Doctrine

The term "prior restraint" (or "previous restraint"), the Supreme Court has stated, is used "to describe administrative and judicial orders forbidding certain communications when issued in advance of the time that such communications are to occur." Alexander v. United States, 509 U.S. 544, 550 (1993).

The *Pentagon Papers Case,* for example, dealt only with a request for an injunction to prevent publication—*not* an attempt to punish a newspaper *after* publication. In his concurring opinion, Justice White (joined by Stewart) emphasized this distinction, pointing out:

> What is more, terminating the ban on publication of the relatively few sensitive documents the Government now seeks to suppress does not mean ... that they will be immune from criminal action. ... [F]ailure by the Government to justify prior restraints does not measure its constitutional entitlement to a conviction for criminal publication. That the Government mistakenly chose to proceed by injunction does not mean that it could not successfully proceed in another way.

White referred to a variety of federal criminal statutes (including the Espionage Act of 1917) prohibiting the publication of classified information and providing criminal sanctions for doing so. "It is thus clear," White continued, "that Congress ... has apparently been satisfied to rely on criminal sanctions and their deterrent effect on the responsible as well as the irresponsible press."

The Court has also considered the prior restraint doctrine in actions to limit newspapers' pretrial press coverage of criminal proceedings. In Nebraska Press Association v. Stuart, 427 U.S. 539 (1976), the Court held that the strong presumption against the validity of prior restraints will bar such "gag orders" except (if at all) in the rarest of circumstances, particularly because of the usual availability of other methods of protecting the defendant's right to a fair trial.

A far more lenient standard is applied to the censorship of movies. In Times Film Corp. v. Chicago, 365 U.S. 43 (1961), and Freedman v. Maryland, 380 U.S. 51 (1965), the Court sustained requirements that movies be prescreened for obscenity before they may be shown to the public. However, the delay caused by the prescreening must be short; the screening procedure must ensure a prompt final judicial decision on whether the speech is obscene; and the burden of proof must be on the censor to show that the speech is unprotected.

---

[1]See Geoffrey Stone, *Perilous Times: Free Speech in Wartime* [Norton 2004]: 500–519.

It seems unlikely that the Court would ever sustain a government requirement that newspapers be prescreened for libel, incitement, or even obscenity, largely because the delay of even a few days would make a much greater difference for the utility of newspapers than of movies.

Where, however, books or photographs that are believed by police to be obscene are offered for sale—*after* their publication—the Court held (5-4) that the materials may be seized before a judicial determination of whether they are obscene. Kingsley Books v. Brown, 354 U.S. 436 (1957).

Prior restraint issues are also raised by requirements for permits to engage in parades or picketing or other forms of speech. If a government agency has unconstrained discretion to deny such a permit, or to delay issuing the permit, then the restriction is unconstitutional because of the danger of denial or delay based on the content of the proposed message. For example, in Lovell v. Griffin, 303 U.S. 444 (1938), the ordinance prohibited the distribution of literature of any kind on public sidewalks without a permit from the city manager, and the requirement was held unconstitutional because it gave the city manager complete discretion to grant or deny the permit.

But if the system is not unacceptably discretionary, and if the law is in furtherance of governmental interests (such as control of automobile and pedestrian traffic) that are unconnected to the content of the proposed message, a permit requirement will not be struck down if the conditions imposed on the grant of the permit are not unreasonable. As the Court stated in Cox v. New Hampshire, 312 U.S. 569 (1941), sustaining a permit requirement to hold a parade in the public streets: "If a municipality has authority to control the use of its public street for parades or processions, as it undoubtedly has, it cannot be denied authority to give consideration, without unfair discrimination, to time, place and manner in relation to the other proper uses of the streets."

12

The Establishment of Religion Clause

The Relationship between the Two Religion Clauses

The First Amendment, in addition to protecting freedom of speech and the press, provides that "Congress shall make no law respecting an establishment of religion, or prohibiting the free exercise thereof."

As already noted, even though the First Amendment expressly refers only to Congress, it has been interpreted to apply also to the States, and not just the federal government. (See comment "'Incorporation' of Rights in Due Process" in Chapter 6.)

The Amendment's two religion clauses—the Establishment Clause (the focus of this chapter) and the Free Exercise Clause (the focus of the next chapter)—normally complement each other. To a great extent, they are two sides of a single coin; both are designed to protect religious freedom. Thus, any government action that violates the Establishment Clause (by, for example, discriminating in favor of one religion) probably also violates the Free Exercise Clause.

However, the two clauses may sometimes conflict because of their somewhat different functions. The Court has noted the difficulty of finding "a neutral course between the two Religion Clauses, both of which are cast in absolute terms, and either of which, if expanded to a logical extreme, would tend to clash with the other." Walz v. Commissioner, 397 U.S. 664, 668-669 (1970).

The Establishment Clause seeks government neutrality, not only between religions but also between religion and nonreligion; but the Free Exercise Clause, by its terms, gives special protection to religion—the very opposite of neutrality. Thus, any government action that supports free exercise (for example, an income tax deduction for contributions to churches) can arguably also be characterized as aiding religion. Because of this tension between the two clauses, neither clause can be read entirely in isolation or as an absolute command, and each must be interpreted in conjunction with the other in order to enable them to coexist.

The next-digested decision, *Everson v. Board of Education,* is a landmark in church-state constitutional law. The case also illustrates the challenge of reconciling the two religion clauses. The Court held that "the clause against establishment of religion by law was intended to erect 'a wall of separation between church and State.'" Yet the Court then proceeded to hold that the challenged law did not violate the Establishment

Clause, relying in part on the ground that the Free Exercise Clause "commands that New Jersey cannot hamper its citizens in the free exercise of their own religion."

Everson v. Board of Education, 330 U.S. 1 (1947)

FACTS: A New Jersey statute authorized school districts to make rules and contracts to transport children to and from school, "including the transportation of school children to and from school other than a public school, except such school as is operated for profit." Pursuant to that law, a local school board adopted a resolution authorizing reimbursement to parents for money spent to transport their children on public buses. A local taxpayer challenged the making of such payments to parents of Roman Catholic parochial school students. The New Jersey Supreme Court upheld the constitutionality of the statute.

ISSUE: Does the statute violate the Establishment Clause of the First Amendment?

DECISION (per *Black*, 5-4): *No.*

The words of the First Amendment reflected in the minds of early Americans a vivid mental picture of conditions and practices that they fervently wished to stamp out in order to preserve liberty for themselves and for their posterity. A large proportion of the early settlers of this country came here from Europe to escape the bondage of laws that compelled them to support and attend government favored churches. The centuries immediately before and contemporaneous with the colonization of America had been filled with turmoil, civil strife, and persecutions, generated in large part by established sects determined to maintain their absolute political and religious supremacy.

These practices of the old world were transplanted to and began to thrive in the soil of the new America. These practices became so commonplace as to shock the freedom-loving colonials into a feeling of abhorrence. No one locality and no one group throughout the Colonies can rightly be given entire credit for having aroused the sentiment that culminated in adoption of the Bill of Rights' provisions embracing religious liberty. But Virginia, where the established church had achieved a dominant influence in political affairs and where many excesses attracted wide public attention, provided a great stimulus and able leadership for the movement.

The movement reached its dramatic climax in Virginia in 1785–1786 when the Virginia legislative body was about to renew Virginia's tax levy for the support of the established church. Thomas Jefferson and James Madison led the fight against this tax. Madison wrote his great "Memorial and Remonstrance" against the law. In it, he eloquently argued that a true religion did not need the support of law; that no person, either believer or nonbeliever, should be taxed to support a religious institution of any kind; that the best interest of a society required that the minds of men always be wholly free; and that cruel persecutions were the inevitable result of government-established religions. Madison's "Remonstrance" received strong support throughout Virginia, with the result that the tax measure died in committee and instead the Assembly enacted the famous Virginia Bill for Religious Liberty, originally written by Thomas Jefferson and providing

That no man shall be compelled to frequent or support any religious worship, place, or ministry whatsoever, nor shall be enforced, restrained, molested, or burthened, in his body or goods, nor shall otherwise suffer on account of his religious opinions or belief.

The provisions of the First Amendment, in the drafting and adoption of which Madison and Jefferson played such leading roles, had the same objective and were intended to provide the same protection against governmental intrusion on religious liberty as the Virginia statute.

In the present case, it is contended that the New Jersey statute and the resolution, insofar as they authorized reimbursement to parents of children attending parochial schools, violate the Constitution by forcing inhabitants to pay taxes to help support and maintain schools that are dedicated to, and that regularly teach, the Catholic faith. This is alleged to be a use of state power to support church schools contrary to the prohibition of the First Amendment that the Fourteenth Amendment made applicable to the states.

In the light of its history and the evils it was designed to suppress, the Establishment of Religion Clause of the First Amendment means at least this: Neither a state nor the federal government can set up a church. Neither can pass laws that aid one religion, aid all religions, or prefer one religion over another. Neither can force or influence a person to go to or to remain away from church against his will or force him to profess a belief or disbelief in any religion. No person can be punished for entertaining or professing religious beliefs or disbeliefs, for church attendance or nonattendance. No tax in any amount, large or small, can be levied to support any religious activities or institutions, whatever they may be called, or whatever form they may adopt to teach or practice religion. Neither a state nor the federal government can, openly or secretly, participate in the affairs of any religious organizations or groups and vice versa. In the words of Jefferson, the clause against establishment of religion by law was intended to erect "a wall of separation between church and state."

We must not strike down the New Jersey law if it is within the State's constitutional power even though it approaches the verge of that power. New Jersey cannot consistently with the Establishment Clause of the First Amendment contribute tax-raised funds to the support of an institution that teaches the tenets and faith of any church. On the other hand, other language of the Amendment commands that New Jersey cannot hamper its citizens in the free exercise of their own religion. Consequently, it cannot exclude individual Catholics, Lutherans, Mohammedans, Baptists, Jews, Methodists, nonbelievers, Presbyterians, or the members of any other faith, *because of their faith, or lack of it,* from receiving the benefits of public welfare legislation. While we do not mean to intimate that a State could not provide transportation only to children attending public schools, we must be careful, in protecting the citizens of New Jersey against state-established churches, to be sure that we do not inadvertently prohibit New Jersey from extending its general state law benefits to all its citizens without regard to their religious belief.

Measured by these standards, we cannot say that the First Amendment prohibits New Jersey from spending tax-raised funds to pay the bus fares of parochial school pupils as a part of a general program under which it pays the fares of pupils attending public and other schools.

It is undoubtedly true that children are helped to get to church schools. There is even a possibility that some of the children might not be sent to the church schools if the parents were compelled to pay their children's bus fares out of their own pockets when transportation to a public school would have been paid for by the state. Similarly, parents might be reluctant to permit their children to attend schools that the State had cut off from such general government services as ordinary police and fire protection, connections for sewage disposal, public highways, and sidewalks.

Of course, cutting off church schools from these services, so separate and so indisputably marked off from the religious function, would make it far more difficult for the schools to operate. But such is obviously not the purpose of the First Amendment. That Amendment requires the state to be a neutral in its relations with groups of religious believers and nonbelievers; it does not require the state to be their adversary. State power is no more to be used so as to handicap religions than it is to favor them.

The State contributes no money to the schools. It does not support them. Its legislation, as applied, does no more than provide a general program to help parents get their children, regardless of their religion, safely and expeditiously to and from accredited schools.

The First Amendment has erected a wall between church and state. That wall must be kept high and impregnable. We could not approve the slightest breach. New Jersey has not breached it here.

Jackson, dissenting (joined by Frankfurter): The Court's opinion marshals every argument in favor of state aid and puts the case in its most favorable light, but much of its reasoning confirms my conclusions that there are no good grounds upon which to support the present legislation. In fact, the undertones of the opinion, advocating complete and uncompromising separation of church from state, seem utterly discordant with its conclusion yielding support to their commingling in educational matters.

Rutledge, dissenting (joined by Frankfurter, Jackson, and Burton): The First Amendment's purpose was to create a complete and permanent separation of the spheres of religious activity and civil authority by comprehensively forbidding every form of public aid or support for religion. Does New Jersey's action furnish support for religion by use of the taxing power? Certainly it does, if the test remains undiluted as Jefferson and Madison made it, that money taken by taxation from one is not to be used or given to support another's religious training or belief, or indeed one's own. The prohibition is absolute.

Two great drives are constantly in motion to abridge, in the name of education, the complete division of religion and civil authority our forefathers made. One is to introduce religious education and observances into the public schools; the other, to obtain public funds for the aid and support of various private religious schools. Both avenues were closed by the Constitution. Neither should be opened by this Court. The matter is not one of quantity, to be measured by the amount of money expended. Now as in Madison's day it is one of principle, to keep separate spheres as the First Amendment drew them.

Early Conceptions of the Establishment of Religion

In his *Everson* opinion, Justice Black quotes Thomas Jefferson's statement that the Establishment Clause was intended to erect "a wall of separation between church and state." The statement appeared in a letter Jefferson wrote in 1802 in response to a letter from Danbury, Connecticut, Baptist ministers complaining of the Connecticut state government's favoritism to the Congregationalist church.

Since the First Amendment at that time applied only to the federal government, the ministers' letter acknowledged "that the national government cannot destroy the laws of each State" but expressed the hope "that the sentiments of our beloved President . . . will shine & prevail through all these States and all the world till Hierarchy and tyranny be destroyed from the Earth." In his response to the ministers, Jefferson did not address their concerns about problems with state establishment of religion, but confined his comment to the national level. Jefferson's letter stated in part:

> I contemplate with sovereign reverence that act of the whole American people which declared that <u>their</u> legislature should make no law respecting an establishment of religion, or prohibiting the free exercise thereof, thus building a wall of separation between church and state." (Underscoring Jefferson's.)[1]

For the next half century there was apparently no further reference to the "wall of separation" until the Supreme Court's opinion in Reynolds v. United States, 98 U.S. 145, 164 (1878), upholding a federal law against polygamy in the territories.

At the time the nation was founded, the term "establishment of religion" referred to a legal affiliation between a State and a particular church that received benefits from the state—in particular, financial support through public taxation. "The classic establishment of religion denoted a legal union between a state and a particular church that benefited from numerous privileges not shared by other churches or unbelievers."[2]

In some States religious tests admitted only Christians or even only Protestants to public office. "More troubling to most dissenters, the constitutions of some states allowed establishment ministers to collect salaries raised by state taxes and permitted laws that gave the established clergy the exclusive right to conduct marriages."[3]

Before the American Revolution, either the Anglican or Congregationalist church was established by law in 9 of the original 13 colonies. By the end of the Revolution, both the nature and number of state establishments of religion had substantially changed. The term "establishment" acquired an additional meaning to reflect the development of "multiple or general" establishments, not limited to a single church.[4] In that sense established churches continued in six States—Massachusetts, Connecticut, New Hampshire, Maryland, Georgia, and South Carolina.[5]

The Anglican Church was everywhere disestablished because of its close relationship to the British Crown. But Congregationalism remained established in Massachusetts, Connecticut, and New Hampshire until the 1830s—nearly half a century after adoption of the Constitution. And until 1877 only Protestants could be members of the New Hampshire state legislature, and until 1876 only Christians could hold public office in North Carolina. The adoption of the First Amendment had no effect on these state restrictions since the Amendment expressly applied only to the national government. The Establishment Clause was added to the Bill of Rights because of concern that Congress might follow the example of the colonies and create a *national* establishment of religion.[6]

The First Amendment became applicable to the States only under the "incorporation" interpretation of the Fourteenth Amendment. In 1925, in Gitlow v. New York, 268 U.S. 652, 666 (1925), the Supreme Court ruled that the Fourteenth Amendment

[1]Philip Hamburger, *Separation of Church and State* [Harvard University Press 2002]: 161.
[2]Leonard W. Levy, *Original Intent and the Founders' Constitution* [Macmillan 1988]: 174.
[3]Hamburger, *Separation of Church and State,* 90.
[4]Levy, *Original Intent and the Founders' Constitution,* 185, 190.
[5]Ibid., 189.
[6]Ibid., 175.

incorporated the free-speech and free-press guarantees of the First Amendment. In 1940, in Cantwell v. Connecticut, 310 U.S. 296 (1940), this doctrine was extended to the religion clauses of the First Amendment.

Government Aid to Religious Schools

The Court's church-state decisions since *Everson* are difficult to reconcile. But the overall trend has been to enlarge the kinds of aid that government can give to religious schools.

In Board of Education v. Allen, 392 U.S. 236 (1968), the Court held that a State could *lend books on secular subjects* to parochial school students.

But three years later, the Court rejected reimbursement of religious schools for the *cost of teachers' salaries, textbooks, and instructional materials,* because of excessive "entanglement" between government and religion, even for the teaching of secular subjects. Lemon v. Kurtzman, 403 U.S. 602 (1971).

Subsequent decisions, however, held it was permissible to provide *sign interpreters* for parochial students, Zobrest v. Catalina Foothills School District, 509 U.S. 1 (1993), and to allow *remedial education instructors* in parochial schools. Agostini v. Felton 521 U.S. 203 (1997).

And in the next-digested case, *Mitchell v. Helms,* the Court (6-3) held that the federal government could loan *equipment and software* to parochial schools as part of a broad program as long as the equipment is not used for religious instruction.

Even more important than the Court's specific holding in *Mitchell* is the rationale of Justice Thomas's plurality opinion, joined by Rehnquist, Scalia, and Kennedy. Under their approach, government aid to religious schools would be *unrestricted—whether direct or indirect*—regardless of how it might be used (even if the aid is "divertible" for religious uses), *provided* that the aid is allocated on the basis of criteria that neither favor nor disfavor religion and is made available to both public and nonpublic schools (including religious schools) on a nondiscriminatory basis.

Two Justices (O'Connor and Breyer) concurred in the result in *Mitchell* but objected to the test advanced by the plurality opinion. In their view, that opinion "foreshadows the approval of direct monetary subsidies to religious organizations, even when they use the money to advance their religious objectives."

The three other Justices (Stevens, Souter, Ginsburg) dissented, contending that government aid to religious schools should be allowed only if it is of a *type* (unlike, for example, cash or buildings) that cannot be "diverted" for religious uses.

Mitchell v. Helms, 530 U.S. 793 (2000)

FACTS: Under Chapter 2 of the Education Consolidation and Improvement Act of 1981, the federal government distributes funds to state and local governmental agencies, which in turn lend educational materials and equipment to public and private schools to implement programs to assist children in elementary and secondary schools. The program provides aid "for the acquisition and use of instructional and educational materials, including library services and materials (including media materials), assessments, reference materials, computer software and hardware for instructional use, and other curricular materials." The enrollment of each participating school determines the amount of aid that it receives. The Act requires that "services, materials, and equipment" provided to private schools must be "secular, neutral, and nonideological." In addition, private schools may not acquire control of Chapter 2 funds or title to Chapter 2 materials, equipment, or property.

For the 1986–1987 fiscal year, 46 private schools in Jefferson Parish, Louisiana, participated in Chapter 2. Of these 46, 34 were Roman Catholic; 7 were otherwise religiously affiliated; and 5 were not religiously affiliated.

The complaint in the case alleged that the Chapter 2 aid received by Roman Catholic schools in Jefferson Parish violates the Establishment Clause of the First Amendment. The Fifth Circuit agreed, holding the federal aid to be unconstitutional.

ISSUE: Does the Chapter 2 program, as applied in Jefferson Parish, violate the Establishment Clause of the First Amendment?

DECISION (*Thomas*, 6-3): *No.*

Thomas (plurality opinion joined by Rehnquist, Scalia, and Kennedy): We conclude that Chapter 2 neither results in religious indoctrination by the government nor defines its recipients by reference to religion. We therefore hold that Chapter 2 is not a "law respecting an establishment of religion."

The question whether governmental aid to religious schools results in governmental indoctrination is ultimately a question whether any religious indoctrination that occurs in those schools could reasonably be attributed to governmental action. In distinguishing between indoctrination that is attributable to government and indoctrination that is not, we have consistently turned to the principle of neutrality, upholding aid that is offered to a broad range of groups or persons without regard to their religion. If the religious, irreligious, and a-religious are all alike eligible for governmental aid, no one could conclude that any indoctrination that any particular recipient conducts has been done at the behest of the government.

As a way of assuring neutrality, we have repeatedly considered whether any governmental aid that goes to a religious institution does so only as a result of the genuinely independent and private choices of individuals. If numerous private choices, rather than the single choice of a government, determine the distribution of aid pursuant to neutral eligibility criteria, then a government cannot, or at least cannot easily, grant special favors that might lead to a religious establishment.

If aid to schools, even "direct aid," is neutrally available and, before reaching or benefiting any religious school, first passes through the hands (literally or figuratively) of numerous private citizens who are free to direct the aid elsewhere, the government has not provided any support of religion. We have departed from the rule relied on in earlier cases that all government aid that directly assists the educational function of religious schools is invalid.

If the government, seeking to further some legitimate secular purpose, offers aid on the same terms, without regard to religion, to all who adequately further that purpose, then it is fair to say that any aid going to a religious recipient only has the effect of furthering that secular purpose.

Our prior decisions have suggested that special Establishment Clause dangers may arise when *money* is given directly to religious schools or entities. But direct payments of money are not at issue in this case, and we refuse to allow a "special" case to create a rule for all cases.

It is also contended that the Establishment Clause requires that aid to religious schools not be divertible to religious use. This "no divertibility" argument, however, is inconsistent with our more recent case law and is unworkable. So long as the governmental aid is not itself unsuitable for use in the public schools because of religious content, and eligibility for aid is determined in a constitutionally permissible manner, any use of that aid to indoctrinate cannot be attributed to the government and is thus not of constitutional concern.

The issue is not divertibility of aid but rather whether the aid itself has an impermissible content. Where the aid would be suitable for use in a public school, it is also suitable for use in any private school. Similarly, the prohibition against the government providing impermissible content resolves the Establishment Clause concerns that exist if aid is actually diverted to religious uses.

A concern for divertibility, as opposed to improper content, is misplaced not only because it fails to explain why the sort of aid that we have allowed is permissible, but also because it is boundless—enveloping all aid, no matter how trivial—and thus has only the most attenuated (if any) link to any realistic concern for preventing an "establishment of religion." Presumably, for example, government-provided lecterns, chalk, crayons, pens, paper, and paintbrushes would have to be excluded from religious schools, but we fail to see how indoctrination by means of (i.e., diversion of) such aid could be attributed to the government.

It is perhaps conceivable that courts could take upon themselves the task of distinguishing among the myriad kinds of possible aid based on the ease of diverting each kind. But it escapes us how a court might coherently draw any such line. It not only is far more workable but also is actually related to real concerns about preventing advancement of religion by government, simply to require that a program of aid to schools not provide improper content and that it determine eligibility and allocate the aid on a permissible basis.

One factor previously given consideration in our application of the Establishment Clause was whether a school that receives aid (or whose students receive aid) is pervasively sectarian. However, the religious nature of a recipient should not matter to the constitutional analysis, so long as the recipient adequately furthers the government's secular purpose. If a program offers permissible aid to the religious (including the pervasively sectarian), the a-religious, and the irreligious, it is a mystery which view of religion the government has established, and thus a mystery what the constitutional violation would be.

Moreover, hostility to aid to pervasively sectarian schools has a shameful pedigree that we do not hesitate to disavow. Opposition to aid to "sectarian" schools acquired prominence in the 1870s with Congress's consideration (and near passage) of the Blaine Amendment, which would have amended the Constitution to bar any aid to sectarian institutions. Consideration of the amendment arose at a time of pervasive hostility to the Catholic Church and to Catholics in general, and it was an open secret that "sectarian" was then code for "Catholic."

We see no basis for concluding that Jefferson Parish's Chapter 2 program has the effect of advancing religion or resulting in governmental indoctrination. The program determines eligibility for aid neutrally, allocates that aid based on the private choices of the parents of schoolchildren, and does not provide aid that has an impermissible content. For the same reasons, Chapter 2 also cannot reasonably be viewed as an endorsement of religion.

Accordingly, we hold that Chapter 2 is not a "law respecting an establishment of religion" and that therefore Jefferson Parish religious schools need not be excluded from Chapter 2.

O'Connor, concurring (joined by *Breyer*): Although I concur in the judgment, I strongly disagree with the rationale of the plurality opinion.

(1) The plurality opinion announces a rule of unprecedented breadth for the evaluation of Establishment Clause challenges to government school-aid programs. That rule is particularly troubling for two reasons.

First, its treatment of neutrality comes close to assigning that factor singular importance in the future adjudication of Establishment Clause challenges to school-aid programs. Although neutrality is important, the Court has never held that a government-aid program passes constitutional muster *solely* because of the neutral criteria it employs as a basis for distributing aid. Rather, neutrality has heretofore been only one of several factors the Court considers.

Second, the plurality's approval of actual diversion of government aid to religious indoctrination is in tension with this Court's precedents. Under our prior decisions, actual diversion is constitutionally impermissible. A per-capita-aid program like Chapter 2 should not be treated the same as a true private choice program.

If, as the plurality contends, the two types of programs are to be treated the same, then there would appear to be no reason why the government should be precluded from providing direct money payments to religious organizations based on the number of persons belonging to each organization. And, if actual diversion is permissible, the participating religious organizations could use that aid to support religious indoctrination. Although the plurality opinion states that it does not reach consideration of standards applicable to direct money payments, the logic of the opinion foreshadows the approval of direct monetary subsidies to religious organizations, even when they use the money to advance their religious objectives.

(2) Nevertheless, I agree that the decision below should be reversed.

In my view, the pertinent inquiry is whether the government acted with the purpose of advancing or inhibiting religion and whether the aid has the effect of doing so. Since Chapter 2 program's secular purpose is not challenged and an excessive entanglement is not alleged, the Court need ask only whether Chapter 2, as applied in Jefferson Parish, results in governmental indoctrination or defines its recipients by reference to religion. Application of that criterion leads me to join in the Court's judgment.

It is clear that Chapter 2 uses wholly neutral and secular criteria to allocate aid to students enrolled in religious and secular schools alike. As to the indoctrination inquiry, aid is allocated on the basis of neutral, secular criteria; it is supplementary to, and does not supplant, nonfederal funds; no Chapter 2 funds reach the coffers of religious schools; the aid is secular; use of the materials is restricted to secular purposes; and evidence of actual diversion is *de minimis*. And because I believe that the Court should abandon the presumption that properly instructed religious-school teachers will use instructional materials and equipment for religious purposes, I see no constitutional need for pervasive monitoring under the Chapter 2 program.

These considerations are sufficient to persuade me that the program does not have the impermissible effect of advancing religion. For the same reasons, the Chapter 2 program cannot reasonably be viewed as an endorsement of religion.

Souter, dissenting (joined by Stevens and Ginsburg): I believe the Court commits error in failing to recognize the divertibility of funds to the service of religious objectives. What is even more troubling is the plurality view espousing a new conception of neutrality as a practically sufficient test of constitutionality; such a conception, if adopted by the Court, would eliminate inquiry into a law's effects.

The nub of the plurality's new position is that, "If the government, seeking to further some legitimate secular purpose, offers aid on the same terms, without regard to religion, to all who adequately further that purpose, then it is fair to say that any aid going to a religious recipient only has the effect of furthering that secular purpose." As a break with consistent doctrine, the plurality's new criterion is unequaled in the history of Establishment Clause interpretation. Simple on its face, it appears to promote evenhandedness neutrality to a single and sufficient test for the constitutionality of school aid.

Under the plurality's regime, little would be left of the right of conscience against compelled support for religion: the more massive the aid, the more potent would be the influence of the government on the teaching mission; the more generous the support, the more divisive would be the resentments of those resisting religious support as well as those religions without school systems ready to claim their fair share.

The plurality would break with the law; the majority misapplies it. That misapplication is, however, the only consolation in the case, which reaches an erroneous result but does not stage a doctrinal coup. But there is no mistaking the abandonment of doctrine that would occur if the plurality were to become a majority. It is beyond question that the plurality's notion of evenhandedness neutrality as a practical guarantee of the validity of aid to sectarian schools would be the end of the principle of no aid to the schools' religious mission. And if that were not so obvious, it would become so after reflecting on the plurality's thoughts about diversion and about giving attention to the pervasiveness of a school's sectarian teaching.

To the plurality there is nothing wrong with aiding a school's religious mission. Under the plurality view, the only question is whether religious teaching obtains its tax support under a formally evenhanded criterion of distribution.

The plurality further attacks the legitimacy of considering a school's pervasively sectarian character when judging whether aid to the school is likely to aid its religious mission. But the relevance of this consideration is simply a matter of common sense: where religious indoctrination pervades school activities of children and adolescents, it takes great care to be able to aid the school without supporting the doctrinal effort.

The plurality nonetheless condemns any inquiry into the pervasiveness of doctrinal content as a remnant of anti-Catholic bigotry (as if evangelical Protestant schools and Orthodox Jewish yeshivas were never pervasively sectarian), and it equates a refusal to aid religious schools with hostility to religion. The plurality's choice to employ imputations of bigotry and irreligion makes clear that, in rejecting the principle of no aid to a school's religious mission, the plurality is attacking the most fundamental assumption underlying the Establishment Clause.

Zelman v. Simmons-Harris, 530 U.S. 640 (2002)

FACTS: Ohio's Pilot Project Scholarship Program provides tuition aid for certain students in the Cleveland City School District to attend participating public or private schools of their parents' choosing and provides tutorial aid for students who choose to remain enrolled in public school. Both religious and nonreligious schools in the district may participate, as may public schools in adjacent school districts. Tuition aid is distributed to parents according to financial need, and where the aid is spent depends solely upon where parents choose to enroll their children.

In the 1999–2000 school year, 82 percent of the participating private schools had a religious affiliation, none of the adjacent public schools participated, and 96 percent of the students participating in the scholarship program were enrolled in religiously affiliated schools. Sixty percent of the students were from families at or below the poverty line. Cleveland schoolchildren also have the option of enrolling in community schools, which are funded under state law but run by their own school boards and receive twice the per-student funding as participating private schools, or magnet schools, which are public schools emphasizing a particular subject area, teaching method, or service, and for which the school district receives the same amount per student as it does for a student enrolled at a traditional public school.

The plaintiffs in the case, Ohio taxpayers, brought suit to enjoin the program on the ground that it violated the Establishment Clause. The District Court granted the plaintiffs' motion for summary judgment, and the Sixth Circuit affirmed.

ISSUE: Does the Cleveland school voucher program violate the Establishment Clause?

DECISION (per *Rehnquist,* 5-4): *No.*

This Court's decisions make clear that a government aid program is permissible under the Establishment Clause if it is neutral with respect to religion and provides assistance directly to a broad class of citizens who, in turn, direct government aid to religious schools wholly as a result of their own genuine and independent private choice. Under such a program, government aid reaches religious institutions only by way of the deliberate choices of numerous individual recipients. Any incidental advancement of a religious mission, or perceived endorsement of a religious message, is attributable to the individual aid recipients—not the government, whose role ends with the disbursement of benefits.

The Cleveland program is one of true private choice and therefore constitutional. It is neutral in all respects towards religion. It confers educational assistance directly to a broad class of individuals defined without reference to religion and permits participation of all schools in the district—religious or nonreligious—and adjacent public schools. The only preference in the program is for low-income families, who receive greater assistance and have priority for admission. Rather than creating financial incentives that skew it towards religious schools, the program creates financial disincentives: Private schools receive only half the government assistance given to community schools and one-third that given to magnet schools, and adjacent public schools would receive two to three times that given to private schools. Families too have a financial disincentive, for they have to co-pay a portion of private school tuition, but pay nothing at a community, magnet, or traditional public school. No reasonable observer would think that such a neutral private choice program carries with it the *imprimatur* of government endorsement.

Nor is there evidence that the program fails to provide genuine opportunities for Cleveland parents to select secular educational options. Their children may remain in public school as before, remain in public school with funded tutoring aid, obtain a scholarship and choose to attend a religious school, obtain a scholarship and choose to attend a nonreligious private school, enroll in a community school, or enroll in a magnet school. The Establishment Clause question must be answered by evaluating *all* options Ohio provides Cleveland schoolchildren, only one of which is to obtain a scholarship and then choose a religious school. Of Cleveland's private schools 82 percent are religious, as are 81 percent of Ohio's private schools. To attribute constitutional significance to the 82 percent figure would lead to the absurd result that a neutral school-choice program might be permissible in parts of Ohio where the percentage is lower, but not in Cleveland, where Ohio has deemed such programs most sorely needed. Likewise, an identical private choice program might be constitutional only in states with a lower percentage of religious private schools.

O'Connor, concurring: While I join the Court's opinion, I write separately for two reasons. First, I do not believe that today's decision, when considered in light of other long-standing government programs that impact religious organizations and our prior Establishment Clause jurisprudence, marks a dramatic break from the past. Second, in verifying that parents of voucher students in religious schools have exercised "true private choice," all reasonable educational alternatives to religious schools that are available to parents must be considered. To do otherwise is to ignore how the educational system in Cleveland actually functions.

There is little question in my mind that the Cleveland voucher program is neutral as between religious schools and nonreligious schools. For nonreligious schools to qualify as genuine options for parents, they need not be superior to religious schools in every respect. They need only be adequate substitutes for religious schools in the eyes of parents. In these cases, parents who were eligible to apply for a voucher also had the option, at a minimum, to send their children to community schools.

Justice Souter seeks to rule out certain nonreligious schools as relevant alternatives to religious schools in the voucher program. But under our Establishment Clause decisions the controlling question is whether parents, after the Cleveland voucher program was enacted, were free to direct state educational aid in either a nonreligious or religious direction. That inquiry requires an evaluation of all reasonable educational options that Ohio provides the Cleveland school system, regardless of whether they are formally made available in the same section of the Ohio Code as the voucher program.

Thomas, concurring: In seeking to bar the Cleveland voucher program, the plaintiffs advocate using the Fourteenth Amendment to handcuff the state's ability to experiment with education. But without education one can hardly exercise the civic, political, and personal freedoms conferred by the Fourteenth Amendment.

Faced with a severe educational crisis, the State of Ohio enacted wide-ranging educational reform that allows voluntary participation of private and religious schools in educating poor urban children otherwise condemned to failing public schools. The program does not force any individual to submit to religious indoctrination or education. It simply gives parents a greater choice as to where and in what manner to educate their children. This is a choice that those with greater means have routinely exercised.

While in theory providing education to everyone, public schools vary significantly in quality. Just as blacks supported public education during Reconstruction, many blacks and other minorities now support school choice programs because they provide the greatest educational opportunities for their children in struggling communities. Opponents of the program raise formalistic concerns about the Establishment Clause but ignore the core purposes of the Fourteenth Amendment.

While the romanticized ideal of universal public education resonates with the cognoscenti who oppose vouchers, poor urban families just want the best education for their children, who will certainly need it to function in our high-tech and advanced society. The failure to provide education to poor urban children perpetuates a vicious cycle of poverty, dependence, criminality, and alienation that continues for the remainder of their lives. If society cannot end racial discrimination, at least it can arm minorities with the education to defend themselves from some of discrimination's effects.

Ten States have enacted some form of publicly funded private school choice as one means of raising the quality of education provided to underprivileged urban children. These programs address the root of the problem with failing urban public schools that disproportionately affect minority students. Converting the Fourteenth Amendment from a guarantee of opportunity to an obstacle against education reform distorts our constitutional values and disserves those with the greatest need.

Stevens, dissenting: In deciding this case, I think we should ignore three factual matters that are discussed at length by my colleagues.

First, the severe educational crisis that confronted the Cleveland City School District when Ohio enacted its voucher program is not a matter that should affect our appraisal of its constitutionality.

Second, the wide range of choices that have been made available to students *within the public school system* has no bearing on the question whether the state may pay the tuition for students who wish to reject public education entirely and attend private schools that will provide them with a sectarian education. The fact that the vast majority of the voucher recipients who have entirely rejected public education receive religious indoctrination at state expense does, however, support the claim that the law is one "respecting an establishment of religion." The State may choose to divide up its public schools into a dozen different options but it is the State's decision to fund private school education over and above its traditional obligation that is at issue here.

Third, the voluntary character of the private choice to prefer a parochial education over an education in the public school system seems to me quite irrelevant to the question whether the government's choice to pay for religious indoctrination is constitutionally permissible. Today, however, the Court seems to have decided that the mere fact that a family that cannot afford a private education wants its children educated in a parochial school is a sufficient justification for this use of public funds.

The Court's decision is profoundly misguided. Whenever we remove a brick from the wall that was designed to separate religion and government, we increase the risk of religious strife and weaken the foundation of our democracy.

Souter, dissenting (joined by Stevens, Ginsburg, and Breyer): It is only by ignoring the meaning of neutrality and private choice themselves that the majority can even pretend to rest today's decision on those criteria.

With respect to both neutrality and choice, the majority looks not to the provisions for tuition vouchers, but to every provision for educational opportunity. However, for the overwhelming number of children in the voucher scheme, the only alternative to the public schools is religious. And it is entirely irrelevant that the State did not deliberately design the network of private schools for the sake of channeling money into religious institutions.

Even if I assumed *arguendo* that the majority's formal criteria were satisfied on the facts, today's conclusion would be profoundly at odds with the Constitution on two levels. The first is circumstantial, in the substantial dimension of the aid. The scale of the aid to religious schools approved today is unprecedented, both in the number of dollars and in the proportion of systemic school expenditure supported. The second is direct, in the defiance of every objective supposed to be served by the bar against establishment. As appropriations for religious subsidy rise, competition for the money will tap sectarian religion's capacity for discord.

Breyer, dissenting (joined by Stevens and Souter): I write separately to emphasize the risk that publicly financed voucher programs pose in terms of religiously based social conflict.

The upshot of prior decisions is the development of constitutional doctrine that reads the Establishment Clause as avoiding religious strife, *not* by providing every religion with an *equal opportunity* (say, to secure state funding or to pray in the public schools), but by drawing fairly clear lines of *separation* between church and state—at least where the heartland of religious belief, such as primary religious education, is at issue.

Under these modern-day circumstances, how is the "equal opportunity" principle to work—without risking the "struggle of sect against sect"? School voucher programs finance the religious education of the young. And, if widely adopted, they may well provide billions of dollars that will do so. Why will different religions not become concerned about, and seek to influence, the criteria used to channel this money to religious schools? Why will they not want to examine the implementation of the programs providing this money—to determine, for example, whether implementation has biased a program toward or against particular sects, or whether recipient religious schools are adequately fulfilling a program's criteria? If so, just how is the State to resolve the resulting controversies without provoking legitimate fears of the kinds of religious favoritism that, in so religiously diverse a nation, threaten social dissension?

I concede that the Establishment Clause currently permits States to channel various forms of assistance to religious schools—for example, transportation costs for students, computers, and secular texts. School voucher programs differ, however, in both *kind* and *degree* from such aid programs. They differ in kind because they direct financing to a core function of the church: the teaching of religious truths to young children. Vouchers also differ in *degree.* The majority's analysis here appears to permit a considerable shift of taxpayer dollars from public secular schools to private religious schools. That fact, combined with the use to which these dollars will be put, exacerbates the conflict problem.

I do not believe that the "parental choice" aspect of the voucher program sufficiently offsets these concerns. The Court, in effect, turns the clock back. This departure risks creating a form of religiously based conflict potentially harmful to the nation's social fabric.

*****

[*Note:* In January 2006, the Florida Supreme Court held that a Florida voucher program violated this provision of the Florida State Constitution: "Adequate provision shall be made by law for a uniform, efficient, safe, secure and high quality system of free public schools."]

Prayer in Public Schools

Except for the infamous 1857 *Dred Scott* decision, probably no decision in the history of the Supreme Court (even *Brown v. Board of Education*) has sparked the same national uproar as Engel v. Vitale, 370 U.S. 421 (1961).[7]

At issue in the *Engel* case was the constitutionality of a school board's direction that each class at the beginning of each school day should recite a brief prayer composed by the New York State Board of Regents: "Almighty God, we acknowledge our dependence upon Thee, and we beg Thy blessings upon us, our parents, our teachers, and our Country." Although the prayer was nondenominational in nature, and although students who wished to do so could remain silent or be excused from the room while the prayer was being recited, the Court (6-1, Frankfurter and White not participating) held that the policy violated the Establishment Clause.

In an opinion by Justice Black (who had also authored the *Everson* opinion), the Court stated:

> [B]y using its public school system to encourage recitation of the Regents' prayer, the State of New York has adopted a practice wholly inconsistent with the Establishment Clause. ...
>
> [T]he constitutional prohibition against laws respecting an establishment of religion must at least mean that in this country it is no part of the business of government to compose official prayers for any group of the American people to recite as a part of a religious program carried on by government.
>
> ...There can be no doubt that New York's state prayer program officially establishes the religious beliefs embodied in the Regents' prayer. ...Neither the fact that the prayer may be denominationally neutral nor the fact that its observance on the part of the students is voluntary can serve to free it from the limitations of the Establishment Clause. ...
>
> It is neither sacrilegious nor antireligious to say that each separate government in this country should stay out of the business of writing or sanctioning official prayers and leave that purely religious function to the people themselves and to those the people choose to look to for religious guidance.

Justice Potter Stewart dissented, denying that "an 'official religion' is established by letting those who want to say a prayer say it" and contending "that to deny the wish of these school children to join in reciting this prayer is to deny them the opportunity of sharing in the spiritual heritage of our Nation."

Two years later, in School District of Abington v. Schempp, 374 U.S. 203 (1963), the Court (8-1) declared unconstitutional state-sponsored Bible readings and recitation of the Lord's Prayer in public schools. The Court emphasized that these religious exercises were prescribed as part of the curricular activities of students, conducted in school buildings, and supervised by teachers. Distinguishing the study of the Bible in a literature or comparative religion course, the Court said that "the exercises here do not fall into those categories. They are religious exercises, required by the States in violation of the command of the First Amendment that the Government maintain strict neutrality, neither aiding nor opposing religion."

In Wallace v. Jaffree, 472 U.S. 38 (1985), the Court (6-3) declared unconstitutional an Alabama law that authorized a moment of silence in public schools for "meditation

---

[7]See Bruce Dierenfield, *The Battle over School Prayer* [Kansas 2007].

or voluntary prayer." In the Court's view, the legislative history of the law was clear that its purpose was to reintroduce prayer into the public schools.

The dissenting opinion of Chief Justice Burger in *Wallace* relied heavily on his opinion for the Court two years earlier in Marsh v. Chambers, 463 U.S. 783 (1983), sustaining (6-3) the Nebraska Legislature's practice of beginning each of its sessions with a prayer by a chaplain paid by the State.

In *Marsh* (without even any reference to *Engel*) the Court held:

> The opening of sessions of legislative and other deliberative public bodies with prayer is deeply embedded in the history and tradition of this country. From colonial times through the founding of the Republic and ever since, the practice of legislative prayer has coexisted with the principles of disestablishment and religious freedom. In the very courtrooms in which the United States District Judge and later three Circuit Judges heard and decided this case, the proceedings opened with an announcement that concluded, "God save the United States and this Honorable Court." The same invocation occurs at all sessions of this Court.
>
> ...[T]he Continental Congress, beginning in 1774, adopted the traditional procedure of opening its sessions with a prayer offered by a paid chaplain. ... [T]he First Congress, as one of its early items of business, adopted the policy of selecting a chaplain to open each session with prayer. ...
>
> Clearly the men who wrote the First Amendment Religion Clauses did not view paid legislative chaplains and opening prayers as a violation of that Amendment, for the practice of opening sessions with prayer has continued without interruption ever since that early session of Congress. It has also been followed consistently in most of the states. ...
>
> This unique history leads us to accept the interpretation of the First Amendment draftsmen who saw no real threat to the Establishment Clause arising from a practice of prayer similar to that now challenged. We conclude that legislative prayer presents no more potential for establishment than the provision of school transportation, Everson v. Board of Education, 330 U.S. 1 (1947), beneficial grants for higher education, Tilton v. Richardson, 403 U.S. 672 (1971), or tax exemptions for religious organizations, Walz v. Tax Comm'n of New York City, 397 U.S. 664 (1970).
>
> ...In light of the unambiguous and unbroken history of more than 200 years, there can be no doubt that the practice of opening legislative sessions with prayer has become part of the fabric of our society. To invoke Divine guidance on a public body entrusted with making the laws is not, in these circumstances, an "establishment" of religion or a step toward establishment; it is simply a tolerable acknowledgment of beliefs widely held among the people of this country.

The Court further rejected the objections "first, that a clergyman of only one denomination—Presbyterian—has been selected for 16 years; second, that the chaplain is paid at public expense; and third, that the prayers are in the Judeo-Christian tradition."

Against this background, the Court in the next two digested cases was confronted with the issue of whether its school prayer decisions should also bar prayers at public school functions *outside* the classroom—graduation ceremonies (*Lee v. Weisman*) and school football games (*Santa Fe Independent School District v. Doe*).

Lee v. Weisman, 505 U.S. 577 (1992)

FACTS: The principal (Lee) of a Providence middle school invited a rabbi to give the traditional prayers at the school's graduation ceremony. The principal provided the rabbi with a copy of a booklet "Guidelines for Civic Occasions" and advised the rabbi that his prayers must be nonsectarian. During both the invocation and benediction delivered by the rabbi, he referred to "God" and the "Lord" while asking for blessing of the graduates, parents, and school officials.

One of those attending was Deborah Weisman, a student who was scheduled to graduate from the school at a future graduation. Deborah and her father sought an injunction barring Lee and other Providence public school officials from inviting clergy to deliver invocations and benedictions at future graduations, including the forthcoming graduation of Deborah Weisman. It was stipulated that attendance at the graduation ceremony was voluntary.

The District Court enjoined petitioners from continuing the practice on the ground that it violated the Establishment Clause of the First Amendment. The Court of Appeals affirmed.

ISSUE: Does a clergyman's delivery of an invocation and benediction at a public school graduation ceremony violate the Establishment Clause?

DECISION (*Kennedy,* 5-4): *Yes.*

The principle that government may accommodate the free exercise of religion does not supersede the fundamental limitations imposed by the Establishment Clause. The State's involvement in the school prayers challenged today violates these limitations.

A school official, the principal, decided that an invocation and a benediction should be given; this is a choice attributable to the state and, from a constitutional perspective, it is as if a state statute decreed that the prayers must occur. The principal chose the religious participant, here a rabbi, and that choice is also attributable to the state.

The state's role did not end with the decision to include a prayer and with the choice of clergyman. The principal provided the rabbi with a copy of "Guidelines for Civic Occasions" and advised him that his prayers should be nonsectarian. Through these means, the principal directed and controlled the content of the prayers. Even if the only sanction for ignoring the instructions were that the rabbi would not be invited back, we think no religious representative who valued his or her continued reputation and effectiveness in the community would incur the State's displeasure in this regard. It is a cornerstone principle of our Establishment Clause jurisprudence that it is no part of the business of government to compose official prayers for any group of the American people to recite as a part of a religious program carried on by government, and that is what the school officials attempted to do.

The First Amendment's Religion Clauses mean that religious beliefs and religious expression are too precious to be either proscribed or prescribed by the State. These concerns have particular application in the case of school officials, whose effort to monitor prayer will be perceived by the students as inducing a participation they might otherwise reject. Though the efforts of the school officials in this case to find common ground appear to have been a good faith attempt to recognize the common aspects of religions, and not the divisive ones, our precedents do not permit school officials to assist in composing prayers as an incident to a formal exercise for their students. Engel v. Vitale, 370 U.S. 421, 425 (1962); School District of Abington v. Schempp, 374 U.S. 203 (1963). And these same precedents caution us to measure the idea of a civic religion against the central meaning of the Religion Clauses of the First Amendment, which is that all creeds must be tolerated, and none favored. The suggestion that government may establish an official or civic religion as a means of avoiding the establishment of a religion with more specific creeds strikes us as a contradiction that cannot be accepted.

It is argued that our constitutional vision of a free society requires confidence in our own ability to accept or reject ideas of which we do not approve, and that prayer at a high school graduation does nothing more than offer a choice. This argument, however, overlooks a fundamental dynamic of the Constitution. The First Amendment protects speech and religion by quite different mechanisms. Speech is protected by ensuring its full expression even when the government participates, for the very object of some of our most important speech is to persuade the government to adopt an idea as its own. The method for protecting freedom of worship and freedom of conscience in religious matters is quite the reverse. The Establishment Clause is a specific prohibition on forms of state intervention in religious affairs, with no precise counterpart in the speech provisions.

The undeniable fact is that the school district's supervision and control of a high school graduation ceremony places public pressure, as well as peer pressure, on attending students to stand as a group or, at least, maintain respectful silence during the invocation and benediction. This pressure, though subtle and indirect, can be as real as any overt compulsion. Wallace v. Jeffree, 472 U.S. 38 (1985). Of course, in our culture, standing or remaining silent can signify adherence to a view or simple respect for the views of others. And no doubt some persons who have no desire to join a prayer have little objection to standing as a sign of respect for those who do. But for the dissenter of high school age, who has a reasonable perception that she is being forced by the state to pray in a manner her conscience will not allow, the injury is no less real. There can be no doubt that for many, if not most, of the students at the graduation, the act of standing or remaining silent was an expression of participation in the rabbi's prayer. That was the very point of the religious exercise. It is of little comfort to a dissenter, then, to be told that, for her, the act of standing or remaining in silence signifies mere respect, rather than participation. What matters is that, given our social conventions, a reasonable dissenter in this milieu could believe that the group exercise signified her own participation or approval of it.

Finding no violation under these circumstances would place objectors in the dilemma of participating, with all that implies, or protesting. We do not address whether that choice is acceptable if the affected citizens are mature adults, but we think the state may not, consistent with the Establishment Clause, place primary and secondary school children in this position. Research in psychology supports the common assumption that adolescents are often susceptible to pressure from their peers towards conformity, and that the influence is strongest in matters of social convention.

Because of the stipulation that attendance at graduation ceremonies is voluntary, it is argued that the option of not attending the graduation excuses any inducement or coercion in the ceremony itself. However, although attendance may not be required by official decree, it is apparent that a graduating student is not free to absent herself from the graduation exercise in any real sense of the term "voluntary," for absence would require forfeiture of those intangible benefits that have motivated the student through all her high school years.

Inherent differences between the public school system and a session of a state legislature distinguish this case from Marsh v. Chambers, 463 U.S. 783 (1983). The atmosphere at the opening of a session of a state legislature, where adults are free to enter and leave with little comment and for any number of reasons, cannot compare with the constraining potential of the one school event most important for the student to attend. By contrast, at a high school graduation, the state-imposed character of an invocation and benediction by clergy selected by the school combine to make the prayer a state-sanctioned religious exercise in which the student was left with no alternative but to submit. This is different from *Marsh,* and suffices to make the religious exercise a First Amendment violation. Our decisions in *Engel v. Vitale* and *School District of Abington v. Schempp* require us to distinguish the public school context.

We do not hold that every state action implicating religion is invalid if one or a few citizens find it offensive. But the conformity required of the student in this case was too high an exaction to withstand the test of the Establishment Clause.

Blackmun, concurring (joined by Stevens and O'Connor): Government pressure to participate in a religious activity is an obvious indication that the government is endorsing or promoting religion. However, our decisions have gone beyond prohibiting coercion, because the Court has recognized that the fullest possible scope of religious liberty entails more than freedom from coercion. The Establishment Clause protects religious liberty on a grand scale; it is a social compact that guarantees for generations a democracy and a strong religious community—both essential to safeguarding religious liberty.

When the government arrogates to itself a role in religious affairs, it abandons its obligation as guarantor of democracy. Democracy requires the nourishment of dialog and dissent, while religious faith puts its trust in an ultimate divine authority above all human deliberation. When the government appropriates religious truth, those who disagree no longer are questioning the policy judgment of the elected but the rules of a higher authority who is beyond reproach.

It is these understandings and fears that underlie our Establishment Clause jurisprudence. We have believed that religious freedom cannot exist in the absence of a free democratic government, and that such a government cannot endure when there is fusion between religion and the political regime. We have believed that religious freedom cannot thrive in the absence of a vibrant religious community, and that such a community cannot prosper when it is bound to the secular. And we have believed that these were the animating principles behind the adoption of the Establishment Clause. To that end, our cases have prohibited government endorsement of religion, its sponsorship, and active involvement in religion, whether or not citizens were coerced to conform.

Souter, concurring (joined by Stevens and O'Connor): I fully agree that prayers at public school graduation ceremonies indirectly coerce religious observance. But in my view coercion of religious conformity, over and above state endorsement of religious exercise or belief, is not a necessary element of an Establishment Clause violation.

It is contended that, whether or not the Establishment Clause permits extensive nonsectarian support for religion, it does not forbid the State to sponsor affirmations of religious belief that coerce neither support for religion nor participation in religious observance. But we could not adopt that reading without abandoning our settled law.

Over the years, this Court has declared the invalidity of many noncoercive state laws and practices conveying a message of religious endorsement. Our precedents may not always have drawn perfectly straight lines, but they simply cannot support the position that a showing of coercion is necessary to a successful Establishment Clause claim.

The First Amendment forbids not just laws "respecting an establishment of religion," but also those "prohibiting the free exercise thereof." Yet laws that coerce non-adherents to support or participate in any religion or its exercise would, virtually by definition, violate their right to religious free exercise. The distinction between the two clauses is apparent—a violation of the Free Exercise Clause is predicated on coercion while the Establishment Clause violation need not be so attended.

That government must remain neutral in matters of religion does not foreclose it from ever taking religion into account. The State may "accommodate" the free exercise of religion by relieving people from generally applicable rules that interfere with their religious callings. But concern for the position of religious individuals in the modern regulatory state cannot justify favoring religion over disbelief. By these lights one easily sees that, in sponsoring the graduation prayers at issue here, the State has crossed the line from permissible accommodation to unconstitutional establishment.

Religious students cannot complain that omitting prayers from their graduation ceremony would, in any realistic sense, interfere with their spiritual callings. To be sure, many of them invest this rite of passage with spiritual significance, but they may express their religious feelings about it before and after the ceremony. Because they have no need for the machinery of the State to affirm their beliefs, the government's sponsorship of prayer at the graduation ceremony is most reasonably understood as an official endorsement of religion and, in this instance, of theistic religion.

It is further argued that graduation prayers are no different from presidential religious proclamations and similar official "acknowledgments" of religion in public life. But religious invocations in Thanksgiving Day addresses and the like, rarely noticed, ignored without effort, conveyed over an impersonal medium, and directed at no one in particular, inhabit a pallid zone worlds apart from official prayers delivered to a captive audience of public school students and their families.

When public school officials, armed with the State's authority, convey an endorsement of religion to their students, they strike near the core of the Establishment Clause. However "ceremonial" their messages may be, they are flatly unconstitutional.

Scalia, dissenting (joined by Rehnquist, White, and Thomas): In holding that the Establishment Clause prohibits invocations and benedictions at public school graduation ceremonies, the Court today lays waste a tradition that is as old as public school graduation ceremonies themselves, and that is a component of an even more longstanding American tradition of nonsectarian prayer to God at public celebrations generally. As its instrument of destruction, the Court invents a boundless, and boundlessly manipulable, test of psychological coercion. Today's opinion shows more forcefully than volumes of argumentation why our Constitution cannot rest upon the changeable philosophical predilections of the Justices of this Court, but must have deep foundations in the historic practices of our people.

The history and tradition of our nation are replete with public ceremonies featuring prayers of thanksgiving and petition. Such supplications have been a characteristic feature of presidential inaugural addresses from the founding of the nation. Our national celebration of Thanksgiving as a day of prayer similarly dates back to President George Washington. Congressional sessions have opened with a chaplain's prayer ever since the First Congress. And this Court's own sessions have opened with the invocation "God save the United States and this Honorable Court" since the days of Chief Justice John Marshall. In addition to this general tradition of prayer at public ceremonies, there exists a more specific tradition of invocations and benedictions at public school graduation exercises.

The Court seeks to distinguish graduation invocations and benedictions on the ground that they involve "psychological coercion." According to the Court, students at graduation who want "to avoid the fact or appearance of participation" in the invocation and benediction are psychologically obligated by "public pressure, as well as peer pressure, . . . to stand as a group or, at least, maintain respectful silence" during those prayers. This assertion—the very linchpin of the Court's opinion—is almost as intriguing for what it does not say as for what it says. It does not say, for example, that students are psychologically coerced to bow their heads, place their hands in a prayer position, pay attention to the prayers, utter "Amen," or in fact pray.

The Court's notion that a student who simply sits in "respectful silence" during the invocation and benediction (when all others are standing) has somehow joined in the prayers is nothing short of ludicrous. Surely our social conventions have not coarsened to the point that anyone who does not stand on his chair and shout obscenities can reasonably be deemed to have assented to everything said in his presence. Although concededly students exposed to prayer at graduation ceremonies retain the free will to sit, it is surely a permissible inference that one who stands is doing so simply out of respect for the prayers of others.

With respect to the school administrators' role, all the record shows is that the principal invited Rabbi Gutterman, provided him a two-page pamphlet (prepared by the National Conference of Christians and Jews) giving general advice on inclusive prayer for civic occasions, and advised him that his prayers at graduation should be nonsectarian. How these facts can fairly be transformed into the Court's charges that the principal "directed and controlled the content of [Rabbi Gutterman's] prayer," that school officials "monitor prayer" and attempted to "compose official prayers," and that the "government involvement with religious activity in this case is pervasive" is difficult to fathom. The Court identifies nothing in the record remotely suggesting that school officials have ever drafted, edited, screened, or censored graduation prayers, or that Rabbi Gutterman was a mouthpiece of the school officials.

The deeper flaw in the Court's opinion is the Court's making violation of the Establishment Clause hinge on the question whether there was state-induced "peer-pressure" coercion. The coercion that was a hallmark of historical establishments of religion was coercion of religious orthodoxy and of financial support by force of law and threat of penalty. The Establishment Clause was adopted to prohibit such an establishment of religion at the federal level. But attendance at graduation is voluntary, and there is nothing in the record to indicate that failure of attending students to take part in the invocation or benediction was subject to any penalty or discipline.

The Court relies on our school prayer cases, Engel v. Vitale, 370 U.S. 421 (1962), and School District of Abington v. Schempp, 374 U.S. 203 (1963). But whatever the merit of those cases, they do not support, much less compel, the Court's psychojourney. In the first place, *Engel* and *Schempp* do not constitute an exception to the rule that public ceremonies may include prayer; rather, they simply do not fall within the scope of the rule, for the obvious reason that school instruction is not a public ceremony. Second, we have made clear our understanding that school prayer occurs within a framework in which attending school is legally required. The question whether forbidden coercion exists in such a framework is quite different from the question whether forbidden coercion exists in an environment utterly devoid of legal compulsion. In addition, the classroom is inherently an instructional setting, and daily prayer might be thought to raise special concerns regarding state interference with the liberty of parents to direct the religious upbringing of their children. Voluntary prayer at graduation—a one-time ceremony at which parents, friends, and relatives are present—can hardly be thought to raise the same concerns.

Santa Fe Independent School District v. Doe, 530 U.S. 290 (2000)

FACTS: Prior to 1995, a student elected as Santa Fe High School's student council chaplain delivered a prayer over the public address system before each home varsity football game. A group of Mormon and Catholic students or alumni sued to challenge this practice under the Establishment Clause.

While the suit was pending, the school district adopted a different policy that authorized two student elections—the first to determine whether "invocations" should be delivered at games, and the second to select the spokesperson to deliver them. After the students held elections authorizing such prayers and selecting a spokesperson, the district court entered an order modifying the policy to permit only a nonsectarian, non-proselytizing prayer before a game.

However, before that policy could be implemented, it was stayed by the District Court. Both sides appealed to the Court of Appeals for the Fifth Circuit, which held that, even as modified by the District Court, the prayer policy was invalid.

ISSUE: Does the school district's policy permitting student-led prayer over the public address system before football games violate the Establishment Clause?

DECISION (per *Stevens*, 6-3): *Yes.*

(a) The Constitution guarantees at a minimum that government may not coerce anyone to support or participate in religion or its exercise, or otherwise act in a way that establishes a state religion or religious faith, or tends to do so. The school district argues unpersuasively that this principle is inapplicable because the policy's messages are private student speech, not public speech. The delivery of a message such as the invocation here—on school property, at school-sponsored events, over the school's public address system, by a speaker representing the student body, under the supervision of school faculty, and pursuant to a school policy that explicitly and implicitly encourages public prayer—cannot be properly characterized as "private" speech.

Unlike this Court's cases dealing with public forums, the school district has not indicated any intent to open its pregame ceremony to nondiscriminatory use by the student body generally. Instead, the policy allows only one student (the same student for the entire season) to give the invocation, which is subject to particular regulations that confine the content and topic of the student's message. The process implemented by the school district guarantees, by definition, that minority candidates will never prevail and that their views will be effectively silenced.

Moreover, the school district has failed to divorce itself from the invocations' religious content. The policy involves both perceived and actual endorsement of religion, declaring that the student elections take place because the school district "has chosen to permit" student-delivered invocations, that the invocation "shall" be conducted "by the high school student council . . . [u]pon advice and direction of the high school principal," and that it must be consistent with the policy's goals, which include "solemniz[ing] the event." A religious message is the most obvious method of solemnizing an event. Indeed, the only type of message expressly endorsed in the policy is an "invocation," a term that primarily describes an appeal for divine assistance and, as used in the past at the school, has always entailed a focused religious message.

A conclusion that the message is not "private speech" is also established by factors beyond the policy's text, including the official setting in which the invocation is delivered, by the policy's sham secular purposes, and by its history, which indicates that the school district intended to preserve its long-sanctioned practice of prayer before football games.

(b) The Court rejects the school district's argument that it does not coerce students to participate in religious observances. The first part of this argument—that there is no impermissible government coercion because the pregame messages are the product of student choices—fails for the reasons already discussed explaining why the mechanism of the dual elections and student speaker do not turn public speech into private speech. Although the ultimate choice of student speaker is attributable to the students, the school district's decision to hold the constitutionally problematic election is clearly a choice attributable to the state.

The second part of the school district's argument—that there is no coercion here because attendance at an extracurricular event, unlike a graduation ceremony, is voluntary—is unpersuasive. For some students, such as cheerleaders, members of the band, and the team members themselves, attendance at football games is mandated, sometimes for class credit. The school district's argument also minimizes the immense social pressure, or truly genuine desire, felt by many students to be involved in the extracurricular event that is American high school football. The Constitution demands that schools not force on students the difficult choice between whether to attend these games or to risk facing a personally offensive religious ritual.

(c) The Court also rejects the school district's argument that the challenge to the policy is premature because no invocation has as yet been delivered under the policy. This argument assumes that the Court is concerned only with the serious constitutional injury that occurs when a student is forced to participate in an act of religious worship because she chooses to attend a school event. But the Constitution also requires that the Court keep in mind the myriad, subtle ways in which Establishment Clause values can be eroded, and guard against other different, yet equally important, constitutional injuries. One is the mere passage by the school district of a policy that has the purpose and perception of government establishment of religion. The policy's text and the circumstances surrounding its enactment reveal that it has such a purpose.

The plain language of the policy clearly spells out the extent of school involvement in both the election of the speaker and the content of the message. Additionally, the text of the policy specifies only one, clearly preferred message—the district's traditional religious "invocation." Finally, the content restrictions of the policy confirm that it is not a content-neutral regulation that creates a limited public forum for the expression of student speech.

Our examination, however, need not stop at an analysis of the text of the policy. This case comes to us as the latest challenge to institutional practices that unquestionably violated the Establishment Clause. One of those practices was the district's long-established tradition of sanctioning student-led prayer at varsity football games.

The district, nevertheless, asks us to pretend that we do not recognize what every Santa Fe High School student understands clearly—that this policy is about prayer. We refuse to turn a blind eye to the context in which this policy arose, and that context quells any doubt that this policy was implemented with the purpose of endorsing school prayer.

Therefore, the simple enactment of this policy, with the purpose and perception of school endorsement of student prayer, was a constitutional violation. We need not wait for the inevitable to confirm and magnify the constitutional injury.

In addition, through its election scheme, the school district has established a governmental mechanism that empowers the student body majority to subject students of minority views to constitutionally improper messages. The award of that power alone is not acceptable.

For the foregoing reasons, the policy is invalid on its face.

Rehnquist, dissenting (joined by Scalia and Thomas): The Court distorts existing precedent to conclude that the school district's student-message program is invalid on its face under the Establishment Clause. But even more disturbing than its holding is the tone of the Court's opinion; it bristles with hostility to all things religious in public life.

The plaintiffs challenged the student-message program at football games before it had been put into practice. Therefore, the question is not whether the policy *may be* applied in violation of the Establishment Clause, but whether it inevitably will be. The Court, venturing into the realm of prophecy, decides that it "need not wait for the inevitable" and invalidates the policy on its face.

The Court holds that merely granting the student body the power to elect a speaker that may choose to pray, "regardless of the students' ultimate use of it, is not acceptable." However, any speech that may occur as a result of the election process here would be *private,* not *government,* speech. The elected student, not the government, would choose what to say. Support for the Court's holding cannot be found in any of our cases. And it essentially invalidates all student elections. A newly elected student body president, or even a newly elected prom king or queen, could use opportunities for public speaking to say prayers. Under the Court's view, the mere grant of power to the students to vote for such offices, in light of the fear that those elected might publicly pray, violates the Establishment Clause.

With respect to the policy's purpose, the Court holds that "the simple enactment of this policy, with the purpose and perception of school endorsement of student prayer, was a constitutional violation." But the policy itself has plausible secular purposes: "[T]o solemnize the event, to promote good sportsmanship and student safety, and to establish the appropriate environment for the competition." The Court grants no deference to—and appears openly hostile toward—the policy's stated purposes, and wastes no time in concluding that they are a sham.

If the policy were implemented, it might possibly be applied in an unconstitutional manner, but it will be time enough to invalidate it if that is found to be the case.

Adding "Under God" to the Pledge of Allegiance

In 1942, in the midst of World War II, Congress adopted a joint resolution officially recognizing the Pledge of Allegiance to the Flag of the United States of America. The pledge then stated: "I pledge allegiance to the flag of the United States of America and to the Republic for which it stands, one Nation indivisible, with liberty and justice for all." In 1954 Congress amended the wording to insert "under God" after "one Nation."

In Elk Grove Unified School District v. Newdow, 542 U.S. 1 (2004), the Supreme Court was asked to consider the applicability of the *Lee* and *Santa Fe* decisions to the "under God" addition. The case, however, ended inconclusively when the Court dismissed the case on the ground that the plaintiff lacked standing to bring the lawsuit.

At issue in the case was a school district's requirement that teachers lead a recitation of the pledge every day in class. California law provides that every public elementary school must begin each day with "appropriate patriotic exercises" and that this require- ment may be satisfied by recitation of the pledge. The Elk Grove Unified School Dis- trict implemented the state law by requiring that "[e]ach elementary school class recite the pledge of allegiance to the flag once each day." Students who objected on religious grounds could abstain.

The plaintiff, an atheist, claimed that the recitation of the pledge in his daughter's elementary school classroom violated the First Amendment. The District Court dis- missed the claim, but the Ninth Circuit (2-1) reversed. The court majority held that, although the plaintiff's daughter was not required to recite the pledge, she was uncon- stitutionally coerced to listen to a religious message during the daily recitation of the pledge by others. The dissenting judge argued that the inclusion of the two words in the pledge was *de minimis* and insufficient to constitute coercion.

After granting review, the Supreme Court (5-3) declined to pass on the constitu- tional issue, holding that the girl's father lacked the requisite standing because of his lack of legal custody of his daughter and the mother's desire to have her continue recit- ing the pledge. Stevens's opinion for the majority was joined by Souter, Kennedy, Ginsburg, and Breyer. Rehnquist, Thomas, and O'Connor wrote separate opinions addressing the merits and rejecting the constitutional challenge. (Scalia recused him- self because he had previously made a speech in which he had stated his view that inclusion of "under God" in the pledge did not violate the Constitution.)

Religious Symbols on Public Property

Religious symbols on public property are frequently challenged under the Establish- ment Clause. Determining their constitutionality is likely to be fact-specific and turn on the particular context and history of the display.

For example, in Capitol Square Review and Advisory Board v. Pinette, 515 U.S. 753 (1995), the issue was whether the Ku Klux Klan (KKK) should be prevented from erecting a large cross in a public park across from the Ohio statehouse. The park, under Ohio law, is designated as a forum for discussion of public questions. In light of the park's designation, seven Justices (although without any opinion joined by a majority) agreed that allowing the cross could not be deemed a governmental endorse- ment of religion and, furthermore, that excluding the cross would violate KKK's free speech rights.

Allegheny County v. Greater Pittsburgh ACLU, 492 U.S. 573 (1989), involved two different religious displays: a nativity scene in a display case in a county courthouse, and a menorah next to a large Christmas tree in front of a city building (with a sign say- ing that the city supports "liberty"). The Court held that the nativity scene violated the Establishment Clause (5-4) because it was inherently a religious symbol implying endorsement of Christianity. On the other hand, the display combining the menorah and the Christmas tree was found permissible (6-3) because it did not endorse any par- ticular religion and was instead a neutral reflection of the holiday season.

In Stone v. Graham, 449 U.S. 39 (1980) (per curiam), the Court (6-3) struck down a Kentucky statute requiring that a copy of the Ten Commandments be posted in every public school classroom in the state. The Court stated:

> The pre-eminent purpose for posting the Ten Commandments on schoolroom walls is plainly religious in nature. The Ten Commandments are undeniably a sacred text in the Jewish and Christian faiths, and no legislative recitation of a supposed secular purpose can blind us to that fact.

In 2005, 25 years later, the Court decided two new cases involving displays of the Ten Commandments. Both cases were decided 5 to 4. In one case, the Court upheld a six-foot-high Ten Commandments monument on the grounds of the Texas Capitol, while ruling in the other case that framed copies of the Commandments on the walls of two Kentucky county courthouses were unconstitutional. The ten individual opinions in the two cases total 136 pages and reflect a wide variety of views—leading one Court of Appeals to describe this area of the law as "Establishment Clause purgatory" (ACLU v. Mercer County, 432 F.23d 624, 626 (6th Cir. 2005)).

In the Kentucky case, McCreary County v. ACLU, 545 U.S. 844 (2005), the Ten Commandments displays were originally placed in the courthouses for the express purpose of demonstrating "America's Christian heritage." After an initial challenge, local officials added copies of the Declaration of Independence, the Mayflower Compact, the Bill of Rights, and other historic documents; the officials called the expanded group of documents the "foundations of American law and government."

In his opinion for the majority holding the displays unconstitutional, Justice Souter emphasized the history of the courthouse displays. The claim that the displays had a secular purpose, he said, "was an apparent sham."

In her concurring opinion in the Kentucky case, Justice O'Connor said, "It is true that many Americans find the Commandments in accord with their personal beliefs. . . . But we do not count heads before enforcing the First Amendment." She said that the country had worked well, when compared with nations gripped by religious violence, by keeping religion "a matter for the individual conscience, not for the prosecutor or bureaucrat."

Dissenting in the Kentucky case, Justice Scalia (joined by Rehnquist and Thomas) accused the majority of demonstrating hostility to religion and departing from the intent of the Constitution's framers:

> How can the Court *possibly* assert that "the First Amendment mandates governmental neutrality between religion and nonreligion," and that "[m]anifesting a purpose to favor adherence to religion generally" is unconstitutional? Who says so? Surely not the words of the Constitution. Surely not the history and traditions that reflect our society's constant understanding of those words. . . .
>
> Nothing stands behind the Court's assertion that governmental affirmation of the society's belief in God is unconstitutional except the Court's own say-so, citing as support only the unsubstantiated say-so of earlier Courts going back no farther than the mid-20th century. And it is, moreover, a thoroughly discredited say-so. It is discredited, to begin with, because a majority of the Justices on the current Court (including at least one Member of today's majority [Justice O'Connor]) have, in separate opinions, repudiated the supposed principle of neutrality between religion and irreligion. And it is discredited because the Court has not had the courage (or the foolhardiness) to apply the neutrality principle consistently.

What distinguishes the rule of law from the dictatorship of a shifting Supreme Court majority is the absolutely indispensable requirement that judicial opinions be grounded in consistently applied principle. That is what prevents judges from ruling now this way, now that—thumbs up or thumbs down—as their personal preferences dictate.

The display upheld in the Texas case, Van Orden v. Perry, 545 U.S. 677 (2005), is one of hundreds of granite monuments that were erected in public places around the country by the Fraternal Order of Eagles in the 1950s and 1960s. The monument is one of 17 monuments and 21 historical markers in the 22-acre park and includes (in addition to the Ten Commandments) an American eagle, two Stars of David, and a symbol of Christ.

In sustaining the constitutionality of the Texas monument, Chief Justice Rehnquist's plurality opinion (joined by Scalia, Kennedy, and Thomas) acknowledged that "Of course, the Ten Commandments are religious" but stated that in addition "the Ten Commandments have an undeniable historical meaning" and that "Simply having religious content or promoting a message consistent with a religious doctrine does not run afoul of the Establishment Clause." Rehnquist pointed to "an unbroken history of official acknowledgment by all three branches of government of the role of religion in American life from at least 1789." He further stated:

We need only look within our own Courtroom. Since 1935, Moses has stood, holding two tablets that reveal portions of the Ten Commandments written in Hebrew, among other lawgivers in the south frieze. Representations of the Ten Commandments adorn the metal gates lining the north and south sides of the Courtroom as well as the doors leading into the Courtroom. Moses also sits on the exterior east facade of the building holding the Ten Commandments tablets. Similar acknowledgments can be seen throughout a visitor's tour of our Nation's Capital.

Rehnquist distinguished *Stone v. Graham,* which struck down the posting of the Commandments in school classrooms, on the ground that the Court has been particularly vigilant in monitoring compliance with the Establishment Clause in public schools.

Justice Breyer (who had voted with the majority in the Kentucky case to invalidate the postings in the courthouses) provided the fifth vote in the Texas case to uphold the validity of the monument. In his opinion concurring in the judgment, Breyer stated that the Texas monument presented a "borderline case" that depended not on any single formula but on context and judgment. Although acknowledging that the text of the Ten Commandments "undeniably has a religious message," he stated that the text itself is not determinative because the Court must examine "the message that the text . . . conveys . . . [in] the context of the display." The monument's physical setting, he said, "suggests little or nothing of the sacred", and the passing of 40 years without any previous dispute about the monument suggested that the public had understood the monument not as a religious object but as part of a "broader moral and historical message reflective of a cultural heritage." Further, he said, a contrary decision would lead to the removal of many long-standing depictions of the Ten Commandments in public places, and "it could thereby create the very kind of religiously based divisiveness that the Establishment Clause seeks to avoid."

In his dissenting opinion (joined by Ginsburg), Justice Stevens agreed that

The wall that separates the church from the State does not prohibit the government from acknowledging the religious beliefs and practices of the American people, nor does it require governments to hide works of art or historic memorabilia from public view just because they also have religious significance.

But he contended that,

Viewed on its face, Texas' display has no purported connection to God's role in the formation of Texas or the founding of our Nation; nor does it provide the reasonable observer with any basis to guess that it was erected to honor any individual or organization.

Instead, "The message transmitted by Texas' chosen display is quite plain: This State endorses the divine code of the 'Judeo-Christian' God." Rejecting Rehnquist's analysis, Stevens stated: "This Nation's resolute commitment to neutrality with respect to religion is flatly inconsistent with the plurality's wholehearted validation of an official state endorsement of the message that there is one, and only one, God."

O'Connor and Souter (joined by Stevens and Ginsburg) also filed dissenting opinions in the Texas monument case. The four dissenters were the four Justices who, along with Breyer, found the Kentucky courthouse displays invalid. Only Breyer voted for the result in both decisions.

Walz v. Tax Comm'n of City of New York, 397 U.S. 664 (1970)

FACTS: The plaintiff is an owner of real estate in New York. He sought an injunction in the New York state courts to prohibit the grant of property tax exemptions to religious organizations. A New York statute exempts

[r]eal property owned by a corporation or association organized exclusively for the moral or mental improvement of men and women, or for religious, bible, tract, charitable, benevolent, missionary, hospital, infirmary, educational, public playground, scientific, literary, bar association, medical society, library, patriotic, historical or cemetery purposes, for the enforcement of laws relating to children or animals, or for two or more such purposes.

The plaintiff (not a member of any religious organization) contended that the exemption for church property indirectly requires him to make an involuntary contribution to religious bodies and thereby violates the Establishment Clause. The trial court's decision rejecting the claim was affirmed by the New York appellate courts.

ISSUE: Does the exemption for religious organizations violate the Establishment Clause?

DECISION (per *Burger*, 8-1): *No.*
The legislative purpose of a property tax exemption is neither the advancement nor the inhibition of religion; it is neither sponsorship nor hostility. New York, in common with the other States, has determined that certain entities that exist in a harmonious relationship to the community at large, and that foster its "moral or mental improvement," should not be inhibited in their activities by property taxation or the hazard of loss of those properties for nonpayment of taxes. It has not singled out one particular church or religious group or even churches as such; rather, it has granted exemption

to all houses of religious worship within a broad class of property owned by nonprofit, quasi-public corporations that include hospitals, libraries, playgrounds, scientific, professional, historical, and patriotic groups. The State has an affirmative policy that considers these groups as beneficial and stabilizing influences in community life and finds this classification useful and desirable, as well as in the public interest.

Governments have not always been tolerant of religious activity, and hostility toward religion has taken many shapes and forms—economic, political, and sometimes harshly oppressive. Grants of exemption historically reflect the concern of authors of constitutions and statutes as to the latent dangers inherent in the imposition of property taxes; exemption constitutes a reasonable and balanced attempt to guard against those dangers. We cannot read New York's statute as attempting to establish religion; it is simply sparing the exercise of religion from the burden of property taxation levied on private profit institutions.

Determining that the legislative purpose of tax exemption is not aimed at establishing, sponsoring, or supporting religion does not end the inquiry, however. We must also be sure that the end result—the effect—is not an excessive government entanglement with religion. The test is inescapably one of degree. Either course, taxation of churches or exemption, occasions some degree of involvement with religion. Elimination of exemption would tend to expand the involvement of government by giving rise to tax valuation of church property, tax liens, tax foreclosures, and the direct confrontations and conflicts that follow in the train of those legal processes.

Granting tax exemptions to churches necessarily operates to afford an indirect economic benefit and also gives rise to some, but yet a lesser, involvement than taxing them. In analyzing either alternative, the questions are whether the involvement is excessive, and whether it is a continuing one calling for official and continuing surveillance leading to an impermissible degree of entanglement. Obviously a direct money subsidy would be a relationship pregnant with involvement and, as with most governmental grant programs, could encompass sustained and detailed administrative relationships for enforcement of statutory or administrative standards, but that is not this case. The hazards of churches supporting government are hardly less in their potential than the hazards of government supporting churches; each relationship carries some involvement rather than the desired insulation and separation.

No one has ever suggested that tax exemption has converted libraries, art galleries, or hospitals into arms of the State or put employees "on the public payroll." There is no genuine nexus between tax exemption and establishment of religion. The exemption creates only a minimal and remote involvement between church and state and far less than taxation of churches.

Separation in this context cannot mean absence of all contact; the complexities of modern life inevitably produce some contact, and the fire and police protection received by houses of religious worship are no more than incidental benefits accorded all persons or institutions within a State's boundaries, along with many other exempt organizations.

All of the 50 States provide for tax exemption of places of worship, most of them doing so by constitutional guarantees. Few concepts are more deeply embedded in the fabric of our national life, beginning with pre-Revolutionary colonial times, than for the government to exercise at the very least this kind of benevolent neutrality toward churches and religious exercise generally so long as none was favored over others and none suffered interference.

No one acquires a vested or protected right in violation of the Constitution by long use, even when that span of time covers our entire national existence and indeed pre-dates it. Yet an unbroken practice of according the exemption to churches, openly and by affirmative state action, not covertly or by state inaction, is not something to be lightly cast aside. As Justice Holmes stated: "If a thing has been practised for two hundred years by common consent, it will need a strong case for the Fourteenth Amendment to affect it." Jackman v. Rosenbaum Co., 260 U.S. 22, 31 (1922).

The adoption of the early exemptions, without any controversy, strongly suggests that they were not thought incompatible with constitutional prohibitions against involvements of church and state. The exemptions have continued uninterrupted to the present day. They are in force in all 50 States. No judicial decision, state or federal, has ever held that they violate the Establishment Clause.

As to the New York statute, we now confirm that view.

Brennan, concurring: The history, purpose, and operation of real property tax exemptions for religious organizations must be examined to determine whether the Establishment Clause is breached by such exemptions.

History is particularly compelling in the present case because of the undeviating acceptance given religious tax exemptions from our earliest days as a nation. Rarely if ever has this Court considered the constitutionality of a practice for which the historical support is so overwhelming.

The exemptions have continued uninterrupted to the present day. They are in force in all 50 States. No judicial decision, state or federal, has ever held that they violate the Establishment Clause. For almost 200 years the view expressed in the actions of legislatures and courts has been that tax exemptions for churches do not threaten the type of interdependence between religion and state that the First Amendment was designed to prevent.

Government has two basic secular purposes for granting real property tax exemptions to religious organizations. First, these organizations are exempted because they, among a range of other private, nonprofit organizations contribute to the well-being of the community in a variety of nonreligious ways, and thereby bear burdens that would otherwise either have to be met by general taxation, or be left undone, to the detriment of the community.

Second, government grants exemptions to religious organizations because they uniquely contribute to the pluralism of American society by their religious activities. To this end, New York extends its exemptions not only to religious and social service organizations but also to scientific, literary, bar, library, patriotic, and historical groups, and generally to institutions "organized exclusively for the moral or mental improvement of men and women." The very breadth of this scheme of exemptions negates any suggestion that the State intends to single out religious organizations for special preference. The scheme is not designed to inject any religious activity into a nonreligious context, as was the case with school prayers.

General subsidies of religious activities would, of course, constitute impermissible state involvement with religion. Tax exemptions and general subsidies, however, are qualitatively different. Though both provide economic assistance, they do so in fundamentally different ways. A subsidy involves the direct transfer of public monies to the subsidized enterprise and uses resources exacted from taxpayers as a whole. An exemption, on the other hand, involves no such transfer. It assists the exempted enterprise only passively, by relieving a privately funded venture of the burden of paying taxes.

Moreover, it cannot realistically be said that termination of religious tax exemptions would quantitatively lessen the extent of state involvement with religion. Such termination, if not impossible, would certainly require extensive state investigation into church operations and finances. It would also give rise to the necessity for tax valuation of church property, tax liens, tax foreclosures, and the direct confrontations and conflicts that follow in the train of those legal processes. Whether government grants or withholds the exemptions, it is going to be involved with religion.

Against this background of the history, purpose, and operation of religious tax exemptions, I cannot find that the exemptions are unconstitutional. To the extent that the exemptions further secular ends, they do not advance essentially religious purposes. To the extent that purely religious activities are benefited by the exemptions, the benefit is passive. Government does not affirmatively foster these activities by exempting religious organizations from taxes, as it would were it to subsidize them.

Harlan, concurring in the result: Two requirements frequently articulated and applied in our cases for achieving this goal are "neutrality" and "voluntarism." While these concepts are at the core of the Religion Clauses, they may not suffice by themselves to achieve in all cases the purposes of the First Amendment. Governmental involvement, while neutral, may be so direct or in such degree as to engender a risk of politicizing religion. Although the very fact of neutrality may limit the intensity of involvement, government participation in certain programs, whose very nature is apt to entangle the state in details of administration and planning, may escalate to the point of inviting undue fragmentation.

This legislation neither encourages nor discourages participation in religious life and thus satisfies the voluntarism requirement of the First Amendment. Unlike the instances of school prayers, or "released time" programs, the State is not utilizing the prestige, power, and influence of a public institution to bring religion into the lives of citizens.

The statute also satisfies the requirement of neutrality. In any particular case the critical question is whether the circumference of legislation encircles a class so broad that it can be fairly concluded that religious institutions could be thought to fall within the natural perimeter. The New York statute has defined a class of nontaxable entities whose common denominator is their nonprofit pursuit of activities devoted to cultural and moral improvement and the doing of "good works" by performing certain social services in the community that might otherwise have to be assumed by government. The statute would appear not to omit any organization that could be reasonably thought to contribute to that goal. As long as the breadth of exemption includes groups that pursue cultural, moral, or spiritual improvement in multifarious secular ways, including, I would suppose, groups whose avowed tenets may be antitheological, atheistic, or agnostic, I can see no lack of neutrality in extending the benefit of the exemption to organized religious groups.

Whether the present exemption entails that degree of involvement with government that presents a threat of fragmentation along religious lines involves, for me, a more subtle question than deciding simply whether neutrality has been violated. That question must be reserved for a later case upon a record that fully develops all the pertinent considerations such as the significance and character of subsidies in our political system and the role of the government in administering the subsidy in relation to the particular program aided.

I do not believe that a "slippery slope" is necessarily without a constitutional toe-hold. It is the task of this tribunal to draw distinctions, including fine ones, in the process of interpreting the Constitution. The prospect of difficult questions of judgment in constitutional law should not be the basis for prohibiting legislative action that is constitutionally permissible. I think this one is, and on the foregoing premises join with the Court in upholding this New York statute.

Douglas, dissenting: In my view the question in the case is whether believers—organized in church groups—can be made exempt from real estate taxes, merely because they are believers, while nonbelievers, whether organized or not, must pay the real estate taxes.

Justice Harlan says he "would suppose" that the tax exemption extends to "groups whose avowed tenets may be antitheological, atheistic, or agnostic." If it does, then the line between believers and nonbelievers has not been drawn. But, with all respect, there is not even a suggestion in the present record that the statute covers property used exclusively by organizations for "antitheological purposes," "atheistic purposes," or "agnostic purposes."

With all due respect, the governing principle is not controlled by Everson v. Board of Education, 330 U.S. 1 (1947). At the parochial schools involved in *Everson,* education in the secular sense was combined with religious indoctrination. Even so, *Everson* was 5 to 4 and, though one of the five, I have since had grave doubts about it, because I have become convinced that grants to institutions teaching a sectarian creed violate the Establishment Clause. This case, however, is quite different. Education is not involved. The financial support rendered here is to the church, the place of worship, and a tax exemption is a subsidy.

The State has a public policy of encouraging private public welfare organizations, which it desires to encourage through tax exemption. Welfare services, whether performed by churches or by nonreligious groups, may well serve the public welfare. Whether a particular church seeking an exemption for its welfare work could constitutionally pass muster would depend on the special facts. Subsidies either through direct grant or tax exemption for sectarian causes, whether carried on by church qua church or by church qua welfare agency, must be treated differently, lest we in time allow the church qua church to be on the public payroll, which, I fear, is imminent.

I conclude that this tax exemption is unconstitutional.

Texas Monthly, Inc. v. Bullock, 489 U.S. 1 (1989)

FACTS: A Texas statute exempted from sales and use taxes "[p]eriodicals . . . published or distributed by a religious faith . . . consist[ing] wholly of writings promulgating the teachings of the faith and books . . . consist[ing] wholly of writings sacred to a religious faith." The plaintiff, the publisher of a nonexempt magazine, *Texas Monthly,* paid under protest sales taxes on its subscription sales and sued to recover those payments in state court. The plaintiff claimed that the tax was unconstitutional on the ground that the exclusive exemption for religious periodicals promoted religion in violation of the Establishment Clause.

The state trial court agreed and struck down the tax as applied to nonreligious periodicals. However, the Texas Court of Appeals reversed, holding that the exemption served the secular purpose of preserving separation between church and state, did not have the primary effect of advancing or inhibiting religion, and did not produce an impermissible government entanglement with religion.

ISSUE: Does the exemption violate the Establishment Clause?

DECISION (6-3): *Yes* (none of the four opinions, however, was joined by a majority of the Court).

Brennan (plurality opinion joined by Marshall and Stevens): In proscribing all laws "respecting an establishment of religion," the First Amendment prohibits, at the very least, legislation that constitutes an endorsement of one or another set of religious beliefs or of religion generally.

It does not follow, of course, that government policies with secular objectives may not incidentally benefit religion. The nonsectarian aims of government and the interests of religious groups often overlap, and this Court has never required that public authorities refrain from implementing reasonable measures to advance legitimate secular goals merely because they would thereby relieve religious groups of costs they would otherwise incur.

Thus, in Mueller v. Allen, 436 U.S. 388 (1983), we upheld a state income tax deduction for the cost of tuition, transportation, and nonreligious textbooks. Although the deduction benefited parochial schools and parents whose children attended them, we concluded that this subsidy did not deprive the law of an overriding secular purpose or effect. Particularly significant in that connection was the availability of the deduction for educational expenses incurred by all parents, including those whose children attend public schools and those whose children attend nonsectarian private schools or sectarian private schools.

And in Walz v. Tax Comm'n of New York City, 397 U.S. 664 (1970), we sustained a property tax exemption that applied to religious properties no less than to real estate owned by a wide array of nonprofit organizations, despite the sizable tax savings it accorded religious groups. The breadth of New York's property tax exemption was essential to our holding that it was not aimed at establishing, sponsoring, or supporting religion.

By contrast, Texas's sales tax exemption for periodicals published or distributed by a religious faith and consisting wholly of writings promulgating the teaching of the faith lacks sufficient breadth to pass scrutiny under the Establishment Clause. Every tax exemption constitutes a subsidy that affects nonqualifying taxpayers, forcing them to become indirect and vicarious donors to the beneficiaries of the tax exemption.

When government grants a subsidy exclusively to religious organizations that is not required by the Free Exercise Clause and that either significantly burdens nonbeneficiaries or cannot reasonably be seen as removing a deterrent to the free exercise of religion, it provides unjustifiable awards of assistance to religious organizations and cannot but convey a message of endorsement to slighted members of the community. It is difficult to view Texas's narrow exemption as anything but state sponsorship of religious belief. This is particularly true where, as here, the subsidy is targeted at writings that *promulgate* the teachings of religious faiths. It is difficult to view Texas's exemption as anything but state sponsorship of religious belief.

Texas claims that the exemption serves a compelling interest in avoiding violations of the Free Exercise Clause. But the State has not presented any evidence that the payment of a sales tax by purchasers of religious periodicals would offend their religious beliefs or inhibit religious activity. No need to accommodate religious activity has been shown.

Contrary to the dissent's claims, we in no way suggest that *all* benefits conferred exclusively upon religious groups are forbidden by the Establishment Clause unless they are mandated by the Free Exercise Clause. Our decisions in Zorach v. Clauson, 343 U.S. 306 (1952), and Corporation of Presiding Bishop v. Amos, 483 U.S. 327 (1987), offer two examples. In *Zorach,* the Court upheld New York City's decision to release students from public schools so that they might obtain religious instruction elsewhere; the practice was found not to coerce students who wished to remain behind, nor did it impose monetary costs on their parents or other taxpayers who opposed, or were indifferent to, the religious instruction given to students who were released. At issue in *Corporation of Presiding Bishop* was the provision of the 1964 Civil Rights Act allowing religious organizations to discriminate on the basis of religion in their employment policies; the Court upheld the exemption, though it had some adverse effect on those holding or seeking employment with those organizations, since it prevented potentially serious encroachments on protected religious freedoms. Texas's tax exemption, by contrast, does not remove a burden on religious activity protected by the Free Exercise Clause.

How expansive the class of exempt organizations or activities must be to withstand constitutional assault depends upon the State's secular aim in granting a tax exemption. If the State chose to subsidize, by means of a tax exemption, all groups that contributed to the community's cultural, intellectual, and moral betterment, then the exemption for religious publications could be retained, provided that the exemption swept as widely as the exemption in *Walz.* In any particular case the critical question is whether the circumference of legislation encircles a class so broad that it can be fairly concluded that religious institutions could be thought to fall within the natural perimeter.

Because Texas's sales tax exemption lacks a secular objective that would justify this preference along with similar benefits for nonreligious publications, and because it effectively endorses religious belief, the exemption manifestly fails this test.

White, concurring, concluded that the Texas law violates the Press Clause of the First Amendment by taxing the appellant while exempting other publishers solely on the basis of the religious content of their publications.

Blackmun, concurring (joined by O'Connor) concluded that the extent to which the Free Exercise Clause requires a tax exemption for the sale of religious literature by a religious organization need not be decided here. Instead, the case should be resolved on the narrow ground that the Establishment Clause is violated by an exemption such as the one at issue that is limited to religious organizations' sales of their religious literature. The Texas statute gives preferential support for the communication of religious messages and offends the most basic understanding of what the Establishment Clause is all about.

Scalia, dissenting (joined by Rehnquist and Kennedy): As a judicial demolition project, today's decision is impressive. The Court today topples an exemption for religious publications of a sort that expressly appears in the laws of at least 15 of the 45 States that have sales and use taxes. And even in States without express exemptions, many churches and tax assessors have understood sales taxes to be inapplicable to the religious literature typically offered for sale in church foyers.

In addition, when one expands the inquiry to other types of taxes such as property, income, amusement, and motor vehicle taxes, the Court's achievement is even more impressive. At least 45 States as well as the federal government provide exemptions for religious groups without analogous exemptions for other types of nonprofit institutions.

I find no basis in the text of the Constitution, this Court's decisions, or the traditions of our people to disapprove this long-standing and widespread practice.

In *Walz,* in sustaining the New York property tax exemption, we recognized that the exemption of religion from various taxes had existed without challenge in the law of all 50 States and the national government before, during, and after the framing of the First Amendment's Religion Clauses, and had achieved "undeviating acceptance" throughout the 200-year history of our nation. Yet in the present case Justice Brennan seeks to explain away *Walz* by asserting that "[t]he breadth of New York's property tax exemption was essential to our holding that it was not aimed at establishing, sponsoring, or supporting religion." Such an interpretation misreads *Walz.* The finding of valid legislative purpose in *Walz* was based on the more direct proposition that "exemption constitutes a reasonable and balanced attempt to guard against" the "latent dangers" of governmental hostility towards religion "inherent in the imposition of property taxes." The Court did not approve an exemption for charities that happened to benefit religion; it approved an exemption for religion as an exemption for religion.

In repudiating what *Walz* plainly approved, the Court achieves a revolution in our Establishment Clause jurisprudence, effectively overruling many other cases that were based, as *Walz* was, on the "accommodation of religion" rationale. It is not always easy to determine when accommodation slides over into promotion, and neutrality into favoritism, but the withholding of a tax upon the dissemination of religious materials is not even a close case.

Today's decision introduces a new strain of irrationality into our Religion Clause jurisprudence. It is not right—it is not constitutionally healthy—that this Court should feel authorized to refashion anew our civil society's relationship with religion, adopting a theory of church and state that is contradicted by current practice, tradition, and even our own case law.

13

The Free Exercise Clause

Compelled Exemptions

Under the Constitution people may think and believe anything that they want. In Reynolds v. United States, 98 U.S. 145, 164 (1878), the first case to construe the Free Exercise Clause, the Court recognized that "Congress was deprived of all legislative power over mere opinion, but was left free to reach actions." Similarly, in Cantwell v. Connecticut, 310 U.S. 296, 303-304 (1940), the Court pointed out that the Free Exercise Clause "embraces two concepts—freedom to believe and freedom to act. The first is absolute but, in the nature of things, the second cannot be."

As those decisions emphasize, one of the key functions of the Free Exercise Clause is to protect the expression of religious beliefs and views. But the more difficult issues involving the Clause arise in connection with the validity of religious *exemptions* from statutes.

These exemptions are of two types: (1) exemptions that the government *may* choose to grant (*permitted* exemptions) and (2) exemptions that the government *must* grant (*compelled* exemptions).

When a legislature enacts a statute such as a tax law, the legislature has broad discretion in choosing whether to grant an exemption that benefits churches and religious groups, *provided* that the exemption is not limited to religion and also includes other educational or cultural organizations. But if the exemption discriminates in favor of religion, a significant question is presented under the Establishment Clause. Thus, as the *Texas Monthly* decision recognized, a tax exemption exclusively for religion is essentially a government subsidy for religion and is therefore invalid.

On the other hand, if the legislature enacts a statute that contains no exemption for religion and either requires or forbids certain conduct (for example, prohibiting polygamy), and if a member of a particular religion claims that complying with the statute would interfere with his or her exercise of the religion, a significant question is presented under the Free Exercise Clause: Does the Clause require the State to accept the claim and refrain from enforcing the statute in that situation—thereby in effect imposing on the State an exemption that its legislature had never granted—or does the statute trump the religious claim?

Early Supreme Court decisions resolved that issue in favor of legislative authority. E.g., Reynolds v. United States, 98 U.S. 145 (1878) (holding that the Free Exercise Clause did not exempt Mormons from complying with a federal law prohibiting polygamy law in the territories).

In later decisions such as Sherbert v. Verner, 374 U.S. 398 (1963) (holding that a State could not deny unemployment benefits to individuals who left their jobs for religious reasons), the Court interpreted the Free Exercise Clause more broadly to impose a heavy burden on government to justify denial of a religious exemption from a generally applicable statute. Under those decisions, the statute was subject to "strict scrutiny" and the government was obliged to carry the burden of demonstrating a compelling governmental interest for refusing to grant the exemption.

But in its 1990 *Smith* decision, the Supreme Court again changed course and instead placed the burden on the person or group seeking the exemption. The decision ignited a national controversy that still continues.

Employment Division, Department of Human Resources of Oregon v. Smith, 494 U.S. 872 (1990)

FACTS: Oregon law prohibits the possession of peyote, a hallucinogen. Alfred Smith and Galen Black are members of the Native American Church, which regards eating peyote as an act of worship and communion. They were both fired from their jobs with a private employer because they had used peyote as part of a religious ceremony of the church. When they applied for state unemployment benefits, the benefits were denied on the ground that they had lost their jobs due to "misconduct."

The Oregon Supreme Court held that the application of Oregon's prohibition of peyote to its use for sacramental purposes was invalid under the Free Exercise Clause of the First Amendment and therefore the State could not withhold benefits from individuals because of their exercise of constitutionally protected rights.

ISSUE: Does the Free Exercise Clause preclude application of the Oregon statute to the sacramental use of peyote?

DECISION (per *Scalia*, 6-3): *No.*

(1) Smith and Black base their Exercise Clause claim on prior decisions of this Court such as Sherbert v. Verner, 374 U.S. 398 (1963), holding that a State could not condition the availability of unemployment insurance on an individual's willingness to forgo conduct required by his religion. In those cases, however, the conduct at issue was not prohibited by law.

In this case, Smith and Black seek to carry the meaning of "prohibiting the free exercise [of religion]" one large step further. They contend that their religious motivation for using peyote places them beyond the reach of a criminal law that is not specifically directed at their religious practice, and that is concededly constitutional as applied to those who use the drug for other reasons.

Our decisions have never held that an individual's religious beliefs excuse him from compliance with an otherwise valid law prohibiting conduct that the State is free to regulate. We first had occasion to assert that principle in Reynolds v. United States, 98 U.S. 145 (1879), where we rejected the claim that criminal laws against polygamy could not be constitutionally applied to those whose religion commanded the practice. We said:

Laws are made for the government of actions, and while they cannot interfere with mere religious belief and opinions, they may with practices.... Can a man excuse his practices to the contrary because of his religious belief? To permit this would be to make the professed doctrines of religious belief superior to the law of the land, and in effect to permit every citizen to become a law unto himself.

The only decisions in which we have held that the First Amendment bars application of a neutral, generally applicable law to religiously motivated action have not involved the Free Exercise Clause alone, but instead have involved the Free Exercise Clause in conjunction with other constitutional protections, such as freedom of speech and of the press (as in Murdock v. Pennsylvania, 319 U.S. 105 (1943), invalidating a tax on solicitation as applied to the dissemination of religious ideas), or the right of parents to direct the education of their children (as in Wisconsin v. Yoder, 406 U.S. 205 (1972), invalidating compulsory school-attendance laws as applied to Amish parents who refused on religious grounds to send their children to school).

The instant case does not present such a hybrid situation, but a free exercise claim unconnected with any communicative activity or parental right. Therefore the rule to which we have adhered ever since *Reynolds* plainly controls.

(2) It is further contended that the claim for a religious exemption must be evaluated under the balancing test set forth in the *Sherbert* case. Under that test, governmental actions that substantially burden a religious practice are presumed to be invalid, are subject to strict scrutiny, and must be justified by a compelling governmental interest.

We conclude today that the sounder approach, and the approach in accord with the vast majority of our precedents, is to hold the *Sherbert* test inapplicable to such claims. The government's ability to enforce generally applicable prohibitions of socially harmful conduct, like its ability to carry out other aspects of public policy, cannot depend on measuring the effects of a governmental action on a religious objector's spiritual development. To make an individual's obligation to obey such a law contingent upon the law's coincidence with his religious beliefs, except where the State's interest can be demonstrated to be "compelling," contradicts both constitutional tradition and common sense.

Nor is it possible to require a "compelling state interest" only when the conduct prohibited is "central" to the individual's religion. It is no more appropriate for judges to determine the "centrality" of religious beliefs before applying a "compelling interest" test in the free exercise field than it would be for them to determine the "importance" of ideas before applying the compelling interest test in the free speech field. What principle of law or logic can be brought to bear to contradict a believer's assertion that a particular act is central to his personal faith? Judging the centrality of different religious practices is akin to the unacceptable business of evaluating the relative merits of differing religious claims.

If the compelling interest test is to be applied at all, moreover, it must be applied across the board to all actions thought to be religiously commanded. Any society adopting such a system would be courting anarchy, but that danger increases in direct proportion to the society's diversity of religious beliefs. Precisely because we are a cosmopolitan nation made up of people of almost every conceivable religious preference, and precisely because we value and protect that religious divergence, we cannot afford the luxury of deeming presumptively invalid every regulation of conduct that is claimed to violate a religious objector's scruples.

Values that are protected against government interference through enshrinement in the Bill of Rights are not thereby banished from the political process. It is therefore not surprising that a number of States have made an exception to their drug laws for sacramental peyote use. But to say that such a religious-practice exemption is permitted, or even that it is desirable, is not to say that courts must require it under the Free Exercise Clause. Although leaving accommodation to the political process will place at a relative disadvantage those religious practices that are not widely engaged in, this is an unavoidable consequence of democratic government that surely must be preferred to a system in which each conscience is a law unto itself or in which judges are obliged to weigh the social importance of all laws against the centrality of all religious beliefs.

The decision of the Oregon Supreme Court is accordingly reversed.

O'Connor, concurring (joined in part by Brennan, Marshall, and Blackmun): Although I agree with the result the Court reaches in this case, I cannot join its opinion.

(1) The First Amendment does not distinguish between laws that are generally applicable and laws that target particular religious practices. If the First Amendment is to have any vitality, it ought not be construed to cover only the extreme and hypothetical situation in which a state directly targets a religious practice.

However, to say that a person's right to free exercise has been burdened does not mean that he has an absolute right to engage in the conduct. Instead, we have required the government to justify any substantial burden on religiously motivated conduct by demonstrating a compelling state interest and a narrowly tailored means to achieve that interest.

We should apply that test in each case to determine whether the burden on the specific plaintiffs before us is constitutionally significant and whether the particular criminal interest asserted by the State before us is compelling. Even if, as an empirical matter, a government's criminal laws might usually serve a compelling interest in health, safety, or public order, the First Amendment at least requires a case-by-case determination of the question. Given the range of conduct that a State might legitimately make criminal, we cannot assume, merely because a law carries criminal sanctions and is generally applicable, that the First Amendment never requires the State to grant a limited exemption for religiously motivated conduct.

The Court suggests that the disfavoring of minority religions is an "unavoidable consequence" under our system of government and that accommodation of such religions must be left to the political process. In my view, however, the First Amendment was enacted precisely to protect the rights of those whose religious practices are not shared by the majority and may be viewed with hostility.

(2) The critical question in this case is whether the claimed exemption will unduly interfere with fulfillment of the governmental interest. Although the question is close, I would conclude that uniform application of Oregon's criminal prohibition is essential to accomplish its overriding interest in preventing the physical harm caused by the use of a controlled substance.

Oregon's criminal prohibition represents that State's judgment that the possession and use of controlled substances, even by only one person, is inherently harmful and dangerous. Because the health effects caused by the use of controlled substances exist regardless of the motivation of the user, the use of such substances, even for religious purposes, violates the very purpose of the laws that prohibit them. Moreover, in view of the societal interest in preventing trafficking in controlled substances, uniform application of the criminal prohibition at issue is essential to the effectiveness of Oregon's stated interest in preventing any possession of peyote. A religious exemption in this case would be incompatible with the State's interest in controlling use and possession of illegal drugs.

It is contended that the sacramental use of peyote is central to the tenets of the Native American Church, but I agree with the Court that our determination of the constitutionality of Oregon's general criminal prohibition cannot, and should not, turn on the centrality of the particular religious practice at issue.

Blackmun, dissenting (joined by Brennan and Marshall): In weighing the interest of Smith and Black in the free exercise of their religion against Oregon's asserted interest in enforcing its drug laws, it is important to articulate in precise terms the State interest involved. It is not the State's broad interest in fighting the critical "war on drugs" that must be weighed against their claim, but the State's narrow interest in refusing to make an exception for the religious, ceremonial use of peyote.

The State's interest in enforcing its prohibition, in order to be sufficiently compelling to outweigh a free exercise claim, cannot be merely abstract or symbolic. In this case, the state actually has not evinced any concrete interest in enforcing its drug laws against religious users of peyote. The State's asserted interest thus amounts only to the symbolic preservation of an unenforced prohibition. But a government interest in symbolism, even symbolism for so worthy a cause as the abolition of unlawful drugs, cannot suffice to abrogate the constitutional rights of individuals.

Similarly, this Court's prior decisions have not allowed a government to rely on mere speculation about potential harms, but have demanded evidentiary support for a refusal to allow a religious exception. In this case, the State's justification for refusing to recognize an exception to its criminal laws for religious peyote use is entirely speculative.

The State proclaims an interest in protecting the health and safety of its citizens from the dangers of unlawful drugs. It offers, however, no evidence that the religious use of peyote has ever harmed anyone. The fact that peyote is classified as a controlled substance does not, by itself, show that any and all uses of peyote, in any circumstance, are inherently harmful and dangerous.

Peyote simply is not a popular drug; its distribution for use in religious rituals has nothing to do with the vast and violent traffic in illegal narcotics that plagues this country. The carefully circumscribed ritual context in which respondents used peyote is far removed from the irresponsible and unrestricted recreational use of unlawful drugs.

Finally, the State argues that granting an exception for religious peyote use would erode its interest in the uniform, fair, and certain enforcement of its drug laws. The State's apprehension of a flood of other religious claims is unfounded. Almost half the States as well as the federal government have maintained an exemption for religious peyote use for many years, and they apparently have not found themselves overwhelmed by claims to other religious exemptions. And allowing an exemption for religious peyote use would not necessarily oblige the State to grant a similar exemption to other religious groups.

Finally, although I agree that courts should refrain from delving into questions whether a particular practice is central to a religion, I do not think this means that the courts must turn a blind eye to the severe impact of a State's restrictions on the adherents of a minority religion such as the Native American Church.

For these reasons, I conclude that Oregon's interest in enforcing its drug laws against religious use of peyote is not sufficiently compelling to outweigh the asserted right to the free exercise of their religion. Since the State could not constitutionally enforce its criminal prohibition in such circumstances, the interests underlying the state's drug laws cannot justify its denial of unemployment benefits in this case.

*****

[*Note:* In 1993, in response to the *Smith* decision and expressly for the purpose of overruling the decision, Congress enacted the Religious Freedom Restoration Act (RFRA). Four years later, in the next digested case, *City of Boerne v. Flores,* the Supreme Court held that Congress exceeded its powers in subjecting States to the requirements of RFRA.

Prior to the *Smith* decision, in addition to the *Reynolds, Yoder,* and *Sherbert* cases cited in the opinions, the Court had considered exemption claims under the Free Exercise Clause in numerous cases, including, e.g., United States v. Lee, 455 U.S. 252 (1982) (rejecting an Amish challenge that their freedom of religion was violated by the requirement that they obtain Social Security numbers and pay Social Security taxes); Goldman v. Weinberger, 475 U.S. 503 (1986) (rejecting a claim by a Jewish army psychologist to wear a yarmulke while on duty); Braunfeld v. Brown, 366 U.S. 599(1961) (rejecting a challenge to Sunday closing laws); Jimmy Swaggart Ministries v. Board of Equalization of California, 493 U.S. 378 (1990) (rejecting a free exercise challenge to the payment of sales and use taxes for the sale of goods and literature by religious groups); Gillette v. United States, 401 U.S. 437 (1971) (denying a conscientious objector exemption to a draft registrant who objected only to a particular war on religious grounds).]

City of Boerne v. Flores, 521 U.S. 507 (1997)

FACTS: In 1993 Congress enacted the Religious Freedom Restoration Act (RFRA). The Act states the following:

(1) [T]he Framers of the Constitution, recognizing free exercise of religion as an unalienable right, secured its protection in the First Amendment to the Constitution;

(2) laws "neutral" toward religion may burden religious exercise as surely as laws intended to interfere with religious exercise;

(3) governments should not substantially burden religious exercise without compelling justification;

(4) in Employment Division v. Smith, 494 U.S. 872 (1990), the Supreme Court virtually eliminated the requirement that the government justify burdens on religious exercise imposed by laws neutral toward religion; and

(5) the compelling interest test as set forth in prior federal court rulings is a workable test for striking sensible balances between religious liberty and competing prior governmental interests.

On the basis of those findings, the Act (42 U.S.C. §2000bb-1) provided that:

- (a) ...Government shall not substantially burden a person's exercise of religion even if the burden results from a rule of general applicability, except as provided in subsection (b) of this section.

- (b) ...Government may substantially burden a person's exercise of religion only if it demonstrates that application of the burden to the person—

(1) is in furtherance of a compelling governmental interest; and

(2) is the least restrictive means of furthering that compelling governmental interest.

The Catholic Archbishop of San Antonio applied for a building permit to enlarge a church in Boerne, Texas. When local zoning authorities denied the permit, relying on an ordinance governing historic preservation in the district, the Archbishop brought suit claiming that the denial of the permit violated RFRA. The District Court held that RFRA exceeded the scope of Congress's enforcement power under §5 of the Fourteenth Amendment. The Fifth Circuit reversed, finding RFRA to be constitutional.

ISSUE: Did Congress have authority under §5 of the Fourteenth Amendment to enact RFRA as applied to the States?

DECISION (per *Kennedy*, 6-3): *No.*

Congress enacted RFRA in response to Employment Division, Department of Human Resources of Oregon v. Smith, 485 U.S. 660 (1990), interpreting the scope of the Free Exercise Clause under the Fourteenth Amendment. It is contended that Congress, in providing that RFRA's requirements shall supersede the Court's interpretation in the *Smith* case, was only "enforcing" the Fourteenth Amendment under §5 by granting further protection to the free exercise of religion.

Congress's §5 power, however, is only preventive or "remedial." The Amendment's design, its history, and §5's text are inconsistent with any suggestion that Congress has the power to decree the substance of the Amendment's restrictions on the states. Legislation that alters the meaning of the Free Exercise Clause cannot be said to be enforcing the Clause. Congress does not enforce a constitutional right by changing what the right is. It has been given the power "to enforce," not the power to determine what constitutes a constitutional violation.

The power to interpret the Constitution in a case or controversy remains in the Judiciary. If Congress could define its own powers by altering the Fourteenth Amendment's meaning, no longer would the Constitution be "superior paramount law, unchangeable by ordinary means." It would be "on a level with ordinary legislative acts, and, like other acts . . . alterable when the legislature shall please to alter it." Marbury v. Madison, 5 U.S. 137, 177 (1803). Under this approach, it is difficult to conceive of a principle that would limit congressional power.

While the line between measures that remedy or prevent unconstitutional actions and measures that make a substantive change in the governing law is not easy to discern, and Congress must have wide latitude in determining where it lies, the distinction exists and must be observed. There must be a congruence and proportionality between the injury to be prevented or remedied and the means adopted to that end. Lacking such a connection, legislation may become substantive in operation and effect.

RFRA is not a proper exercise of Congress's §5 enforcement power because it contradicts vital principles necessary to maintain separation of powers and the federal-state balance. In contrast to the record of widespread and persisting racial discrimination that confronted Congress and the Judiciary in cases supporting voting rights legislation, RFRA's legislative record lacks examples of any instances of generally applicable laws passed because of religious bigotry in the past 40 years. Rather, the emphasis of the RFRA hearings was on laws like the one at issue that place incidental burdens on religion. It is difficult to maintain that such laws are based on animus or hostility to the burdened religious practices or that they indicate some widespread pattern of religious discrimination in this country.

RFRA's most serious shortcoming, however, lies in the fact that it is so out of proportion to a supposed remedial or preventive object that it cannot be understood as responsive to, or designed to prevent, unconstitutional behavior. It appears, instead, to attempt a substantive change in constitutional protections, proscribing State conduct that the Fourteenth Amendment itself does not prohibit. Its sweeping coverage ensures its intrusion at every level of state and local government, displacing laws and prohibiting official actions of almost every description and regardless of subject matter. It makes any law subject to challenge at any time by any individual who claims a substantial burden on his or her free exercise of religion. And requiring a State to demonstrate a compelling interest and further show that it has adopted the least restrictive means of achieving that interest is the most demanding test known to constitutional law.

RFRA is an unconstitutional intrusion by Congress into the States' traditional prerogatives and general authority to regulate for the health and welfare of their citizens.

Stevens, concurring: RFRA is a "law respecting an establishment of religion" that violates the First Amendment. If the historic landmark on the hill in Boerne happened to be a museum or an art gallery owned by an atheist, it would not be eligible for an exemption from the city ordinances that forbid an enlargement of the structure. Because the landmark is owned by the Catholic Church, it is claimed that RFRA gives its owner a federal statutory entitlement to an exemption from a generally applicable, entirely neutral civil law. Thus the statute has provided the church with a legal weapon that no atheist or agnostic can obtain. This governmental preference for religion, as opposed to irreligion, is forbidden by the First Amendment.

Scalia (joined by Stevens), concurring in part: I disagree with the claim of Justice O'Connor's dissent that historical materials support a result contrary to the one reached in the *Smith* case. The material that the dissent claims is at odds with *Smith* either has little to say about the issue or is, in fact, more consistent with *Smith* than with the dissent's interpretation of the Free Exercise Clause.

O'Connor, dissenting (joined by Breyer in part): I remain of the view that *Smith* was wrongly decided, and I would use this case to reexamine the Court's holding there. Therefore, I would direct the parties to brief the question whether *Smith* represents the correct understanding of the Free Exercise Clause and set the case for reargument. If the Court were to correct the misinterpretation of the Free Exercise Clause set forth in *Smith,* it would simultaneously put our First Amendment jurisprudence back on course and allay the legitimate concerns of a majority in Congress who believed that *Smith* improperly restricted religious liberty. We would then be in a position to review RFRA in light of a proper interpretation of the Free Exercise Clause.

Souter, dissenting: I have serious doubts about the precedential value of the *Smith* rule and its entitlement to adherence. But, without briefing and argument on the merits of that rule, I am not now prepared to join in rejecting it or join the majority in assuming it to be correct. In order to provide full adversarial consideration, this case should be set down for reargument permitting plenary reexamination of the issue. Since the

Court declines to follow that course, the constitutionality of the law cannot now be soundly decided. I would therefore dismiss the writ of certiorari as improvidently granted, and I accordingly dissent from the Court's disposition of this case.

*****

[*Note:* Justice Kennedy's opinion is premised on the doctrine of judicial supremacy and the twentieth-century conflation of *Marbury v. Madison*. As pointed out in the comment "Judicial Review and Judicial Supremacy" in Chapter 2, Chief Justice Marshall's opinion in *Marbury* held only that the Court was not precluded from considering the Constitution in cases before it. But the case is invoked in *City of Boerne* as authority to preclude Congress from implementing the Fourteenth Amendment—notwithstanding an express constitutional grant of power to Congress to "enforce" the Amendment.]

The Aftermath of the *City of Boerne* Decision

In response to the *City of Boerne* decision, holding that §5 of the Fourteenth Amendment did not authorize Congress to enact RFRA as applied to the States, a dozen States enacted so-called "little RFRAs." These statutes restored in their jurisdictions the pre-*Smith* test, requiring proof of a compelling interest to overcome the assertion of a religious free exercise claim in those States.

Congress also responded to the *City of Boerne* decision by enacting in 2000 the Religious Land Use and Institutionalized Persons Act (RLUIPA)—this time invoking (instead of the Fourteenth Amendment) Congress's authority under its spending and commerce powers.

§3 of the RLUIPA prohibits federally funded programs (including state prisons and mental hospitals) from burdening the religious exercise of prisoners without a "compelling government interest." In Cutter v. Wilkinson, 544 U.S. 709 (2005), five Ohio prison inmates, adherents of "non-mainstream" religions such as Wicca and Asatru, invoked §3 to protest denial of access to ceremonial items and opportunities for group worship. The State contended that enforcement of §3 would compromise prison security and violates the Establishment Clause. Rejecting that contention, the Court unanimously held that §3 on its face is compatible with the Establishment Clause because it alleviates exceptional government-created burdens on private religious exercise. In addition, the Court held that religious accommodations need not "come packaged with benefits to secular entities"; if it were otherwise, all manner of religious accommodations would fall (such as, for example, providing chaplains and allowing worship services).

While the *City of Boerne* decision precludes application of the federal RFRA to the States, it did not affect the validity of RFRA as applied to free exercise claims asserted against the federal government. In *Gonzales v. O Centro Espirita Beneficiente Uniao,* 546 U.S. 418 (2006), it was contended that RFRA requires an exception to the Controlled Substances Act for the use of a hallucinogenic tea (hoasca) by a small church in its religious ceremonies. After the government had seized a shipment of hoasca and threatened prosecution, the church obtained a preliminary injunction prohibiting enforcement of the act against the church. In a unanimous decision, the Supreme Court sustained the preliminary injunction, holding that under RFRA the government had failed to demonstrate, at the preliminary injunction stage, a compelling interest that outweighed the church's religious exercise claim.

Locke v. Davey, 540 U.S. 712 (2004)

FACTS: Washington State established its Promise Scholarship Program to assist academically gifted students with postsecondary education expenses. Under the Program, however, because of a provision in the State Constitution prohibiting government aid to religion, such a scholarship may not be used to pursue a degree in devotional theology.

Joshua Davey was awarded a Promise Scholarship and chose to attend Northwest College, a private, church-affiliated institution that is eligible under the program. When he enrolled, Davey elected to pursue a degree in pastoral ministries and business administration. It is undisputed that a pastoral ministries degree is devotional in nature.

After learning that he would not be allowed to use his scholarship to pursue that degree, Davey brought this action for an injunction and damages, arguing that the State's action was discriminatory and violated his rights under the Free Exercise Clause of the First Amendment. The Court of Appeals for the Ninth Circuit upheld Davey's constitutional claim.

The Court of Appeals held that, because Washington State had singled out religion for unfavorable treatment, its exclusion of devotional theology majors had to be narrowly tailored to achieve a compelling state interest under the Supreme Court's decision in Church of Lukumi Babalu Aye, Inc. v. Hialeah, 508 U.S. 520 (1993), and that the State's policy against government aid to religion did not meet that standard.

ISSUE: Does the State's exclusion of devotional theology majors from the Promise Scholarship Program violate the Free Exercise Clause?

DECISION (per *Rehnquist,* 7-2): *No.*

Under our precedents construing the Establishment Clause—notably the *Zelman* decision sustaining the constitutionality of the Cleveland voucher program—the link between government funds and religious training is broken by the independent and private choice of recipients. Thus, there is no doubt that Washington State could, consistent with the federal constitution, choose to permit Promise Scholars to pursue a degree in devotional theology, and the State does not contend otherwise. The question before us, however, is whether Washington, under its own constitution, can deny them such funding without violating the First Amendment's Free Exercise Clause. We hold that Washington may do so.

We reject Davey's contention, relying on the *Church of Lukumi Babalu* case, that the program is presumptively unconstitutional because it is not facially neutral with respect to religion. To accept such a sweeping presumption of unconstitutionality would extend our prior decisions well beyond not only their facts but their reasoning.

Washington's program imposes neither criminal nor civil sanctions on any type of religious service or rite. It does not interfere with the right of ministers to participate in community political affairs. And it does not require students to choose between their religious beliefs and receiving a government benefit. The State has merely chosen not to fund a distinct category of instruction.

Because the Promise Scholarship Program funds training for all secular professions, Justice Scalia in his dissent contends the State must also fund training for religious professions. But training for religious professions and training for secular professions are not fungible. Training someone to lead a congregation is an essentially religious endeavor. Indeed, majoring in devotional theology is akin to a religious calling as well as an academic pursuit. That a state would deal differently with religious education for the ministry than with education for other callings is a product of these differences, not evidence of hostility toward religion.

Even though the differently worded Washington Constitution draws a more stringent antiestablishment line than does the federal Constitution, the interest it seeks to further is scarcely novel. Since this country's founding, there have been popular uprisings against using taxpayer funds to support church leaders, which was one of the hallmarks of an "established" religion. Most States that sought to avoid such an establishment around the time of the founding placed in their constitutions formal prohibitions against using tax funds to support the ministry.

Moreover, the entirety of the Promise Scholarship Program goes a long way toward including religion in its benefits, since it permits students to attend accredited religious schools, and students are still eligible to take devotional theology courses under the program's current guidelines.

In short, we find neither in the history or text of the Washington Constitution, nor in the operation of the Promise Scholarship Program, anything that suggests animus towards religion. Given the historic and substantial State interest at issue, we therefore cannot conclude that the denial of funding for vocational religious instruction alone is inherently constitutionally suspect.

In view of our rejection of a presumption of unconstitutionality in this situation, Davey's claim must fail. The State's interest in not funding the pursuit of devotional degrees is substantial, and the exclusion of such funding places a relatively minor burden on Promise Scholars.

Scalia, dissenting (joined by Thomas): In Church of Lukumi Babalu Aye, Inc. v. Hialeah, 508 U.S. 520 (1993), the majority opinion held that "[a] law burdening religious practice that is not neutral . . . must undergo the most rigorous of scrutiny," and that "the minimum requirement of neutrality is that a law not discriminate on its face." The concurrence of Justices Blackmun and O'Connor stated that "[w]hen a law discriminates against religion as such . . . it automatically will fail strict scrutiny." And the concurrence of Justice Souter endorsed the "noncontroversial principle" that "formal neutrality" is a "necessary conditio[n] for free-exercise constitutionality." These opinions are irreconcilable with today's decision, which sustains a public benefits program that facially discriminates against religion.

When the State makes a public benefit generally available, that benefit becomes part of the baseline against which burdens on religion are measured; and when the State withholds that benefit from some individuals solely on the basis of religion, it violates the Free Exercise Clause no less than if it had imposed a special tax.

That is precisely what the State of Washington has done here. It has created a generally available public benefit, whose receipt is conditioned only on academic performance, income, and attendance at an accredited school. It has then carved out a solitary course of study for exclusion: theology. Davey is not asking for a special benefit to which others are not entitled. He seeks only *equal* treatment—the right to direct his scholarship to his chosen course of study, a right every other Promise Scholar enjoys.

What is the nature of the State's asserted interest here? The interest to which the Court defers is not fear of a conceivable Establishment Clause violation, budget limitations, avoidance of endorsement, or substantive neutrality—none of these. It is a pure philosophical preference: the State's opinion that it would violate taxpayers' freedom of conscience *not* to discriminate against candidates for the ministry. This sort of protection of "freedom of conscience" has no logical limit and can justify the singling out of religion for exclusion from public programs in virtually any context.

The Court makes no serious attempt to defend the program's neutrality, and instead identifies two features thought to render its discrimination less offensive. The first is the lightness of Davey's burden. However, the indignity of being singled out for special burdens on the basis of one's religious calling is so profound that the harm can never be dismissed as insubstantial.

The other reason the Court thinks this particular facial discrimination less offensive is that the scholarship program was not motivated by animus toward religion. I fail to see why the legislature's motive matters. When we declared racial segregation unconstitutional, we did not ask whether the state had originally adopted the regime, not out of "animus" against blacks, but because of a well-meaning but misguided belief that the races would be better off apart. It is sufficient that the citizen's rights have been infringed.

Today's holding is limited to training the clergy, but its logic is readily extendible. What next? Having accepted the State's justification in this case, the Court is less well equipped to fend it off in the future. I respectfully dissent.

Thomas, dissenting: On the assumption (undisputed by the parties) that the State denies Promise Scholarships only to students who pursue a degree in devotional theology, I believe that Justice Scalia's application of our precedents is correct and join his dissent.

*****

[*Note:* In the *Church of Lukumi Babalu Aye* case, cited in the majority and dissenting opinions, ordinances enacted by the City of Hialeah, Florida, that criminalized ritualistic animal sacrifices were held unconstitutional under the Free Exercise Clause. The Court held (9-0) that the texts and operation of the Hialeah ordinances demonstrated that they were specifically designed to suppress a particular religious practice of the Santeria religion.]

Cantwell v. State of Connecticut, 310 U.S. 296 (1940)

FACTS: Newton Cantwell and his two sons, Jesse and Russell, members of a group known as Jehovah's Witnesses, and claiming to be ordained ministers, were convicted of violating §6294 of the Connecticut Statutes:

> No person shall solicit money, services, subscriptions or any valuable thing for any alleged religious, charitable or philanthropic cause, from other than a member of the organization for whose benefit such person is soliciting or within the county in which such person or organization is located unless such cause shall have been approved by the secretary of the public welfare council. Upon application of any person in behalf of such cause, the secretary shall determine whether such cause is a religious one or is a bona fide object of charity or philanthropy and conforms to reasonable standards of efficiency and integrity, and, if he shall so find, shall approve the same and issue to the authority in charge a certificate to that effect. Such certificate may be revoked at any time. Any person violating any provision of this section shall be fined not more than one hundred dollars or imprisoned not more than thirty days or both.

In addition, Jesse Cantwell was convicted of committing the common law offense of inciting a breach of the peace.

On the day of their arrest the three defendants were engaged in going singly from house to house in New Haven. They were individually equipped with a bag containing books and pamphlets on religious subjects, a portable phonograph, and a set of phonograph records that described the books. They asked each resident they called upon if they could play one of the records. If permission was granted, the resident was asked to buy the book described in the record and, upon refusal, was asked to make a contribution towards the publication of the pamphlets. About 90 percent of the residents in the neighborhood are Roman Catholics. One of the phonograph records (describing a book entitled *Enemies*) included an attack on the Catholic religion.

In the course of the solicitation Jesse Cantwell stopped two men in the street, received their permission to play a phonograph record, and played the record *Enemies,* which attacked the religion and church of the two men, who were Catholics. Both were incensed by the contents of the record and were tempted to strike Cantwell unless he went away. On being told to leave, he departed. There was no evidence that he was personally offensive or entered into any argument with those he interviewed.

On appeal, the defendants' convictions were sustained by the Connecticut Supreme Court.

ISSUE: Was the defendants' conduct protected by the Constitution?

DECISION (per *Roberts,* 9-0): *Yes.*

(1) *The convictions under §6924*—We hold that §6924, as applied to the defendants, deprives them of their liberty without due process of law in contravention of the Fourteenth Amendment.

The fundamental concept of liberty embodied in the Fourteenth Amendment embraces the liberties guaranteed by the First Amendment. The First Amendment declares that Congress shall make no law respecting an establishment of religion or prohibiting the free exercise thereof. The Fourteenth Amendment has rendered the legislatures of the States as incompetent as Congress to enact such laws.

The constitutional inhibition of legislation on the subject of religion has a double aspect. On the one hand, it forestalls compulsion by law of the acceptance of any creed or the practice of any form of worship. Freedom of conscience and freedom to adhere to such religious organization or form of worship as the individual may choose cannot be restricted by law. On the other hand, it safeguards the free exercise of the chosen form of religion.

Thus the Amendment embraces two concepts—freedom to believe and freedom to act. The first is absolute but, in the nature of things, the second cannot be. Conduct remains subject to regulation for the protection of society. The freedom to act must have appropriate definition to preserve the enforcement of that protection. In every case the power to regulate must be so exercised as not, in attaining a permissible end, unduly to infringe the protected freedom. No one would contest the proposition that a State may not wholly deny the right to preach or to disseminate religious views. Plainly such a restraint would violate the terms of the guarantee. It is equally clear that a State may by general and nondiscriminatory legislation regulate the times, the places, and the manner of soliciting upon its streets, and of holding meetings thereon, and may in other respects safeguard the peace, good order, and comfort of the community, without unconstitutionally invading the liberties protected by the Fourteenth Amendment. Clearly §6924 is not such a regulation; if a certificate is procured, solicitation is permitted without restraint but, in the absence of a certificate, solicitation is altogether prohibited.

The State insists that the statute is merely designed to guard against the perpetration of frauds under the cloak of religion. Even if that is so, the question remains whether the method adopted by Connecticut to that end transgresses the liberty safeguarded by the Constitution. Generally the regulation of solicitation, when it does not involve any religious test and does not unreasonably obstruct or delay the collection of funds, is not open to any constitutional objection, even though the collection be for a religious purpose. Such regulation would not constitute a prohibited previous restraint on the free exercise of religion or interpose an inadmissible obstacle to its exercise. It will be noted, however, that the statute challenged in this case requires an application to the secretary of the public welfare council of the State; that he is empowered to determine whether the cause is a religious one, and that the issue of a certificate depends upon his affirmative action. If he finds that the cause is not that of religion, to solicit for it becomes a crime. He is not to issue a certificate as a matter of course. His decision to issue or refuse it involves appraisal of facts, the exercise of judgment, and the formation of an opinion. He is authorized to withhold his approval if he determines that the cause is not a religious one. Such a censorship of religion as the means of determining its right to survive is a denial of liberty protected by the First Amendment and included in the liberty within the protection of the Fourteenth Amendment.

Nothing we have said is intended even remotely to imply that, under the cloak of religion, persons may, with impunity, commit frauds upon the public. Certainly penal laws are available to punish such conduct. Even the exercise of religion may be at some slight inconvenience in order that the State may protect its citizens from injury. Without doubt a State may protect its citizens from fraudulent solicitation by requiring a stranger in the community, before permitting him publicly to solicit funds for any purpose, to establish his identity and his authority to act for the cause he purports to represent. The State is likewise free to regulate the time and manner of solicitation generally, in the interest of public safety, peace, comfort, or convenience. But to condition the solicitation of aid for the perpetuation of religious views or systems upon a license, the grant of which rests in the exercise of a determination by state authority as to what is a religious cause, is to lay a forbidden burden upon the exercise of liberty protected by the Constitution. But to condition the solicitation of aid for the perpetuation of religious views or systems upon a license, the grant of which rests in the exercise of a determination by state authority as to what is a religious cause, is to lay a forbidden burden upon the exercise of liberty protected by the Constitution.

(2) *The conviction for inciting a breach of the peace*—We hold that, in the circumstances disclosed, the conviction of Jesse Cantwell for inciting a breach of the peace must also be set aside.

Determining the lawfulness of the conviction demands the weighing of two conflicting interests. The Constitution requires that the free exercise of religion be not prohibited and that freedom to communicate information and opinion be not abridged. The State of Connecticut has an obvious interest in the preservation and protection of peace and good order within her borders. We must determine whether the alleged protection of the State's interest, means to which end would, in the absence of limitation by the federal Constitution, lie wholly within the State's discretion, has been pressed, in this instance, to a point where it has come into fatal collision with the overriding interest protected by the federal compact.

The breach of peace conviction was not pursuant to a statute evincing a legislative judgment that street discussion of religious affairs, because of its tendency to provoke disorder, should be regulated, or a judgment that the playing of a phonograph on the streets should in the interest of comfort or privacy be limited or prevented. Violation of a statute exhibiting such a legislative judgment and narrowly drawn to prevent the supposed evil would pose a question differing from that we must here answer. Such a declaration of the State's policy would weigh heavily in any challenge of the law as infringing constitutional limitations. Here, however, the judgment is based on a common law concept of the most general and undefined nature.

The offense known as breach of the peace embraces a great variety of conduct destroying or menacing public order and tranquility. It includes not only violent acts but acts and words likely to produce violence in others. No one would have the hardihood to suggest that the principle of freedom of speech sanctions incitement to riot or that religious liberty connotes the privilege to exhort others to physical attack upon those belonging to another sect. When clear and present danger of riot, disorder, interference with traffic upon the public streets, or other immediate threat to public safety, peace, or order, appears, the power of the State to prevent or punish is obvious. Equally obvious is it that a State may not unduly suppress free communication of views, religious or other, under the guise of conserving desirable conditions. Here we have a situation analogous to a conviction for an offense embracing a great variety of conduct under a general and indefinite characterization, and leaving to the executive and judicial branches too wide a discretion in its application.

Having these considerations in mind, we note that Jesse Cantwell, on April 26, 1938, was upon a public street, where he had a right to be, and where he had a right peacefully to impart his views to others. There is no showing that his deportment was noisy, truculent, overbearing or offensive. He requested of two pedestrians permission to play to them a phonograph record. The permission was granted. It is not claimed that he intended to insult or affront the hearers by playing the record. It is plain that he wished only to interest them in his propaganda. The sound of the phonograph is not shown to have disturbed residents of the street, to have drawn a crowd, or to have impeded traffic. Thus far he had invaded no right or interest of the public or of the men accosted. The record played by Cantwell embodies a general attack on all organized religious systems as instruments of Satan and injurious to man; it then singles out the Catholic Church for strictures couched in terms that naturally would offend not only persons of that persuasion, but all others who respect the honestly held religious faith of their fellows. The hearers were in fact highly offended. One of them said he felt like hitting Cantwell and the other that he was tempted to throw Cantwell off the street. The one who testified he felt like hitting Cantwell said, in answer to the question "Did you do anything else or have any other reaction?" "No, sir, because he said he would take the victrola and he went." The other witness testified that he told Cantwell he had better get off the street before something happened to him and that was the end of the matter as Cantwell picked up his books and walked up the street.

As the Connecticut Supreme Court acknowledged, Jesse Cantwell's conduct, considered apart from the effect of his communication upon his hearers, did not amount to a breach of the peace, but his conviction was sustained on the basis that he engaged in conduct likely to incite violence by others, even though he had not intended such an eventuality. But examination discloses that, in practically all cases upholding such a theory, the provocative language that was held to amount to a breach of the peace consisted of profane, indecent, or abusive remarks directed to the person of the hearer. We find in the instant case no assault or threatening of bodily harm, no truculent bearing, no intentional discourtesy, no personal abuse. On the contrary, we find only an effort to persuade a willing listener to buy a book or to contribute money in the interest of what Jesse Cantwell, however misguided others may think him, conceived to be true religion.

In the realm of religious faith, and in that of political belief, sharp differences arise. In both fields the tenets of one man may seem the rankest error to his neighbor. To persuade others to his own point of view, the pleader, as we know, at times resorts to exaggeration, to vilification of men who have been, or are, prominent in church or state, and even to false statement. But the people of this nation have ordained in the light of history, that, in spite of the probability of excesses and abuses, these liberties are, in the long view, essential to enlightened opinion and right conduct on the part of the citizens of a democracy.

The essential characteristic of these liberties is that under their shield many types of life, character, opinion, and belief can develop unmolested and unobstructed. Nowhere is this shield more necessary than in our own country for a people composed of many races and of many creeds. There are limits to the exercise of these liberties. The danger in these times from the coercive activities of those who in the delusion of racial or religious conceit would incite violence and breaches of the peace in order to deprive others of their equal right to the exercise of their liberties is emphasized by events familiar to all. These and other transgressions of those limits the States appropriately may punish. Although the contents of the record not unnaturally aroused animosity, we think that, in the absence of a statute narrowly drawn to define and punish specific conduct as a clear and present danger to a substantial interest of the State, and in the light of the constitutional guarantees, Jesse Cantwell's communication raised no such clear and present menace to public peace and order as to render him liable to conviction of the common law offense in question.

The judgment affirming the convictions is reversed.

*****

[*Note:* Post-*Cantwell* decisions protecting religious solicitation have similarly relied on both the Free Exercise and Freedom of Speech Clauses of the First Amendment. In Murdock v. Pennsylvania, 319 U.S. 105 (1943), and Follett v. Town of McCormick, 321 U.S. 573 (1944), the Court struck down the application of license taxes to Jehovah's Witnesses engaged in door-to-door solicitation. In Watchtower Bible & Tract Society v. Village of Stratton, 536 U.S. 150 (2002), the Court invalidated an ordinance prohibiting door-to-door solicitation without first registering with the mayor and receiving a permit, to the extent the ordinance applied to religious proselytizing, anonymous political speech, and the distribution of handbills.]

14

Executive Powers

The Rise of the "Imperial Presidency"

Article II of the Constitution (§1) begins: "The executive Power shall be vested in a President of the United States of America." Article II (§2) then enumerates specific powers of the President (pages 8–9).

But are these specifically enumerated powers the President's only powers? Or does the President have, in addition, certain "inherent powers" by the very nature of the office?

As the *Youngstown* and *Hamdi* cases illustrate, many Presidents have asserted such inherent powers or—much the same—have simply chosen to act without regard to the limitations of Article II. The result has been to substantially enlarge the *de facto* powers of the Executive.

Although Thomas Jefferson was known as a strict constructionist, his experience as President markedly changed his views. He wrote that "On great occasions, every good officer must be ready to risk himself in going beyond the strict line of the law, when the public preservation requires it; his motives will be a justification." Similarly, he declared that

> The laws of necessity, of self-preservation, of saving our country when in danger, are of a higher obligation. . . . To lose our country by a scrupulous adherence to written law, would be to lose the law itself, with life, liberty, property and all those who are enjoying them with us; thus absurdly sacrificing the end to the means.

In the agreement Jefferson made with France to buy the Louisiana territory (consisting of nearly one million square miles, and doubling the size of the United States, for only about four cents per acre), he promised that the territory would eventually become States of the Union and that the inhabitants would have the rights of American citizens. The Constitution said nothing about acquiring territory or promising statehood or citizenship, or about the President's having such authority. But because of his concern that Napoleon would back out of the agreement, Jefferson barreled ahead, solely on the basis of Senate ratification and despite his previous conclusion that a constitutional amendment was essential. ("I infer that the less we say about the constitutional difficulties respecting Louisiana the better," he wrote James Madison, his Secretary of State, "and that what is necessary for surmounting them must be done sub silentio.") Jefferson thus "performed the most aggressive executive action ever by an American

President, a projection of executive authority that would stand the test of time as perhaps the boldest in American history." [1]

In the Civil War, Abraham Lincoln suspended the right of habeas corpus—a right that under the Constitution only Congress can suspend—and refused to obey a habeas corpus order issued by the Chief Justice of the Supreme Court. In addition, Lincoln on his own authorized the trial of hundreds of civilians by military tribunals, extended the period of voluntary enlistment to three years, and increased the size of the army and navy—all without first obtaining Congress's approval.

Relying on his status as commander in chief, Lincoln issued the Emancipation Proclamation. He acknowledged that the Proclamation was without "constitutional or legal justification, except as a military measure" but added that "I conceive that I may in an emergency do things on military grounds which cannot constitutionally be done by Congress."

In 1940, when Adolf Hitler had conquered France and apparently was on the verge of invading Great Britain, Franklin Roosevelt transferred 50 old destroyers to the British before Congress could reject it. The then Republican presidential candidate, Wendell Willkie (although a strong supporter of aid to Britain), called it "the most arbitrary and dictatorial action ever taken by the President in the history of the United States." And Roosevelt himself (according to his secretary) feared that the deal could result in his impeachment.

And that same year, without getting Congress's approval—which he knew he could not get—Roosevelt ordered American planes and ships to accompany British convoys and alert them to the presence of German submarines.

In 1984, even though Congress had specifically prohibited further funding of the Contras (an anti-communist guerrilla organization in Nicaragua), President Ronald Reagan authorized secret funding of the Contras by using the proceeds of arm sales to Iran. According to the *New York Times* of December 9, 2006, Secretary of State George Schultz called the plan "an impeachable offense," and President Reagan warned that, if the story leaked, "we'll all be hanging by our thumbs in front of the White House."

The administration of George W. Bush has gone further than any previous administration, not only in asserting presidential prerogatives, but also in claiming *exclusive* authority to act notwithstanding any limitation imposed by Congress. Three examples:

- The original purpose of "signing statements" (issued by a President when approving bills enacted by Congress) was fairly innocuous—to include the President's interpretation of the law as part of the law's legislative history. But in recent years signing statements have been used as a kind of backdoor line-item veto—to enable a President to sign a bill that he accepts only in part and yet avoid a veto, by designating sections of the bill that he claims unconstitutionally infringe Executive powers and that he will therefore neither enforce nor obey. Presidents of both parties have employed the practice (William Clinton did so to challenge the validity of 140 provisions), but the number of provisions challenged by the current President's signing statements (over 1,100 provisions, including, e.g., restrictions in the Patriot Act and the McCain Torture Ban) exceed the total number of provisions (600) challenged in signing statements by all of his predecessors combined.
- In 1978, Congress enacted the Foreign Intelligence Surveillance Act (FISA), which prohibits government "electronic surveillance" of any person in the United States except as authorized

---

[1] Joseph Ellis, *American Creation* [Knopf 2007]: 224. See also Arthur Schlesinger, Jr., The Imperial Presidency [Houghton Mifflin 1973]: 23–24, 108.

by a warrant obtained from a special court established for that purpose. In 2002 President Bush authorized the National Security Agency, without obtaining a warrant as required by FISA, to monitor international telephone calls and emails to and from individuals within the United States. The government sought to justify this warrantless surveillance on the grounds (1) that Congress cannot limit the President's inherent power under the Constitution to take action he believes necessary to protect the nation's security and (2) that the FISA warrant requirement was repealed by Congress's general grant of authority in the September 2001 "Authorization for Use of Military Force" (reproduced later in this chapter).

- President Bush also asserted the inherent power to indefinitely detain incommunicado anyone (even a U.S. citizen seized in this country) that he designates as an "enemy combatant." See comments "The Detention of Enemy Combatants" and "Prosecuting Enemy Combatants for War Crimes" in this chapter.[2]

Many Presidents have also often acted unilaterally to engage the Nation in armed conflicts, as summarized in the next comment, "Authorizing Acts of War."

Authorizing Acts of War

Article I of the Constitution (§8) explicitly assigns to Congress the power "To declare War." It also grants Congress the power "To raise and support Armies" and "To provide and maintain a Navy." Article II (§2) provides that "The President shall be Commander in Chief of the Army and Navy of the United States."

Notwithstanding the designation of the President as Commander in Chief, the Framers clearly contemplated, and the early Presidents acknowledged, that Congress's power to declare war was exclusive and that all military operations (except to repel surprise attacks) must be authorized by Congress. James Madison, for example, declared that "In no part of the Constitution is more wisdom to be found than in the clause which confides the question of war and peace to the legislature, and not to the executive department."

In later years, however, as recounted by Arthur Schlesinger, Jr. in *The Imperial Presidency,* Presidents have ordered dozens of acts of war without congressional authorization.

But it was not until 1950 that a President took the country into a major overseas conflict solely on the basis of his unilateral decision. Without asking Congress for authority to do so, President Harry Truman sent troops to fight North Korea, claiming that he had inherent power to do so as commander in chief.

In 1964, President Lyndon Johnson similarly denied that he needed congressional authorization to engage in war, but he obtained enactment of the Gulf of Tonkin resolution to provide further support for his decision to send large forces to Vietnam. The resolution (based on later discredited reports of an attack on an American destroyer) stated that Congress "approves and supports the determination of the President, as Commander in Chief, to take all necessary measures to repel any armed attack against the forces of the United States and to prevent further aggression."

In 1970, to justify extending the war to Cambodia, President Richard Nixon stated that he was acting as Commander in Chief to ensure the safety of American armed forces in Vietnam.

---

[2]See also, e.g., Charles Savage, *Takeover: The Return of the Imperial Presidency and the Subversion of American Democracy* [Little Brown 2007].

In 1973, Congress adopted—over Nixon's veto—the War Powers Resolution, seeking to limit the authority of the President, "[i]n the absence of a declaration of war, in any case in which United States Armed Forces are introduced . . . into hostilities or into situations where imminent involvement in hostilities is clearly indicated by the circumstances." The Resolution requires the President to withdraw the forces within 60 days "unless the Congress (1) has declared war or has enacted a specific authorization for such use of United States Armed Forces, (2) has extended by law such sixty-day period, or (3) is physically unable to meet as a result of an armed attack upon the United States."

Nixon and all subsequent Presidents have taken the position that the War Powers Resolution is an unconstitutional invasion of the President's powers.[3] And, as a practical matter, Presidents have generally ignored it.

Some recent examples: The first President Bush invaded Panama and sent U.S. forces to resist Iraq's invasion of Kuwait, and President Clinton bombed Kosovo, Iraq, Afghanistan, and Sudan—all without obtaining any congressional authorization.

But in some instances, beginning with the 1953 resolution authorizing President Dwight Eisenhower "to employ the Armed Forces . . . as he deems necessary" in defense of Formosa, Presidents have obtained from Congress advance grants of discretionary authority to use military force. The Formosa resolution, as Schlesinger points out in *The Imperial Presidency* (p. 160), "committed Congress to the approval of hostilities without knowledge of the specific situation in which the hostilities would begin. It was therefore a contingency authorization of the sort . . . that Madison had declined in 1810 as an unconstitutional delegation of the war-making power."

On September 14, 2001, three days after the "9/11" attack, a resolution entitled "Authorization for Use of Military Force" was passed authorizing the President to "use all necessary and appropriate force against those nations, organizations, or persons he determines planned, authorized, committed, or aided the terrorist attacks" or "harbored such organizations or persons." On October 7, 2001, the attack on Afghanistan was launched. In his letter to Congress announcing this action, while expressing his appreciation for the September 14 resolution, President Bush stated that he had acted "pursuant to my constitutional authority to conduct U.S. foreign relations as Commander in Chief and Chief Executive."

On October 10, 2002, Congress approved the "Iraq Military Force Resolution" authorizing the President "to use the Armed Forces of the United States as he determines to be necessary and appropriate in order to defend the national security of the United States against the continuing threat posed by Iraq." On March 3, 2003, the attack on Iraq was commenced. In his letter to Congress, although noting the October 10 resolution, President Bush stated that he had ordered the action "pursuant to my authority as Commander in Chief."

The 2001 (Afghanistan) and 2002 (Iraq) resolutions are set forth in the following pages.

---

[3]The objection is that the provision allowing Congress to require the President to remove troops from combat by merely passing a concurrent resolution violates the requirement that a congressional action, if it is to have the force of law, must be presented to the President for signature or veto. Reliance is placed on the Supreme Court's decision in Immigration and Naturalization Service v. Chadha, 462 U.S. 919 (1983), holding (7-2) unconstitutional the use of a "legislative veto" to control the Executive by the device of congressional resolutions without submitting the action to the President for his approval. In his dissent in *Chadha,* Justice White referred to the War Powers Resolution as one of the many congressional actions invalidated by the majority's decision.

Authorization for Use of Military Force
(Joint Congressional Resolution, September 14, 2001)

To authorize the use of United States Armed Forces against those responsible for the recent attacks launched against the United States.

Whereas, on September 11, 2001, acts of treacherous violence were committed against the United States and its citizens; and

Whereas, such acts render it both necessary and appropriate that the United States exercise its rights to self-defense and to protect United States citizens both at home and abroad; and

Whereas, in light of the threat to the national security and foreign policy of the United States posed by these grave acts of violence; and

Whereas, such acts continue to pose an unusual and extraordinary threat to the national security and foreign policy of the United States; and

Whereas, the President has authority under the Constitution to take action to deter and prevent acts of international terrorism against the United States:

Now, therefore, be it

Resolved by the Senate and House of Representatives of the United States of America in Congress assembled,

*****

(a) IN GENERAL—That the President is authorized to use all necessary and appropriate force against those nations, organizations, or persons he determines planned, authorized, committed, or aided the terrorist attacks that occurred on September 11, 2001, or harbored such organizations or persons, in order to prevent any future acts of international terrorism against the United States by such nations, organizations, or persons.

(b) War Powers Resolution Requirements—

1. SPECIFIC STATUTORY AUTHORIZATION—Consistent with section 8(a)(1) of the War Powers Resolution, the Congress declares that this section is intended to constitute specific statutory authorization within the meaning of section 5(b) of the War Powers Resolution.

2. APPLICABILITY OF OTHER REQUIREMENTS—Nothing in this resolution supercedes any requirement of the War Powers Resolution.

Iraq Military Force Resolution
(Joint Congressional Resolution, October 10, 2002)

Section 1. Short Title.

This joint resolution may be cited as the "Authorization for the Use of Military Force Against Iraq."

Sec.2. Support for United States Diplomatic Efforts.

The Congress of the United States supports the efforts by the President to

(1) strictly enforce through the United Nations Security Council all relevant Security Council resolutions applicable to Iraq and encourages him in those efforts; and

(2) obtain prompt and decisive action by the Security Council to ensure that Iraq abandons its strategy of delay, evasion and noncompliance and promptly and strictly complies with all relevant Security Council resolutions.

Sec. 3. Authorization for Use of United States Armed Forces.

(a) AUTHORIZATION—The President is authorized to use the Armed Forces of the United States as he determines to be necessary and appropriate in order to

(1) defend the national security of the United States against the continuing threat posed by Iraq; and

(2) enforce all relevant United Nations Security Council resolutions regarding Iraq.

(b) PRESIDENTIAL DETERMINATION—In connection with the exercise of the authority granted in subsection (a) to use force the President shall, prior to such exercise or as soon thereafter as may be feasible, but no later than 48 hours after exercising such authority, make available to the Speaker of the House of Representatives and the President pro tempore of the Senate his determination that

(1) reliance by the United States on further diplomatic or other peaceful means alone either (A) will not adequately protect the national security of the United States against the continuing threat posed by Iraq or (B) is not likely to lead to enforcement of all relevant United Nations Security Council resolutions regarding Iraq; and

(2) acting pursuant to this resolution is consistent with the United States and other countries continuing to take the necessary actions against international terrorists and terrorist organizations, including those nations, organizations, or persons who planned, authorized, committed, or aided the terrorists attacks that occurred on September 11, 2001.

(c) WAR POWERS RESOLUTION REQUIREMENTS—

(1) SPECIFIC STATUTORY AUTHORIZATION—Consistent with section 8(a)(1) of the War Powers Resolution, the Congress declares that this section is intended to constitute specific statutory authorization within the meaning of section 5(b) of the War Powers Resolution.

(2) APPLICABILITY OF OTHER REQUIREMENTS—Nothing in this resolution supersedes any requirement of the War Powers Resolution.

Sec. 4. Reports to Congress.

(a) The President shall, at least once every 60 days, submit to the Congress a report on matters relevant to this joint resolution, including actions taken pursuant to the exercise of authority granted in section 3 and the status of planning for efforts that are expected to be required after such actions are completed, including those actions described in section 7 of Public Law 105-338 (the Iraq Liberation Act of 1998).

*****

United States v. Curtiss-Wright Export Corporation, 299 U.S. 304 (1936)

FACTS: A Joint Resolution of Congress authorized President Roosevelt to prohibit sales of arms and munitions to Bolivia and Paraguay (then engaged in armed conflict) if he made a finding (as he then did) that the prohibition would contribute to establishing peace. The Resolution provided that any sale in violation of the prohibition was punishable by a fine not exceeding $10,000 or by imprisonment not exceeding two years or both.

Curtiss-Wright Corporation was indicted under the resolution for selling guns to Bolivia. Curtiss-Wright challenged the Resolution, claiming it constituted an unconstitutional delegation of lawmaking power to the President and an abdication by Congress of its essential functions. The District Court agreed, and the government appealed to the Supreme Court.

ISSUE: Was the delegation to the President unconstitutional?

DECISION (per *Sutherland,* 7-1, Stone not participating): *No.*

Whether, if the Joint Resolution had related solely to internal affairs, it would be open to the challenge that it constituted an unlawful delegation, we find it unnecessary to determine. The whole aim of the resolution is to affect a situation entirely external to the United States and falling within the category of foreign affairs.

The two classes of powers are different, in respect of both their origin and their nature. The broad statement that the federal government can exercise no powers except those specifically enumerated in the Constitution, and such implied powers as are necessary and proper to carry into effect the enumerated powers, is categorically true only in respect of our internal affairs. In that field, the primary purpose of the Constitution was to carve from the general mass of legislative powers then possessed by the States such portions as it was thought desirable to vest in the federal government, leaving those not included in the enumeration still in the States. As a result of the separation from Great Britain by the colonies, acting as a unit, the powers of external sovereignty passed from the Crown not to the colonies severally, but to the colonies in their collective and corporate capacity as the United States of America.

Not only is the federal power over external affairs in origin and essential character different from that over internal affairs, but Congress's participation in the exercise of the power is significantly limited. In this vast external realm, with its important, complicated, delicate, and manifold problems, the President alone has the power to speak or listen as a representative of the nation. He makes treaties with the advice and consent of the Senate, but he alone negotiates. Into the field of negotiation the Senate cannot intrude, and Congress itself is powerless to invade it.

We are here dealing not alone with an authority vested in the President by an exertion of legislative power, but with such an authority plus the very delicate, plenary, and exclusive power of the President as the sole organ of the federal government in the field of international relations. If, in the maintenance of our international relations, serious embarrassment is to be avoided and success for our aims achieved, congressional legislation that is to be made effective through negotiation and inquiry within the international field must often accord to the President a degree of discretion and freedom from statutory restriction that would not be admissible were domestic affairs alone involved.

Moreover, he, not Congress, has the better opportunity of knowing the conditions that prevail in foreign countries, and especially is this true in time of war. He has his confidential sources of information. He has his agents in the form of diplomatic, consular, and other officials. Secrecy in respect of information gathered by them may be highly necessary, and the premature disclosure of it productive of harmful results.

The principles that justify such legislation also find overwhelming support in the unbroken legislative practice that has prevailed almost from the inception of the national government to the present day. The result of holding that the joint resolution here under attack is an unlawful delegation of legislative power would be to stamp a multitude of comparable acts and resolutions as likewise invalid. And while this Court may not, and should not, hesitate to declare acts of Congress, however many times repeated, to be unconstitutional if beyond all rational doubt it finds them to be so, an impressive array of legislation enacted by nearly every Congress from the beginning of our national existence to the present day must be given unusual weight in the process of reaching a correct determination of the problem.

We accordingly conclude, both upon principle and in accordance with precedent, that there is sufficient warrant for the broad discretion vested in the President to determine whether the enforcement of the statute will have a beneficial effect upon the reestablishment of peace in the affected countries; whether he shall make proclamation to bring the resolution into operation; and whether and when the resolution shall cease to operate.

McReynolds, dissenting, does not agree. He is of opinion that the court below reached the right conclusion and its judgment ought to be affirmed.

Monitoring Foreign Communications

In accord with the dichotomy recognized in the *Curtiss-Wright* case, the Executive also has broader powers to monitor foreign communications than those involving "internal affairs."

In United States v. United States District Court, 407 U.S. 297 (1972), the Court (8-0) rejected the government's claim that electronic surveillance for domestic intelligence purposes was lawful as a reasonable exercise of presidential authority to protect the national security. However, the Court emphasized that the case before it "require[d] no judgment on the scope of the President's surveillance power with respect to the activities of foreign powers, within or without the country," and expressed no opinion as to "the issues which may be involved with respect to activities of foreign powers or their agents."

In 1978, in response to the Court's decision, Congress enacted the Foreign Intelligence Surveillance Act (FISA), which prohibits government "electronic surveillance" except as authorized by statute and established a special court to consider warrants required under the act. "Electronic surveillance" is defined in the act to include the acquisition of the contents of any wire communication "to or from a person in the United States, without the consent of any party thereto, if such acquisition occurs in the United States." Notwithstanding that requirement, as pointed out in the comment "The Rise of the 'Imperial Presidency' " at the beginning of this chapter, President George W. Bush claimed that as Commander in Chief he had authority to monitor international telephone calls and emails to and from individuals within the United States.

In August 2007, Congress passed temporary legislation amending FISA for a period of six months. The amendment removed the prohibition on warrantless spying on Americans abroad and gave the government broad powers to order telecommunication companies to make their networks available to government investigators. The amendment expired in February 2008 because the Senate and House could not agree on conditions of renewal, particularly concerning whether telecommunications companies should be immune from civil liability for taking part in the administration's program of eavesdropping without warrants after the 9/11 terrorist attacks.

In June 2008, after a four-month deadlock on the issue, Congress amended FISA to overhaul the rules on the government's wiretapping powers and grant the companies the immunity proposed by the administration. The amendment (which expires in 2012 unless Congress renews it) provides that the civil damage suits pending against the companies "shall be promptly dismissed" if the court finds that the companies received legitimate requests from the government directing their participation in the program.

Other key features of the legislation: Individual warrants are no longer required to monitor purely foreign communications that pass through American telecommunications switches. The government may now use broad warrants to eavesdrop on large groups of foreign targets at once. In targeting and wiretapping Americans, the government must obtain individual court orders from the FISA court, but in "exigent" or emergency circumstances it will be able to proceed for at least seven days without a court order if it certifies that "intelligence important to the national security of the United States may be lost." Another provision affirms that the statute's restrictions constitute the "exclusive" means for the executive branch to conduct wiretapping operations in terrorism and espionage cases.

Youngstown Sheet & Tube Co. v. Sawyer, 343 U.S. 579 (1952)

FACTS: During the Korean War, a dispute arose between American steel companies and their employees over the terms of new collective bargaining agreements. After efforts to resolve the dispute failed, the Steelworkers Union gave notice of a nationwide strike. In response, President Harry Truman determined that a strike in the steel industry would jeopardize the national defense because steel was essential in the production of nearly all weapons and other war materials.

A few hours before the strike was to begin, the President issued an Executive Order directing Sawyer, the Secretary of Commerce, to take possession of the steel mills and keep them running. The next morning the President sent a message to Congress reporting his executive order.

The heads of the various steel mills protested but obeyed, staying on as operating managers for the government. But within a few weeks the steel companies sued Sawyer in the federal district court, claiming that the seizure was unlawful and requesting injunctive relief.

The mill owners argued that the President's order amounted to lawmaking, a legislative function that the Constitution granted to Congress and not to the President. The government contended that the President's action was necessary to avert a national catastrophe which would inevitably result from a stoppage of steel production, and that in meeting this grave emergency the President was acting within the aggregate of his constitutional powers as the nation's chief executive and the Commander in Chief of the Armed Forces. The government argued that a strike disrupting steel production for even a brief period would so endanger the well-being and safety of the nation that the President had "inherent power" to do what he had done.

The District Court issued a preliminary injunction, which the Court of Appeals stayed while the government appealed to the Supreme Court.

ISSUE: Did the President have the authority to seize the nation's steel mills?

DECISION (per *Black*, 6-3): *No.*

The President's power, if any, to issue the order must stem either from an act of Congress or from the Constitution itself. There is no statute that expressly authorizes the President to take possession of property as he did here. Nor is there any act of Congress to which our attention has been directed from which such a power can fairly be implied.

There are two statutes that do authorize the president to take both personal and real property under certain conditions. However, the government states that the seizure provisions of those statutes were "much too cumbersome, involved, and time-consuming for the crisis which was at hand."

Moreover, the use of the seizure technique to solve labor disputes in order to prevent work stoppages was not only unauthorized but furthermore Congress had refused to adopt that method of settling labor disputes. When the Taft-Hartley Act was under consideration in 1947, Congress specifically rejected an amendment that would have authorized such governmental seizures.

It is therefore clear that, if the President had authority to issue the order, it must be found in some provision of the Constitution. And it is not claimed that express constitutional language grants this power to the President. The contention is that presidential power should be implied from the aggregate of his powers under the Constitution. Particular reliance is placed on provisions in Article II stating that "The executive Power shall be vested in a President. . ."; that "he shall take Care that the Laws be faithfully executed"; and that he "shall be Commander in Chief of the Army and Navy of the United States."

The order cannot properly be sustained as an exercise of the President's power as Commander in Chief. The government cites cases upholding broad powers in military commanders engaged in day-to-day fighting in a theater of war. However, we cannot with faithfulness to our constitutional system hold that the Commander in Chief is empowered by his position to take possession of private property in order to keep labor disputes from stopping production. That is a job for the Nation's lawmakers, not for its military authorities.

Nor can the seizure order be sustained because of provisions granting executive power to the President. In the framework of our Constitution, the President's power to see that the laws are faithfully executed refutes the idea that he is to be a lawmaker. And the Constitution is neither silent nor equivocal about who shall make laws that the president is to execute. The first section of the first article says that "All legislative Powers herein granted shall be vested in a Congress of the United States."

The founders of this nation entrusted the lawmaking power to the Congress alone in both good and bad times. This seizure order cannot stand.

Frankfurter, concurring: We must put to one side consideration of what powers the President would have had if there had been no legislation whatever bearing on the authority asserted by the seizure, or if the seizure had been only for a short, explicitly temporary period, to be terminated automatically unless Congressional approval were given. These and other questions are not now before us.

Congress has frequently—at least 16 times since 1916—specifically provided for executive seizure of production, transportation, communications, or storage facilities.

In every case it has qualified this grant of power with limitations and safeguards. This demonstrates that Congress deemed seizure so drastic a power as to require that it be carefully circumscribed whenever the President was vested with this extraordinary authority.

Congress in 1947 was again called upon to consider whether governmental seizure should be used to avoid serious industrial shutdowns. In adopting the provisions that it did, for dealing with a "national emergency" arising out of a breakdown in peaceful industrial relations, Congress was very familiar with governmental seizure as a protective measure. On a balance of considerations, Congress chose not to lodge this power in the President.

Nothing can be plainer than that Congress made a conscious choice of policy. It could not more clearly and emphatically have withheld seizure authority than it did in 1947.

Douglas, concurring: There can be no doubt that the emergency that caused the President to seize these steel plants was one that bore heavily on the country. But the emergency did not create power; it merely marked an occasion when power should be exercised. And the fact that it was necessary that measures be taken to keep steel in production does not mean that the President, rather than the Congress, had the constitutional authority to act. The Congress, as well as the President, is trustee of the national welfare.

The method by which industrial peace is achieved is of vital importance not only to the parties but to society as well. A determination that sanctions should be applied, that the hand of the law should be placed upon the parties, and that the force of the courts should be directed against them, is an exercise of legislative power. In this nation the legislative power of the federal government is in the Congress.

The legislative nature of the action taken by the President seems to me to be clear. When the United States takes over an industrial plant to settle a labor controversy, it is condemning property. The seizure of the plant is a taking in the constitutional sense. A permanent taking would amount to the nationalization of the industry. A temporary taking falls short of that goal. But though the seizure is only for a week or a month, the condemnation is complete and the United States must pay compensation for the temporary possession.

If we sanctioned the present exercise of power by the President, we would be expanding Article II of the Constitution and rewriting it to suit the political conveniences of the present emergency. Article II provides that the President "shall take Care that the Laws be faithfully executed." But the power to execute the laws starts and ends with the laws Congress has enacted.

We pay a price for our system of checks and balances, for the distribution of power among the three branches of government. It is a price that today may seem exorbitant to many. Today a kindly President uses the seizure power to effect a wage increase and to keep the steel furnaces in production. Yet tomorrow another President might use the same power to prevent a wage increase, to curb trade-unionists, to regiment labor as oppressively as the steel industry thinks it has been regimented by this seizure.

Jackson, concurring: We may well begin by a somewhat oversimplified grouping of practical situations in which a President may doubt, or others may challenge, his powers.

1. When the President acts pursuant to an express or implied authorization of Congress, his authority is at its maximum, for it includes all that he possesses in his own right plus all that Congress can delegate. If his act is held unconstitutional under these circumstances, it usually means that the federal government as an undivided whole lacks power. A seizure executed by the President pursuant to an Act of Congress would be supported by the strongest of presumptions and the widest latitude of judicial interpretation, and the burden of persuasion would rest heavily upon any who might attack it.

2. When the President acts in absence of either a congressional grant or denial of authority, he can only rely upon his own independent powers, but there is a zone of twilight in which he and Congress may have concurrent authority, or in which its distribution is uncertain. Therefore, congressional inertia, indifference, or quiescence may sometimes, at least as a practical matter, enable, if not invite, measures on independent presidential responsibility. In this area, any actual test of power is likely to depend on the imperatives of events and contemporary imponderables rather than on abstract theories of law.

3. When the President takes measures incompatible with the expressed or implied will of Congress, his power is at its lowest ebb, for then he can rely only upon his own constitutional powers minus any constitutional powers of Congress over the matter. Courts can sustain exclusive presidential control in such a case only by disabling the Congress from acting upon the subject. Presidential claim to a power at once so conclusive and preclusive must be scrutinized with caution, for what is at stake is the equilibrium established by our constitutional system.

Into which of these classifications does this executive seizure of the steel industry fit? It is eliminated from the first by admission, for it is conceded that no congressional authorization exists for this seizure. That takes away also the support of the many precedents and declarations that were made in relation, and must be confined, to this category.

Can it then be defended under flexible tests available to the second category? It seems clearly eliminated from that class because Congress has not left seizure of private property an open field but has covered it by statutory policies inconsistent with this seizure. In choosing a different and inconsistent way of his own, the President cannot claim that it is necessitated or invited by failure of Congress to legislate upon the occasions, grounds, and methods for seizure of industrial properties.

This leaves the current seizure to be justified only by the severe tests under the third grouping, where it can be supported only by any remainder of executive power after subtraction of such powers as Congress may have over the subject. In short, we can sustain the President only by holding that seizure of such strike-bound industries is within his domain and beyond control by Congress.

It is now a settled principle of constitutional law that the executive branch, like the federal government as a whole, possesses only delegated powers. The purpose of the Constitution was not only to grant power, but to keep it from getting out of hand.

Nothing in our Constitution is plainer than that the power to declare war is entrusted only to Congress. Of course, a state of war may, in fact, exist without a formal declaration. But no doctrine that the Court could promulgate would seem to me more sinister and alarming than that a President whose conduct of foreign affairs is so largely uncontrolled, and often even is unknown, can vastly enlarge his mastery over the internal affairs of the country by his own commitment of the nation's armed forces to some foreign venture.

That the military powers of the Commander in Chief were not to supersede representative government of internal affairs seems obvious from the Constitution and from elementary American history. They demonstrate that Congress, not the Executive, should control utilization of the war power as an instrument of domestic policy.

We should not use this occasion to circumscribe, much less to contract, the lawful role of the President as Commander in Chief. I should indulge the widest latitude of interpretation to sustain his exclusive function to command the instruments of national force, at least when turned against the outside world for the security of our society. But, when it is turned inward, not because of rebellion but because of a lawful economic struggle between industry and labor, it should have no such indulgence.

The government seeks to support the seizure upon nebulous, inherent powers never expressly granted but said to have accrued to the office from the customs and claims of preceding administrations. The plea is for a resulting power to deal with a crisis or an emergency according to the necessities of the case, the unarticulated assumption being that necessity knows no law.

Loose and irresponsible use of adjectives colors much of the discussion of presidential powers. "Inherent" powers, "implied" powers, "incidental" powers, "plenary" powers, "war" powers, and "emergency" powers are used, often interchangeably and without fixed or ascertainable meanings.

The Framers of the Constitution, however, knew what emergencies were, knew the pressures they engender for authoritative action, knew too how they afford a ready pretext for usurpation. Aside from suspension of the privilege of the writ of habeas corpus in time of rebellion or invasion, when the public safety may require it, they made no express provision for exercise of extraordinary authority because of a crisis. I do not think we rightfully may so amend their work, and, if we could, I am not convinced it would be wise.

The Executive, except for his authority to recommend and veto legislation, has no legislative power. The executive action here originates in the individual will of the President and represents an exercise of authority without law.

Burton, concurring: The President chose not to use the Taft-Hartley procedure provided by Congress. Now it is contended that, although the President chose not to follow the statutory procedure, his substituted procedure must be accepted as its equivalent. Those circumstances distinguish this emergency from one in which Congress takes no action.

The present situation is not comparable to that of an imminent invasion or threatened attack. We do not face the issue of what might be the President's constitutional power to meet such catastrophic situations. Nor is it claimed that the current seizure is in the nature of a military command addressed by the President, as Commander in Chief, to a mobilized nation waging, or imminently threatened with, total war.

The controlling fact here is that Congress, within its constitutionally delegated power, has prescribed for the President specific procedures, exclusive of seizure, for his use in meeting the present type of emergency. Under these circumstances, the President's order invaded the jurisdiction of Congress and violated the essence of the principle of the separation of governmental powers.

Clark, concurring: In my view, the Constitution does grant to the President extensive authority in times of grave and imperative national emergency. In fact, such a grant may well be necessary to the very existence of the Constitution itself. As Lincoln aptly said, "[is] it possible to lose the nation and yet preserve the Constitution?" In describing this authority I care not whether one calls it "residual," "inherent," "moral," "implied," "aggregate," "emergency," or otherwise.

I conclude that, where Congress has laid down specific procedures to deal with the type of crisis confronting the President, he must follow those procedures in meeting the crisis, but that in the absence of such action by Congress, the President's independent power to act depends upon the gravity of the situation confronting the nation. I cannot sustain the seizure in question because here Congress had prescribed methods to be followed by the President in meeting the emergency at hand.

Vinson, dissenting (joined by Reed and Minton): The power of eminent domain, invoked in this case, is an essential attribute of sovereignty and has long been recognized as a power of the federal government. However, plaintiffs claim that the power of eminent domain can be exercised only under an Act of Congress; under no circumstances, they say, can that power be exercised by the President unless he can point to an express provision in enabling legislation. Under this view, the President is left powerless at the very moment when the need for action may be most pressing and when no one, other than he, is immediately capable of action.

Cases often arise presenting questions that could not have been foreseen by the Framers. In such cases, the Constitution has been treated as a living document adaptable to new situations. But we are not called upon today to expand the Constitution to meet a new situation. For, in this case, we need only look to history and time-honored principles of constitutional law. It is those who assert the invalidity of the Executive Order who seek to amend the Constitution in this case.

Our Presidents have on many occasions, with or without explicit statutory authorization, dealt with national emergencies by acting promptly and resolutely to enforce legislative programs, at least to save those programs until Congress could act. Congress and the courts have responded to such executive initiative with consistent approval.

The absence of a specific statute authorizing seizure of the steel mills has not until today been thought to prevent the President from taking such action. Unlike an administrative commission confined to the enforcement of the statute under which it was created, or the head of a department when administering a particular statute, the President is a constitutional officer charged with taking care that a "mass of legislation" be executed. Flexibility as to mode of execution to meet critical situations is a matter of practical necessity.

The single presidential purpose disclosed on this record is to faithfully execute the laws by acting in an emergency to maintain the status quo. In his "Message to Congress" immediately following the seizure, the President explained the necessity of his action and expressed his desire to cooperate with any legislative proposals approving, regulating, or rejecting the seizure of the steel mills. Consequently, there is no evidence of any presidential purpose to defy Congress or act in any way inconsistent with the legislative will.

The diversity of views expressed in the six opinions of the majority, the lack of reference to authoritative precedent, the complete disregard of the uncontroverted facts showing the gravity of the emergency, and the temporary nature of the taking all serve to demonstrate how far afield one must go to affirm the District Court's injunction.

According to the opinions of the majority, the broad executive power granted by Article II to an officer on duty 365 days a year cannot be invoked to avert disaster. Instead, the President must confine himself to sending a message to Congress recommending action. Under this messenger-boy concept of the office, the President cannot even act to preserve legislative programs from destruction so that Congress will have something left to act upon.

Faced with the duty of executing the defense programs that Congress had enacted and the disastrous effects that any stoppage in steel production would have on those programs, the President acted to preserve those programs by seizing the steel mills. There is no question that the possession was temporary in character and subject to congressional direction. No basis for claims of arbitrary action, unlimited powers or dictatorial usurpation of congressional power appears from the facts of this case. On the contrary, the president acted in full conformity with his duties under the Constitution.

*****

[*Note:* Of the seven opinions in the *Youngstown* case, Justice Jackson's concurring opinion is clearly the most well-known because of his frequently cited categorization of three types of conflict between Congress and the President.

In *Dames & Moore v. Regan,* 453 U.S. 654 (1981), in commenting on Justice Jackson's three categories, the Court pointed out "that executive action in any particular instance falls, not neatly in one of three pigeonholes, but rather at some point along a spectrum running from explicit congressional authorization to explicit congressional prohibition." In an opinion by Justice Rehnquist (who coincidentally had been Jackson's law clerk when the *Youngstown* case was decided), the Court stated: "we cannot ignore the general tenor of Congress' legislation . . . in trying to determine whether the President is acting alone or at least with the acceptance of Congress. . . . Congress cannot anticipate and legislate with regard to every possible action the President may find it necessary to take or every possible situation in which he might act. Such failure of Congress specifically to delegate authority does not, 'especially . . . in the areas of foreign policy and national security,' imply congressional disapproval of action taken by the Executive. On the contrary, the enactment of legislation closely related to the question of the President's authority in a particular case which evinces legislative intent to accord the President broad discretion may be considered to 'invite' 'measures on independent presidential responsibility.' At least this is so where there is no contrary indication of legislative intent and when, as here, there is a history of congressional acquiescence in conduct of the sort engaged in by the President."]

The Detention of Enemy Combatants

On September 18, 2001, one week after the 9/11 attack, Congress passed a joint resolution ("Authorization for Use of Military Force" (AUMF), reproduced earlier in this chapter) permitting the President "to use all necessary and appropriate force against those nations, organizations, or persons he determines planned, authorized, committed, or aided the terrorist attacks that occurred on September 11, 2001, or harbored such organizations or persons."

Shortly thereafter, President Bush signed an executive order providing that any person he designated as an "enemy combatant" would be held without trial indefinitely and incommunicado in a military prison unless and until the government determined that access to counsel or further process is warranted.

The President's authority to take such action was immediately challenged in habeas corpus actions filed in the federal courts. In response, relying on the President's authority as Commander in Chief under Article II and the September 18, 2001, resolution (AUMF), the government contended that prisoners designated by the President as "enemy combatants" have no constitutional or statutory rights to obtain review of their detention in the civilian courts.

In a series of decisions since 2004, the Supreme Court has repeatedly rejected the President's claim that his authority to detain "enemy combatants" is unreviewable by the federal courts. These decisions have involved both (1) "enemy combatants" who are U.S. citizens imprisoned in the United States and (2) alien "enemy combatants" imprisoned outside the borders of the United States.

(1) U.S. Citizens Imprisoned in the United States as Enemy Combatants

In Hamdi v. Rumsfeld, 542 U.S. 507 (2004) and Rumsfeld v. Padilla, 542 U.S. 426 (2004), two United States *citizens* (one captured on an Afghanistan battlefield, the other arrested on his return to the United States at O'Hare Airport) were designated "enemy combatants" by the President, held incommunicado in a military prison *in the United States,* and denied many of the protections (including access to counsel) enjoyed by defendants in ordinary civilian and military courts.

In *Hamdi,* the Court concluded (5-4) that Hamdi's detention was authorized under Congress's AUMF resolution, thereby making it unnecessary to pass on the President's claim of inherent power. But the Court rejected (8-1) the government's argument that the civilian courts have no role at all to review the detention of a citizen enemy combatant. Instead, according to the Court, Hamdi was entitled at least to notice of the factual basis for his classification as an enemy combatant and a "fair opportunity" to rebut the government's factual assertions before a neutral decision maker. The Court noted, however, that an adequate form of military review might make unnecessary any review by the civilian courts.

On remand of the *Hamdi* case, before any hearing was held, Hamdi's lawyers and the government reached an agreement to release Hamdi in Saudia Arabia. The agreement required Hamdi to renounce any claim to U.S. citizenship and to abide by travel restrictions (including not traveling to the United States, Afghanistan, Iraq, Israel, Pakistan, Syria, the West Bank, or the Gaza Strip). Hamdi also promised that he will not engage in any acts of terrorism, will not engage in any combatant activities against the United States, and will not assist or affiliate with either the Taliban or the al Qaeda. Pursuant to the agreement, Hamdi was flown to Saudia Arabia and released.

The *Padilla* case also involves a U.S. citizen detained in the United States, but Padilla—unlike Hamdi—was apprehended in the United States. The Supreme Court (5-4) dismissed Padilla's case on the procedural ground that Padilla's habeas corpus petition had been filed in the wrong federal district (New York) and should instead have been filed in South Carolina where Padilla was imprisoned.

Subsequently, Padilla filed a new habeas corpus action in South Carolina. After the Court of Appeals for the Fourth Circuit upheld the government's authority to hold Padilla as an enemy combatant, Padilla petitioned the Supreme Court for certiorari. However, just before the government was to file its response to the petition, a federal grand jury in Florida indicted Padilla for violating federal antiterrorism laws, and Padilla was transferred to a civilian prison. On that basis, the government opposed Padilla's petition for certiorari as moot, arguing that he was no longer being detained as an enemy combatant since he was now charged with civilian crimes. The Court

(6-3) denied certiorari on the ground of mootness. In August 2007 in the criminal case, Padilla was found guilty; his appeal is now pending.

(2) Alien Enemy Combatants Imprisoned at Guantánamo

Starting in January 2002, the U.S. transported more than 800 foreign nationals to the U.S. naval base at Guantánamo Bay, Cuba, for detention as enemy combatants to be held there indefinitely until the end of hostilities or unless the government chose to release or transfer them elsewhere. Although a 1903 treaty with Cuba gives the United States "complete jurisdiction and control" over the base, the treaty also provides that Cuba retains "ultimate sovereignty" over the area.

Some of the 800 detainees had been captured on the battlefield in Afghanistan, but the majority were not. Some had been turned over by Afghan warlords in exchange for rewards. Many others were taken into custody in various countries located far from Afghanistan.

About 270 detainees still remain at Guantánamo. Many have been held there since 2002. They deny that they have ever committed acts of war or terrorism against the United States, and they claim that they have never been given a fair opportunity to rebut their characterization as enemy combatants.

In Rasul v. Bush, 542 U.S. 466 (2004), the Supreme Court (6-3) broadly construed the habeas corpus statute (28 U.S.C. 2241) to hold that the Guantánamo detainees could challenge their detention in a habeas corpus action in the federal courts.

The majority held that the detainees' claims were not precluded by the Court's decision in Johnson v. Eisentrager, 339 U.S. 763 (1950), which held that habeas corpus was not available to nonresident enemy aliens outside the territorial jurisdiction of any American civil court. The *Eisentrager* decision, in the view of the *Rasul* majority, was distinguishable because it was "relevant only to the question of the prisoners' *constitutional* entitlement to habeas corpus" and had little bearing "on the question of the petitioners' *statutory* entitlement to habeas review." (Italics the Court's.)

The Court concluded: "Petitioners contend that they are being held in federal custody in violation of the laws of the United States. No party questions the District Court's jurisdiction over petitioners' custodians. .. .. Section 2241, by its terms, requires nothing more." In addition, the majority held that, "Whatever traction the presumption against extraterritoriality might have in other contexts, it certainly has no application to the operation of the habeas statute with respect to persons detained within 'the territorial jurisdiction' of the United States," and that the Guantánamo base should be regarded as part of U.S. territory because (under the terms of the U.S. lease from Cuba) it was under the government's "complete jurisdiction and control."

Three Justices dissented in an opinion by Justice Scalia, who contended that,

> In abandoning the venerable statutory line drawn in *Eisentrager,* the Court boldly extends the scope of the habeas statute to the four corners of the earth. . . . The consequence of this holding, as applied to aliens outside the country, is breathtaking. It permits an alien captured in a foreign theater of active combat to bring a §2241 petition against the Secretary of Defense.

The Congressional Response to the *Rasul* Decision

In December 2005, Congress enacted the Detainee Treatment Act (DTA), which, in large measure, overturned the Court's *Rasul* decision. The DTA amended the federal habeas corpus statute to strip the federal courts of jurisdiction to adjudicate claims of detainees (other than U.S. citizens) held outside U.S. borders. The Act, however, authorized an appeal to the Court of Appeals for the District of Columbia Circuit from a final decision of a military tribunal finding a detainee to be an enemy combatant. The scope of such an appeal is limited to the question whether the military tribunal's decision was consistent with required standards and procedures and, where applicable, "the Constitution and the laws of the United States."

Except for the appeal procedure in the Court of Appeals for the District of Columbia, DTA prohibits the federal courts from hearing or considering any action

> relating to any aspect of the detention, transfer, treatment, trial, or conditions of confinement of an alien who is or was detained by the United States and has been determined by the United States to have been properly detained as an enemy combatant or is awaiting such determination.

In Hamdan v. Rumsfeld, 548 U.S. 557 (2006) (discussed more fully in the comment "Prosecuting Enemy Combatants for War Crimes" at the end of this chapter), the Court held that the DTA jurisdiction-stripping provision did not apply to detainees' habeas corpus petitions that were pending when the DTA was enacted.

In October 2006, in response to *Hamdan v. Rumsfeld,* Congress enacted the Military Commissions Act. §7 of the Act reaffirmed the DTA limitation on federal courts' habeas corpus jurisdiction and specifically provided that the limitation applied to habeas corpus petitions filed before as well as after enactment of DTA.

In June 2008, in the next-digested case, *Boumediene v. Bush,* the Supreme Court held (5-4) that Congress's limitation on the federal courts' habeas corpus jurisdiction is unconstitutional. The decision is nearly unprecedented in rejecting a major assertion of wartime power backed by both of the other branches of the federal government.

Boumediene v. Bush, ___U.S.___, 128 S.Ct. 2229 (2008)

FACTS: Following the Court's decision in Hamdi v. Rumsfeld, 542 U.S. 507 (2004), the Defense Department established Combatant Status Review Tribunals (CSRTs) to determine whether individuals detained at the U.S. Naval Station at Guantánamo Bay, Cuba, were appropriately classified as "enemy combatants."

The petitioners in this case are 37 aliens detained at Guantánamo after being captured in Afghanistan or elsewhere abroad and found to be enemy combatants by CSRTs. Each petitioner sought a writ of habeas corpus in the District Court, which ordered the cases dismissed for lack of jurisdiction because Guantánamo is outside sovereign U.S. territory. The Court of Appeals affirmed, but the Supreme Court reversed in Rasul v. Bush, 542 U.S. 466 (2004), holding that 28 U.S.C. §2241 extended statutory habeas jurisdiction to Guantánamo, and remanded petitioners' cases to the lower courts for reconsideration.

Subsequently Congress passed the Detainee Treatment Act of 2005 (DTA) and the Military Commissions Act of 2006 (MCA). (These statutes are summarized in the preceding comment "The Detention of Enemy Combatants.")

In reconsidering petitioners' cases in light of *Rasul* and the new legislation, the D.C. Court of Appeals concluded that MCA §7 stripped all federal courts of jurisdiction to consider petitioners' habeas applications; that petitioners are not entitled to habeas or the protections of the Suspension Clause, U. S. Const., Art. I, §9, cl. 2; and that it was therefore unnecessary to consider whether the DTA appeal procedure provided an adequate and effective substitute for habeas.

ISSUE: Is the Act of Congress stripping the federal courts of habeas corpus jurisdiction constitutional?

DECISION (per *Kennedy,* 5-4): *No.*

Petitioners present the question whether they have the constitutional privilege of habeas corpus, a privilege that can only be withdrawn except in conformance with the Suspension Clause, Art. I, §9, cl. 2 (which provides that "[t]he Privilege of the Writ of Habeas Corpus shall not be suspended, unless when in Cases of Rebellion or Invasion the public Safety may require it"). We hold these petitioners do have the habeas corpus privilege and that the procedures provided in DTA for review of the detainees' status are not an adequate and effective substitute for habeas corpus. Therefore §7 of the Military Commissions Act of 2006 operates as an unconstitutional suspension of the writ.

We do not address whether the President has authority to detain these petitioners, nor do we hold that the writ must issue. These and other questions regarding the legality of the detention are to be resolved in the first instance by the District Court.

(The Detainees' Eligibility for Habeas Corpus)

In deciding the constitutional questions now presented, we must determine whether petitioners are barred from seeking the writ or invoking the protections of the Suspension Clause either because of their status, i.e., petitioners' designation by the Executive Branch as enemy combatants, or their physical location, i.e., their presence at Guantánamo Bay. The Government contends that noncitizens designated as enemy combatants and detained in territory located outside our Nation's borders have no constitutional rights and no privilege of habeas corpus. Petitioners contend they do have cognizable constitutional rights and that Congress, in seeking to eliminate recourse to habeas corpus as a means to assert those rights, acted in violation of the Suspension Clause.

Guantánamo Bay is not formally part of the United States. And under the terms of the lease between the United States and Cuba, Cuba retains "ultimate sovereignty" over the territory while the United States exercises "complete jurisdiction and control." We do not question the Government's position that Cuba, not the United States, maintains sovereignty, in the legal and technical sense of the term, over Guantánamo Bay. But this does not end the analysis. As we did in *Rasul,* we take notice of the obvious and uncontested fact that the United States, by virtue of its complete jurisdiction and control over the base, maintains *de facto* sovereignty over this territory.

Practical considerations weighed heavily in Johnson v. Eisentrager, 339 U.S. 763 (1950), where the Court addressed whether habeas corpus jurisdiction extended to enemy aliens who had been convicted of violating the laws of war. The prisoners were detained at Landsberg Prison in Germany during the Allied Powers' postwar occupation. The Court stressed the difficulties of ordering the Government to produce the prisoners in a habeas corpus proceeding. It "would require allocation of shipping space, guarding personnel, billeting and rations" and would damage the prestige of military commanders at a sensitive time. True, the Court in *Eisentrager* denied access to the writ, and it noted the prisoners "at no relevant time were within any territory over which the United States is sovereign, and [that] the scenes of their offense, their capture, their trial and their punishment were all beyond the territorial jurisdiction of any court of the United States." The Government seizes upon this language as proof positive that the *Eisentrager* Court adopted a formalistic, sovereignty-based test for determining the reach of the Suspension Clause. We reject this reading for three reasons.

First, we do not accept the idea that the above-quoted passage from *Eisentrager* is the only authoritative language in the opinion and that all the rest is dicta. The Court's further determinations, based on practical considerations, were integral to its opinion.

Second, because the United States lacked both *de jure* sovereignty and plenary control over Landsberg Prison, it is far from clear that the *Eisentrager* Court used the term "sovereign" only in the narrow technical sense. In any event, even if we assume the *Eisentrager* Court considered the United States' lack of formal legal sovereignty over Landsberg Prison as the decisive factor in that case, its holding is not inconsistent with a functional approach to questions of extraterritoriality.

Third, if the Government's reading of *Eisentrager* were correct, the opinion would have marked not only a change in but a complete repudiation of the functional approach of previous decisions to questions of extraterritoriality. We cannot accept the Government's view. Nothing in *Eisentrager* says that *de jure* sovereignty is or has ever been the only relevant consideration in determining the geographic reach of the Constitution or of habeas corpus.

The Government's formal sovereignty-based test also raises troubling separation-of-powers concerns. The necessary implication of the argument is that by surrendering formal sovereignty over any unincorporated territory to a third party, while at the same time entering into a lease that grants total control over the territory back to the United States, it would be possible for the political branches to govern without legal constraint. Our basic charter cannot be contracted away like this. To hold the political branches have the power to switch the Constitution on or off at will would permit a striking anomaly in our tripartite system of government, leading to a regime in which Congress and the President, not this Court, say "what the law is." Marbury v. Madison, 5 U.S. 137 (1803).

Like the *Eisentrager* petitioners, the sites of these detainees' apprehension and detention are technically outside the sovereign territory of the United States. But, unlike Landsberg Prison, Guantánamo Bay is no transient possession. In every practical sense Guantánamo is not abroad; it is within the constant jurisdiction of the United States.

We recognize, as the Court did in *Eisentrager,* that there are costs to holding the Suspension Clause applicable in a case of military detention abroad. Habeas corpus proceedings may require expenditure of funds by the Government and may divert the attention of military personnel from other pressing tasks. While we are sensitive to these concerns, we do not find them dispositive. Compliance with any judicial process requires some incremental expenditure of resources. Yet civilian courts and the armed forces have functioned alongside each other at various points in our history. The government presents no credible arguments that the military mission at Guantánamo would be compromised if habeas corpus courts had jurisdiction to hear the detainees' claims.

The situation in *Eisentrager* was far different, given the historical context and nature of the military's mission in postwar Germany. When hostilities in the European

Theater came to an end, in addition to supervising massive reconstruction and aid efforts, the American forces stationed in Germany faced potential security threats from a defeated enemy. Similar threats are not apparent here. In addition, there is no indication that adjudicating a habeas corpus petition would cause friction with the host government.

It is true that before today the Court has never held that noncitizens detained by our Government in territory over which another country maintains *de jure* sovereignty have any rights under our Constitution. But the cases before us lack any precise historical parallel. They involve individuals detained by executive order for the duration of a conflict that, if measured from September 11, 2001, to the present, is already among the longest wars in American history. The detainees, moreover, are held in a territory that, while technically not part of the United States, is under the complete and total control of our Government. Under these circumstances the lack of a precedent on point is no barrier to our holding.

We hold that Article I, §9, cl. 2, of the Constitution has full effect at Guantánamo Bay. If the privilege of habeas corpus is to be denied to the detainees now before us, Congress must act in accordance with the requirements of the Suspension Clause. This Court may not impose a *de facto* suspension by abstaining from these controversies. The MCA does not purport to be a formal suspension of the writ; and the Government, in its submissions to us, has not argued that it is. Petitioners, therefore, are entitled to the privilege of habeas corpus to challenge the legality of their detention.

(Adequacy of the DTA Alternative to Habeas Corpus)

In light of this holding, the question becomes whether the statute stripping jurisdiction to issue the writ avoids the Suspension Clause mandate because Congress has provided adequate substitute procedures for habeas corpus. In the ordinary course we would remand to the Court of Appeals to consider this question in the first instance. However, the gravity of the separation-of-powers issues raised by these cases and the fact that these detainees have been denied meaningful access to a judicial forum for a period of years render these cases exceptional. In all likelihood a remand simply would delay ultimate resolution of the issue by this Court.

The DTA's jurisdictional grant for review of a CSRT finding is quite limited. The Court of Appeals has jurisdiction not to inquire into the legality of the detention generally but only to assess whether the CSRT complied with the "standards and procedures specified by the Secretary of Defense" and whether those standards and procedures are lawful.

We do not endeavor to offer a comprehensive summary of the requisites for an adequate substitute for habeas corpus. We do consider it uncontroversial, however, that the privilege of habeas corpus entitles the prisoner to a meaningful opportunity to demonstrate that he is being held pursuant to "the erroneous application or interpretation" of relevant law. And the habeas court must have the power to order the conditional release of an individual unlawfully detained—though release need not be the exclusive remedy and is not the appropriate one in every case in which the writ is granted. These are the easily identified attributes of any constitutionally adequate habeas corpus proceeding. But, depending on the circumstances, more may be required.

To determine the necessary scope of habeas corpus review, we must assess the CSRT process, the mechanism through which petitioners' designation as enemy combatants became final. The most relevant of the alleged CSRT deficiencies for our purposes are the constraints upon the detainee's ability to rebut the factual basis for the government's assertion that he is an enemy combatant. At the CSRT stage the detainee has limited means to find or present evidence to challenge the Government's case against him. He does not have the assistance of counsel and may not be aware of the most critical allegations that the Government relied upon to order his detention. The detainee can confront witnesses that testify during the CSRT proceedings. But given that there are in effect no limits on the admission of hearsay evidence—the only requirement is that the tribunal deem the evidence "relevant and helpful"—the detainee's opportunity to question witnesses is likely to be more theoretical than real.

The Government defends the CSRT process, arguing that it was designed to conform to the procedures suggested by the plurality in Hamdi v. Rumsfeld, 542 U.S. 507 (2004). Setting aside the fact that the relevant language in *Hamdi* did not garner a majority of the Court, it does not control the matter at hand. There was no question in that case of a suspension of habeas corpus. Instead, the plurality concentrated on whether the Executive had the authority to detain and, if so, what rights the detainee had under the Due Process Clause.

Although we make no judgment as to whether the CSRTs, as currently constituted, satisfy due process standards, we agree with petitioners that, even when all the parties involved in this process act with diligence and in good faith, there is considerable risk of error in the tribunal's findings of fact. And given that the consequence of error may be detention of persons for the duration of hostilities that may last a generation or more, this is a risk too significant to ignore.

For the writ of habeas corpus, or its substitute, to function as an effective and proper remedy in this context, the court that conducts the habeas proceeding must have the means to correct errors that occurred during the CSRT proceedings. This includes some authority to assess the sufficiency of the Government's evidence against the detainee. It also must have the authority to admit and consider relevant exculpatory evidence that was not introduced during the earlier proceeding. Here that opportunity is constitutionally required.

The extent of the showing required of the Government in these cases is a matter to be determined. We need not explore it further at this stage. We do hold that, when the judicial power to issue habeas corpus properly is invoked, the judicial officer must have adequate authority to make a determination in light of the relevant law and facts and to formulate and issue appropriate orders for relief, including, if necessary, an order directing the prisoner's release.

We now consider whether the DTA allows the Court of Appeals to conduct a proceeding meeting these standards. We see no way to construe the statute to allow what is also constitutionally required in this context—an opportunity for the detainee to present relevant exculpatory evidence that was not made part of the record in the earlier proceedings.

If the Court of Appeals determines that the CSRT followed appropriate and lawful standards and procedures, it will have reached the limits of its jurisdiction. There is no language in the DTA that can be construed to allow the Court of Appeals to admit and consider newly discovered evidence that could not have been made part of the CSRT record because it was unavailable to either the government or the detainee when the CSRT made its findings. This evidence, however, may be critical to the detainee's argument that he is not an enemy combatant and there is no cause to detain him. By foreclosing consideration of evidence not presented or reasonably available to the detainee at the CSRT proceedings, the DTA disadvantages the detainee by limiting the scope of collateral review to a record that may not be accurate or complete.

We do not imply DTA review would be a constitutionally sufficient replacement for habeas corpus but for these limitations on the detainee's ability to present exculpatory evidence. For even if it were possible, as a textual matter, to read into the statute each of the necessary procedures we have identified, we could not overlook the cumulative effect of our doing so. Petitioners have met their burden of establishing that the DTA review process is, on its face, an inadequate substitute for habeas corpus.

MCA §7 thus effects an unconstitutional suspension of the writ.

(Consideration of Prudential Barriers to Habeas Corpus Review)

In light of our conclusion that there is no jurisdictional bar to the district court's entertaining petitioners' claims, the question remains whether there are prudential barriers to habeas corpus review under these circumstances.

In cases involving foreign citizens detained abroad by the Executive, it likely would be both an impractical and unprecedented extension of judicial power to assume that habeas corpus would be available at the moment the prisoner is taken into custody. If and when habeas corpus jurisdiction applies, as it does in these cases, then proper deference can be accorded to reasonable procedures for screening and initial detention under lawful and proper conditions of confinement and treatment for a reasonable period of time. Domestic exigencies, furthermore, might also impose such onerous burdens on the Government that here, too, the Judicial Branch would be required to devise sensible rules for staying habeas corpus proceedings until the Government can comply with its requirements in a responsible way. Here, as is true with detainees apprehended abroad, a relevant consideration in determining the courts' role is whether there are suitable alternative processes in place to protect against the arbitrary exercise of governmental power.

The cases before us, however, do not involve detainees who have been held for a short period of time while awaiting their CSRT determinations. Were that the case, or were it probable that the Court of Appeals could complete a prompt review of their applications, the case for requiring temporary abstention or exhaustion of alternative remedies would be much stronger. These qualifications no longer pertain here. In some of these cases, six years have elapsed without the judicial oversight that habeas corpus or an adequate substitute demands. And there has been no showing that the Executive faces such onerous burdens that it cannot respond to habeas corpus actions. To require these detainees to complete DTA review before proceeding with their habeas corpus actions would be to require additional months, if not years, of delay. While some delay in fashioning new procedures is unavoidable, the costs of delay can no longer be borne by those who are held in custody. The detainees in these cases are entitled to a prompt habeas corpus hearing.

Our decision today holds only that the petitioners before us are entitled to seek the writ; that the DTA review procedures are an inadequate substitute for habeas corpus; and that the petitioners in these cases need not exhaust the review procedures in the court of appeals before proceeding with their habeas actions in the District Court. The only law we identify as unconstitutional is MCA §7. Accordingly, both the DTA and the CSRT process remain intact. Our holding with regard to exhaustion should not be read to imply that a habeas court should intervene the moment an enemy combatant steps foot in a territory where the writ runs. The Executive is entitled to a reasonable period of time to determine a detainee's status before a court entertains that detainee's habeas corpus petition. The CSRT process is the mechanism Congress and the President set up to deal with these issues. Except in cases of undue delay, federal courts should refrain from entertaining an enemy combatant's habeas corpus petition at least until after the Government, acting via the CSRT, has had a chance to review his status.

*****

In considering both the procedural and substantive standards used to impose detention to prevent acts of terrorism, proper deference must be accorded to the political branches. The law must accord the Executive substantial authority to apprehend and detain those who pose a real danger to our security.

Security depends upon a sophisticated intelligence apparatus and the ability of our Armed Forces to act and to interdict. Security subsists, too, in fidelity to freedom's first principles. Chief among these are freedom from arbitrary and unlawful restraint and the personal liberty that is secured by adherence to the separation of powers. It is from these principles that the judicial authority to consider petitions for habeas corpus relief derives.

Our opinion does not undermine the Executive's powers as Commander in Chief. On the contrary, the exercise of those powers is vindicated, not eroded, when confirmed by the Judicial Branch. Within the Constitution's separation-of-powers structure, few exercises of judicial power are as legitimate or as necessary as the responsibility to hear challenges to the authority of the Executive to imprison a person. Some of these petitioners have been in custody for six years with no definitive judicial determination as to the legality of their detention. Their access to the writ is a necessity to determine the lawfulness of their status, even if, in the end, they do not obtain the relief they seek.

Because our Nation's past military conflicts have been of limited duration, it has been possible to leave the outer boundaries of war powers undefined. If, as some fear, terrorism continues to pose dangerous threats to us for years to come, the Court might not have this luxury. This result is not inevitable, however. The political branches, consistent with their independent obligations to interpret and uphold the Constitution, can engage in a genuine debate about how best to preserve constitutional values while protecting the nation from terrorism.

It bears repeating that our opinion does not address the content of the law that governs petitioners' detention. That is a matter yet to be determined. We hold that petitioners may invoke the fundamental procedural protections of habeas corpus. The laws and Constitution are designed to survive, and remain in force, in extraordinary times. Liberty and security can be reconciled; and in our system they are reconciled within the framework of the law. The Framers decided that habeas corpus, a right of first importance, must be a part of that framework, a part of that law.

Souter, concurring (joined by Ginsburg and Breyer):

I join the Court's opinion in its entirety and add this afterword only to emphasize two things one might overlook after reading the dissents.

Justice Scalia is correct that here, for the first time, this Court holds there is (he says "confers") constitutional habeas jurisdiction over aliens imprisoned by the military outside an area of *de jure* national sovereignty. But no one who reads the Court's opinion in *Rasul* could seriously doubt that the jurisdictional question must be answered the same way in purely constitutional cases, given the Court's reliance in *Rasul* on the historical background of habeas generally in answering the statutory question. But whether one agrees or disagrees with today's decision, it is no bolt out of the blue.

A second fact insufficiently appreciated by the dissents is the length of the disputed imprisonments, some of the prisoners represented here today having been locked up for six years. Hence the hollow ring when the dissenters suggest that the Court is somehow precipitating the judiciary into reviewing claims that the military (subject to appeal to the Court of Appeals for the District of Columbia Circuit) could handle within some reasonable period of time. It is, in fact, the very lapse of four years from the time *Rasul* put everyone on notice that habeas process was available to Guantánamo prisoners, and the lapse of six years since some of these prisoners were captured and incarcerated, that stand at odds with the repeated suggestions of the dissenters that these cases should be seen as a judicial victory in a contest for power between the Court and the political branches.

Roberts, dissenting (joined by Scalia, Thomas, and Alito):

Today the Court strikes down as inadequate the most generous set of procedural protections ever afforded aliens detained by this country as enemy combatants. The political branches crafted these procedures amidst an ongoing military conflict, after much careful investigation and thorough debate. The Court rejects them today out of hand, without bothering to say what due process rights the detainees possess, without explaining how the statute fails to vindicate those rights, and before a single petitioner has even attempted to avail himself of the law's operation. And to what effect? The majority merely replaces a review system designed by the people's representatives with a set of shapeless procedures to be defined by federal courts at some future date. One cannot help but think, after surveying the modest practical results of the majority's ambitious opinion, that this decision is not really about the detainees at all, but about control of federal policy regarding enemy combatants.

(1) The majority is adamant that the Guantánamo detainees are entitled to the protections of habeas corpus. I regard the issue as a difficult one, primarily because of the unique and unusual jurisdictional status of Guantánamo Bay. I nonetheless agree with Justice Scalia's analysis of our precedents and the pertinent history of the writ, and accordingly join his dissent. The important point for me, however, is that the Court should have resolved these cases on other grounds. Habeas is most fundamentally a procedural right, a mechanism for contesting the legality of executive detention. The critical threshold question in these cases, prior to any inquiry about the writ's scope, is whether the system the political branches designed protects whatever rights the detainees may possess. If so, there is no need for any additional process, whether called "habeas" or something else.

Congress entrusted that threshold question in the first instance to the Court of Appeals for the District of Columbia Circuit. But before the D.C. Circuit has addressed the issue, this Court cashiers the statute, and without answering this critical threshold question itself. The Court does eventually get around to asking whether review under the DTA is, as the Court frames it, an "adequate substitute" for habeas, but even then its opinion fails to determine what rights the detainees possess and whether the DTA system satisfies them. The majority instead compares the undefined DTA process to an equally undefined habeas right—one that is to be given shape only in the future by district courts on a case-by-case basis. This whole approach is misguided.

It is also fruitless. How the detainees' claims will be decided now that the DTA is gone is anybody's guess. But the habeas process the Court mandates will most likely end up looking a lot like the DTA system it replaces, as the district court judges shaping it will have to reconcile review of the prisoners' detention with the undoubted need to protect the American people from the terrorist threat—precisely the challenge Congress undertook in drafting the DTA. All that today's opinion has done is shift responsibility for those sensitive foreign policy and national security decisions from the elected branches to the federal Judiciary.

I believe the system the political branches constructed adequately protects any constitutional rights aliens captured abroad and detained as enemy combatants may enjoy. I therefore would dismiss these cases on that ground. With all respect for the contrary views of the majority, I must dissent.

The political branches created a two-part, collateral review procedure for testing the legality of the prisoners' detention: It begins with a hearing before a CSRT followed by review in the D.C. Circuit. As part of that review, Congress authorized the D.C. Circuit to decide whether the CSRT proceedings are consistent with "the Constitution and laws of the United States." No petitioner, however, has invoked the D.C. Circuit review the statute specifies. As a consequence, that court has had no occasion to decide whether the CSRT hearings, followed by review in the Court of Appeals, vindicate whatever constitutional and statutory rights petitioners may possess.

Remarkably, this Court does not require petitioners to exhaust their remedies under the statute; it does not wait to see whether those remedies will prove sufficient to protect petitioners' rights. Instead, it not only denies the D.C. Circuit the opportunity to assess the statute's remedies, it refuses to do so itself: the majority expressly declines to decide whether the CSRT procedures, coupled with Article III review, satisfy due process.

It is grossly premature to pronounce on the detainees' right to habeas without first assessing whether the remedies the DTA system provides vindicate whatever rights petitioners may claim. The plurality in Hamdi v. Rumsfeld, 542 U.S. 507, 533 (2004), explained that the Constitution guaranteed an American *citizen* challenging his detention as an enemy combatant the right to "notice of the factual basis for his classification, and a fair opportunity to rebut the Government's factual assertions before a neutral decisionmaker." The plurality specifically stated that constitutionally adequate collateral process could be provided "by an appropriately authorized and properly constituted military tribunal," given the "uncommon potential to burden the Executive at a time of ongoing military conflict." This point is directly pertinent here, for surely the Due Process Clause does not afford *noncitizens* in such circumstances greater protection than citizens are due.

If the CSRT procedures meet the minimal due process requirements outlined in *Hamdi,* and if an Article III court is available to ensure that these procedures are followed in future cases, there is no need to reach the Suspension Clause question. Detainees will have received all the process the Constitution could possibly require, whether that process is called "habeas" or something else. The question of the writ's reach need not be addressed.

This is why the Court should have required petitioners to exhaust their remedies under the statute. Because the majority refuses to assess whether the CSRTs comport with the Constitution, it ends up razing a system of collateral review that it admits may, in fact, satisfy the Due Process Clause and be "structurally sound." But if the collateral review procedures Congress has provided—CSRT review coupled with Article III scrutiny—are sound, interference by a federal habeas court may be entirely unnecessary.

In the absence of any assessment of the DTA's remedies, the question whether detainees are entitled to habeas is an entirely speculative one. Our precedents have long counseled us to avoid deciding such hypothetical questions of constitutional law. The Court acknowledges that "the ordinary course" would be not to decide the constitutionality of the DTA at this stage, but abandons that ordinary course in light of the "gravity" of the constitutional issues presented and the prospect of additional delay. It is, however, precisely when the issues presented are grave that adherence to the ordinary course is most important. A principle applied only when unimportant is not much of a principle at all, and charges of judicial activism are most effectively rebutted when courts can fairly argue they are following normal practices.

The Court is also concerned that requiring petitioners to pursue "DTA review before proceeding with their habeas corpus action" could involve additional delay. The nature of the habeas remedy the Court instructs lower courts to craft on remand, however, is far more unsettled than the process Congress provided in the DTA. There is no reason to suppose that review according to procedures the federal Judiciary will design, case by case, will proceed any faster than the DTA process petitioners disdained. On the contrary, the system the Court has launched (and directs lower courts to elaborate) promises to take longer. The Court assures us that, before bringing their habeas petitions, detainees must usually complete the CSRT process. Then they may seek review in federal district court. Either success or failure there will surely result in an appeal to the D.C. Circuit—exactly where judicial review *starts* under Congress's system. The effect of the Court's decision is to add additional layers of quite possibly redundant review. And because nobody knows how these new layers of "habeas" review will operate, or what new procedures they will require, their contours will undoubtedly be subject to fresh bouts of litigation. If the majority were truly concerned about delay, it would have required petitioners to use the DTA process that has been available to them for 2-1/2 years, with its Article III review in the D.C. Circuit. That system might well have provided petitioners all the relief to which they are entitled long before the Court's newly installed habeas review could hope to do so.

(2) The majority's overreaching is particularly egregious given the weakness of its objections to the DTA. Simply put, the Court's opinion fails on its own terms. The majority strikes down the statute because it is not an "adequate substitute" for habeas review, but fails to show what rights the detainees have that cannot be vindicated by the DTA system.

Hamdi concluded that American citizens detained as enemy combatants are entitled to only limited process, and that much of that process could be supplied by a military tribunal, with review to follow in an Article III court. That is precisely the system we have here. It is adequate to vindicate whatever due process rights petitioners may have.

The *Hamdi* plurality declared that the due process rights enjoyed by *American citizens* detained as enemy combatants could be vindicated "by an appropriately authorized and properly constituted military tribunal." The DTA represents Congress's considered attempt to provide the accused alien combatants detained at Guantánamo a constitutionally adequate opportunity to contest their detentions before just such a tribunal.

But Congress went further in the DTA. CSRT review is just the first tier of collateral review in the DTA system. The statute provides additional review in an Article III court. The statute directs the D.C. Circuit to consider whether a particular alien's status determination "was consistent with the standards and procedures specified by the Secretary of Defense" *and* "whether the use of such standards and procedures to make the determination is consistent with the Constitution and laws of the United States." That is, a *court* determines whether the CSRT procedures are constitutional, and a *court* determines whether those procedures were followed in a particular case. Congress followed the Court's lead, only to find itself the victim of a constitutional bait and switch.

Hamdi further suggested that this "basic process" on collateral review could be provided by a military tribunal. It pointed to prisoner-of-war tribunals as a model that would satisfy the Constitution's requirements. Only "[i]n the *absence* of such process" before a military tribunal, the Court held, would Article III courts need to conduct full-dress habeas proceedings to "ensure that the minimum requirements of due process are achieved" (emphasis added). And even then, the petitioner would be entitled to no more process than he would have received from a properly constituted military review panel, given his limited due process rights and the government's weighty interests.

Hamdi is of pressing relevance here because it establishes the procedures American *citizens* detained as enemy combatants can expect from a habeas court proceeding under §2241. The DTA system of military tribunal hearings followed by Article III review looks a lot like the procedure *Hamdi* blessed. If nothing else, it is plain from the design of the DTA that Congress, the president, and this nation's military leaders have made a good-faith effort to follow our precedent.

(3) For all its eloquence about the detainees' right to the writ, the Court makes no effort to elaborate how exactly the remedy it prescribes will differ from the procedural protections detainees enjoy under the DTA. The Court objects to the detainees' limited access to witnesses and classified material, but proposes no alternatives of its own. Indeed, it simply ignores the many difficult questions its holding presents. What, for example, will become of the CSRT process? The majority says federal courts should *generally* refrain from entertaining detainee challenges until after the petitioner's CSRT proceeding has finished. But to what deference, if any, is that CSRT determination entitled?

There are other problems. Take witness availability. What makes the majority think witnesses will become magically available when the review procedure is labeled "habeas"? Will the location of most of these witnesses change—will they suddenly become easily susceptible to service of process? Or will subpoenas issued by American habeas courts run to Basra? And if they did, how would they be enforced? Speaking of witnesses, will detainees be able to call active-duty military officers as witnesses? If not, why not?

The majority has no answers for these difficulties. What it does say leaves open the distinct possibility that its habeas remedy will, when all is said and done, end up looking a great deal like the DTA review it rejects.

The majority rests its decision on abstract and hypothetical concerns. The DTA satisfies the majority's own criteria for assessing adequacy. This statutory scheme provides the combatants held at Guantánamo greater procedural protections than have ever been afforded alleged enemy detainees—whether citizens or aliens—in our national history.

*****

So who has won? Not the detainees. The Court's analysis leaves them with only the prospect of further litigation to determine the content of their new habeas right, followed by further litigation to resolve their particular cases, followed by further litigation before the D.C. Circuit—where they could have started had they invoked the DTA procedure. Not Congress, whose attempt to determine—through democratic means——how best to balance the security of the American people with the detainees' liberty interests has been unceremoniously brushed aside. Not the Great Writ, whose majesty is hardly enhanced by its extension to a jurisdictionally quirky outpost, with no tangible benefit to anyone. Not the rule of law, unless by that is meant the rule of lawyers, who will now arguably have a greater role than military and intelligence officials in shaping policy for alien enemy combatants. And certainly not the American people, who today lose a bit more control over the conduct of this nation's foreign policy to unelected, politically unaccountable judges.

Scalia, dissenting (joined by Roberts, Thomas, and Alito):

Today, for the first time in our nation's history, the Court confers a constitutional right to habeas corpus on alien enemies detained abroad by our military forces in the course of an ongoing war. The Chief Justice's dissent, which I join, shows that the procedures prescribed by Congress in the Detainee Treatment Act provide the essential protections that habeas corpus guarantees; there has thus been no suspension of the writ, and no basis exists for judicial intervention beyond what the act allows. My problem with the majority opinion is more fundamental still: The writ of habeas corpus does not, and never has, run in favor of aliens abroad; the Suspension Clause thus has no application, and the Court's intervention in this military matter is entirely *ultra vires.*

America is at war with radical Islamists. The game of bait and switch that today's opinion plays upon the Nation's Commander in Chief will make the war harder on us. It will almost certainly cause more Americans to be killed. That consequence would be tolerable if necessary to preserve a time-honored legal principle vital to our constitutional Republic. But it is this Court's blatant *abandonment* of such a principle that produces the decision today. The President relied on our settled precedent in Johnson v. Eisentrager, 339 U.S. 763 (1950), when he established the prison at Guantánamo Bay for enemy aliens. Had the law been otherwise, the military surely would not have transported prisoners there, but would have kept them in Afghanistan, transferred them to another of our foreign military bases, or turned them over to allies for detention. Those other facilities might well have been worse for the detainees themselves.

In the long term, then, the Court's decision today accomplishes little, except perhaps to reduce the well-being of enemy combatants that the Court ostensibly seeks to protect. In the short term, however, the decision is devastating. At least 30 of those prisoners hitherto released from Guantánamo Bay have returned to the battlefield. Some have been captured or killed. But others have succeeded in carrying on their atrocities against innocent civilians. In one case, a detainee released from Guantánamo Bay masterminded the kidnapping of two Chinese dam workers, one of whom was later shot to death when used as a human shield against Pakistani commandoes. Another former detainee promptly resumed his post as a senior Taliban commander and murdered a

UN engineer and three Afghan soldiers. Still another murdered an Afghan judge. It was reported only last month that a released detainee carried out a suicide bombing against Iraqi soldiers in Mosul, Iraq.

These, mind you, were detainees whom *the military* had concluded were not enemy combatants. Their return to the kill illustrates the incredible difficulty of assessing who is and who is not an enemy combatant in a foreign theater of operations where the environment does not lend itself to rigorous evidence collection. Astoundingly, the Court today raises the bar, requiring military officials to appear before civilian courts and defend their decisions under procedural and evidentiary rules that go beyond what Congress has specified. As the Chief Justice's dissent makes clear, we have no idea what those procedural and evidentiary rules are, but they will be determined by civil courts and (in the Court's contemplation at least) will be more detainee-friendly than those now applied, since otherwise there would no reason to hold the congressionally prescribed procedures unconstitutional. If they impose a higher standard of proof (from foreign battlefields) than the current procedures require, the number of the enemy returned to combat will obviously increase.

But even when the military has evidence that it can bring forward, it is often fool-hardy to release that evidence to the attorneys representing our enemies. And one escalation of procedures that the Court *is* clear about is affording the detainees increased access to witnesses (perhaps troops serving in Afghanistan?) and to classified information. During the 1995 prosecution of Omar Abdel Rahman, federal prosecutors gave the names of 200 unindicted coconspirators to the "Blind Sheik's" defense lawyers; that information was in the hands of Osama bin Laden within two weeks. In another case, trial testimony revealed to the enemy that the United States had been monitoring their cellular network, whereupon they promptly stopped using it, enabling more of them to evade capture and continue their atrocities.

And today it is not just the military that the Court elbows aside. A mere two terms ago in Hamdan v. Rumsfeld, 548 U.S. 557 (2006), when the Court held that the Detainee Treatment Act of 2005 had not stripped habeas jurisdiction over Guantánamo petitioners' claims, four members of today's five-justice majority joined an opinion saying the following:

> Nothing prevents the President from returning to Congress to seek the authority [for trial by military commission] he believes necessary. Where, as here, no emergency prevents consultation with Congress, judicial insistence upon that consultation does not weaken our Nation's ability to deal with danger. To the contrary, that insistence strengthens the Nation's ability to determine—through democratic means—how best to do so. The Constitution places its faith in those democratic means. [548 U.S. at 636 (Breyer, J., concurring).]

Turns out they were just kidding. For in response, Congress, at the President's request, quickly enacted the Military Commissions Act, emphatically reasserting that it did not want these prisoners filing habeas petitions. It is therefore clear that Congress and the Executive—*both* political branches—have determined that limiting the role of civilian courts in adjudicating whether prisoners captured abroad are properly detained is important to success in the war that some 190,000 of our men and women are now fighting. As the Solicitor General argued, the Military Commissions Act and the Detainee Treatment Act . . . represent an effort by the political branches to strike an appropriate balance between the need to preserve liberty and the need to accommodate the weighty and sensitive governmental interests in ensuring that those who have in fact fought with the enemy during a war do not return to battle against the United States.

But it does not matter. The Court today decrees that no good reason to accept the judgment of the other two branches is "apparent." What competence does the Court have to second-guess the judgment of Congress and the President on such a point? None whatever. But the Court blunders in nonetheless. Henceforth, as today's opinion makes unnervingly clear, how to handle enemy prisoners in this war will ultimately lie with the branch that knows least about the national security concerns that the subject entails.

What drives today's decision is neither the meaning of the Suspension Clause, nor the principles of our precedents, but rather an inflated notion of judicial supremacy. The Court says that, if the extraterritorial applicability of the Suspension Clause turned on formal notions of sovereignty, "it would be possible for the political branches to govern without legal constraint" in areas beyond the sovereign territory of the United States. That cannot be, the Court says, because it is the duty of this Court to say what the law is. It would be difficult to imagine a more question-begging analysis: our power "to say what the law is" is circumscribed by the limits of our statutorily and constitutionally conferred jurisdiction. And that is precisely the question in these cases: whether the Constitution confers habeas jurisdiction on federal courts to decide petitioners' claims. It is both irrational and arrogant to say that the answer must be yes because otherwise we would not be supreme. The "functional" test usefully evades the precedential land mine of *Eisentrager* but is so inherently subjective that it clears wide brainstormed separation-of-powers principles to establish a manipulable functional test for the extraterritorial reach of habeas corpus (and, no doubt, for the extraterritorial reach of other constitutional protections as well).

The majority blatantly misdescribes important precedents, most conspicuously Justice Jackson's opinion for the Court in *Johnson v. Eisentrager*. It breaks a chain of precedent as old as the common law that prohibits judicial inquiry into detentions of aliens abroad absent statutory authorization. And, most tragically, it sets our military commanders the impossible task of proving to a civilian court, under whatever standards this Court devises in the future, that evidence supports the confinement of each and every enemy prisoner.

The nation will live to regret what the Court has done today.

*****

[*Note:* In July 2008, only a few weeks after the Supreme Court's *Boumediene* decision, the Court of Appeals for the Fourth Circuit (sitting *en banc*) issued a very important decision in Al-Marri v. Pucciarelli, 534 F.3d 213 (4th Cir. 2008), involving elements of both *Boumediene* and *Hamdi*.

The detainees in all three cases were imprisoned as "enemy combatants," but there are several major differences: (1) Al-Marri—unlike Hamdi and the *Boumediene* detainees, who were apprehended in foreign countries—was taken into custody in the United States; (2) Al-Marri and Hamdi—unlike the *Boumediene* detainees in Guantánamo—were held in military prisons in the United States; and (3) Al-Marri—unlike the *Boumediene* detainees, who are nonresident aliens, and unlike Hamdi, who was a nonresident U.S. citizen—was on his arrest a lawful resident of the United States.

Ali Al-Marri is a Qatar citizen who attended Bradley University in Peoria, Illinois, in the late 1980s and early 1990s. He graduated from Bradley in 1991 and returned to Qatar. On September 10, 2001, together with his wife and children, he returned to the United States, for the stated purpose of attending graduate school at Bradley. In December 2001 Al-Marri was arrested in Peoria, charged with credit card fraud, and held in civilian jails until 2003, when President Bush signed an order designating Al-Marri as an "enemy combatant," and he was then transferred to a military prison in South Carolina, where he has since been detained. The government alleges that Al-Marri is an Al-Qaeda member who was to be part of the "second wave" of terror attacks following 9/11.

Seven of the nine Fourth Circuit judges participating in the case wrote individual opinions totaling 216 pages. The court (5-4) held that Al-Marri—although lawfully residing in the United States at the time of his arrest—could be detained indefinitely as an "enemy combatant." At the same time, a somewhat differently constituted majority (5-4) held that Al-Marri was entitled to broad habeas corpus review of the government's claimed basis for his designation as an "enemy combatant." A petition for certiorari to review the decision was filed in the Supreme Court on September 23, 2008.]

Prosecuting Enemy Combatants for War Crimes

In addition to the issues presented by the *detention* of prisoners at Guantánamo, other issues arise from the prosecution of a small number of these detainees for war crimes in violation of the laws of war.

Ahmad Hamdan was captured in Afghanistan and eventually detained at Guantánamo Bay. Hamdan admittedly was Osama bin Laden's personal driver in Afghanistan between 1996 and November 2001. While detained at Guantánamo, Hamdan (as well as nine other detainees) was charged with conspiracy to commit attacks on civilians and civilian objects, murder and destruction of property by an unprivileged belligerent, and terrorism.

Before his trial by a military commission, Hamdan filed a habeas corpus petition in a federal district court, contending that the military commission procedures authorized by the President violate both the Uniform Code of Military Justice (UCMJ) and the Geneva Conventions. Hamdan's claims were rejected by the Court of Appeals for the District of Columbia. (The panel included then Circuit Judge John Roberts, subsequently appointed Chief Justice of the United States.)

The Supreme Court reversed, Hamdan v. Rumsfeld, 548 U.S. 557 (2006) (5-3, Roberts not participating). The controlling opinion, written by Stevens, was joined by Breyer, Souter, and Ginsburg. Kennedy and Breyer filed concurring opinions. Scalia, Thomas, and Alito dissented.

Initially the Court rejected the Government's argument that the DTA, barring detainee access to habeas corpus, applied to cases like Hamdan's that were already pending at the time DTA was enacted. On the merits, the Court sustained Hamdan's claims (1) that the AUMF resolution did not expand the president's power to prosecute detainees for war crimes and (2) that the rules of the special military commissions convened by President Bush violated both the court-martial standards of UCMJ and the Geneva Conventions.

The Court held that the commissions authorized in 2001 violated UCMJ Article 36 (b), which provides that "All rules and regulations made under this article shall be uniform insofar as practicable." The majority construed this provision to mean that the rules for a military commission trying a detainee in Guantánamo must, "insofar as practicable," be the same as those for a court-martial of an American soldier.

Unlike court-martial rules, the rules for the commissions established in 2001 provide, for example, that an accused and his civilian counsel may be excluded from, and precluded from ever learning what evidence was presented during, any part of the proceeding that the presiding officer decides to "close" for the protection of classified information or "other national security interests." In addition, the commission rules permit the admission of *any* evidence that, in the presiding officer's opinion, would have probative value to a reasonable person. Because of these variances, and in the absence of any determination by the president that it is impracticable to apply court-martial rules to commission proceedings, the Court held that the uniformity requirement of Article 36(b) had not been satisfied.

In concluding that the procedures also violated the Geneva Conventions, the Court rejected the Government's argument that the Conventions applied only to signatory nations and therefore not to organizations such as al Qaeda. In war crimes prosecutions to which it is applicable, Article 3 of the Geneva Conventions requires trials "by a regularly constituted court affording all the judicial guarantees which are recognized as indispensable by civilized peoples."

The *Hamdan* decision, it should be noted, was not based on *constitutional* grounds. Instead, the Court relied on its interpretation of a federal statute (UCMJ) and the Geneva Conventions. And Justice Breyer's concurring opinion, joined by three other justices, stated that "Nothing prevents the president from returning to Congress to seek the authority he believes necessary."

In October 2006, Congress enacted the Military Commissions Act that, in effect, overruled the Court's *Hamdan* decision. The Act bars the federal courts from hearing claims based on the Geneva Conventions, and the Act rejects the Court's ruling in *Hamdan* that military commission procedures must comply with the requirements applicable to court-martials of American soldiers.

(In addition, §7 of the Act provided that decisions of military commissions can be reviewed only by an appeal to the Court of Appeals for the District of Columbia and that otherwise "no court, justice, or judge shall have jurisdiction to hear or consider any claim or cause of action whatsoever, ... relating to the prosecution, trial, or judgment of a military commission." §7 was held unconstitutional in the last-digested case, *Boumediene v. Bush*.)

15

Voting and Elections

Discrimination in Voting

The Constitution does not itself confer the right to vote. With some exceptions, the determination of voting eligibility is left in the control of the States—even in elections for the President.

It is only because of legislation adopted by the States that citizens are allowed to vote in presidential elections. And they do not actually vote for presidential candidates but instead they vote for a slate of electors.

Article II (§1) provides that each State shall appoint electors "in such manner as the [State] Legislature . . . may direct," and the electors from all the States then vote to select the President. The winner of the popular vote in each State receives all the State's electoral votes, except in Maine and Nebraska, where the state legislatures have adopted legislation allocating the electoral votes. In 26 of the States and the District of Columbia, the electors are legally bound to vote for the winner of the State's popular vote and are subject to penalties if they do not; in the other 24 States, electors are not legally bound to vote for a specific candidate but in practice they almost always do so.

Voting, although left largely in the control of the States, is subject to restrictions imposed by several Amendments of the federal Constitution (and federal statutes enacted pursuant to those Amendments). The Fourteenth Amendment prohibits discrimination in violation of the equal protection of the laws, and the Fifteenth Amendment prohibits the denial of the right to vote "on account of race, color, or previous condition of servitude." Other pertinent Amendments include: the Nineteenth Amendment extending the right to vote to women; the Twenty-Fourth Amendment prohibiting poll taxes in federal elections; and the Twenty-Sixth Amendment fixing 18 as the voting age.

The Fourteenth and Fifteenth Amendments prohibit two types of voting discrimination: (1) discrimination that *prevents* certain citizens from voting and (2) discrimination *among voters* in the *exercise* of their right to vote.

Vote Prevention

The most egregious form of the first type of discrimination took place in the South. After the Civil War, to prevent Negroes from voting, Southern States employed a variety of techniques, including literacy tests, grandfather clauses, property qualifications, "good character" tests, and the requirement that registrants "understand" or "interpret" certain matters. Many of these techniques were held unconstitutional by the Supreme

Court. Thus, for example, grandfather clauses were invalidated in Guinn v. United States, 238 U.S. 347 (1915), and the white primary was nullified in Smith v. Allwright, 321 U.S. 649 (1944).

Nevertheless, Negroes in many States continued to be effectively disenfranchised. Even when Negroes obtained injunctions against such practices, some States merely switched to discriminatory devices not covered by the federal decrees.

Frustration with that case-by-case approach led in 1965 to the enactment of the landmark legislation summarized in the next comment "The Federal Voting Rights Act." The Act and its later amendments have made it much easier to establish a voting rights violation. As a result, the stricter standard imposed by the Act (instead of the Equal Protection Clause and other provisions of the Constitution) has become the governing test for this kind of discrimination.

Vote Dilution

Constitutional issues, however, remain particularly important in connection with the second type of discrimination—where, even though citizens are not prevented from voting, there is still discrimination *among* voters, so that the votes of some are far more effective than the votes of others.

This type of discrimination takes three main forms: (1) malapportionment of districts on a population basis; (2) gerrymandering of district lines; and (3) discrimination in the standards for counting votes

(1) *Malapportionment*—Even when qualified voters are not prevented from voting, their votes may be discriminatorily "diluted" (or devalued) because of the way that the boundaries of voter districts in a State have been drawn, with the result that voters in some districts have greater influence in the selection of representatives than voters in other districts.

A key precedent is the first digested case in this chapter, *Reynolds v. Sims,* expounding the "one person, one vote" principle.

(2) *Gerrymandering*—Even if the population of a district is approximately equal to the population of each other district in the State (and thus complies with the "one person, one vote" requirement), a legislature may still be able to predetermine (or at least strongly influence) the results of voting in that district by gerrymandering the district's lines—by the device of placing certain groups of voters inside or outside the district on the basis of how they are likely to vote.

Such gerrymandering may be either racial or political in nature: (a) Racial gerrymandering may be employed either to *limit* minority representation, e.g., Gomillion v. Lightfoot, 364 U.S. 339 (1960), or to *increase* minority representation, e.g., *Shaw v. Reno,* digested later in this chapter. (b) Political gerrymandering may involve, for example, drawing the lines of a district to provide a safe seat for an incumbent or drawing lines on a statewide basis to retain or increase control of a state legislature or congressional delegation. Efforts to impose judicial controls on political gerrymandering have so far been unsuccessful (e.g., *Vieth v. Jubelirer,* digested later in this chapter).

(3) *Discrimination in the standards used for counting votes*—Even in a situation in which districts were neither malapportioned nor gerrymandered, it might still be claimed that the votes were *counted* in an unconstitutionally discriminatory manner.

That was the type of voting discrimination found in 2000 in *Bush v. Gore,* the last-digested case in this chapter. In that highly controversial decision, the Supreme Court held that the Equal Protection Clause was violated by a state voting system that sanctioned sharply differing standards for counting votes from district to district.

The Federal Voting Rights Act

The constitutionality of the Voting Rights Act of 1965 was sustained in South Carolina v. Katzenbach, 383 U.S. 301 (1966) (8-1), and Katzenbach v. Morgan, 384 U.S. 641 (1966) (7-2).

§2 of the Voting Rights Act, as originally enacted, stated, "No voting qualification or prerequisite to voting, or standard, practice, or procedure shall be imposed or applied by any State or political subdivision to deny or abridge the right of any citizen of the United States to vote on account of race or color." §2 also authorized the Attorney General as well as private citizens to sue in the federal courts to enforce the Act's provisions.

§4 of the Act empowered the Attorney General to suspend literacy tests and other restrictions on voting in any State or political subdivision (the "covered jurisdictions") where on November 1, 1964, less than 50 percent of citizens had voted or were registered to vote.

§5 provided that, for a period of five years, all "covered jurisdictions" (all then in the Deep South) were prohibited from implementing any changes in their voting procedures without obtaining "preclearance" from either the Attorney General or the District Court for the District of Columbia. Such changes range from moving a polling place or keeping polls open an hour longer to redrawing district lines after a census. §5 places the burden of proof on a covered government entity to demonstrate that the change does not have a racially discriminatory purpose or effect. No change can be precleared if it "would lead to a retrogression in the position of racial minorities with respect to their effective exercise of the electoral franchise." Beer v. United States, 425 U.S. 130 (1976).

In 1970, Congress extended §5 for five more years, suspended the use of literacy tests on a nationwide basis, and added November 1, 1968, as an alternate date for determining what jurisdictions are covered.

A 1975 amendment extended §5 to 1982, added November 1, 1972, as an alternate coverage date, and expanded the scope of the Act to include citizens with limited English proficiency—speakers of Spanish, Asian, Native American, and Alaskan Native languages. The use of ballots and other election materials only in English was prohibited in any State or political subdivision where members of a single language minority constituted more than five percent of the citizens of voting age. In addition, in jurisdictions (approximately 450) with a significant number of voting age citizens with limited English proficiency and who speak a covered minority language, assistance in that language must be provided at all stages of the electoral process.

As a result of the changes made in the 1970 and 1975 amendments, the preclearance requirement was extended to political subdivisions in a number of additional States outside the Deep South, including Alaska, Arizona, and Texas in their entirety, and one or more counties or townships in California, Florida, Michigan, New Hampshire, New York, and South Dakota. (Today 16 States in whole or part remain subject to the preclearance requirement.)

Efforts began in Congress in early 1981 to renew the Act once again. The focus of controversy became the issue of the appropriate standard of proof for identifying practices that "deny or abridge" the right to vote under §2. Supreme Court decisions had held that establishing a violation of the Equal Protection Clause required proof of discriminatory *purpose* in addition to discriminatory *effects*. Civil rights groups, claiming that the purpose test imposed an unduly burdensome litigation obstacle, argued that the Act should be amended to adopt a more lenient "results" standard. Supporters of the purpose test countered that the "results" standard would lead to the establishment of racial quotas and proportional representation in elections.

Finally a compromise was reached that in effect endorsed "results" as the primary criterion, and the Act was renewed for 25 more years. As amended, §2 is violated when, based on "the totality of circumstances," the political process is "not equally open to participation" by members of a protected class and they "have less opportunities than other members of the electorate to participate in the electoral process and to elect representatives of their choice." §2(a) further provides that "The extent to which members of a protected class have been elected to office [is] one circumstance which may be considered" in evaluating "the totality of circumstances."

In 2006, it was proposed to again renew the Act (due to expire in 2007). Opponents contended that black voter registration and participation rates, along with the growth of minority officeholders, demonstrated blacks were no longer disenfranchised and that therefore the Act's onerous preclearance requirements were no longer necessary or appropriate to protect voting rights. In July 2006, after extensive debate, Congress voted to renew the Act for an additional 25 years.

Overcoming the "Political Question" Barrier

Invoking the so-called (and somewhat misnamed) "political question" doctrine, the Supreme Court has from time to time held that the federal courts should decline to rule on certain types of constitutional issues on the ground that the issue should be more appropriately resolved in the political process. When the political question doctrine is applied, even though it is alleged that the Constitution has been violated, the result is dismissal of the case—leaving the constitutional question to be decided (if at all) by the legislative or executive bodies of government.

Until relatively recently, one of the categories of cases held to be nonjusticiable under the political question doctrine involved the apportionment of population within a State's voting districts. In States where voting districts had not been reapportioned for many years, even though in the interim there had been substantial growth in urban areas, the result was that rural residents were overrepresented and urban dwellers were underrepresented in both the state legislatures and Congress. Not surprisingly, since (with few exceptions) redistricting is performed by the state legislatures themselves, those who benefited from this system generally had little incentive to voluntarily redraw districts at the expense of their own seats or power.

In Colegrove v. Green, 328 U.S. 549 (1946), the Supreme Court declared nonjusticiable a challenge to the congressional districting in Illinois. The Court concluded that "[c]ourts ought not to enter this political thicket" because "effective working of our government revealed this issue to be of a peculiarly political nature and therefore not fit for judicial determination." Only in cases charging racial discrimination in the drawing of election districts or in holding elections did the Supreme Court approve federal court involvement. E.g., Gomillion v. Lightfoot, 364 U.S. 339 (1960) (redrawing of Tuskegee, Alabama, districts to disenfranchise blacks); Smith v. Allwright, 321 U.S. 649 (1944) (discrimination against blacks in political primaries).

But in 1962, in the landmark decision of Baker v. Carr, 369 U.S. 186 (1962), the Supreme Court changed course and held that malapportionment claims could be adjudicated under the Equal Protection Clause. The case involved a particularly egregious set of facts: Between 1901 and 1961, in addition to a substantial growth in its population, Tennessee experienced a major redistribution of population from rural areas to large urban centers. Yet, representation of each county in the Tennessee General Assembly was still determined according to an allocation based on 1900 population figures. A group of Tennessee voters brought suit in a federal district court, seeking a declaratory judgment that the Tennessee General Assembly's failure to reapportion resulted in the "debasement of their votes" and the denial of equal protection of the laws under the Fourteenth Amendment. The Court (6-2, Whittaker not participating) held that the equal protection claim was justiciable and remanded the case to the district court for determination of the merits of the claim.

The following year, the Court in Gray v. Sanders, 372 U.S. 368 (1963), upheld a challenge to Georgia's use of a county-unit system to select statewide officers. Each county was assigned a specified number of unit votes, ranging from two unit votes for the least populated counties to only six unit votes for the most populated counties. Because of the large disparity in the populations of the counties and the discriminatory effect of the Georgia system on voters in the larger urban counties, the Court held that in a statewide election the Equal Protection Clause required counting each person's vote equally with those of all other voters in the state. Douglas, writing for the Court, stated:

> Once the geographical unit for which a representative is to be chosen is designated, all who participate in the election are to have an equal vote: whatever their race, whatever their sex, wherever their occupation, whatever their income, and whatever their home may be in that geographic unit.

Douglas' opinion further declared that "The conception of political equality from the Declaration of Independence, to Lincoln's Gettysburg Address, to the Fifteenth, Seventeenth, and Nineteenth Amendments can mean only one thing—one person, one vote."

The following year, in Wesberry v. Sanders, 376 U.S. 1 (1964), Georgia districts for the election of members of the U.S. House of Representatives were held unconstitutional because of the large disparity in the populations of the districts; some congressional districts had twice as large a population as others. Relying on Article I, §2 of the Constitution, providing that members of the House of Representatives be chosen "by the People of the several States," the Court again concluded that the rule is "one person, one vote." The Court declared: "While it may not be possible to draw congressional districts with mathematical precision, that is no excuse for ignoring our Constitution's plain objective of making equal representation for equal numbers of people the fundamental goal for the House of Representatives."

A few months after *Wesberry* was decided, the Court announced its decision in the next-digested case, *Reynolds v. Sims*.

Reynolds v. Sims, 377 U.S. 533 (1964)

FACTS: The Alabama legislature, like the legislatures of every State except Nebraska, consists of two houses. The Alabama legislature consisted of 106 representatives and 35 senators.

Although Alabama's Constitution required legislative representation based on population and a reapportionment every ten years, the State still utilized a districting plan based upon its 1900 census to allocate representation. As a result, because of intervening changes of population, districts that had a large increase in population (proportionate to the other districts) did not have a corresponding increase in representation. Thus, the State's senate districts (each electing one senator) varied in population from 15,417 to 934,864, and the house districts (each electing one representative) varied in population from 31,175 to 634,864.

Claiming that this malapportionment of the legislature deprived them of rights under the Equal Protection Clause of the Fourteenth Amendment, voters in several Alabama counties brought suit against Alabama officials responsible for conducting elections. Their complaints sought an injunction requiring that the 1962 election for the legislature be held at large over the entire State.

In response to the litigation, the legislature adopted two redistricting plans. The District Court, holding that neither plan would cure the gross discrimination of the existing representation, ordered temporary reapportionment for the 1962 election on the basis of a combination of features of the two plans.

The officials appealed, claiming that the District Court erred in holding unconstitutional the legislature's reapportionment plans and that a federal court lacks power affirmatively to reapportion a legislature. The plaintiffs also appealed, claiming that the plan adopted by the District Court had failed to reapportion both houses of the legislature on a population basis.

ISSUE: Must a State apportion both houses of a bicameral legislature according to population?

DECISION (per *Warren*, 8-1): *Yes.*

We are faced with the problem of implementing our decision in Baker v. Carr, 369 U.S. 186 (1962), holding that the apportionment of representation in a state legislature does not present a political question beyond the proper province of the federal courts.

The Equal Protection Clause requires substantially equal legislative representation for all citizens in a State regardless of where they reside. Legislators represent people, not trees or acres. Legislators are elected by voters, not farms or cities or economic interests.

If it were alleged that certain otherwise qualified voters had been entirely prohibited from voting for members of their state legislature, clearly a serious constitutional claim would be presented. And, if a State should provide that the votes of citizens in one part of the State should be given two times, or five times, or ten times the weight of votes of citizens in another part of the State, it could hardly be contended that the right to vote of those residing in the disfavored areas had not been effectively diluted. It would appear extraordinary to suggest that a State could be constitutionally permitted to enact a law providing that certain of the State's voters could vote two, five, or ten times for their legislative representatives, while voters living elsewhere could vote only once. And it is inconceivable that a state law to the effect that, in counting votes for legislators, the votes of citizens in one part of the State would be multiplied by two, five, or ten, while the votes of persons in another area would be counted only at face value, could be constitutionally sustainable. The effect of state legislative districting schemes that give the same number of representatives to unequal numbers of constituents is identical.

The Equal Protection Clause guarantees the opportunity for equal participation by all voters in the election of state legislators. Diluting the weight of votes because of place of residence impairs basic constitutional rights under the Fourteenth Amendment just as much as invidious discriminations based upon factors such as race, Brown v. Board of Education, 347 U.S. 483 (1954), or economic status, Griffin v. Illinois, 351 U.S. 12 (1956).

We hold that, as a basic constitutional standard, the Equal Protection Clause requires that the seats in both houses of a bicameral state legislature must be apportioned on a population basis. Under both the existing and proposed apportionment plans, neither house of the Alabama Legislature was apportioned on a population basis. The District Court therefore correctly held that all three of these schemes were constitutionally invalid.

One of the proposed plans—the so-called 67-Senator Amendment—at least superficially resembles the scheme of legislative representation followed in the federal Congress. Under this plan, each of Alabama's 67 counties is allotted one senator, and no counties are given more than one Senate seat. Arguably, this is analogous to the allocation of two Senate seats in the federal Congress, to each of the 50 States, regardless of population. Seats in the Alabama House, under the proposed constitutional amendment, are distributed by giving each of the 67 counties at least one, with the remaining 39 seats being allotted among the more populous counties on a population basis. This scheme, at least at first glance, appears to resemble that prescribed for the federal House of Representatives, where the 435 seats are distributed among the States on a population basis, although each State, regardless of its population, is given at least one congressman. Thus, although there are substantial differences in underlying rationale and result, the 67-Senator Amendment, as proposed by the Alabama Legislature, at least arguably presents for consideration a scheme analogous to that used for apportioning seats in Congress.

We find the federal analogy inapposite and irrelevant to state legislative districting schemes. The Founding Fathers clearly had no intention of establishing a pattern or model for the apportionment of seats in state legislatures when the system of representation in the Federal Congress was adopted.

The system of representation in the two Houses of the federal Congress was conceived out of compromise and concession indispensable to the establishment of our federal republic. Arising from unique historical circumstances, it is based on the consideration that in establishing our type of federalism a group of formerly independent States bound themselves together under one national government. The resulting agreement between the larger and smaller States on this matter averted a deadlock in the Constitutional Convention that had threatened to abort the birth of our nation.

Political subdivisions of States—counties, cities, or whatever—never were and never have been considered as sovereign entities. Rather, they have been traditionally regarded as subordinate governmental instrumentalities created by the State to assist in the carrying out of state governmental functions. These governmental units are created as convenient agencies for exercising such of the governmental powers of the State as may be entrusted to them, and the number, nature and duration of the powers conferred upon them and the territory over which they shall be exercised rests in the absolute discretion of the State. The relationship of the States to the federal government could hardly be less analogous.

Since we find the so-called federal analogy inapposite to a consideration of the constitutional validity of state legislative apportionment schemes, we necessarily hold that the Equal Protection Clause requires both houses of a state legislature to be apportioned on a population basis. The right of a citizen to equal representation and to have his vote weighted equally with those of all other citizens in the election of members of one house of a bicameral state legislature would amount to little if States could effectively submerge the equal-population principle in the apportionment of seats in the other house.

By holding that both houses of a state legislature must be apportioned on a population basis, we mean that the Equal Protection Clause requires that a State make an honest and good faith effort to construct districts, in both houses of its legislature, as nearly of equal population as is practicable. We realize that it is a practical impossibility to arrange legislative districts so that each one has an identical number of residents, or citizens, or voters.

So long as the divergences from a strict population standard are based on legitimate considerations incident to the effectuation of a rational state policy, some deviations from the equal-population principle are constitutionally permissible. But neither history alone, nor economic or other sorts of group interests, are permissible factors in attempting to justify disparities from population-based representation. Citizens, not history or economic interests, cast votes. Considerations of area alone provide an insufficient justification for deviations from the equal-population principle. Again, people, not land or trees or pastures, vote. Modern developments and improvements in transportation and communications make rather hollow, in the mid-1960s, most claims that deviations from population-based representation can validly be based solely on geographical considerations. And arguments for allowing such deviations in order to ensure effective representation for sparsely settled areas and to prevent legislative districts from becoming so large that the availability of access of citizens to their representatives is impaired are today, for the most part, unconvincing.

The action taken by the District Court in this case, in ordering into effect a reapportionment of both houses of the Alabama Legislature for purposes of the 1962 primary and general elections, was an appropriate and well-considered exercise of judicial power. Accordingly we affirm the judgment below and remand the cases for further proceedings consistent with the views stated in this opinion.

Clark, concurring in the judgment: The Court goes much beyond the necessities of this case in laying down a new "equal population" principle for state legislative apportionment. It seems to me that all that the Court need say in this case is that each plan considered by the trial court is "a crazy quilt," clearly revealing invidious discrimination in each house of the Legislature and therefore violative of the Equal Protection Clause. I, therefore, do not reach the question of the so-called "federal analogy." But in my view, if one house of the State Legislature meets the population standard, representation in the other house might include some departure from it so as to take into account, on a rational basis, other factors in order to afford some representation to the various elements of the State.

Stewart, concurring in the judgment: All of the parties agree with the District Court's finding that legislative inaction for some 60 years in the face of growth and shifts in population has converted Alabama's legislative apportionment plan enacted in 1901 into one completely lacking in rationality. Accordingly, I would affirm the judgment of the District Court holding that this apportionment violated the Equal Protection Clause.

Harlan, dissenting: The Court's decision is remarkable for its failure to address itself at all to the Fourteenth Amendment as a whole or to the legislative history of the Amendment pertinent to the matter at hand.

Stripped of aphorisms, the Court's argument boils down to the assertion that the plaintiffs' right to vote has been invidiously "debased" or "diluted" in violation of the Equal Protection Clause. However, the terms of the Fourteenth Amendment and its history [detailed at length in Justice Harlan's opinion] provide conclusive evidence that neither those who proposed nor those who ratified the Amendment believed that equal protection limited the power of the States to apportion their legislatures as they saw fit. Indeed, the only remedy allowed by the Amendment for a State's regulation of voting was set forth in Section 2 of the Amendment. Section 2 provides that a State's representation in the House of Representatives shall be proportionately reduced if the right to vote "is denied to any of the male inhabitants of such State, being twenty-one years of age, and citizens of the United States, or in any way abridged, except for participation in rebellion, or other crime. . ." Moreover, the history demonstrates that the intention to leave undisturbed the State's power to control suffrage was deliberate and was widely believed to be essential to the adoption of the Amendment.

Although the Court provides only generalities in elaboration of its main thesis, its opinion nevertheless fully demonstrates how far removed these problems are from fields of judicial competence. Under the Court's decision, it is unconstitutional for a State to give consideration to any of the following in establishing legislative districts: (1) history; (2) "economic or other sorts of group interests"; (3) area; (4) geographical considerations; (5) a desire "to insure effective representation for sparsely settled areas"; (6) "availability of access of citizens to their representatives"; (7) theories of bicameralism (except those approved by the Court); (8) occupation; (9) "an attempt to balance urban and rural power"; (10) the preference of a majority of voters in the State.

So far as now appears, the *only* factor a State may consider, apart from numbers, is political subdivisions. But, according to the majority opinion, even "a clearly rational state policy" recognizing this factor is unconstitutional if "population is submerged as the controlling consideration." I know of no principle of logic or practical or theoretical politics, still less any constitutional principle, which establishes all or any of these exclusions.

The Court says only that "legislators represent people, not trees or acres." This may be conceded. But it is surely equally obvious and, in the context of elections, more meaningful to note that people are not ciphers and that legislators can represent their electors only by speaking for their interests—economic, social, political—many of which do reflect the place where the electors live. The Court does not establish, or indeed even attempt to make a case for the proposition that conflicting interests within a State can only be adjusted by disregarding them when voters are grouped for purposes of representation.

"One Person, One Vote" Issues

In a companion case decided the same day as *Reynolds,* the Court struck down Colorado's districting plan even though it had been approved by Colorado citizens in a referendum (and indeed by a majority of Colorado voters in every county in the State). Lucas v. Forty-Fourth General Assembly, 377 U.S. 713 (1964). The plan provided that only one house of Colorado's legislature would be apportioned by population. The Court concluded: "An individual's constitutionally protected right to cast an equally weighed vote cannot be denied *even by a vote of a majority of a State's electorate,* if the apportionment scheme adopted by the voters fails to measure up to the requirements of the Equal Protection Clause." Similarly, the Court stated: "We hold that the fact that a challenged legislative apportionment plan was approved by the electorate *is without federal constitutional significance,* if the scheme adopted fails to satisfy the basic requirements of the Equal Protection Clause." (Italics added.)

In subsequent cases, the Court has sought to resolve the myriad issues involved in implementing the "one person, one vote" principle.

One such issue is what units are covered by the principle. The Court held that, whenever a State chooses to vest "governmental functions" in a body (whether the functions are labeled "legislative" or "administrative") and to elect its members from districts, the districts must have must have substantially equal populations. E.g., Avery v. Midland County, 390 U.S. 474 (1968) (applying the principle to the selection of county commissioners); Hadley v. Junior College District, 397 U.S. 50 (1970) (applying the principle to an elected body governing a junior college district).

Another key issue is what degree of exactness is required. Congressional districts are held to a virtually zero deviation standard. For example, Karcher v. Daggett, 462 U.S. 725 (1983) (even less than one percent requires further justification). More latitude is given for state and local offices, but the governmental body must demonstrate a good-faith effort to achieve equality. E.g., White v. Regester, 412 U.S. 755 (1973) (deviation of 9.9 percent allowed between the largest and smallest districts).

How should population be measured for apportionment purposes? All persons in the area (the census standard), or all citizens, or all potential voters, or all registered voters? In Burns v. Richardson, 384 U.S. 73 (1966), the Court held that States are not required to use total population figures as the standard and sustained a limitation to registered voters in that case since the distribution of registered voters approximated the distribution of state citizens.

Drawing Black-Majority Districts

In 1969, the Supreme Court held that the preclearance requirement of the Federal Voting Rights Act applied not only to the use of discriminatory devices such as literacy tests but also to changes in voting procedures that limited the ability of black voters to elect black candidates.

In Allen v. State Board of Elections, 393 U.S. 544 (1969), it was contended that several amendments to the Mississippi Election Code did not require preclearance since they did not prescribe who may register to vote. One amendment provided for at-large election of county supervisors instead of election by districts; another amendment provided that superintendents of education shall be appointed rather than elected; and a third amendment changed the requirements for independent candidates running in general elections. The Court held (7-2) that each of the amendments required pre-clearance under §5. In addition, with respect to the change from district to at-large voting for county supervisors, the Court declared:

> The right to vote can be affected by a dilution of voting power as well as by an absolute prohibition on casting a ballot. See Reynolds v. Sims, 377 U.S. 533, 555 (1964). Voters who are members of a racial minority might well be in the majority in one district, but in a decided minority in the county as a whole. This type of change could therefore nullify their ability to elect the candidate of their choice just as would prohibiting some of them from voting.

The Court thus transferred the concept of vote "dilution" from the one person, one vote context to the "dilution" of influence of a racial bloc.[1]

In 1982, Congress amended the Voting Rights Act to eliminate the need for proof of discriminatory purpose in challenging an election system as being racially discriminatory. (See comment "The Federal Voting Rights Act" in this chapter.)

The combination of the *Allen* decision and the 1982 amendment led to the Department of Justice's policy to block proposed election changes that did not include, in the Department's view, a sufficient number of black-majority districts to ensure the election of black representatives. The policy was resisted under the Equal Protection Clause, as in the next-digested case, *Shaw v. Reno,* and its progeny.

Shaw v. Reno, 509 U.S. 630 (1993)

FACTS: The eligible voting population of North Carolina is approximately 20 percent black. The black population is relatively dispersed and constitutes a majority of the general population in only 5 of the State's 100 counties.

§5 of the Voting Rights Act of 1965 prohibits political subdivisions covered by the Act from implementing changes in a "standard, practice, or procedure with respect to voting" without federal authorization. Forty of North Carolina's counties are covered by the Act. To comply with §5, North Carolina submitted to the U.S. Attorney General a congressional reapportionment plan with one majority-black district (District 1).

The Attorney General objected to the plan on the ground that the creation of a single majority-black district in the State was insufficient and that a second majority-black district should also have been created. In response, the North Carolina legislature revised its proposal to include a second majority-black district (District 12).

Both of the proposed majority-black districts had dramatically irregular boundaries. District 1 was compared to a "Rorschach ink-blot test," and a "bug splattered on a windshield." District 12 was even more unusually shaped. It was approximately 160 miles long and, for much of its length, no wider than the I-85 corridor. It was described as winding in snake-like fashion through tobacco country, financial centers, and manufacturing areas "until it gobbles in enough enclaves of black neighborhoods." Northbound and southbound drivers on I-85 sometimes found themselves in separate districts in one county, only to change districts when they entered the next county. According to one state legislator, "[i]f you drove down the interstate with both car doors open, you'd kill most of the people in the district." Of the ten counties through which District 12 passed, five were cut into three different districts; even towns were

---

[1]See Andrew Kull, *The Color-Blind Constitution* [Harvard University Press 1992]: 214–216.

divided. At one point, the area in the district remained contiguous only because it intersected at a single point with two other districts before crossing over them. [See the map of District 12 at the end of this case digest.]

Plaintiffs, five white North Carolina residents, filed this action claiming that the State had created an unconstitutional racial gerrymander in violation of the Equal Protection Clause. They alleged that the two districts concentrated a majority of black voters arbitrarily without regard to considerations such as compactness, contiguousness, geographical boundaries, or political subdivisions, in order to create congressional districts along racial lines and to assure the election of two black representatives.

The District Court held that the redistricting plan did not violate the Equal Protection Clause because favoring minority voters did not constitute unconstitutional discrimination and because the plan did not lead to proportional underrepresentation of white voters on a statewide basis.

ISSUE: Does the creation of a majority-black district having dramatically irregular boundaries require the State to justify the redistricting under the strict scrutiny standard?

DECISION (per *O'Connor*, 5-4): *Yes.*

The plaintiffs claim that the deliberate segregation of voters into separate districts on the basis of race violated their constitutional right to participate in a "color-blind" electoral process. The plaintiffs allege that the redistricting legislation is so extremely irregular on its face that it rationally can be viewed only as an effort to segregate the races for purposes of voting, without sufficiently compelling justification. We conclude that this allegation is sufficient to state a claim that the reapportionment statute violates equal protection.

Although we have never held that race-conscious state decision making is impermissible in all circumstances, our voting rights precedents support the conclusion that state laws classifying citizens according to race require strict scrutiny. Redistricting does differ in some ways from other kinds of state decision making in that race as well as age, economic status, political persuasion, and other demographic considerations are taken into account when district lines are drawn. This sort of race consciousness does not necessarily lead to impermissible race discrimination. However, a redistricting plan may be so highly irregular that, on its face, it rationally cannot be understood as anything other than an effort to segregate voters on the basis of race.

Reapportionment is one area where appearances do matter. Compactness and contiguity are objective factors that may be considered (though they are not constitutionally required) to defeat a claim that a district has been gerrymandered on racial lines. A reapportionment plan that includes in one district individuals who belong to the same race, but who are otherwise widely separated by geographical and political boundaries, and who may have little in common with one another but the color of their skin, bears an uncomfortable resemblance to political apartheid. It reinforces the stereotype that members of the same racial group necessarily think alike, share the same political interests, and, thus, will prefer the same candidate at the polls. We have rejected such perceptions elsewhere as impermissible racial stereotypes.

It may be that North Carolina has a sufficient reason for creating the districts as it did. North Carolina argues that it was attempting to comply with the Voting Rights Act and, in the alternative, that it had a significant interest in eradicating the effects of past racial discrimination. But racial gerrymandering, even for remedial purposes, may balkanize us into competing racial factions; it threatens to carry us further from the goal of a political system in which race no longer matters. It is for these reasons that race-based districting by our state legislatures demands close judicial scrutiny. We hold that the plaintiffs have stated a claim under the Equal Protection Clause by alleging that North Carolina adopted a reapportionment scheme so irrational on its face that it can be understood only as an effort to segregate voters into separate voting districts because of their race.

If, on remand, the allegations of a racial gerrymander are not contradicted, the District Court must determine whether the plan is narrowly tailored to further a compelling governmental interest. Reversed and remanded for further proceedings.

White, dissenting (joined by Blackmun and Stevens): As the majority recognizes, a legislature always is aware of race when it draws district lines, just as it is aware of age, economic status, religious and political persuasion, and a variety of other demographic factors. As a result, lawmakers are quite aware that the districts they create will have a white or a black majority, and so the creation of each new district presents the unavoidable choice as to the racial composition of the district. To allow judicial interference whenever this occurs would be to invite constant and unmanageable intrusion.

As I understand the majority's theory, a redistricting plan that uses race to "segregate" voters by drawing odd-shaped lines is harmful in a way that a plan that uses race to distribute voters differently is not, for the former "bears an uncomfortable resemblance to political apartheid." The distinction is without foundation. By focusing on the shape of the new district—by focusing on looks rather than impact—the majority's approach will unnecessarily hinder to some extent a State's voluntary effort to ensure a modicum of minority representation where the minority population is geographically dispersed.

Furthermore, it is evident that North Carolina had a compelling interest to comply with the Attorney General's requirements under the Voting Rights Act. North Carolina's plan was narrowly tailored to fit those requirements.

Blackmun, dissenting: It is particularly ironic that the case in which the majority chooses to abandon settled law and to recognize for the first time this "analytically distinct" constitutional claim is a challenge by white voters to the plan under which North Carolina has sent black representatives to Congress for the first time since Reconstruction.

Stevens, dissenting: First, there is no independent constitutional requirement of how a State must draw its electoral districts, and, despite the majority's references to the odd shape of the new district, it does not suggest otherwise.

Second, although the Equal Protection Clause does forbid a State from drawing district lines for the purpose of making it more difficult for members of a minority group to win an election, it does not forbid the majority from facilitating the election of a member of a group (whether the group is based on race, religion, or political party) that lacks such power because it remains underrepresented in the state legislature.

Third, redistricting to benefit an underrepresented group does not become impermissible when the minority group is defined by race. If it is permissible to draw boundaries to provide adequate representation for rural voters, for union members, for Hasidic

Jews, for Polish Americans, or for Republicans, it necessarily follows that it is permissible to do the same thing for members of the very minority group whose history in the United States gave birth to equal protection.

Souter, dissenting: Until today, the Court has analyzed equal protection claims involving race in electoral districting differently from equal protection claims involving other forms of governmental conduct. Unlike other contexts in which we have addressed a state's conscious use of race (see, e.g., Richmond v. J.A. Croson Co., 488 U.S. 469 (1989) [city contracting]; Wygant v. Jackson Bd. of Ed., 476 U.S. 267 (1986) [teacher layoffs]), electoral districting calls for decisions that nearly always require some consideration of race for legitimate reasons where there is a racially mixed population. As long as members of racial groups have the commonality of interest implicit in our ability to talk about concepts like "minority voting strength" and "dilution of minority votes," and as long as racial bloc voting takes place, legislators will have to take race into account in order to avoid dilution of minority voting strength in the districting plans they adopt.

A second distinction between districting and most other governmental decisions in which race has figured is that those other decisions using racial criteria characteristically occur in circumstances in which the use of race to the advantage of one person is necessarily at the obvious expense of a member of a different race. Thus, for example, awarding government contracts on a racial basis excludes certain firms from competition on racial grounds. See Richmond v. J. A. Croson Co., supra, at 493. And when race is used to supplant seniority in layoffs, someone is laid off who would not be otherwise. Wygant v. Jackson Board of Education, supra, at 282-283 (plurality opinion). The same principle pertains in nondistricting aspects of voting law, where race-based discrimination places the disfavored voters at the disadvantage of exclusion from the franchise without any alternative benefit. See, e.g., Gomillion v. Lightfoot, 364 U.S. 339, 341 (1960) (voters alleged to have been excluded from voting in the municipality).

In districting, by contrast, the mere placement of an individual in one district instead of another denies no one a right or benefit provided to others. All citizens may register, vote, and be represented. In whatever district, the individual voter has a right to vote in each election, and the election will result in the voter's representation. As we have held, one's constitutional rights are not violated merely because the candidate one supports loses the election or because a group (including a racial group) to which one belongs winds up with a representative from outside that group. See Whitcomb v. Chavis, 403 U.S. 124, 153-155 (1971). It is true, of course, that one's vote may be more or less effective depending on the interests of the other individuals who are in one's district, and our cases recognize the reality that members of the same race often have shared interests. "Dilution" thus refers to the effects of districting decisions not on an individual's political power viewed in isolation, but on the political power of a group. This is the reason that the placement of given voters in a given district, even on the basis of race, does not, without more, diminish the effectiveness of the individual as a voter.

In my view, there is no justification for the Court's determination to depart from our prior decisions by carving out this narrow group of cases for strict scrutiny in place of the review customarily applied in cases dealing with discrimination in electoral districting on the basis of race.

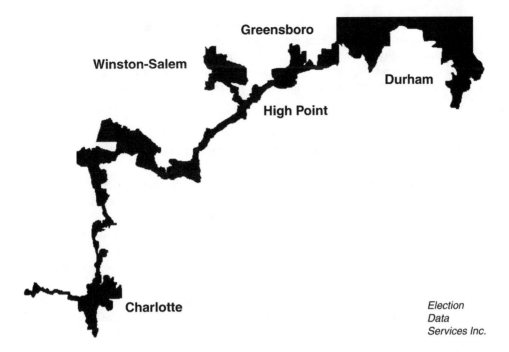

Congressional District 12, 1992

The Aftermath of *Shaw v. Reno*

The North Carolina Redistricting

On remand, although applying the strict scrutiny standard, the District Court found that creation of the majority-black districts was justified as an effort to obtain approval of the Department of Justice under the Voting Rights Act.

But, on appeal, the Supreme Court (again by a 5-4 vote) rejected that justification, concluding that the plan for District 12 violated the Equal Protection Clause. The Court found that race was the predominant factor in creating the district and held that a second majority black district was not narrowly tailored to comply with the Voting Rights Act. Shaw v. Hunt, 517 U.S. 899 (1996) (known as "Shaw II").

In response, the North Carolina legislature (1997) redrew the boundaries, but the revised district lines were again challenged under the Equal Protection Clause. The District Court, without holding a trial, found the plan to be unconstitutional.

On appeal, this decision was also reversed by the Supreme Court, which held (this time unanimously) that a trial of the factual issues was necessary. Hunt v. Cromartie, 526 U.S. 541 (1999). The Court held that the plaintiffs had introduced only "circumstantial evidence" in support of their claim that race had been the predominant factor in creating District 12 and that therefore summary judgment was inappropriate because of evidence that the legislature's principal goals were the protection of incumbents and preservation of a 6-6 split between Republicans and Democrats.

The majority opinion (written by Justice Thomas and joined by Rehnquist, O'Connor, Scalia, and Kennedy) noted that

> [o]ur prior decisions have made clear that a jurisdiction may engage in constitutional political gerrymandering, even if it so happens that the most loyal Democrats happen to

be black Democrats and even if the State were *conscious* of that fact. . . . Evidence that blacks constitute even a supermajority in one congressional district while amounting to less than a plurality in a neighboring district will not, by itself, suffice to prove that a jurisdiction was motivated by race in drawing its district lines when the evidence also shows a high correlation between race and party preference." [Pages 551–552 (italics the Court's).]

Stevens (joined by Souter, Ginsburg, and Breyer) dissented.

On remand, this time after trial, the District Court again held that the districting was race-motivated and unconstitutional.

But on appeal the Supreme Court (also 5 to 4) again reversed, holding that the District Court's findings of facts were "clearly erroneous." Easley v. Cromartie, 532 U.S. 234 (2001). The majority opinion (written by Justice Breyer and joined by the other dissenters in the 1999 decision as well as Justice O'Connor) concluded that, "The evidence taken together, however, does not show . . . that racial considerations predominated in the drawing of District 12's boundaries" (p. 257). According to the majority, since African Americans in North Carolina vote Democratic about 95 percent of the time, the legislature's creation of a majority black district could rationally be seen as using race for a constitutional political objective—the creation of a safe Democratic seat.

The Court stated that,

given the fact that the party attacking the legislature's decision bears the burden of proving that racial considerations are "dominant and controlling," given the "demanding" nature of that burden of proof, and given the sensitivity, the "extraordinary caution," that district courts must show to avoid treading upon legislative prerogatives, the attacking party has not successfully shown that race, rather than politics, predominantly accounts for the result. [Page 257.]

Thomas (who had written the 1999 *Hunt v. Cromartie* decision) dissented, joined by Rehnquist, Scalia, and Kennedy.

The practical effect of this series of the Court's decisions is to substantially increase the burden of establishing that a black-majority district was created for a "predominantly" racial purpose. But a correlative effect is to accord greater legitimacy to traditional political tactics as an alternative explanation for gerrymandering a district.

The Georgia Redistricting

Two years after the decision in *Shaw v. Reno,* the decision was applied by the Supreme Court in Miller v. Johnson, 515 U.S. 900 (1995), to reject (5-4) a Georgia plan providing for three majority-black congressional districts.

The Georgia Legislature adopted the plan after the Justice Department refused to preclear, under §5 of the Voting Rights Act, two earlier plans that each contained only two majority-black districts. Voters in the new Eleventh District (which joined metropolitan black neighborhoods together with the poor black population of coastal areas 260 miles away) challenged the plan on the ground that the district was a racial gerrymander in violation of the Equal Protection Clause.

The Supreme Court declared that, "Just as the State may not, absent extraordinary justification, segregate citizens on the basis of race in its public parks, . . . buses, . . . golf courses, . . . beaches, . . . and schools, . . . so did we recognize in *Shaw* that it may not separate its citizens into different voting districts on the basis of race" (page 911). Further, "When the State assigns voters on the basis of race, it engages in the offensive and demeaning assumption that voters of a particular race, because of their race, 'think alike, share the same political interests, and will prefer the same candidates at the polls' " (pages 911–912).

Turning then to the record in the case, the Court found it unnecessary to base its decision on the district's shape, considered separately, since there was substantial additional evidence showing that the Georgia Legislature was motivated by a predominant, overriding purpose to create a third majority-black district in order to comply with the Justice Department's preclearance demands. There was little doubt, the Court held, that Georgia's true interest was to satisfy the Justice Department's preclearance demands and that, in utilizing §5 to require the maximization of majority-minority districts whenever possible, the Department had exceeded its authority under the Voting Rights Act.

The Court's decision was bitterly condemned by civil rights leaders on the ground that it would reduce the number of black representatives in Congress. Yet, as related by sociologist Orlando Patterson, "when the same Afro-American candidates ran in non-gerrymandered districts with majority Euro-American electors in the 1996 elections, *every single one was re-elected*" (italics in original). Recent elections, according to Professor Patterson, show that "even a small proportion of Afro-American voters can powerfully influence the elected leaders of both parties—whatever their ethnic ancestry—to vote in a manner that advances the interests of Afro-Americans and the less privileged," and that "the practice of specially concentrating electors into minority districts so as to ensure the election of a minority representative almost always makes all the other voting districts of such a gerrymandered state not only more conservative, but more self-consciously hostile to the interests of the Afro-American minorities in their midst." [2]

In Georgia v. Ashcroft, 539 U.S. 461 (2003), the Court considered a Georgia Senate proposal that would reduce the number of majority-black districts but would increase the number of majority-Democratic districts. The proposal was supported by leading Georgia black legislators since it would increase the influence of black voters, who were overwhelmingly Democrats. However, the Department of Justice refused to preclear the change under §5 of the Voting Rights Act because it would likely reduce the number of black representatives in the legislature. The Court (5-4) sustained the Georgia Senate proposal, holding that it would protect the interests of black voters even if the elected representatives in the affected districts were white.

Vieth v. Jubelirer, 541 U.S. 267 (2004)

FACTS: Population figures derived from the 2000 census showed that Pennsylvania was entitled to only 19 Representatives in the U.S. House of Representatives, thereby requiring a decrease of two Representatives and a decrease of two congressional districts. Republicans, controlling a majority of both State Houses, drew new boundaries for the congressional districts. Under the plan, Democratic incumbent congressmen were placed in the same congressional district in two instances, and another Democratic representative was placed in a heavily Republican district.

---

[2] *The Ordeal of Integration: Progress and Resentment in America's "Racial" Crisis* [Civitas 1997]: 67.

Plaintiffs, registered Democrats who vote in Pennsylvania, brought suit to enjoin implementation of the plan on the ground that it both created malapportioned districts and constituted a political gerrymander in violation of the Constitution.

On defendants' motion to dismiss, the District Court dismissed the political gerrymandering claim, but declined to dismiss the malapportionment claim. The plaintiffs appealed the dismissal of their gerrymander claim.

ISSUE: Did the District Court err in declining to consider a claim that the proposed redistricting plan was gerrymandered for partisan political purposes?

DECISION: *No* (5-4, but none of the opinions was joined by a majority of the Justices).

Scalia (joined by Rehnquist, O'Connor, and Thomas): Political gerrymandering claims are nonjusticiable because no judicially discernible and manageable standards for adjudicating such claims exist. The Court should overrule Davis v. Bandemer, 478 U.S. 109 (1986), in which the Court held that political gerrymandering claims are justiciable but could not agree upon a standard for assessing political gerrymandering claims.

In *Bandemer,* the Court was "not persuaded" that there are no such standards, but the six-justice majority could not discern what the standards might be. For the past 18 years, the decisions of the lower courts seeking to apply the test stated in *Bandemer* plurality opinion have almost invariably produced the same result as would have obtained had the question been held nonjusticiable—judicial intervention has been refused.

The *Bandemer* plurality's test—that a political gerrymandering claim can succeed only where the plaintiffs show "both intentional discrimination against an identifiable political group and an actual discriminatory effect on that group"—has proved unmanageable. Because that test was misguided when proposed, has not been improved in subsequent application, and is not even defended by the plaintiffs here, it should not be affirmed.

Plaintiffs' proposed two-pronged test is no more acceptable. Plaintiffs are mistaken when they contend that their intent prong ("predominant intent") is no different from that which this Court has applied in racial gerrymandering cases. In those cases, the predominant intent test is applied to the challenged district in which the plaintiffs voted, whereas here plaintiffs assert that their test is satisfied only when partisan advantage was the predominant motivation *behind the entire statewide plan.* Vague as a predominant-motivation test might be if used to evaluate single districts, it all but evaporates when applied statewide.

The effects prong of the plaintiffs' proposal requires that the plaintiffs show that the rival party's voters are systematically "packed" or "cracked," and that the map can thwart the plaintiffs' ability to translate a majority of votes into a majority of seats. The Constitution, however, provides no right to proportional representation, and in any event such a test is not judicially manageable. There is no effective way to ascertain a party's majority status, and, in any event, majority status in statewide races does not establish majority status for particular district contests. Moreover, even if a majority party could be identified, it would be impossible to ensure that it won a majority of seats unless the states' traditional election structures were radically revised.

For many of the same reasons, Justice Powell's *Bandemer* test—a totality-of-the-circumstances analysis that evaluates districts with an eye to ascertaining whether the particular gerrymander is "fair"—must also be rejected. "Fairness" is not a judicially manageable standard. Some criterion more solid and more demonstrably met than that is necessary to enable state legislatures to discern the limits of their districting discretion, to meaningfully constrain the courts' discretion, and to win public acceptance for the courts' intrusion into a process that is the very foundation of democratic decision making.

Kennedy, concurring: While agreeing with the conclusion of the plurality opinion that the complaint must be dismissed, I do not believe that all possibility of judicial relief should be foreclosed in cases such as this, since a limited and precise rationale may yet be found for measuring a gerrymander's burden on representational rights.

Courts confront two obstacles when presented with a claim of injury from partisan gerrymandering. First is the lack of comprehensive and neutral principles for drawing electoral boundaries. No substantive definition of fairness in districting commands general assent.

Second is the absence of rules to limit and confine judicial intervention. That courts can grant relief in districting cases involving race does not answer the need for fairness principles, since those cases involve sorting permissible districting classifications from impermissible ones. Politics is a different matter. A determination that a gerrymander violates the law must rest on something more than the conclusion that political classifications were applied. It must rest instead on a conclusion that the classifications, though generally permissible, were applied in an invidious manner or in a way unrelated to any legitimate legislative objective. However, with no agreed upon substantive principles of fair districting, there is no basis on which to define clear, manageable, and politically neutral standards for measuring the burden a given partisan classification imposes on representational rights. Suitable standards for measuring this burden are critical to our intervention.

In this case, the plurality convincingly demonstrates that the standards proposed by the Court in *Bandemer,* by the parties here, and by the dissents are either unmanageable or inconsistent with precedent, or both. There are, then, weighty arguments for holding cases like these to be nonjusticiable. However, they are not so compelling that they require the Court now to bar all future partisan gerrymandering claims. That a workable standard for measuring a gerrymander's burden on representational rights has not yet emerged does not mean that none will emerge in the future. The Court should adjudicate only what is in the case before it.

Stevens, dissenting: The central question presented by this case is whether political gerrymandering claims are justiciable. Although our reasons for coming to this conclusion differ, five Justices are convinced that the plurality's answer to that question is erroneous. That we have somewhat differing views—particularly concerning the standard that should be applied—should not obscure the fact that the areas of our agreement are of far greater significance.

Plaintiffs urge us to craft new rules that in effect would authorize judicial review of statewide election results to protect the democratic process from a transient majority's abuse of its power to define voting districts. I agree with the Court's refusal to undertake that ambitious project. I am persuaded, however, that the District Court failed to apply well-settled propositions of law when it granted the motion to dismiss plaintiff Susan Furey's gerrymandering claim with respect to the specific district in which she lives.

The problem in the plurality's view is not that there is no judicially manageable standard to fix an unconstitutional partisan gerrymander, but rather that the judiciary lacks the ability to determine when a state legislature has violated its duty to govern impartially. Quite obviously, however, several standards for identifying impermissible partisan influence are available to judges who have the will to enforce them. We could hold that every district boundary must have a neutral justification; we could apply the predominant motivation standard fashioned by the Court in its racial gerrymandering cases; or we could endorse either of the approaches advocated today by Justices Souter and Breyer. What is clear is that it is not the unavailability of judicially manageable standards that drives today's decision. It is, instead, a failure of judicial will to condemn even the most blatant violations of a state legislature's fundamental duty to govern impartially.

Souter, dissenting (joined by Ginsburg): I would preserve the holding in *Bandemer* that political gerrymandering is a justiciable issue, but otherwise start anew. I would adopt a political gerrymandering test analogous to the standard applicable to summary judgments, calling for a plaintiff to satisfy elements of a prima facie cause of action, at which point the State would have the opportunity not only to rebut the evidence supporting the plaintiff's case but to offer an affirmative justification for the districting choices. My own judgment is that we would have better luck at devising a workable prima facie case if we concentrated as much as possible on suspect characteristics of individual districts instead of statewide patterns.

Breyer, dissenting: At least one circumstance exists where use of purely political boundary-drawing factors can amount to a serious, and remediable, abuse, namely the *unjustified* use of political factors to entrench a minority in power. By entrenchment I mean a situation in which a party that enjoys only minority support among the populace has nonetheless contrived to take, and hold, legislative power. By *unjustified* entrenchment I mean that the minority's hold on power is purely the result of partisan manipulation.

We cannot always count on a severely gerrymandered legislature itself to find and implement a remedy. The party that controls the process has no incentive to change it. And, as a result of increasingly precise map-drawing technology, a party may be able to bring about a gerrymander that is virtually impossible to dislodge. Thus, court action may prove necessary.

The bottom line is that courts should be able to identify the presence of one important gerrymandering evil, the unjustified entrenching in power of a political party that the voters have rejected. They should be able to separate the unjustified abuse of partisan boundary-drawing considerations to achieve that end from their more ordinary and justified use. And they should be able to design a remedy for extreme cases.

In the case before us I would authorize the plaintiffs to proceed, and I dissent from the majority's contrary determination.

Seeking a Test for Political Gerrymanders

In 2006, in a case involving Texas redistricting, the Court again was unable to come up with a "workable test" for deciding "how much partisan dominance is too much."

League of United Latin American Citizens v. Perry, ___ U.S. ____, 126 S.Ct. 2594 (2006).

Following the 2000 census, when the sharply divided Texas legislature (then under the control of the Democratic Party) could not agree on a redistricting plan, the district lines were redrawn in accordance with an order of the federal district court. In 2003, just three years after the court-ordered redistricting, and after control of the Texas legislature had shifted to the Republican Party, a new redistricting plan was adopted that increased Republican congressional seats by six. The plan was challenged in a federal court action alleging a host of constitutional and statutory violations, including the claim that the mid-decade redistricting constituted an unconstitutional political gerrymander.

In upholding (7-2) the Texas mid-decade redistricting, the Supreme Court stated: "We do not revisit the justiciability holding [in *Vieth v. Jubelirer*] but do proceed to examine whether appellants' claims offer the Court a manageable, reliable measure of fairness for determining whether a partisan gerrymander violates the Constitution." (126 S.Ct. at 2607.) On that issue, the Court concluded that a districting plan is not rendered invalid even when partisan advantage is the sole motivation for adopting the plan. The majority held (id. at 2609):

> Evaluating the legality of acts arising out of mixed motives can be complex, and affixing a single label to those acts can be hazardous. When the actor is a legislature and the act is a composite of manifold choices, the task can be even more daunting. . . . [T]here is nothing inherently suspect about a legislature's decision to replace mid-decade a court-ordered plan with one of its own. And even if there were, the fact of mid-decade redistricting alone is no sure indication of unlawful political gerrymanders.

As the Texas case demonstrates, courts are often ill-equipped to determine what is "fair" in politics, particularly in analyzing each party's strategies and counterstrategies in responding to the other party's moves. Courts lack any neutral yardstick (such as a basically mathematical one-person, one-vote rule) to measure how much is too much. This has led to support for removing redistricting authority from politicians and instead transferring it to a neutral body. In Iowa, for example, district lines are drawn by the nonpartisan Legislative Services Bureau (an agency similar to the federal Congressional Research Service); consideration of political factors such as location of incumbents, previous boundary locations, and voters' party affiliations is specifically forbidden. Another approach has been adopted in California, where voters in 2008 approved transfer of the redistricting function from the legislature to a bipartisan commission.

The Statutory Context of *Bush v. Gore*

The much-debated *Bush v. Gore,* the next-digested case, can be fully understood only in the framework of the applicable federal and state deadlines for the conduct of the election.

The Constitution provides that "Each State shall appoint, *in such Manner as the Legislature thereof may direct,* a Number of Electors." (Article II, §1, italics added.)

Prior to the 2000 presidential election, as part of the state's election code, the Florida Legislature had provided that "Returns *must be filed* [in the Florida Department of State] by 5 p.m. on the 7th day following the . . . election"—i.e., November

14—and that "If the returns are not received . . . by the time specified, *such returns may be ignored and the results on file at that time may be certified by the department.*" (§102.112, italics added.) The election law further provided that "If the county returns are not received by the Department of State by . . . [November 14], all missing counties *shall be ignored,* and the results shown by the returns on file *shall be certified.*" (§102.111, italics added.)

The Florida election law authorized several successive steps for challenging an election result:

(1) *Machine recount*—If the margin of victory was less than one-half of a percent of the votes cast, an automatic machine recount was conducted.

(2) *Manual recount*—The unsuccessful candidate could, within 72 hours after the election, request a county canvassing board to make a manual recount, which the board "may" authorize. (§102.166(4).)

(3) *Contest of the certification*—After the results are certified by the Florida Department of State, the candidate could commence a suit in the circuit court to contest the certification on the ground of "[r]eceipt of a number of illegal votes or rejection of a number of legal votes sufficient to change or place in doubt the result of the election." (§102.168(3)(c).)

However, the entire state vote-counting process was subject to time schedules established by federal law: The 2000 election was held on November 7; the electors of each State were to be determined by December 12; and the electors of all States were scheduled to meet in Washington on December 18 to determine the winner.

In addition, a federal statute provides that a State's determination of its electors—if made by the December 12 deadline and "made pursuant to [the State's election] law so existing on said day"—"shall be conclusive, and shall govern in the counting of the electoral votes . . . so far as the ascertainment of the electors appointed by each State is concerned." (3 U.S.C. §5.)

Bush v. Gore, 531 U.S. 98 (2000)

FACTS: On November 8, 2000, the day following the presidential election, the Florida Division of Elections reported that Bush's statewide total votes exceeded Gore's by 1,784 votes.

The Machine Recount: Because the margin of victory was less than one-half of a percent of the votes cast, an automatic machine recount was conducted. The machine recount showed Bush still winning but by a smaller margin.

The Protest Proceeding: Gore then filed protests with canvassing boards in four heavily Democratic counties (Palm Beach, Broward, Miami-Dade, and Volusia), requesting them to conduct manual recounts of the ballots.

The Florida statute provided that "Returns *must be filed*" in the Florida Department of State by November 14 and that otherwise "*such returns may be ignored and the results on file at that time may be certified by the department.*" (§102.112, italics added.) The statute further provided that "If the county returns are not received by the Department of State by . . . [November 14], all missing counties *shall be ignored,* and the results shown by the returns on file *shall be certified.*" (§102.111, italics added.)

Because the manual recounts had not been completed, Gore requested the Florida Secretary of State (Kathleen Harris) to waive the November 14 filing deadline imposed by the statute. The Secretary ordered that any county desiring to forward late returns should submit a written statement of the facts and circumstances justifying a later filing. After reviewing their submissions, the Secretary determined that they did not justify an extension.

Gore then brought an action in the Florida courts to require inclusion of the hand recounts that had not been filed by the statutory deadline. After a hearing, the trial court dismissed Gore's action, concluding that the Secretary of State had exercised "reasoned judgment" and had not abused her discretion under the statute. Gore then appealed to the Florida Supreme Court.

On its own motion, the Florida Supreme Court enjoined certification of the results until further order of the court. On November 21 the Florida Supreme Court reversed the trial court and ordered acceptance of the hand recounts if completed by 5 p.m. on November 26. Although the Florida statute provided that late-filed returns "shall be ignored," the Florida Supreme Court held that the returns must be accepted unless "the returns are submitted so late that their inclusion will preclude a candidate from contesting the certification or preclude Florida's voters from participating fully in the federal electoral process."

The November 21 decision was vacated by the U.S. Supreme Court on December 4 in a *per curiam* opinion. The Florida court was directed to clarify its November 21 decision in two respects—the extent to which the Florida court regarded the Florida Constitution as limiting the Florida Legislature's authority under the U.S. Constitution; and the extent to which the Florida court gave consideration to 3 U.S.C. §5.

The First Manual Recount: In the interim, because of the extension ordered by the Florida Supreme Court on November 21, the recount continued.

The results from Broward County's hand recount were submitted to the Secretary of State on November 25. On November 22, the Miami-Dade canvassing board unanimously decided to halt its recount, after counting only 136 of the 635 precincts. The Palm Beach canvassing board began a hand recount, but did not complete its work by the November 26 deadline set by the Florida Supreme Court and instead submitted only partial returns.

When the November 26 deadline arrived, after inclusion of the additional hand recounts, Bush was still ahead by 537 votes, and accordingly the Florida Elections Canvassing Commission certified the results of the election and declared Bush the winner of Florida's 25 electoral votes.

The Contest Proceeding: To contest the certification, Gore then filed another lawsuit, claiming the "[r]eceipt of a number of illegal votes or rejection of a number of legal votes sufficient to change or place in doubt the result of the election." (§102.168(3)(c).)

Gore's complaint alleged that the certified results did not include the partial recount of ballots in Miami-Dade County and the incomplete hand recount in Palm Beach County. Gore further asked the court to evaluate "chad" and "dimple" ballots in Palm Beach and Miami-Dade—ballots on which voting machines had failed to detect any vote for president (so-called "undervotes").

On December 4, 2000, following a two-day trial, the trial court rejected the Gore claims. The court found that there was no credible evidence establishing a reasonable probability that the election results would be different if the requested relief was granted; that the Palm Beach board did not abuse its discretion in rejecting the 3,300 ballots Gore sought to have reviewed again; and that the Miami-Dade canvassing Board did not abuse its discretion in deciding not to perform a complete manual recount.

Appeal to the Florida Supreme Court: On December 8, a 4-to-3 majority of the Florida Supreme Court reversed.

The Florida Supreme Court ordered the trial court to include in the certified vote totals a net gain of 215 votes for Gore that had been submitted by Palm Beach past the November 26 deadline; to include a net gain of 168 votes for Gore in a partial recount in Miami-Dade; and to make a manual recount of 9,000 Miami-Dade "undervote" ballots.

In addition, rejecting Gore's position that the recount should be limited to the four counties whose votes Gore had challenged, the court held that the trial court should order

> the Supervisor of Elections and the Canvassing Boards, as well as the necessary public officials, in all counties that have not conducted a manual recount or tabulation of the undervotes . . . to do so forthwith, said tabulation to take place in the individual counties where the ballots are located.

The court stated that "a final decision as to the result of the statewide election should only be determined upon consideration of the legal votes contained within the undervote . . . ballots of all Florida counties, as well as the legal votes already tabulated."

The Florida Supreme Court, however, did not address the question of what standards should be applied to determine whether an "undervote" ballot expressed the intention of the voter to vote for one candidate or another. Nor did the court address the subject of "overvote" ballots (ballots that the machines rejected because more than one candidate for president was marked).

The court did, however, recognize that the statewide recount it ordered had to be accomplished speedily to comply with the federal statute requiring completion of the state's selection of electors six days prior to the meeting of the Electoral College. The court acknowledged that the "need for prompt resolution and finality is especially critical in presidential elections where there is an outside deadline established by federal law," and that, "because the selection and participation of Florida's electors in the presidential election process is subject to a stringent calendar controlled by federal law, the Florida election law scheme must yield in the event of a conflict."

Dissenting together with two other justices, Florida Supreme Court Chief Justice Charles Wells stated that "[c]ontinuation of [a] system of county-by-county decisions regarding how a dimpled chad is counted is fraught with equal protection concerns" and that

> many times a reading of a ballot by a human will be subjective [and] [t]his subjective counting is only compounded where no standards exist or, as in this statewide contest, where there are no statewide standards for determining voter intent by the various canvassing boards, individual judges, or multiple unknown counters who will eventually count these ballots.

In addition, in his view, the majority ignored the fact that "overvotes" as well as "undervotes" result in a vote not being counted, and "not to count all of the ballots if any were to be recounted would plainly be changing the rules after the election and would be unfairly discriminatory against votes in the precincts in which there was no manual recount."

The case was immediately appealed to the U.S. Supreme Court.

The December 11 Florida Supreme Court decision. On December 11, while the appeal from its December 8 decision was pending in the U.S. Supreme Court (and in response to the U.S. Supreme Court's December 4 opinion), the Florida Supreme Court issued a supplemental opinion, stating that late filing of returns would not be permitted where it would "result in Florida voters not participating fully in the federal electoral process, as provided in 3 U.S.C. §5 [the 'safe harbor' provision of federal law]" and that Florida law "required that there be time . . . to accommodate the outside deadline set forth in 3 U.S.C. §5 of *December 12, 2000*." (Italics added.)

On December 12, the U.S. Supreme Court issued its decision.

ISSUES: (1) whether the recount ordered by the Florida Supreme Court, permitting each canvassing board to determine its own standards to count "undervotes" and excluding any recount of "overvotes," violates the Equal Protection Clause; (2) whether the Florida Supreme Court applied new post-election standards for resolving presidential election contests, thereby violating Article II, §1, clause 2, and failing to comply with 3 U.S.C. §5; and (3) if a constitutional violation is found, whether the case should be remanded to the Florida Supreme Court for continuation of the manual recount.

DECISION: On the merits, the Court (7-2) held that the recount directed by the Florida Supreme Court violated the Equal Protection Clause.

Three Justices (Rehnquist, Scalia, Thomas) also found a violation of Article II.

On the remedy issue, holding that any further recount could not be completed by the December 12 "safe harbor" date (the same date as the Court's decision), the Court (5-4) reversed the Florida Supreme Court decision directing the recount to proceed. The dissenting Justices (Stevens, Ginsburg, Souter, and Breyer) concluded that the Florida Supreme Court, irrespective of the December 12 safe harbor date, should be ordered to devise a recount that would meet equal protection requirements.

The Equal Protection Issue: In a *per curiam* opinion (joined by Rehnquist, Scalia, Kennedy, O'Connor, and Thomas), the Court stated that, "[w]hen the state legislature vests the right to vote for President in its people, the right to vote as the legislature has prescribed is fundamental, and one source of its fundamental nature lies in the equal weight accorded to each vote and the equal dignity owed to each voter." The central problem, the Court held, was that similar ballots in a statewide election would be treated differently, depending on the standards applied in each county and the personnel applying those varying standards:

> As seems to have been acknowledged at oral argument, the standards for accepting or rejecting contested ballots might vary not only from county to county but indeed within a single county from one recount team to another.
>
> The record provides some examples. A monitor in Miami-Dade County testified at trial that he observed that three members of the county canvassing board applied different standards in defining a legal vote. And testimony at trial also revealed that at least one county changed its evaluative standards during the counting process. Palm Beach County, for example, began the process with a 1990 guideline which precluded counting completely attached chads, switched to a rule that considered a vote to be legal if any light could be

seen through a chad, changed back to the 1990 rule, and then abandoned any pretense of a per se rule, only to have a court order that the county consider dimpled chads legal. This is not a process with sufficient guarantees of equal treatment.

In addition, the Florida Supreme Court, while ordering a statewide hand recount of all "undervotes," had omitted any consideration of an estimated 110,000 "overvote" ballots:

> As a result, the citizen whose ballot was not read by a machine because he failed to vote for a candidate in a way readable by a machine may still have his vote counted in a manual recount; on the other hand, the citizen who marks two candidates in a way discernable by the machine will not have the same opportunity to have his vote count, even if a manual examination of the ballot would reveal the requisite indicia of intent.

The Remedy Issue—The *per curiam* opinion, relying on the Florida Supreme Court's repeated statements that the recount had to be concluded by the December 12 safe harbor date, reversed the Florida Supreme Court decision ordering the recount to proceed:

> The Supreme Court of Florida has said that the legislature intended the State's electors to "participat[e] fully in the federal electoral process," as provided in 3 U.S.C. §5. That statute, in turn, requires that any controversy or contest that is designed lo lead to a conclusive selection of electors be completed by December 12. That date is upon us, and there is no recount procedure in place under the State Supreme Court's order that comports with minimal constitutional standards. Because it is evident that any recount seeking to meet the December 12 date will be unconstitutional for the reasons we have discussed, we reverse the judgment of the Supreme Court of Florida ordering a recount to proceed.
>
> Seven Justices of the Court agree that there are constitutional problems with the recount ordered by the Florida Supreme Court that demand a remedy. The only disagreement is as to the remedy. Because the Florida Supreme Court has said that the Florida Legislature intended to obtain the safe-harbor benefits of 3 U.S.C. §5, Justice Breyer's proposed remedy—remanding to the Florida Supreme Court for its ordering of a constitutionally proper contest until December 18—contemplates action in violation of the Florida election code, and hence could not be part of an "appropriate" order authorized by Fla. Stat. §102.168(8) (2000).

Four Justices (Stevens, Breyer, Souter, and Ginsburg) dissented on the remedy issue.

Rehnquist, concurring (joined by Scalia and Thomas), urged that reversal was also required by 3 U.S.C. §5, providing that the state's selection of electors "shall be conclusive, and shall govern in the counting of the electoral votes" if the electors are chosen under laws enacted prior to the federal election day. This statute, Rehnquist contended, prevents a state from changing its electoral process after the election, and the Florida Supreme Court had done this by "significantly depart[ing] from the statutory framework in place on November 7, and [by] authoriz[ing] open-ended further proceedings which could not be completed by December 12, thereby preventing a final determination by that date" in accordance with the mandate of the Florida legislature.

Souter, although dissenting on the remedy issue, acknowledged that the recount ordered by the Florida Supreme Court should be reversed: "I can conceive of no legitimate state interest served by these differing treatments of the expressions of voters' fundamental rights. The differences appear wholly arbitrary." But Souter agreed with

Stevens, Breyer, and Ginsburg that the case should be remanded to the Florida courts to afford them the opportunity to establish appropriate uniform standards for the recount.

Breyer, although dissenting on the remedy issue, joined Souter's opinion with respect to the equal protection issue and the need for uniform standards. But he agreed with Stevens, Souter, and Ginsburg that the majority was wrong in ending the counting and failing to remand the case for resumption of the recount under appropriate standards. In his view, there was nothing magical about the December 12 deadline and Florida could still choose its electors after that date. Breyer stated:

> I fear that in order to bring this agonizingly long election process to a definitive conclusion, we have not adequately attended to that necessary "check upon our own exercise of power," "our own sense of self-restraint." I would repair the damage done as best we now can, by permitting the recount to continue under uniform standards.

Stevens, dissenting, challenged the Court's holding on equal protection. He acknowledged that "the use of differing substandards for determining voter intent in different counties employing similar voting systems may raise serious concerns," but contended that "Those concerns are alleviated—if not eliminated—by the fact that a single impartial magistrate will ultimately adjudicate all objections arising from the recount process." In his view, the case should be sent back to Florida for the establishment of standards and the subsequent counting. He concluded: "Although we may never know with complete certainty the identity of the winner of this year's Presidential election, the identity of the loser is perfectly clear. It is the Nation's confidence in the judge as an impartial guardian of the rule of law."

Ginsburg, dissenting, disagreed with the majority's finding a denial of equal protection, rejected Rehnquist's Article II analysis, and agreed with Stevens, Breyer, and Souter that the case should be returned to Florida for resumption of the recount.

16

Cruel and Unusual Punishment

The Death Penalty Reconsidered

The Eighth Amendment prohibits inflicting "cruel and unusual punishments."

Other provisions of the Constitution demonstrate that the Framers clearly contemplated the use of the death penalty in certain cases. The Fifth Amendment requires a grand jury indictment for "a capital ... offense," and both the Fifth and Fourteenth Amendments prohibit depriving "any person of life ... without due process of law."

In Trop v. Dulles, 356 U.S. 86, 101 (1958), the plurality opinion of Chief Justice Earl Warren (speaking for himself and three other Justices) stated that "The [Eighth] Amendment must draw its meaning from the evolving standards of decency that mark the progress of a maturing society." But (although the death penalty was not directly an issue in that case) the opinion acknowledged that, "Whatever the arguments may be against capital punishment ... the death penalty has been employed throughout our history, and, in a day when it is still widely accepted, it cannot be said to violate the constitutional concept of cruelty."

In McGautha v. California, 402 U.S. 183 (1971), the Court (6-3) upheld the constitutionality of the death penalty against claims that due process required States to prescribe legislative standards for a jury's exercise of discretion in determining whether to impose a death penalty. In his concurring opinion, Justice Black commented:

> In my view, [the Eighth Amendment] cannot be read to outlaw capital punishment because that penalty was in common use and authorized by law here and in the countries from which our ancestors came at the time the Amendment was adopted. It is inconceivable to me that the framers intended to end capital punishment by the Amendment. Although some people have urged that this Court should amend the Constitution by interpretation to keep it abreast of modern ideas, I have never believed that lifetime judges in our system have any such legislative power.

Nevertheless, the following year in 1972 in the next-digested case, *Furman v. Georgia,* the Court abruptly changed course. The Court (5-4) held that the death penalty, at least as administered in the three cases before the Court, constituted "cruel and unusual punishment." The *Furman* decision and its progeny reflect a major revolution in the interpretation of the Eighth Amendment.

Furman v. Georgia, 408 U.S. 238 (1972)

On June 29, 1972, the Court entered the following order:

> PER CURIAM.
>   Petitioner in No. 69-5003 was convicted of murder in Georgia and was sentenced to death pursuant to Ga. Code Ann. 26-1005 (Supp. 1971) (effective prior to July 1, 1969). 225 Ga. 253, 167 S. E. 2d 628 (1969). Petitioner in No. 69-5030 was convicted of rape in Georgia and was sentenced to death pursuant to Ga. Code Ann. 26-1302 (Supp. 1971) (effective prior to July 1, 1969). 225 Ga. 790, 171 S. E. 2d 501 (1969). Petitioner in No. 69-5031 was convicted of rape in Texas and was sentenced to death pursuant to Tex. Penal Code, Art. 1189 (1961). 447 S. W. 2d 932 (Ct. Crim. App. 1969). Certiorari was granted limited to the following question: "Does the imposition and carrying out of the death penalty in [these cases] constitute cruel and unusual punishment in violation of the Eighth and Fourteenth Amendments?"
>   The Court holds that the imposition and carrying out of the death penalty in these cases constitute cruel and unusual punishment in violation of the Eighth and Fourteenth Amendments. The judgment in each case is therefore reversed insofar as it leaves undisturbed the death sentence imposed, and the cases are remanded for further proceedings.
>   So ordered.

Each of the nine Justices filed a separate opinion expressing his individual views. The opinions totaled 243 pages in the official reports—the longest decision at that time in the Court's history.[1]

Five Justices (Douglas, Brennan, Stewart, White, and Marshall) concurred in the judgment, and four (Burger, Blackmun, Powell, and Rehnquist) dissented.

Each of the five Justices in the majority approached the matter from a different viewpoint. Two Justices concluded that the death penalty is "cruel and unusual" because the imposition of capital punishment "does not comport with human dignity" (Brennan) or because it is "morally unacceptable" and "excessive" (Marshall). One Justice concluded that the death penalty violates the Eighth Amendment because it is inflicted on the poor and hapless defendant but not the affluent and socially better defendant (Douglas). Two Justices concluded that capital punishment is applied in an arbitrary, "wanton," and "freakish" manner (Stewart) and so infrequently that it serves no justifying end (White).

The four dissenters, in four separate opinions, argued with different emphases that the Constitution itself recognizes capital punishment in the Fifth and Fourteenth Amendments, that the death penalty was not cruel and unusual when the Eighth and Fourteenth Amendments were proposed and ratified, that the Court was engaging in a wholly unjustified legislative act to strike it down now, and that even under modern standards it could not be considered cruel and unusual. Each of the dissenters joined each of the other dissenting opinions.

The Aftermath of the *Furman* Decision

In *Furman,* only two of the Justices in the majority concluded that the death penalty was *per se* invalid. The other three Justices in the majority based their views on the adequacy of the standards and procedures used in death penalty cases. In response,

---

[1] The background of the Court's decision is related in detail in Bob Woodward and Scott Armstrong, *The Brethren: Inside the Supreme Court* [Simon & Schuster 1979]: 205–220, 430–441.

35 state legislatures sought to overcome that objection by enacting new death penalty statutes, which were immediately also attacked as unconstitutional.

While the validity of these new statutes was being challenged, there was in effect a virtual national moratorium on executions. Between 1972 and 1982, only six executions were carried out in the United States.

In the 1975 term, the Court was confronted with 50 certiorari petitions from defendants appealing their death penalty sentences. Five cases, reflecting the principal types of amendments adopted by the States, were selected for review. In their decisions in these cases, the Justices (except for Brennan and Marshall) agreed that capital punishment for murder was not inherently unconstitutional and instead focused on sentencing procedures.

In two of the cases, involving statutes requiring an automatic death penalty for murder, the statutes were struck down: Woodson v. North Carolina, 428 U.S. 280 (1976); Roberts v. Louisiana, 428 U.S. 325 (1976). The Court (5-4) held that individualized consideration of the facts concerning the murder was essential.

The statutes in the other three 1975 term cases were sustained (7-2): Gregg v. Georgia, 428 U.S. 153 (1976) (statute providing for a separate hearing on sentencing and requiring the jury to find at least one of ten statutory aggravating factors); Proffitt v. Florida, 428 U.S. 242 (1976) (statute generally similar to Georgia's, except that the trial judge, rather than jury, was directed to weigh statutory aggravating and mitigating factors); Jurek v. Texas, 428 U.S. 262 (1976) (statute construed as requiring consideration of mitigating factors).

In 1988, the Court held that it was unconstitutional to impose a death sentence on a murder defendant who was 15 at the time of the murder—regardless of any aggravating circumstances of the crime. Thompson v. Oklahoma, 487 U.S. 815 (1988). The Court relied on what it considered to be a national consensus of "the evolving standards of decency that mark the progress of a maturing society" since half of the States permitting a death penalty had adopted such a policy.

The following year, in Stanford v. Kentucky, 492 U.S. 361 (1989), the Court in an opinion written by Justice Scalia (joined by Rehnquist, O'Connor, Kennedy, and White) held that there was no national consensus opposed to the death penalty for a murder defendant below 18, since at that time 22 of 37 death penalty States permitted that penalty for 16-year-olds and 25 permitted it for 17-year-olds. A separate plurality opinion written by Justice Scalia (joined by the other majority justices except O'Connor) rejected the dissenters' reliance on "other indicia, including public opinion polls, the views of interest groups and the positions adopted by various professional associations" and opposed the dissenters' position that the Court should bring its own judgment to bear on the acceptability of the death penalty for juvenile offenders.

In an opinion written by Justice Brennan (joined by Marshall, Blackmun, and Stevens), the dissenters contended that the plurality's exclusive focus on the laws enacted and applied by the States "would largely return the task of defining the contours of Eighth Amendment protection to political majorities." According to Justice Brennan, "it is for [the Court] ultimately to judge whether the Eighth Amendment permits imposition of the death penalty in a particular class of cases," and the "inquiry must also encompass what Justice Scalia calls, with evident but misplaced disdain, 'socioscientific' evidence."

In that same term, in Penry v. Lynaugh, 492 U.S. 302 (1989), the Court (5-4) vacated Penry's death sentence on the ground that the jury had not been instructed that it could consider mental retardation as a mitigating factor. However, the Court (5-4) rejected the claim that mental retardation categorically precludes a death sentence. Speaking for the majority, Justice O'Connor stated:

> In sum, mental retardation is a factor that may well lessen a defendant's culpability for a capital offense. But we cannot conclude today that the Eighth Amendment precludes the execution of any mentally retarded person of Penry's ability convicted of a capital offense simply by virtue of his or her mental retardation alone.

She added that in her view "the two state statutes prohibiting execution of the mentally retarded, even when added to the 14 States that have rejected capital punishment completely, do not provide sufficient evidence at present of a national consensus" (page 334). Justices Scalia, Rehnquist, Kennedy, and White concurred on the ground that execution of mentally retarded offenders did not contravene either prevailing standards at the time the Bill of Rights was adopted or the "evolving standards of decency."

It was not long before the *Penry* and *Stanford* decisions were reconsidered in the next two digested cases, *Atkins v. Virginia* (2002) and *Roper v. Simmons* (2005).

*****

Today the laws of 36 States still provide for imposition of the death penalty. But in the last few years the number of death sentences in the country has fallen drastically. Through the 1990s, about 300 prisoners a year were sentenced to death; since then the number has steadily dropped to 110 in 2007, when death sentences were imposed in only 18 States. Even in Texas, the State where death sentences have been most common, the number of death sentences has dropped 65 percent in the past ten years.

Not only has there been a drop in the number of death *sentences,* but it has become increasingly rare for death sentences *to be carried out.*

In 2007, 42 inmates (slightly more than 1 percent of those on death row) were executed—a 10-year low. The number dropped from 53 in 2006, but a principal reason for the reduction was that for several months many executions were stayed to await the decision of the Supreme Court in Baze v. Rees, __ U.S. __, 128 S.Ct. 1520 (2008), concerning the validity of the lethal injection method used by nearly all of the States allowing the death penalty (all except Nebraska). On April 16, 2008, by a 7-2 vote, the Court ruled that the legal injection method does not violate the Eighth Amendment. Following the announcement of the decision, a substantial number of previously stayed executions were rescheduled to be carried out.

The 42 executions in 2007 took place in 10 States; 26 of the 42 were executed in Texas. All of the 42 were men, and 22 were white, 14 black, and 6 Hispanic.

The 42 had, on the average, been on death row for over 10 years. Some had been on death row for as long as 15 to 25 years. (One Texas prisoner still awaiting execution has been on death row for 30 years.)

At the end of 2006, there were 3,350 inmates on death row: 660 in California, 397 in Florida, 393 in Texas; 3,300 men and 50 women; 1,517 white, 1,397 black, 359 Hispanic, and 77 others. At the end of 2007, the number had dropped only slightly to 3,263.

Executions in California are so backed up that the State would have to execute five prisoners a month for the next 10 years just to carry out the death sentences of those already on death row. The average wait for execution in the State is 17.2 years. Thirty prisoners have been on the California death row for more than 25 years, 119 for more than 20 years, and 408 for more than 10 years. Four times as many California death row prisoners have died from causes like suicide and AIDS than from execution.

Federal laws also provide for the death penalty for certain crimes. While State executions have been declining, federal executions have increased. From 1963 to 2001, there were none; since 2001, there have been three. Federal death rows now house 48 inmates, compared with 19 in 2000.

Atkins v. Virginia, 536 U.S. 304 (2002)

FACTS: Daryl Atkins was found guilty by a Virginia jury of abduction, armed robbery, and murder.

In the penalty hearing that followed, in support of the imposition of the death penalty, the State proved two aggravating circumstances—future dangerousness and vileness of the offense. To prove future dangerousness, the State relied on Atkins's 16 prior felony convictions as well as the testimony of four victims of his earlier robberies and assaults. To prove the vileness of the offense, the State relied upon the trial record, including pictures of the deceased's body that had been shot eight times. The defense relied on one witness, a psychologist, who testified that Atkins had an IQ of 59 and was in his opinion mildly retarded. In response, the State presented the testimony of another psychologist, who opined that Atkins was not mentally retarded but rather was of average intelligence. The jury sentenced Atkins to death.

On appeal, it was again contended that Atkins was retarded and on that ground cannot be sentenced to death. The Virginia Supreme Court rejected that contention, relying on Penry v. Lynaugh, 492 U.S. 302 (1989). Atkins's low IQ score, the Virginia Supreme Court held, was insufficient to warrant reduction of his sentence to life imprisonment.

Atkins appealed, claiming a violation of the Eighth Amendment (as incorporated in the Fourteenth Amendment Due Process Clause).

ISSUE: Does the death penalty for a mentally retarded offender constitute cruel and unusual punishment under the Eighth Amendment?

DECISION (per *Stevens,* 6-3): *Yes.*

In the 13 years since we decided *Penry,* the American public, legislators, scholars, and judges have deliberated over the question whether the death penalty should ever be imposed on a mentally retarded criminal. The consensus reflected in those deliberations informs our answer to the question presented by this case: whether such executions are "cruel and unusual punishments" prohibited by the Eighth Amendment.

As Chief Justice Warren stated in his opinion in Trop v. Dulles, 356 U.S. 86 (1958): "The basic concept underlying the Eighth Amendment is nothing less than the dignity of man. . . . The Amendment must draw its meaning from the evolving standards of decency that mark the progress of a maturing society."

The *Penry* decision recognized that the "clearest and most reliable objective evidence of contemporary values is the legislation enacted by the country's legislatures." But such objective evidence, though of great importance, does not wholly determine the controversy, for the Constitution contemplates that in the end our own judgment will be brought to bear on the question of the acceptability of the death penalty.

(1) In 1986 in *Penry,* the Court held that the enactment by two States of legislation prohibiting the imposition of the death penalty on mentally retarded offenders, "even when added to the 14 States that have rejected capital punishment completely, do not provide sufficient evidence at present of a national consensus."

Much has changed since then. Fifteen additional States have adopted such legislation. It is not so much the number of these States that is significant, but the consistency of the direction of change. The large number of States prohibiting the execution of mentally retarded persons (and the complete absence of States passing legislation reinstating the power to conduct such executions) provides powerful evidence that today our society views mentally retarded offenders as categorically less culpable than the average criminal. Moreover, even in those States that allow the execution of mentally retarded offenders, only a small number of such executions have taken place. The practice, therefore, has become truly unusual, and it is fair to say that a national consensus has developed against it.

[The opinion at this point includes a lengthy footnote contending that "Additional evidence makes it clear that this legislative judgment reflects a much broader social and professional consensus," citing the views of various psychologist organizations and religious groups. The footnote further states that "within the world community, the imposition of the death penalty for crimes committed by mentally retarded offenders is overwhelmingly disapproved" and that "polling data shows a widespread consensus among Americans, even those who support the death penalty, that executing the mentally retarded is wrong." According to the footnote, "Although these factors are by no means dispositive, their consistency with the legislative evidence lends further support to our conclusion that there is a consensus among those who have addressed the issue." (536 U.S. at 316 n. 21.)]

(2) Our own judgment also supports what we find to be a national consensus against the death penalty for mentally retarded persons.

Such persons frequently know the difference between right and wrong and are competent to stand trial. Because of their impairments, however, they have diminished capacities to understand and process information, to communicate, to abstract from mistakes and learn from experience, to engage in logical reasoning, to control impulses, and to understand the reactions of others. There is no evidence that they are more likely to engage in criminal conduct than others, but there is abundant evidence that they often act on impulse rather than pursuant to a premeditated plan, and that in group settings they are followers rather than leaders. Their deficiencies do not warrant an exemption from criminal sanctions, but they do diminish their personal culpability.

In light of these deficiencies, our death penalty jurisprudence provides two reasons consistent with the legislative consensus that the mentally retarded should be categorically excluded from execution.

(a) There is a serious question whether either of the two justifications we have recognized as a basis for the death penalty—retribution and deterrence—applies to mentally retarded offenders. With respect to retribution by society, the severity of the appropriate punishment necessarily depends on the culpability of the offender. With respect to deterrence of capital crimes by prospective offenders, the same cognitive and behavioral impairments that make mentally retarded defendants less morally culpable also make it less likely that their conduct will be influenced by awareness of the possibility of capital punishment.

(b) In addition, the risk that the death penalty will be imposed is enhanced by their lesser ability to make a persuasive showing of mitigation in the face of prosecutorial evidence of one or more aggravating factors. Mentally retarded defendants may be less able to give meaningful assistance to their counsel and are typically poor witnesses, and their demeanor may create an unwarranted impression of lack of remorse for their crimes.

Our independent evaluation of the issue reveals no reason to disagree with the judgment of the legislatures that have recently addressed the matter and concluded that death is not a suitable punishment for a mentally retarded criminal. Construing and applying the Eighth Amendment in the light of our "evolving standards of decency," we therefore conclude that such punishment is excessive and prohibited by the Eighth Amendment.

(3) To the extent there is serious disagreement about the execution of mentally retarded offenders, it is in determining which offenders are, in fact, retarded. Not all people who claim to be mentally retarded will be so impaired as to fall within the range of mentally retarded offenders about whom there is a national consensus. As was our approach in Ford v. Wainwright, 477 U.S. 399 (1986), with regard to determination of insanity, "we leave to the State[s] the task of developing appropriate ways to enforce the constitutional restriction upon its execution of sentences."

The judgment of the Virginia Supreme Court is reversed and the case is remanded for further proceedings not inconsistent with this opinion.

Scalia, dissenting (joined by Rehnquist and Thomas): Today's decision is the pinnacle of our Eighth Amendment death-is-different jurisprudence. Not only does it, like all of that jurisprudence, find no support in the text or history of the Eighth Amendment, it does not even have support in current social attitudes regarding the conditions that render an otherwise just death penalty inappropriate. Seldom has an opinion of this Court rested so obviously upon nothing but the personal views of its members.

Before today, our opinions consistently emphasized that Eighth Amendment judgments regarding the existence of social "standards" "should be informed by objective factors to the maximum possible extent" and should not be merely the subjective views of individual Justices. First in importance among such objective factors are the statutes passed by society's elected representatives. In this case, the Court pays lip service to these precedents as it miraculously extracts a "national consensus" forbidding execution of the mentally retarded from the fact that 18 States—less than *half* (47 percent) of the 38 States that permit capital punishment—have enacted legislation barring execution of the mentally retarded.

Our prior cases have generally required a much higher degree of agreement before finding a punishment cruel and unusual on "evolving standards" grounds. For example, we proscribed the death penalty for rape of an adult woman after finding that only one jurisdiction (Georgia) authorized such a punishment, and we supported the common-law prohibition of execution of the insane since not a single State authorizes such punishment. Similarly, *we invalidated* a life sentence without parole under a statute under which the criminal was treated more severely than he would have been in any other State.

What the Court calls evidence of "consensus" in the present case more closely resembles evidence that we found *inadequate* to establish consensus in earlier cases. For example, the Court in *Stanford* in 1989 upheld a state law permitting execution of defendants who committed a capital crime at age 16 where only 15 of the 36 death penalty States (42 percent) prohibited death for such offenders.

But the prize for the "Court's Most Feeble Effort" to fabricate "national consensus" must go to its appeal to the views of assorted professional and religious organizations, members of the so-called "world community," and respondents to opinion polls. As Chief Justice Rehnquist points out, the views of professional and religious organizations and the results of opinion polls are irrelevant in this case. Equally irrelevant are the practices of the "world community," whose notions of justice are (thankfully) not always those of our people. We must never forget that it is a Constitution for the United States of America that we are expounding.

Rehnquist, dissenting (joined by Scalia and Thomas): The question presented by this case is whether a national consensus deprives Virginia of the constitutional power to impose the death penalty on capital murder defendants like petitioner, i.e., those defendants who indisputably are competent to stand trial, aware of the punishment they are about to suffer and why, and whose mental retardation has been found an insufficiently compelling reason to lessen their individual responsibility for the crime. The Court pronounces the punishment cruel and unusual primarily because 18 States have passed laws limiting the death eligibility of certain defendants based on mental retardation alone, despite the fact that the laws of 19 other States besides Virginia continue to leave the question of proper punishment to the individuated consideration of sentencing judges or juries familiar with the particular offender and his or her crime.

I agree with Justice Scalia that the Court's assessment of the current legislative judgment regarding the execution of defendants like petitioner more resembles a *post hoc* rationalization for the majority's subjectively preferred result rather than any objective effort to ascertain the content of an evolving standard of decency. I write separately, however, to call attention to the defects in the Court's decision to place weight on foreign laws, the views of professional and religious organizations, and opinion polls in reaching its conclusion.

In making determinations about whether a punishment is cruel and unusual under the evolving standards of decency embraced by the Eighth Amendment, we ascribe primacy to legislative enactments because of the constitutional role legislatures play in expressing policy of a State. In a democratic society, the legislatures—not the courts—are constituted to respond to the will and consequently the moral values of the people.

Our opinions have also recognized that data concerning the actions of sentencing juries, though entitled to less weight than legislative judgments, is a significant and reliable index of contemporary values, because of the jury's function of maintaining a link between contemporary community values and the penal system.

In my view, these two sources—the work product of legislatures and sentencing jury determinations—ought to be the sole indicators by which courts ascertain the contemporary American conceptions of decency for purposes of the Eighth Amendment. They are the only objective indicia of contemporary values firmly supported by our precedents. More importantly, however, they can be reconciled with the undeniable precepts that the democratic branches of government and sentencing juries are, by design, better suited than courts to evaluating and giving effect to the complex societal and moral considerations that inform the selection of publicly acceptable criminal punishments.

Completely absent from the record in this case are any comprehensive statistics that would prove (or disprove) whether juries routinely consider death a disproportionate punishment for mentally retarded offenders. Instead, the majority adverts to the fact that other countries have disapproved imposition of the death penalty for crimes committed by mentally retarded offenders. I fail to see, however, how the views of other countries regarding the punishment of their citizens provide any support for the Court's ultimate determination. Our prior decisions have explicitly rejected the idea that the sentencing practices of other countries could serve to establish whether a practice is accepted or not accepted among our people. To resolve that question, as the *Stanford* opinion pointed out, "*American* conceptions of decency . . . are dispositive" (emphasis in original). If it is evidence of a *national* consensus for which we are looking, then the viewpoints of other countries simply are not relevant.

To further buttress its appraisal of contemporary societal values, the Court marshals the statements of several professional organizations and religious groups opposing the death penalty for mentally retarded offenders. In my view, none of these statements should be accorded any weight on the Eighth Amendment scale when the elected representatives of a State's populace have not deemed them persuasive enough to prompt legislative action. For the Court to rely on such data today serves only to illustrate its willingness to proscribe by judicial fiat—at the behest of private organizations speaking only for themselves—a punishment about which no across-the-board consensus has developed through the workings of normal democratic processes in the States.

Even if I were to accept the legitimacy of the Court's decision to reach beyond the product of legislatures and practices of sentencing juries to discern a national standard of decency, I would take issue with the blind-faith credence it accords opinion polls. An extensive body of social science literature describes how methodological and other errors can affect the reliability and validity of estimates about the opinions and attitudes of a population derived from various sampling techniques. Everything from variations in the survey methodology, such as the choice of the target population, the sampling design used, the questions asked, and the statistical analyses used to interpret the data can skew the results.

There are strong reasons for limiting our inquiry into what constitutes an evolving standard of decency under the Eighth Amendment to the laws passed by legislatures and the practices of sentencing juries in America. Here, the majority goes beyond these well-established objective indicators of contemporary values. It finds further support for its conclusion in international opinion, the views of professional and religious organizations, and opinion polls not demonstrated to be reliable. Believing this view to be seriously mistaken, I dissent.

The Aftermath of the *Penry* and *Atkins* Cases

In holding that mental retardation precludes the death penalty, *Atkins* overruled Penry v. Lynaugh, 492 U.S. 302 (1989). In *Penry,* although rejecting mental retardation as a bar to the death penalty, the Supreme Court nevertheless had vacated Penry's death sentence on the ground that the jury had not been told that it could consider retardation as a mitigating factor. On retrial of the punishment issue, Penry was again sentenced to death, but in 2001 the Supreme Court reversed that sentence, again because of faulty jury instructions. In 2002 in his third punishment trial, following the *Atkins* decision, the jury decided that Penry's impairment did not reach the level of mental retardation and again sentenced him to death. In October 2005 that ruling was reversed by a sharply divided Texas Court of Criminal Appeals, which held (5-4) that the trial judge's instructions to the jury were deficient and ordered a fourth trial to determine Penry's punishment. Ultimately, Penry was spared the death penalty because of the Supreme Court's ruling in the *Atkins* case.

In *Atkins,* the Court placed reliance on the testimony of a psychologist who had testified on behalf of the defense that Atkins had an IQ of only 59. However, when the case was remanded to the state courts for a new trial on the retardation issue, experts for both the prosecution and defense testified that Atkins's IQ was between 74 and 76. The jury rejected the claim of mental retardation and again sentenced him to death, but the Virginia Supreme Court reversed Atkins's death sentence again, this time on the ground that the jury had been told that another jury had previously upheld Atkins's death sentence. Subsequently, it was learned that the prosecution had improperly withheld evidence suggesting that it was Atkins's accomplice in the murder who had actually pulled the trigger. Instead of ordering a third trial on the retardation issue, the trial judge commuted Atkins's sentence to life imprisonment.

It is generally recognized that no single criterion can be utilized to diagnose mental retardation and that three criteria must be met: (1) an IQ below 70, (2) significant limitations in the ability to function at age level in an ordinary environment, and (3) evidence that the limitations became apparent in childhood. Mild retardation (IQ 60–70) may not be obvious in early years; even when poor academic performance is considered, expert assessment may be necessary to distinguish mild retardation from learning disability or behavior problems. By contrast, moderate retardation (IQ 50–60) is nearly always obvious in early years; these individuals will encounter difficulty in school, at home, and in the community, and may require special classes. Severe retardation (IQ below 50) will require more intensive support and supervision throughout the person's life.

Roper v. Simmons, 543 U.S. 551 (2005)

FACTS: Christopher Simmons, then 17, discussed with two friends his plan to burglarize a house and then commit a murder by tying up the victim and pushing the victim from a bridge. Simmons said they could "get away with it" because they were minors. Several days later, Simmons and one of the friends broke into Shirley Crook's home in the middle of the night, forced her from her bed, bound her, and drove her to a state park. There, they walked her to a railroad trestle spanning a river, "hog-tied" her with electrical cable, bound her face completely with duct tape, and pushed her, still alive, from the trestle. She drowned in the water below.

At Simmons's trial, after the jury found Simmons guilty of murder, the trial then proceeded to the penalty phase. The State sought the death penalty. Among the aggravating factors relied on, the State contended that the murder involved depravity of mind and was outrageously and wantonly vile, horrible, and inhuman.

The defense contended that the death penalty for Simmons would, because of his age, constitute cruel and unusual punishment. In response, the State relied on Stanford v. Kentucky, 492 U.S. 361 (1989), holding that the death penalty for a murder committed by an under-18 offender was not barred by the Eighth Amendment.

The jury recommended the death penalty after finding that the State had proved the required aggravating factors. Accepting the jury's recommendation, the trial judge imposed the death penalty.

Simmons obtained new counsel, who moved in the trial court to set aside the conviction and sentence. In the postconviction hearing, testimony was presented that

Simmons was "very immature," "very impulsive," and "very susceptible to being manipulated or influenced." Clinical psychologists testified about Simmons's background, including a difficult home environment and dramatic changes in behavior, accompanied by poor school performance in adolescence. The trial judge denied the motion for postconviction relief.

In a consolidated appeal from Simmons's conviction and the denial of postconviction relief, the Missouri Supreme Court affirmed Simmons's sentence. The federal courts denied Simmons's petition for a writ of habeas corpus.

Subsequently the U.S. Supreme Court held in Atkins v. Virginia, 536 U.S. 304 (2002), that the Eighth Amendment prohibits the execution of a mentally retarded person. Relying on *Atkins* and its reasoning, Simmons filed a new petition for postconviction relief in the Missouri courts, contending that there was now a national consensus against the execution of a juvenile offender under 18 and that *Stanford v. Kentucky* was therefore no longer controlling.

The Missouri Supreme Court sustained Simmons's contention and held that his death sentence was barred by the Eighth Amendment. The State appealed to the U.S. Supreme Court.

ISSUE: Does the Eighth Amendment prohibit capital punishment of juvenile offenders under 18 at the time of the crime?

DECISION (per *Kennedy,* 5-4): *Yes.*

(a) The Eighth Amendment's prohibition against "cruel and unusual punishments" must be interpreted by considering history, tradition, and precedent, and with due regard for its purpose and function. To implement this framework this Court has established the propriety and affirmed the necessity of referring to "the evolving standards of decency that mark the progress of a maturing society" to determine which punishments are so disproportionate as to be "cruel and unusual." Trop v. Dulles, 356 U.S. 86 (1958).

In Thompson v. Oklahoma, 487 U.S. 815 (1958), a plurality determined that national standards of decency did not permit the execution of any offender under age 16 at the time of the crime. The next year, in *Stanford,* the Court held that there was no national consensus against the execution of offenders over 15 because 22 of 37 death penalty States permitted that penalty for 16-year-old offenders and 25 permitted it for 17-year-olds.

On the same day that *Stanford* was decided, the Court in Penry v. Lynaugh, 492 U.S. 302 (1989), rejected a categorical exemption from the death penalty for mentally retarded persons because only two States had enacted laws banning such executions. But three terms ago in *Atkins,* the Court held that standards of decency had evolved since *Penry* and now demonstrated that the execution of the mentally retarded is cruel and unusual punishment. After observing that mental retardation diminishes personal culpability even if the offender can distinguish right from wrong, and that mentally retarded offenders' impairments make it less defensible to impose the death penalty as retribution for past crimes or as a real deterrent to future crimes, the Court ruled that the death penalty constitutes an excessive sanction for the entire category of mentally retarded offenders.

Just as the *Atkins* Court reconsidered the issue decided in *Penry,* the Court now reconsiders the issue decided in *Stanford.*

(b) Both objective indicia of consensus, as expressed in particular by the enactments of legislatures that have addressed the question, and the Court's own determination in the exercise of its independent judgment, demonstrate that the death penalty is a disproportionate punishment for juveniles.

(1) As in *Atkins,* the objective indicia of national consensus here—the rejection of the juvenile death penalty in the majority of States; the infrequency of its use even where it remains on the books; and the consistency in the trend toward abolition of the practice—provide sufficient evidence that today society views juveniles, in the words *Atkins* used respecting the mentally retarded, as "categorically less culpable than the average criminal." The evidence of such consensus is similar, and in some respects parallel, to the evidence in *Atkins:* 30 States prohibit the juvenile death penalty, including 12 that have rejected it altogether and 18 that maintain it but, by express provision or judicial interpretation, exclude juveniles from its reach. Moreover, even in the 20 States without a formal prohibition, the execution of juveniles is infrequent.

There is, to be sure, at least one difference between the evidence of a national consensus in *Atkins* and in this case. Impressive in *Atkins* was the rate of abolition of the death penalty for the mentally retarded. Sixteen States that permitted the execution of the mentally retarded at the time of *Penry* had prohibited the practice by the time we heard *Atkins.* By contrast, five States that allowed the juvenile death penalty at the time of *Stanford* have abandoned it in the intervening 15 years—four through legislative enactments and one through judicial decision.

Although the rate of change in reducing the incidence of the juvenile death penalty has been less dramatic, the difference between this case and *Atkins* in that respect is counterbalanced by the consistent direction of the change toward abolition. Indeed, the slower pace here may be explained by the simple fact that the impropriety of executing juveniles between 16 and 18 years old gained wide recognition earlier than the impropriety of executing the mentally retarded.

(2) Rejection of the imposition of the death penalty on juvenile offenders under 18 is required by the Eighth Amendment.

Three general differences between juveniles under 18 and adults demonstrate that juvenile offenders cannot with reliability be classified among the worst offenders. Juveniles' susceptibility to immature and irresponsible behavior means their irresponsible conduct is not as morally reprehensible as that of an adult. Their own vulnerability and comparative lack of control over their immediate surroundings mean juveniles have a greater claim than adults to be forgiven for failing to escape negative influences in their whole environment. And the reality that juveniles still struggle to define their identity means it is less supportable to conclude that even a heinous crime committed by a juvenile is evidence of irretrievably depraved character.

The *Thompson* plurality recognized the import of these characteristics with respect to juveniles under 16. The same reasoning applies to all juvenile offenders under 18. Once juveniles' diminished culpability is recognized, it is evident that neither of the two penological justifications for the death penalty—retribution and deterrence of capital crimes by prospective offenders—provides adequate justification for imposing that penalty on juveniles.

Although the Court cannot deny or overlook the brutal crimes too many juvenile offenders have committed, it disagrees with the State's contention that, given the Court's own insistence on individualized consideration in capital sentencing, it is arbitrary and unnecessary to adopt a categorical rule barring imposition of the death penalty on an offender under 18. An unacceptable likelihood exists that the brutality or cold-blooded nature of any particular crime would overpower mitigating arguments based on youth as a matter of course, even where the juvenile offender's objective immaturity, vulnerability, and lack of true depravity should require a sentence less severe than death. When a juvenile commits a heinous crime, the State can exact forfeiture of some of the most basic liberties, but the State cannot extinguish his life and his potential to attain a mature understanding of his own humanity.

While drawing the line at 18 is subject to the objections always raised against categorical rules, that is the point where society draws the line for many purposes between childhood and adulthood and the age at which the line for death eligibility ought to rest. *Stanford* should be deemed no longer controlling.

(c) Our determination that the death penalty is disproportionate punishment for offenders under 18 finds confirmation in the stark reality that the United States is the only country in the world that continues to give official sanction to the juvenile death penalty. This reality does not become controlling, for the task of interpreting the Eighth Amendment remains our responsibility. Nevertheless, the Court's opinions have referred to the laws of other countries and to international authorities as instructive for its interpretation of the Eighth Amendment's prohibition of cruel and unusual punishments.

Article 37 of the United Nations Convention on the Rights of the Child, which every country in the world has ratified save for the United States and Somalia, contains an express prohibition on capital punishment for crimes committed by juveniles under 18. Parallel prohibitions are contained in other significant international covenants. Even before these covenants came into being, the United Kingdom abolished the juvenile death penalty,

The opinion of the world community, while not controlling our outcome, does provide respected and significant confirmation for our own conclusions. It does not lessen our fidelity to the Constitution or our pride in its origins to acknowledge that the express affirmation of certain fundamental rights by other nations and peoples simply underscores the centrality of those same rights within our own heritage of freedom.

Stevens, concurring (joined by Ginsburg): Perhaps even more important than our specific holding today is our reaffirmation of the basic principle that informs the Court's interpretation of the Eighth Amendment. If the meaning of that amendment had been frozen when it was originally drafted, it would impose no impediment to the execution of 7-year-old children today. The evolving standards of decency that have driven our construction of this critically important part of the Bill of Rights foreclose any such reading of the Amendment. In the best tradition of the common law, the pace of that evolution is a matter for continuing debate; but that our understanding of the Constitution does change from time to time has been settled since John Marshall breathed life into its text. If great lawyers of his day—Alexander Hamilton, for example—were sitting with us today, I would expect them to join Justice Kennedy's opinion for the Court. In all events, I do so without hesitation.

O'Connor, dissenting: The Court's decision today establishes a categorical rule forbidding the execution of any offender for any crime committed before his eighteenth birthday, no matter how deliberate, wanton, or cruel the offense, and regardless of the degree of the individual offender's maturity and capacities. Neither the objective evidence of contemporary societal values, nor the Court's moral proportionality analysis, nor the two in tandem, suffice to justify this ruling.

Although the Court finds support for its decision in the fact that a majority of the States now disallow capital punishment of 17-year-old offenders, it refrains from asserting that its holding is compelled by a genuine national consensus. Indeed, the evidence before us fails to demonstrate conclusively that any such consensus has emerged in the brief period since we upheld the constitutionality of this practice in *Stanford*.

Instead, the rule decreed by the Court rests, ultimately, on its independent moral judgment that death is a disproportionately severe punishment for any 17-year-old offender. I do not subscribe to this judgment. Adolescents *as a class* are undoubtedly less mature, and therefore less culpable for their misconduct, than adults. But the Court has adduced no evidence impeaching the seemingly reasonable conclusion reached by many state legislatures: that at least *some* 17-year-old murderers are sufficiently mature to deserve the death penalty in an appropriate case. Nor has it been shown that capital sentencing juries are incapable of accurately assessing a youthful defendant's maturity or of giving due weight to the mitigating characteristics associated with youth.

The Court's analysis is premised on differences *in the aggregate* between juveniles and adults, which frequently do not hold true when comparing individuals. Although it may be that many 17-year-old murderers lack sufficient maturity to deserve the death penalty, some juvenile murderers may be quite mature. Chronological age is not an unfailing measure of psychological development, and common experience suggests that many 17-year-olds are more mature than the average young "adult." In short, the class of offenders exempted from capital punishment by today's decision is too broad and too diverse to warrant a categorical prohibition. Indeed, the age-based line drawn by the Court is indefensibly arbitrary—it quite likely will protect a number of offenders who are mature enough to deserve the death penalty and may well leave vulnerable many who are not.

On this record—and especially in light of the fact that so little has changed since our recent decision in *Stanford*—I would not substitute our judgment about the moral propriety of capital punishment for 17-year-old murderers for the judgments of the nation's legislatures. Rather, I would demand a clearer showing that our society truly has set its face against this practice before reading the Eighth Amendment categorically to forbid it.

With respect to the Court's discussion of foreign and international law, because I do not believe that a genuine *national* consensus against the juvenile death penalty has yet developed, the evidence of an *international* consensus does not alter my determination that the Eighth Amendment does not, at this time, forbid capital punishment of 17-year-old murderers in all cases. Nevertheless, I disagree with Justice Scalia's contention in his dissenting opinion that foreign and international law has no place in our Eighth Amendment jurisprudence.

Scalia, dissenting (joined by Rehnquist and Thomas): In reaching its decision, the Court adverts to "the evolving standards of decency" of our national society. It then finds, on the flimsiest of grounds, that a national consensus that could not be perceived in our people's laws barely 15 years ago now solidly exists. Worse still, the Court says in so many words that what our people's laws say about the issue does not, in the last analysis, matter: "[I]n the end our own judgment will be brought to bear on the question of the acceptability of the death penalty under the Eighth Amendment." The Court thus proclaims itself sole arbiter of our nation's moral standards—and in the course of discharging that awesome responsibility purports to take guidance from the views of foreign courts and legislatures. I do not believe that the meaning of our Eighth Amendment, any more than the meaning of other provisions of our Constitution, should be determined by the subjective views of five members of this Court and like-minded foreigners.

Words have no meaning if the views of less than 50 percent of death penalty States can constitute a national consensus. In *Atkins,* the Court found additional support in the fact that 16 States had prohibited execution of mentally retarded individuals since *Penry.* Now, the Court says a legislative change in just *four* States is "significant" enough to trigger a constitutional prohibition. (Washington State's decision to prohibit executions of offenders under 18 was made by a judicial, not legislative, decision, that did not purport to reflect popular sentiment and is irrelevant to the question of changed national consensus.)

Our previous cases have required overwhelming opposition to a challenged practice, generally over a long period of time. And *none* of our cases dealing with an alleged constitutional limitation upon the death penalty has counted (as States supporting a consensus in favor of that limitation) States that have eliminated the death penalty entirely, and with good reason. Including States that bar the death penalty concerning the necessity of making an exception to the penalty for offenders under 18 is rather like including old-order Amishmen in a consumer-preference poll on the electric car. *Of course* they do not like it, but that sheds no light whatever on the point at issue. That 12 States favor *no* executions says something about consensus against the death penalty, but nothing—absolutely nothing—about consensus that offenders under 18 deserve special immunity from such a penalty. In repealing the death penalty, those 12 States considered *none* of the factors that the Court puts forth as determinative of the issue before us today—lower culpability of the young, inherent recklessness, lack of capacity for considered judgment, etc.

Since *Stanford,* moreover, a number of legislatures and voters have *affirmed* their support for capital punishment of 16- and 17-year-old offenders. Though the Court is correct that no State has lowered its death penalty age, both the Missouri and Virginia Legislatures—which, at the time of *Stanford,* had no minimum age requirement— expressly established 16 as the minimum. The people of Arizona and Florida have done the same by ballot initiative.

The Court's reliance on the alleged infrequency of executing under-18 murderers credits an argument that this Court considered and explicitly rejected in *Stanford.* That infrequency is explained, we accurately said, both by the undisputed fact that a far smaller percentage of capital crimes are committed by persons under 18 than over, and by the fact that juries are required at sentencing to consider the offender's youth as a mitigating factor. Thus, as pointed out in *Stanford*, "it is not only possible, but overwhelmingly probable, that the very considerations which induce [Simmons] and [his] supporters to believe that death should *never* be imposed on offenders under 18 cause prosecutors and juries to believe that it should *rarely* be imposed."

Of course, the real force driving today's decision is not the actions of four state legislatures, but the Court's "own judgment" that murderers younger than 18 can never be as morally culpable as older counterparts. Having declared reliance on "the evolving standards of decency" of our society, it makes no sense for the Court then to *prescribe* those standards rather than discern them from the practices of our people. By what conceivable warrant can nine lawyers presume to be the authoritative conscience of the nation?

Today's opinion provides a perfect example of why judges are ill-equipped to make the type of legislative judgments the Court insists on making here. To support its opinion that States should be prohibited from imposing the death penalty on anyone who committed murder before age 18, the Court looks to scientific and sociological studies, picking and choosing those that support its position. It never explains why those particular studies are methodologically sound; none was ever entered into evidence or tested in an adversarial proceeding. In other words, all the Court has done today, to borrow from another context, is to look over the heads of the crowd and pick out its friends.

We need not look far to find studies contradicting the Court's conclusions. For example, the American Psychological Association (APA), which claims in this case that scientific evidence shows persons under 18 lack the ability to take moral responsibility for their decisions, has previously taken precisely the opposite position before this very Court. In its brief in Hodgson v. Minnesota, 497 U.S. 417 (1990), the APA found a "rich body of research" showing that juveniles are mature enough to decide whether to obtain an abortion without parental involvement. Given the nuances of scientific methodology and conflicting views, courts—which can only consider the limited evidence on the record before them—are ill-equipped to determine which view of science is the right one. Legislatures are better qualified to weigh and evaluate the results of statistical studies in terms of their own local conditions and with a flexibility of approach that is not available to the courts.

Even putting aside questions of methodology, the studies cited by the Court offer scant support for a categorical prohibition of the death penalty for murderers under 18. At most, these studies conclude that, *on average,* or *in most cases,* persons under 18 are unable to take moral responsibility for their actions. Not one of the cited studies opines that all individuals under 18 are unable to appreciate the nature of their crimes.

The studies the Court cites in no way justify a constitutional imperative that prevents legislatures and juries from treating exceptional cases in an exceptional way—by determining that some murders are not just the acts of happy-go-lucky teenagers, but heinous crimes deserving of death.

That "almost every State prohibits those under 18 years of age from voting, serving on juries, or marrying without parental consent," is patently irrelevant—and is yet another resurrection of an argument that this Court gave a decent burial in *Stanford.* As we explained in *Stanford,* it is "absurd to think that one must be mature enough to drive carefully, to drink responsibly, or to vote intelligently, in order to be mature enough to understand that murdering another human being is profoundly wrong, and to conform one's conduct to that most minimal of all civilized standards." Serving on a jury or entering into marriage also involves decisions far more sophisticated than the simple decision not to take another's life.

Moreover, the age statutes the Court lists set the appropriate ages for the operation of a system that makes its determinations in gross, and that does not conduct individualized maturity tests. The criminal justice system, by contrast, provides for individualized consideration of each defendant. In capital cases, this Court requires the sentencer to make an individualized determination, which includes weighing aggravating factors and mitigating factors, such as youth. In other contexts where individualized consideration is provided, we have recognized that at least some minors will be mature enough to make difficult decisions that involve moral considerations. For instance, we have struck down abortion statutes that do not allow minors deemed mature by courts to bypass parental notification provisions. It is hard to see why this context should be any different. Whether to obtain an abortion is surely a much more complex decision for a young person than whether to kill an innocent person in cold blood.

The Court concludes, however, that juries cannot be trusted with the delicate task of weighing a defendant's youth along with the other mitigating and aggravating factors of his crime. This startling conclusion undermines the very foundations of our capital sentencing system, which entrusts juries with making the difficult and uniquely human judgments that defy codification and that build discretion, equity, and flexibility into a legal system. The Court suggests that juries will be unable to appreciate the significance of a defendant's youth when faced with details of a brutal crime. This assertion is based on no evidence; to the contrary, the Court itself acknowledges that the execution of under-18 offenders is "infrequent" even in the States "without a formal prohibition on executing juveniles," suggesting that juries take seriously their responsibility to weigh youth as a mitigating factor.

To the extent our Eighth Amendment decisions constitute something more than a show of hands on the current justices' current personal views about penology, they purport to be nothing more than a snapshot of American public opinion at a particular point in time (with the time frames now apparently shortened to a mere 15 years). The "evolution" of the Eighth Amendment is no longer determined by objective criteria, and the result will be to crown arbitrariness with chaos.

The Death Penalty in Non-Murder Cases

In Coker v. Georgia, 433 U.S. 584 (1977), the Court held (7-2) that a State may not impose a death sentence for rape of an adult woman. The Eighth Amendment, the Court stated, bars not only punishments that are "barbaric" but also those that are "excessive" in relation to the crime committed, and a "punishment is 'excessive' and unconstitutional if it (1) makes no measurable contribution to acceptable goals of punishment and hence is nothing more than the purposeless and needless imposition of pain and suffering; or (2) is grossly out of proportion to the severity of the crime." In rejecting the death penalty for the rape of an adult woman, the Court concluded that

> Rape is without doubt deserving of serious punishment; but in terms of moral depravity and of the injury to the person and to the public, it does not compare with murder, which does involve the unjustified taking of human life. Although it may be accompanied by another crime, rape by definition does not include the death of or even the serious injury to another person. The murderer kills; the rapist, if no more than that, does not. Life is over for the victim of the murderer; for the rape victim, life may not be nearly so happy as it was, but it is not over and normally is not beyond repair.

The Court also emphasized that "Georgia is the sole jurisdiction in the United States at the present time [1977] that authorizes a sentence of death when the rape victim is an adult woman, and only two other jurisdictions provide capital punishment when the victim is a child."

In Enmund v. Florida, 458 U.S. 782 (1982), the Court applied its *Coker* analysis to the death penalty for conviction of "felony murder"—the crime of participating with others in a felony (such as a robbery) that results in a murder, even though the defendant did not personally commit the murder. The Court (5-4) ruled that death is an unconstitutional penalty for felony murder if the defendant did not himself kill, or attempt to take life, or intend that anyone be killed. The Court emphasized that most states did not allow capital punishment in felony murder cases and that evidence of jury decisions and other consensus indicia also showed an opposition to the death penalty in such circumstances.

However, in Tison v. Arizona, 481 U.S. 137 (1987), the Court backtracked somewhat from *Enmund*. Relying on an "apparent consensus" among the States, the Court held (5-4) that "major participation in the felony committed, combined with reckless indifference to human life, is sufficient to satisfy the *Enmund* culpability requirement."

How should these precedents be applied to capital punishment for the rape of a *child?* That was the issue in the recent case of Kennedy v. Louisiana, __ U.S. __, 128 S.Ct. 2641 (2008), concerning the constitutionality of a Louisiana statute permitting the death penalty for the rape of a child under the age of 12. After the Louisiana statute was enacted in 1995, five other States (Georgia, Montana, Oklahoma, South Carolina, and Texas) also passed legislation making child rape a capital offense, but (unlike Louisiana) only for a defendant who had committed a previous sex crime. No one has been sentenced to death under any of these laws.

The defendant in the case, Patrick Kennedy, was sentenced to death for the rape of his 8-year-old stepdaughter. In a 5 to 4 decision having the effect of invalidating all six statutes, the Supreme Court ruled that imposing the death penalty for raping a child is unconstitutional if the victim was not killed. In an opinion by Justice Kennedy, the Court held that "The death penalty is not a proportional punishment for the rape of a child" under "the evolving standards of decency that mark the progress of a maturing society" and that "the death penalty should not be expanded to instances where the victim's life was not taken." (128 S.Ct. at 2659, 2664.) According to the Court, "Thirty-seven jurisdictions—36 States plus the Federal Government—have the death penalty. [But] only six of these jurisdictions authorize the death penalty for rape of a child." (Id. at 2653.) This, the Court concluded, demonstrates a "national consensus" against it.[2]

In an opinion by Justice Alito (joined by Roberts, Scalia, and Thomas), the dissenters contended that "The harm that is caused to the victims and to society at large by the worst child rapists is grave," and that the Court should sustain "the judgment of the Louisiana lawmakers and those in an increasing number of other States that these harms justify the death penalty." (Id. at 2677.) The dissent also protested that the majority had ruled out executing someone for raping a child "no matter how young the child, no matter how many times the child is raped, no matter how many children the perpetrator rapes, no matter how sadistic the crime, no matter how much physical or psychological trauma is inflicted, and no matter how heinous the perpetrator's prior criminal record may be." (Id. at 2665.)

*****

[*Note:* After the decision, it was pointed out that the majority's statement concerning federal law (quoted above) is incorrect. In fact, Congress in 2006 amended the sex

---

[2]The Court added, however, that "Our concern here is limited to crimes against individual persons. We do not address, for example, crimes defining and punishing treason, espionage, terrorism, and drug kingpin activity, which are offenses against the State." (128 S.Ct. at 2659.)

crimes section of the Uniform Code of Military Justice to allow the death penalty for child rape. See, for example, Linda Greenhouse, "In Court Ruling on Executions, a Factual Flaw," *New York Times,* July 2, 2008. Although supporting the Court's conclusion in the case that the death penalty should be limited to homicides, the *Washington Post* editorialized that the Court should grant rehearing because "The Supreme Court's legitimacy depends not only on the substance of its rulings but also on the quality of its deliberation." The *Post* noted "that the various parties failed to identify the recently enacted UCMJ provision," as did "the mainstram media, which only picked up the story after a blogger noted the mistake." Editorial, "Supreme Slip-Up," *Washington Post,* July 5, 2008. Among others, constitutional law professor Lawrence Tribe joined in the criticism, calling the Court's *Kennedy* decision "its seriously misinformed as well as morally misguided ruling." Lawrence Tribe, "The Supreme Court Is Wrong on the Death Penalty," *Wall Street Journal,* July 31, 2008. On October 1, 2008, the Court denied the State's petition for rehearing and modified the Court's opinion by adding a footnote stating that, "we find that the military penalty does not affect our reasoning or conclusions."]

Proportionality in Non-Capital Cases

Cruel and unusual punishment issues may arise not only in challenges to the death penalty but also in claims in non-capital cases that long prison sentences are "grossly disproportionate" to the crimes committed. Such claims are common under state recidivist statutes that impose increased punishment on defendants who have committed three or more felonies.

In Rummel v. Estelle, 445 U.S. 263 (1980), the Court (5-4) upheld a mandatory life sentence under a recidivist statute following a third felony conviction. The Court rejected the defendant's reliance on the nonviolent nature of the felonies and the small amount of money involved in the felonies ($230).

Rummel was distinguished in Solem v. Helm, 463 U.S. 277 (1983). Helm, like Rummel, had been sentenced to life imprisonment under a recidivist statute following conviction for a nonviolent felony involving a small amount of money. Helm's sentence, however, was held (5-4) to be disproportionate and therefore cruel and unusual because Helm's sentence was life imprisonment without possibility of parole, whereas Rummel was eligible for parole after 12 years. In only one other State, according to the Court, could he have received so harsh a sentence, and in no other State was it mandatory.

But in Harmelin v. Michigan, 501 U.S. 957 (1991), the Court held (5-4) that a mandatory term of life imprisonment without possibility of parole was not cruel and unusual as applied to the crime of possession of more than 650 grams of cocaine. Three of the five Justices in the majority (Kennedy, O'Connor, and Souter) concluded that the sentence was not disproportionate; two (Scalia and Rehnquist) contended that there are no adequate textual or historical standards to enable judges to determine whether a particular penalty is disproportionate.

In Ewing v. California, 538 U.S. 11 (2003), the Court affirmed (5-4) a sentence of 25 years to life under California's "Three Strikes, You're Out" law. After numerous previous felony convictions (grand theft, battery, burglary, appropriating lost property, firearms violation, and other offenses), the defendant's conviction that led to application of the "Three Strikes" law was a conviction of felony grand theft for stealing three golf clubs, worth $399 apiece. Three of the five Justices in the majority (O'Connor, Rehnquist, and Kennedy) concluded that the sentence was not grossly disproportionate and therefore did not violate the Eighth Amendment; two (Scalia and Thomas) rejected use of a judicial proportionality standard altogether. Justices Breyer, Stevens, Souter, and Ginsburg dissented.

17

Property Rights

From Locke to *Kelo*

The ideas underlying the Declaration of Independence and the Constitution reflected, in large measure, the writings of the English philosophers——particularly John Locke, in many respects the intellectual father of the American Revolution.

Locke's central political principle was that the right of property is the very basis of human freedom and the primary right on which all others rested. He maintained that both society and government primarily exist to protect the preexisting natural right of property.

So when this nation was founded, the Framers viewed the protection of property as a key priority. According to James Madison, persons and property were "both essential objects of government," and John Adams expressed a common view when he said that "Property is surely a right of mankind as [much] as liberty."

Reflecting that view, several provisions were included in the Constitution to specifically protect property rights. One provision (Article I, §10) prohibits a State from enacting "any . . . Law impairing the Obligation of Contracts." The Fifth and Fourteenth Amendments prohibit depriving a person of "property" (as well as "life" and "liberty") without due process of law. And the Fifth Amendment requires not only "just compensation" for any taking of private property but also that the taking must be "for public use."

The Court has acknowledged that

> the dichotomy between personal liberties and property rights is a false one. Property does not have rights. People have rights. The right to enjoy property without unlawful deprivation, no less than the right to speak or the right to travel, is, in truth, a "personal" right. . . .
> In fact, a fundamental interdependence exists between the personal right to liberty and the personal right in property. Neither could have meaning without the other. That rights in property are basic civil rights has long been recognized [citing Locke, Adams, and Blackstone].

Lynch v. Household Finance Corp., 405 U.S. 538, 552 (1972).

But over the years, in the constellation of constitutional values, property rights have been accorded a distinctly inferior position in comparison with other personal rights. As Judge Learned Hand observed: "it began to seem, as though, when 'personal rights' were in issue, something strangely akin to the discredited attitude towards the Bill of

Rights of the old apostles of the institution of property, was regaining recognition. Just why property was not a 'personal right' nobody took the time to explain." [1]

The Court has relied on the "liberty" component of the Fourteenth Amendment Due Process Clause as the foundation for establishing rights that are otherwise unsupported in the Constitution. E.g., Roe v. Wade, 410 U.S. 113 (1973); Lawrence v. Texas, 539 U.S. 558 (2003). In addition, to assess the violation of "personal liberties," the Court has applied the most rigorous standard of review ("strict scrutiny"), thereby imposing on governmental bodies a heavy burden to justify their conduct. (See comments "Overview of the Equal Protection Clause" in Chapter 3 and "The Substantive Due Process Doctrine" in Chapter 6.)

In contrast, the property guarantees in the Constitution—particularly the Takings Clause—have been diluted by judicial interpretation.

A prime example has been the Supreme Court's classification of the taking of private property as merely another manifestation of so-called "police power"—an almost undefinable reservoir of authority exercised by a state or municipal government to protect safety, health, and morals and promote the public interest, and extending to an infinite variety of matters routinely involved in the management of government such as building codes and the hours of labor. Such police power matters can scarcely be equated with the taking of one's private property in terms of either historical status or impact on the dispossessed owner.

Nevertheless, by characterizing takings in that way, the Court thereby consigned takings to review by the lowest possible standard of judicial review—the "rational basis" test. The effect has been virtually automatic endorsement of whatever "public use" a state or city designates for a taking of private property. Among all the guarantees of the Bill of Rights, only the public use limitation is singled out for such extraordinary deference.

In Berman v. Parker, 348 U.S. 26 (1954), the Court stated:

> We deal, in other words, with what traditionally has been known as the police power. . . .
> In such cases, the legislature, not the judiciary, is the main guardian of the public needs to be served by societal legislation. . . . *This principle admits of no exception merely because the power of eminent domain is involved.* The role of the judiciary in determining whether that power is being exercised for a public purpose is an extremely narrow one. (Italics added.)

In Hawaii Housing Authority v. Midkiff, 467 U.S. 229 (1984), after quoting *Berman,* the Court stated that "[t]he 'public use' requirement is thus coterminous with the scope of a sovereign's police powers" and that the Court has never struck down an exercise of eminent domain power where the use of that power is "*rationally related* to a conceivable public purpose." (Italics added.)

In the next-digested case, *Kelo v. City of New London,* the Court again rejected any "heightened form of review" on the public use issue.

Kelo v. City of New London, 545 U.S. 524 (2005)

FACTS: In February 1998, the pharmaceutical company Pfizer Inc. announced that it would build a $300 million research facility on a site immediately adjacent to the Fort Trumbull area of New London, Connecticut. Local leaders hoped that Pfizer would

---

[1] Learned Hand, *The Spirit of Liberty* [Chicago 3d ed. 1960]: 205–206.

draw new business to the area, and this led to a plan for private development of 90 acres of the Fort Trumbull area. In addition to creating jobs, generating tax revenue, and helping to "build momentum for the revitalization of downtown New London," the plan was also designed to make the city more attractive and to create leisure and recreational opportunities on the waterfront and in the park. Included in the plan would be a waterfront conference hotel, offices, condominiums, restaurants, shopping, and parking.

Under the plan, the land would be acquired by the city for purchase by one or more private developers. The city bought most of the property earmarked for the project from willing sellers, but initiated condemnation proceedings when the owners of the rest of the property refused to sell. The objecting owners filed a state-court action claiming that the taking of their properties by eminent domain would not be for a "public use" and would therefore violate the Fifth Amendment Takings Clause (incorporated in the Due Process Clause of the Fourteenth Amendment).

Plaintiff Susette Kelo has lived in the Fort Trumbull area since 1997. Plaintiff Wilhelmina Dery was born in her Fort Trumbull house in 1918 and has lived there her entire life. Her husband Charles has lived in the house since they married some 60 years ago. In all, the nine plaintiffs own 15 properties in Fort Trumbull. Ten of the parcels are occupied by the owner or a family member; the other five are held as investment properties. There is no allegation that any of these properties is blighted or otherwise in poor condition; rather, they were condemned only because they happen to be located in the development area.

The Connecticut Supreme Court (by a 4-3 vote) upheld the proposed takings. The three dissenters found the takings unconstitutional because the city had failed to adduce "clear and convincing evidence" that the economic benefits of the plan would, in fact, come to pass.

ISSUE: Would the condemnation of the plaintiffs' property violate the Takings Clause?

DECISION (per *Stevens,* 5-4): *No.*

The city's proposed disposition of petitioners' property qualifies as a "public use" within the meaning of the Takings Clause.

Two polar propositions are perfectly clear. On the one hand, it has long been accepted that the sovereign may not take the property of *A* for the sole purpose of transferring it to another private party *B,* even though *A* is paid just compensation. On the other hand, it is equally clear that a state may transfer property from one private party to another if future "use by the public" is the purpose of the taking; the condemnation of land for a railroad with common-carrier duties is a familiar example. Neither of these propositions, however, determines the disposition of this case.

As for the first proposition, the city would no doubt be forbidden from taking petitioners' land for the purpose of conferring a private benefit on a particular private party. Nor would the city be allowed to take property under the mere pretext of a public purpose, when its actual purpose was to bestow a private benefit. In the present case, the takings would be executed pursuant to a carefully considered development plan, and the trial judge and all the members of the Supreme Court of Connecticut agreed that there was no evidence of an illegitimate purpose in this case. On the other hand, this is not a case in which the city is planning to open the condemned land to use by the general public. Nor will the private lessees of the land in any sense be required to operate like common carriers, making their services available to all comers.

Those who govern the city were not confronted with the need to remove blight in the Fort Trumbull area, but their determination that the area was sufficiently distressed to justify a program of economic rejuvenation is entitled to our deference. The city has carefully formulated an economic development plan that it believes will provide appreciable benefits to the community, including—but by no means limited to—new jobs and increased tax revenue. As with other exercises in urban planning and development, the city is endeavoring to coordinate a variety of commercial, residential, and recreational uses of land, with the hope that they will form a whole greater than the sum of its parts. Given the comprehensive character of the plan, the thorough deliberation that preceded its adoption, and the limited scope of our review, we conclude that the plan unquestionably serves a public purpose and therefore the takings challenged here satisfy the public use requirement of the Fifth Amendment.

To avoid this result, the plaintiffs urge us to adopt a new bright-line rule that economic development does not qualify as a public use. Neither precedent nor logic supports plaintiffs' proposal. Promoting economic development is a traditional and long accepted function of government. There is, moreover, no principled way of distinguishing economic development from the other public purposes that we have recognized. In our cases, for example, in Berman v. Parker, 348 U.S. 26 (1954), we endorsed the purpose of transforming a blighted area into a "well-balanced" community through redevelopment, and in Hawaii Housing Authority v. Midkiff, 467 U.S. 229 (1984), we upheld the interest in breaking up a land oligopoly that "created artificial deterrents to the normal functioning of the State's residential land market."

It is further argued that without a bright-line rule nothing would stop a city from transferring citizen A's property to citizen B for the sole reason that citizen B will put the property to a more productive use and thus pay more taxes. Such a one-to-one transfer of property, executed outside the confines of an integrated development plan, is not presented in this case. While such an unusual exercise of government power would certainly raise a suspicion that a private purpose was afoot, hypothetical cases of that nature can be confronted if and when they arise. They do not warrant the crafting of an artificial restriction on the concept of public use.

Alternatively, plaintiffs maintain that for takings of this kind we should require a "reasonable certainty" that the expected public benefits will actually accrue. Such a rule, however, would represent an even greater departure from our precedent. The disadvantages of a heightened form of review are especially pronounced in this type of case. Orderly implementation of a comprehensive redevelopment plan obviously requires that the legal rights of all interested parties be established before new construction can be commenced. A constitutional rule that required postponement of the judicial approval of every condemnation until the likelihood of success of the plan had been assured would unquestionably impose a significant impediment to the successful consummation of many such plans.

In affirming the city's authority to take plaintiffs' properties, we do not minimize the hardship that condemnations may entail, notwithstanding the payment of just compensation. This Court's authority, however, extends only to determining whether the city's proposed condemnations are for a public use within the meaning of the Fifth Amendment to the federal Constitution. The judgment of the Supreme Court of Connecticut is affirmed.

Kennedy, concurring: I join the opinion for the Court and add these further observations.

This Court has declared that a taking should be upheld as consistent with the Public Use Clause as long as it is rationally related to a conceivable public purpose. However, the determination that a rational-basis standard of review is appropriate does not alter the fact that transfers intended to confer benefits on particular, favored private entities, and with only incidental or pretextual public benefits, are forbidden by the Public Use Clause.

A court applying rational-basis review under the Public Use Clause should strike down a taking that, by a clear showing, is intended to favor a particular private party, with only incidental or pretextual public benefits. A court confronted with a plausible accusation of impermissible favoritism to private parties should treat the objection as a serious one and review the record to see if it has merit, though with the presumption that the government's actions were reasonable and intended to serve a public purpose. Here, the trial court conducted a careful and extensive inquiry into "whether, in fact, the development plan is of primary benefit to ... the [private] developer and private businesses which may eventually locate in the plan area [e.g., Pfizer], and in that regard, only of incidental benefit to the city." The trial court concluded that benefiting Pfizer was not "the primary motivation or effect of this development plan"; instead, "the primary motivation for [defendants] was to take advantage of Pfizer's presence." Likewise, the trial court concluded that "[t]here is nothing in the record to indicate that ... [defendants] were motivated by a desire to aid [other] particular private entities." This case, then, survives the meaningful rational basis review that in my view is required under the Public Use Clause.

The taking in this case occurred in the context of a comprehensive development plan meant to address a serious citywide depression, and the projected economic benefits of the project cannot be characterized as *de minimis.* The identity of most of the private beneficiaries were unknown at the time the city formulated its plans. The city complied with elaborate procedural requirements that facilitate review of the record and inquiry into the city's purposes. In sum, while there may be categories of cases in which the transfers are so suspicious, or the procedures employed are so prone to abuse, or the purported benefits are so trivial or implausible, that courts should presume an impermissible private purpose, no such circumstances are present in this case.

O'Connor, dissenting (joined by Rehnquist, Scalia, and Thomas): Under the banner of economic development, all private property is now vulnerable to being taken and transferred to another private owner, so long as it might be upgraded—i.e., given to an owner who will use it in a way that the legislature deems more beneficial to the public—in the process. To reason, as the Court does, that the incidental public benefits resulting from the subsequent ordinary use of private property render economic development takings "for public use" is to wash out any distinction between private and public use of property—and thereby effectively to delete the words "for public use" from the Takings Clause of the Fifth Amendment. Accordingly I dissent.

The Fifth Amendment to the Constitution, made applicable to the States by the Fourteenth Amendment, provides that "private property [shall not] be taken for public use, without just compensation." Thus the Fifth Amendment's language imposes two distinct conditions on the exercise of eminent domain: "the taking must be for a 'public use' and 'just compensation' must be paid to the owner." These two limitations serve to protect "the security of Property," which Alexander Hamilton described to the

Philadelphia Convention as one of the "great obj[ects] of Gov[ernment]." Together they ensure stable property ownership by providing safeguards against excessive, unpredictable, or unfair use of the government's eminent domain power—particularly against those owners who, for whatever reasons, may be unable to protect themselves in the political process against the majority's will.

The Takings Clause permits the taking of private property without the owner's consent only for the *public's* use, not for the benefit of another private person. Where is the line between "public" and "private" property use? We give considerable deference to legislatures' determinations about what governmental activities will advantage the public. But if the political branches were the sole arbiters of the public-private distinction, the Public Use Clause would amount to little more than hortatory fluff. An external, judicial check on how the public use requirement is interpreted, however limited, is necessary if this constraint on government power is to retain any meaning.

The facts of this case present an issue of first impression: Are economic development takings constitutional? I would hold that they are not. We are guided by two precedents about the taking of real property by eminent domain. In *Berman v. Parker,* we upheld takings within a blighted neighborhood of Washington, D.C. The neighborhood had so deteriorated that, for example, 64.3 percent of its dwellings were beyond repair. It had become burdened with "overcrowding of dwellings," "lack of adequate streets and alleys," and "lack of light and air." Congress had determined that the neighborhood had become "injurious to the public health, safety, morals, and welfare" and that it was necessary to "eliminat[e] all such injurious conditions by employing all means necessary and appropriate for the purpose," including eminent domain.

In *Hawaii Housing Authority v. Midkiff,* we upheld a land condemnation scheme in Hawaii whereby title in real property was taken from lessors and transferred to lessees. At that time, the state and federal governments owned nearly 49 percent of the state's land, and another 47 percent was in the hands of only 72 private landowners. Concentration of land ownership was so dramatic that on the state's most urbanized island, Oahu, 22 landowners owned 72.5 percent of the fee simple titles. The Hawaii Legislature had concluded that the oligopoly in land ownership was "skewing the State's residential fee simple market, inflating land prices, and injuring the public tranquility and welfare," and therefore enacted a condemnation scheme for redistributing title.

The Court's holdings in *Berman* and *Midkiff* were true to the principle underlying the Public Use Clause. In both those cases, the extraordinary precondemnation use of the targeted property inflicted affirmative harm on society—in *Berman* through blight resulting from extreme poverty and in *Midkiff* through oligopoly resulting from extreme wealth. And in both cases, the relevant legislative body had found that eliminating the existing property use was necessary to remedy the harm. Thus a public purpose was realized when the harmful use was eliminated. Because each taking *directly* achieved a public benefit, it did not matter that the property was turned over to private use. Here, in contrast, New London does not claim that Susette Kelo's and Wilhelmina Dery's well-maintained homes are the source of any social harm. Indeed, it could not so claim without adopting the absurd argument that any single-family home that might be razed to make way for an apartment building, or any church that might be replaced with a retail store, or any small business that might be more lucrative if it were instead part of a national franchise, is inherently harmful to society and thus within the government's power to condemn.

In moving away from our decisions sanctioning the condemnation of harmful property use, the Court today significantly expands the meaning of "public use." It holds that the sovereign may take private property currently put to ordinary private use, and give it over for new, ordinary private use, so long as the new use is predicted to generate some secondary benefit for the public—such as increased tax revenue, more jobs, maybe even aesthetic pleasure. But nearly any lawful use of real private property can be said to generate some incidental benefit to the public. Thus, if predicted (or even guaranteed) positive side effects are enough to render transfer from one private party to another constitutional, then the words "for public use" do not realistically exclude *any* takings, and thus do not exert any constraint on the eminent domain power.

The Court protests that it does not sanction the bare transfer from *A* to *B* for *B*'s benefit. It suggests a role for courts in future cases in ferreting out takings whose sole purpose is to bestow a benefit on the private transferee—without detailing how courts are to conduct that complicated inquiry. For his part, Justice Kennedy suggests that courts may divine illicit purpose by a careful review of the record and the process by which a legislature arrived at the decision to take—without specifying what courts should look for in a case with different facts, how they will know if they have found it, and what to do if they do not. Whatever the details of Justice Kennedy's as-yet-undisclosed test, it is difficult to envision anyone so inept as to fail it. The trouble with economic development takings is that private benefit and incidental public benefit are, by definition, merged and mutually reinforcing. In this case, for example, any boon for Pfizer or the plan's private developer is difficult to disaggregate from the promised public gains in taxes and jobs.

The Court also puts special emphasis on the particular facts in this case concerning the deliberative process that was followed. Justice Kennedy, too, takes great comfort in these facts. But none has any legal significance to blunt the force of today's holding. If legislative prognostications about the secondary public benefits of a new use can legitimate a taking, there is nothing in the Court's rule or in Justice Kennedy's gloss on that rule to prohibit property transfers generated with less care, that are less comprehensive, that happen to result from less elaborate process, whose only projected advantage is the incidence of higher taxes, or that hope to transform an already prosperous city into an even more prosperous one.

Berman and *Midkiff* endorsed government intervention when private property use had veered to such an extreme that the public was suffering as a consequence. Today, on the Court's theory, any property may be taken for the benefit of another private party, but the fallout from this decision will not be random. The beneficiaries are likely to be those citizens with disproportionate influence and power in the political process, including large corporations and development firms. As for the victims, the government now has license to transfer property from those with fewer resources to those with more. The Founders cannot have intended this perverse result.

Thomas, dissenting: Long ago, William Blackstone wrote that "the law of the land . . . postpone[s] even public necessity to the sacred and inviolable rights of private property." The Framers embodied that principle in the Constitution, allowing the government to take property not for "public necessity" but instead for "public use." Defying this understanding, the Court replaces the Public Use Clause with a "[P]ublic [P]urpose" Clause, a restriction that is satisfied, the Court instructs, so long as the purpose is "legitimate" and the means "not irrational." This deferential shift in phraseology enables the Court to hold, against all common sense, that a costly urban-renewal project whose stated purpose is a vague promise of new jobs and increased tax revenue (but which is also suspiciously agreeable to the Pfizer Corporation) is for a public use.

Today's decision is simply the latest in a string of our cases construing the Public Use Clause to be a virtual nullity, without the slightest nod to its original meaning. In my view, the Public Use Clause, originally understood, is a meaningful limit on the government's eminent domain power. Our cases have strayed from the Clause's original meaning, and I would reconsider them.

The most natural reading of the Clause is that it authorizes the taking of property only if the public has a right to employ it, not if the public realizes any conceivable benefit from the taking. When the government takes property and gives it to a private individual, and the public has no right to use the property, it strains language to say that the public is employing the property, regardless of the incidental benefits that might accrue to the public from the private use. Tellingly, the phrase "public use" contrasts with the very different phrase "general Welfare" used elsewhere in the Constitution. The Framers would surely have used some such broader term if they had meant the Public Use Clause to have a similarly sweeping scope.

The Court has previously recognized the overriding respect for the sanctity of the home that has been embedded in our traditions since the origins of the Republic, when the issue is only whether the government may search a home. Yet today the Court tells us that we are not to "second-guess the City's considered judgments," when the issue is, instead, whether the government may take the infinitely more intrusive step of tearing down petitioners' homes. Something has gone seriously awry with this Court's interpretation of the Constitution. Though citizens are safe from the government in their homes, the homes themselves are not. Once one accepts, as the Court at least nominally does, that the Public Use Clause is a limit on the eminent domain power of the Federal Government and the States, there is no justification for the almost complete deference it grants to legislatures as to what satisfies it.

In *Berman v. Parker,* the Court proclaimed that, "Subject to specific constitutional limitations, when the legislature has spoken, the public interest has been declared in terms well-nigh conclusive. In such cases the legislature, not the judiciary, is the main guardian of the public needs to be served by social legislation." That reasoning was question-begging, since the question to be decided was whether the "specific constitutional limitation" of the Public Use Clause prevented the taking of the owner's department store. *Berman* also appeared to reason that any exercise by Congress of an enumerated power (in this case, its plenary power over the District of Columbia) was *per se* a "public use" under the Fifth Amendment. But the very point of the Public Use Clause is to limit that power.

More fundamentally, *Berman* and *Midkiff* erred by equating the eminent domain power with the police power of States. See *Midkiff,* 467 U.S. at 240 ("The 'public use' requirement is ... coterminous with the scope of a sovereign's police powers"); *Berman,* 348 U.S. at 32. Traditional regulation under a state's police power, such as the power to abate a nuisance, required no compensation whatsoever, in sharp contrast to the takings power, which has always required compensation. The question whether the state can take property using the power of eminent domain is therefore distinct from the question whether it can regulate property pursuant to the police power. To construe the Public Use Clause to overlap with the states' police power conflates these two categories.

The "public purpose" test applied by *Berman* and *Midkiff* also cannot be applied in a principled manner. Once one permits takings for public purposes in addition to public uses, no coherent principle limits what could constitute a valid public use—at least none beyond the text of the Constitution itself. I share the Court's skepticism about second-guessing a legislature's decision. But the public purpose standard this Court has adopted demands the use of such judgment, for the Court concedes that the Public Use Clause would forbid a purely private taking and it is difficult to imagine how a court could find that a taking was purely private except by determining that the taking did not, in fact, rationally advance the public interest. The Court is therefore wrong to criticize the "actual use" test as "difficult to administer." On the contrary, it is far easier to analyze whether the government owns or the public has a legal right to use the taken property than to ask whether the taking has a "purely private purpose."

The consequences of today's decision are not difficult to predict and promise to be harmful. So-called "urban renewal" programs provide some compensation for the properties they take, but no compensation is possible for the subjective value of these lands to the individuals displaced and the indignity inflicted by uprooting them from their homes. Allowing the government to take property solely for public purposes is bad enough, but extending the concept of public purpose to encompass any economically beneficial goal guarantees that these losses will fall disproportionately on poor communities. Those communities are not only systematically less likely to put their lands to the highest and best social use, but are also the least politically powerful. If ever there were justification for intrusive judicial review of constitutional provisions that protect "discrete and insular minorities," United States v. Carolene Products Co., 304 U.S. 144, 152 n.4 (1938), surely that principle would apply with great force to the powerless groups and individuals the Public Use Clause protects. The deferential standard this Court has adopted for the Public Use Clause is therefore deeply perverse. As Justice O'Connor points out, it encourages "those citizens with disproportionate influence and power in the political process, including large corporations and development firms," to victimize the weak.

The principles this Court should employ to decide this case are found in the Public Use Clause itself. When faced with a clash of constitutional principle and a line of unreasoned cases wholly divorced from the text, history, and structure of our founding document, we should not hesitate to resolve the tension in favor of the Constitution's original meaning.

The Anti-*Kelo* Backlash

Very few Supreme Court decisions have aroused the same degree of public outrage as the *Kelo* decision, holding that the Takings Clause permits government seizure of private property for private development.

Action by State Legislatures—In response to the backlash against *Kelo,* and despite intense opposition by local municipalities and developers, the legislatures in 35 States have adopted legislation ostensibly limiting the use of eminent domain for private development.

Critics, however, have charged that most of these statutes are largely symbolic in nature, providing little or no protection for property owners. It is also contended that the States that enacted the most meaningful reforms (e.g., Georgia and South Dakota) have only rarely permitted eminent domain for private development, and that the States where the practice has been common (e.g., New York, New Jersey, and California) have enacted only cosmetic reforms or none at all.

Action by Voter Referendums—In contrast to the post-*Kelo* reforms adopted by state legislatures, those adopted by voter referendums are for the most part much stronger.

In September and November 2006, there were property rights referendums in 13 States. Nine of the 13 dealt exclusively with proposals to prohibit or limit the use of eminent domain for private development. Each of the nine was approved by the voters: Florida, Georgia, Louisiana, Michigan, Nevada, New Hampshire, North Dakota, Oregon, and South Carolina.[2]

The other four referendums—in Arizona, California, Idaho, and Washington—also included (in addition to public use limitations) more controversial requirements that States compensate citizens for regulations that devalue property. Of these four measures, only the Arizona referendum passed. No "stand-alone" post-*Kelo* referendum on public use was defeated anywhere in the country.

"Regulatory Takings"

Generally "takings" have been recognized only in situations where (as in *Kelo*) the government acquires private property or physically occupies it.

But in a landmark decision, Pennsylvania Coal v. Mahon, 260 U.S. 393 (1922), in an opinion by Justice Oliver Wendell Holmes, the Court held that a taking might also be found if a government regulation of the use of property went "too far." The case involved a Pennsylvania statute that prohibited the mining of coal in any manner that would cause the subsidence of property; the effect of the law was to prevent companies from exercising their mining rights since the statute required them to leave columns of coal underground to support the surface. Although the statute did not authorize the government to confiscate, occupy, destroy, or invade the property, the Court found that the regulation constituted a taking because "mak[ing] it commercially impracticable to mine certain coal has nearly the same effect for constitutional purposes as appropriating or destroying it."

The *Pennsylvania Coal* case has spawned hundreds—perhaps thousands—of claims that other government regulations have also gone too far and therefore constitute takings requiring the payment of compensation. Such claims have involved, for example, zoning ordinances, conditions on development of property, limits on conveyance of property, and rent controls.

Only a handful of these claims have been upheld by the Supreme Court. The Court's decisions do not offer a formula or rule for determining when a government regulation constitutes a taking. However, one important principle that has emerged from the Court's decisions is that a government regulation is not a taking simply because it decreases the value of a person's property so long as the owner retains reasonable economically viable uses of the property.

Penn Central Transportation Co. v. New York, 438 U.S. 104 (1978), involved a challenge to the New York City Landmarks Preservation Law. Under that law, over

---

[2]For example, the Florida referendum amended the Florida Constitution to strengthen the state's legislatively adopted post-*Kelo* law, already one of the strongest in the country. The constitutional amendment prohibits the transfer of private property taken by eminent domain to another person or private entity, except that "that the Legislature may by general law passed by a three-fifths vote of the membership of each house of the Legislature permit exceptions allowing the transfer of such private property."

the opposition of Penn Central, the New York City Preservation Commission designated the Grand Central railroad terminal as an architectural landmark. Subsequently Penn Central requested commission approval of a plan to leave the terminal intact but construct over it a 50-story office building (which would net Penn Central an annual guaranteed fee of $3 million). The law required advance commission approval to any proposal "to alter the exterior architectural features of the landmark or to construct any exterior improvement on the landmark site." When the Commission rejected the proposal, Penn Central sued, claiming that the Commission's action constituted a taking without just compensation. The Supreme Court (6-3) held that the development restriction was not a taking because it did not impede existing uses or prevent a reasonable return on investment or "frustrate distinct investment-backed expectations." The majority commented that "this Court, quite simply, has been unable to develop any 'set formula' for determining when 'justice and fairness' require that economic injuries caused by public action be compensated by the government, rather than remain disproportionately concentrated on a few persons."

In Lingle v. Chevron U.S.A. Inc., 544 U.S. 528 (2005), decided in the same term as *Kelo,* Chevron contended that the Hawaii Legislature had "taken" its property by enacting a statute limiting the rent that oil companies may charge dealers who lease company-owned service stations. The district court upheld Chevron's claim, holding that the rent cap constituted an uncompensated taking, and the Ninth Circuit affirmed, but the Supreme Court unanimously reversed. In an opinion by Justice O'Connor (who dissented in *Kelo*), the Court rejected the taking claim, holding that the impact of the Hawaii law on Chevron could not be deemed functionally equivalent to the acquisition of its private property.

In February 2006, the Oregon Supreme Court upheld a unique referendum designed to curb regulatory takings. The measure, approved by 61 percent of Oregon voters, requires state and local governments to either (1) compensate landowners for any reduction in the value of their property as a result of a governmental regulation or (2) exempt the landowners from the regulation.[3]

The Decline of the Contracts Clause

Article I, §10, provides that "No *State* shall ... pass any ... law impairing the Obligation of Contracts." (Italics added.) The Clause therefore does not apply to federal laws. In addition, the Clause does not limit regulation of the terms of future contracts; it applies only to state laws "impairing" contracts that are already in existence.

The Clause was primarily aimed at debtor relief laws—laws postponing payments of debts and laws authorizing payments in installments or in commodities. For nearly a century, the Court aggressively used the Contracts Clause to invalidate a variety of such state laws.

However, starting in the late 1900s, reliance on the Clause was largely superseded by the Court's development of the doctrine of substantive due process, which expanded the Due Process Clause of the Fourteenth Amendment to require not only procedural ("process") fairness but also the substantive "reasonableness" of state laws.

---

[3]The *New York Times* of July 25, 2006, reported that 2,755 claims had already been filed, covering 150,455 acres. According to the *Times,* "If all the claims were paid, state officials say, it could amount to more than $3 billion in compensation.... Instead of paying property owners, local government agencies have routinely chosen to waive the regulations, clearing the way for numerous developments in rural areas."

(See comment "The Substantive Due Process Doctrine" in Chapter 6.) And, when due process review of economic regulation became more deferential in the 1930s, the role of the Contracts Clause also diminished.

In 1934, in Home Building & Loan Association v. Blaisdell, 290 U.S. 398 (1934), the Court (5-4) held that the Contracts Clause was not violated by a Minnesota law that prevented mortgage holders from foreclosing on mortgages for a two-year period, even though this was the very kind of debtor relief legislation that the Contracts Clause was meant to forbid.

In an opinion by Chief Justice Hughes, the majority acknowledged that "Emergency does not increase granted power or remove or diminish the restrictions imposed upon power granted or reserved" but stated that "While emergency does not create power, emergency may furnish the occasion for the exercise of power" and "it does not follow that conditions may not arise in which a temporary restraint of enforcement may be consistent with the spirit and purpose of the constitutional provision and thus be found to be within the range of the reserved power of the state to protect the vital interests of the community." (Pages 425, 439.) In this case, according to the majority (page 442):

> there has been a growing appreciation of public needs and of the necessity of finding ground for a rational compromise between individual rights and public welfare. The settlement and consequent contraction of the public domain, the pressure of a constantly increasing density of population, the interrelation of the activities of our people and the complexity of our economic interests, have inevitably led to an increased use of the organization of society in order to protect the very bases of individual opportunity. Where, in earlier days, it was thought that only the concerns of individuals or of classes were involved, and that those of the state itself were touched only remotely, it has later been found that the fundamental interests of the state are directly affected; and that the question is no longer merely that of one party to a contract as against another, but of the use of reasonable means to safeguard the economic structure upon which the good of all depends.
>
> It is no answer to say that this public need was not apprehended a century ago, or to insist that what the provision of the Constitution meant to the vision of that day it must mean to the vision of our time. If by the statement that what the Constitution meant at the time of its adoption it means to-day, it is intended to say that the great clauses of the Constitution must be confined to the interpretation which the framers, with the conditions and outlook of their time, would have placed upon them, the statement carries its own refutation. It was to guard against such a narrow conception that Chief Justice Marshall uttered the memorable warning: "We must never forget, that it is a constitution we are expounding"—"a constitution intended to endure for ages to come, and, consequently, to be adapted to the various crises of human affairs." (McCulloch v. Maryland, 4 Wheat. 316, 407.)

The Court concluded (page 447) "that the contract clause is not an absolute and utterly unqualified restriction of the state's protective power" and "this legislation is clearly so reasonable as to be within the legislative competency."

In his dissent joined by three other Justices, Justice Sutherland contended (pages 448–449, 483):

> A provision of the Constitution, it is hardly necessary to say, does not admit of two distinctly opposite interpretations. It does not mean one thing at one time and an entirely different thing at another time. If the contract impairment clause, when framed and adopted, meant that the terms of a contract for the payment of money could not be altered in invitum by a state statute enacted for the relief of hardly pressed debtors to the end and with

the effect of postponing payment or enforcement during and because of an economic or financial emergency, it is but to state the obvious to say that it means the same now. . . .

The only legitimate inquiry we can make is whether it is constitutional. If it is not, its virtues, if it have any, cannot save it; if it is, its faults cannot be invoked to accomplish its destruction.

Since *Blaisdell,* the Court has invalidated only two laws under the Clause. United States Trust Co. v. New Jersey, 431 U.S. 1 (1977); Allied Structural Steel Co. v. Spannaus, 438 U.S. 234 (1978).

In the *United States Trust* case, the Court (4-3) struck down a state law repealing an earlier state covenant to bondholders that limited subsidies to certain kinds of rail operations. The majority concluded that a State, in impairing a state obligation, was acting in the State's own self-interest and was therefore not entitled to as much deference as a State's impairment of an obligation arising from a *private* contract.

In the *Allied* case, the Minnesota Private Pension Benefits Protection Act was found to violate the Clause by retroactively modifying the payment obligations assumed by a private employer under its voluntarily established pension plan. Although conceding that the Clause had "receded into comparative desuetude," the Court majority (5-3) denied that the Clause had become "a dead letter" and struck down the challenged law on the ground that it nullified "express terms of the company's contractual obligations and impose[d] a completely unexpected liability in potentially disabling amounts."

Under the present interpretation of the Contracts Clause, a state law interfering with a private contract will be struck down only if the law fails to reasonably serve a "significant and legitimate public purpose"—a test quite similar to the minimalist "rational basis" test applied to economic regulation under the Due Process Clause. But a state law that impairs a contractual obligation of the state itself (such as the bond covenant in the *United States Trust* case) may be subjected to a more rigorous standard of review.

18

The Second Amendment

The Background of the *Heller* Case

The subject of guns evokes passionate debate, particularly over the extent to which guns should be regulated by the government and the extent to which such regulation is permitted by the Constitution.

At the heart of the controversy is the Second Amendment:

> *A well regulated Militia, being necessary to the security of a free State, the right of the people to keep and bear Arms, shall not be infringed.*

The words of the Amendment raise many questions, including: What is a "militia"? What is a "right of the people"? What does it mean to "keep and bear arms"? What kinds of "arms" are permissible? What types of infringements on the right are prohibited?

For over two centuries until its decision in the next-digested case, *District of Columbia v. Heller,* the Supreme Court never resolved any of these questions. Although *Heller* defers some of these questions for future resolution, the decision is the Court's first authoritative interpretation of the Second Amendment.

The Court's only previous extended discussion of the subject is United States v. Miller, 307 U.S. 174 (1939). The case involved a challenge to the National Firearms Act of 1934, which sharply limited private ownership of such gangster-associated weapons as sawed-off shotguns and submachine guns. The defendants were indicted for possession of a sawed-off shotgun in violation of the act, and they successfully claimed in the District Court that a sawed-off shotgun was a "militia weapon" and hence protected by the Second Amendment. The case went to the Supreme Court on only one question: whether it was proper to take "judicial notice" that a sawed-off shotgun was a "militia weapon," or whether such a finding required evidentiary proceedings.

The Supreme Court reversed, concluding that evidentiary hearings were required. In its opinion, the Court reviewed the early history of the militia and stated that it had been made up of "all males physically capable of acting in concert for the common defense. ... And further, that ordinarily when called for service these men were expected to appear bearing arms supplied by themselves and of the kind in common use at the time" (307 U.S. at 178-79). In light of that history, the Court held (*id.*):

> In the absence of any evidence tending to show that possession or use of "a shotgun having a barrel of less than eighteen inches in length" at this time has some reasonable

relationship to the preservation or efficiency of a well regulated militia, we cannot say that the Second Amendment guarantees the right to keep and bear such an instrument. Certainly it is not within judicial notice that this weapon is any part of the ordinary military equipment or that its use could contribute to the common defense.

Accordingly, the Court remanded the case to the District Court for further fact-finding proceedings.

In its opinion, the Supreme Court commented that the "obvious purpose" of the Second Amendment was "to assure the continuation and render possible the effectiveness of" the militia when called upon to carry out its constitutional mandate "to execute the Laws of the Union, suppress Insurrections and repel Invasions" and that the Amendment "must be interpreted and applied with that end in view." The Court further stated (307 U.S. at 178):

> The signification attributed to the term Militia appears from the debates in the Convention, the history and legislation of Colonies and States, and the writings of approved commentators. These show plainly enough that the Militia comprised all males physically capable of acting in concert for the common defense. "A body of citizens enrolled for military discipline." And further, that ordinarily when called for service these men were expected to appear bearing arms supplied by themselves and of the kind in common use at the time.

The holding of *Miller*—that a factual inquiry was necessary to determine whether a particular firearm was of the sort employed by a colonial militia—was essentially procedural in nature. However, the decision emphasizes that "militia" as used in the Amendment refers to the entire armed citizenry. In addition, since the Court considered Mr. Miller's Second Amendment claim without suggesting (much less holding) that he had no basis to press such a claim, and since the Court did not place any significance on whether Miller was involved in any military or militia service, it arguably provides support for inferring that the Court viewed the Second Amendment as protecting at least some type of individual right to keep and bear arms.[1]

Nevertheless, in subsequent years, the *Miller* decision was widely accepted by the federal courts of appeals as evidencing a *rejection* of an individual right to keep and bear arms. The largely settled consensus of the Circuits was that the right only applies to participants in an organized state militia. In United States v. Parker, 362 F.3d 1279, 1284 (10th Cir. 2004), for example, the Tenth Circuit held that "an individual has a right to bear arms, but only in direct affiliation with a well-organized state-supported militia." The First, Third, Eighth, and Eleventh Circuits were in accord.[2] Similarly emphasizing that the Second Amendment's purpose is to protect state militias, the Fourth, Sixth, Seventh, and Ninth Circuits held that only States may enforce the Second Amendment.[3]

This consensus was sharply challenged by what became a flood of scholarly articles based on new analysis of the history and purpose of the Second Amendment. In the

---

[1]See, e.g., Glenn H. Reynolds, "A Critical Guide to the Second Amendment," 62 *Tennessee Law Review* 461, 500 (1995).

[2]Cases v. United States, 131 F.2d 916, 923 (1st Cir. 1942); United States v. Rybar, 103 F.3d 273, 286 (3d Cir. 1996); United States v. Hale, 978 F.2d 1016, 1020 (8th Cir. 1992); United States v. Wright, 117 F.3d 1265, 1274 (11th Cir. 1997).

[3]United States v. Johnson, 497 F.2d 548, 550 (4th Cir. 1974) (per curiam); United States v. Warin, 530 F.2d 103, 106 (6th Cir. 1976); Gillespie v. City of Indianapolis, 185 F.3d 693, 710 (7th Cir. 1999); Silveira v. Lockyer, 312 F.3d 1052, 1087 (9th Cir. 2002).

view of these scholars—on both the left and the right[4]—the Amendment did indeed protect an individual right. This reconsideration of the issue led to the effort to seek Supreme Court clarification and ultimately to the Court's decision in *District of Columbia v. Heller.*

District of Columbia v. Heller, ___ U.S. ___, 128 S.Ct. 2783 (2008)

In 1973 the District of Columbia enacted a gun ordinance as part of an effort to address the District's violent crime problem. The ordinance, one of the strictest in the country, prohibits handgun possession by making it a crime to carry an unregistered firearm and prohibiting the registration of handguns; provides separately that no person may carry an unlicensed handgun, but authorizes the police chief to issue one-year licenses; and requires residents to keep lawfully owned firearms unloaded and dissembled or bound by a trigger lock or similar device.

Dick Heller, a District of Columbia special policeman, applied to register a handgun he wished to keep at home, but his application was denied. He filed this suit seeking, on Second Amendment grounds, to enjoin the city from enforcing the bar on handgun registration, the licensing requirement insofar as it prohibits carrying an unlicensed firearm in the home, and the trigger-lock requirement insofar as it prohibits the use of functional firearms in the home.

The District Court dismissed the suit, but the Court of Appeals for the District of Columbia Circuit reversed, holding by a 2-to-1 vote that "the right in question is individual," not tied to membership in a state militia, and that the city's total ban on handguns, as well as its requirement that firearms in the home be kept nonfunctional even when necessary for self-defense, violated that right. The court left the door open to "reasonable regulations," such as prohibiting the carrying of concealed weapons, or weapons in particular locations, or the ownership of guns by felons.

In appealing to the Supreme Court, the District of Columbia principally argued (1) that the Second Amendment's text and history show that the amendment grants a right that "may be exercised only in connection with service in a state-regulated militia" and (2) that, even if gun ownership is an individual right, the handgun ban is amply justified as a reasonable regulation by considerations of public safety and health.

The Supreme Court reversed 5 to 4 in a lengthy (65 pages) opinion by Justice Scalia, joined by Justices Roberts, Kennedy, Thomas, and Alito. The Court held that the Second Amendment recognized an individual right to possess and carry a firearm unconnected with militia service. Justices Stevens, Breyer, Ginsburg, and Souter dissented in opinions by Stevens and Breyer.

---

[4]Perhaps the most influential of these articles were by Don B. Kates, Jr., "Handgun Prohibition and the Original Meaning of the Second Amendment," 82 *Michigan Law Review* 204 (1983), and Sanford Levinson, "The Embarrassing Second Amendment," 99 *Yale Law Journal* 637 (1989). See also, e.g., Akhil R. Amar, "The Bill of Rights and the Fourteenth Amendment," 101 *Yale Law Journal* 1193, 1205-11, 1261-62 (1992); Eugene Volokh, "The Commonplace Second Amendment," 73 *New York University Law Review* 793 (1998); Glenn H. Reynolds, "A Critical Guide to the Second Amendment," 62 *Tennessee Law Review* 461 (1995). Professor Lawrence Tribe, author of a leading treatise on constitutional law, "said he had come to believe that the Second Amendment protected an individual right. 'My conclusion came as something of a surprise to me, and an unwelcome surprise,' Professor Tribe said. 'I have always supported as a matter of policy very comprehensive gun control.' The first two editions of Professor Tribe's influential treatise on constitutional law, in 1978 and 1988, endorsed the collective rights view. The latest, published in 2000, sets out his current interpretation." Adam Liptak, "A Liberal Case for the Individual Right to Own Guns Helps Sway the Federal Judiciary," *New York Times,* May 7, 2007.

The decision is unquestionably a constitutional landmark. But its practical consequences should not be overstated. It is neither a Magna Carta for pro-gun enthusiasts nor a return to the Wild West feared by gun control proponents.

Although the opinion does not offer a general test for what is within and what is outside of the individual right to possess and carry weapons, the Court cautioned that "The Court's opinion should not "be taken to cast doubt on longstanding prohibitions on the possession of firearms by felons and the mentally ill, or laws forbidding the carrying of firearms in sensitive places such as schools and government buildings, or laws imposing conditions and qualifications on the commercial sale of arms" or prohibiting the carrying of "dangerous and unusual weapons." Nor does the decision cast doubt on nondiscriminatory requirements for licensing of firearms.

The decision does not pass on the question whether the Second Amendment has been "incorporated" into the Due Process Clause of the Fourteenth Amendment so as to be applicable to the States as well as the federal government. (See comment "'Incorporation' of Rights in Due Process" in Chapter 6.) However, since most of the other provisions of the Bill of Rights have been held to be "incorporated," it is generally assumed that ultimately the Supreme Court would accord the same status to the Second Amendment.

The full effect of the decision cannot, of course, be predicted. But its greatest impact is likely to be on the relatively few cities (such as several in Illinois like Chicago, Morton Grove, Wilmette, and Winnetka) that, like the District of Columbia, enacted flat prohibitions on handguns.

The Meaning of "Militia"

The linchpin of the majority opinion is Scalia's analysis of the prefatory clause of the Amendment: "A well regulated militia being necessary to the security of a free State."

It is this clause that led many to believe that the "right" established by the balance of the Amendment—the operative clause—is limited to members of a state "militia." The prefatory clause, Scalia held, may be relevant to clarify ambiguity in the balance of the Amendment, but otherwise "does not limit or expand the scope of the operative clause."

In defining the terms in the prefatory clause, the Court reaffirmed the *Miller* definition of "militia" as "all males physically capable of acting in concert for the common defense." However, according to the Court:

Unlike armies and navies, which Congress is given the power to create ("to raise . . . Armies"; "to provide . . . a Navy," Art. I, §8, cls. 12-13), the militia is assumed by Article I already to be *in existence*. Congress is given the power to "provide for calling forth the militia," §8, cl. 15; and the power not to create, but to "organiz[e]" it—and not to organize "a" militia, which is what one would expect if the militia were to be a federal creation, but to organize "the" militia, connoting a body already in existence.

"The Right of the People"

The opinion construes "right of the people" to refer to individual members of "people"—not the right of a collective body:

The first salient feature of the operative clause is that it codifies a "right of the people." The unamended Constitution and the Bill of Rights use the phrase "right of the people" two other times, in the First Amendment's Assembly-and-Petition Clause and in the Fourth Amendment's Search-and-Seizure Clause. The Ninth Amendment uses very similar terminology ("The enumeration in the Constitution, of certain rights, shall not be construed to deny or disparage others retained by the people"). All three of these instances unambiguously refer to individual rights, not "collective" rights, or rights that may be exercised only through participation in some corporate body.

In short, the right attaches to persons and not to corporate entities (States, militias, or otherwise).

The Meaning of the Operative Phrase

After "[p]utting all of these textual elements together," the Court finds:

> that they guarantee the individual right to possess and carry weapons in case of confrontation. This meaning is strongly confirmed by the historical background of the Second Amendment. We look to this because it has always been widely understood that the Second Amendment, like the First and Fourth Amendments, codified a *pre-existing* right. The very text of the Second Amendment implicitly recognizes the pre-existence of the right and declares only that it "shall not be infringed." ...
>
> There seems to us no doubt, on the basis of both text and history, that the Second Amendment conferred an individual right to keep and bear arms. Of course the right was not unlimited, just as the First Amendment's right of free speech was not.... Thus, we do not read the Second Amendment to protect the right of citizens to carry arms for *any sort* of confrontation, just as we do not read the First Amendment to protect the right of citizens to speak for *any purpose*. [Italics the Court's.]

Prior Decisions of the Supreme Court

The majority concluded "that nothing in our precedents forecloses our adoption of the original understanding of the Second Amendment." *United States v. Miller* was distinguished on the ground that it held only that short-barreled shotguns were not shown to have relationship to "the preservation or efficiency of a well-regulated militia." In the majority's view, *Miller* assumes an individual rights reading of the Amendment while recognizing that only certain types of weapons are within the scope of the individual right: "We therefore read *Miller* to say only that the Second Amendment does not protect those weapons not typically possessed by law-abiding citizens for lawful purposes, such as short-barreled shotguns."

Application to the D.C. Ordinance and the Level of Review

Finally, Justice Scalia applied the Court's interpretation to the D.C. ordinance. According to the opinion, "Few laws in the history of our Nation have come close to the severe restriction of the District's handgun ban." The Court stated:

> The handgun ban amounts to a prohibition of an entire class of "arms" that is overwhelmingly chosen by American society for that lawful purpose. The prohibition extends, moreover, to the home, where the need for defense of self, family, and property is most acute. Under any of the standards of scrutiny that we have applied to enumerated constitutional rights, banning from the home "the most preferred firearm in the nation to 'keep' and use for protection of one's home and family," ... would fail constitutional muster.

While holding that the D.C. ordinance would be unconstitutional "[u]nder any of the standards of scrutiny that we have applied to enumerated constitutional rights," and although clearly rejecting a "rational basis" standard, the majority does not explicitly determine what other standard should be applied in evaluating a restriction under the Second Amendment.[5] That question is left for decision in a future case. Clearly, however, the majority would require either "strict scrutiny" (the standard applicable, for example, to reviewing claims under the First Amendment) or some other standard that would also require a substantial showing of justification.

Scalia rejected the proposal in Justice Breyer's for "a judge-empowering 'interest balancing inquiry' that 'asks whether the statute burdens a protected interest in a way or to an extent that is out of proportion to the statute's salutary effects upon other important governmental interests.' " Scalia stated:

> We know of no other enumerated constitutional right whose core protection has been subjected to a freestanding "interest-balancing" approach. The very enumeration of the right takes out of the hands of government—even the Third Branch of Government—the power to decide on a case-by-case basis whether the right is really worth insisting upon. A constitutional guarantee subject to future judges' assessments of its usefulness is no constitutional guarantee at all. Constitutional rights are enshrined with the scope they were understood to have when the people adopted them, whether or not future legislatures or (yes) even future judges think that scope too broad. We would not apply an "interest-balancing" approach to the prohibition of a peaceful neo-Nazi march through Skokie. See National Socialist Party of America v. Skokie, 432 U.S. 43 (1977) (per curiam). The First Amendment contains the freedom-of-speech guarantee that the people ratified, which included exceptions for obscenity, libel, and disclosure of state secrets, but not for the expression of extremely unpopular and wrong-headed views. The Second Amendment is no different. Like the First, it is the very product of an interest-balancing by the people —which Justice Breyer would now conduct for them anew. And whatever else it leaves to future evaluation, it surely elevates above all other interests the right of law-abiding, responsible citizens to use arms in defense of hearth and home.

The Court's Conclusion

The Court stated:

> In sum, we hold that the District's ban on handgun possession in the home violates the Second Amendment, as does its prohibition against rendering any lawful firearm in the home operable for the purpose of immediate self-defense. Assuming that Heller is not disqualified from the exercise of Second Amendment rights, the District must permit him to register his handgun and must issue him a license to carry it in the home.
>
> We are aware of the problem of handgun violence in this country, and we take seriously the concerns raised by the many *amici* who believe that prohibition of handgun ownership is a solution. The Constitution leaves the District of Columbia a variety of tools for combating that problem, including some measures regulating handguns.... But the enshrinement of constitutional rights necessarily takes certain policy choices off the table. These include the absolute prohibition of handguns held and used for self-defense in the home. Undoubtedly some think that the Second Amendment is outmoded in a society where our standing army is the pride of our Nation, where well-trained police forces provide personal security, and where gun violence is a serious problem. That is perhaps

---

[5]Concerning the different standards of scrutiny applied by the Court, see comments "Overview of the Equal Protection Clause" in Chapter 3 and "The Substantive Due Process Doctrine" in Chapter 6.

debatable, but what is not debatable is that it is not the role of this Court to pronounce the Second Amendment extinct.

Stevens's Dissent

Justice Stevens's opinion begins by denying the case presents a question of "collective" or "individual" right. He states:

> The question presented by this case is not whether the Second Amendment protects a "collective right" or an "individual right." Surely it protects a right that can be enforced by individuals. But a conclusion that the Second Amendment protects an individual right does not tell us anything about the scope of that right.

Reading *United States v. Miller* quite differently than the majority, Stevens contended that "our decision in *Miller* was faithful to the text of the Second Amendment and the purposes revealed in its drafting history." Furthermore, according to Stevens,

> Even if the textual and historical arguments on both sides of the issue were evenly balanced, respect for the well-settled views of all of our predecessors on this Court, and for the rule of law itself, ... would prevent most jurists from endorsing such a dramatic upheaval in the law.

Stevens argued that "the postratification history of the Amendment ... makes abundantly clear that the Amendment should not be interpreted as limiting the authority of Congress to regulate the use or possession of firearms for purely civilian purposes."

Breyer's Dissent

Justice Breyer, like Stevens, declined to defend a "collective" right; instead, like Stevens, he agreed that "The Amendment protects an 'individual' right——i.e., one that is separately possessed, and may be separately enforced, by each person on whom it is conferred." But he argues that the right is conferred only on those in a narrowly defined militia. According to Breyer, "the Second Amendment protects militia-related, not self-defense-related, interests" and "self-defense alone, detached from any militia-related objective, is not the Amendment's concern."

The larger part of Breyer's dissent is devoted to his contention

> that the District's law is consistent with the Second Amendment even if that Amendment is interpreted as protecting a wholly separate interest in individual self-defense ... because the District's regulation, which focuses upon the presence of handguns in high-crime urban areas, represents a permissible legislative response to a serious, indeed life-threatening, problem.

To determine the validity of such restrictions, Breyer acknowledged that a rational-basis standard would be inappropriate but opposed the application of the more rigorous "strict scrutiny" standard. Instead, he urged "an interest-balancing inquiry, with the interests protected by the Second Amendment on one side and the governmental public-safety concerns on the other, the only question being whether the regulation at issue impermissibly burdens the former in the course of advancing the latter."

Appendix A: United States Constitution

Note: Certain pertinent provisions have been italicized.

We the People of the United States, in Order to form a more perfect Union, establish Justice, insure domestic Tranquillity, provide for the common defence, promote the general Welfare, and secure the Blessings of Liberty to ourselves and our Posterity, do ordain and establish this Constitution for the United States of America.

Article I (Congress)

Section 1

All legislative Powers herein granted shall be vested in a Congress of the United States, which shall consist of a Senate and House of Representatives.

Section 2 (House of Representatives)

The House of Representatives shall be composed of Members chosen every second Year by the People of the several States, and the Electors in each State shall have the Qualifications requisite for Electors of the most numerous Branch of the State Legislature.

No Person shall be a Representative who shall not have attained to the age of twenty five Years, and been seven Years a Citizen of the United States, and who shall not, when elected, be an Inhabitant of that State in which he shall be chosen.

Representatives and direct Taxes shall be apportioned among the several States which may be included within this Union, according to their respective Numbers, which shall be determined by adding to the whole Number of free Persons, including those bound to Service for a Term of Years, and excluding Indians not taxed, three fifths of all other Persons. The actual Enumeration shall be made within three Years after the first Meeting of the Congress of the United States, and within every subsequent Term of ten Years, in such Manner as they shall by Law direct. The Number of Representatives shall not exceed one for every thirty Thousand, but each State shall have at Least one Representative; and until such enumeration shall be made, the State of New Hampshire shall be entitled to chuse three, Massachusetts eight, Rhode-Island and Providence Plantations one, Connecticut five, New-York six, New Jersey four, Pennsylvania eight, Delaware one, Maryland six, Virginia ten, North Carolina five, South Carolina five, and Georgia three.

When vacancies happen in the Representation from any State, the Executive Authority thereof shall issue Writs of Election to fill such Vacancies.

The House of Representatives shall chuse their Speaker and other Officers; and shall have the sole Power of Impeachment.

Section 3 (Senate)

The Senate of the United States shall be composed of two Senators from each State, chosen by the Legislature thereof, for six Years; and each Senator shall have one Vote.

Immediately after they shall be assembled in Consequence of the first Election, they shall be divided as equally as may be into three Classes. The Seats of the Senators of the first Class shall be vacated at the Expiration of the second Year, of the second Class at the Expiration of the fourth Year, and of the third Class at the Expiration of the sixth Year, so that one third may be chosen every second Year; and if Vacancies happen by Resignation, or otherwise, during the Recess of the Legislature of any State, the Executive thereof may make temporary Appointments until the next Meeting of the Legislature, which shall then fill such Vacancies.

No Person shall be a Senator who shall not have attained to the Age of thirty Years, and been nine Years a Citizen of the United States, and who shall not, when elected, be an Inhabitant of that State for which he shall be chosen.

The Vice President of the United States shall be President of the Senate but shall have no Vote, unless they be equally divided.

The Senate shall chuse their other Officers, and also a President pro tempore, in the Absence of the Vice President, or when he shall exercise the Office of President of the United States.

The Senate shall have the sole Power to try all Impeachments. When sitting for that Purpose, they shall be on Oath or Affirmation. When the President of the United States is tried the Chief Justice shall preside: And no Person shall be convicted without the Concurrence of two thirds of the Members present.

Judgment in Cases of Impeachment shall not extend further than to removal from Office, and disqualification to hold and enjoy any Office of honor, Trust or Profit under the United States: but the Party convicted shall nevertheless be liable and subject to Indictment, Trial, Judgment and Punishment, according to Law.

Section 4

The Times, Places and Manner of holding Elections for Senators and Representatives, shall be prescribed in each State by the Legislature thereof; but the Congress may at any time by Law make or alter such Regulations, except as to the Places of chusing Senators.

The Congress shall assemble at least once in every Year, and such Meeting shall be on the first Monday in December, unless they shall by Law appoint a different Day.

Section 5

Each House shall be the Judge of the Elections, Returns and Qualifications of its own Members, and a Majority of each shall constitute a Quorum to do Business; but a smaller Number may adjourn from day to day, and may be authorized to compel the Attendance of absent Members, in such Manner, and under such Penalties as each House may provide.

Each House may determine the Rules of its Proceedings, punish its Members for disorderly Behaviour, and, with the Concurrence of two thirds, expel a Member.

Each House shall keep a Journal of its Proceedings, and from time to time publish the same, excepting such Parts as may in their Judgment require Secrecy; and the Yeas and Nays of the Members of either House on any question shall, at the Desire of one fifth of those Present, be entered on the Journal.

Neither House, during the Session of Congress, shall, without the Consent of the other, adjourn for more than three days, nor to any other Place than that in which the two Houses shall be sitting.

Section 6

The Senators and Representatives shall receive a Compensation for their Services, to be ascertained by Law, and paid out of the Treasury of the United States. They shall in all Cases, except Treason, Felony and Breach of the Peace, be privileged from Arrest during their Attendance at the Session of their respective Houses, and in going to and returning from the same; and for any Speech or Debate in either House, they shall not be questioned in any other Place.

No Senator or Representative shall, during the Time for which he was elected, be appointed to any civil Office under the Authority of the United States, which shall have been created, or the Emoluments whereof shall have been encreased during such time; and no Person holding any Office under the United States, shall be a Member of either House during his Continuance in Office.

Section 7

All Bills for raising Revenue shall originate in the House of Representatives; but the Senate may propose or concur with amendments as on other Bills.

Every Bill which shall have passed the House of Representatives and the Senate, shall, before it become a law, be presented to the President of the United States: If he approve he shall sign it, but if not he shall return it, with his Objections to that House in which it shall have originated, who shall enter the Objections at large on their Journal, and proceed to reconsider it. If after such Reconsideration two thirds of that House shall agree to pass the Bill, it shall be sent, together with the Objections, to the other House, by which it shall likewise be reconsidered, and if approved by two thirds of that House, it shall become a Law. But in all such Cases the Votes of both Houses shall be determined by Yeas and Nays, and the Names of the Persons voting for and against the Bill shall be entered on the Journal of each House respectively. If any Bill shall not be returned by the President within ten Days (Sundays excepted) after it shall have been presented to him, the Same shall be a Law, in like Manner as if he had signed it, unless the Congress by their Adjournment prevent its Return, in which Case it shall not be a Law

Every Order, Resolution, or Vote to which the Concurrence of the Senate and House of Representatives may be necessary (except on a question of Adjournment) shall be presented to the President of the United States; and before the Same shall take Effect, shall be approved by him, or being disapproved by him, shall be repassed by two thirds of the Senate and House of Representatives, according to the Rules and Limitations prescribed in the Case of a Bill.

Section 8

The Congress shall have Power To lay and collect Taxes, Duties, Imposts and Excises, to pay the Debts and provide for the common Defence and general Welfare of the United States; but all Duties, Imposts and Excises shall be uniform throughout the United States;

To borrow Money on the credit of the United States;

To regulate Commerce with foreign Nations, and among the several States, and with the Indian Tribes;

To establish an uniform Rule of Naturalization, and uniform Laws on the subject of Bankruptcies throughout the United States;

To coin Money, regulate the Value thereof, and of foreign Coin, and fix the Standard of Weights and Measures;

To provide for the Punishment of counterfeiting the Securities and current Coin of the United States;

To establish Post Offices and post Roads;

To promote the Progress of Science and useful Arts, by securing for limited Times to Authors and Inventors the exclusive Right to their respective Writings and Discoveries;

To constitute Tribunals inferior to the supreme Court;

To define and punish Piracies and Felonies committed on the high Seas, and Offences against the Law of Nations;

To declare War, grant Letters of Marque and Reprisal, and make Rules concerning Captures on Land and Water;

To raise and support Armies, but no Appropriation of Money to that Use shall be for a longer Term than two Years;

To provide and maintain a Navy;

To make Rules for the Government and Regulation of the land and naval Forces;

To provide for calling forth the Militia to execute the Laws of the Union, suppress Insurrections and repeal Invasions;

To provide for organizing, arming, and disciplining, the Militia, and for governing such Part of them as may be employed in the Service of the United States, reserving to the States respectively, the Appointment of the Officers, and the Authority of training the Militia according to the discipline prescribed by Congress;

To exercise exclusive Legislation in all Cases whatsoever, over such District (not exceeding ten Miles square) as may, by Cession of Particular States, and the Acceptance of Congress, become the Seat of the Government of the United States, and to exercise like Authority over all Places purchased by the Consent of the Legislature of the State in which the Same shall be, for the Erection of Forts, Magazines, Arsenals, dock-Yards and other needful Buildings;—And

To make all Laws which shall be necessary and proper for carrying into Execution the foregoing Powers and all other Powers vested by this Constitution in the Government of the United States, or in any Department or Officer thereof.

Section 9

The Migration or Importation of such Persons as any of the States now existing shall think proper to admit, shall not be prohibited by the Congress prior to the Year one thousand eight hundred and eight, but a Tax or duty may be imposed on such Importation, not exceeding ten dollars for each Person.

The Privilege of the Writ of Habeas Corpus shall not be suspended, unless when in Cases of Rebellion or Invasion the public Safety may require it.

No Bill of Attainder or ex post facto Law shall be passed.

No Capitation, or other direct, Tax shall be laid, unless in Proportion to the Census of Enumeration herein before directed to be taken. [*Modified in 1913 by Amendment XVI*]

No Tax or Duty shall be laid on Articles exported from any State.

No Preference shall be given by any Regulation of Commerce or Revenue to the Ports of one State over those of another: nor shall Vessels bound to, or from, one State, be obliged to enter, clear or pay Duties in another.

No Money shall be drawn from the Treasury, but in Consequence of Appropriations made by Law; and a regular Statement and Account of the Receipts and Expenditures of all public Money shall be published from time to time.

No Title of Nobility shall be granted by the United States: And no Person holding any Office of Profit or Trust under them, shall, without the Consent of the Congress, accept of any present, Emolument, Office, or Title, of any kind whatever, from any King, Prince or foreign State.

Section 10

No State shall enter into any Treaty, Alliance, or Confederation; grant Letters of Marque and Reprisal; coin Money; emit Bills of Credit; make any Thing but gold and silver Coin a Tender in Payment of Debts; *pass any Bill* of Attainder, ex post facto Law, or Law *impairing the Obligation of Contracts,* or grant any Title of Nobility.

No State shall, without the Consent of the Congress, lay any Imposts or Duties on Imports or Exports, except what may be absolutely necessary for executing it's inspection Laws: and the net Produce of all Duties and Imposts, laid by any State on Imports or Exports, shall be for the Use of the Treasury of the United States; and all such Laws shall be subject to the Revision and Controul of the Congress.

No State shall, without the Consent of Congress, lay any Duty of Tonnage, keep Troops, or Ships of War in time of Peace, enter into any Agreement or Compact with another State, or with a foreign Power, or engage in War, unless actually invaded, or in such imminent Danger as will not admit of delay.

Article II (Executive Branch)

Section 1

The executive Power shall be vested in a President of the United States of America. He shall hold his Office during the Term of four Years, and, together with the Vice President, chosen for the same Term, be elected, as follows:

Each State shall appoint, in such Manner as the Legislature thereof may direct, a Number of Electors, equal to the whole Number of Senators and Representatives to which the State may be entitled in the Congress: but no Senator or Representative, or Person holding an Office of Trust or Profit under the United States, shall be appointed an Elector.

The Electors shall meet in their respective States, and vote by Ballot for two Persons, of whom one at least shall not be an Inhabitant of the same State with themselves. And they shall make a List of all the Persons voted for, and of the Number of Votes for each; which List they shall sign and certify, and transmit sealed to the Seat of the Government of the United States, directed to the President of the Senate. The President of the Senate shall, in the Presence of the Senate and House of Representatives, open all the Certificates, and the Votes shall then be counted. The Person having the greatest Number of Votes shall be the President, if such Number be a Majority of the whole Number of Electors appointed; and if there be more than one who have such Majority, and have an equal Number of Votes, then the House of Representatives shall immediately chuse by Ballot one of them for President; and if no Person have a Majority, then from the five highest on the List the said House shall in like Manner chuse the President. But in chusing the President, the Votes shall be taken by States, the Representatives from each State having one Vote; a quorum for this Purpose shall consist of a Member or Members from two thirds of the States, and a Majority of all the States shall be necessary to a Choice. In every Case, after the Choice of the President, the Person having the greatest Number of Votes of the Electors shall be the Vice President. But if there should remain two or more who have equal Votes, the Senate shall chuse from them by Ballot the Vice President. [*Modified in 1804 by Amendment XII*]

The Congress may determine the Time of chusing the Electors, and the Day on which they shall give their Votes; which Day shall be the same throughout the United States.

No Person except a natural born Citizen, or a Citizen of the United States, at the time of the Adoption of this Constitution, shall be eligible to the Office of President; neither shall any person be eligible to that Office who shall not have attained to the Age of thirty five Years, and been fourteen Years a Resident within the United States.

In Case of the Removal of the President from Office, or of his Death, Resignation, or Inability to discharge the Powers and Duties of the said Office, the Same shall devolve on the Vice President, and the Congress may by Law provide for the Case of Removal, Death, Resignation or Inability, both of the President and Vice President, declaring what Officer shall then act as President, and such Officer shall act accordingly, until the Disability be removed, or a President shall be elected.

The President shall, at stated Times, receive for his Services, a Compensation, which shall neither be encreased nor diminished during the Period for which he shall have been elected, and he shall not receive within that Period any other Emolument from the United States, or any of them.

Before he enter on the Execution of his Office, he shall take the following Oath or Affirmation: —"I do solemnly swear (or affirm) that I will faithfully execute the Office of President of the United States, and will to the best of my Ability, preserve, protect and defend the Constitution of the United States."

Section 2

The President shall be Commander in Chief of the Army and Navy of the United States, and of the Militia of the several States, when called into the actual Service of the United States; he may require the Opinion, in writing, of the principal Officer in each of the executive Departments, upon any Subject relating to the Duties of their respective Offices, and he shall have Power to Grant Reprieves and Pardons for Offences against the United States, except in Cases of Impeachment.

He shall have Power, by and with the Advice and Consent of the Senate, to make Treaties, provided two thirds of the Senators present concur; and he shall nominate, and by and with the Advice and Consent of the Senate, shall appoint Ambassadors, other public Ministers and Consuls, Judges of the supreme Court, and all other Officers of the United States, whose Appointments are not herein otherwise provided for, and which shall be established by Law; but the Congress may by Law vest the Appointment of such inferior Officers, as they think proper, in the President alone, in the Courts of Law, or in the Heads of Departments.

The President shall have Power to fill up all Vacancies that may happen during the Recess of the Senate, by granting Commissions which shall expire at the End of their next Session.

Section 3

He shall from time to time give to the Congress Information on the State of the Union, and recommend to their Consideration such Measures as he shall judge necessary and expedient; he may, on extraordinary Occasions, convene both Houses, or either of them, and in Case of Disagreement between them, with Respect to the Time of Adjournment, he may adjourn them to such Time as he shall think proper; he shall receive Ambassadors and other public Ministers; *he shall take Care that the Laws be faithfully executed,* and shall Commission all the Officers of the United States.

Section 4

The President, Vice President and all Civil Officers of the United States, shall be removed from Office on Impeachment for and Conviction of, Treason, Bribery, or other high Crimes and Misdemeanors.

Article III (Judiciary)

Section 1

The judicial Power of the United States, shall be vested in one supreme Court, and in such inferior Courts as the Congress may from time to time ordain and establish. The Judges, both of the supreme and inferior Courts, shall hold their Offices during good Behaviour, and shall, at stated Times, receive for their Services, a Compensation, which shall not be diminished during their Continuance in Office.

Section 2

The judicial Power shall extend to all Cases, in Law and Equity, arising under this Constitution, the Laws of the United States, and Treaties made, or which shall be made, under their Authority;—to all Cases affecting Ambassadors, other public ministers and Consuls;—to all Cases of admiralty and maritime Jurisdiction;—to Controversies to which the United States shall be a Party;—to Controversies between two or more States;—between a State and Citizens of another State;—between Citizens of different States;—between Citizens of the same State claiming Lands under Grants of different States, and between a State, or the Citizens thereof, and foreign States, Citizens or Subjects.

In all Cases affecting Ambassadors, other public Ministers and Consuls, and those in which a State shall be Party, the supreme Court shall have original Jurisdiction. In all the other Cases before mentioned, the supreme Court shall have appellate Jurisdiction, both as to Law and Fact, with such Exceptions, and under such Regulations as the Congress shall make.

The Trial of all Crimes, except in Cases of Impeachment, shall be by Jury; and such Trial shall be held in the State where the said Crimes shall have been committed; but when not committed within any State, the Trial shall be at such Place or Places as the Congress may by Law have directed.

Section 3

Treason against the United States, shall consist only in levying War against them, or in adhering to their Enemies, giving them Aid and Comfort. No Person shall be convicted of Treason unless on the Testimony of two Witnesses to the same overt Act, or on Confession in open Court.

The Congress shall have Power to declare the Punishment of Treason, but no Attainder of Treason shall work Corruption of Blood, or Forfeiture except during the Life of the Person attainted.

Article IV

Section 1

Full Faith and Credit shall be given in each State to the public Acts, Records, and judicial Proceedings of every other State. And the Congress may by general Laws prescribe the Manner in which such Acts, Records and Proceedings shall be proved, and the Effect thereof.

Section 2

The Citizens of each State shall be entitled to all Privileges and Immunities of Citizens in the several States.

A Person charged in any State with Treason, Felony, or other Crime, who shall flee from Justice, and be found in another State, shall on Demand of the executive Authority of the State from which he fled, be delivered up, to be removed to the State having Jurisdiction of the Crime.

No Person held to Service or Labour in one State, under the Laws thereof, escaping into another, shall, in Consequence of any Law or Regulation therein, be discharged from such Service or Labour, but shall be delivered up on Claim of the Party to whom such Service or Labour may be due.

Section 3

New States may be admitted by the Congress into this Union; but no new State shall be formed or erected within the Jurisdiction of any other State; nor any State be formed by the Junction of two or more States, or Parts of States, without the Consent of the Legislatures of the States concerned as well as of the Congress.

The Congress shall have Power to dispose of and make all needful Rules and Regulations respecting the Territory or other Property belonging to the United States; and nothing in this Constitution shall be so construed as to Prejudice any Claims of the United States, or of any particular State.

Section 4

The United States shall guarantee to every State in this Union a Republican Form of Government, and shall protect each of them against Invasion; and on Application of the Legislature, or of the Executive (when the Legislature cannot be convened) against domestic Violence.

Article V (Amending the Constitution)

The Congress, whenever two thirds of both Houses shall deem it necessary, shall propose Amendments to this Constitution, or, on the Application of the Legislatures of two thirds of the several States, shall call a Convention for proposing Amendments, which, in either Case, shall be valid to all Intents and Purposes, as Part of this Constitution, when ratified by the Legislatures of three fourths of the several States, or by Conventions in three fourths thereof, as the one or the other Mode of Ratification may be proposed by the Congress; Provided that no Amendment which may be made prior to the Year One thousand eight hundred and eight shall in any Manner affect the first and fourth Clauses in the Ninth Section of the first Article; and that no State, without its Consent, shall be deprived of its equal Suffrage in the Senate.

Article VI

All Debts contracted and Engagements entered into, before the Adoption of this Constitution, shall be as valid against the United States under this Constitution, as under the Confederation.

This Constitution, and the Laws of the United States which shall be made in Pursuance thereof; and all Treaties made, or which shall be made, under the Authority of the United States, shall be the supreme Law of the Land; and the Judges in every State shall be bound thereby, any Thing in the Constitution or Laws of any state to the Contrary notwithstanding.

The Senators and Representatives before mentioned, and the Members of the several State Legislatures, and all executive and judicial Officers, both of the United States and of the several States, shall be bound by Oath or Affirmation, to support this Constitution; but no religious Test shall ever be required as a Qualification to any Office or public Trust under the United States.

Article VII

The Ratification of the Conventions of nine States, shall be sufficient for the Establishment of this Constitution between the States so ratifying the same.

Amendment I (1791)

Congress shall make no law respecting an establishment of religion, or prohibiting the free exercise thereof; or abridging the freedom of speech, or of the press; or the right of the people peaceably to assemble, and to petition the Government for a redress of grievances.

Amendment II (1791)

A well regulated Militia, being necessary to the security of a free State, the right of the people to keep and bear Arms, shall not be infringed.

Amendment III (1791)

No Soldier shall, in time of peace be quartered in any house, without the consent of the Owner, nor in time of war, but in a manner to be prescribed by law.

Amendment IV (1791)

The right of the people to be secure in their persons, houses, papers, and effects, against unreasonable searches and seizures, shall not be violated, and no Warrants shall issue, but upon probable cause, supported by Oath or affirmation, and particularly describing the place to be searched, and the persons or things to be seized.

Amendment V (1791)

No person shall be held to answer for a capital, or otherwise infamous crime, unless on a presentment or indictment of a Grand Jury, except in cases arising in the land or naval forces, or in the Militia, when in actual service in time of War or public danger; nor shall any person be subject for the same offence to be twice put in jeopardy of life or limb; nor shall be compelled in any criminal case to be a witness against himself, nor be deprived of life, liberty, or property, without due process of law; nor shall private property be taken for public use, without just compensation.

Amendment VI (1791)

In all criminal prosecutions, the accused shall enjoy the right to a speedy and public trial, by an impartial jury of the State and district wherein the crime shall have been committed, which district shall have been previously ascertained by law, and to be informed of the nature and cause of the accusation; to be confronted with the witnesses against him; to have compulsory process for obtaining witnesses in his favor, and to have the Assistance of Counsel for his defence.

Amendment VII (1791)

In Suits at common law, where the value in controversy shall exceed twenty dollars, the right of trial by jury shall be preserved, and no fact tried by a jury, shall be otherwise re-examined in any Court of the United States, than according to the rules of the common law.

Amendment VIII (1791)

Excessive bail shall not be required, nor excessive fines imposed, nor cruel and unusual punishments inflicted.

Amendment IX (1791)

The enumeration in the Constitution, of certain rights, shall not be construed to deny or disparage others retained by the people.

Amendment X (1791)

The powers not delegated to the United States by the Constitution, nor prohibited by it to the States, are reserved to the States respectively, or to the people.

Amendment XI (1795)

The Judicial power of the United States shall not be construed to extend to any suit in law or equity, commenced or prosecuted against one of the United States by Citizens of another State, or by Citizens or Subjects of any Foreign State.

Amendment XII (1804)

The Electors shall meet in their respective states and vote by ballot for President and Vice-President, one of whom, at least, shall not be an inhabitant of the same state with themselves; they shall name in their ballots the person voted for as President, and in distinct ballots the person voted for as Vice-President, and they shall make distinct lists of all persons voted for as President, and of all persons voted for as Vice-President, and of the number of votes for each, which lists they shall sign and certify, and transmit sealed to the seat of the government of the United States, directed to the President of the Senate;—The President of the Senate shall, in the presence of the Senate and House of Representatives, open all the certificates and the votes shall then be counted;—The person having the greatest Number of votes for President, shall be the President, if such number be a majority of the whole number of Electors appointed; and *if no person have such majority, then from the persons having the highest numbers not exceeding three on the list of those voted for as President, the House of Representatives shall choose immediately, by ballot, the President. But in choosing the President, the votes shall be taken by states, the representation from each state having one vote;* a quorum for this purpose shall consist of a member or members from two-thirds of the states, and a majority of all the states shall be necessary to a choice. And if the House of Representatives shall not choose a President whenever the right of choice shall devolve upon them, before the fourth day of March next following, then the Vice- President shall act as President, as in the case of the death or other constitutional disability of the President—The person having the greatest number of votes as Vice-President, shall be the Vice-President, if such number be a majority of the whole number of Electors appointed, and if no person have a majority, then from the two highest numbers on the list, the Senate shall choose the Vice-President; a quorum for the purpose shall consist of two-thirds of the whole number of Senators, and a majority of the whole number shall be necessary to a choice. But no person constitutionally ineligible to the office of President shall be eligible to that of Vice-President of the United States.

Amendment XIII (1865)

Section 1. Neither slavery nor involuntary servitude, except as a punishment for crime whereof the party shall have been duly convicted, shall exist within the United States, or any place subject to their jurisdiction.

Section 2. Congress shall have power to enforce this article by appropriate legislation.

Amendment XIV (1868)

Section 1. All persons born or naturalized in the United States and subject to the jurisdiction thereof, are citizens of the United States and of the State wherein they reside. No State shall make or enforce any law which shall abridge the privileges or immunities of citizens of the United States; nor shall any State deprive any person of life, liberty, or property, without due process of law; nor deny to any person within its jurisdiction the equal protection of the laws.

Section 2. Representatives shall be apportioned among the several States according to their respective numbers, counting the whole number of persons in each State, excluding Indians not taxed. But when the right to vote at any election for the choice of electors for President and Vice President of the United States, Representatives in Congress, the Executive and Judicial officers of a State, or the members of the Legislature thereof, is denied to any of the male inhabitants of such State, being twenty-one years of age, and citizens of the United States, or in any way abridged, except for participation in rebellion, or other crime, the basis of representation therein shall be reduced in the proportion which the number of such male citizens shall bear to the whole number of male citizens twenty-one years of age in such State.

Section 3. No person shall be a Senator or Representative in Congress, or elector of President and Vice President, or hold any office, civil or military, under the United States, or under any State, who, having previously taken an oath, as a member of Congress, or as an officer of the United States, or as a member of any State legislature, or as an executive or judicial officer of any State, to support the Constitution of the United States, shall have engaged in insurrection or rebellion against the same, or given aid or comfort to the enemies thereof. But Congress may by a vote of two-thirds of each House, remove such disability.

Section 4. The validity of the public debt of the United States, authorized by law, including debts incurred for payment of pensions and bounties for services in suppressing insurrection or rebellion, shall not be questioned. But neither the United States nor any State shall assume or pay any debt or obligation incurred in aid of insurrection or rebellion against the United States, or any claim for the loss or emancipation of any slave; but all such debts, obligations and claims shall be held illegal and void.

Section 5. The Congress shall have power to enforce, by appropriate legislation, the provisions of this article.

Amendment XV (1870)

Section 1. The right of citizens of the United States to vote shall not be denied or abridged by the United States or by any State on account of race, color, or previous condition of servitude.

Section 2. The Congress shall have power to enforce this article by appropriate legislation.

Amendment XVI (1913)

The Congress shall have power to lay and collect taxes on incomes, from whatever source derived, without apportionment among the several States, and without regard to any census or enumeration.

Amendment XVII (1913)

The Senate of the United States shall be composed of two Senators from each State, elected by the people thereof, for six years; and each Senator shall have one vote. The electors in each State shall have the qualifications requisite for electors of the most numerous branch of the State legislatures.

When vacancies happen in the representation of any State in the Senate, the executive authority of such State shall issue writs of election to fill such vacancies: Provided, That the legislature of any State may empower the executive thereof to make temporary appointments until the people fill the vacancies by election as the legislature may direct.

This amendment shall not be so construed as to affect the election or term of any Senator chosen before it becomes valid as part of the Constitution.

Amendment XVIII (1919)

Section 1. After one year from the ratification of this article the manufacture, sale, or transportation of intoxicating liquors within, the importation thereof into, or the exportation thereof from the United States and all territory subject to the jurisdiction thereof for beverage purposes is hereby prohibited.

Section 2. The Congress and the several States shall have concurrent power to enforce this article by appropriate legislation.

Section 3. This article shall be inoperative unless it shall have been ratified as an amendment to the Constitution by the legislatures of the several States, as provided in the Constitution, within seven years from the date of the submission hereof to the States by the Congress.

Amendment XIX (1920)

The right of citizens of the United States to vote shall not be denied or abridged by the United States or by any State on account of sex. Congress shall have power to enforce this article by appropriate legislation.

Amendment XX (1933)

Section 1. The terms of the President and Vice President shall end at noon on the 20th day of January, and the terms of Senators and Representatives at noon on the 3d day of January, of the years in which such terms would have ended if this article had not been ratified; and the terms of their successors shall then begin.

Section 2. The Congress shall assemble at least once in every year, and such meeting shall begin at noon on the 3d day of January, unless they shall by law appoint a different day.

Section 3. If, at the time fixed for the beginning of the term of the President, the President elect shall have died, the Vice President elect shall become President. If a President shall not have been chosen before the time fixed for the beginning of his term, or if the President elect shall have failed to qualify, then the Vice President elect shall act as President until a President shall have qualified; and the Congress may by law provide for the case wherein neither a President elect nor a Vice President elect shall have qualified, declaring who shall then act as President, or the manner in which one who is to act shall be selected, and such person shall act accordingly until a President or Vice President shall have qualified.

Section 4. The Congress may by law provide for the case of the death of any of the persons from whom the House of Representatives may choose a President whenever the right of choice shall have devolved upon them, and for the case of the death of any of the persons from whom the Senate may choose a Vice President whenever the right of choice shall have devolved upon them.

Section 5. Sections 1 and 2 shall take effect on the 15th day of October following the ratification of this article.

Section 6. This article shall be inoperative unless it shall have been ratified as an amendment to the Constitution by the legislatures of three-fourths of the several States within seven years from the date of its submission.

Amendment XXI (1933)

Section 1. The eighteenth article of amendment to the Constitution of the United States is hereby repealed.

Section 2. The transportation or importation into any State, Territory, or possession of the United States for delivery or use therein of intoxicating liquors, in violation of the laws thereof, is hereby prohibited.

Section 3. This article shall be inoperative unless it shall have been ratified as an amendment to the Constitution by conventions in the several States, as provided in the Constitution, within seven years from the date of the submission hereof to the States by the Congress.

Amendment XXII (1951)

Section 1. No person shall be elected to the office of the President more than twice, and no person who has held the office of President, or acted as President, for more than two years of a term to which some other person was elected President shall be elected to the office of the President more than once. But this Article shall not apply to any person holding the office of President, when this Article was proposed by the Congress, and shall not prevent any person who may be holding the office of President, or acting as President, during the term within which this Article becomes operative from holding the office of President or acting as President during the remainder of such term.

Section 2. This article shall be inoperative unless it shall have been ratified as an amendment to the Constitution by the legislatures of three-fourths of the several States within seven years from the date of its submission to the States by the Congress.

Amendment XXIII (1961)

Section 1. The District constituting the seat of Government of the United States shall appoint in such manner as the Congress may direct: A number of electors of President and Vice President equal to the whole number of Senators and Representatives in Congress to which the District would be entitled if it were a State, but in no event more than the least populous State; they shall be in addition to those appointed by the States, but they shall be considered, for the purposes of the election of President and Vice President, to be electors appointed by a State; and they shall meet in the District and perform such duties as provided by the twelfth article of amendment.

Section 2. The Congress shall have power to enforce this article by appropriate legislation.

Amendment XXIV (1964)

Section 1. The right of citizens of the United States to vote in any primary or other election for President or Vice President, for electors for President or Vice President, or for Senator or Representative in Congress, shall not be denied or abridged by the United States or any State by reason of failure to pay any poll tax or other tax.

Section 2. The Congress shall have power to enforce this article by appropriate legislation.

Amendment XXV (1967)

Section 1. In case of the removal of the President from office or of his death or resignation, the Vice President shall become President.

Section 2. Whenever there is a vacancy in the office of the Vice President, the President shall nominate a Vice President who shall take office upon confirmation by a majority vote of both Houses of Congress.

Section 3. Whenever the President transmits to the President pro tempore of the Senate and the Speaker of the House of Representatives has written declaration that he is unable to discharge the powers and duties of his office, and until he transmits to them a written declaration to the contrary, such powers and duties shall be discharged by the Vice President as Acting President.

Section 4. Whenever the Vice President and a majority of either the principal officers of the executive departments or of such other body as Congress may by law provide, transmit to the President pro tempore of the Senate and the Speaker of the House of Representatives their written declaration that the President is unable to discharge the powers and duties of his office, the Vice President shall immediately assume the powers and duties of the office as Acting President.

Thereafter, when the President transmits to the President pro tempore of the Senate and the Speaker of the House of Representatives has written declaration that no inability exists, he shall resume the powers and duties of his office unless the Vice President and a majority of either the principal officers of the executive department or of such other body as Congress may by law provide, transmit within four days to the President pro tempore of the Senate and the Speaker of the House of Representatives their written declaration that the President is unable to discharge the powers and duties of his office. Thereupon Congress shall decide the issue, assembling within forty-eight hours for that purpose if not in session. If the Congress, within twenty-one days after receipt of the latter written declaration, or, if Congress is not in session, within twenty-one days after Congress is required to assemble, determines by two-thirds vote of both Houses that the President is unable to discharge the powers and duties of his office, the Vice President shall continue to discharge the same as Acting President; otherwise, the President shall resume the powers and duties of his office.

Amendment XXVI (1971)

Section 1. The right of citizens of the United States, who are eighteen years of age or older, to vote shall not be denied or abridged by the United States or by any State on account of age.

Section 2. The Congress shall have power to enforce this article by appropriate legislation.

Amendment XXVII (1992)

No law varying the compensation for the services of the Senators and Representatives shall take effect, until an election of Representatives shall have intervened.

Appendix B: Index of Case Digests

Appendix C: Table of Case References by Justice

Note: Cases are listed in the order in which they are discussed.

Alito, Samuel A., Jr.

Parents Involved in Community Schools v. Seattle School District No. 1 (2007), joined in part Chief Justice Roberts's opinion

Rumsfeld v. Forum for Academic and Institutional Rights, Inc. (2006), did not participate

Davenport v. Washington Education Association (2007), joined in part Justice Scalia's opinion; joined in Justice Breyer's concurrence in part and concurrence in the judgment

Federal Election Commission v. Wisconsin Right to Life, Inc. (2008), joined Chief Justice Roberts's opinion

Boumediene v. Bush (2008), joined Chief Justice Roberts's dissent; joined Justice Scalia's dissent

Hamdan v. Rumsfeld (2006), dissent

Black, Hugo L.

Ferguson v. Skrupa (1963), opinion

Korematsu v. United States (1944), opinion

New York Times Co. v. Sullivan (1964), joined Justice Brennan's opinion

Bell v. Maryland (1964), dissent

Heart of Atlanta Motel, Inc. v. United States (1964), concurrence

Katzenbach v. McClung (1964), concurrence

Griswold v. Georgia (1965), dissent; joined Justice Potter's dissent

Planned Parenthood of S. E. Pennsylvania v. Casey (1992), concurrence in the judgment

Brandenburg v. Ohio (1969), concurrence

Dennis v. United States (1951), dissent

Cohen v. California (1971), joined Justice Blackmun's dissent

New York Times Co. v. United States (1971), concurrence; joined Justice Douglas's concurrence

Cox v. New Hampshire (1941), joined Chief Justice Hughes's opinion

Everson v. Board of Education (1947), opinion

Engel v. Vitale (1961), opinion

Abington School District v. Schempp (1963), joined Justice Clark's opinion

Youngstown Sheet and Tube Co. v. Sawyer (1952), opinion
Lucas v. Forty-Fourth General Assembly of Colorado (1964), joined Chief Justice Warren's opinion

Blackmun, Harry A.

Batson v. Kentucky (1986), joined in Justice Powell's opinion
Regents of the University of California v. Bakke (1978), concurrence in part, dissent in part
Roe v. Wade (1973), opinion
Eisenstadt v. Baird (1972), joined Justice White's concurrence in the judgment
Thornburgh v. American College of Obstetricians and Gynecologists (1986), opinion
Planned Parenthood of S. E. Pennsylvania v. Casey (1992), concurring in part and dissenting in part
Webster v. Reproductive Health Services (1989), concurring in part and dissenting in part
Akron v. Akron Center for Reproductive Health (1983), joined Justice Powell's opinion
R. A. V. v. St. Paul (1992), concurrence; joined Justice White's concurrence
Cohen v. California (1971), dissent
Branzburg v. Hayes (1972), joined Justice White's opinion
New York Times Co. v. United States (1971), joined Justice Harlan's dissent
Wallace v. Jaffree (1985), joined Justice Stevens's opinion
Stone v. Graham (1989), dissent
Lee v. Weisman (1992), concurrence
Texas Monthly, Inc. v. Bullock (1989), concurrence
Employment Division, Department of Human Resources of Oregon v. Smith (1990), dissent; concurrence in part in Justice O'Connor's opinion
United States v. U.S. District Court (1972), joined Justice Powell's opinion
Beer v. United States (1976), joined Justice Stewart's opinion
Shaw v. Reno (1993), dissented and joined Justice White's dissent
Furman v. Georgia (1972), dissent
Harmelin v. Michigan (1991), joined dissents of Justices White and Stevens

Bradley, Joseph P.

Slaughter-House Cases (1873), dissent
Civil rights cases (1883), opinion

Brandeis, Louis D.

Abrams v. United States (1919), joined Justice Holmes's dissent

Brennan, William J.

Ferguson v. Skrupa (1963), joined Justice Black's opinion
New York Times Co. v. Sullivan (1964), opinion
Batson v. Kentucky (1986), joined in Justice Powell's opinion; joined in Justice Stevens's concurrence
Bell v. Maryland (1964), opinion; joined Justice Goldberg's concurrence
Regents of the University of California v. Bakke (1978), concurring in part and dissenting in part
Griswold v. Connecticut (1965), joined concurrence by Justice Goldberg
Eisenstadt v. Baird (1972), opinion
Webster v. Reproductive Health Services (1989), joined Justice Blackmun's concurrence in part, dissent in part
Akron v. Akron Center for Reproductive Health (1983), joined Justice Powell's opinion
Texas v. Johnson (1989), opinion
New York Times Co. v. United States (1971), concurrence
Abington School District v. Schempp (1963), joined Justice Clark's opinion; concurrence
Wallace v. Jaffree (1985), joined Justice Stevens's opinion
Texas Monthly, Inc. v. Bullock (1989), opinion

Employment Division, Department of Human Resources of Oregon v. Smith (1990), joined Justice
    O'Connor's concurrence in part; joined Justice Blackmun's dissent
United States v. U.S. District Court (1972), joined Justice Powell's opinion
Beer v. United States (1976), joined Justice Marshall's dissent
Lucas v. Forty-Fourth General Assembly of Colorado (1964), joined Chief Justice Warren's opinion
Furman v. Georgia (1972), concurrence

Brewer, David J.

Lochner v. New York (1905), joined Justice Peckham's opinion

Breyer, Stephen G.

United States v. Virginia (1996), joined Justice Ginsburg's opinion
Gonzales v. Raich (2005), joined Justice Stevens's opinion
Adarand Constructors, Inc. v. Peña (1995), joined Justice Souter's dissent
Grutter v. Bollinger (2003), joined Justice Ginsburg's concurrence
Parents Involved in Community Schools v. Seattle School District No. 1 (2007), dissent
Washington v. Glucksberg (1997), concurrence; joined Justice O'Connor's concurrence in part
Vacco v. Quill (1997), concurrence
Virginia v. Black (2003), joined Justice O'Connor's opinion in part
Boy Scouts of America v. Dale (2000), joined Justice Stevens's dissent
Davenport v. Washington Education Association (2007), concurrence in part with Justice Scalia's
    opinion; concurrence in the judgment
Federal Election Commission v. Wisconsin Right to Life, Inc. (2008), dissent
Mitchell v. Helms (2000), joined Justice O'Connor's concurrence in the judgment
Zelman v. Simmons-Harris (2002), dissent; joined Justice Souter's dissent
Van Orden v. Perry (2005), joined Justice Rehnquist's opinion
City of Boerne v. Flores (1997), dissent; joined Justice O'Connor's dissent in part
Hamdi v. Rumsfeld (2004), joined Justice O'Connor's opinion
Rasul v. Bush (2004), joined Justice Stevens's opinion
Boumediene v. Bush (2008), joined Justice Kennedy's opinion; joined Justice Souter's concurrence
Hamdan v. Rumsfeld (2006), joined Justice Stevens's opinion; concurrence
Vieth v. Jubelirer (2004), dissent
Bush v. Gore (2000), dissent and joined Justice Souter's dissent
Ewing v. California (2003), dissent

Brown, Henry B.

Plessy v. Ferguson (1896), opinion
Lochner v. New York (1905), joined Justice Peckham's opinion

Burger, Warren E.

Batson v. Kentucky (1986), dissent
Regents of the University of California v. Bakke (1978), concurring in part and dissenting in part
Eisenstadt v. Baird (1972), dissent
Roe v. Wade (1973), concurrence
Thornburgh v. American College of Obstetricians and Gynecologists (1986), dissent
Akron v. Akron Center for Reproductive Health (1983), joined Justice Powell's opinion
Cohen v. California (1971), joined Justice Blackmun's dissent
Branzburg v. Hayes (1972), joined Justice White's opinion
New York Times Co. v. United States (1971), dissent and joined Justice Harlan's dissent
Wallace v. Jaffree (1985), dissent
Stone v. Graham (1980), dissent
United States v. U.S. District Court (1972), concurrence in the judgment

Beer v. United States (1976), joined in Justice Stewart's opinion
Furman v. Georgia (1972), dissent

Butler, Pierce

Near v. Minnesota (1931), dissent

Burton, Harold H.

Everson v. Board of Education (1947), joined Justice Rutledge's dissent
Youngstown Sheet and Tube Co. v. Sawyer (1952), concurrence

Clark, Tom C.

Ferguson v. Skrupa (1963), joined Justice Black's opinion
New York Times Co. v. Sullivan (1964), joined Justice Brennan's opinion
Heart of Atlanta Motel, Inc. v. United States (1964), opinion
Katzenbach v. McClung (1964), opinion
Dennis v. United States (1951), did not participate
Abington School District v. Schempp (1963), opinion
Youngstown Sheet and Tube Co. v. Sawyer (1952), concurrence
Reynolds v. Sims (1964), concurrence in the judgment
Lucas v. Forty-Fourth General Assembly of Colorado (1964), dissent; joined Justice Stewart's
    dissent

Day, William R.

Lochner v. New York (1905), joined Justice Peckham's opinion

Douglas, William O.

Hirabayashi v. United States (1943), concurrence
New York Times Co. v. Sullivan (1964), joined Justice Brennan's opinion; concurrence; joined in
    Justice Goldberg's concurrence
Bell v. Maryland (1964), concurrence
Heart of Atlanta Motel, Inc. v. United States (1964), concurrence
Katzenbach v. McClung (1964), concurrence
Griswold v. Connecticut (1965), opinion
Eisenstadt v. Baird (1972), joined Justice Brennan's opinion; concurrence
Roe v. Wade (1973), concurrence
Brandenburg v. Ohio (1969), concurrence
Dennis v. United States (1951), dissent
United States v. O'Brien (1968), dissent
Branzburg v. Hayes (1972), dissent
New York Times Co. v. United States (1971), concurrence; joined Justice Black's concurrence
Cox v. New Hampshire (1941), joined Chief Justice Hughes's opinion
Abington School District v. Schempp (1963), joined Justice Clark's opinion; concurrence
United States v. U.S. District Court (1972), joined Justice Powell's opinion; concurrence
Youngstown Sheet and Tube Co. v. Sawyer (1952), concurrence
Gray v. Sanders (1963), opinion
Lucas v. Forty-Fourth General Assembly of Colorado (1964), joined Chief Justice Warren's opinion
Furman v. Georgia (1972), per curiam

Frankfurter, Felix

Korematsu v. United States (1944), concurrence
Cooper v. Aaron (1958), concurrence

Dennis v. United States (1951), concurrence in the judgment
Cox v. New Hampshire (1941), joined Chief Justice Hughes's opinion
Everson v. Board of Education (1947), joined dissents of Justices Jackson and Rutledge
Youngstown Sheet and Tube Co. v. Sawyer (1952), concurrence

Fuller, Melville

Lochner v. New York (1905), joined Justice Peckham's opinion

Ginsburg, Ruth Bader

United States v. Virginia (1996), opinion
Gonzales v. Raich (2005), joined Justice Stevens's opinion
Adarand Constructors, Inc. v. Peña (1995), joined dissents of Justices Souter and Stevens
Gratz v. Bollinger (2003), dissent
Grutter v. Bollinger (2003), concurrence
Parents Involved in Community Schools v. Seattle School District No. 1 (2007), joined Justice
        Breyer's dissent
Gonzales v. Carhart (2007), dissent
Washington v. Glucksberg (1997), joined Justice O'Connor's concurrence in part
Virginia v. Black (2003), dissent in part and joined Justice Souter's concurrence in part
Boy Scouts of America v. Dale (2000), joined Justice Stevens's dissent
Davenport v. Washington Education Association (2007), joined Justice Scalia's opinion
Federal Election Commission v. Wisconsin Right to Life, Inc. (2008), dissent
Mitchell v. Helms (2000), joined Justice Souter's dissent
Zelman v. Simmons-Harris (2002), joined Justice Souter's dissent
Van Orden v. Perry (2005), joined Justice Stevens's dissent
Hamdi v. Rumsfeld (2004), joined Justice Souter's opinion concurring in part and dissenting in part
Rasul v. Bush (2004), joined Justice Stevens's opinion
Boumediene v. Bush (2008), joined Justice Kennedy's opinion; joined Justice Souter's concurrence
Hamdan v. Rumsfeld (2006), joined Justice Stevens's opinion; joined Justice Breyer's concurrence
Vieth v. Jubelirer (2004), joined Justice Souter's dissent
Bush v. Gore (2000), dissent; joined Justice Stevens's dissent; joined Justice Souter's dissent in part
Roper v. Simmons (2005), joined Justice Stevens's concurrence
Ewing v. California (2003), dissent

Goldberg, Arthur J.

Ferguson v. Skrupa (1963), joined Justice Black's opinion
New York Times Co. v. Sullivan (1964), joined Justice Brennan's opinion
Bell v. Maryland (1964), concurrence; joined Justice Douglas's concurrence in part
Heart of Atlanta Motel, Inc. v. United States (1964), concurrence
Katzenbach v. McClung (1964), concurrence
Griswold v. Connecticut (1965), concurrence
Abington School District v. Schempp (1963), joined Justice Goldberg's concurrence
Lucas v. Forty-Fourth General Assembly of Colorado (1964), joined Chief Justice Warren's opinion

Harlan, John Marshall (1833–1911)

Plessy v. Ferguson (1896), dissent
Civil Rights Cases (1883), dissent
Lochner v. New York (1905), joined Justice Peckham's opinion

Harlan, John Marshall, II (1899–1971)

Ferguson v. Skrupa (1963), joined Justice Black's opinion
New York Times Co. v. Sullivan (1964), joined Justice Brennan's opinion
Bell v. Maryland (1964), joined Justice Black's dissent

Griswold v. Connecticut (1965), concurrence in the judgment
United States v. O'Brien (1968), concurrence
Cohen v. California (1971), opinion
New York Times Co. v. United States (1971), dissent
Abington School District v. Schempp (1963), joined majority opinion and Justice Goldberg's
    concurrence
Reynolds v. Sims (1964), dissent

Holmes, Oliver Wendell, Jr.

Lochner v. New York (1905), dissent
Schenck v. United States (1919), opinion
Pennsylvania Coal v. Mahon (1922), opinion

Hughes, Charles Evans

West Coast Hotel Co. v. Parrish (1937), opinion
Near v. Minnesota (1931), opinion
Cox v. New Hampshire (1941), opinion

Jackson, Robert H.

Korematsu v. United States (1944), dissent
Shelley v. Kraemer (1948), did not participate
Dennis v. United States (1951), concurrence in the judgment
Everson v. Board of Education (1947), dissented and joined Justice Rutledge's dissent
Youngstown Sheet and Tube Co. v. Sawyer (1952), concurrence

Kennedy, Anthony M.

United States v. Virginia (1996), joined Justice Ginsburg's opinion
Gonzales v. Raich (2005), joined Justice Stevens's opinion
Grutter v. Bollinger (2003), dissent; joined Chief Justice Rehnquist's dissent
Parents Involved in Community Schools v. Seattle School District No. 1 (2007), concurrence; joined
    in part Chief Justice Roberts's opinion
Webster v. Reproductive Health Services (1989), joined in part Chief Justice Rehnquist's opinion
Planned Parenthood of S. E. Pennsylvania v. Casey (1992), co-authored plurality opinion with Justice
    O'Connor and Justice Souter
Stenberg v. Carhart (2000), dissent
Gonzales v. Carhart (2007), opinion
Romer v. Evans (1996), opinion
Lawrence v. Texas (2003), opinion
Texas v. Johnson (1989), concurrence
Virginia v. Black (2003), joined Justice Souter's opinion concurring in part and dissenting in part
Federal Election Commission v. Wisconsin Right to Life, Inc. (2008), joined Chief Justice Roberts's
    opinion in part
Davenport v. Washington Education Association (2007), joined Justice Scalia's opinion
Mitchell v. Helms (2000), joined Justice Thomas's opinion
Lee v. Weisman (1992), opinion
Texas Monthly, Inc. v. Bullock (1989), joined Justice Scalia's dissent
City of Boerne v. Flores (1997), opinion
Hamdi v. Rumsfeld (2004), joined Justice O'Connor's opinion
Rasul v. Bush (2004), concurrence in the judgment
Boumediene v. Bush (2008), opinion
Hamdan v. Rumsfeld (2006), concurrence; joined Justice Breyer's concurrence
Vieth v. Jubelirer (2004), concurrence
Bush v. Gore (2000), per curiam

Stanford v. Kentucky (1989), joined in Justice Scalia's opinion
Penry v. Lynaugh (1989), joined Justice O'Connor's opinion
Roper v. Simmons (2005), opinion
Harmelin v. Michigan (1991), joined in part Justice Scalia's opinion; concurrence in part; concurrence in the judgment
Ewing v. California (2003), joined Justice O'Connor's opinion
Kelo v. City of New London (2005), joined Justice Stevens's opinion; concurrence

Marshall, John

Marbury v. Madison (1803), opinion

Marshall, Thurgood

Batson v. Kentucky (1986), joined Justice Powell's opinion; concurrence
Regents of the University of California v. Bakke (1978), concurring in part and dissenting in part
Eisenstadt v. Baird (1972), joined Justice Brennan's opinion
Webster v. Reproductive Health Services (1989), joined Justice Blackmun's concurrence in part, dissent in part
Akron v. Akron Center for Reproductive Health (1983), joined Justice Powell's opinion
United States v. O'Brien (1968), did not participate
Branzburg v. Hayes (1972), joined Justice Stewart's dissent
New York Times Co. v. United States (1971), concurrence
Wallace v. Jaffree (1985), joined Justice Stevens's opinion
Texas Monthly, Inc. v. Bullock (1989), joined in Justice Brennan's opinion
Employment Division, Department of Human Resources of Oregon v. Smith (1990), joined in Justice O'Connor's concurrence in part, dissent in part
United States v. U.S. District Court (1972), joined Justice Powell's opinion
Furman v. Georgia (1972), concurrence
Beer v. United States (1976), dissent

McKenna, Joseph

Lochner v. New York (1905), joined Justice Peckham's opinion

McReynolds, James C.

Near v. Minnesota (1931), joined Justice Butler's dissent
United States v. Curtiss-Wright Export Corp. (1936), dissent
Cox v. New Hampshire (1941), joined Chief Justice Hughes's opinion

Miller, Samuel F.

Slaughter-House Cases (1873), opinion

Minton, Sherman

Dennis v. United States (1951), joined Chief Justice Vinson's opinion
Youngstown Sheet and Tube Co. v. Sawyer (1952), joined Chief Justice Vinson's dissent

Murphy, Frank

Korematsu v. United States (1944), dissent
Hirabayashi v. United States (1943), concurrence
Cox v. New Hampshire (1941), joined Chief Justice Hughes's opinion

O'Connor, Sandra Day

United States v. Virginia (1996), joined Justice Ginsburg's opinion

Batson v. Kentucky (1986), joined Justice Powell's opinion; concurrence
Gonzales v. Raich (2005), dissent
Adarand Constructors, Inc. v. Peña (1995), opinion
Grutter v. Bollinger (2003), opinion
Akron v. Akron Center for Reproductive Health (1983), dissent
Thornburgh v. American College of Obstetricians and Gynecologists (1986), dissent
Webster v. Reproductive Health Services (1989), concurrence
Planned Parenthood of S. E. Pennsylvania v. Casey (1992), co-authored plurality opinion with Justices Kennedy and Souter
Washington v. Glucksberg (1997), concurrence
Lawrence v. Texas (2003), concurrence in the judgment
Texas v. Johnson (1989), joined in Chief Justice Rehnquist's dissent
R. A. V. v. St. Paul (1992), joined Justice White's concurrence
Virginia v. Black (2003), opinion
Mitchell v. Helms (2000), concurrence in the judgment
Zelman v. Simmons-Harris (2002), joined Chief Justice Rehnquist's opinion; concurrence
Wallace v. Jaffree (1985), concurrence
Lee v. Weisman (1992), joined Justice Blackmun's concurrence; joined Justice Souter's concurrence
McCreary Co. v. American Civil Liberties Union (2005), concurrence
Van Orden v. Perry (2005), dissent
Texas Monthly, Inc. v. Bullock (1989), joined Justice Blackmun's concurrence
Employment Division, Department of Human Resources of Oregon v. Smith (1990), concurrence in the judgment
City of Boerne v. Flores (1997), dissent
Hamdi v. Rumfeld (2004), opinion
Rasul v. Bush (2004), joined Justice Stevens's opinion
Shaw v. Reno (1993), opinion
Vieth v. Jubelirer (2004), joined Justice Scalia's opinion
Bush v. Gore (2000), per curiam
Stanford v. Kentucky (1989), joined Justice Scalia's opinion
Penry v. Lynaugh (1989), opinion
Roper v. Simmons (2005), dissent
Harmelin v. Michigan (1991), joined Justice Scalia's opinion in part; joined Justice Kennedy's concurring in part; concurrence in the judgment
Ewing v. California (2003), opinion
Lingle v. Chevron (2005), opinion
Kelo v. City of New London (2005), dissent

Peckham, Rufus

Lochner v. New York (1905), opinion

Powell, Lewis F.

Batson v. Kentucky (1986), opinion
Regents of the University of California v. Bakke (1978), opinion
Eisenstadt v. Baird (1972), did not participate
Akron v. Akron Center for Reproductive Health (1983), opinion
Branzburg v. Hayes (1972), joined Justice White's opinion; concurrence
Wallace v. Jaffree (1985), joined Justice Stevens's opinion; concurrence
United States v. U.S. District Court (1972), opinion
Beer v. United States (1976), joined in Justice Stewart's opinion
Furman v. Georgia (1972), dissent

Reed, Stanley F.

Shelley v. Kraemer (1948), did not participate

Dennis v. United States (1951), joined Chief Justice Vinson's opinion
Cox v. New Hampshire (1941), joined Chief Justice Hughes's opinion
Youngstown Sheet and Tube Co. v. Sawyer (1952), joined in Chief Justice Vinson's dissent

Rehnquist, William H.

United States v. Virginia (1996), concurrence
Batson v. Kentucky (1986), joined Justice Burger's dissent
Gonzales v. Raich (2005), joined in part Justice O'Connor's dissent
Regents of the University of California v. Bakke (1978), concurring in part and dissenting in part
Gratz v. Bollinger (2003), opinion
Eisenstadt v. Baird (1972), did not participate
Roe v. Wade (1973), dissent; joined Justice White's dissent
Webster v. Reproductive Health Services (1989), opinion
Akron v. Akron Center for Reproductive Health (1983), joined Justice O'Connor's dissent
Planned Parenthood of S. E. Pennsylvania v. Casey (1992), concurrence in part, dissent in part;
        joined in Justice Scalia's concurrence in part, dissent in part
Washington v. Glucksberg (1997), opinion
Vacco v. Quill (1997), opinion
Romer v. Evans (1996), joined Justice Scalia's dissent
Lawrence v. Texas (2003), joined Justice Scalia's dissent
Texas v. Johnson (1989), dissent
Virginia v. Black (2003), joined in part Justice O'Connor's opinion
Wisconsin v. Mitchell (1993), opinion
Boy Scouts of America v. Dale (2000), opinion
Branzburg v. Hayes (1972), joined Justice White's opinion
Mitchell v. Helms (2000), joined Justice Thomas's opinion
Zelman v. Simmons-Harris (2002), opinion
Wallace v. Jaffree (1985), dissent
Lee v. Weisman (1992), joined Justice Scalia's dissent
Stone v. Graham (1980), dissent
Santa Fe Independent School District v. Doe (2000), dissent
McCreary Co. v. American Civil Liberties Union (2005), joined Justice Scalia's dissent
Van Orden v. Perry (2005), opinion
Texas Monthly, Inc. v. Bullock (1989), joined Justice Scalia's dissent
Locke v. Davey (2004), opinion
United States v. U.S. District Court (1972), did not participate
Dames and Moore v. Regan (1981), opinion
Hamdi v. Rumsfeld (2004), joined Justice O'Connor's opinion
Rasul v. Bush (2004), joined Justice Scalia's dissent
Beer v. United States (1976), joined Justice Stewart's opinion
Vieth v. Jubelirer (2004), joined Justice Scalia's opinion
Bush v. Gore (2000), concurrence
Furman v. Georgia (1972), dissent
Stanford v. Kentucky (1989), joined Justice Scalia's opinion
Penry v. Lynaugh (1989), joined Justice O'Connor's opinion
Atkins v. Virginia (2002), dissent; joined Justice Scalia's dissent
Roper v. Simmons (2005), joined Justice Scalia's dissent
Harmelin v. Michigan (1991), joined Justice Scalia's opinion
Ewing v. California (2003), joined Justice O'Connor's opinion
Kelo v. City of New London (2005), joined Justice O'Connor's dissent

Roberts, John G., Jr.

Parents Involved in Community Schools v. Seattle School District No. 1 (2007), opinion
Rumsfeld v. Forum for Academic and Institutional Rights, Inc. (2006), opinion

Davenport v. Washington Education Association (2007), joined in part Justice Scalia's opinion; joined in Justice Breyer's concurrence in part and concurrence in the judgment

Federal Election Commission v. Wisconsin Right to Life, Inc. (2008), opinion

Boumediene v. Bush (2008), dissent; joined Justice Scalia's dissent

Hamdan v. Rumsfeld (2006), did not participate

Roberts, Owen J.

Korematsu v. United States (1944), dissent

Cox v. New Hampshire (1941), joined Chief Justice Hughes's opinion

Cantwell v. State of Connecticut (1940), opinion

Rutledge, Wiley B.

Hirabayashi v. United States (1943), concurrence

Shelley v. Kraemer (1948), did not participate

Everson v. Board of Education (1947), dissent

Scalia, Antonin G.

United States v. Virginia (1996), dissent

Gonzales v. Raich (2005), concurrence in the judgment

Adarand Constructors, Inc. v. Peña (1995), concurrence

Grutter v. Bollinger (2003), dissent; joined in Chief Justice Rehnquist's dissent; joined in Justice Thomas's dissent

Parents Involved in Community Schools v. Seattle School District No. 1 (2007), joined in part Chief Justice Roberts's opinion

Webster v. Reproductive Health Services (1989), joined Chief Justice Rehnquist's opinion; concurrence

Planned Parenthood of S. E. Pennsylvania v. Casey (1992), concurrence in part, dissent in part; joined Chief Justice Rehnquist's concurrence in part, dissent in part

Romer v. Evans (1996), dissent

Lawrence v. Texas (2003), dissent

R. A. V. v. St. Paul (1992), opinion

Virginia v. Black (2003), joined Justice O'Connor's opinion in part; concurrence in part, dissent in part

Davenport v. Washington Education Association (2007), opinion

Federal Election Commission v. Wisconsin Right to Life, Inc. (2008), joined in part Chief Justice Roberts's opinion

Mitchell v. Helms (2000), joined Justice Thomas's opinion

Lee v. Weisman (1992), dissent

Santa Fe Independent School District v. Doe (2000), joined Chief Justice Rehnquist's dissent

McCreary Co. v. American Civil Liberties Union (2005), dissent

Van Orden v. Perry (2005), joined in Chief Justice Rehnquist's opinion; concurrence

Texas Monthly, Inc. v. Bullock (1989), dissent

Employment Division, Department of Human Resources of Oregon v. Smith (1990), opinion

City of Boerne v. Flores (1997), concurrence in part

Locke v. Davey (2004), dissent

Hamdi v. Rumsfeld (2004), dissent

Rasul v. Bush (2004), dissent

Boumediene v. Bush (2008), dissent; joined Chief Justice Roberts's dissent concurrence

Hamdan v. Rumsfeld (2006), dissent

Vieth v. Jubelirer (2004), opinion

Bush v. Gore (2000), joined Chief Justice Rehnquist's concurrence

Stanford v. Kentucky (1989), opinion

Penry v. Lynaugh (1989), joined Justice O'Connor's opinion

Atkins v. Virginia (2002), dissent; joined Chief Justice Rehnquist's dissent

Rope v. Simmons (2005), dissent
Harmelin v. Michigan (1991), opinion
Ewing v. Michigan (2003), joined Justice O'Connor's opinion
Kelo v. City of New London (2005), joined Justice O'Connor's dissent

Souter, David H.

United States v. Virginia (1996), joined Justice Ginsburg's opinion
Gonzales v. Raich (2005), joined Justice Stevens's opinion
Adarand Constructors, Inc. v. Peña (1995), dissent
Planned Parenthood of S. E. Pennsylvania v. Casey (1992), co-authored plurality opinion with
    Justices Kennedy and O'Connor
Washington v. Glucksberg (1997), concurrence in the judgment
Virginia v. Black (2003), concurrence in part, dissent in part
Boy Scouts of America v. Dale (2000), joined Justice Stevens's dissent
Davenport v. Washington Education Association (2007), joined Justice Scalia's opinion
Federal Election Commission v. Wisconsin Right to Life, Inc. (2008), dissent
Mitchell v. Helms (2000), dissent
Zelman v. Simmons-Harris (2002), dissent; joined Justice Breyer's dissent
Lee v. Weisman (1992), concurrence
McCreary Co. v. American Civil Liberties Union (2005), opinion
Van Orden v. Perry (2005), dissent
City of Boerne v. Flores (1997), dissent
Hamdi v. Rumsfeld (2004), concurrence in part, dissent in part
Rasul v. Bush (2004), joined Justice Stevens's opinion
Boumediene v. Bush (2008), joined Justice Kennedy's opinion; concurrence
Hamdan v. Rumsfeld (2006), joined Justice Stevens's opinion; joined Justice Breyer's concurrence
Shaw v. Reno (1993), dissent
Vieth v. Jubelirer (2004), dissent
Bush v. Gore (2000), dissent
Harmelin v. Michigan (1991), joined in part Justice Scalia's opinion; joined in part Justice Kennedy's
    concurrence in part; concurrence in the judgment
Ewing v. California (2003), dissent

Stevens, John Paul

United States v. Virginia (1996), joined Justice Ginsburg's opinion
Batson v. Kentucky (1986), joined Justice Powell's opinion; concurrence
Gonzales v. Raich (2005), opinion
Regents of the University of California v. Bakke (1978), concurrence in part, dissent in part
Adarand Constructors, Inc. v. Peña (1995), dissent
Parents Involved in Community Schools v. Seattle School District No. 1 (2007), dissent; joined
    Justice Breyer's dissent
Planned Parenthood of S. E. Pennsylvania v. Casey (1992), concurrence in part, dissent in part
Webster v. Reproductive Health Services (1989), concurrence in part, dissent in part
Akron v. Akron Center for Reproductive Health (1983), joined Justice Powell's opinion
Washington v. Glucksberg (1997), concurrence in the judgment
Bowers v. Hardwick (1986), dissent (referenced in Justice Kennedy's opinion in Lawrence v. Texas
    [2003])
Texas v. Johnson (1989), dissent
R. A. V. v. St. Paul (1992), joined in part Justice White's concurrence
Virginia v. Black (2003), concurrence in part Justice O'Connor's opinion; concurrence
Boy Scouts of America v. Dale (2000), dissent
Davenport v. Washington Education Association (2007), joined Justice Scalia's opinion
Federal Election Commission v. Wisconsin Right to Life, Inc. (2008), dissent
Wallace v. Jaffree (1985), opinion

Mitchell v. Helms (2000), joined Justice Souter's dissent
Zelman v. Simmons-Harris (2002), dissent; joined dissents of Justices Souter and Breyer
Lee v. Weisman (1992), joined Justice Blackmun's concurrence; joined Justice Souter's concurrence
Santa Fe Independent School District v. Doe (2000), opinion
Van Orden v. Perry (2005), dissent; joined dissents of Justices O'Connor and Souter
Texas Monthly, Inc. v. Bullock (1989), joined Justice Brennan's opinion
City of Boerne v. Flores (1997), concurrence; joined in part Justice Scalia's concurrence
Hamdi v. Rumsfeld (2004), joined Justice Scalia's dissent
Rasul v. Bush (2004), opinion
Boumediene v. Bush (2008), joined Justice Kennedy's opinion
Hamdan v. Rumsfeld (2006), plurality opinion
Beer v. United States (1976), did not participate
Shaw v. Reno (1993), dissent; joined Justice White's dissent
Vieth v. Jubelirer (2004), dissent
Bush v. Gore (2000), dissent
Atkins v. Virginia (2002), opinion
Roper v. Simmons (2005), concurrence
Harmelin v. Michigan (1991), dissent; joined Justice White's dissent
Ewing v. California (2003), dissent
Kelo v. City of New London (2005), opinion

Stewart, Potter

New York Times Co. v. Sullivan (1964), joined Justice Brennan's opinion
Regents of the University of California v. Bakke (1978), concurring in part and dissenting in part
Griswold v. Connecticut (1965), dissent; joined Justice Black's dissent
Eisenstadt v. Baird (1972), joined Justice Brennan's opinion
Roe v. Wade (1973), concurrence
Branzburg v. Hayes (1972), dissent
New York Times Co. v. United States (1971), concurrence; joined Justice White's concurrence
Abington School District v. Schempp (1963), dissent
Stone v. Graham (1980), dissent
United States v. U.S. District Court (1972), joined Justice Powell's opinion
Beer v. United States (1976), opinion
Lucas v. Forty-Fourth General Assembly of Colorado (1964), dissent
Reynolds v. Sims (1964), concurrence in the judgment
Furman v. Georgia (1972), concurrence

Stone, Harlan Fiske

Hirabayashi v. United States (1943), opinion
Cox v. New Hampshire (1941), joined Chief Justice Hughes's opinion
United States v. Curtiss-Wright Export Corp. (1936), did not participate

Sutherland, George

Near v. Minnesota (1931), joined Justice Butler's dissent
United States v. Curtiss-Wright Export Corp. (1936), opinion

Swayne, Noah

Slaughter-House Cases (1873), dissent

Taney, Roger B.

Dred Scott v. Sandford (1857), opinion

Thomas, Clarence

United States v. Virginia (1996), did not participate
Gonzales v. Raich (2005), dissent; joined in part Justice O'Connor's dissent
Adarand Constructors, Inc. v. Peña (1995), concurrence
Grutter v. Bollinger (2003), dissent; joined dissents by Chief Justice Rehnquist and Justice Scalia
Parents Involved in Community Schools v. Seattle School District No. 1 (2007), joined in part Chief
     Justice Roberts's opinion; concurrence
Planned Parenthood of S. E. Pennsylvania v. Casey (1992), joined Chief Justice Rehnquist's concur-
     rence in part, dissent in part; joined Justice Scalia's concurrence in part, dissent in part
Gonzales v. Carhart (2007), concurrence
Romer v. Evans (1996), joined Justice Scalia's dissent
Lawrence v. Texas (2003), dissent; joined Justice Scalia's dissent
Virginia v. Black (2003), dissent; joined Justice Scalia's dissent in part
Federal Election Commission v. Wisconsin Right to Life, Inc. (2008), joined in part Chief Justice
     Roberts's opinion
Mitchell v. Helms (2000), opinion
Zalman v. Simmons-Harris (2002), concurrence
Lee v. Weisman (1992), joined Justice Scalia's dissent
Santa Fe Independent School District v. Doe (2000), joined Chief Justice Rehnquist's dissent
McCreary Co. v. American Civil Liberties Union (2005), joined Justice Scalia's dissent
Van Orden v. Perry (2005), joined Chief Justice Rehnquist's opinion; concurrence
Locke v. Davey (2004), joined Justice Scalia's dissent
Hamdi v. Rumsfeld (2004), dissent
Rasul v. Bush (2004), joined Justice Scalia's dissent
Boumediene v. Bush (2008), joined dissents by Chief Justice Roberts and Justice Scalia
Hamdan v. Rumsfeld (2006), dissent
Hunt v. Cromartie (1999), opinion
Vieth v. Jubelirer (2004), joined Justice O'Connor's opinion
Bush v. Gore (2000), joined per curiam and Chief Justice Rehnquist's concurrence
Atkins v. Virginia (2002), joined dissents by Chief Justice Rehnquist and Justice Scalia
Roper v. Simmons (2005), joined Justice Scalia's dissent
Ewing v. California (2003), joined Justice O'Connor's opinion
Kelo v. City of New London (2005), dissent; joined Justice O'Connor's dissent

Van Devanter, Willis

Near v. Minnesota (1931), joined Justice Butler's dissent

Vinson, Frederick M.

Shelley v. Kraemer (1948), opinion
Barrows v. Jackson (1953), dissent
Dennis v. United States (1951), opinion
Youngstown Sheet and Tube Co. v. Sawyer (1952), dissent

Warren, Earl

Ferguson v. Skrupa (1963), joined Justice Black's opinion
New York Times Co. v. Sullivan (1964), joined Justice Brennan's opinion
Brown v. Board of Education (1954), opinion
Bell v. Maryland (1964), joined Justice Goldberg's concurrence
Griswold v. Connecticut (1965), joined Justice Goldberg's concurrence
United States v. O'Brien (1968), opinion
Abington School District v. Schempp (1963), joined Justice Clark's opinion
Reynolds v. Sims (1964), opinion

Lucas v. Forty-Fourth General Assembly of Colorado (1964), opinion
Trop v. Dulles (1958), opinion

White, Byron R.

Ferguson v. Skrupa (1963), joined Justice Black's opinion
New York Times Co. v. Sullivan (1964), joined Justice Brennan's opinion
Batson v. Kentucky (1986), joined Justice Powell's concurrence
Bell v. Maryland (1964), joined Justice Black's dissent
Regents of the University of California v. Bakke (1978), concurrence in part, dissent in part
Griswold v. Connecticut (1965), concurrence in the judgment
Eisenstadt v. Baird (1972), concurrence in the judgment
Roe v. Wade (1973), dissent
Webster v. Reproductive Health Services (1989), joined in part Chief Justice Rehnquist's opinion
Akron v. Akron Center for Reproductive Health (1983), joined Justice O'Connor's dissent
Planned Parenthood of S. E. Pennsylvania v. Casey (1992), concurrence in part, dissent in part; joined opinions of Chief Justice Rehnquist and Justice Scalia concurring in part and dissenting in part
Texas v. Johnson (1989), joined Chief Justice Rehnquist's dissent
R. A. V. v. St. Paul (1992), concurrence
Cohen v. California (1971), joined in part Justice Blackmun's dissent
New York Times Co. v. United States (1971), concurrence
Branzburg v. Hayes (1972), opinion
Abington School District v. Schempp (1963), joined Justice Clark's opinion
Wallace v. Jaffree (1985), dissent
Lee v. Weisman (1992), joined Scalia's dissent
Stone v. Graham (1980), per curiam
Texas Monthly, Inc. v. Bullock (1989), concurrence
United States v. U.S. District Court (1972), concurrence in the judgment
Beer v. United States (1976), dissent
Lucas v. Forty-Fourth General Assembly of Colorado (1964), joined Chief Justice Warren's opinion
Shaw v. Reno (1993), dissent
Furman v. Georgia (1972), concurrence
Stanford v. Kentucky (1989), joined Justice Scalia's opinion
Penry v. Lynaugh (1989), joined Justice O'Connor's opinion
Hamelin v. Michigan (1991), dissent

White, Edward D.

Lochner v. New York (1905), joined Justice Harlan's dissent

Acknowledgments

This book is the unintended product of my having agreed several years ago to teach a Supreme Court course designed for a general audience. In attempting to select a text for the course, I was unable—despite the abundance of literature on the Court—to find a book that I felt would be suitable for a class of this nature. The only alternative, I concluded, was to develop my own materials. With each revision, I have added my extensive commentary on a variety of topics, particularly to assist the reader in understanding some of the occasionally challenging concepts and doctrines of constitutional law.

I am indebted to Joel Larus, the founder and original director of the Pierian Springs Academy in Sarasota, Florida, for inducing me to teach the course; to the Academy administrative staff for their assistance; and to my many students whose cogent questions and comments in class helped shape the contents of the book. Finally, but most importantly, my thanks to my wife, Betty, for her constant support.

Selected Bibliography

Amar, Akhil Reed. *America's Constitution: A Biography*. New York: Random House, 2005. The "life story" of the Constitution, emphasizing the author's emphasis on the Constitution's text and structure as the appropriate primary foundation for its interpretation.

Barnett, Randy. *Restoring the Lost Constitution: The Presumption of Liberty*. Princeton, NJ: Princeton University Press, 2004. Advances an originalist and libertarian approach to constitutional interpretation.

Belz, Herman. *A Living Constitution or Fundamental Law? American Constitutionalism in Historical Perspective*. Lanham, MD: Rowman & Littlefield, 1998. An extended attack on the broad judicial discretion permitted by "living constitutionalism."

Bickel, Alexander. *The Least Dangerous Branch: The Supreme Court at the Bar of Politics*. Indianapolis, IN: Bobbs-Merrill, 1962. An inquiry into the "counter-majoritorian difficulty"—the domination of popularly elected political branches by an unelected judiciary.

Caplan, Lincoln. *The Tenth Justice: The Solicitor General and the Rule of Law*. New York: Vintage, 1987. Study of the important role of the Office of Solicitor General, the division of the Department of Justice that represents the United States in the Supreme Court.

Cardozo, Benjamin. *The Nature of the Judical Process*. Mineola, NY: Dover Publications, 2005. Famous 1921 lectures by Cardozo (then on the New York Court of Appeals) on how judges do and should decide cases.

Dierenfield, Bruce. *The Battle over School Prayer: How Engel v. Vitale Changed America*. Lawrence, KS: University of Kansas Press, 2007. Describes the impact of the Court's 1962 decision forbidding school prayer in the public schools.

Farber, Daniel, and Suzanna Sherry. *Desperately Seeking Certainty: The Misguided Quest for Constitutional Foundations*. Chicago: University of Chicago Press, 2002. A critique of a variety of "grand theories" offered by judges and philosophers on how the Constitution ought to be interpreted.

Fehrenbacher, Don. *The Dred Scott Case: Its Significance in American Law and Politics*. New York: Oxford, 1978. The classic history of the 1857 decision that divided the nation.

Fried, Charles. *Saying What the Law Is: The Constitution in the Supreme Court*. Cambridge, MA: Harvard University Press, 2004. The author (a former U.S. Solicitor General) reviews the Court's recent decisions in several controversial areas.

Garrow, David. *Liberty and Sexuality: The Right to Privacy and the Making of Roe v. Wade*. Berkeley, CA: University of California Press, 1994. As Fehrenbacher did with the *Dred Scott* case and Kluger did with *Brown v. Board of Education,* Garrow traces in detail the background and decisions in *Griswold v. Connecticut* and *Roe v. Wade*.

Greenburg, Jan Crawford. *Supreme Conflict: The Inside Story of the Struggle for Control of the United States Supreme Court.* New York: Penguin, 2007. A fascinating and well-balanced "inside" account of the making of recent key decisions.

Greenhouse, Linda. *Becoming Justice Blackmun: Harry Blackmun's Supreme Court Journey.* New York: Times Books, 2005. The book (by the Supreme Court reporter for the *New York Times* and based on Justice Blackmun's papers at the Library of Congress) is particularly valuable for the description of the background of Blackmun's opinion in *Roe v. Wade.*

Haines, Charles Grove. *The American Doctrine of Judicial Supremacy.* New York: Russell & Russell, 1959. Relates the historical development of the doctrine of judicial review in the United States.

Hamburger, Philip. *Separation of Church and State.* Cambridge, MA: Harvard University Press, 2002. An important book examining the church-state relationship from the colonial period to the present.

Hand, Learned. *The Spirit of Liberty.* Chicago: University of Chicago Press, 1977. Essays and lectures by Hand, who is widely regarded as one of the greatest judges of the twentieth century (but who was never appointed to the Supreme Court)

Hyman, Harold, and William Wiecek. *Equal Justice under Law: Constitutional Development 1835–1875.* New York: Harper & Row, 1982. An incisive history of constitutional change in the pre-Civil War and crucial Reconstruction period.

Jackson, Robert. *The Struggle for Judicial Supremacy: A Study of a Crisis in American Power Politics.* New York: Knopf, 1941. A critical account of the Supreme Court's gradual increase of power in relation to Congress and the Executive; published while Jackson was finishing his year as FDR's Attorney General before being appointed to the Supreme Court, where he served with great distinction (1941–1954).

Klarman, Michael. *From Jim Crow to Civil Rights: The Supreme Court and the Struggle for Racial Equality.* New York: Oxford, 2004. An incisive account of constitutional law concerning race from the late nineteenth century through the 1960s.

Kluger, Richard. *Simple Justice: The History of Brown v. Education.* New York: Knopf, 1976. A moving history of the background and drama of the most important Supreme Court case of the century.

Kull, Andrew. *The Color-Blind Constitution.* Cambridge, MA: Harvard University Press, 1992. Traces the changing views toward "color blindness" in the application of the Equal Protection Clause.

Levy, Leonard. *Original Intent and the Framers' Constitution.* London: Macmillan, 1988. An expert historian's analysis of the background and legislative history of the original Constitution and the Bill of Rights.

Marin, Patricia, and Catherine Horn (eds.). *Realizing Bakke's Legacy: Affirmative Action, Equal Opportunity, and Access to Higher Education.* Sterling, VA: Stylus Publishing, 2008. Although polemical in viewpoint, contains up-to-date data on the racial achievement gap and minority education.

Mason, Alpheus. *Brandeis: A Free Man's Life.* New York: Viking Press, 1946. An excellent biography of Louis D. Brandeis, social reformer and (after a tumultuous confirmation battle) Justice of the Supreme Court (1916–1939).

McWhorter, John. *Losing the Race: Self-Sabotage in Black America.* New York: Free Press, 2000. A black educator's analysis of explanations offered for racial disparities.

Murphy, Bruce Allen. *Wild Bill: The Legend and Life of William O. Douglas.* New York: Random House, 2003. Sets the record straight on the controversial justice who served on the Court longer than any other justice in the Court's history (1939–1975).

Newton, Jim. *Justice for All: Earl Warren and the Nation He Made.* New York: Penguin, 2006. Despite the title, Newton's book is an impartial and illuminating biography of an extraordinary Chief Justice (1953–1969).

Posner, Richard. *Law, Pragmatism, and Democracy.* Cambridge, MA: Harvard University Press, 2003. A provocative account by one of the nation's leading judges of the decision-making process.

Rae, Douglas. *Equalities.* Cambridge, MA: Harvard University Press, 1981. An eye-opening explanation of the almost infinite number of definitions of "equality."

Rothstein, Richard. *Class and Schools: Using Social, Economic, and Educational Reform to Close the Black-White Achievement Gap.* New York: Teachers College Press, 2004. Analysis of the causes and possible remedies for the marked disparities in the racial achievement gap.

Savage, Charlie. *Takeover: The Return of the Imperial Presidency and the Subversion of American Democracy.* New York: Little Brown, 2007. A powerful book detailing the efforts by the Bush-Cheney administration to enhance presidential powers.

Scalia, Antonin. *A Matter of Interpretation.* Princeton, NJ: Princeton University Press, 1997. Justice Scalia and other contributors argue the merits and demerits of textualism as a basis for constitutional interpretation.

Schuck, Peter. *Diversity in America: Keeping Government at a Distance.* Cambridge, MA: Belknap Press, 2003. Analyzes the controversial policy areas where politics and diversity intersect.

Schwartz, Bernard. *Super Chief: Earl Warren and His Supreme Court—A Judicial Biography.* New York: New York University Press, 1983. A biography of Chief Justice Earl Warren and history of the "Warren Court" (1953–1969).

Smith, Jean Edward. *John Marshall: Definer of a Nation.* New York: Henry Holt, 1996. An excellent biography of Marshall, who, probably more than any other person, molded the Supreme Court into the powerful institution it is today.

Stone, Geoffrey. *Perilous Times: Free Speech in Wartime.* New York: Norton, 2004. A comprehensive history of the nation's successes and failures in meeting wartime challenges to the First Amendment.

Swisher, Carl Brent. *American Constitutional Development.* Cambridge, MA: Riverside Press, 1943. A good (although now somewhat outdated) one-volume constitutional history by a prominent political scientist.

Thernstrom, Stephan, and Abigail Thernstrom. *America in Black and White.* New York: Simon & Schuster, 1997. The authors focus on key aspects of the race issue, including recent social and economic trends and the changing racial climate regarding preferences.

Thernstrom, Abigail, and Stephan Thernstrom. *No Excuses: Closing the Racial Gap in Learning.* New York: Simon & Schuster, 2003. The authors explore the troubling racial gap in academic performance and what can be done about it.

Wills, Garry. *"Negro President": Jefferson and the Slave Power.* New York: Houghton Mifflin, 2003. Relates the impact of the slave power on Jefferson's 1800 election and his administration.

Woodward, Bob, and Scott Armstrong. *The Brethren: Inside the Supreme Court.* New York: Simon & Schuster, 1979. A ground-breaking (at the time) "inside story" of the Court's deliberations, notably concerning the 1972 death penalty cases.

Index

About the Author

After graduation from Northwestern University Law School, **Earl E. Pollock** was Law Clerk to both Chief Justice Fred Vinson and Chief Justice Earl Warren of the United States Supreme Court. He then joined the Department of Justice and served as Assistant to the Solicitor General. On leaving government, he became a partner in a Chicago-based national law firm, heading the firm's antitrust group and later co-chairing the firm's litigation department. With his wife, Betty, he now lives in Sarasota, Florida.